An Introduction to the **AMERICAN ECONOMY**
Analysis and Policy

Sanford D. Gordon

Professor of Economics
Chairman, Department of Economics
State University College
Oneonta, New York

Jess Witchel

Chairman, Social Studies Department
Washington Irving High School
New York City

Instructor, Department of History
The City College
City University of New York
New York City

An Introduction to the

American Economy
Analysis and Policy

D. C. HEATH AND COMPANY

BOSTON

iv

D. C. Heath and Company   Boston
Library of Congress Catalog Card Number: 67–15651

Preface

This book is designed as an introduction to the fundamental concepts and principles of economics and, in particular, to those that are basic to the American economic system. However, to study only theory, without reference to actual economic conditions, would be like working in a vacuum. Consequently, the book also seeks to explain, in terms of theory and principle, how our economic system operates. Wherever possible, the problem-solving approach is used to identify continuing economic problems and the various solutions proposed.

The major concepts emphasized in AN INTRODUCTION TO THE AMERICAN ECONOMY—ANALYSIS AND POLICY are consistent with the recommendations of the National Task Force on Economic Education published in 1961. Both the microeconomic approach (the study of the individual and of business) and the macroeconomic approach (the study of aggregates, the nation's economy as a whole) are analyzed, and each is illustrated by means of specific examples. When controversial questions are introduced, there is recognition that solutions are likely to represent a spectrum of opinion rather than a choice between two clear alternatives. In dealing with problems, a deliberate effort has been made to avoid the "either-or" approach; instead, whenever feasible, a range of possible alternatives is considered. Sufficient descriptive material is introduced to provide the background necessary for a sophisticated consideration of the major problems of contemporary economic development.

Unit I considers what economics is, what questions it seeks to answer, what the purpose of an economic system is, and how the model of classical capitalism answers the major questions of economics. The approach is analytical rather than descriptive; however, materials and examples for illustrating principles and theories are drawn from the economic environment and from experiences familiar to most individuals. At the same time that classical theory is explored, the existence of other theories and models is recognized.

Unit II deals with the factors that business uses in producing goods and services: labor, natural resources, capital, and management. The roles of government and consumers are also considered. The two chapters on government stress the increasing part government plays in the economy and the ways in which its decisions affect the consumer and producer markets. A chapter on the consumer examines his role in determining production and raises questions concerning his freedom of choice.

The chapters on the factors of production are organized in similar fashion: the role of each factor in the American economy is analyzed and its part in providing answers to the basic questions of *How, What,* and *For Whom* is discussed. In relation to each factor the classical theory and its model are considered, together with certain departures from them. Finally, in the chapters on government and the consumer, some of the problems faced by our society are identified, and potential solutions are considered. Whenever possible, these solutions are evaluated in terms of the classical model.

Unit III introduces a second model, that of macroeconomic theory. In this unit fundamentals of national income accounting, income flow, money, banking, income determination, and the role of government policy as an active influence on the economy are discussed. The theories and concepts developed here are focused on the Keynesian model. The authors believe that the material included here on the fundamentals of income analysis, although by nature theoretical and abstract, provides a valuable new dimension for understanding economics. With details and qualifications held to a minimum, an adequate understanding of the national income approach can be achieved. The fact that some of this material is controversial in nature provides an opportunity for examining different viewpoints concerning our nation's economic development.

In Chapter 14, "Formulating Modern Economic Policy," the new model and the classical model are brought together into what economists call the *neoclassical synthesis.* The roles of modern monetary and fiscal policy, which have already been identified and evaluated, are discussed within the framework of this new model. Again, existing problems of our economy are identified, and a number of possible solutions are considered.

Unit IV views the American economy in relation to the world scene. Chapter 15 identifies the theories fundamental to international economics, the existing barriers to trade and to its future expansion, and recent developments aimed at removing such barriers. Chapter 16 focuses attention on major economic systems other than our own—socialism, communism, and fascism. With each of these systems care is taken to distinguish between the theory and actual practice. Recognition is given to the existence of competition in the world between these different economic systems and different ways of life, and to the fact that uncommitted nations have several alternatives from which to choose.

Unit V identifies and analyzes major contemporary problems of the American economy. Three of these deal with segments of the economy; the others are concerned with the national economy as a whole.

These particular problems have been selected not only because they are constantly discussed by the professional economist and the conscientious citizen but also because the traditional solutions are being questioned in the light of continuing change. An awareness of the meaning of alternative courses of action should help in the making of informed decisions.

The authors believe that the following features of AN INTRODUCTION TO THE AMERICAN ECONOMY—ANALYSIS AND POLICY are most significant to the development of a fresh approach to the study of economics:

1. Greater emphasis is placed on the analytical than on the descriptive approach to the subject. This approach encourages understanding of economic principles instead of mere rote memorization.

2. Orientation is directed toward basic economic theory, with conscious effort to avoid endless details and qualifications. This simplification, however, does not mean oversimplification to the point of distortion; rather it represents a focus on major principles and their relation to our nation's economic system.

3. Consideration is given to the "ideal" (the model or theory) and to the "real" (actual practice as carried on in the economy).

4. The problem-solving approach is used both in the presentation of ideas and in the organization of content.

5. Recognition is given to the problems of the contemporary economic scene. Among these are questions related to economic growth, the public versus the private sector, education as a factor in economic growth, and the appropriate goals of an affluent society. These problems are just beginning to receive from leaders in government, education, and economics the attention they deserve. They are likewise appropriate for consideration in the classroom.

6. Abstract ideas are explained and illustrated by means of specific examples based on familiar circumstances. In addition the classical and Keynesian models are illustrated by means of inserts, using a step-by-step visual and explanatory analysis and including transparent overlays to demonstrate conclusions. These models summarize the presentation of theory and provide a new and unique dimension for understanding abstract materials.

7. Much of the content and many of the visual materials, as well as approaches and methods, have been tested by actual use in class and have been refined by continuing experience.

It is the sincere hope of the authors that this book provides a conceptual framework for thinking about our changing economic world. In a democratic country with a traditional emphasis on the private sector of the economy and a growing importance of the public sector, it is essential for citizens to understand the nature of economics and of the issues with which that subject is concerned, since it is their decisions that determine economic policy.

Although this book is fully the responsibility of the authors, it is, nevertheless, the product of many minds and many influences. Our first acknowledgment rightfully belongs to the thousands of students whose insights and experience have guided us. They have helped in defining the suitability of particular materials, the effectiveness of different presentations, the directions of student interest and concern, and less obvious aspects of the "new economics."

Special thanks must be given to our colleagues who lived through this project with us. Their criticisms and suggestions were invaluable. Professors Walter Baumgartner and Philip Robbins of State University College at Oneonta, New York, offered specific suggestions that have added clarity to the presentation. Dr. Royal Netzer, President of State University College, and Dr. James Frost, Executive Dean of the State University of New York, gave the sympathetic encouragement necessary to make this book a reality. Professor Gerald Fabiano deserves special mention for the help he provided on Chapters 1, 2, 3, 10, and 11. Mrs. George Waddington, our typist, has not only met every deadline but has been a valuable critic as well.

Most of all, we are grateful to our families—parents, wives, and children—who have assumed many of our responsibilities and who have sustained us by their interest and understanding.

Sanford D. Gordon
Jess Witchel

Contents

Tables

Figures (charts and graphs)

Maps

ACKNOWLEDGMENTS

ILLUSTRATIONS AND CARTOONS: Austin Stevens; GRAPHS: Winston Allen; CARTOGRAPHY: Arthur Turner

Grateful acknowledgment is made to the following sources for their permission to reproduce the following material:

xviii	TWA Photo by Ezra Stoller Associates	179	E. I. DuPont de Nemours and Company
9	DuPont, "The Profit Motive"	190	International Business Machines Corporation
16	Bettmann Archive	224	United Press International
17	DuPont, "The Profit Motive"	238	*Straight Herblock*, Simon & Schuster, 1964
22	Jordan Marsh Company	259	Shoemaker in *Chicago's American*
38	Allis Chalmers	274	Kansas Power & Light Company
43	U. S. Steel Corporation	274	Radio Corporation of America
47	New York Stock Exchange	276	New York *Daily News* photo
50	General Motors Corporation	308	Jacob Burck, Chicago *Sun-Times*
70	H. M. Lambert (E. P. Jones)	308	Drawing by William Hamilton © 1966 The New Yorker Magazine, Inc.
84	Culver Pictures		
98	Edmund Valtman, The Hartford *Times*	317	Wide World
111	Black Star	319	Parker Allen
130	Atomic Energy Commission	332	Valtman, The Hartford *Times*
132	North American Aviation Inc., Space & Information System Division	333	The European Community Information Service
		341	New York *World-Telegram*
133	Allied Radio Corporation, Chicago	363	Wide World
135	United States Air Force	364	Sovfoto
148	Don Orehek, *Look* magazine	379	© 1964 by The New York Times Company. Reprinted by permission.
154	Photo by Leo Durling. Graph from Committee on Public Affairs of the American Petroleum Institute and Platt's Oilgram Service	387	Franklynn Peterson Associates
		394	Wide World
		395	Wide World
162	Bureau of Reclamation	405	*The Herblock Book*, Beacon Press, 1952
179	Reprinted by permission of Humble Oil & Refining Company © 1965.	412	Gordon Converse, The *Christian Science Monitor*

Graphic material credited to the New York *Times* is copyright © 1933; 1963, 4, 5, 6 by The New York Times Company. Reprinted by permission.

ILLUSTRATIONS AND CARTOONS: Austin Stevens
GRAPHS: Winston Allen,
CARTOGRAPHY: Arthur Turner

UNIT I
The Framework of Our Economy

1 Economics—What It Is and What It Tries to Do

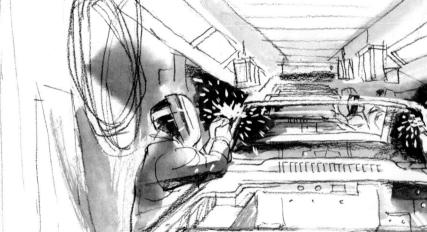

Preview

Chapter 1 introduces you to the subject of economics. It explains what economics is and explores the central questions which economics seeks to answer. Furthermore, it examines the kind of economic system we have in this country. You will learn what an economic model is and what part such a model can play in answering the questions of *What? How?* and *For Whom?* Finally, you will be introduced to the approach and pattern of organization that will be followed in this study of economics.

At the beginning of each chapter there is a short introduction explaining in general terms what the chapter is about. Questions are raised as a frame of reference for considering new ideas. Exploring new ideas is easier if you have some idea of what to expect.

Overview

What does economics deal with?

What is an economic system?

What questions are answered by the study of economics?

In what way will the study of economics help you?

Part A Economics as a Discipline

Why should you study economics?

As you skim through the pages of this book, you will see graphs and charts, facts and figures. As you examine some sections more closely, you will probably ask the questions "Why should I study economics? Will this study help me in any way?" Psychologists have found that students are better able to learn when they can see a purpose in learning. There is good reason, then, to begin by examining possible answers to these questions.

CITIZENS INFLUENCE ECONOMIC POLICIES OF GOVERNMENT

In a democracy we, as citizens, are expected to participate, at least indirectly, in decision making. In voting for our representatives or in supporting a political party, we are endorsing certain principles and supporting particular solutions to problems. How far should the government go in providing medical care? Should taxes be raised or lowered? Are greater curbs needed on big business and big labor? Are my tax dollars being spent wisely? Is our tariff policy in need of a change? These few questions, although they are usually asked within a political framework, have an economic nature. They are as important as the money in your pocket, and just as personal. Their answers will affect the amount of money you make and the amount of money you have to spend. There is little government activity that does not have an economic origin, and no one can avoid the influence of government in his life.

CONSUMERS AND PRODUCERS INFLUENCE ECONOMIC POLICIES OF BUSINESS

Even though the influence of government policy on your life may seem remote at the present time, you are nevertheless deeply involved in economics. As you go shopping, you are interested in the kinds of goods you get and the prices you pay for them. When you go to work, you will be concerned about the amount of compensation you receive. The purchases that you make as a consumer and the income that you receive as a producer or worker help to shape the economic decisions and policies made by American businesses. Although the study of economics may not provide you with a method of earning a living, it can help you to understand better your role as a consumer and a producer. It can also increase your ability to make decisions that are best for you as individual and citizen.

What economics is

Economics is one of the social sciences. Like political science, sociology, and geography it is concerned with the study of man's attempt to organize his environment

Opportunities for economists are to be found in business, government, and teaching.

to satisfy his needs. Economics concentrates on the satisfaction of man's material needs, such as food and shelter. Specifically, *it concerns itself with the study of production, distribution, and consumption of goods and services.*

If we picture man in an economic sense, we think of him as trying to make a living. He works to produce goods or services that people want and are willing to pay for. In return for the value he creates, he gets paid so that he can buy the things he and his family want. In the simplest society he works to produce the things he and his family want and will consume directly. In a more complex society he is more specialized and must exchange the goods or services he produces for goods and services that other people produce. This allows him to satisfy many more wants than if he himself had to create everything he needs and wants. Whether we look at man as part of a family or as part of a great nation, we know that he has material wants which he seeks to satisfy. Economics is the study of how man tries to satisfy these wants. In studying economics you may at times pause to evaluate how successful we in America have been in satisfying these wants.

The central problem of economics

Though definitions are very useful in delineating the scope of an academic discipline like economics, they are sometimes weak in pointing out the purpose and direction of the discipline. In the course of living, man is faced with certain basic problems. In trying to find answers, he gathers facts, organizes them, discovers related questions, and develops methods for solving problems. Collectively, these procedures, the body of knowledge, and the attitudes developed add up to a discipline, e.g., *economics.* However, the discipline develops because man is searching for answers.

WHAT DO ECONOMISTS DO?

Economists are concerned with the ways in which man satisfies his material wants. They must know what resources exist to produce goods and services; they must be able to determine what goods and services man wants. They must also consider the problem of utilizing resources most effectively to provide maximum satisfaction. For this purpose they study the supply of and demand for commodities, as well as their production, distribution, and consumption.

In performing their job, economists must develop certain skills and learn to use particular tools of analysis. They must learn how to gather and organize information and to interpret the data needed to solve economic problems. The study of problems such as price rises, unstable market trends, employment, and monetary and tariff policies occupies the time of professional economists. Theories, systems, and models are used to help explain how our whole economy or portions of it have worked, are working, or may work under certain conditions. Since quantitative relationships are extremely important, tools for statistical analysis may also be needed.

In 1963 about 20,000 people were employed primarily as economists. Of these, the largest number — about half — held teaching positions at the upper secondary, college, and university levels. Government, particularly the federal government, is the second largest employer. Private industry and research organizations are hiring an increasingly large number of economists. Some economists are self-employed, supplying their services to businesses for a fee.

Although a bachelor's degree with a major in economics is satisfactory for beginning jobs, a master's degree, or preferably a Ph.D., is required for advanced teaching and for more responsible jobs in government and industry.

SOURCE: U.S. Department of Labor, Bureau of Labor Statistics, *Occupational Outlook Handbook,* 1963–64 edition

Let us review briefly the questions that economics seeks to answer.

FOR INDIVIDUALS

All of us, at some time or other, allow ourselves the luxury of daydreaming. A common subject for these dreams is to picture ourselves as able to afford all the things we associate with wealth. A look through a mail-order catalogue or a visit to a large department store whets our appetite for a never-ending list of products. However, nothing can bring us back to reality sooner than reaching into our pockets and finding how little we have to work with. *The problem we are faced with is that our resources, usually identified as money, are limited.* The only way we can resolve our problem is to make choices. After looking at our resources, we must examine our list of wants and identify the things that we need immediately, those that we can postpone, and those that we cannot afford. As individuals we are faced with the central problem involved in economics: *deciding just how to allocate our limited resources to fulfill as many unlimited wants as we can.*

FOR NATIONS

Nations face the same problem. As a country's population grows, the need for more goods and services grows correspondingly. Resources necessary to production may increase, but there never are enough resources to satisfy the total desires of a nation. Whether the budget meeting is taking place in the family living room, in the city hall, in the conference room of the corporation board of directors, or in the chamber of the House of Representatives in Washington, D.C., the basic problem still exists. We need to find methods of allocating our limited resources in order to satisfy our unlimited wants.

Some of the things we want are of no concern to the economist. These are things, like air and sunshine, which exist in such abundance that we call them *free goods.* We also have psychological needs, such as the need to feel wanted. These, too, the economist ignores. It is the relative scarcity of goods and services that creates our central economic problem and forces us to make choices—to decide what we will have and what we will do without. Such scarce goods are called *economic goods,* and they can be obtained only by effort and money. These are the goods with which the economist is concerned. Meeting the needs of people and nations from the supply of resources available leads to the basic activity called *production.* In the course of trying to meet unlimited wants from limited economic goods, production leads to new problems in economics.

The big questions: What? How? For Whom?

There are three questions that are closely associated with the central problem of unlimited wants and limited resources.

Production involves four factors, all of which contribute value to the final product and must be paid for.

We shall call them the problems of *What? How?* and *For Whom?* Whether we study the simple subsistence economy of a South Pacific island or the complex system of an industrialized nation, we must see how the problem of *What* to produce is solved. If economics deals with the study of the satisfaction of material wants, then the student may well ask what material wants shall be met. Should the people submit an annual list? Should a central planning committee decide? How much freedom should the people have in deciding? The question of what to produce is basic and exists because we have limited resources and unlimited wants.

If we answer the question of *What,* we must then consider the question of *How:* how do we produce the goods and services we have decided upon? Production, even in a simple society, can be difficult to achieve. It involves getting the right kind and amount of "ingredients" together at the right time and place to produce the things we want. We have to be careful not to waste these ingredients, since they are usually in limited supply. Inefficient production will mean that there will not be enough resources left over to satisfy other wants. We will have more to say about these ingredients shortly.

After deciding what to produce and how to produce it, we still have a major question to answer: *For Whom* is this production meant? The *For Whom* is a question of *distribution.* Shall everyone get an equal portion? Should production be distributed according to need? If so, how do we determine need? The problem of who gets steak and who gets hamburger is as basic as the *What* and the *How.*

Factors of production

Although nations may choose different economic systems, all must be concerned with producing. Before proceeding with our discussion of economic systems, we must first understand what we have described as the ingredients of production. All production involves four separate *factors:* natural resources, labor, capital, and management.

NATURAL RESOURCES

Natural resources — the materials nature provides — are necessary to the production of the things we want. Some economists prefer to call this factor *land.* The minerals in the ground, forests, waterfalls, and fertile soil are all examples of a nation's resources; they are important in determining its production.

LABOR

To adapt natural resources for human use, we must apply work. This is done by *labor,* the second factor of production. Here, too, the skill and the amount of labor will be important in determining production. India has more than twice the labor force that we have in the United States, but the greater skill of the American worker makes him far more productive. Superior education has allowed him to utilize machines.

CAPITAL

The third factor of production is *capital.* Most people think of capital as money. To the economist *capital is any man-made instrument of production,* that is, a good used to further production. Frequently this will mean a tool or a machine. It can also mean the rolled steel that is used in automobile production. By placing great amounts of capital in skilled hands, productivity can be increased tremendously.

MANAGEMENT

The fourth factor of production is *management.* People engaged in this function are referred to as *entrepreneurs* (enterprisers). It is the responsibility of the manager to initiate production, to organize the other factors of production, and to operate the productive establishment. If he produces goods and services efficiently, he contributes a valuable service in satisfying people's wants. When we have the four factors mentioned previously, we have the ingredients of production.

The need for an economic system

In order to answer the central problem of limited resources and unlimited wants and the related questions of *What? How?* and *For Whom?* we need some rules or guiding principles. Such principles usually reflect the values that people hold. We find a broad range of values held by the American people. Most students of American history would agree that individual freedom and the sanctity of private property rank among the highest. Some people today would place equality and the general welfare high on the list. In Russia the best interests of the state and collective ownership of property are emphasized. Values such as these, and more specifically the principles that stem from them, provide the direction for answering the big questions in economics. The method a nation uses in answering these questions we call its *economic system.*

WHAT KIND OF ECONOMIC SYSTEM?

An economic system must provide an answer to the question of who is to produce the goods and services. If businessmen produce all, we have an exclusively private enterprise system which we classify as *capitalism.* The emphasis of this system is on the private ownership and operation of the factors of production. If, on the other hand, the means of production and distribution are owned and operated by government, the system is labeled *socialism.*

Actually, since no country has all its production coming exclusively from either the private or the public (government) sector, all countries may be said to have more or less mixed economies. However, this does not mean they are the same. Far from it. In the United States the largest portion of our goods and services comes from businesses — private enterprises — and a much smaller, though important, portion (primarily services) comes from government. Some of these services with which we come in close contact are educational and library facilities and the postal system. Although our economy is mixed, we usually label it *capitalism, mixed capitalism, private enterprise,* or *free enterprise.* These terms are characteristic of economies in which production stems primarily from business, and in which government plays a lesser role.

In the Soviet Union most means of production are owned and operated by the government, and very little originates with private enterprise. Because of this emphasis on government production, the U.S.S.R. calls its system socialism. Most economically developed countries of the world have economic systems which are somewhere between that found in the United States and that of the Soviet Union.

Part B   An Overview of the American Economic System

Production — What?

With most of our production coming from business enterprises consisting of about five million privately owned firms, how do we decide what to produce? In a country with over 190,000,000 people, each of whom has a variety of wants larger than the inventory list of a supermarket, the question of *What* seems overwhelming. Even the thousands of items listed in mail-order catalogues do not begin to cover the numerous wants of people. Deciding what to produce under these circumstances would appear impossible. Yet this is being done all the time, along with decisions about how much of each product to make. Not only have we been finding answers to these questions, but the indication is that our system is working comparatively well. It is a fact that we Americans produce, and that our people consume, more goods and services than any other country in the world.

Every day businessmen throughout the country make decisions about what and how much to produce. They are very careful in their estimates because they realize that if their decisions are wrong they will lose money. They also realize that those who make the most accurate decisions will make the most money. What guidelines do we have to follow?

INDIVIDUAL CHOICES DETERMINE PRODUCTION

Businessmen watch carefully what customers buy. Every time you buy something in a store you are casting your dollar vote for that particular good. Actually you vote many hundreds of times a year for the various products you buy. If very few people buy a product, that product will be defeated at the polls; that is, it will not be produced or it will be produced in a smaller quantity. The storekeeper does not order it

again, and the producer knows that he will have to cut down his production, change his product, or stop producing it. However, if a great many people buy a product, the casting of these many votes will result in the storekeeper's increasing his order and the producer's increasing the amount he manufactures. The buyers tell the sellers what they want, and the sellers in turn tell the producers.

You cast votes indicating your choice whenever you obtain something that is produced. Consider how many times you have purchased a phonograph record at your favorite music store. If you and your friends are particularly interested in a special record, the owner of the music store will have to increase his order for records to satisfy this single want of many people. You

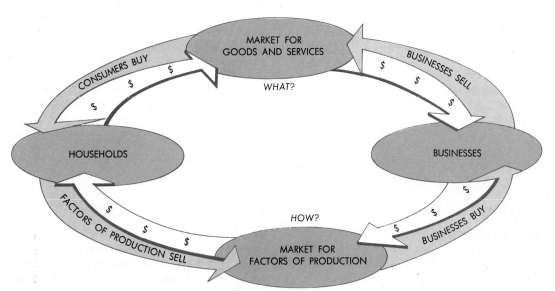

Figure 1–1 The Circular Flow of the Economy

This simplified circular flow model of pure capitalism shows how a free-enterprise economic system answers the questions of what to produce and how to produce. People from households go to the market as consumers to buy and they go to the market as suppliers of the factors of production to sell. Businesses go to the market to sell

their production, but they must first go to the market as buyers in order to get the factors of production necessary to produce. The inner lines show the flow of money payments. The outer lines show the flow of economic resources, that is, production and factors of production. The flow of money thus determines the allocation of resources.

also find this same principle—of supply meeting demand—in a library. If a librarian has a number of requests for one book, she may have to order additional copies. Her second order to the book publisher tells him of an additional demand. These examples help us to see that both the kind and the amount of our production are determined by the choices which people make in buying goods and services.

Production—How?

You will recall our previous mention of the fact that all production involves four factors: natural resources, labor, capital, and management. If producers and sellers are to increase their business, they need to employ more of the factors of production—more iron ore, more machinists, more machines, and more foremen. How can these factors be obtained? They can be secured from producers facing reduced demand or from money not currently in use. Producers who are increasing their business need more of the factors; they usually take them from those whose business is declining; they do so by offering more money.

THE DIRECTING SATELLITE: A GUIDE TO PRODUCTION

An example may help you to understand the relationships indicated in Figure 1–1. Try to imagine that floating above our country is a directing satellite carrying a sensitive antenna. This instrument records every single purchase that is made by every single buyer in the entire country. It is registering the votes of people for the goods and services they want. This scientific instrument then transfers the results to a computer, which determines whether the factors of production are going in the right amount to the places that are producing the goods and services.

Let us suppose that Americans indicate an increasing interest in new automobiles and a decreasing interest in new appliances. This change would be shown by the purchase of more automobiles and fewer appliances. Our satellite, having registered this change, would indicate that some of the steel and the workers and the foremen now producing appliances should be shifted to producing cars.

The allocation of our resources is determined by buyers and sellers at the market as if their wants were registered by our imaginary satellite.

INCENTIVES INFLUENCE PRODUCTION

A logical question which you might ask at this point is how, in a democracy, you can shift people from one industry to another. You cannot force people to move, nor can you arbitrarily order that materials be redirected from one producer to another. This is where our wonderful instrument comes to the rescue. Signals to offer more dollars are transmitted from our satellite to the factors of production. The greater the need for factors of production to move from one industry to another — as from appliances to automobiles — the more dollars will be offered to speed the change.

You know that, as a worker, the more you earn, the more satisfactions you can derive from your income. Therefore, you will try to work at the job that will pay you the most. Since fewer appliances are being bought, fewer appliance workers will be needed. Some of these workers will find themselves looking for another means of earning a living. Since demand for cars has increased, thereby requiring more labor, we will find our workers following the signals — moving where more dollars are offered. The same would be true of steel and machines.

The satellite, after recording the kind and quantity of our purchases, also determines the kind and amount of production needed to meet our demands. Its computer determines whether the factors of production are going in the correct combination to the right place to produce the goods and services we want. It then suggests the necessary adjustments in the flow of our resources to the right place, in the right amounts, and at the right time. This is accomplished by directing additional resources where they are needed, and redirecting resources when they are not needed, by adjusting the amount of dollars offered. This payment provides incentive for change.

Consumer choices are important in determining the *What* of production.

Distribution — For Whom?

Why is our satellite so successful? We are able to understand its success when we answer the question of *For Whom.* The production is there. For whom is it meant? The tall? The strong? The fair? No! With some exceptions, to be mentioned later, it will go to those who have the money — the dollars — to buy it. Businessmen want to make big profits, workers want high wages, landlords want to collect as much rent as possible, just as you want your income raised in order to buy more of the things you want.

It would be nice if everyone could have all the things he wanted. However, you will recall that we said that our needs seem unlimited — never ending — and our resources to produce are definitely limited. If we agree that everyone cannot have everything he wants, or even most of the things he wants, and we know that we have to figure out some system of distributing the production, why should it be decided on the basis of who has the most money? There are some people who have a great need for goods and services but do not have the money to obtain them.

OUR SYSTEM PROVIDES ANSWERS

American economic practices do provide us with some answers to the question of meeting our needs, although not everyone considers these the best ways of distributing goods and services. Money payments are used as incentives to reward people for making contributions to the well-being of our country. Workers may toil in order to earn money to satisfy their needs; and although they are working with their own self-interest in mind, they are also adding production that our people want. The more they produce, the better they serve society. The more their services are in demand, the higher their wages will be. Businessmen try to produce the best possible products most efficiently. As a result they will try to increase their profits by producing at as low a cost as they can and selling as much of their product as possible at the highest acceptable price. Since other businessmen are also trying to produce efficiently the things that people want, there is competition for the buyer's dollars. Those who make the best products—the products that people want most—at the lowest price will get most of the dollars. The people of the country are being served by this competition because they are getting what they want. Although the successful businessman may be doing his job for his personal gain—earning more money—society benefits by his efforts. Thus, the worker and the businessman, motivated largely by self-interest and the desire for profit, both contribute to the material growth of the country.

Adam Smith and the theory of classical capitalism

Most of the theory behind classical capitalism comes from a book, *The Wealth of Nations,* published the year our country declared its political independence—1776.

In it Adam Smith, a professor at the University of Glasgow, Scotland, described and advocated the system of classical capitalism. The system which Smith described and which became the basis of our economic system depends on the *market* to answer the basic economic questions. The market is the place where buyers and sellers meet and where prices placed on the goods we want to sell and buy will determine how we allocate our resources. The things we buy determine the *What*—buying the best products at the lowest prices. Those who have taken the factors of production and put them together in the most economical way to produce the goods the public wants, determine the *How.* The money that goes to those who do the jobs that we indicate we want done and do those jobs better than others, indirectly answers the question *For Whom.*

THE LIMITED ROLE OF GOVERNMENT

What part does the government play in Smith's plan? The answer is: almost none. As a matter of fact we frequently refer to this system as *laissez-faire,* a French expression meaning "hands off." It is expected that government will protect us from invasion by foreign countries, and will protect our freedoms and our property. However, the original plan contemplated no interference with the free flow of the factors of production and the production itself. The directing satellite—or the "invisible hand," as Smith called it—was responsible for guiding everything to the places that needed it most. Remember that need was determined by the most money offered. Only if the government stayed out of the marketplace could the questions *What, How,* and *For Whom* be answered in such a way as to insure the most good for the most people concerned.

The classical model: theory and practice

Is the economic system we now have in this country the one just described? Is the

ADAM SMITH AND THE THEORY OF LAISSEZ-FAIRE

Adam Smith (1723–90) lived at a time when England's economy was undergoing a significant transition. During the seventeenth century the Netherlands led England in commerce and France led her in manufacturing; in the next century England surpassed both.

During this time the economic philosophy dominant among the nations of western Europe was mercantilism. This system, designed to increase a nation's supply of precious metals, required extensive government controls. Monopoly privileges, subsidies, and tariff protection were granted to a select few in order to encourage investment in new business ventures bringing monetary return.

By the middle of the eighteenth century the conditions on which the mercantile system was based had begun to change in England. As businesses grew in power with the increase of trade and manufacturing, government protection was no longer so essential to them. At the same time, the Industrial Revolution was shaping a new era of production. It was on these new conditions that Adam Smith based his theories of laissez-faire.

Smith believed that individual initiative, motivated by the desire for profits, could result in a healthier national economy. If the economy

was freed from the restraints of government interference, the factors of production could seek their maximum return. With supply and demand operating in a free competitive market, the problems of production and distribution could be solved most effectively. And since England was stronger than her neighbors and more efficient in production, she could afford to encourage free competition at home and overseas.

Smith is usually referred to as the father of modern economics. In giving meaning and order to the environment he lived in, he reflected the changes taking place in his day, and his ideas influenced the direction of future change and development.

---

system that Adam Smith described as existing in 18th-century England the system we have? Do workers and businessmen determine their wages and prices in the marketplace according to the dollars suggested by the satellite? Does the government really stay out of the marketplace?

The answer to all these questions is *no*. Businessmen do not always compete with one another. Neither do workers or landlords. We must also note that the government does not always stay out of the marketplace.

This functioning system — laissez-faire, or classical capitalism — which Adam Smith

and others described is what economists sometimes call a *theory* or a *model*. A model is developed to help analyze or understand the economy better. It is like models you are familiar with, a set of plans designed to work in a particular way. You have probably seen people look at a set of plans and remark, "It looks good on paper, but . . ." This means that things in real life do not seem to work out quite the way they are planned. Similarly, economists' models do not seem to work out exactly as planned. Not every situation can be anticipated, nor all details included. When theories or plans are made involving people, too many things can go wrong. This does not mean that we throw away our plans. Since we know of little involving man that is perfect, we make plans with the hope that they will be as close to perfect as possible. However, we should recognize our limitations and make changes accordingly.

The classical model as described by Adam Smith has to a great extent served as the basis for our nation's economic system. However, the model as originally set forth by Adam Smith was further defined and amplified as a result of continued study of its operation. Other economists, such as Jean Baptiste Say, a French economist writing at the beginning of the 19th century, and Alfred Marshall, a British professor of political economy writing at the end of the same century, took Smith's model and added to it or changed it.

The classical model: practice and change

The classical model—sometimes called capitalism, sometimes laissez-faire—developed as the private enterprise system which ultimately became characteristic of our economy. We will have to examine this model more closely. It is important to know about this model because it has guided us in the past as well as in the present, and it will probably continue to guide us in the future. In addition, we must try to answer the questions of how and why we have changed the model; we have not become slaves to blueprints, but rather have changed the blueprints somewhat to meet our needs.

There were many things that Adam Smith, writing over 180 years ago, could not have foreseen in our modern atomic age. There are times when economists expect that people will behave in certain ways and they do not. When these things happen, we need to alter our plans to allow for the unexpected or for new developments. If our model is really a good one and seems to do most of the things it is designed to do, we do

NO "CONSENSUS" ON ECONOMIC POLICY

WASHINGTON — Reports from Washington indicate that there is no solid agreement on President Johnson's economic policies. Disagreement comes from both the left and right of the Administration's middle-of-the-road position.

Gardner Ackley, chairman of the President's Council of Economic Advisers, favors generous tax reductions and mild spending restraints. Leon H. Keyserling, who held the same post as Mr. Ackley under President Truman, favors increased government spending for recovery. Raymond J. Saulnier, President Eisenhower's chief economist, sees the need for restraint in spending and credit. Ackley is continuing the policies of the previous chairman, Walter W. Heller, who was appointed by the late President Kennedy.

Economics is not an exact science, and much controversy centers around economic policy.

not dispose of it when we have trouble. Rather, we modify it in an effort to make it a better model, one which will meet our current demands.

As an example, big business and big labor unions have at times interfered with the operation of the free market—of the directing satellite—and we have had to make adjustments. We have sometimes needed things in this country, but businessmen have either not had enough money to provide them or have not wanted to do so because of fear that they might lose money trying! At times, through no fault of their own, some people have been unable to create enough value in the marketplace to support themselves and their families. These are just a few of the examples which have influenced us to alter our model and to consider further changes.

In Chapter 11 you will be introduced to another model which uses a different approach to answer the big questions of our economy. Those who favor the new approach criticize the classical model as being too far removed from the reality of the world that is. However, the defenders of this model claim it has not been given a fair chance, and some of them say we need to return to it rather than continue altering it.

Reasons for economic controversy

From this discussion it is obvious that economics, like other disciplines, has unresolved problems. Just as you find disagreements about values and interpretations among physicians, biologists, historians, and art critics, so there are differences among economists. If economists disagree, how can a student who is just being introduced to the subject draw his own conclusions about economic problems? Although this question may be answered by pointing out that the same problems of disagreement exist in all subjects, there are at least two better answers. First, the tools, the method of approach, the facts, and the problems that all economists deal with are the same. Differences most frequently arise because of disagreements concerning values and judgments. These differences will be pointed out at the end of some chapters after the problems have been identified, the facts presented, and the tools given for analyzing the problem. Second, the areas of agreement are far greater than the areas of disagreement. For these reasons economists are able to function within the discipline and provide the student with the tools to make intelligent decisions as a consumer, a producer, and a citizen.

Looking ahead

We will now take a closer look at parts of the American economy, examining the classical model, some of its modifications, and some unanswered questions. In Unit III we will look at another model — the Keynesian — and discuss its application to the American economy as a whole. Then we will see the part which the economy of our country has played and can continue to play in the world. We will conclude with a brief look at some of the economic problems we are facing in this decade.

In each instance we will try to use the following approach:

1. In what way does this answer the big questions: *What? How? For Whom?*
2. If the model applies, what does it prescribe? Has it undergone any particular changes? Does it differ appreciably from conditions in the real world?
3. Are there major problems that have to be solved? What are they, and what are some possible solutions?

REVIEW: the highlights of the chapter

1. The study of economics helps you to understand your role as a consumer and producer and provides you with tools to make wiser decisions as a citizen.
2. Economics is a social science that concerns itself with the production, distribution, and consumption of goods and services.
3. The central problem in economics stems from the fact that there are limited resources to satisfy man's unlimited wants. To solve this problem he must make choices.
4. Three related problems that every society must find answers to are: *What* shall we produce? *How* shall we produce it? *For Whom* shall we produce it?

5. All production involves four basic factors: natural resources, labor, capital, and management. Natural resources are the materials nature provides, labor is work applied to production, and capital is the man-made instruments used in production. Finally, management initiates and organizes the other factors.

6. An economic system provides rules and guiding principles to help answer the central and related questions. An economic system that depends primarily on private enterprise to supply production is called capitalism. When production comes mainly from government enterprise, it is socialism. Most countries have mixed economies, although they may emphasize business or government.

7. The American economy emphasizes production by private enterprise. Under this system the *What* is determined by businessmen who are influenced in their decisions by what consumers purchase in the market for goods and services. In order to produce these goods, the businessman goes to the market to buy the factors of production. Money payments are used as incentives to reward people for supplying the services that society wants.

8. Adam Smith, in *The Wealth of Nations*, set forth what has come to be known as the classical model. This model depends on a market free from government interference to answer the major questions. Government's role is to protect freedom and property and to defend against foreign invasion.

9. Many forces have worked to interfere with the freedom of the market and to cause alteration of the model. Though some disagreement exists among economists as to whether to go back to the original model, alter it further, or substitute a new model, they are in general agreement on facts, methods, and approaches to problems.

2 Demand and Supply— An Answer to Resource Allocation

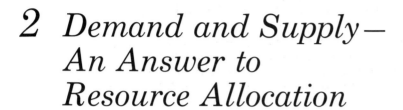

Preview

In the first chapter, after identifying what economics is and what problems it seeks to solve, we sketched the model that has guided a great deal of the development of the American economy. In this and succeeding chapters we will take a closer look at this classical model and see how it provides answers to the central problem of the allocation of our resources. Since our resources are limited and our wants are not, we must make decisions as to how we use what we have. In our economic system these choices should be determined by what people want and by the efficiency of the producing unit.

The *market* is the place or condition in which buyers and sellers meet to exchange commodities for the prices they agree upon. The buyers' willingness and ability to purchase at certain prices is called *demand*. The sellers' offer to part with goods at certain prices is known as *supply*. The numbers and independence of buyers and sellers determine the kind of competition there is. In this chapter we will study our market structure and show how this method, with its price system, is used to allocate our resources. We will then consider whether this model shows how resources are actually allocated under our present system.

Overview

What is the difference between utility, value, and price?

What is a market? What kinds of markets are there?

How are supply and demand important in allocating resources?

What causes prices to change?

Part A   The Market

Price: an important economic influence

Price is a primary influence in determining the allocation of resources in our free enterprise system. It determines what goods and services will be produced and in what quantity. It influences the use of the four factors of production. In addition it is most important in determining who gets what. A different way of stating this idea is to say that the price system answers the questions *What? How?* and *For Whom?*

When we think of price we often also think of value, and when we think of value we may think of usefulness or utility. The student of economics must distinguish between price, value, and utility. Although none of the three is exactly the same as the others, it is easy to see that they are closely related. *Utility* relates to the satisfaction that a good or service can provide. If, in addition to its usefulness, it is also relatively scarce, it has *economic value*. When we measure that value with other goods and

Markets have existed in a variety of forms at different periods of history. Local and seasonal markets and country auctions all have counterparts in the present-day economy.

COMPETITION CUTS RETAIL PROFITS

NEW YORK — Presidents of some of the largest New York City retail stores are reporting that despite consecutive annual sales peaks they have been fighting declining profits. They attribute this to the fierce competition that exists to attract the more than one million shoppers they deal with daily.

Efforts are made to keep expenses as low as possible in an effort to raise gross margins. One president characterized the competitive situation as the "survival of the fittest."

Competition makes the consumer "king."

services, we call it *exchange value*. When we measure its value in money we call it *price*.

Conditions of pure competition

A market is a place or situation where buyers and sellers meet. It can be a market for goods and services where consumers meet suppliers or a market where suppliers come to bid for the factors of production (see Fig. 2–10 on p. 30.) In order for the classical model to work as planned, certain market conditions must be met:

1. There must be enough buyers and enough sellers acting independently so that the entry or exit of any one buyer or seller will not affect price.

2. The products offered for sale should be sufficiently alike so that buyers will feel free to choose the product offered by any seller.

3. New sellers should be able to enter and existing sellers should be able to leave the market freely.

When these three conditions exist, we have what economists call a *purely competitive market* or *pure competition*.

Consumers benefit from competitive prices

Pure competition serves the consumer well because, if sellers are to be successful, they must offer their products at the lowest prices. Charging one penny more than any other seller will mean no sales, since it is assumed there is no difference between the quality of one product and that of another.

Society progresses by means of improved efficiency

To obtain higher profits, sellers are encouraged to improve their products and increase the efficiency of their production. The better their product and the lower their cost, the more money they will make. Their action, which at first appears to have only a selfish motive for making the greatest profit, actually serves the best interests of the consumer, too. Those who favor this classical model call the desire to make more money by increasing efficiency and improving products "incentive". They consider this a step toward a better society because it induces us to perform at our most efficient level. There are others who think that such motivation runs counter to the spirit of brotherhood, pits man against his fellowman, and is not a fair method of distributing production. The clash between several sets of values has resulted in the modification of the classical model. We will examine this synthesis after we have examined the classical model more closely and after we have taken a look at the market situations that actually exist.

Market conditions other than pure competition

All competition which is not pure is called *imperfect competition*. There are few places in the United States where a market with the three conditions usually considered as basic to pure competition exists. Agriculture, textiles, and certain retail fields come closest to meeting the criteria for pure competition. Yet even in these areas there is some interference with the freedom needed in the marketplace as called for in the classical model.

Pure monopoly

The opposite of pure competition is *pure monopoly*. It exists when the following conditions prevail:

1. Only one seller offers the product for sale, allowing him to exercise considerable control over price.
2. There is no close substitute to which the buyer can turn.
3. Other businesses may not enter the field.

A condition of pure monopoly places the consumer at the mercy of the monopolist. With no place to turn, he must deprive himself of the product or pay the price the monopolist charges. These prices are unchecked by competition, so that more of the consumer's limited resources are used. The consumer's position is further weakened

In some industries competition is wasteful or not feasible. Consumers are protected by government supervision and regulation.

in that the monopolist lacks incentive to improve his product, and the consumer has no alternative but to buy from him. In this case, monopoly interferes with progress.

Fortunately for the consumer there are today no major privately owned monopolies that are not regulated by government in our country. Thus, in *public utilities* and transportation the protective measures of the government safeguard the consumer. Public monopolies, such as the post office, mint, and fire department, are owned by the people.

Before World War II, the Aluminum Company of America had a virtual monopoly on primary aluminum. The Pullman Standard Company still makes all sleeping cars for our railroads. In some cases, government action has helped to establish competition by creating an environment which has brought additional producers into the market. We can still find certain businesses which have a virtual monopoly in their own geographic areas—television stations, newspapers, and cement plants, for instance. The effect of these local monopolies on prices is debatable.

MONOPOLISTIC COMPETITION

Most markets are found to be somewhere between pure competition and pure monopoly. When there are a large number of sellers acting independently, with each trying to convince the buyer that his product is different from that of other sellers, we have a market condition known as *monopolistic competition*. The manufacturers of name-brand aspirin plead with buyers not to ask simply for aspirin or for a combination-of-ingredients tablet, but to ask for their aspirin by name. The implication is that their aspirin is a special product. The consumer can substitute a different brand tablet, but will he be getting the same product? Because substitution is not as easy under monopolistic competition as under pure competition, the seller has some control over price.

OLIGOPOLY

The remaining market situations are classified as *oligopoly*. The prefix *oligo*, meaning "a few," gives us a clue to its meaning. An oligopoly exists when a few sellers have sufficient control over the market for a product so that changes in price by one will affect all other sellers. Examples of oligopolies are the "Big Three" in automobiles and the "Big Four" in rubber tires, linoleum, tin cans, and cigarettes. Although it is difficult to differentiate between products like tin cans, copper, and steel, there is an attempt to do so wherever possible. Serious barriers to entering the market exist, and little attempt is made to bring about changes in price, particularly in lowering price. The absence of pure competition does not eliminate changes in price resulting from changes in the supply of goods offered, but it does lessen such an effect. The producer, under conditions of oligopoly, must be very careful that any action he takes will not bring retaliatory action by others in the field.

Competition among buyers

Just as there are situations involving sellers that deviate from the classical model, so pure competition is not always found on the buyers' side. Frequently, suppliers of goods not used directly by consumers—tobacco farmers and ranchers, for instance—find themselves in market situations with few buyers or even in a condition of *monopsony*, where there is only one buyer. In some industries a few buyers meet a few sellers. Although the rubber tire industry is an oligopoly, it must sell a major share of its product to automobile manufacturers, whose industry is also oligopolistic. When large retail chain stores contract with producers to manufacture an item under their name, they exercise considerable control over price. Though competition among buyers has not been reduced as much as it has among sellers, we cannot ignore it as a factor in influencing price.

Part B   How Demand Functions in the Classical Model

In our discussion of different market conditions we showed that prices were influenced by the number of buyers and sellers. Under pure competition price is determined by demand and supply. While most market situations are not purely competitive, it is nevertheless important for us to know how such a market determines price. The competitive market is important for three reasons:

1. Competition is a condition which most Americans consider desirable, and we have pursued a policy to make our market more competitive.
2. Imperfect competition is affected, but to a lesser degree, by the same forces.
3. We are all consumers and are affected by price.

The nature of demand

In Chapter 1 we spoke about the satellite's registering the wants of consumers. It did not register the daydreams that people have about the things they would buy if they had more money. Only when consumers are willing to part with their limited resources to obtain a good or service at a given price did the computer in the satellite react. This willingness on the part of consumers to purchase certain amounts of a product at given prices at a particular time and place is called *demand.*

Consumers will purchase products based on (1) the urgency of their need for the product, (2) the price of the product, (3) the price of the substitutes, and (4) their income. The general rule of the *law of demand* is that the lower the price of a given product, the more of it consumers will buy. Conversely, the higher the price, the less consumers will buy.

DEMAND IS SUBJECT TO THE LAW OF DIMINISHING MARGINAL UTILITY

Why do consumers buy products? They usually buy to satisfy a want. The utility of a product depends on its ability to satisfy wants. The greater the want-satisfaction, the greater the utility. However, the utility for a number of units of a given product, let us say candy bars, is not the same. If you have eight candy bars, each candy bar you eat may increase your total satisfaction. However, the satisfaction you derive from the first candy bar is likely to be greater than that from the second bar. The third will probably give you less satisfaction than the second, and the fourth less than the third, and so on. Even if you are particularly fond of candy, it is unlikely that you would wish to consume the total number of candy bars that you have available. Once your hunger for candy is satisfied, each unit that you consume will at a certain point give you an ever-diminishing satisfaction, and therefore will have an ever-decreasing utility.

The word *marginal* is frequently used in economics. It refers to one more unit or one less unit. The marginal utility of candy bars would be the degree of satisfying power — utility — of eating the last candy bar you have had or the next candy bar you will have. The *law of diminishing marginal utility* states that as the supply of a product a consumer has increases, its satisfying power for each extra unit decreases. You may be willing to pay 20 cents for the first bar of a candy that usually sells for 10 cents, but you will buy additional candy bars only at lower prices as your desire for them declines.

OTHER FACTORS ALSO INFLUENCE DEMAND

Although the law of diminishing marginal utility explains consumer purchases based on the urgency of the need and the price of the product, the use of substitutes and the level of income of buyers also affect demand. If you are in a theater and want something to eat while watching the movie, you will probably go to the refreshment stand and see what is for sale. Candy might be your first choice, but the 20-cent price seems too high. A small bag of popcorn costs only 15 cents. While the popcorn is not quite as satisfying as the candy to you, it is cheaper and will last twice as long. The price of the substitute may cause you and other candy lovers to buy popcorn in spite of your preference for candy.

Suppose that you are in the situation described above but that this time your funds are greater. Your added resources allow you to satisfy more of your wants. This phenomenon was observed on the national scene after World War II. The American consumer increased his consumption of meat and decreased his purchases of wheat, even though the price of the former had gone up considerably. Increased income made it possible to satisfy more wants. The same principle is seen to operate in the efforts of merchandisers to capture the teen-age market.

Demand schedule

In our discussion of demand some students may have received the impression that demand referred only to how much of a product consumers would buy at a particular price. This is not the correct impression. Our definition said a "willingness" on the part of consumers to buy certain amounts of products at given prices. This means that at 20 cents only a few candy lovers will buy candy that is associated with a price of 10 cents. This does not mean that many have no desire for the candy. They just do not want to part with that much of their limited resources. However, if the price is dropped to 15 cents, you and others who were not willing to buy before may now want to purchase candy bars. If the price is reduced to 12 cents, a greater quantity of candy bars will be sold. At a still lower price a still larger number will be sold, perhaps also to popcorn lovers buying candy as a substitute.

When we speak of the quantity of a product that consumers will buy at varied price levels, we are making use of the economist's concept of demand. When we list in a table the amounts consumers will buy of a product at various prices, in a particular market, and at a given point in time, we have a *demand schedule*. Table 2–1 is an example of a demand schedule.

Table 2–1   Demand Schedule for Candy Bars for One Week

PRICE	QUANTITY
$.20	50
.15	200
.12	275
.10	350
.05	500

Increasing the price causes consumers to switch their purchases to other goods.

Demand curve

Let us see what the demand schedule for candy bars looks like when we place it on a graph. Figure 2–1 illustrates graphically the demand schedule in Table 2–1. The vertical axis shows us the five different price levels; the horizontal axis shows us quantities at intervals of 100. We draw our demand curve (or line) by locating points on our graph for each of the different price levels. We go up the vertical axis, measuring price, until we come to 20 cents. We then follow the horizontal line to the right until we come to the right quantity for 20 cents—50. Since we have quantities identified only in intervals of 100 units, we locate our point halfway between 0 and 100. Point A on Figure 2–1 shows us the demand for candy bars at the price of 20 cents. We now locate our points for 15 cents (B), 12 cents (C), 10 cents (D), and 5 cents (E). Now we connect points A, B, C, D, and E, and we can see what the demand schedule in Table 2–1 looks like on a graph. Can we tell how many candy bars will be sold at 14 cents? Our demand schedule does not give us this information; but if we measure on the vertical axis four fifths of the way between 10 cents and 15 cents and draw a horizontal line to the right, we can get an estimate. The point at which our 14-cent price line crosses our demand curve gives us an approximation of the quantity that could be sold. Is it closest to 225, 250, or 275?

Notice how the demand curve slopes downward as we follow it to the right. This helps explain the buying habits of consumers. Can you explain the economics of a sale held by a retail merchant? As you move from left to right on our demand curve, you should be able to explain how the downward slope explains the law of diminishing marginal utility.

Elasticity of demand

Not all demand curves look like the one shown in Figure 2–1. Let us look at the

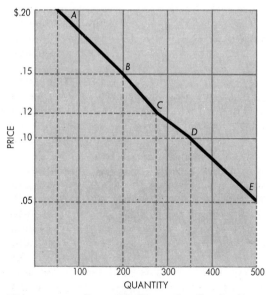

Figure 2–1 Demand Curve for Candy Bars for One Week

The downward-sloping curve shows consumers buying more candy bars as the price is reduced.

demand for salt rather than candy bars. The price of salt may vary from 10 cents a pound to 20 cents a pound. If your family uses between one and two pounds of salt a month, its expenditure for salt could fluctuate from 10 to 40 cents a month, depending on the extremes in the quantities used and the prices paid. Another way of looking at it is to say that the cost of satisfying your family's need for salt can fluctuate from $\frac{1}{3}$ cent to $1\frac{1}{3}$ cents per day, a 400 percent variation in price. There would probably be a very small decline in the sale of salt if the price increased 50 percent, or even 100 percent. The cost is so low, even at the highest price, that few people would deprive themselves. When a relatively large change in price brings about only a small change in the quantity purchased, we say that the demand for a product is *inelastic*. In other words, the demand for salt is inelastic. Another aspect to consider is what you could use in place of salt. A comparison of a curve plotted for candy bars and of one for salt would show a vast difference, the latter being far steeper.

If a seller has no competition and no fear of government's controlling the price, any increase he makes in the price of an inelastic product will increase his revenue from that product. What factors might restrain such a seller from using such power excessively? What considerations will determine where the price is eventually set?

AN EXAMPLE OF ELASTIC DEMAND

The demand curve for expensive meats is quite different from that for salt. When sirloin steak goes on sale, reduced from $1.35 a pound to $1 a pound, purchases are likely to increase by a far greater percentage than the percentage of the reduction in the price. Many shoppers who know that their families like steak seldom buy it because the high price would mean they would have to sacrifice too many other wants. However, a drop in price changes the whole situation. Fewer wants will have to be given up in order to obtain the satisfaction that steak provides. We can conclude that the demand for steak, being very responsive to a change in price, is elastic.

When a relatively small change in price brings about a large change in the quantity bought, we have a product with *elastic* demand. Think of elastic as stretching. A change in price that brings about little stretching (change) in the quantity bought is inelastic; a lot of stretching of quantity bought is elastic. Compare the curve of an elastic demand with that of an inelastic demand. Is it more important to have vigorous competition when a product is elastic or when it is inelastic?

A word of caution is in order before you try to analyze the elasticity of a product. In the case of most products the elasticity

Style changes usually influence demand.

changes over a very broad price range. Steak may be quite elastic when its price fluctuates between 80 cents and $1.50. As the price goes above $1.50, it becomes less and less elastic. There will be a relatively small change in the quantity of steak sold when the price goes above $2. The relatively few who can afford to pay such a high price, or the few who feel they must have steak because of their dietary habits or the high want-satisfaction from eating steak, will probably pay the additional money no matter what the price.

FACTORS DETERMINING ELASTICITY

What makes the demand for a product inelastic? Usually the demand is inelastic when (1) it is difficult to find a substitute, (2) it represents a small portion of an individual's budget, and (3) it is considered a necessity. Any one or a combination of these reasons will tend to make demand inelastic. Conversely, products for which there are many substitutes, which represent a large portion of the budget, and which are considered luxuries tend to be elastic in demand.

Most products will not fit neatly into either category, and what may have an elastic demand in one family may have an inelastic demand in another. Evaluate the elasticity of the demand for milk, a television set, your favorite magazine, a second car in a suburban family, and a first car for a low-income family in a metropolitan center. The influence of elasticity of demand may be seen in Cases I and II of the classical model insert following page 44.

Changes in demand

A change in demand means an increase or a decrease in the number of units of a product that could be sold throughout the range of prices at which they are offered. It does *not*, however, mean changing the number of units sold by changing the price. An example may clarify this difference. Assume that your school has recently conducted a vigorous campaign to improve dental hygiene. There may well have been an emphasis on avoiding sweets, particularly candy, between meals. It is possible, if not probable, that the demand for candy has declined. On the other hand, a campaign urging young people to take some sweets for sustaining energy shortly after midday would probably result in an increase in demand for candy. The increase or decrease in sales did not come about by a change in price. The price remained the same, but the units sold changed.

CAUSES FOR A CHANGE IN DEMAND

Changes in demand may be caused by a change in people's taste, a change in consumer income, and a change in the market for substitutes. An important change has taken place in the demand for butter, particularly in the last ten years. Advertising, inventions, and style changes affect demand by changing people's tastes. How can a producer protect himself from a change in demand?

A change in demand will result in a new set of figures on the demand schedule. When we plot a new demand curve, we find the curve shifting either to the right or to the left of the original demand curve. In Figure 2–2 which curve illustrates an increase in demand? Which curve illustrates a decrease? If you follow one price level, such as 10 cents, through all three demand curves, you can easily find the answer.

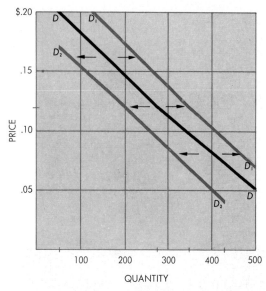

Figure 2–2 Changes in the Demand Curve

Changes in demand are shown by shifting the curve to the right (D_1) or left (D_2) from the original demand (D). Explain how you can determine which of the two curves that have shifted represents an increase in demand.

Part C   How Supply Functions in the Classical Model

What is supply?

Just as demand deals with the consumer's willingness to buy, supply concerns itself with producers or sellers and their willingness to offer products for sale. Like demand it refers to a particular product offered in a given market at a given time and at different prices. We may define supply as the various amounts of products that a seller will offer for sale at specific prices at a specified time and place. When we have this information, we can prepare a supply schedule, just as we did for demand.

Factors influencing supply

Supply, like demand, is subject to change under a variety of conditions. These changes occur not in relation to price but as a response to other circumstances of the market.

SUPPLY AND THE TIME FACTOR

In considering supply, we must recognize that the time factor has an important effect on availability. For an accurate analysis of supply we must know whether reference is being made to what will be offered for sale under the following conditions:

ALFRED MARSHALL AND HIS CONTRIBUTION TO PRICE THEORY

Alfred Marshall (1842–1924), for many years professor of economics at Cambridge University in England, is most noted for his contributions to the theory of price. Believing strongly that the best of all economic worlds is one in which the forces of supply and demand are able to operate in a free competitive market with a minimum of government interference, Marshall focused attention on the individual firm and the ways in which prices for its goods are determined. Borrowing from the classical economists Smith and Ricardo the concept of the importance of cost on the supply side, and from the marginalists, of whom he was the greatest (see p. 106), the concept of marginal utility determining demand, he created a new synthesis for interpreting price formation. An expert mathematician, he developed diagrams as an aid to economic analysis.

Perhaps the greatest contribution of Marshall was the recognition that the time element is extremely important in determining supply. For the immediate period, demand is the major factor determining price because the supply is fixed. As the time interval is lengthened, supply can be adapted to changes in demand, keeping in mind the cost of production. For the short run a business can alter its quantity by using existing facilities of production. In the long run a business is able to change its production facilities, as by adding new plant and equipment. Therefore, the supply side becomes more important as the interval of time is increased.

Marshall was not only an original thinker and a great synthesizer, but he was also a great teacher. His most famous pupil was John Maynard Keynes, the most influential economist of the twentieth century (see p. 225).

1. the product presently available

2. the short run, where producers or sellers can utilize their present facilities to increase or decrease the amount of the product

3. the long run, where producers and sellers can increase their facilities so as to produce or sell more or less of the product, and where either additional producers or sellers or fewer producers or sellers are in the market

When stretch pants for girls and continental pants for boys were first introduced into the market, a very few firms devoted a small part of their production facilities to them. No one could possibly know how well these products would catch on. A supply curve for the existing stretch or continental pants could be drawn. When it was apparent that these items were going to be very popular, the producers already involved in making them used their existing facilities

to turn out more. The supply curve for this situation is for the short run. When enthusiasm continued to mount, other producers decided that they should enter the production of the new fashions, and so additional facilities were used. This last situation would call for a supply curve for the long run.

Let us once again turn back to our satellite. The intensity of the demand for new-fashioned pants is picked up on the antenna and registered on the computer. This information is relayed to the businessman, who then realizes that he can earn additional dollars if he will turn his efforts to producing these pants. However, such action takes time and reflects our three possible supply situations—present, short run, and long run.

THE LAW OF SUPPLY

There is a direct relationship between price and the quantity supplied. When a supplier can get a higher price for his product, he has incentive to go to the market for additional factors of production so that he can offer more of his product on the goods and services market. The general rule for supply states that *producers will offer more of their product for sale as price rises and will offer less as price falls.*

COST AS A FACTOR RELATING TO SUPPLY

In a purely competitive market the supplier of goods and services has no control over the market price, since he produces too little to influence market conditions. With no difference between his product and that of his competitors, he will sell nothing if he charges above the market price and he will sell all if he charges below the market price. However, in considering the price, he must take into account his cost of production. There are times when he may be willing to sell below his cost. This might happen when prices tumble for what he believes will be a short time. However, no businessman can afford to lose money for a prolonged period of time. He must be constantly aware of his costs in relationship to the market price if he is to compete successfully and earn a profit.

Many people are under the impression that as production increases, costs per unit decrease. Though mass production has made this true in certain industries and at certain levels of production, both logic and evidence from practical experience have shown that costs per unit begin to rise beyond a certain level of production. Some economists refer to this as the *law of increasing costs.*

The reason costs rise as production goes up is complex, and we cannot go into a complete answer to the question here. However, it is easy to recognize that, as production goes up, the need for additional factors of production will also grow. This will involve competitive bidding in the marketplace for the factors of production. If we need more skilled labor to produce more, and none of this labor is unemployed, we will have to get it from other sources. This can be done by offering higher wages. Higher bidding would also apply to the other factors of production. We should also recognize that not all labor is equally productive, just as not all land is equally fertile and not all ore is equally rich in the mineral wanted.

When output is low, producers will use the most efficient factors of production. As these factors of production grow scarcer, they will have to use the less productive factors. Only when prices rise does it pay to employ these less productive factors. Otherwise, the additional costs will be greater than the additional revenue received. We will consider the nature of cost of each factor of production in greater detail in subsequent chapters.

SUPPLY SCHEDULE AND SUPPLY CURVE

A *supply schedule* is a table listing the amount of a product sellers will offer for sale at various prices in a particular market and at a given time. From the data in a supply schedule we can draw a supply curve. Table 2-2 shows a supply schedule for candy bars for a week. Figure 2-3 shows the supply curve drawn from the supply schedule. This schedule may be compared with the demand schedule on page 20, and the supply curve compared with the demand curve on page 21.

Table 2-2 Supply Schedule for Candy Bars for One Week

PRICE	QUANTITY
$.20	500
.15	350
.12	275
.10	200
.05	50

When the market price increases, suppliers can afford to increase the quantity they offer for sale.

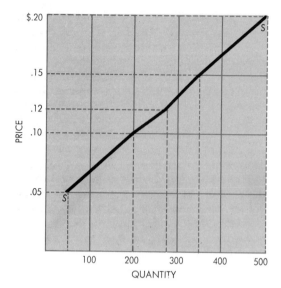

Figure 2–3 Supply Curve for Candy Bars for One Week

The upward-sloping curve shows that the seller will offer more candy bars as price is increased.

Elasticity of supply

Supply, like demand, may be *elastic* or *inelastic*. When the quantity of a product offered for sale varies little although major changes in price are made, the supply is inelastic. An inelastic supply curve appears as a steeply sloping or vertical curve because the quantity offered changes relatively little with price changes.

If the quantity of a product offered for sale varies greatly when small changes in price are made, the supply is elastic. An elastic curve appears as a gently sloping or horizontal curve.

The causes for elasticity of supply are complex, but as a general rule any good whose supply can be increased in a short time is said to be elastic. If there is a longer time period producers have the opportunity of changing production facilities, and market conditions can change. Identify on Figure 2–4 the elastic and the inelastic supply curves.

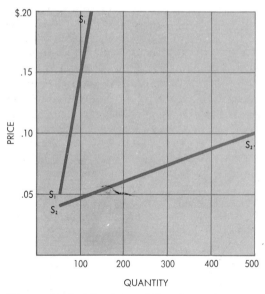

Figure 2–4 Elasticity of Supply

The two curves shown here illustrate elastic and inelastic supply. Identify each curve.

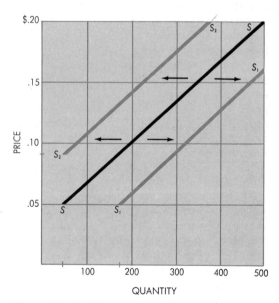

Figure 2–5 Changes in the Supply Curve

Changes in supply are shown by shifting the original curve (S) to the right (S_1) or left (S_2).

Changes in supply

A change in supply, like a change in demand, is a change in the quantity of the product at the different price levels. It is *not* a change in the quantity offered resulting from a change in price. As we have previously seen, cost is a major factor in determining supply. Changes in the cost of production, such as wage increases or technological advances in machinery, will usually result in a change in supply.

Another factor is the expectation of future prices. Businessmen do not know what prices will be; they only know what prices are. They plan their production on what they expect prices to be. If they anticipate prices to be above their costs, they produce with confidence. Falling prices will tend to discourage production.

A change in the demand for other goods can result in a change in supply. When stretch pants became fashionable, the manufacturers shifted more of their facilities into the production of this popular product.

Figure 2–5 shows changes in supply. Examine the curves and note which ones show the increase. Follow one price through all curves and see what quantities are offered.

Part D   How Price Is Determined

Interaction of supply and demand

Supply and demand take on real significance when they are put together. Sellers offer products for sale when they anticipate demand. Buyers can convert their wants into demand only if there is supply. The two interact to create the market price and provide an answer to our basic question of allocating our resources.

Let us put our supply schedule and demand schedule side by side and see how the laws of supply and demand determine price. The illustration given assumes a purely competitive market for a given period of time. As we look at Table 2–3, we see that at prices above 12 cents dealers will offer more candy bars than consumers will buy, resulting in a surplus of candy bars. Having a surplus means wasting our limited resources. Sellers have a choice of cutting back their production, stopping production of candy bars for a while, or cutting their price.

Below the price of 12 cents consumers want more candy bars than are offered for sale. Some who want candy bars will not be able to buy them, even if they are willing to pay more. Only at 12 cents do the number of candy bars offered for sale and the number of candy bars buyers wish to purchase equal each other. Where supply and demand equal each other, the market is at *equilibrium,* and the price at this point is the *equilibrium price.*

Table 2–3   Supply and Demand Schedules for Candy Bars for One Week

QUANTITY BUYERS WOULD PURCHASE	PRICE	QUANTITY SELLERS WOULD OFFER	SURPLUS (+) OR SHORTAGE (−)
50	$.20	500	+450
200	.15	350	+150
275	.12	275	0
350	.10	200	−150
500	.05	50	−450

What is the equilibrium price?

We can show the supply and demand schedules in Table 2–3 graphically by drawing the supply and demand curves (see Figure 2–6). The equilibrium point is where the supply and demand curves intersect. Any point above that would leave a surplus; any point below would be a shortage. When the forces of supply and demand are allowed to operate freely without any interference from government or groups formed to control prices, the *market will be cleared;* that is, there will be no shortage of buyers willing to pay the freely-arrived-at market price and there will be no surplus of producers willing to sell at the freely-arrived-at market price.

Changes in supply and demand

Changes in price and quantity will occur when changes in supply or demand, or both, take place. This can be seen most easily in Figures 2–7, 2–8, and 2–9.

Figure 2–7 illustrates the effect of a given supply and changes in demand. An increase in demand shifts the curve to the right, as shown by the movement of the original demand, D, to the increased demand, D_1. The intersection, which tells us the equilibrium price and quantity, shifts along the supply curve, showing a higher price and a greater quantity of the product bought. The broken line connecting the new intersection with the vertical axis mea-

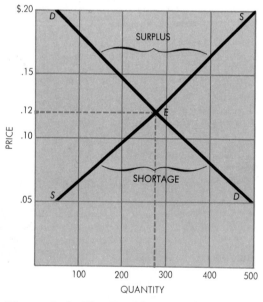

Figure 2–6 The Equilibrium Price and the Quantity Exchanged for Candy Bars for One Week

The price of candy bars for one week in a purely competitive market will be at the intersection of the supply curve and the demand curve (E). At this equilibrium point, the market will be cleared. Any price above E will leave sellers with a surplus. Any price below E will produce a shortage for buyers.

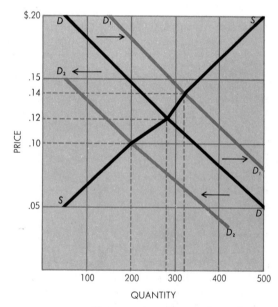

Figure 2–7 Change in Demand and Its Effect on Price and Quantity

An increase in demand, supply remaining the same, results in an increase in price and an increase in quantity. A decrease in demand, supply remaining the same, results in a decrease in price and a decrease in quantity. These examples show the direct relationship between changes in demand and changes in the equilibrium price and quantity exchanged.

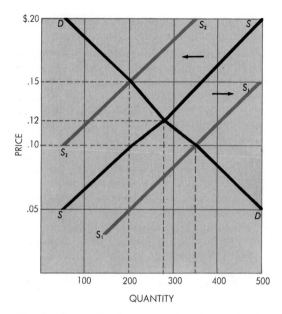

Figure 2–8 Change in Supply and Its Effect on Price and Quantity

An increase in supply, demand remaining the same, results in a decrease in price and an increase in quantity. A decrease in supply, demand remaining the same, results in an increase in price and a decrease in quantity. These examples show the inverse relationship between changes in supply and changes in the equilibrium price, and the direct relationship between changes in supply and changes in quantity exchanged.

suring price and the horizontal axis measuring quantity shows the new market condition, 325 units sold at 14 cents. Both price and quantity have increased with an increase in demand. A decrease in demand is shown by D_2. What are the new equilibrium price and quantity with D_2 as demand? Compare the market situations between popular and classical records. Which record dealer has to be more alert to changes in demand?

Figure 2–8 illustrates the effect of a given demand and changes in supply. An increase in supply shifts the supply curve to the right, creating a new equilibrium price

and quantity. The intersection of S_1 (the increased supply curve) and D (the unchanged demand curve) lowers the market price to 10 cents and increases the quantity sold to 350 units. Whether we increase supply or demand, there will be an increase in quantity. It is easier to learn how to draw and interpret supply and demand curves than to memorize the relationships involved. The classical model insert, following page 44, will explain further the effect of changes in supply and demand.

A decrease in supply is shown in Figure 2–8 by S_2. What influence can a new, more efficient machine have on the market? It can be seen how successful research helps the producer and the consumer.

Figure 2–9 illustrates the effect of equal increases in supply and demand. The

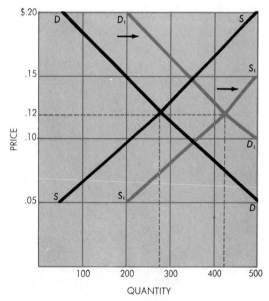

Figure 2–9 Change in Supply and Demand and the Effects on Price and Quantity

An increase in supply and demand will result in an increase in the quantity exchanged. The equilibrium price will change when the changes in supply and demand are not equal.

equal shifting of both curves to the right results in an increase in the number of units sold at the marketplace, but there is no change in price. If demand increases more than supply, both quantity and price will increase. Is the illustration in Figure 2–9 more likely to be characteristic of a short time period or a long time period? Why?

Resource allocation and the classical model

We are now in a better position to see how the classical model provides an answer to the allocation of our limited resources to meet our unlimited wants. In Chapter 1, Figure 1–1, we showed a simplified model of how our economic system is supposed to operate. In Figure 2–10 we have added to the original model the forces of supply and demand in our market for goods and services and our market for the factors of production. How are resources allocated by this system? How are prices determined?

If we turn once again to our satellite, we now can see that the measurements made by the computer are measurements of demand—by consumers in the marketplace for goods and services and by businesses in the marketplace for the factors of production. After figuring out demand, the computer relays the amount of dollars that would be enough to induce businesses to offer sufficient supply in the marketplace to satisfy the wants of consumers. It also tries to bring enough factors of production into the marketplace to supply the ingredients necessary for production.

In Figure 2–10 we can see how the consumers and businesses with dollars go to their respective markets representing demand. When households represent factors of production and businesses have goods to offer, they both represent supply in their respective markets. The amount of money offered—prices in the market for goods and services and payments for rent,

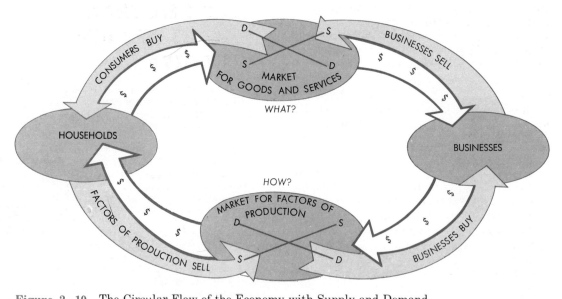

Figure 2–10 The Circular Flow of the Economy with Supply and Demand

The classical model's answer to resource allocation is the market mechanism. Through the interaction of supply and demand, price determines the answers to our basic questions *What?* and *How?*

PRICES OF COPPER NEAR RECORD LEVEL

NEW YORK — The recent jump in copper prices is attributed to the Kennecott strike, which cut about a third of the nation's output. Strikes in the Rhodesian Copper Belt and in Chile have reduced output sharply. Fears that the civil war in the Congo may affect the Katanga mines have also influenced the world market price for copper.

According to the Bureau of Mines, United States copper mines yielded three percent less copper than last year, while consumption rose one percent for the same period.

Prices are a reflection of the interaction of supply and demand.

wages, and interest for the factors of production—is the key to the allocation of our resources. Because it is the interaction of supply and demand in a purely competitive market that determines price, we can now see the importance of studying those forces.

Conditions necessary for making the classical model work

If the classical model is to work as its creators intended, certain conditions must be met and certain assumptions must be made. If they are not, modifications in the model may be needed. What conditions and assumptions are necessary?

1. Man is primarily an economic being with an incentive to make money in order to satisfy his wants. He will take the highest paying job he can get, go into the most profitable business, sell what the public wants most and, at least in the long run, sell at the highest price that will give him the greatest profit. He will buy products at the lowest price without showing favoritism to any seller.

2. The factors of production, including labor, are mobile and can be readily moved to the place which will offer the highest return. As consumers' wants change, the allocation of resources must shift to meet these new needs.

3. Both the market for goods and services and the market for the factors of production are free from control whether by government, by buyers, or by sellers. Nothing must interfere with the freedom of consumers and the factors of production. Business, too, must be free to enter or leave the market and to act independently in the market.

4. Knowledge must be available to consumers so that they may determine what products can best serve their needs and can thus make wise decisions.

5. Society will achieve its maximum happiness by allowing individuals to make most of the decisions on what to produce and how to produce it. This system contrasts with one in which society, acting

GLASS FIBER FABRIC FIRMS CHARGED WITH PRICE-FIXING

NEW YORK — The Justice Department filed criminal and civil antitrust suits against six textile companies for fixing prices of industrial glass fiber fabrics.

The action was taken on the grounds of violation of the Sherman Act. The Justice Department maintained that the defendants, as well as their alleged conspirators, acted "to restrain, suppress, avoid and eliminate price competition in the sale of glass fiber industrial fabrics." The report says that secret meetings were held on one or more occasions at various hotels and restaurants in New York and that the defendants used a secret code or veiled terminology, in writing or orally, to camouflage price-fixing agreements.

The government tries to maintain competition.

collectively through government, makes the decisions about production.

While the five conditions stated above do not exist in our environment in pure form, they are present to a far greater degree than in most other nations. Many people in our society think, talk, believe, and behave as if the classical model does exist in pure, or nearly pure, form. As a result the classical model influences much of our behavior as consumers, as owners of the factors of production, and as citizens trying to influence economic policy. We often refer to incentives for producing, such as commissions to salesmen, bonuses for managers, and higher pay for extra hours of work.

We have antitrust laws to keep the market competitive. Both state and national governments make information easily available to the consumer so that he can be a more effective buyer. Not only do most Americans resent the government's going into business, but loud complaints are heard when the government's budget is increased, since such action often results in individuals having fewer free choices.

The classical model, with its emphasis on a free market, cannot be dismissed merely because some controls have been instituted. Some of these controls, such as antitrust action, have helped to keep the market free. The classical model is a major factor in determining our country's answers to the big economic questions, although modifications of it and substitutions from other models have added flexibility to our economic system.

Part E   The Problem: To What Degree Should Man Follow His Economic Self-interest?

At the end of most chapters we will present a problem involving the materials covered in the chapter. The points of view given will be those held by many people, but they must not be interpreted as being the sole truth or as necessarily being the right answers. There are in economics many controversial questions about which even the "experts" disagree. Using the information and the "tools" learned in the chapter and the positions stated in the problem, see if you can arrive at a conclusion which you consider best for you and the society in which you live. Let your conclusions be tentative ones, since additional information, other "tools," and different points of view will be introduced in later chapters and may cause you to change your mind.

Turning now to the problem, we may ask to what extent man should follow his economic self-interest. An observer trying to analyze the American society's system of values would encounter difficulty. He would soon find numerous examples which would be hard to explain. While we extol the virtues of individualism and independence and admire the "self-made man," we also give praise for cooperation and teamwork and show compassion for the less fortunate. Advertising frequently tries to persuade consumers to buy high-priced goods in order to show their success, and one famous economist pointed out that "keeping up with the Joneses" is part of the American way of life. At the same time we are told from the pulpit that we are too obsessed with materialism and that character is the true measure of a man.

The classical model depends on man's desire to acquire goods and services as an incentive. Is this materialistic motivation necessary? Does this kind of behavior represent only man's selfish, acquisitive motives, disregarding his altruistic and other non-material values?

The classical model defended

The classical model works as intended when man pursues his own economic gain. As a producer, man is keenly aware of the effect of the satellite and the number of dollars it assigns to the various jobs on the market for the factors of production. The jobs in which demand is greatest and supply the least will offer him the biggest dollar rewards. Thus, as he follows his own self-interest he is also helping to fulfill the wants of consumers.

As a consumer man also seeks his economic welfare. He tries to get the largest number of products that will satisfy his wants best and at the lowest prices. In this way his limited resources will provide him with the most want-satisfaction. When emotions and ideals that are inconsistent with the classical model are allowed to exert undue influence on man's behavior, the entire society suffers. The things men want most, as they express their wants at the market, will not be available in the kind and quantity they wish.

Every society must provide its workers and businessmen with an incentive to produce efficiently. What serves this purpose better than offering money as a reward? Money can be converted into whatever want-satisfactions the possessors wish. Acquisition of power, contributions to charities, and purchase of the things we want are all made possible by money. Workers will put forth greater effort when overtime pay is the reward. Profit spurs businessmen to produce better goods more efficiently. Everyone benefits, except those who are lazy, because society has more of the things it wants.

The classical model under attack

Many people believe that man is more than an economic animal—that he does not live by bread alone. His behavior is influenced by many things, including the fact that he is a member of society. The values that he holds cannot always be measured by a price tag. Man's primary aim in life is to seek happiness. He can do this in many ways, but few would accept mere material satisfaction as the sole, or even the primary, means. Man has a need to create, to serve, to show fellowship and compassion, to gain recognition for achievement in ways apart from financial gain.

When we consider man as a producer, we must, as the classical economist would insist, recognize incentive as a means of insuring that the things society needs will be produced. However, money need not be the only incentive. The artist or writer does not usually express himself primarily for the sake of the money he will make. Clergymen, doctors, lawyers, teachers, and social workers frequently enter their professions because they have purposes and ideals above and beyond merely earning dollars. Do the athletes on your school teams try less hard than the professionals because they are not paid for their efforts? There are many situations in society in which money is only a secondary consideration.

Does man, acting as a consumer, consider price and quality alone? An examination of shopping habits reveals conflicting evidence. Studies by consumer organizations have shown that consumers frequently fail to look at prices—that they buy at a particular place or buy a particular brand out of habit or because of location, service, or friendship. Other studies show that advertising appeals to many emotions, not all of them of an economic nature.

If we are to achieve a better society, we must curb our material considerations and encourage man to produce and achieve for human betterment. This cannot be done if man seeks only financial rewards.

Considering an answer

What disagreements do you have with the two positions just stated? Are they different because of the facts or the values presented? Can you think of a third or fourth position? Does the favoring of one position mean that the other position is entirely wrong?

In what way does this problem relate to supply and demand? How does it relate to the questions *What? How?* and *For Whom?* How is this problem important to you?

The positions given here represent only one part of the conflict between those who believe in following the classical model closely, those who believe we should modify it, and those who want a new model. They show that economics has unresolved problems which frequently reflect conflicting values.

As you proceed with your study of economics, you will acquire additional information and learn about other tools for analyzing problems. You will also become acquainted with issues related to these problems. It will be interesting to see whether you change your conclusions about some of the problems as you consider them and other related questions.

REVIEW: *the highlights of the chapter*

1. Price measures values in money. Goods and services have economic value when they satisfy want (utility) and are relatively scarce. Price plays a very important part in determining the allocation of our resources.

2. A market is a place where buyers and sellers meet. There are markets for goods and services, and markets for the factors of production. Markets can be classified as having pure competition, pure monopoly, monopolistic competition, and oligopoly. The number of buyers and sellers and their ability to influence price distinguish the type of market. Most markets fall somewhere between pure competition and pure monopoly. The classical model assumes pure competition. All competition that is not pure is called imperfect competition.

3. Demand is the willingness on the part of consumers to buy certain amounts of a product at certain prices in a given market. The general rule for demand is that the lower the price of a given product, the more of it consumers will buy. This rule is explained by the law of diminishing marginal utility. The use of substitutes and the level of buyers' income also influence demand. A demand schedule lists the quantities of a product consumers will buy at various prices, and can be plotted on a graph as a demand curve. The elasticity of demand is determined by the way price changes affect quantity. Changes in demand can be brought about in a number of ways.

4. Supply is the willingness of sellers to offer certain amounts of products at certain prices in a given market. Supply schedules will differ for products available immediately, for the short run, and for the long run. The general rule for supply states that producers will offer more of their product for sale as price rises. This is because costs, which have a great influence on supply, will begin to rise beyond a certain level of production. Supply schedules can

be plotted on graphs to give supply curves. They may be elastic or inelastic and may change because of costs.

5. When we put supply and demand together we get the equilibrium price, which will clear the market of products. Changes in supply and demand will bring about changes in price and the quantity bought.

6. The classical model explains that it is the laws of supply and demand interacting at the market that determine the allocation of our resources.

7. Certain conditions must be met if the classical model is to work. They include the economic motivation of man, mobility of the factors of production, pure competition, and freedom for consumers and producers.

IN CONCLUSION: some aids to understanding

Terms for review

demand	economic value
market	exchange value
supply	incentive
utility	pure competition
price	monopolistic competition
monopoly	imperfect competition
oligopoly	equilibrium
monopsony	change in demand
elasticity	classical model
clearing the market	law of diminishing marginal
increasing costs	utility

Questions for review

1. Classical capitalism depends on the market for answers to the basic economic questions.
   (a) What is the major function of the market in the American economy?
   (b) What are the important considerations that determine the kind of competition which develops?
   (c) List and explain the various kinds of markets we have.

2. Since resources are usually limited, what are the factors which determine the allocation of these resources?

3. The terms *value, price,* and *utility* are all interdependent.
   (a) What is the basic economic meaning of each?
   (b) How are they interdependent?

4. The idea of competition is one of the keystones of the capitalist system.
   (a) What is the meaning of *competition*?

(b) What are the various kinds of competition which may develop?

(c) Why is competition essential to this system?

5. "Monopoly may be both a blessing and a curse to the producer and to the consumer." Give examples to demonstrate the validity of this statement.

6. In our economy, supply and demand are important factors in determining price.

   (a) Draw a graph which will demonstrate the result of price increase on demand and another graph to demonstrate the opposite effect.

   (b) What factors besides price will determine the shape of the demand curve?

   (c) What influences are present in our economy to determine the supply of any commodity or service?

7. Present arguments to uphold the thesis that our democratic society will achieve maximum happiness and success if it permits the individual to decide what to produce and how to produce it.

Additional questions and problems

1. Products have value for a variety of reasons. Sometimes the value of a product will change with circumstances. We identify value in prices. Account for the prices of the following: (a) roses in February, (b) ice skates in May, (c) diamonds, (d) bread, (e) a day-old newspaper.

2. In what kind of market would you place each of the following? (a) A gas and electric company, (b) an orange grower, (c) a local automobile dealer, (d) an appliance-manufacturer, (e) the Boston Symphony Orchestra.

3. Check the general rule for demand by interviewing a local merchant on the effect of a sale. What happens to demand for a product when it is no longer on sale?

4. Make a list of five products with elastic demand and five with inelastic demand. What accounts for this elasticity?

5. Over the years the demand for products changes. Ask an older person if he can identify some changes in consumer preferences. Explain why you think these changes have taken place.

6. Do men or women bring about a greater change in demand? Give reasons to support your answer.

7. Explain the relationship between cost and supply. Why does the time period influence supply?

8. What factors are most likely to bring about a change in supply?

9. Explain why, under pure competition, the market price will have to be the equilibrium price.

10. Draw supply and demand curves and consider them your original supply and demand. Then determine whether price and quantity will increase or decrease in the following situations:
   (a) Demand increases and supply remains the same
   (b) Supply increases and demand remains the same
   (c) Demand decreases and supply remains the same
   (d) Demand and supply both decrease, but demand decreases more than supply.

11. On graph paper, plot the following supply and demand schedules. Let each interval (box) represent one cent for price (start with 20) and let each interval represent 300 cans for quantity.

Demand and Supply Schedules for 6-ounce Cans of Frozen Orange Juice

Price per can	Demand	Supply
$ .32	1,000	5,500
.31	1,100	4,800
.30	1,200	4,300
.29	1,400	3,800
.28	1,600	3,200
.27	1,900	2,700
.26	2,300	2,300
.25	2,600	1,900
.24	3,000	1,700
.23	3,500	1,500
.22	4,100	1,300
.21	4,700	1,100
.20	5,500	1,000

   (a) What is the market price for 6-ounce cans of frozen orange juice?
   (b) If oranges are hurt by a frost and the supply drops 400 cans at each price level, what will be the new price?

UNIT II

The Factors Responsible for Producing Our Goods and Services

Chapter 3.
Business Enterprise

Chapter 4.
Labor: Its Uses and Rewards

Chapter 5.
Labor: Its Organization and Development

Chapter 6.
Natural Resources, Capital,
and Management:
Their Uses and Rewards

Chapter 7.
Government and Its Developing
Role in the Economy

Chapter 8.
Government and Public Finance

Chapter 9.
The Consumer and His Role in
the American Economy

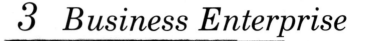

3 Business Enterprise

Preview

The focus of Unit II is on *microeconomics*, the study of individual units of the economy. Unit III, in turn, will deal with *macroeconomics*, the study of the nation's economy as a whole. Actually, our study of microeconomics began in Chapter 2 with an analysis of how demand and supply determine price. It continues in this unit with a consideration of the factors in the economy that are responsible for production.

In a *private enterprise* economy the decisions on what and how to produce are determined mainly by businessmen. Businessmen ascertain the probable trend of consumer wants and then proceed to organize the factors of production in order to satisfy these wants. Their motivation is profit; and if their decisions on the *What* and the *How* are correct, they will probably do well.

American businesses vary in size, organization, and product according to the many diverse needs of the consumer. Businesses are organized as single proprietorships, partnerships, or corporations, each having certain advantages and limitations. The Industrial Revolution, with its change in the methods of production, gave an impetus to the modern corporation. It also led to business combinations that changed the pattern of competition away from the classical model. Government has responded to this change by trying to keep competition as close to the original model as possible. Where competition has been impractical, the consumer has been protected by government regulation of business.

Overview

What do the giant corporations and the neighborhood grocery store have in common? What differences exist between them?

What is the importance of large corporations to our nation's modern industrial economy?

In what ways are stocks and bonds important to business?

40

Part A   Characteristics of Business Enterprise

Production in the United States

The primary concern that we, as individuals, have with economics lies in deciding how well we can afford to live. If we are to achieve a high *standard of living*, it is necessary that the production of goods and services be maintained at a high level. In 1966 the market value of all the production in the United States, called the *gross national product* (GNP), is expected to be about $725 billion. This is equal to almost one third of the value of all the world's production. This achievement is even more remarkable when you consider that it was actually carried out by only one sixteenth of the world's population. Most of this production came from America's businesses.

The role of business

You will recall from the preceding chapters that the classical model calls for businessmen to go to the market for goods and services to find out what consumers want and then, spurred on by the profit motive, go to the market for the factors of production in order to produce the goods. About three fourths of the value of the total GNP resulted from the decisions made by private enterprise. Although the decisions on the remainder of our production were determined by governments at the local, state, and national levels, most of this production came from business enterprise. Our schools, our weapons of defense, and most of the purchased items in government budgets were produced by business. Throughout our history we have remained fairly consistent in favoring private enterprise over government enterprise regarding the *What* and the *How* of production.

VARIETY OF BUSINESS ENTERPRISES

With almost five million separate businesses in our country their size and

Table 3–1 Business Population

(in thousands of concerns)

ITEM	1929	1933	1941	1943	1946	1949	1953	1960	1962	1963
Total Operating Businesses[1]	3,029	2,782	3,276	3,030	3,242	3,984	4,188	4,658	4,755	4,797
Manufacturing	257	167	230	243	264	322	331	323	317	313
Wholesale Trade	148	142	190	182	209	260	283	317	327	332
Retail Trade	1,327	1,291	1,561	1,401	1,458	1,783	1,846	1,997	2,022	2,032
Service Industries	591	575	615	579	614	739	750	872	918	942
Contract Construction	234	185	194	164	199	339	405	476	473	470
All Other[5]	472	422	486	461	498	541	573	674	698	708
New Entrants[2]	([3])	([3])	290	146	617	331	352	438	430	([3])
Discontinued Businesses[2]	([3])	([3])	271	337	209	306	299	384	387	([3])
Commercial and Industrial Failures[4]	22.9	19.9	11.8	3.2	1.1	9.2	8.9	15.4	15.8	14.4

[1]1929–33, annual average; 1941–60, as of Jan. 1. [2]Annual total. [3]Not available. [4]Closures resulting in a known loss to creditors. [5]Includes transportation, communications, public utilities, finance, insurance, real estate and mining and quarrying.

The information given in this table applies only to certain kinds of businesses. The total number of business organizations is much larger. In 1962, according to the information then available, it included 9,183,000 sole proprietorships, 932,000 active partnerships, and 1,268,000 active corporations. SOURCES: U.S. Department of Commerce; U.S. Treasury Department, Internal Revenue Service, *Statistics of Income*, 1962, *U.S. Business Tax Returns*

organization vary greatly. The man who sells popcorn, ice cream, and hot dogs from his cart is in business, although his total sales may amount to only a few thousand dollars a year. In contrast, we have giant corporations that do more business than the value of all goods and services produced in many countries. In 1965 General Motors sold more goods and services—almost $21 billion worth—than the total combined production of Greece, Ireland, Norway, and Portugal.

Both the street vendor and General Motors are producing what they think their customers want. They are both in business to make as large a profit as they can; they both must take risks, invest money, and organize the factors of production. While they have much in common, they are organized quite differently. In order to get a better understanding of business and the part that the form of organization of a business plays, we will take a hypothetical venture into business ourselves.

Starting a business

Our chief purpose in going into business is to make a profit. This can be done by supplying to consumers something they want but do not have, or something that is better than what they now have. If there are mice but no mousetraps, build a trap. If there is a mousetrap, build a better one or build a cheaper one.

WHAT TO PRODUCE

First we shall call a meeting to discuss the *What*. After listening to many suggestions, all of which prove unsatisfactory for one reason or another, we finally hit upon the idea of a wooden construction set for a model city. The demand for construction games, according to the latest toy trade journals, appears on the increase. In the past, plastics and steel have been used, but wood is more versatile. It can be painted easily; also, we have ready access to it. A model city, in contrast to a model house, is novel. Let's give it a try! After organizing

ourselves into a business firm, sometimes called an enterprise, we adopt the name "Build-a-City." As the organizers of the business we are known as entrepreneurs or, more simply, managers.

HOW TO PRODUCE

We are now ready to consider means of producing—the *How* of business enterprise. Our responsibility is to collect the other factors of production and assemble them in the right amount, at the right time, and in the right place.

The major natural resource we need is lumber. There is a mill nearby, but it is presently selling all the lumber it produces. If we are to divert the wood from its present use to our business, we must offer a slightly higher price than the present market price. We have increased the demand, but the supply of materials on hand remains the same.

In the labor market we may attract workers by offering them jobs that will pay at least as much as, if not more than, they are currently earning. However, if there is unemployment in the area—if the supply of workers is greater than the demand—labor costs may be low, and we may hire workers at the going market rate.

We will also need machinery and a factory. Usually, the more and better the machinery available to workers, the more they can produce. Because machinery is not used to satisfy the consumer's needs but rather to make the goods that the consumer wants, it is called a *capital good* or a *producer good*. Goods used directly by the consumer to satisfy his needs are called *consumer goods*.

To buy machinery and a building we obviously need money. Money, when it is used by business to buy the things needed in production, is called capital. When people ask us, "How much capital do you have?" they are not referring to the actual number of machines. They mean how much money we have for man-made instruments of production, i.e., machines, buildings, and goods made by others that are necessary for production.

RAISING CAPITAL

At a meeting to discuss the cost of equipment we soon discover that we do not have enough capital. The decision is made to go to a commercial bank to see if the officials there will lend us the amount of money we need. A major function of commercial banks is to provide short-term capital to businesses. If we obtain a loan, we will have to pay a price for its use, *interest*. Interest is expressed as a rate in percentage. If we borrow one hundred thousand dollars at six percent interest for one year,

it means that we pay six thousand dollars for the money we borrow. Although interest is paid for the money borrowed, in the long run it is for the equipment and other things needed for our business.

Money is used in many other ways in the marketplace. The money we pay for the wood from the forest (natural resources) is called *rent*, and the money we pay our workers is called *wages*. We, the entrepreneurs, receive the money that is left, the *profits*. Payments to each of the factors of production are subject, at least in part, to supply and demand. Each of these factors of production will be discussed more fully in succeeding chapters.

Part B   Forms of Business Organization

Although we have proceeded with the initial steps in starting a business, we have neglected to answer one of the first and most important questions facing any businessman. What kind of business organization shall we choose? There are three forms of organization from which to select: a *single proprietorship*, a *partnership*, and a *corporation*. Since each form has particular advantages and disadvantages, our choice can best be made after an examination of each form.

Single proprietorship

To illustrate the various forms of organization possible, let us suppose that you alone are the one who thought of the idea of producing "Build-a-City" sets and want to start a company by yourself. Such a business is classified as a single proprietorship, the most common type of business and the easiest to organize. Over 80 percent of all firms use this form. You, as owner, are the boss, and need not consult with others in making your business decisions. You cannot be fired. If you fail, it will be your own fault. On the other hand, if there is a profit you will receive it all—a great incentive. Another advantage is that you do not have to pay a corporation income tax.

At first you may be happy to be the sole owner of a business. However, you soon recognize that there are serious drawbacks to such an organization. If your business is

Business represents many different kinds of enterprise.

Table 3−2 Comparison of Forms of Business Organization

	SINGLE PROPRIETORSHIP	PARTNERSHIP	CORPORATION
Ease of organization	Easiest	Moderately difficult	Most difficult
Capital generally available for operation	Least	Intermediate	Most (best able to raise capital)
Responsibility	Centered in one person	Spread among partners	Policy set by directors; president supervises day-to-day operation
Incentive to succeed	Centered in one person	Spread among partners	Spread among many people
Flexibility	Greatest	Intermediate	Least
Ability to perform varied functions (production or purchasing, accounting, selling, etc.)	Dependent on one individual's versatility	Dependent on capabilities of two or more individuals	Best able to employ individuals with different capabilities
Possibility of conflict among those in control	None	Most prone to conflict, especially if partners have equal interest in business	Chain of command reduces internal conflict; wide ownership minimizes disagreement
Taxation	No corporate income tax	No corporate income tax	Corporate income tax
Distribution of profits or losses	All to proprietor	Distributed to partners in accordance with terms of partnership agreement	Profits retained or to stockholders as dividends; losses reduce price of stock
Liability for debts in event of failure	Unlimited	Unlimited, but spread among partners	Limited to each stockholder's investment
Length of life	Limited by one individual's life span (or until he goes out of business)	Limited (partnership is reorganized upon death or withdrawal of any partner)	Unlimited (with ownership of shares readily transferable)

After studying this table, discuss which form of organization would be best for our "Build-a-City" company. Remember that there is no single right answer. Depending on the circumstances, however, some answers will be better than others. Be sure that you consider all possibilities before you make your decision.

like many single proprietorships, you are likely to be bothered by a shortage of cash. This shortage may not be caused by incompetence or carelessness. Deficits are most likely to occur when you attempt to meet the constant expenditures of the business. If business had been bad, this would be easy to understand. Actually, business has been almost too good. You have had so many requests for "Build-a-City" sets that in order to meet this demand, you have had to employ more of the factors of production. In addition, your financial situation has been hurt because the merchants buying your sets have been slow in paying their bills. You might solve your problem by en-

SUPPLY AND DEMAND:
THE CLASSICAL MODEL'S ANSWER TO THE ALLOCATION OF RESOURCES

This is an exercise in the functioning of the price system: the classical model's answer to the question of allocating our limited resources. Its purpose is to review how, in a free market, the forces of supply and demand determine price and the distribution of our resources. We are going to review these concepts graphically.

Consumers make their wants known by showing a willingness and an ability to purchase certain quantities of a product at different prices. This is known as demand, and it can be shown graphically. Business offers for sale certain quantities of a product at different prices. This is known as supply, and it can also be shown graphically.

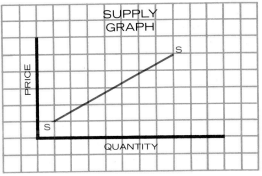

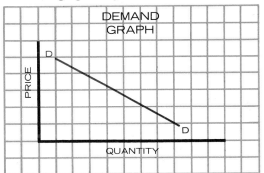

Consumers and businesses meet at the market, where the demand for goods interacts with the supply of goods. The intersection of demand and supply is the *equilibrium price*. This will clear the market. Any price higher than this will leave a surplus of goods. Any price below this point will leave consumers wanting more. Note that the intersection of demand and supply shows (1) price and (2) quantity exchanged. If we change the price we will vary the quantity exchanged, altering our resource allocation.

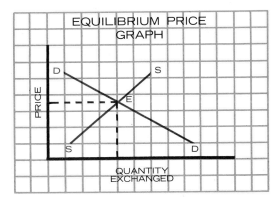

A change in demand is an increase or a decrease in the number of units that will be sold throughout the range of prices offered. It can be caused by (1) a change in consumers' income, (2) a change in taste, and (3) a change in the market for substitutes.

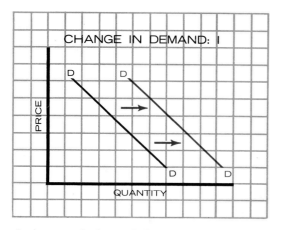

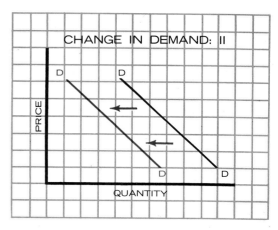

An increase in demand shifts the demand curve to the right.

A decrease in demand shifts the demand curve to the left.

A change in supply is an increase or a decrease in the number of units offered throughout the range of prices. Changes in supply are caused by (1) changes in cost, (2) expectations of profit, and (3) changes in the demand for other goods.

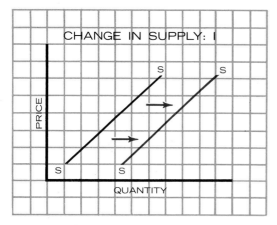

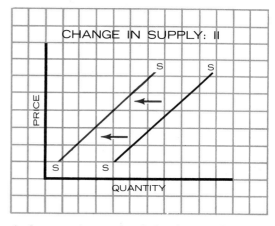

An increase in supply shifts the supply curve to the right.

A decrease in supply shifts the supply curve to the left.

Some products are very responsive to price changes. A small change in price will bring about a major change in the quantity that is bought or offered for sale. Such products are said to have an *elastic demand* or an *elastic supply*. Shown graphically, the curves are more horizontal than vertical.

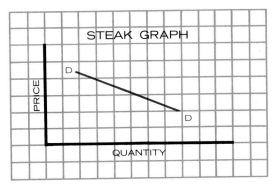

The demand for sirloin steak is highly elastic because substitutes can easily be found, it is not a necessity, and it may represent a large share of the food budget.

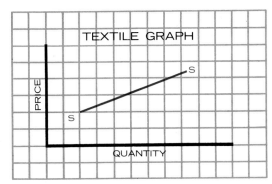

The supply of textiles is highly elastic because it is easy to increase production in a short time.

Products that respond very little to price changes are said to have an *inelastic demand* or an *inelastic supply*. Shown graphically, the curves are more vertical than horizontal.

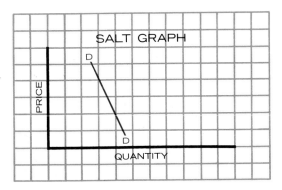

The demand for salt is highly inelastic because it represents a small share of the food budget and substitution is difficult.

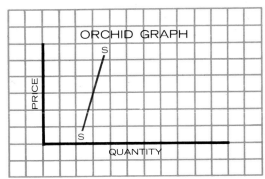

The supply of orchids is highly inelastic because of the time and difficulty involved in cultivating new plants.

Before proceeding with our case studies, a word of caution is necessary. The models that are shown above and on the transparent overlays are not accurate pictures of the real world. They are simplified in order to help you understand better how elasticity and changes in demand and supply affect distribution and price.

Few products have supply and demand schedules that fit neatly into linear patterns. Most products have schedules that are graphically expressed by curves with changing slopes, particularly at the upper and lower price ranges. This simplification does not distort the basic ideas of the functioning of the price system.

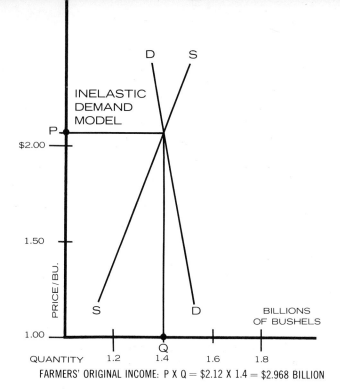

INELASTIC
DEMAND
MODEL

FARMERS' ORIGINAL INCOME: P X Q = $2.12 X 1.4 = $2.968 BILLION

On these pages are two case studies from "the world that is," showing graphically the importance of changes in supply and demand and of the elasticity of demand. Complete Case I on the overlay before starting Case II.

CASE I: Agriculture

The demand (D) for most agricultural products tends to be highly inelastic. Thus a change in price will make little difference in the quantity consumers buy. The point where supply (S) and demand (D) intersect is the equilibrium price (P), at which the market will be cleared (Q).

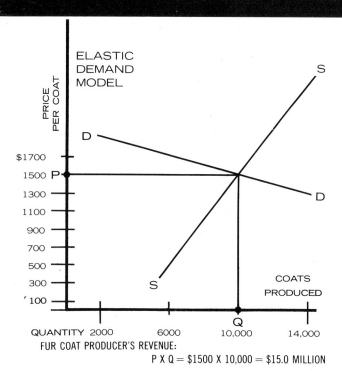

ELASTIC
DEMAND
MODEL

FUR COAT PRODUCER'S REVENUE:
P X Q = $1500 X 10,000 = $15.0 MILLION

CASE II: Excise tax on fur coats

The demand for many kinds of fur coats is highly elastic. A small change in price will bring about a major change in the quantity bought. The equilibrium price is P and the quantity exchanged is Q.

larging your factory, buying a few more machines, and hiring additional men. This would allow you to increase the size of your business sufficiently to meet the demand. If only you had more capital!

As you consider enlarging your business, you may become aware of another disadvantage of the single proprietorship. It is nice to be your own boss, but it also means that all the responsibility is on your shoulders. You never seem to have any free time and are required to be a specialist in such diverse activities as buying, producing, and merchandising. You may hire a managerial assistant to help share your responsibilities, but his interest in the business is not as personal as if he were an owner. Two additional disadvantages, unlimited liability and limited life, which apply to both proprietorships and partnerships, will be considered in connection with partnerships. It occurs to you that, although a partnership also has disadvantages, perhaps it would be a better form of organization for your purposes.

Partnership

What your business needs, if it is to expand more quickly, is additional capital and perhaps additional talent. As the present owner, you might interest several people in investing their money in your business and becoming partners. A partnership might also relieve you of some of the responsibilities, and the skills of several others might be pooled to help the business develop. Like a single proprietorship, a partnership does not have to pay a corporate income tax. This is a tax which is paid to the national government on the profits of the corporation. It is in addition to the tax you pay on the income you draw from the company.

Along with their advantages, partnerships have problems. Although partners will share the profits according to a prearranged plan, you are not sure that each partner will devote his fair share of time and effort to the business. Partners do not always agree on methods and policies to be used in operating a business.

Once the decision to form a partnership is made, a competent attorney will draw up the articles of partnership. This is a necessary legal document, a *contract,* which will specify the rights and duties of all partners. With all the effort you have put into the business, you do not want to leave anything to chance.

About nine percent of all firms in our country are partnerships. Of these, small businesses account for the largest number. Other than some professional firms — such as law, investment, accounting, and medical partnerships — the million- and multimillion-dollar firms stay away from both the proprietorship and the partnership.

There are two other serious drawbacks, mentioned under proprietorships, which you must consider. Both single proprietorships and partnerships are subject to *unlimited liability* and to *limited life.* Unlimited liability would become important to you if your business were deteriorating and you found that you owed a great deal more money to your creditors than your debtors owed to you. If you thought that you could not reverse the downward trend of your business and if your creditors threatened legal action, you would probably want to dissolve your business. Unlimited liability makes this difficult. Not only are the *assets* (those things that have market value) of your business subject to loss, but your personal property could also be taken to pay your debts. In the case of a partnership each partner would be subject to this same kind of liability. Instead of your business becoming a means of supporting you, it could become a hazard capable of wiping out all your savings.

"Limited life" refers to the fact that the business will end if one of the partners leaves the company. In such an event a new partnership agreement must be drawn up. The same would apply if one partner died or if the owner of a single proprietorship died. The business and the owners are co-existent.

The corporation

A third type of business organization is the corporation. It is usually more difficult to organize than the other two forms. First you must go to a lawyer, who draws up the necessary papers asking the state for the powers you will need to establish your business. He submits these papers to the state government, which will grant you a charter. The charter gives you the right to do business; it also makes that business separate from you before the law. Separating you from the business is an important advantage. It means that your business now has *limited liability:* you and other stockholders can lose only the money you have put into the business, and not your personal possessions. Let us suppose that a purchaser of your product injured himself because of a defective part in the "Build-a-City" set that he bought. If he decided to sue for the damages he sustained, he would not sue you or any stockholders as persons. Instead, he would file his suit against the corporation.

Unlike the single proprietorship and partnership, the corporation has *perpetual life.* No matter how many of its stockholders die, the corporation will continue to exist. Such continuity is of particular value to businesses with heavy fixed costs and capital investment.

Probably the greatest advantage of a corporate form of business organization is its great ability to raise capital. After the

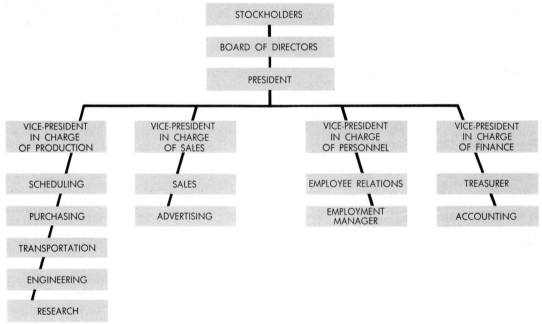

Figure 3–1 The Structure of a Typical Corporation

In the typical corporation the stockholders elect the board of directors. The board of directors sets general policy, makes decisions on declaring dividends, and elects the officers. The officers carry out day-to-day operations and administer policy.

The New York Stock Exchange is one of the busiest markets in the world.

corporation is chartered, a primary consideration will be to determine approximately how much money your business needs and how much it is currently worth. Let us assume that you evaluate your present business at $150,000. You would like an additional $350,000 to expand your facilities and have some money to take care of your operating expenses in the transitional stage of your business. To raise this additional money you issue 50,000 shares of stock. You retain 15,000 shares and attempt to sell the remaining 35,000. A share of stock represents ownership. In your particular case each share of stock will represent one fifty-thousandth ownership of the proposed corporation. If each share of stock is sold for $10 a share, the proposed corporation would now be worth $500,000. You would have the $150,000 business in addition to the $350,000 in cash for the sale of your stock for expansion and operation.

SELLING STOCK

How can you sell your stock? Many people will think immediately of the New York Stock Exchange as the best place. You may already be somewhat familiar with this famous stock exchange and the millions of shares of stock traded there every business day. After checking, you would soon find that only very large, long-established companies worth many millions of dollars can be listed on the New York Stock Exchange, or even on the smaller exchanges located throughout the country. A second possibility is to try to sell the stock yourself. Initially the idea might sound appealing as you think of a few people who might be able to buy stock. However, $350,000 is a great deal of money, and you soon realize that you have neither the time nor the ability to raise the money through personal sales of stock. When you talk this problem over with a business acquaintance, he tells you about an investment banker. As he explains the procedure, it sounds as if this third possibility might be your answer.

THE INVESTMENT BANKER

An investment banker is in the business of selling securities. Although many people who have savings put their money in a savings account in order to receive interest, others are not satisfied with the interest that a bank pays them. They think that their money will bring a greater return if it is invested in some business. They may not want to organize a business themselves, but they might be willing to take a chance on a business that is already operating. They may buy *bonds* or *stock*.

If people buy shares of stock in a business, they become owners and share in the returns; however, they do not have to worry about day-to-day management. They may buy shares in a big corporation through a stock exchange, or they might go to investment bankers or stockbrokers to see what stock is available there. There is a bigger risk involved when one buys stock in a small company like ours as compared to investing in a large, well-established firm. Yet, there is also the chance of a big return on the money invested in a new organization. Many businesses that depend upon making money with money will frequently go to investment banks and buy stock in a growing company.

You decide to go to an *investment bank* and discuss the prospect of its selling your stock. The investment bank is responsible for examining your business and deciding whether it has a reasonably good chance for future development. If the investment banker thinks it has a chance to grow, he will agree to try to sell the stock.

Let us assume that the investment bank

READING STOCK MARKET REPORTS

Most city newspapers publish daily stock market reports providing their readers with information on what is happening to the stock of major corporations of the United States. The accompanying illustration is an example of a report of a few New York Stock Exchange transactions. Let us see if we can learn to "read" the stock market report.

The stocks of corporations are listed alphabetically by the names of the corporations so as to make it easy to locate the name of the stock you are looking for. Find "Acme Markets" on the list. At the extreme left of the name is the number 73½ and next to it 64. At the top of the columns of figures you will find the labels "High" and "Low" bracketed by "1965." This means that the highest price paid for a share of Acme Markets stock thus far in 1965 was $73.50 (not including the broker's commission and taxes). The lowest price paid was $64.

Just to the right of Acme Markets you find "2b." The title of this column is labeled "Stock and div in $." Stock merely means the name of the corporation. The "div in $" is an abbreviation for "dividends in dollars." The 2 means that Acme pays $2 a share as its annual rate. The *b* that follows the 2 means that you must turn to the footnote explanation, usually at the bottom of the page. The footnote reads, "Annual rate plus stock dividend," meaning that a stock dividend was paid in addition to the $2. The next column is labeled "Sales in 100s." There were 1,100 shares of Acme traded on the New York Stock Exchange for the day. "Open" (sometimes called "First") refers to the price paid for Acme when the market opened, $67.87½. The price of a stock listed on the New York Stock Exchange moves in eighths of a point, a point being one dollar. This is followed by the highest price for the day ($67.87½), the lowest price ($67.37½), and the closing (sometimes called "Last"), $67.75. The last column, net change, is the difference between the closing price of the previous day's trading and the closing price of the day's trading being reported, in this case −¼. Thus, the price of Acme Markets has gone down $.25 a share.

is willing. You inform its representative that you want to get $10 a share. The bank will then try to sell your stock for as much as possible. If the stock sells for $11.00 a share, the bank keeps the $1.00 and you receive $10.

What happens if the bank cannot sell the 35,000 shares you have offered for sale? In this case you would get back the unsold shares and have to work with the capital you raised, or try to borrow the rest. Large, well-established businesses may make an arrangement with the investment bank to have it *underwrite* the stock. This means that if the investment bank cannot sell all the stock, the business would still get the agreed amount. Naturally, this is a better arrangement, but there is no way to force the bank to make such an agreement.

TRANSFERRING OWNERSHIP

People can buy or sell their ownership in the corporation quite easily. They do so by putting their stock up for sale. Suppose you decided on the corporate form for your business and it has expanded just as you

have planned. The value of your business has doubled, so that it is now approximately one million dollars. Since there are still 50,000 shares, each share should be worth about double its original price. Some of the owners may think that their stock will not increase further in value and will want to sell it. There are others who admire the rapid expansion and would like to "buy in." The bigger corporations handle this exchange by having the sale of their stocks take place in the stock market.

In this case, however, the owners of "Build-a-City" stock wishing to sell would either try to arrange the sale themselves or have a brokerage house do this. A *stock-broker* is in the business of buying and selling shares of stock for others. Our stock would be an *over-the-counter* sale because it is not listed on a stock exchange. The broker differs from the investment banker in that he sells stock that is already owned, rather than new issues. Some indirect safeguards to buyers of stock, or securities, are provided by regulation through the Securities and Exchange Commission, an agency of the federal government.

PERPETUAL LIFE

If the owner of stock in a corporation dies, the stock he owns passes on to his heirs. Unlike the proprietorship or partnership, the corporation continues as if nothing had happened. This characteristic of a corporation, known as perpetual life, is possible because a corporation is considered a person in the eyes of the law. It can sue and be sued without the owners' becoming involved beyond the possible fluctuation of the value of their stock. However, the officers of the corporation, who might also be owners, may be held responsible for certain acts of the corporation specified by law. To the owner of shares of stock in the corporation, limited liability provides an important safeguard; his personal responsibility and financial liability are limited to the value of the stock that he owns.

1965 High	Low	Stock and div in $	Sales in 100s	Open	High	Low	Close	Net chg
45	41½	Abacus 1.52f	2	42½	42½	42¼	42½	-⅜
50	44½	Abbott L .90	40	44¾	44⅜	44¼	44⅜	......
23⅝	17½	ABC Con .70	65	19	19⅜	18⅜	19⅜	+½
93	77⅞	ACF Ind 3a	40	79⅜	81½	79	81½	+1
73½	64	Acme Mkt 2b	11	67⅝	67⅝	67¼	67⅝	-⅛
28½	26½	AdamE 2.05g	12	26½	27	26½	27	+⅜
18½	12¾	Ad Millis .40a	30	13	13½	13	13½	+¾
55⅝	44½	Address 1.40	93	44½	45¼	44	45½	-⅛
33½	15⅞	Admiral	280	26½	27⅝	25⅞	27½	+1½
33½	27⅞	Aeroquip .70	15	28	28½	27½	28⅛	+⅝
63⅝	51¼	Air Prod .20b	44	57½	57½	56¼	57½	+⅝
66½	53⅞	Air Red 2.50	93	56½	58⅛	56⅛	58⅜	+⅜
3½	2⅞	AJ Industries	16	2½	2⅞	2½	2½	......
39⅜	35	Ala Gas 1.70	3	35½	35½	35½	35½	......
25¼	24¼	AlbertoCu .28	78	24	24	22⅝	23½	-⅞
12	9½	Alleg Cp .20e	29	9⅜	9½	9⅜	9½	......
40½	31¼	Alleg 6pf .60	5	31½	32	31½	32	+¼
47¼	39⅜	Alleg Lud 2	23	42	42	41¼	41⅜	-⅜
31	26½	Alleg Pw 1.06	13	28	28	27⅞	28	-½
31½	27½	Allenln 1.40a	7	29⅜	29⅜	29½	29⅜	-½
58¼	47½	Allied C 1.90b	188	47⅜	48¼	47⅜	48	+⅜
20½	14¾	AlliedKid .85	8	17½	17½	17¼	17½	-⅜
45½	39	Allied Mills 2	13	40	40½	39½	40½	......
30½	10⅛	Allied Pd .40	85	23½	24⅜	22½	24⅜	+⅞
89½	68⅜	Allied Strs 3	x38	77½	77⅜	75⅞	77⅜	-¼
94½	90½	Allied St pf4	z40	90⅜	90⅜	90⅜	90⅜	......
17	14½	AlliedSup .60	84	14	14⅜	13¾	14	-⅛
26½	19½	AllisChal .50	104	20½	21⅛	20½	21⅛	+½
15⅜	12½	AlphaPC .50	17	12½	12½	12½	12½	-¼
13½	9⅜	Alside Inc	17	10	10¼	9⅞	10¼	+⅜
32½	26⅜	Alum Ltd .80	165	27⅜	27⅝	27¼	27⅝	+⅛
79⅜	60⅜	Alcoa 1.40	161	72½	73⅞	72¼	73⅞	+⅞
24¾	21½	AmalSug .80a	3	21⅛	21⅞	21½	21⅞	+⅛

DISADVANTAGES OF A CORPORATION

Before you become too impressed with the advantages of a corporation and make a hasty decision, you should consider its disadvantages. Besides having to pay a corporation income tax, which was mentioned earlier, you will have to consider that the corporation may fall out of your control. In your business you own 30 percent of the stock—15,000 shares of a total of 50,000. In practically none of the large corporations in this country does any single person own as much as 30 percent of the stock. Such a large block would almost certainly mean control, since most stockholders are not interested in controlling policy and give their proxy (right to vote) to the directors of the corporation. Since your corporation would be a small one with few shares of stock, there is a real possibility of several stockholders' getting together to vote you out.

You can try to avoid this difficulty in several ways. One method of keeping control would be to limit your expansion so that you always own at least 51 percent of the stock. However, such a move may not give you the money you need to develop as you have planned. Another alternative is to try to sell a different kind of stock, one that does not carry voting rights. The stock we have been referring to is known as *common* stock, and each share carries with it the right to one vote on matters concerning the control of the company. The holder of common stock also takes a chance on a return on his money because *dividends,* the money paid to the owners of this stock, are paid only after the corporation has taken care of all its other obligations. If the corporation makes a big profit, the common stockholder does well; but if business is poor, there may be no dividends. In addition, the value of the stock, which reflects the earning power of the business, may drop and discourage future buying.

PREFERRED STOCK

A different type of stock—one having less risk but also fewer rights—is known as *preferred* stock. Although preferred stock represents ownership, it might better be

Stock, which represents ownership, is becoming widely distributed among the American public.

called a second-class ownership. Rarely does it carry the right to vote. The corporation has an obligation to pay its preferred stockholders a stated dividend before it pays anything to those holding common stock. Therefore, if the corporation earns only a small profit, the preferred stockholder will get his dividend and the chances are that the common stockholder will be left without one. On the other hand, a large profit will not give the owner of preferred stock any additional reward, whereas the common stockholder may receive a substantial dividend.

If you are able to sell preferred stock rather than common stock to raise the capital you need, you will be sure of maintaining control. However, you will probably find that those who buy preferred stock are not willing to take great risks, and therefore they will favor large corporations that have been in business for years and have a long record of paying dividends. Still less risk is found in *cumulative preferred stock;* to holders of this kind of stock a corporation that fails to pay dividends for one or several years will have to pay accumulated dividends when profits are made.

SELLING BONDS

You might also try selling bonds to raise money. A bond does not represent partial ownership of a corporation, but stands for a loan of a specified amount, often $1,000. The loan of $1,000 is referred to as the principal. The bondholder receives a specified rate of interest, usually every six months, on the principal invested. Whether the business makes money or not, the corporation must pay interest to bondholders or risk being sued. At the end of a stated period the company must pay the principal to the bondholder. The bondholder runs the least risk of losing his money, but he also makes the least return on his investment if the corporation makes a substantial profit.

It would be nice if you could sell bonds, but why should a person worried about taking a risk put money into a new company? After considering the possible alternatives, you decide to go to an investment banker and ask him to sell the common stock necessary to raise the money you need.

Part C   Evolution and Concentration of Business

The Industrial Revolution brings changes in methods of production

After looking at the classical model and going through the process of organizing a business unit within the framework of this theory, we now must pause to consider a historical force that brought about a change in the real world not completely anticipated by such classical economists as Adam Smith.

One of the most important revolutions in the history of mankind was the Industrial Revolution, which occurred in western Europe and America after 1750. In the course of the Industrial Revolution waterpower, steam, and later electricity were harnessed to run new and complex machines. This in turn brought about great changes in the production and distribution of goods, involving different uses of the factors of production. In the next chapter we will examine the changes which the Industrial Revolution brought to the workingman. Here we will examine the changes it brought to ways of producing goods and services.

FIXED AND VARIABLE COSTS

One change was a greater demand for capital because the businessman's costs tended to increase. These costs may be divided into two categories, *fixed costs* and *variable costs.* Fixed costs are those expenses which do not change with changes in production or sales. They pertain only to the short run, since all costs may fluctuate in the long run. The owner of the hardware

store on Main Street pays his landlord $200 a month in rent. He pays that amount whether his sales are $5,000 a month or $35,000 a month. He sometimes refers to these fixed costs as his overhead.

Expenses which change with the volume of business are known as variable costs. As sales go up, variable costs will also go up. The hardware store owner will have to hire additional employees if his business gets significantly better. What other examples of variable costs can you think of?

THE EFFECT OF HIGH FIXED COSTS

Before the Industrial Revolution, fixed costs were far less important than they are today. Imagine that your "Build-a-City" business was operating in the eighteenth century. How do you think it would be organized? In all probability the actual building would be very small. In most cases the material would be distributed to workers who would return to their homes and carve the models with their own tools. Your fixed expenses would be small. You would hire workers as you needed them. If business was poor, some labor could be eliminated and your costs would decrease. If sales declined, you could close the business completely without losing much money. When economic conditions improved, you would be able to reopen your business with very little expense. The system described here

The use of water and steam for power to drive machines led to the Industrial Revolution. With such power man was able to use larger and more complex machinery. This development resulted in the factory system and led to a change in the status of the worker.

operated very well for businessmen. They were able to open or close their businesses as the need for their products changed.

Now suppose that a large and costly machine is invented to produce "Build-a-City" sets. Not only would your methods of production change, but so would the basis on which you would make your decisions for the business as a whole. No longer would the workmen supply the tools. Now you would supply them. The cost of going into your kind of business would be increased considerably due to the expense of machines and a factory located in a place convenient for workers to reach. In the same way, changed methods of production led to the factory system in the course of the Industrial Revolution.

Under these new conditions, if business declined, you might still cut costs by discharging some of your employees. However, the fixed costs for the machines and the factory would remain constant. What would happen if business declined to a level at which you were losing money? Would it pay to continue producing? If you decided to go out of business, you would lose the entire sum you invested. Also remember that if at some time you decided to come back into the business when business prospects looked better, the cost of starting again might be more than you could afford. The Industrial Revolution, by increasing fixed costs largely through the introduction of machinery and factories, greatly limited the opportunities for entering or leaving the business community. If your business has high fixed costs, the only way to pay them is to make sure your production is high enough to spread the costs over the many things you produce.

Let us suppose you have two machines, each capable of producing 100 "Build-a-City" sets an hour. You find it easy to pay for the cost of the machines and the factory when they are in operation for eight hours a day and five days a week. If business de-

clines, however, and you have only enough orders to require the production of 800 sets a day you will have a problem. You could cut your variable costs by letting one of your machine operators go and using just one machine for the eight hours. However, the cost to cover both machines and the factory would have to come from the sale of 800 sets rather than 1,600 sets, hardly a bright prospect for making a profit.

COMPETITION UNDER NEW CIRCUMSTANCES

The answer to operating a high fixed-cost business successfully is to make sure that sales are kept reasonably high at all times. After the Civil War the maturation of the American Industrial Revolution and the spread of a fine system of transportation gave American business a huge market. Producers in Boston could easily sell to buyers in St. Louis. What happened, however, when the national demand for a product declined? Each producer of that article did everything in his power to keep his sales up in order to pay for his fixed costs. This usually meant cutting his price to keep his own customers and also attract some of his competitors' customers. When his competitors followed his example, the battle to obtain a bigger portion of the market led to price wars, or "cutthroat competition." Prices fell even below the cost of production. Why? Because businessmen who spent staggering amounts of money developing their businesses could no longer afford to move. They needed to have income in order to meet their fixed costs, even if they had to dip into their past earnings or borrow money to pay for their variable costs. They would rather lose money for a short time in the hope either that business for the whole industry would improve or that some of their competitors would falter.

There were some economists, perhaps influenced by the concept of survival of the fittest, who thought that this fierce competition during a slowdown in business was in the long run beneficial. The weaker, less efficient businesses would not survive and the consumer would be left with the strongest, most efficient businessmen to serve him. Some economists still believe that this so-called social Darwinism is best. Critics of these economists point out that with fewer business opportunities and with greater requirements for capital, competition is bound to be lessened. With few producers it is easy to get together and agree on a price that would be higher than it would be if the market were free, with the price more affected by supply and demand.

Establishing production for maximum profit

Every business seeks to make the largest profit it can. In doing so it must consider the revenue it receives from the sale of its goods and the cost of producing and selling those goods. It can make its greatest profit when the difference between its total revenue and its total cost is greatest.

MARGINAL COST

We have already seen in Chapter 2 that costs for each unit produced are not the same at all levels of production. At very low levels of production the fixed costs have to be shared by relatively few units, making costs high for each unit. At very high levels of production the law of increasing costs (variable costs) makes unit costs very high. Thus the businessman must decide on some in-between level of production to make his greatest profit.

The *marginal cost* is the additional cost of adding one more unit of production to the total cost. This can be seen in Table 3–3. To illustrate, the marginal cost for expanding production from four units to five units is obtained by subtracting the total costs for producing four units from the costs for producing five ($115 – $85).

THE MOST PROFIT POSSIBLE UNDER PURE COMPETITION

Under pure competition no producer is able to influence the market price no matter

how few or how many units he offers for sale. The revenue he gets for each additional unit he sells is the same. Explaining this same idea in economic terms, we would say that under pure competition the market price and the marginal revenue are the same. *Marginal revenue* is the additional income the seller gets by the sale of an additional unit.

If the market price, or marginal revenue, is $35, our businessman in the situation described in Table 3–3 would set his production at six units. If he produced the seventh unit, he would lose $15 (seventh unit: the marginal revenue of $35 minus marginal cost of $50 equals −$15). When he produced his fifth unit, he would note that his marginal cost ($30) was $5 less than his marginal revenue ($35). He would, therefore, try to produce an additional unit in the hope that there would still be a favorable difference between marginal cost and marginal revenue.

We may conclude that under pure competition the firm can make the most profit (in the short run) by setting production at the level where marginal cost and marginal revenue are equal to each other.

Table 3–3   Total and Marginal Costs

UNITS PRODUCED	TOTAL COST	MARGINAL COST
1	$ 30	$20
2	50	15
3	65	20
4	85	30
5	115	35
6	150	50
7	200	

Marginal costs are determined by subtracting the total cost for *n* units from the total cost of *n* + 1 units.

THE MOST PROFIT POSSIBLE IN OTHER MARKET CONDITIONS

When the businessman holds a partial monopoly, he has more freedom in controlling both his production and his price.

Since he has some control over the setting of price, marginal revenue will not remain the same at all levels of production. Like those operating under pure competition he will try to make the most profit, and this will be at the point where the difference between total revenue and total cost is greatest. By restricting production he is able to keep his prices slightly above what they would be under pure competition. Thus the consumer is forced to pay a higher price, production levels may be set at less than their optimum efficiency, and the businessman will not be utilizing all the resources he might if the market were operating under pure competition. This explains why economists generally favor pure competition, or at least highly competitive conditions, and why they urge vigorous *antitrust* action by government to enforce competition. Let us see some of the methods used to interfere with the free market.

Changes in production bring about concentration of business

If we examine the development of American industry, we find that those industries subject to high fixed costs have moved through the stages previously described. As the cost of machinery, research, and factories increased, it became difficult for new firms to enter the market. In the 1870's and 1880's, as the impact of the American Industrial Revolution made itself felt, the average size of the business unit increased. It was at this time that the corporation became more common; for as we have discovered, it was the kind of business best suited to raising large amounts of capital. Prior to this time a special act of the legislature was needed to grant a charter. Passage of general incorporation acts after 1875 simplified that process. When business conditions declined, fierce competition developed, and often only the strongest firms survived. These price wars were often disastrous for small businesses, and costly for the giants of industry as well.

PRICE-FIXING AND LOOSE COMBINATIONS

To prevent the effects of excessive competition, some leaders of American industry reasoned that cooperation and agreement served their interests better than competition. What do you think would happen if all firms in an industry agreed to charge a particular price? If this price were higher than the prices of a competitive market, profits of each producer would increase. This technique, known as "price-fixing," forces the consumer to pay a higher price than he would under competition. Another technique was for producers to divide the market among themselves, with each producer having the exclusive right to sell in his portion of the market. These methods did not work well in the 1880's or 1890's because the agreements were not committed to legal documents. At a time in our history identified with "rugged individualism," when faith and trust were not relied upon, too many businessmen hedged on their agreements whenever it was possible to make more money. These oral agreements were known as *loose combinations* because they were not binding on the participants.

CLOSED COMBINATIONS

In time more formal agreements known as *closed combinations* developed. One kind was known as a *trust*. It was formed when producing companies surrendered their common stock and voting control in their own companies to a board of trustees of a new company. In turn the owners of the producing companies were given the equivalent of their stock in trust certificates. The new company then controlled the entire market and was usually able to make a large profit because of the high prices resulting from the absence of competition. The profit was then divided and the owners of the trust certificates received dividends.

One trust that forced people to pay artificially high prices was the sugar trust. It illustrates the harm a trust can do. Most sugarcane used in the making of sugar was imported. However, before the consumer bought it, it had to be refined. Competition among sugar refiners was intense as each struggled to gain a dominant position in the industry. Distributors and consumers benefited by the low prices that resulted. When the sugar trust was organized in 1887, there were twenty-three sugar companies in operation. Seventeen of these companies exchanged their stock for trust certificates, thereby coming under the single control of a giant trust called the Sugar Refineries Company. The trust certificate assured the owner dividends in the same manner as when he had common stock; but unlike the stock it was traded for, there was no voting right. The votes, and therefore the control, were in the hands of the board of trustees (the directors) of the sugar trust.

By having control over seventeen of the twenty-three refineries, the trust was able to control the supply of sugar and thereby raise the price. The first action the trust took was to close all but four of its factories. With only a limited supply available, sugar buyers had to bid against each other to get the sugar they needed. Thus, the trust

forced consumers to pay higher prices and caused workers to lose their jobs. The sugar trust was interfering with competition, an essential part of our economic system. Without competition the buyer was largely at the mercy of the seller.

HOLDING COMPANIES

Another form of closed corporation that became popular after trusts started to disappear was the *holding company*. Such a company gains control by buying up enough stock of other companies to control them. In Figure 3–2 we can see how such a company can gain control of a large industrial empire with relatively little capital. Companies A through I are producing companies, each worth $10 million. Company J buys more than 50 percent of the stock of Companies A, B, and C so as to be able to control them. Company K does the same to D, E, and F; and Company L, to G, H, and I. Companies J, K, and L are holding companies. They are created not to produce but only to hold stock of other companies for the purpose of controlling A through I. For $45 million they control a $90-million industrial empire.

Company M, a higher-level holding company, is formed to gain control of Com-

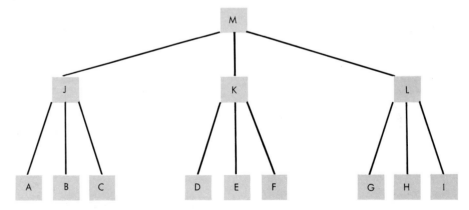

Figure 3–2   A Small Holding Company

Companies A through I are producing companies. Companies J, K, and L are first-level holding companies, and Company M is a second-level holding company.

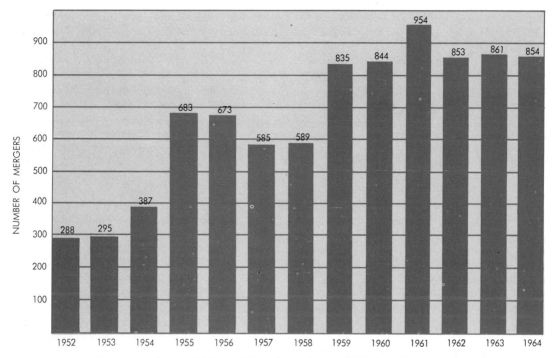

Figure 3–3 Mergers and Acquisitions – Manufacturing and Mining Concerns
Acquired: 1952 to 1964   SOURCE: *Statistical Abstract*

panies J, K, and L. It buys up 50 percent of the stock of each of the holding companies. Company M can now control the $90-million empire for less than $23 million. If any of the producing companies or first-level holding companies have preferred stock, Company M needs far less capital for control. Having holding companies at additional levels can also reduce the capital needed for control. It is also well to remember that control can almost always be achieved with far less than 50 percent ownership because of the many stockholders who have no interest in voting.

Before the passage of the Public Utility Holding Company Act of 1935, huge holding companies existed. The Associated Gas and Electric Company, a billion-dollar establishment, was controlled by a promoter who owned about $100,000 of voting stock.

Samuel Insull and his associates in a giant utility holding company were able to control their producing companies with far less than one percent of the stated value of securities of their producing companies.

MERGERS

The most common kind of consolidation today is the *merger*. When two or more companies get together to form one company, a merger is created. An example is the case of the Nash and Hudson automobile companies, which joined to form the American Motors Corporation. Stockholders of each company had to approve the transaction.

Mergers have, on occasion, been formed by smaller companies in an industry dominated by a few giant firms. These smaller companies claim that they need to merge in order to become more efficient so

Controversy continues over how vigorous an antitrust policy the government should follow.

that they can compete more effectively against the biggest corporations. They maintain that such action increases competition rather than reducing it. The Antitrust Division of the Justice Department has not always agreed with them.

The most recent type of merger movement has been characterized by giant firms in one industry diversifying their holdings by buying into unrelated industries. These have been called *conglomerations*. The Columbia Broadcasting System's acquisition of the New York Yankees baseball team is an example of this kind of merger.

Reaction to combinations

Interfering with the trading of goods and services is contrary to the model designed by Adam Smith and other classical economists. Obstructions to the market, such as monopolies, loose combinations, trusts, holding companies, and oligopolies, brought protests from many Americans. They wanted the government to do something to insure competition and help keep prices low. In 1890 Congress passed the Sherman Antitrust Act, which outlaws monopolies, attempts to form monopolies, and combinations and conspiracies in restraint of trade. Because the Sherman Act contained no definitions, did not indicate the meaning of "restraint," and did not clearly

express whether labor as well as capital was to be included, much of its meaning remained for the courts to interpret.

In 1914 Congress passed the Clayton Act. This act spelled out its purpose and meaning. Among other things, it prohibited *interlocking directorates* in competing companies, discriminatory price-cutting, tying contracts (contracts which force buyers to purchase items they may not want), and the forming of holding companies. In the same year Congress created a Federal Trade Commission to help enforce the antitrust acts. A strong effort was made to keep the market free and competitive. In subsequent years other laws have been passed, and the Supreme Court has handed down rulings relative to how much competition should exist. With few exceptions our government has expressed its approval of competition. Has this government policy worked? Do we now have the competitive society expressed in the model and sought after by our laws?

Separation of ownership and control

Several of our largest corporations are owned by more than a million people, and there are a great many more with over 100,000 different stockholders. In very few of these firms does any one stockholder own more than 10 percent of the outstanding stock. Studies have shown that this wide

MERGERS, LAWS, AND THE HIGH COURT: THREE VIEWPOINTS

**Robert H. Bork, Associate Professor,
Yale Law School:**

"The laws are generally clear—but this is not to say they're good. The Court has always tried to simplify, to push toward automaticity—partly because it doesn't feel at ease dealing with economics, and partly because this Court doesn't have a firm grasp on the nature of competition and a free market. It sees anti-competitive tendencies even where they don't exist. Half the laws themselves are anti-competitive. The real problem of mergers lies with horizontal mergers. That's where the only intelligent fear lies and that's where the enforcement drive should be. Congress went too far in amending Section 7; the Supreme Court has pushed even further."

George J. Stigler, Professor, University of Chicago Graduate School of Business:

"Businessmen have always said that [the laws are confused]. It's a big game they play. They love to run behind this so-called cloud of confusion—but it's a cloud they make themselves. The antitrust laws are as good as I could expect. In general, they heighten competition—and anything that does that is good. On the other hand, when it comes to concentration in specific industries, I would not say that we're teetering on the dangerous brink. There are an immense number of fields where significantly increased concentration would not hurt. I'm not prepared to say that the Justice Department is administering the law with unbounded skill—but, in general, the laws are doing what they're supposed to be doing."

Donald F. Turner, professor of law and public administration, Harvard University:

"Any company can get competent legal advice that will indicate the outcome of a vertical or horizontal merger. But in regard to conglomerate mergers, the law is not predictable because it is in a very primitive stage. There have been no Supreme Court decisions in this area. If a company is failing, it is generally held that there are no holds barred. If the conglomerate law gets awfully tough then [competition will suffer]. In general, though, the area of industry mergers is clearly one in which there hasn't been much thinking. But I disagree with those who think the antitrust laws generally are a barrier to business growth, progress, and efficiency."

SOURCE: *Newsweek,* June 29, 1964, p. 77

---

diversification of ownership has brought about a separation of ownership and control. It is rare for the entire management of such companies to own more than a fifth of all voting stock. Do you think this loss of control by the majority of the ownership in a corporation holds any danger? If so, to whom?

Natural monopolies

There appears to be little disagreement among economists regarding the formation of natural monopolies. In some industries it is not economical to have competition. These industries—utilities and transportation companies, for instance—are usually characterized by their extremely high fixed costs. Consider how costly it would be to have three different sets of railroad tracks running side by side from New York to Chicago for three competing companies. Consider the inefficiency and inconvenience of having many competing telephone companies each with its own telephone poles, telephone books, and dial systems. Such industries are called *natural monopolies,* and an appropriate level of government grants a franchise to such businesses giving them exclusive rights to do business in a given area. If there is no competition, you may ask, how are we protected? The federal government has set up commissions, such as the Interstate Commerce Commission, to regulate those industries that engage in interstate commerce and to protect consumers. State and local governments also have commissions which regulate natural monopolies under their jurisdiction. If a company wants to increase its rate (price) it must get permission from the commission in charge. If a company does not present a good reason for raising rates, such as failing to earn a fair return on its investment, chances are slight that such increases will be granted.

Part D   The Problem: How Much Economic Competition Is Desirable?

There is a difference of opinion among economists, responsible citizens, and public officials regarding the amount of competition we should have. No other country in the world has committed itself as much as we have to promoting competition and to curbing monopolistic practices. Our sympathy has usually been for the "underdog," namely, small business, even when it could not compete effectively. However, our dependence on and support of giant corporations leaves considerable room for variation in the determination of our public policy. What follows is an examination of several points of view, each designed to show the rationale of the position taken. Each statement contains values, facts, and generalizations. This is followed by a list of facts (p. 64) which seem to lead to differing conclusions. There are, next, four groups of

Table 3-4   Sales of Leading U.S. Retail Outlets

	1963 sales (in thousands)		1963 sales (in thousands)
DEPARTMENT STORES		Jewel Tea	788,409
J. C. Penney Co.	$1,834,318	First National	723,402
Federated Department Stores	932,777	Grand Union	667,417
Allied Stores Corp.	829,807		
May Department Stores	723,714	**DRUG STORES**	
Macy's	582,906	Walgreen Co.	$336,748
Gimbel Bros., Inc.	492,386	Rexall Drug	280,511
Marshall Field & Co.	256,615	Sterling Drug Co.	252,451
VARIETY STORES		**SHOE STORES**	
F. W. Woolworth Co.	$1,183,002	Brown Shoe	$316,867
W. T. Grant Co.	698,673	International Shoe Co.	295,615
McCrory	569,116	Melville Shoe Co.	182,403
S. S. Kresge Co.	510,531	Edison Bros. Stores, Inc.	145,329
J. J. Newberry Co.	319,344	Endicott Johnson Corp.	118,405
G. C. Murphy Co.	267,837	U.S. Shoe	90,824
S. H. Kress & Co.	154,931		
		MAIL-ORDER HOUSES	
GROCERY STORES		Sears, Roebuck & Co.	$5,115,767
Great Atlantic & Pacific Tea Co.	$5,189,188	Montgomery Ward & Co.	1,500,112
Safeway Stores, Inc.	2,649,712	Spiegel, Inc.	300,341
Kroger Co.	2,102,106		
Acme Markets	1,118,686	**FURNITURE STORES**	
National Tea (Chicago)	1,056,919	Larchfield Corp.	$61,896
Food Fair	1,003,344	Reliable Stores Corp.	30,970
Winn-Dixie	831,323	Haverty Furniture Co., Inc.	25,724

SOURCE: *Fortune Magazine.* Reprinted by special permission from the *1965 Fortune Directory;* © 1965 Time, Inc.

questions, which may be called subproblems. Answers to these subproblems should help you in arriving at an answer to the main problem: How much competition should there be? Keep in mind the material presented in this chapter that is related to the problem.

The classical viewpoint

We have seen that the classical economist calls for a highly competitive economy. He elevates the consumer to the highest position on the economic ladder and organizes an economic system to serve him. Production is created for the consumer, and the economy should be organized to produce the goods he wants at the lowest cost. This can be done only by having strong competition among the producers of goods and services—the businessmen. They recognize that by producing only the best goods in the most efficient way and offering them at the lowest prices will the consumer buy their products and allow them to make money.

If there is only one producer of a good, there is no need to improve it, to increase efficiency, or to lower price. The consumer is compelled to buy whatever product is offered. If there are only a few producers, it is a simple matter for them to cooperate with one another and to sell the product at a price high enough for the least efficient producer to make money. The more efficient producers are willing to go along at the high price, since their profits will be greater. Even if there are quite a few producers, one large company can influence the supply of the product on the market and affect the price. If the small producers try to lower the price in an effort to attract business, the giant can force them to close by lowering the price below cost for a short time. After he has destroyed them, he can raise the price to make up for his losses.

JOSEPH A. SCHUMPETER AND DYNAMIC CAPITALISM

Joseph A. Schumpeter (1883–1950), a professor of economics in Austria and later in the United States, is known for his studies of capitalism. Although he admired the institutions of capitalism, he prophesied their ultimate destruction. His theories on the stages of capitalism have greatly influenced subsequent economic thinking.

Schumpeter was concerned with capitalism primarily as a means of economic development. His hero was the entrepreneur, the key figure whose innovations benefit society. Driven by the desire for profit, the true entrepreneur introduces new products and methods, creates new markets, and explores new systems of organization. Schumpeter also recognized certain limitations in classical capitalism. The conditions for perfect competition are found in very few industries, and monopolistic competition, oligopoly, and monopolistic practices are common.

Schumpeter's greatest contribution was in the analysis of capitalism as an evolutionary process. He saw that innovation, the dynamic factor in economic development, was also a source of weakness. Innovations tend to occur in clusters, creating an imbalance which leads to business cycles. Just as innovation theory explains economic development, so it also explains periodic depressions.

Eventually, in the course of business cycles, the entrepreneurial function becomes obsolete and is replaced by bureaucratic committees and teams of experts who lack the drive and imagination to move the society forward. Some of capitalism's basic institutions, such as private property, are undermined as the government comes to depend for support on inducements and popular appeal. Eventually, Schumpeter predicted, some form of "state capitalism," with its accompanying inefficiency and stagnation, will become the basis of our nation's economic system.

With many producers, no one business can control enough of the supply to affect the price. Only within this framework can the consumer take advantage of a free-trade market.

What would the classical economist's answer be for the little businessman who cannot compete? Does he make any special provision for him? Remember, there are millions of little businesses and only a few giants. Our defender of the classical model might remind us of the basic problem in economics: the efficient allocation of our limited resources to meet our unlimited wants. Special consideration given to any group might encourage waste. If we allow artificially high prices, we permit resources to flow to less efficient producers. In addition, we ask the consumer to pay more and deprive him of buying other things with the money he would have had left over if he had bought in a competitive market. The inefficient producer should move into more profitable work and thereby be of greater service to society. We are all consumers, and a highly competitive society will keep prices low and allow us to get the most goods for our money. Isn't that what we all want from our economic system? Or will the elimination of the small and inefficient business eventually eliminate too much competition and result in inefficiency or exploitation of the consumer?

The case for limited competition

Although economists of many different viewpoints would be eager to answer the arguments presented above and give their own pet theories, we can examine only some of the more popular positions.

REWARDING THE EFFICIENT

One of the first limitations that most critics of the classical position would point to is its self-defeating features. If we permit the existence of a free marketplace with unlimited competition, the most efficient producers will soon emerge as the victors in the economic struggle. Eventually only a few producers would be competing with one another. This in itself would not do any harm if it were easy for more producers to enter the market. This would be possible when the demand for a product increased or the producers already in the market started to make such high profits as to attract more businessmen into the field. However, with the great increase in fixed costs, businessmen cannot move in and out of an industry so easily.

BIGNESS MAKES PROGRESS EASIER

The successful businesses acquire the best machinery for efficient production, build large research laboratories to help them improve their products, and engage in big advertising programs to help sell their products to the consumers. When new ideas are developed for better products, isn't it easier to sell them to the big, established companies than to try to compete in the field? Considering the amount of money needed to start a new business, few people are willing to take the great risk involved. Our antitrust laws cannot force people to go into business to compete, and we cannot break up the big producers if we are to reward those who are most efficient.

DIVERSIFICATION

The most successful businesses have become so powerful and have acquired so much money that they have been able to branch out into many different industries. During World War II, General Motors went into the diesel locomotive business because of the great demand and limited supply. Within a few years General Motors was producing more diesel locomotives than any other company. It is also one of the largest manufacturers of household appliances. General Motors is not alone in diversifying its holdings. The American Motors Corporation and the Ford Motor Company also are in the appliance business. Chrysler Corporation is a large manufacturer of air conditioners. Each of these corporations is also in the finance business.

ADVANTAGES OF GIANT CORPORATIONS

Should we try to break up these huge corporations and penalize them for their success? If we break them up into smaller units, how will we be able to carry out costly research to improve our products? Those who favor large corporations would present the following evidence to support their viewpoint.

These corporations are owned by millions of stockholders, who are also consumers. The profits distributed by these companies help to raise the standard of living. The millions of workers employed by the giant industries earn higher wages than those in industries in which there are many producers. By providing steady employment for their millions of workers, these corporations tend to have a stabilizing effect on the entire national economy.

By diversifying their interests, large corporations do a better job of allocating resources from one product to another. Competition can and does exist among giants. When competition within an industry is largely eliminated, there may be competition between industries, as in the aluminum and stainless steel industries. Although prices have not declined, income has risen faster than prices; a high income is as important to encourage competition as a low price, particularly if it rises faster than prices.

Government action keeps big business in line and prevents it from disregarding the consumer. It would be more advantageous for the small businessman, as well as

Table 3–5 Largest U.S. and Foreign Corporations, 1963
(millions of dollars)

TEN LARGEST U. S. INDUSTRIAL CORPORATIONS			FIVE LARGEST FOREIGN INDUSTRIAL CORPORATIONS		
	Sales	Assets[1]		Sales	Assets[1]
General Motors	$16,495	$10,785	Royal Dutch-Shell		
Standard Oil (N. J.)	10,264	11,997	(Britain-Holland)	$6,521	$10,651
Ford Motor	8,743	5,949	Unilever (Britain-		
General Electric	4,919	3,015	Holland)	4,297	2,720
Socony Mobil Oil	4,352	4,660	National Coal Board		
U. S. Steel	3,599	5,139	(Britain)	2,520[2]	3,017
Chrysler	3,505	2,124	British Petroleum		
Texaco	3,416	4,455	(Britain)	2,172[2]	3,144
Gulf Oil	2,978	4,549	Nestlé (Switzerland)	1,852	300
Western Electric	2,833	1,981			

FIVE LARGEST U. S. COMMERCIAL BANKS		FIVE LARGEST U. S. TRANSPORTATION COMPANIES		
	Assets[1]		Operating revenues (1963)	Assets[1]
Bank of America	$14,694	Southern Pacific	$906	$2,595
Chase Manhattan Bank	12,118	Pennsylvania Railroad	858	2,846
First National City Bank	11,798	New York Central Railroad	706	2,362
Manufacturers Hanover Trust	6,540	United Air Lines	623	635
Chemical Bank New York Trust	5,831	Atchison, Topeka & Santa		
		Fe Railway	616	1,658

FIVE LARGEST U. S. LIFE INSURANCE COMPANIES		FIVE LARGEST U. S. UTILITIES	
	Assets[1]		Assets[1]
Metropolitan	$20,466	American Tel. & Tel.	$28,275
Prudential	19,781	Consolidated Edison of N. Y.	2,986
Equitable Life Assurance	11,271	Pacific Gas & Electric	2,979
New York Life	8,070	Tennessee Gas	2,234
John Hancock Mutual	7,194	Commonwealth Edison (Chicago)	1,894

[1]As of December 31, 1963. [2]Estimate by *Fortune Magazine*.
  SOURCE: *Fortune Magazine.* Reprinted by special permission from the *1965 Fortune Directory*; © 1965 Time, Inc.

for the economy, if he worked for a large company. Finally, the American standard of living is higher than that of any other nation in the world, and it keeps getting higher. By its efficiency and its constant increasing of productivity, big business has made a significant contribution to our standard of living. Since big business has proved itself successful in meeting our economic needs and contributing to our progress, why threaten to do away with "a good thing"?

Considering an answer

The following statements contain facts, of which some favor a policy of greater competition, some support the present condition of our economy, and some suggest the desirability of a move toward less competition. Examine these facts carefully. Identify the policy concerned and evaluate its advantages and disadvantages in each case.

The five hundred largest corporations, less than one tenth of one percent of our total enterprises, control approximately sixty percent of the nation's assets in all fields of production.

Research now requires team effort, and only big business or government has the means to support it.

Prices have risen much faster in industries with few producers than in those with many producers.

Wages are higher in industries with few producers than in those with many.

Decision-making power in the largest corporations is in the hands of a small minority of the stockholders. Their power is so great that some might threaten our democratic way of life.

Chain stores and mail-order houses sell at lower prices than independents.

As more and more Americans own stock in large enterprises, decisions regarding those companies and earnings from them are more widely spread throughout our population.

The Senate Subcommittee on Antitrust and Monopoly in 1956 reported that giant corporations make their huge profits not from efficiency or the best allocation of the nation's resources, but rather from their great power in the marketplace.

Big corporations have given generously to support our colleges and universities in research and in scholarships to help develop human resources.

MAKING THE POLICY

With these facts and arguments in mind, try to decide what our country's economic policy ought to be regarding the amount of competition we should have. Should we:

1. Go back to our original model by having a government policy of vigorous antitrust action? Should we break up our biggest corporations and thereby increase the number of producers?

2. Allow our economic system to develop as it has in the past, making sure that government, under the watchful eye of the Federal Trade Commission, the Antitrust Division of the Justice Department, and congressional investigating committees, guards the consumers' interests from abuse?

3. Forget about competition and our classical capitalistic model? Should we encourage combinations, but give the government greater control over business—as much as it has over natural monopolies? Should we substitute government control over prices for the market control?

4. Follow different policies for different industries? Should we use competition in industries which are most efficient producing as small units, and should we use regulation in cases where bigness is most economical?

As a policymaker, which alternative would you select?

REVIEW: the highlights of the chapter

1. About three fourths of the value of our goods and services results from decisions made by private enterprise. An even greater percentage of our gross national product (GNP) is produced by our businesses.

2. Sometimes a business firm is called an enterprise. Those who organize the enterprise are called entrepreneurs.

3. Collecting and organizing the factors of production is an essential function of business management.

4. Goods used to make other goods (tools) are called capital goods. Goods used directly by the consumer to satisfy his needs are called consumer goods.

5. Interest is money paid for the use of money, rent for the use of natural resources, and wages for labor performed; profit is money received for risks taken in organizing a business and operating it efficiently.

6. A business can be organized as a single proprietorship, a partnership, or a corporation. Each has advantages and disadvantages.

7. Unlimited liability and limited life are two serious drawbacks of both the single proprietorship and the partnership in contrast to the corporation.

8. The biggest advantage of a corporation form of business organization is its great ability to raise capital. Ownership in a corporation is easily transferable.

9. An investment banker is in the business of selling new issues of securities.

10. Common stock is characterized by voting rights and greater risk, while preferred stock usually carries a stated dividend and has no voting rights.

11. Bonds represent a loan rather than ownership. A corporation must pay interest to bondholders or risk being sued.

12. The Industrial Revolution was the result of the application of waterpower and steam power to the operation of machinery, largely replacing the use of man power.

13. Fixed costs are those expenses which do not change, regardless of the volume of sales. These have become more important since the Industrial Revolution.

14. Variable costs are those directly related to the volume of a particular business.

15. Under pure competition a firm can make its greatest profit by setting production where marginal cost is equal to marginal revenue (market price). Where partial monopoly exists, the firm

has some control over price and may restrict production, thereby raising price above the price in the free market.

16. The cost of machinery, research, and factories makes it difficult for new firms to enter an industry. Price-fixing occurs when a group of firms agrees to charge the same price.

17. A trust is a closed combination in which producing companies exchange their control and stock for trust certificates. These certificates do not carry voting rights. A trust generally forces people to pay higher prices. Holding companies are another form of closed combination.

18. The national government attempted to solve the problem of business combinations by passing the Sherman Antitrust Act (1890), the Clayton Act (1914), and the Federal Trade Commission Act (1914). Additional legislation has been passed since then.

19. Separation of ownership and control in our largest corporations has developed because stockholders have little interest in a business other than in its dividends.

20. Natural monopolies are encouraged and regulated by the federal government.

21. A major controversy that remains unresolved is how much competition we should have in our economy.

IN CONCLUSION: some aids to understanding

Terms for review

GNP	corporation
single proprietorship	partnership
capital goods	consumer goods
interest	rent
wages	profit
factors of production	liability
limited life	investment bank
cumulative preferred stock	common stock
cutthroat competition	bonds
price-fixing	social Darwinism
holding company	trusts
conglomeration	merger
variable costs	natural monopoly
fixed costs	dividend
loose combinations	closed combinations

Names to know

Sherman Antitrust Act	Federal Trade Commission
Clayton Act	Interstate Commerce Commission

Questions for review

1. Imagine yourself as a businessman starting a new enterprise.
   (a) What forms of organization are available to you?
   (b) What factors will determine your choice?
   (c) What are the advantages and disadvantages of each kind of organization?
2. What form of business organization would you recommend for each of the following?
   (a) a physician
   (b) an appliance company
   (c) a restaurant
   (d) a grocery store
   (e) a wheat farmer
   (f) a barbershop
   (g) an automobile repair shop
   (h) a professional baseball team
3. A business which is being organized must utilize all the factors of production.
   (a) What are these factors?
   (b) Where may the businessman turn to raise funds for developing or expanding his business?
   (c) What are the various payments he must make for use of the factors of production?
   (d) What is the reward left for him?
4. Business has found a variety of ways to gain advantage in a competitive market.
   (a) What are the historic methods used by American business to control the market?
   (b) Explain the essential differences in these methods.
   (c) What is the most common method today?
5. Since the Industrial Revolution, most large businesses have turned to the corporate form of organization.
   (a) Draw a chart of the structure of a modern corporation.
   (b) Label the following parts: board of directors, officers, owners, creditors.
   (c) Define the function of each as well as the control each exercises.
   (d) Describe the methods available to double the financial worth of this corporation.
6. Explain: "The control of a giant corporation may be exercised by a well-organized group of stockholders with minor stock holdings."

Additional questions and problems

1. What effects do proxy votes have upon the decisions made by the management of a large corporation? Why?
2. List a number of business establishments that are representative of your community and categorize them under the three types of

business organization. Which form is most common? Can you give reasons for this?

3. Select five stocks from those listed on the New York Stock Exchange. Follow their daily progress in a newspaper for a period of two weeks and try to identify some of the factors that contribute to fluctuations in the stocks which you selected.

4. Why are overhead costs such as rent, taxes, interest on capital investments, and insurance considered as fixed costs whereas wages, raw materials, and freight charges are variable costs?

5. What decision would you make in the following problem?

John is a junior in high school and has received $2,000 in the will of a close relative. The will states that the money must be invested in either stocks or bonds to help pay the cost of John's college education. What kind of investment should John make—common stocks, preferred stocks, or bonds? Consider the following factors before arriving at a decision:

John's family income is $6,500.

John hopes to go to a private liberal arts college.

John is an average student and is athletic, but it appears unlikely that he will win a scholarship to go to school.

John's family does not have money saved for his future education.

There are three children in the family, and John is the oldest.

6. In order to check the growing power of business, the federal government has found it necessary to establish certain controls on business.

(a) Trace the growth of federal controls over business by means of a chronological table listing the major regulatory agencies and the laws restricting corporations.

(b) What circumstances caused the various changes in government policy?

(c) What present business practices might require additional controls?

4 Labor: Its Uses and Rewards

Preview

Production of goods results from putting the factors of production together to turn out the materials and services wanted by society. We have just seen how business, when it goes to the market with goods and services, represents supply; and when it goes to the market for the factors of production, it represents demand. Here we are interested in the market concerned with the factors of production, and in one particular factor, labor.

In addition to its human value, labor represents, in dollars, our most valuable resource. Since we know from our central problem that resources are limited, we must make choices on how to allocate them. Just as price, resulting from interaction of supply and demand, helps to solve the problem of allocating our production, so wages (the price for labor) help to allocate our supply of labor. There are many factors that influence the demand and supply of labor. Some of these factors interfere with the mechanism of the classical model. In Chapter 5 we will examine the causes and the consequences of changes in the status of labor, with particular reference to the roles of government and labor unions.

Overview

How is labor unique in comparison with the other three factors of production?

What considerations determine wage rates?

What influence does a labor union have on working conditions?

Should we increase government's regulation of unions?

Part A   The Role of Labor in Production

What is labor?

Labor is one of the four factors of production. Its responsibility is to take natural resources and man-made instruments of production, or either of these, and fashion them into products that businessmen want for sale to consumers. It is human effort used in creating value to satisfy consumer wants. The value created by labor varies from country to country, region to region, and job to job. Value from labor can be increased by providing tools (capital) and skills (education) for workers to use. It is the human effort, shaped by the skill for producing, that businessmen bid for when they seek labor's services in the market for the factors of production.

It is important that you should not think of labor only as a factor involving physical effort. The role of labor has changed as manufactured energy, such as electricity and steam, has been substituted for human energy in producing goods.

Managers who receive salaries and people who are self-employed must also be considered labor. The economist insists that the self-employed man pay himself a wage or salary, since if he performed the same work for someone else he would be paid.

THE UNIQUE QUALITIES OF LABOR

The foregoing description of labor places it in the classical model without differentiating it from other factors of production. Actually, labor has at least two characteristics that make it unique. First of all, labor stems from and cannot be separated from human beings. This means that, as a factor of production, labor has feelings and is capable of independent action. Secondly, labor has the means of buying back the goods and services produced. Machines are not sensitive to the surroundings in which

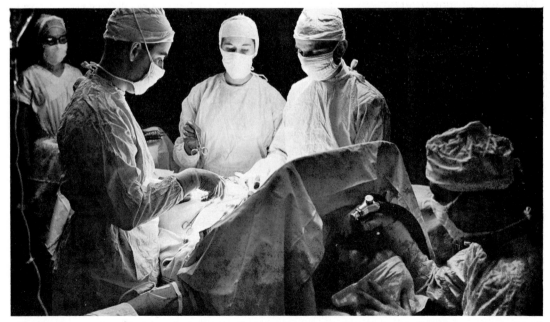

Differences in wages that people receive reflect investment in their training, the degree of scarcity of their skill, and factors such as government and union influence.

they are used, and if they are not used today they can frequently make up for the lost output at some other time. The same may be said about most natural resources. Moreover, neither of these other factors is playing the additional role of consumer.

The supply of labor tends to be quite inelastic, particularly for a short period of time. This is less true for unskilled labor than for skilled labor, since several years may be needed to develop the talent necessary to perform skilled work acceptably. Another factor contributing to the inelasticity of labor is the low degree of mobility of the worker. Returning to our satellite, we find that the computer may suggest offering the worker more dollars than he is presently earning to induce him to move from one section of the country to another. However, the worker may prefer to remain where he is because he has established roots in the community. In trying to analyze labor's role in the classical model as well as in the American economy today, we must take these characteristics into consideration.

Characteristics of the American labor force

Of the 195 million people in the United States, approximately 80 million are counted as members of the *labor force*. While this represents only 40 percent of our total population, a closer look reveals that 90 percent of the men between the ages of 20 and 65 consider themselves as part of the labor force and that 40 percent of the women in this age group do the same. The percentage of our labor force under 20 and over 65 has been growing smaller each year. This is so for our younger people because of the value placed on higher education and the difficulty they have in obtaining employment without training and skills. Our older people are retiring earlier, partially because our productivity per worker has increased sufficiently to keep our standard of living high without their efforts. Our Social Security system, the addi-

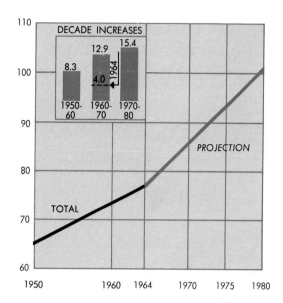

Figure 4-1 Additions to the Labor Force

An annual average addition of 1½ million persons to the labor force is expected for the period 1964–1970. (The civilian labor force consists of those persons 14 years of age and over who are employed or are looking for work.) This increase represents a substantial change from our 1960–64 experience, when annual additions to the labor force averaged under 1 million. The 1964–70 rate of addition is expected to carry over into the 1970–80 decade. SOURCES: N.I.C.B., *Road Maps of Industry* No. 1520; U.S. Department of Labor, Bureau of Labor Statistics

tional income from pensions from both public and private employment, and savings and investments are an effect of this high productivity and allow some to retire in relative comfort. The fact that our labor force is small in proportion to our population and that our standard of living is high is proof of the high productivity of American labor. Figure 4-2 compares our production of selected items with that of the Soviet Union. The lower production in the U.S.S.R. is achieved with a work force considerably larger than that of our own country.

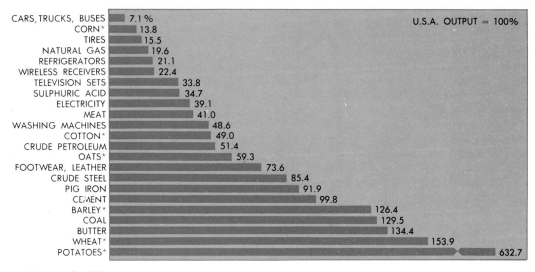

*Data are for 1961

Figure 4-2   U.S.S.R. Production as Percent of U.S.A., 1962: Selected Items
SOURCES: N.I.C.B., *Road Maps of Industry* No. 1428; United Nations; U.S. Department of Commerce; U.S. Department of the Interior; *Electrical Merchandising*

Table 4-1   Composition of the Employed Labor Force in the United States in 1900 and 1964
(as percentage of total)

	1900	1964
WHITE-COLLAR	17.6	42.7
Professional, Technical, and Kindred	4.3	10.9
Managers, Officials, and Proprietors (except farm)	5.8	10.3
Clerical and Kindred	3.0	15.2
Sales	4.5	6.3
MANUAL	35.8	36.8
Craftsmen, Foremen, and Kindred	10.5	12.9
Operatives and Kindred	12.8	18.1
Laborers (except farm and mine)	12.5	5.8
SERVICE	9.0	13.0
Private Household	5.4	3.2
Service (except private household)	3.6	9.8
FARM	37.6	7.5
Farmers and Farm Managers	19.9	3.4
Farm Laborers and Foremen	17.7	4.1
TOTAL	100.0	100.0

SOURCE: Bureau of Labor Statistics

An interesting and useful way of measuring a nation's productivity and standard of living is to look at the distribution of its labor force among the categories of occupation. Table 4–1 shows major occupations in 1900 contrasted with 1964.

The occupational distribution of the labor force has changed radically from 1900 to the present time. The tremendous increase in the white-collar occupations and the equally dramatic reduction in number of those engaged in agriculture shows that we have far less need for workers to engage in the physical aspects of production and far more need for workers who supply primarily services rather than goods.

IMPORTANCE OF CAPITAL TO LABOR PRODUCTIVITY

In countries which are underdeveloped, most workers must use a large amount of their energy in providing for the physical necessities of life. Without modern equipment (capital) to work with or the skills for using such tools, few workers can be freed to provide luxury goods or extra services associated with a high standard of living. With 40 percent of the Soviet Union's labor force engaged in agriculture and very little of the total output available for export, it is easy to see why their standard of living and average productivity of workers are so much lower than ours.

Part B   How Wages Are Determined

Wages: reward for labor

Wages are the prices management pays for human effort. When expressed as the price of labor per hour, per week, or for some other period of time, payment is called a "wage rate." Whether it is called a wage or a salary or a commission, the payment to labor represents a cost to the employer in return for value created. Wages also represent an income to the worker. In addition to being the most costly factor in production, payment to labor is the source of about three fourths of the nation's income. To see how labor earns wages by creating value in the market for the factors of production and then spends these wages in the market for goods and services, refer to the chart of the model in Figure 2–10 on page 30.

DIFFERENCES IN WAGES

When you enter the market as a potential wage earner, you are interested in getting the highest price for the efforts you will perform. If you turn to the "help wanted" section of your newspaper or visit an employment agency, you can get some idea of the wage rate (price for labor for some unit of time, e.g., per hour) for various jobs. As you begin to study the job market, the following questions may come to mind: Why is there so much difference in pay for different jobs? Why is it that similar jobs may pay different wages? Wouldn't everyone be better off if all jobs paid more?

Suppose you reverse your role and enter the market as a businessman seeking to hire workers. You are now concerned with costs. If you can keep the cost of production down, you can offer your products for sale at a lower price and make a larger profit. Since labor is likely to be your most expensive cost, you want to employ your workers at the lowest wage possible. You will probably ask yourself: What will determine how much I will have to pay to get the help I need? How free am I to determine what wages I will pay? Can higher wages provide labor that can create greater value?

REAL WAGES AND MONEY WAGES

Before we answer the question of what determines wages, we must distinguish the difference between money wages and real wages. The term *money wages* refers to the amount of dollars paid for a given amount of work. *Real wages* tell what your money will buy in the market for goods and services at a given time. It is in the latter that you as a worker are most interested. If all

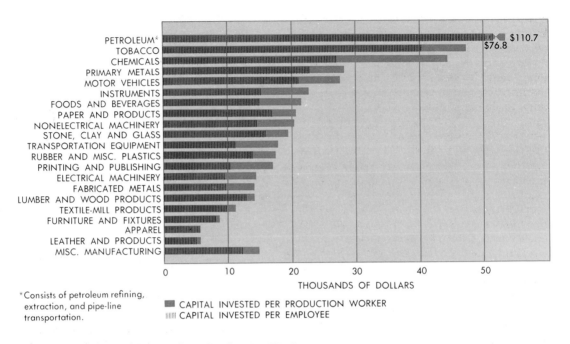

*Consists of petroleum refining, extraction, and pipe-line transportation.

Figure 4–3   Capital Invested per Production Worker

Capital invested is total assets less investments in government obligations and securities of other corporations. Since it is stated at book value, capital invested reflects the price underlying the original cost of the assets and not the cost of these assets in current prices. It is stated after deducting all reserves such as for depreciation, etc. The figures for production workers are annual averages for those actually employed in industries in 1962, as reported by the Bureau of Labor Statistics. The amount of capital invested per production worker, therefore, is affected by the total of capital invested and the level of employment in any year. SOURCES: N.I.C.B., *Road Maps of Industry* No. 1526; U.S. Department of Labor, Bureau of Labor Statistics

laborers who sought employment were working, and demanded and received a 10 percent increase in their money wages but did *not* create any additional goods and services, would they be any better off? What would happen to the few exceptions whose wages remained the same?

Wages under the classical model

In Chapter 2 we learned that the laws of supply and demand determine the allocation of our resources by interacting to determine price. Here our resource is labor and our price is wages. Let us see how these tools help determine wages.

It is obvious that wages must be related to the value that labor creates. An employer cannot afford to pay his workers more than the value they create for him, for to do so would mean losing money. We must, therefore, consider labor's productivity. To do so we will assume that the cost of our other factors of production remains the same and that each worker has the same ability.

THE LAW OF DIMINISHING RETURNS INFLUENCES WAGES

Let us use for our illustration the business we started in Chapter 3, "Build-a-City." Our factory has a fixed number of machines, a fixed amount of materials for making our sets coming in each week, and a certain number of hours per week for work. As we start to add workers we find that, even though each worker may have the same ability, the value that each worker adds to the total product is not the same. At low levels of production each additional worker adds more value to the total value of the product than the preceding worker did; e.g., the tenth worker might add $160 while the ninth might add only $150. However, we soon see a change. We reach a point where additional units of labor will yield decreasing value; for example, the eleventh worker might add $157 and the twelfth worker might add only $154. When we increase quantities of one factor of production (in this case labor) and keep other factors the same, a point is reached at which the value of additional units of the increasing factor (labor) will cost more, proportionately, than the value of the additional production added. Economists call this phenomenon the *law of diminishing returns*.

Marginal productivity related to wage rates

Because of the law of diminishing returns, an employer will hire workers up to the point where the wage received by the last worker equals the value that he creates for his employer. We call this the *marginal productivity wage theory*. Marginal productivity may be expressed as "marginal physical product" when referring to additional unit output, or as "marginal revenue product" when the additional output is stated in money value.

In our own business, if we keep a record of what each additional worker adds to the value of the total product, we can discover what each worker's marginal productivity is. Figure 4–4 shows the marginal productivity of our workers after the law of diminishing returns has set in. It is also a demand schedule for labor. Under pure

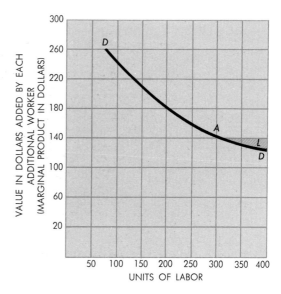

Figure 4–4   Marginal Productivity Theory Applied to Labor

Under pure competition wage rates are determined by marginal productivity. Demand Schedule *D* shows the marginal productivity of workers after the law of diminishing returns has set in. With 300 workers (*A*), the employer can afford to pay $140. Because each additional worker would create a lesser value than $140, the employer must cease hiring or lower wages to the level of the marginal product of the last worker hired. Area *L* is where marginal productivity is below the wage rate ($140).

competition we, as an employer, will hire additional labor as long as it will not cost us more in wages than the additional value we will receive. If we hire more than 300 workers, we will have to pay them less than $140 because they add less than $140 of value to our total product.

MAXIMUM WAGE

At this point you might ask why we, as employers, cannot pay a higher wage, since the value added by workers before the 300th worker is greater than $140. Are these workers being cheated? The answer is *no*. Since every worker in the force of 300

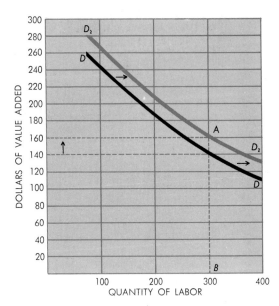

Figure 4–5 Marginal Productivity of Labor

By increasing demand, with supply of labor remaining the same (*A*), wages are increased. Increasing marginal productivity will bring about an increase in demand.

has equal ability and can be interchanged with every other worker, the marginal product of the last worker sets the maximum wage the employer can pay. Under pure competition, where the employer must meet the competitive market price of others, he cannot afford to lose money on any worker.

As with other aspects of the economy we have studied, the theory or model of marginal productivity sets the pattern for the way in which wages should be determined. Remember, however, that a model is an abstraction of the real world, not the real world itself. Even if we had pure competition, the value added by the last worker could be only an estimate of the employer and employee as they seek an agreement, since neither knows the exact value created by each worker. It is to the worker's interest to have that estimate set high and to the employer's to have it set low.

The effect of supply and demand on wage rates

Let us return to the economic tools that we studied in Chapter 2 for explaining the interaction of supply and demand. They will help to explain the equilibrium point for wage rates and the number of workers employed. In Figure 4–4 we saw the marginal productivity of workers. This is our demand for labor. With a given supply of 300 workers the equilibrium point for wage rate is $140 per week. If supply remains the same (*A*), how can wages increase? In Figure 4–5 we see that by increasing demand (D_2), supply remaining the same (inelastic), we can increase wages to $160 per week. How can demand for the product, and consequently wages, be increased? Although using such methods as increasing the demand for the product through advertising and reducing foreign competition by raising tariffs will help, the most reliable way would be to increase the productivity of the worker. Our marginal productivity curve, which is our demand curve, shifts upward to show the greater productivity per worker. Figure 4–6 shows that as output per man-hour goes up, so do wages.

Factors affecting the supply of labor

The factors affecting the supply of labor are numerous and very complex. We can consider only a few of the most important influences. When we seek to hire workers for our "Build-a-City" plant, we will need many different kinds of talent. We may need skilled operators of complicated machinery, as well as electricians, plumbers, painters, bookkeepers, salesmen, foremen, and unskilled workers. When we enter the labor market, we are seeking particular kinds of labor, not labor generally. The unskilled worker without a job may want to be employed as a machine operator; however, unless he trains for this job, he does not count as part of supply in the market for machine operators.

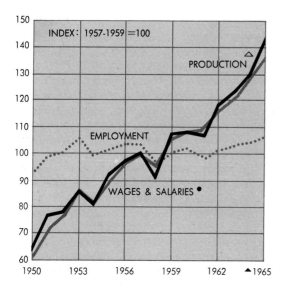

150
140
130
120
110
100
90
80
70
60

INDEX: 1957-1959 = 100

PRODUCTION

EMPLOYMENT

WAGES & SALARIES •

1950   1953   1956   1959   1962   ▲1965

▲ 1st half seasonally adjusted annual rate
△ Based on constant dollar national income originating in manufacturing
• Based on payments in current dollars

Figure 4–6   Labor Costs and Output in Manufacturing

Total manufacturing employment is barely higher now than in 1950. But output has boomed and has been closely followed on a year-to-year basis by employee wages and salaries, exclusive of fringe payments, for which revised data are not now available. The postwar influence of labor-saving capital on the nation's manufacturing complex is apparent in the chart. In contrast to manufacturing, employment has risen rapidly in some other groups, notably wholesale and retail trade, finance, real estate, and services. SOURCE: N.I.C.B., *Road Maps of Industry* No. 1534

SKILL OF THE WORKER

One of the major problems we face in our country today stems from the fact that we do not have merely a general labor market. We have many different supplies of labor. For the last decade we have had a continuing problem of unemployment averaging about 5 percent of our labor force. During this same time we have had shortages of engineers, teachers, nurses, doctors,

SHORTAGE OF TOOLMAKERS BRINGS FEDERAL AID

CLEVELAND — A critical shortage of tool and die makers has spurred the federal government to contribute $4 million for a nationwide training program.

The program was initiated by the Labor Department's Bureau of Apprenticeship and Training, and the funds were made available under the Manpower Development and Training Act.

James A. Gray, executive vice-president of the National Tool, Die and Precision Machining Association, says that in spite of the present training program the shortage of skilled craftsmen is critical. He forecasts the need for 50,000 more journeyman toolmakers by 1970.

Training programs in local trade and high schools have already been started in Rochester, N.Y., Hartford, Conn., and Dayton, Ohio, and future plans call for programs in cities located in 13 other states.

There are many labor markets. Skilled workers are usually low on the supply side and high on the demand side. For unskilled workers the market situation is just the opposite.

and many others whose skills all require long periods of training. Unemployment among unskilled workers, particularly those who drop out of school early, and among members of minority groups averages two to three times higher than the national rate of unemployment. While skilled workers can move into the unskilled labor market (obviously, few would ever want to), the unskilled worker has difficulty moving into the skilled labor market without further training or experience.

MOBILITY

The supply of labor is affected by the lack of mobility among many workers. Those who have pleasant associations with

STEEL COMPANIES SEEKING WORKERS

BALTIMORE — Scouts have been sent out by United States Steel Corporation and Youngstown Sheet and Tube Company to recruit workers for plants in Pittsburgh, Chicago, and Gary. So far the recruiting program has yielded too few employees in the immediate area of the plants to satisfy demand.

Interviews are now taking place in communities several hundred miles from these plants in order to obtain new workers.

Labor mobility is important if we are to maximize the use of our resources.

a particular job, frequently because of the security of a known position as compared to the risk of moving to a new situation, will tend to stay where they are, even though the wage rate might be higher in some other place. After working for a firm for several years, a worker builds up seniority, which protects him from being one of the first laid off when business declines. He may also build up funds in a pension plan and other benefits that companies offer after a certain number of years of service. This lack of mobility is even more limiting when moving involves settling in a new region. For example, the need for labor has dropped in West Virginia because the demand for coal has declined, and not enough demand for labor has come from other industries in the region. Since many workers have been unwilling to leave their homes here, the result has been a higher rate of unemployment in West Virginia than for the nation as a whole.

MINIMUM WAGES AND SUPPLY

Since 1938 we have had laws putting a "floor" under wage rates. The *minimum wage* law passed by the national government in 1961 made it unlawful to pay workers less than $1.25 an hour if they are

engaged in work that may in any way be interpreted as interstate commerce. The coverage of this law has been extended to include a majority of jobs. State governments have passed their own minimum wage laws to cover those not included in the federal law, although the minimum rate of such laws is usually lower.

Figure 4–7 shows graphically what happens to the supply curve when minimum wage laws exist. Note how the increase in the minimum wage rate has decreased the number of workers that employers will demand.

Economists do not agree on the value of minimum wage laws to labor. Those who argue against these laws point out that such restrictions encourage unemployment. Many employers might want to hire addi-

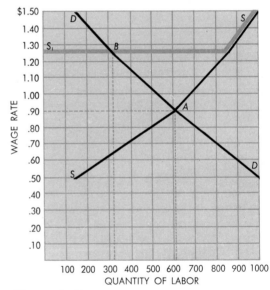

Figure 4–7 Effect of a Minimum Wage Law

A minimum wage law shifts the supply curve from SS to $S'S$. Although the wage rate has moved up from what it would be under purely competitive conditions from $.90 (A) to $1.25 (B), the number of workers employed has declined from 610 to 320. If the demand curve were more elastic, would the decline in the quantity of labor be as great, the same, or greater?

tional workers, but they can do so only if these workers produce at least as much value as they receive. Those who are just entering the labor market or who have very little skill may not be worth the minimum wage rate because they would add less value to the employer's product than they would receive. Since no employer will knowingly hire a worker for more than he is worth, the minimum wage law can cause unemployment for those whose productivity is below the general level.

Those who favor the minimum wage claim that the lowest-paid wage earners have no one to bargain for them and that they are easily imposed upon by employers. Any worker who cannot create sufficient value to be paid the minimum wage rate should not be considered part of the labor force and should qualify for public assistance or training to make him more productive. Wage rates that are so very low tend to discourage employers from making their firms more efficient, thus retarding technological progress. Such rates also tend to reduce incentive among employees.

LABOR UNIONS AND THE SUPPLY OF LABOR

Labor unions can influence wages by controlling the supply of labor. Some unions, mainly those with highly skilled workers, restrict their membership, thus causing the supply curve to shift to the left. Other unions may be successful in organizing almost all the workers; they will try to set a wage rate higher than what it might be under purely competitive conditions. Figure 4–8 shows graphically what happens when membership is restricted, with Figure 4–7 illustrating that an effect like that of the minimum wage is equally applicable in the case of the other unions.

What happens in both cases to the number of workers employed? Do you think that this shifting of the supply curve, causing a change in employment, acts as a check on how far unions go to raise wages? Explain the reasons for your answer.

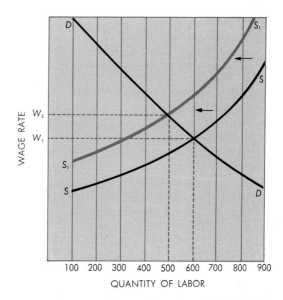

Figure 4–8 Effect of Union Membership Restrictions on Wage Rates

Unions that restrict their membership can increase the wage rate by shifting the supply curve to the left. What has happened to the number of people employed?

OTHER FACTORS INFLUENCING SUPPLY

A number of laws have been passed which have had the effect of reducing the supply of labor that is available. While we will deal with specific labor legislation later, it is important to point out here some conditions which affect the supply of labor:

1. Prohibiting children under a certain age from working reduces the labor force.

2. Social Security payments allow older members of the labor force to retire.

3. Fixing a standard work week of 40 hours with a higher wage rate for overtime (more than 40 hours) encourages employers to hire more workers rather than have present workers put in longer hours.

Explain what happens to the supply curve for labor in each of the cases given.

Summing up wages under the classical model

Under conditions of pure competition, where workers and employers act independently and are willing to move from market to market and have a complete knowledge of the labor market, wage rates and the number of workers employed will be determined by the interaction of demand and supply. The productivity that the last worker adds determines the maximum wage that the employer can pay.

Since the conditions of pure competition rarely exist, other factors influencing wages must be considered. Markets with a single large employer, unions, and government laws bring about changes in demand and supply, changing the equilibrium point for wage rates and the quantity of labor from what it might be under conditions of pure competition.

In the next chapter we will turn our attention to two of the most important influences affecting the classical model: labor unions and government. When the development of these factors has been traced, we will consider a problem significant to the future of labor.

REVIEW: the highlights of the chapter

1. Labor is one of the four factors of production. It represents human effort used in the creation of value. This value varies with the skill and tools of the worker.
2. Labor differs from other factors of production because it can act on its own initiative and because it buys back what it helps to produce.
3. The American labor force of about 80 million workers is highly skilled, and an increasing number are engaged in white-collar jobs.
4. Wages are prices management pays for human effort. In addition to being income for the worker, wages are the most costly factor of production.
5. Money wages refer to the amount of money paid for a given amount of work. Real wages tell what the money will buy.
6. The demand schedule for labor is determined by the marginal productivity of workers.
7. Under conditions of pure competition, wage rates and the quantity of labor are determined by the interacting of supply and demand. Minimum wage laws and unions change the supply curve and, at certain levels, tend to reduce the number of workers hired.

IN CONCLUSION: some aids to understanding

Terms for review

labor	law of diminishing returns
labor force	marginal productivity theory of wages
wage rate	mobility of labor
real wages	minimum wage
money wages	demand for labor

Questions for review

1. Labor is one of the integral parts of the productive process, yet it is sometimes called a "unique" or "peculiar" factor. What differentiates it from the other three?
2. Explain why a profile of the labor force would show that the vast majority are in the 20-to-65 age group and very few in the younger and older groups.
3. Labor has been called a commodity subject to the law of supply and demand in the marketplace. Do you agree? Why or why not?
4. To insure maximum profit, an employer will be guided, in hiring new workers and in setting wages, by the following factors: labor's productivity, its marginal productivity, and its supply and skills. Explain how each factor influences wage payments.
5. Explain why the percentage of our labor force engaged in the physical aspects of production has declined from 1900 to 1964.
6. Considering the general labor market, explain the advantage a skilled worker has as compared to an unskilled worker.
7. Explain how a minimum wage can be both a blessing and a curse to workers.
8. What factors other than minimum wages and unions influence the supply of labor?

Additional questions and problems

1. Draw an imaginary supply and demand graph for labor, labeling wage rates and number of workers. Show what happens when worker output per man-hour increases. Explain the changes.
2. Explain how an unskilled worker receiving $2 per hour might be overpaid whereas a toolmaker receiving $3 might be underpaid.
3. Turn to the "help wanted" section of a newspaper. List in descending order the wages paid for different jobs. Explain the reasons for the differences in wages offered.
4. "Labor benefits most when it cooperates fully with management." Explain why you agree or disagree with this statement.
5. Why does the elasticity in demand for labor affect the power of a union in influencing wages?

5 Labor: Its Organization and Development

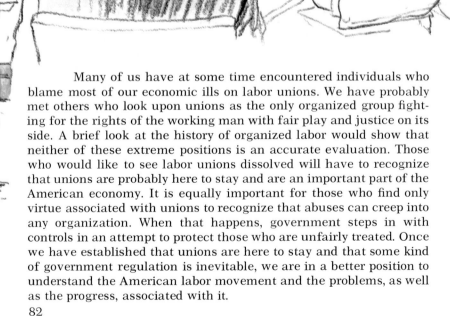

Many of us have at some time encountered individuals who blame most of our economic ills on labor unions. We have probably met others who look upon unions as the only organized group fighting for the rights of the working man with fair play and justice on its side. A brief look at the history of organized labor would show that neither of these extreme positions is an accurate evaluation. Those who would like to see labor unions dissolved will have to recognize that unions are probably here to stay and are an important part of the American economy. It is equally important for those who find only virtue associated with unions to recognize that abuses can creep into any organization. When that happens, government steps in with controls in an attempt to protect those who are unfairly treated. Once we have established that unions are here to stay and that some kind of government regulation is inevitable, we are in a better position to understand the American labor movement and the problems, as well as the progress, associated with it.

82

Part A   A Sketch of the Labor Movement

Causes of union development

The history of the labor movement can be traced back to the Industrial Revolution and the establishment of the factory system in the latter part of the eighteenth century in England. With the introduction of the factory system, the worker was placed in a new position. No longer could the worker provide his own tools and move from employer to employer or set up his own business. He became dependent on the owner of the new and expensive tools. He received wages; but, since he no longer supplied any capital, he had to forgo interest (payment for capital). Labor was the only thing the worker could offer the employer. This placed the worker in a poor bargaining position, since he had to accept whatever wage the employer offered. Having been downgraded from a relatively independent craftsman to a mere factory hand subject to the decisions of the employer, his discontent grew.

THE START OF COLLECTIVE BARGAINING

Whether workers were getting a fair rate for their efforts, considering that productivity tended to be low, is not certain. However, we are sure that workers suffered from poverty, long hours of work, and poor working conditions. When they compared their miserable existence with that of their employer, they decided that they were not getting a fair share of the returns. Working together in a factory made it easy for them to communicate their mutual discontent to one another. If they could unite and agree on what changes they wanted, they could face their employer with strength. They could then send a representative to bargain with the employer concerning wages, hours, and conditions of work. The procedure by which a representative of workers and a representative of employers fixed the terms of employment was slow in developing. However, it marks the beginning of *collective bargaining*, which was to become the major source of union strength.

Slow growth of early unionism

Although labor unions can be traced back to the 1790's in the United States, their growth was slow and their strength weak until the 1930's. Five major factors are largely responsible for this slow growth:

1. The lack of any federal policy recognizing unions as collective bargaining agents for workers
2. The hostility of the courts, which prosecuted unions under conspiracy laws
3. The strong resistance on the part of American businessmen to accepting unions
4. The individualism of the American worker
5. The lack of effective communications necessary to the success of mass movements

The effects of these factors will be seen as we trace the growth of unions.

Before the Civil War unions were primarily local craft or trade unions made up of skilled workers. These groups rarely had any affiliation with unions in other cities. With no federal legislation and with few state laws recognizing the existence of unions, the courts had to decide most disputes between labor and management. Unfortunately for the unions, the courts turned to common law. Accordingly, they held that combinations of workmen that sought to raise wages were criminal conspiracies and hence illegal. Although the decision in the case of *Commonwealth* v. *Hunt* in 1842 ended the conspiracy interpretation, the courts in general continued to discourage the growth of unions by refusing to concede their legality and by declaring illegal the methods, such as strikes, used by unions to obtain their demands.

TERENCE V. POWDERLY, G. M. W.

Powderly's leadership in the Knights of Labor did much to advance the cause of labor.

The Knights of Labor: first national union

The first important national union was the Knights of Labor. It was organized in 1869 by Philadelphia garment workers, under the leadership of Uriah S. Stephens, as a secret society. It tried to include farmers, small merchants, and even professional people as well as manual workers. Besides seeking to accomplish the traditional objectives of labor—higher pay, shorter hours, and better working conditions—it showed interest in extending public education, prohibiting child labor, establishing an income tax, having government ownership of the railroads, and many other causes. Because of these broad interests, it was called a reform union. After dropping its secrecy, it grew quickly, reaching a membership of 700,000 in 1886. Although its avowed method of reaching its goals was political

action, its progress is usually attributed to several successful strikes and to the great energy of its most important grand master, Terence V. Powderly.

Because the Knights of Labor was composed of many different elements seeking many different objectives, its success was inevitably of short duration. Several unsuccessful strikes and a weakening of Powderly's leadership hastened the decline. Although the career of the Knights of Labor was short, its contributions cannot be dismissed. It helped to reorganize some weak existing unions and assisted in the formation of other unions. It brought the problems of labor to the attention of Congress and the President, and because of its diverse membership won support from outside the field of labor.

American Federation of Labor: a modern labor union

The modern labor movement in America can be traced back more directly to the formation of the American Federation of Labor. Started in 1881 as the Federation of Organized Trades and Labor Unions, and more formally organized in 1886 in Columbus, Ohio, as the American Federation of Labor, its character and approach to labor problems differed markedly from the reform and political nature of the Knights. Reflecting the thinking of its leader, Samuel Gompers, for over a third of a century, the AF of L tried to bring trade unions together in a loose federation. Gompers' approach has been called "bread-and-butter" or "business" unionism because he steered his organization away from any idealistic policies or political entanglements and emphasized the immediate economic gains of higher pay, shorter hours, and better working conditions.

Instead of trying to embrace as many workers as possible in one big union, Gompers preferred the more conservative approach of craft organization, in which those doing the same kind of skilled work (plumbers, for instance) are organized into the same union. These craft or trade unions would then affiliate with the AF of L, retaining a great deal of autonomous power. Craft organization leaves little room for the unskilled worker. You will recall that it is far easier to control the supply of skilled workers than that of unskilled workers.

GOMPERS' PHILOSOPHY

Gompers ran his union as a "hardheaded businessman" would run his business. He refused to commit his union to the support of a political party, preferring to reward the friends and punish the enemies of labor at the ballot box. He wanted government to stay out of all union-management negotiations, being more fearful of what an unfriendly government might do to hamper the organized labor movement than optimistic about what good a friendly government might do. Some radical thinkers, including Marxists, crept into the union, but Gompers showed no sympathy for them or their doctrines. Perhaps the best illustration of the Gompers philosophy was expressed in his reply to an inquiry as to what labor's ultimate goals were. He replied simply, "More, more, and more."

We can sum up the following guiding principles of the AF of L under Gompers' leadership: (1) Concentrate only on direct economic benefits for the worker. (2) Have no alliances with any political groups or party. (3) Organize along craft lines, allowing freedom for the unions within the federation. (4) Keep government out of labor-management affairs.

Progress and reverses in union growth, 1898–1947

The AF of L grew slowly from its birth until 1898, at which time its membership numbered 278,000, slightly more than one percent of the labor force. However, the six years from 1898 to 1904, sometimes referred to as the "honeymoon period of capital and labor," saw the membership jump more than six times to 1,676,000, more than

5 percent of the labor force. A second period of rapid growth took place during the period of the first World War, rising from 2,000,000 in 1914 to 4,078,000 in 1920, or one out of every ten workers.

DECLINE IN THE 1920's

During the 1920's a number of important factors combined to cause a serious decline in the influence and membership of unions. In the course of this setback the AF of L was reduced to 2,532,261 members. Among the causes of decline were:

1. Vigorous antiunion activity by businessmen under the leadership of the National Association of Manufacturers
2. Lack of good public relations, resulting in loss of middle-class sympathy
3. Blame placed on unions for the rising cost of living
4. Use by management of labor spies and *strikebreakers*
5. Use by courts of injunctions (p. 89), based on the principles that property rights must be protected and that law and order must be maintained at all costs
6. Use of police and militia to limit strikes

In addition, labor leaders themselves must share the blame. Their insistence on trying to organize skilled workers at a time when assembly-line production increased the demand for unskilled workers caused a large segment of the labor force to be neglected.

YEARS OF RAPID GROWTH, 1933 – 1947

The period from 1933 until 1947 was the most fruitful in all the history of American organized labor. Membership in all organized labor groups grew from about 3,000,000 to over 15,000,000, approximately one out of every four workers. Three principal factors were responsible for this remarkable growth: (1) new federal legislation, (2) new leadership and a revitalization within unions, and (3) World War II and the expansion of industry.

From the passage of the Norris-La-Guardia Act of 1932 until the passage of the Taft-Hartley Act of 1947 the federal government encouraged union development as never before. Injunctions were limited, yellow-dog contracts (p. 89) were made unenforceable, and collective bargaining rights and minimum wages were made part of federal legislation. These acts reflected a growing sentiment in favor of labor; their effect was to make it easier for labor leaders to organize workers.

THE CIO AND INDUSTRIAL ORGANIZATION

After the death of Samuel Gompers (1924), William Green became the leader of the AF of L. His policies were generally considered conservative; and he, along with the majority of the leadership, continued to place greatest emphasis on *craft* (or trade) organization. Although *industrial unions* – in which all workers in an industry, regardless of their job, belong to the same union – were always permitted in the AF of L, they were given little encouragement.

However, many of the leaders of industrial unions felt that the best opportunities for further organization were in the steel and automobile industries, which were better suited for industrial organization. Under the leadership of John L. Lewis, president of the United Mine Workers, a Committee for Industrial Organization was created in 1935 to encourage the formation of industrial unions within the AF of L.

A conflict between those favoring industrial organization (sometimes referred to as "vertical organization") and those preferring craft organization (sometimes referred to as "horizontal organization") led to the formation of a new and separate union, known after 1938 as the Congress of Industrial Organizations. After several successful strikes the workers in the steel and automobile industries were organized. As the CIO gained prestige, union membership increased rapidly. When the AF of L saw

Craft unions are sometimes called horizontal because they include workers with the same or similar skills, no matter what industry they work in. Industrial unions may be called vertical, since all workers in an industry, no matter what their skill, are in the same union.

the success of its rival in organizing workers in mass-production industries, it too began to press for industrial organization.

UNION STRENGTH INCREASES DURING WORLD WAR II

By the beginning of World War II organized labor had over 10 million members. The CIO's share was only slightly less than that of the AF of L. With many new workers joining the industrial work force, membership jumped to approximately 15 million by the end of the war. Unions gave a no-strike pledge for the duration of the war and had, in general, an excellent production record.

Even before the war was over, however, the public's favorable image of labor had begun to change. Several strikes in 1944 and a record high number of strikes immediately following the war contributed to the change. Strikes in such key industries as meat-packing, coal, steel, and even transportation caused major inconvenience to the public. In addition, the cost of living

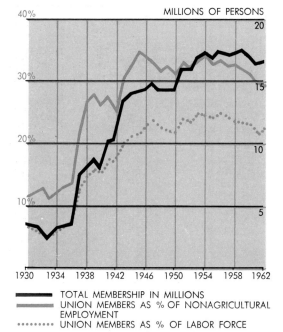

40%   MILLIONS OF PERSONS

1930 1934 1938 1942 1946 1950 1954 1958 1962

▬▬▬▬▬ TOTAL MEMBERSHIP IN MILLIONS
▬▬▬▬▬ UNION MEMBERS AS % OF NONAGRICULTURAL
        EMPLOYMENT
········· UNION MEMBERS AS % OF LABOR FORCE

Figure 5–1 Changes in Union Membership

Union membership increased in 1962 for the first time since 1959. A downward drift has been evident in the importance of union membership in relation to the labor force and to nonagricultural employment. The declining percentage of nonfarm members belonging to labor unions is partially explained by the increasing percentage of the work force engaged in service industries and white-collar jobs. These groups are less inclined to join unions. SOURCE: N.I.C.B., *Road Maps of Industry* No. 1487

skyrocketed and many people preferred to place the blame directly on labor rather than on the removal of price and wage controls. The pendulum, which had seemed to swing in favor of labor for a number of years, was now moving against it. Shortly, this change was reflected in legislation.

Postwar conditions bring reform and consolidation

Labor had hailed the passage of the National Labor Relations Act of 1935 (known popularly as the Wagner Act), but it resented bitterly the passage of the Labor-Management Relations Act of 1947 (known popularly as the Taft-Hartley Act). It is difficult to give an unbiased appraisal of an act that has caused such emotional controversy. Most impartial observers would agree on the following:

1. The Taft-Hartley Act reversed the trend by which government bolstered the power of unions and it applied controls over unions as well as management.

2. It tried to establish standards for the internal management and operation of unions, although it had difficulty in securing compliance.

3. It sought, with only limited success, to avoid the undesirable effects of major strikes on the economy.

While labor seems to have learned to live with what it originally called a "slave-labor act," those who expected the Taft-Hartley Act to be a cure-all soon discovered its weaknesses. Investigations by Congress which disclosed corrupt practices of some union officials, including unauthorized use of union funds and undemocratic methods of getting and maintaining control of the union, led to the passage of the Labor-Management Reporting and Disclosure Act of 1959 (popularly known as the Landrum-Griffin Act). A weakness of regulatory legislation was shown by the inability of the Railroad Labor Act (in any other industry it would have been the Taft-Hartley Act) to avert a threatened major railroad strike in 1963. On that occasion, presidential and congressional intervention introduced compulsory arbitration on some issues.

THE GREAT MERGER

Early in the 1950's the AF of L and CIO began talking about merging. The major influences that acted to bring the two giant unions together were:

1. The feeling that unity might provide organized labor with greater political power to stem legislative attacks

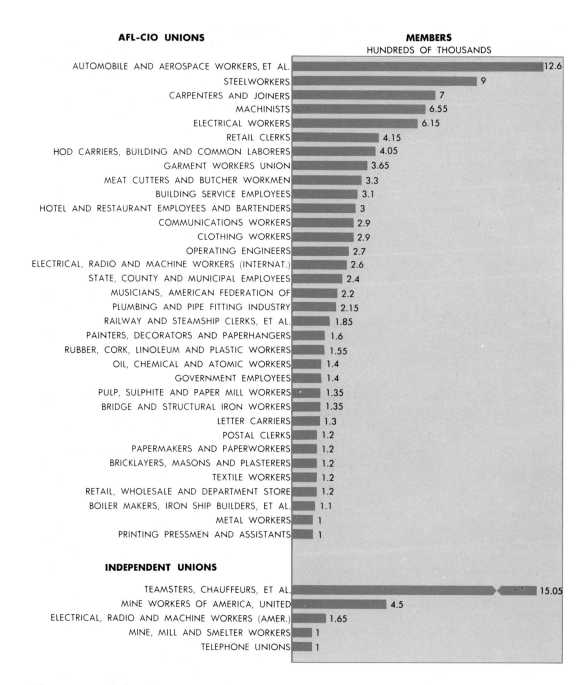

Figure 5-2 Labor Union Memberships: Unions with a Membership of 100,000 or over as of July 1, 1965.   SOURCE: *World Almanac*

2. The fact that leadership within the unions had changed hands, eliminating some of the personal animosities that had been an obstacle to a merger
3. The slow growth in membership that set in after the close of World War II
4. The increasing interest on the part of the AF of L in using industrial organization

In 1955 the two unions were joined, resulting in a giant association representing the common interests of almost sixteen million workers.

INDEPENDENT UNIONS

Outside the AFL–CIO are about three million workers organized in independent unions. The largest of these is the International Brotherhood of Teamsters, which was expelled from the AFL–CIO in 1957 because of dissatisfaction with the activities of some of the Teamster leaders. The four railroad brotherhoods and the United Mine Workers make up most of the remaining independent union membership.

Recent history

The last decade has produced little that labor can cheer about. Membership in unions has remained almost the same in spite of the increase in the labor force. Legislation has placed greater control over unions and their leaders; investigations by Senator McClellan's Labor Committee have uncovered corrupt practices, and several prolonged strikes and threats of strikes have made the public and its representatives less than friendly. In addition, the number of manual workers, who are most likely to join unions, has not increased as fast as has the number of white-collar workers. The latter identify more with management and are less inclined to join unions. However, organized labor is no longer the weak "underdog" that enlists the sympathy and energies of outsiders looking for a righteous cause. It is recognized as part of the American way of life. Whether the pendulum will again swing in its favor in the future remains in doubt.

Part B   Labor–Management Relations—Focus for Conflict

Although labor and management both profit by prosperity, since a "big pie" allows everyone to have larger portions, conflicts about the distribution of the "pie" arise. Each side tries to make sure that its position and demands will prevail. To do so, both management and labor use methods they consider necessary to "win."

Weapons used by management

Weapons used by employers to combat unions have frequently been very effective, but some have been considered extremely harsh by labor. In addition to the methods previously described, management has used the following devices:

Company unions were set up by management to discourage or prevent workers from joining an existing union or starting a union of their own. These unions were largely dominated by management.

Yellow-dog contracts made workers sign a contract not to join a union as a condition of employment. If they did join a union, they violated the contract and were subject not only to being discharged but to being sued as well.

Blacklists containing the names of union organizers were circulated among employers to prevent these men from getting jobs and to warn employers of what these men might try to do if hired to work for a company.

A *lockout*, an employer's strike, was also used. By closing his business, or threatening to close it, the employer could bring great pressure to bear on workers to agree to his demands.

An *injunction*, a court order restraining some person or group from particular actions, was sometimes used. Employers would request judges to issue injunctions to prevent unions from striking or picketing, claiming such action threatened their property. Although the union could defend itself, judges were often less than sympathetic with the workers' cause, and frequently the issuance of a temporary injunction was enough to break a strike.

All of these devices have been declared illegal or have been sufficiently limited in use to render them ineffective.

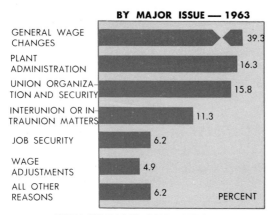

TOTAL STOPPAGES, 3,362 = 100%

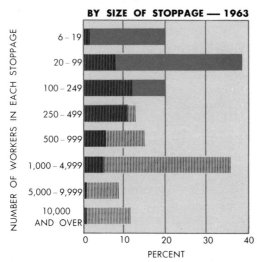

‖‖‖ TOTAL WORKERS INVOLVED, 941,000 = 100%
■ NUMBER OF STOPPAGES, 3,362 = 100%

Weapons used by unions

Unions also have weapons which have been used to win demands. The heart of unionism is collective bargaining, in which union officials negotiate with representatives of management to secure such benefits as higher wages, shorter hours, improved working conditions, longer vacations and sick leaves, and better retirement benefits. Because employees are many and employers few, only by uniting do members of unions feel they can compete successfully with management in bargaining. In order to achieve this equality, the union seeks to be recognized as the bargaining agent for the workers in the making of a labor contract. This is a legal agreement between labor and management covering all conditions of work and labor relations for a specific period of time. To represent the workers more effectively, the union tries to enlist all the workers in the company. It does this by one of the following means, listed in order of preference:

The *closed shop* makes it a requirement of employment that the worker be a member of the union. By limiting membership, the union can control the supply of workers. This practice is now illegal.

The *union shop* allows the employer to hire anyone, but the new worker must join

Figure 5–3   Work Stoppages in the United States

Work stoppages as shown on this chart include all strikes and lockouts occurring during the year involving six workers or more for one full shift or longer. Stoppages in 1963 totaled 3,362, the second lowest during the postwar period. The number of workers involved and the number of mandays of idleness during the year were the lowest of the postwar years. The major issues for over 70 percent of the stoppages in 1963 were: general wage changes, 39 percent; plant administration, 16 percent; and union organization and security, 16 percent. SOURCES: N.I.C.B., *Road Maps of Industry* No. 1496; U.S. Department of Labor, Bureau of Labor Statistics

the union within a specified period — usually between thirty and sixty days.

The *agency shop* requires all workers to pay dues to the union because the union acts as their agent in bargaining, but workers are not required to join the union. This arrangement reduces the tension among those who feel that a worker should have a right to join or not to join a union without being discriminated against in employment.

The union may ask the employer for a *checkoff* agreement, whereby the employer deducts from the employee's paycheck his union dues. This insures continuity of membership and protects union authority.

The *open shop* is far less acceptable to unions because it allows the employers to hire nonunion workers and the workers are not required to join the union at any time during their employment. Under an open-shop agreement the union may be the bargaining agent for all the workers or only for those who are members of the union, as stated in the contract.

Two variations of the above conditions have developed within recent years. The *maintenance-of-membership shop* requires workers to continue their membership in the union for the duration of the contract under which they are working. If they are not members of the union, they do not have to join. The *preferential shop* exists when management agrees to hire union members as long as they are available, in preference to nonunion workers.

The *strike* is a work stoppage organized by the union. It is most likely to be used at the time of expiration of an existing labor contract. If the stoppage is not sanctioned by the union, it is called a *wildcat strike*. Without the power to strike, unions would be in an extremely weak bargaining position. Not only is the employer faced with the loss of income but he may lose some of his customers permanently. In addition, his fixed costs, which in some cases may be substantial, will continue.

Strikes are very costly for workers as well. Though the union often compensates

Table 5–1 Work Stoppages, Selected Years, 1885–1964

Year	Strikes and lockouts	Workers involved (thousands)	Man-days idle (thousands)	Year	Strikes and lockouts	Workers involved (thousands)	Man-days idle (thousands)
1885	695	258	n.a.	1933	1,695	1,168	16,872
1890	1,897	373	n.a.	1935	2,014	1,117	15,456
1895	1,255	407	n.a.	1939	2,613	1,171	17,812
1900	1,839	568	n.a.	1943	3,752	1,981	13,501
1905	2,186	302	n.a.	1945	4,750	3,470	38,025
1915	1,593	n.a.	n.a.	1949	3,606	3,030	50,500
1917	4,450	1,227	n.a.	1952	5,117	3,540	59,100
1920	3,411	1,463	n.a.	1957	3,673	1,390	16,500
1925	1,301	428	n.a.	1960	3,333	1,320	19,100
1929	921	289	5,352	1961	3,367	1,450	16,300
1930	637	183	3,317	1962	3,614	1,230	18,600
1932	841	324	10,502	1963	3,362	941	16,100
				1964	3,655	1,640	22,900

n.a. = not available

More man-days of work are lost because of accidents, illness, and absenteeism than because of strikes. Although wages remain the single most important issue, other factors are becoming increasingly important. SOURCE: U. S. Department of Labor, Bureau of Labor Statistics, *Analysis of Work Stoppages*

for loss of pay by providing strike benefits and some states give unemployment benefits, a prolonged strike will force most workers to dip into their savings or to borrow money. Even when a strike results in the workers' winning most of their demands, it may take years for the workers to make up for the lost income. This has led some to believe that a strike is never worthwhile. Others point out that the threat of a strike would be ineffective if strikes did not take place. Still others base their argument on principles, claiming the strike to be the only real weapon labor has in its struggle for its rights.

Because strikes may cause inconveniences to the public and receive a great deal of newspaper coverage, many people get a false impression of their number and severity. Less than one half of one percent of man-days of work have been lost because of strikes, considerably less than the amount of time lost due to accidents, illness, and absenteeism.

Picketing is an activity carried on by unions during a strike. By placing picket lines around a business, the workers hope that their presence and their signs will prevent nonunion men (scabs) from taking their jobs. They also try to persuade customers to avoid doing business with the company. In many parts of the country people have respected picket lines, and the weapon of picketing has helped unions win their strikes.

A *boycott* is a refusal by a union to patronize a business with which it is having a dispute. A *secondary boycott*, now illegal, occurs when a nonstriking union prohibits its members from dealing in any way with a company whose workers are on strike or from purchasing its products.

A *union label* signifies that the product was made by union workers and according to union standards. Organized labor has tried to make consumers conscious of buying only goods with such labels.

The *slowdown* occurs when workers purposely reduce the speed at which they work. This increases the cost of production to the employer and will reduce his profits. As a form of protest it represents the direct action occasionally used by workers during the early growth of unions.

Political action has been an important method by which labor has sought to accomplish its aims. Financial contributions, together with meeting halls, posters, and sound trucks, are used to help candidates who are "friends of labor." While it is highly debatable whether the unions have any considerable control over their members when they go to the polls, few politicians, particularly from highly industrialized states, are willing to risk the antagonism of organized labor.

Part C   Governmental Influence on Union Development

Labor legislation

One of the major factors in determining the pattern of union development has been labor legislation. As you know, laws passed by the Congress are subject to the interpretation of the courts. Until the late 1930's the courts were frequently unfriendly to labor unions.

EARLY LABOR LAWS

The Sherman Antitrust Act, aimed at business combinations, was more fre-quently used against labor unions in the 1890's than against business. In part to correct this situation, Congress passed the Clayton Act in 1914, exempting labor unions from prosecution under the antitrust laws. However, judicial interpretation still persisted in restricting the growth and activities of unions.

It was not until the 1930's that labor was able to feel the benefits of legislation passed in its behalf. In 1932 the Norris-

LaGuardia Act made the yellow-dog contract unenforceable in federal courts and placed restrictions on the use of injunctions in labor-management disputes.

WAGNER ACT

The most important law passed in labor's behalf was the National Labor Relations Act, or Wagner Act, of 1935. Labor frequently refers to it as the Magna Carta of the labor movement. It recognized labor's right to bargain collectively. To implement this, it set up the National Labor Relations Board (NLRB). Among its duties the Board supervises elections, determining who will represent the workers in their bargaining with employers. The NLRB also investigates any complaints concerning violation of contracts. The Act prohibits management from interfering with attempts of unions to organize, from having any part in the administration of the union, and from practicing discrimination in the hiring or retaining of an employee because of membership in a union. Many students of the labor movement think that labor could not have achieved its present strength without the favorable provisions of the Wagner Act.

FAIR LABOR STANDARDS ACT

The Fair Labor Standards Act of 1938 established minimum wages and maximum hours in industries engaged in interstate commerce. It also called for overtime pay with double pay for Sundays and holidays when not part of the regular work week for the particular job.

TAFT-HARTLEY ACT

The Labor-Management Relations Act, or Taft-Hartley Act, of 1947 amended the Wagner Act. In the eyes of its supporters, the Taft-Hartley Act brought about a better balance between labor and management. Just as the Wagner Act specifies unfair practices of management and makes them unlawful, so the Taft-Hartley Act specifies unfair practices of labor. It prohibits unions from coercing workers to join, *featherbedding* (forcing employers to hire more work-

COURT DELAYS DOCK STRIKE UNDER TAFT-HARTLEY LAW FOR 80 DAYS

NEW YORK — The ban against a longshoremen's strike along the East and Gulf coasts was extended to the full 80 days allowed under the Taft-Hartley Law by Federal Judge Irving Ben Cooper.

Judge Cooper said the strike would "imperil the national health and safety," echoing the words of President Johnson.

The dockworkers are ordered to stay on the job under the terms of the expired contract until December 19 unless a new contract is agreed upon before that date.

The Taft-Hartley Act aims at preventing strikes by delaying them through a court order. How successful it has been is a matter of controversy.

ers than they need), calling secondary boycotts, calling a *jurisdictional strike* (one called by rival unions, each seeking authority), or failing to bargain with employers in good faith. In addition, it outlaws the closed shop and allows the government to suspend for eighty days (the "cooling-off period") a strike which may "imperil the national health or safety." Unions are required to give a sixty-day notice of their intention to strike.

One of the most dramatic controversies over the Taft-Hartley Act has been over Section 14(b), which permits states to pass laws prohibiting the union shop. These "right-to-work" laws have been passed in nineteen states, primarily in the Deep South, the Southwest, and the farm belt, where union organization is least extensive. Labor claims that these laws seriously hamper its attempts to recruit members. Those in favor of these laws and of the right of states to pass such laws insist that union membership should never be made a condition of employment.

LANDRUM-GRIFFIN ACT

The Labor-Management Reporting and Disclosure Act, or Landrum-Griffin Act, of 1959 was designed to reform corrupt unions and make their practices more democratic. It regulates union elections and also restricts some undesirable people—communists and former convicts—from holding union offices. In addition it places a tight control on the reporting of union finances, and guarantees the individual worker's right to participate in all proceedings of the union. The effectiveness of this legislation is open to question. However, organized labor has accepted most of the law without vigorous protests.

An example of collective bargaining: focus on agreement

To explain how the process of collective bargaining works, let us return to the example of developing our own business, "Build-a-City," which we used in Chapter 3. We have about 100 workers who until now have shown no desire to join a union. However, a member of the United Toy Workers Union, a national union organized along industrial lines and affiliated with the AFL–CIO, has spoken to some of our workers about the advantages of union membership. This labor organizer points out to our employees that wages of workers in organized industries are higher than in nonorganized ones, that working conditions and *fringe benefits* such as insurance benefits, sick time, and vacations are better, and that the individual worker can feel more secure with the great power and resources of a huge organization protecting his rights. Alone he is at the mercy of the employer, who can dismiss him without any cause. Since most of our workers seem to agree with these arguments, the United Toy Workers Union petitions the National Labor Relations Board (NLRB) to become the exclusive bargaining agent for the workers in our factory. A date for voting on whether this union should be designated the official bargaining agent for the workers is set.

We in management are unhappy with these developments and feel that our employees are being ungrateful in showing their lack of confidence in our attempts to treat them fairly. We believe that we are paying our workers for their full marginal revenue product. If we are forced to pay higher wages than this, either we will have to cut down on the number of workers so as to move to a higher marginal revenue product (see p. 75) or, if our competition will permit, we will have to pass the cost on to the consumer. However, raising the price will reduce our sales as consumers find substitutes. In turn, a decline in sales will reduce the number of workers we need. If wage demands become excessive we, as a new firm unable to withstand any long periods of losses, may be forced out of business. The union, having monopoly power, can force its demands on us and prevent us from exercising our right to operate and control our business as we think it should be run. Our only alternative may be to join with other employers to meet power with power.

When the votes are counted, the NLRB declares the United Toy Workers Union to be the sole bargaining agent at our plant. We may not like the results, but we call together our lawyer and economist and sit down at the bargaining table with a representative of the union, the union's lawyer, and the union's economist. It is not essential that lawyers and economists be brought in, but it is likely that persons skilled in both professions will have prepared position papers presenting reasons for the acceptance or rejection of demands. We are determined to draw up a labor contract, listing the conditions of work and the methods for settling differences. Such a contract usually ends disagreements for its duration.

METHODS OF REACHING AGREEMENT

Many hours of discussion narrow the disagreements down to two:

1. Should the company pay the entire cost of a medical insurance policy or only half?
2. Should workers with less than one year of working time for the company be entitled to a week's vacation with pay?

So far we have used *conciliation*, with only our company's representative and the union's representative present, to settle our differences. Since this has not worked in resolving the two problems listed above, we now try mediation.

Mediation is settlement with the help of an impartial person having no connection with either side. The mediator may be a professional, trained in bringing dispu-

CITIZENS' COMMISSION RECOMMENDS PLAN TO SETTLE DETROIT NEWSPAPER STRIKE

DETROIT — Gov. Romney's three-man commission recommended a three-step procedure for settling the three-months-old newspaper strike in Detroit. Although the Governor endorsed the plan, it remains for the two striking unions and the two struck newspapers to agree to the proposal.

The first step calls for the two sides to first reconsider their positions and resume negotiations. If by October 26 no settlement is reached, the commission recommends that mediators enter the talks, with authority to arbitrate if the strike continues until November 1. The arbitration would be binding on both sides.

Neither the newspapers nor the union have had any comment on the commission's recommendation.

Arbitration is usually resorted to when mediation fails to bring about agreement.

tants together and trusted by each side, or a prominent person acceptable to both parties. The mediator does not provide an answer. He merely helps to bring the two sides together.

If mediation fails, both sides may turn to *voluntary arbitration*. Unlike mediation, voluntary arbitration commits the disputants to abide by the arbitrator's decision. This agreement is morally binding but not legally enforceable. *Compulsory arbitration* requires the disputants to submit disagreements to an arbitrator. While this method has been used in Australia and New Zealand, and in the United States during the second World War and during the threatened railroad strike of 1963, neither American labor nor American business approves of it. Both groups consider compulsory arbitration a threat to free collective bargaining.

Since both union and management recognize that industrial peace is important for our company, our differences are finally settled and the contract signed. The agreement (contract) is for three years, with negotiations for a new contract to be started three months before the old one expires. Any disagreements in the interpretation of the provisions of the contract are to be handled by a selected labor-management committee. If this committee fails to reach a satisfactory decision within a month, the disagreement is to be turned over to an arbitrator agreeable to both sides.

Once an agreement is completed, our attitude toward the union undergoes a change. The union leaders, while tough and demanding at times, are responsible men who recognize that only a strong, healthy, and profitable firm can provide workers with security. The union has existed for many years and has a reputation of driving hard bargains but of always being fair. We can also take some satisfaction in knowing that, signing with this union reduces the chance that some irresponsible or corrupt organizers might seek to gain short-range benefits for themselves is greatly lessened.

The classical model and labor today

From the example of union organizing and labor contract negotiations in our company, it is evident that the classical model is no longer the exclusive guide in determining wage policy. The reasons for departing from this model are many and complex, but all the causes may be traced back to (1) the Industrial Revolution, (2) the development of organized labor, and (3) the realization that labor is not merely a factor of production to be bought in the marketplace. The number of persons employed in industries where individual workers can draw up separate contracts with their employers has been reduced considerably in all fields and to almost nothing in our mass-production industries. Organized labor, while making up only about 25 percent of our labor force, has a definite influence on wage rates of unorganized workers. State and federal legislation on minimum wage rates, maximum hours, child labor laws, and conditions of work has brought about changes in the supply and demand curves as applied to labor.

NEW TRENDS IN LABOR RELATIONS

Historians frequently refer to the last hundred years as the era of the "rise of the common man." More specifically, they point to the increased dignity associated with labor. Papal encyclicals, the spread of liberal ideas, and state and federal legislation have emphasized the importance of humanism in labor relations. In more recent times, economic thinking has emphasized the importance of the purchasing power of the general public. In keeping with this trend, Henry Ford recognized that the automobile industry could be a huge success only if his workers could afford to buy the products that they made. Labor has been recognized as a very significant consumer in the economy. In Chapter 11 we shall see the relation of income to consumer spending.

INDUSTRY-WIDE BARGAINING

If you refer to your newspaper, you can probably find that bargaining between labor and management is going on in a way that would have been difficult for economists to anticipate only a few years ago. Sitting around a bargaining table might be the representatives of the steelworkers or automobile workers on the one side and those of a great corporation such as United States Steel or General Motors on the other. The contract that they sign will probably apply not only to the workers of the corporation concerned but also to labor throughout that particular industry. Negotiating labor contracts which will set a pattern for workers in an entire industry is known as *industry-wide bargaining.*

Settlements arrived at in key industries frequently set a pattern for settlements in many other mass-production industries. New kinds of agreements often become widely accepted, too. Establishment of a 3.2 percent wage increase based on an estimate of a 3.2 percent increase in productivity per worker, an *escalator clause* which provides workers with automatic increases and decreases based on fluctuations in the cost of living, or using the principle of profits as a basis for determining wage increases will, when gained in one contract, probably be applied to other contracts. Even the wages of those not organized are eventually affected.

THE CLASSICAL MODEL IS STILL IMPORTANT

Although all the evidence presented here indicates a change from the classical model, it is still doubtful that we have departed greatly from that model. The productivity of labor is, in the long run, the major factor in determining real wage rates. While unions may limit the supply of labor available, causing wages to rise, these wages can come only from increased productivity. Let us consider further the effect of a change in wage rates.

Suppose that a strong union is able to bargain for an increase in wages of five percent when productivity has gone up only three percent. Such a change will increase the cost of production per unit and force the employer to pay for it by cutting into his profits or by raising prices to the consumer. In industries where there is little competition the additional cost will probably be passed on to the consumer immediately. In competitive industries prices will rise eventually because of the additional purchasing power in the hands of the workers, who are also consumers. However, in the interim some of the weakest firms will be forced out of business. Under these conditions unemployment will probably rise and thereby cause wages to fall.

If prices rise two percent to pay for the additional cost, the five percent increase in wages will have a purchasing power of only three percent, the same as the increase in productivity. Some critics of labor use the illustration just given as proof that labor is responsible for what is called a *cost-push* inflation. They maintain that wage increases that are in excess of increased productivity per man-hour have raised costs and forced prices up. Defenders of labor reply that the cost for additional wages should come from excessively high profits. In the negotiation for a new contract in the automotive industry in 1964, Walter Reuther, head of the United Auto Workers, argued that the higher wages he asked for could be paid from the huge earnings which the automobile manufacturers were making and even allow for prices on cars to be lowered. Some critics of industry go a step further and say that business welcomes the opportunity to give a wage increase because such action permits raising prices not only high enough to pay for the additional cost but even higher, so that profits will be larger than ever.

Do unions raise wages?

The debate on the influence of unions in raising wages will undoubtedly continue with no definite answer. Variations will be found from industry to industry. We do know that monopoly power in both industry and labor has brought about changes in the supply and demand for labor. We also know that labor as a whole cannot long receive wages in excess of the value it produces, and that probably some government regulation is necessary to make sure that no segment of the economy will disrupt the development of the American economy as a whole. Equally important, we can all agree that if we can make the "pie" (the total goods and services produced) grow faster than the mouths that will consume it, everyone can have a bigger portion. A highly skilled labor force, characterized by a high degree of productivity, has been one of our country's chief assets in giving us a high standard of living. There can be no substitute for it.

Part D   The Problem: Is Automation a Blessing or a Curse to Labor?

Labor has always been interested in a market in which the demand for labor is high and the supply small. Such a market condition will allow wages to remain high or move still higher. If, on the other hand, large numbers of people move into the labor market without a corresponding increase in the number of jobs, wage rates are threatened. As we scan the papers we find that employment seems to be going up steadily, with few interruptions, but that the percentage of people unemployed has only recently declined, due largely to the increased expenditures for the Viet Nam war. The major explanation for this seemingly odd phenomenon is that more people are joining the labor force than are leaving it. This means that we have to increase the number

"Hey, Joe! It says our jobs are next!"

of jobs available just to prevent the number of unemployed from going up, to say nothing of reducing the number of jobless.

LABOR AND TECHNOLOGICAL CHANGE

An additional complication that poses a threat which many consider more serious is illustrated by a cartoon showing machinery replacing human labor. This is an old problem that has always concerned labor, and it has been identified in many ways, most frequently by the term *technological unemployment.* Today we usually refer to the introduction of machines to replace human labor as *automation.*

Although there are many definitions of automation, the major element distinguishing it from the meaning given in the paragraph above is that it involves a continuous operation of production linking together the several or many different jobs to be performed, usually by some feedback system. In the 1920's and 1930's the assembly-line production technique was greatly refined and extended in this country. A product would start at one end of an assembly line and would be conveyed, frequently by a belt, past many workmen, each of whom would add to or perform some kind of operation to make the finished product. Automation differs from the described assembly-line technique in that machines control machines. Through a system of feeding back information, the machines on the assembly line are told when they are to perform their job on the product passing by and what that operation will be.

Automation has already been developed to a great degree in the production of petroleum, chemicals, and certain phases of steel, paper, plastics, and even automobiles. In the office and research laboratory the computer can perform many kinds of operations, store tremendous amounts of information, and, most important for our study, replace workers. Management uses automation or any other kind of mechanization when doing so will reduce costs and perform the job as well as or better than human beings will do it.

MANAGEMENT AND TECHNOLOGICAL CHANGE

While we are focusing our attention on the effects of automation on employment, it is important to recognize the far-reaching problems which this new development in technology presents to management and education. Investment in machinery, research, and education takes on new significance as both firms and workers struggle for positions on a more flexible economic ladder. It is true that firms with large amounts of capital can support large research staffs, but ideas that change production techniques or consumer demand can and do come from small businesses. No firm, no manager, and no worker can afford to take success for granted. Rapid technological progress in today's world may very well make present standards of production obsolete for tomorrow's market.

To understand better the effect of automation on unemployment, let us look at the problem from three different points of view. Do not assume that the "truth" is to be found in any one position. While some viewpoints may be more politically expedient, they may not be characteristic of the real world in which we live. Examine the questions that remain to be answered after reading the three viewpoints presented. Your answers to these questions may help you arrive at a conclusion of what policy, if any, we should have in trying to resolve the problems that automation may create. Make sure that you understand when you are expressing value judgments, when you are stating facts, and when you are using economic reasoning.

Automation as a threat to labor

Testifying before the Joint Economic Committee of Congress, two of the most prominent labor leaders in the country pointed out some of the problems which automation and other technological changes pose for labor. Certainly the most serious threat has been the replacement of human labor by machines. A few facts illustrate this change. For the period between 1953 and 1960 the food and beverage industry increased its production 20 percent but decreased the number of workers in production and maintenance by eight percent. Textile mills had a similar rise in production during this period but dropped 22 percent of their workers in production and maintenance. In basic steel, production increased only slightly during this period, but production and maintenance jobs declined by 52,600.

Although it is true that white-collar jobs in the chemical and electrical machinery industries have increased faster than blue-collar jobs have decreased, opportunities for those discharged have been very small. Many skilled and semiskilled workers have seen their jobs downgraded or eliminated. They have found that their skills are obsolete and that new training and experience are necessary.

The much-publicized retraining and relocation program can help, but it does not bring about a solution to the problem. A study of a well-financed retraining program set up after a plant had been closed showed that of the 431 production workers who could have benefited from the program, only thirteen completed the course and only seven found jobs involving their new skills. Few workers appear anxious to take a retraining course, and many are either too old or do not have the ability to learn the kinds of skills that are in demand.

Wages will decline in jobs where technological changes reduce demand. The general wage level is likely to go down as displaced workers try to find new jobs. It is estimated that some two and a half million jobs will have to be found each year in the decade ahead to take care of those who are replaced by technological developments and new workers looking for their first job.

A world-famous mathematician who has contributed much to the development of automatic control machines predicted that if we were to have an all-out effort in producing automated equipment, we would have a depression that would be far worse than the Great Depression of the thirties. Furthermore, human labor would be competing with machinery, which is the equivalent of slave labor. Only if we are willing to abandon our worship of progress and our willingness to allow the few to benefit at the expense of the many can our new knowledge be a blessing rather than a curse.

Automation as a blessing to labor

The major reason for the remarkable advance in man's standard of living is the increase in his productive capacity. Behind this increased productive capacity is the technological progress that has given man tools that perform more efficiently. The latest development in the Industrial Revolution is automation. It promises to help man achieve an even higher standard of living by producing goods more cheaply, reducing hours of work, and allowing man more leisure to develop his talents and enjoy the fruits of his labor. Nowhere is this better illustrated than in the United States, where technological progress has been the greatest and the standard of living the highest.

The fear that automation will bring widespread unemployment is unfounded. There has never been as much automation as we have today, and there have never been so many people employed. In an interview on the subject of automation a labor leader representing a lithographers' union said that his union was in favor of automation because it brought down unit costs sufficiently to allow employers to pay higher wages with a 35-hour week, three-week vacations, ten paid holidays, and many other benefits. Membership in his union has increased at a far faster rate than the general population. While admitting that some workers may have some difficulty for short periods of time in retraining or in relocating, these inconveniences are more than offset by the widespread long-range benefits which reduced costs bring.

A representative of one of America's major corporations pointed out to a congressional committee that automation can provide new and increased employment opportunities by (1) lower-cost, higher-volume business, (2) the expansion of service industries, (3) the supplying of automated equipment, and (4) the development of new products, leading to the expansion of existing firms and the creation of new enterprises.

The same arguments which carriage makers advanced when the automobile was introduced are being used by those who fear the computer and other automatic control machines. Looking back with historical perspective, we should welcome this revolution as something positive in man's effort to free himself from drudgery and provide himself with more of the things he wants.

A moderate position

Between the two extreme positions stated above is one that recognizes the advantages of technological progress but seeks to avoid the hardships that come to many in the transition process. In many industries management and labor have developed elaborate plans to ease the adjustment of workers who are replaced by machines. These plans include the establishment of job retraining programs financed by management, with some of the money coming from savings realized by using new machinery. Other programs include the introduction of new equipment in a slow and orderly way to prevent mass layoffs, the reduction of hours by increasing vacation periods, and the establishment of funds to be given to discharged workers for a period of time to lessen the hardships of the period of unemployment. The federal government, in its manpower and redevelopment program and its program to make "war on poverty," is helping to alleviate the burdens of those affected.

Considering an answer

In spite of the efforts just described, a study by the Bureau of Labor Statistics indicates that over one million workers lost their jobs in the period from 1953 to 1959 because of technological changes. This leaves us with the following problems that you, the citizen, will have to decide.

Can we rely on the classical model to provide answers to the problem? Will the absence of any government aid, or even aid from business, make the worker more mobile in seeking a job, even if he may suffer hardships in the period between jobs?

Can labor and management work out solutions together without the aid of government? What is management's responsibility, if any, to displaced workers? What is management's responsibility to its stockholders in trying to maximize profits by cutting costs? What is management's responsibility to the consumer in passing on reduced costs in the form of lower prices?

Can management, in conjunction with labor, ease the difficulties of automating without reducing competition? Under conditions of pure competition, won't the firm which automates first and to the greatest extent, disregarding the hardships that may result to its workers, be in the best position to make the most profits?

If the government must give assistance, as it has now done, how far can it go without interfering with our free-enterprise tradition? Will government interference lessen the mobility of labor, and thereby delay the long-range solutions to the problem? Does government have a responsibility to protect workers from the hardships of technological changes over which the worker has no control?

REVIEW: *the highlights of the chapter*

1. Labor unions are organized to improve the bargaining position of workers. The history of organized labor has moved like a pendulum, with progress made from 1898 to 1904, 1914 to 1920, and 1933 to 1947. The periods before, in between, and after were characterized by unfriendly courts, unfavorable legislation, and conflicts with employers.

2. The Knights of Labor, the American Federation of Labor, and the Congress of Industrial Organizations were the major labor organizations shaping American labor policy.

3. Unions are organized along both craft and industrial lines.

4. Both employers and unions have used many weapons to win their demands. Many of the most severe practices of both groups have now been outlawed.

5. The federal government gave its official endorsement to unions in the Wagner Act. The Taft-Hartley Act attempted to balance the power of unions and management.

6. Collective bargaining is the heart of unionism. Conciliation, mediation, and arbitration are methods of reaching agreement.

7. Automation is the latest technological change to threaten the employment opportunities of workers.

IN CONCLUSION: *some aids to understanding*

Terms for review

injunction	lockout
closed shop	union shop
collective bargaining	open shop
reform union	maintenance-of-membership shop
craft union	preferential shop
industrial union	boycott
company union	conciliation
yellow-dog contract	compulsory arbitration
blacklist	featherbedding
jurisdictional strike	"right-to-work" laws

Names to know

Knights of Labor	CIO
Norris-LaGuardia Act	Taft-Hartley Act
Landrum-Griffin Act	Wagner Act
AF of L	National Labor Relations Board

Questions for review

1. What changes did the Industrial Revolution bring about in regard to the position of labor?
2. What major factors impeded the growth of the labor movement in the United States?
3. Contrast the objectives of the Knights of Labor and the American Federation of Labor. Justify the labels "reform union" and "bread-and-butter union" as applied to each of them.
4. Compare the position of organized labor in the 1920's with its position in the 1930's. Explain the reasons for the difference.
5. Make a list of the weapons used by management and the weapons used by unions. Which ones have been declared illegal?
6. Why has organized labor sometimes referred to the Wagner Act as the "Magna Carta of the labor movement"? What were the objectives of the Taft-Hartley Act with regard to the unions?
7. "In spite of many factors interfering with the classical model's approach to wage determination, the theory it offers is still important in explaining wage rates." Explain the meaning of this statement.

Additional questions and problems

1. In a brief essay, justify the demands of labor for the following:
   (a) An increase in wages coupled with a demand that prices of the produced article remain the same.
   (b) A share in the profits of industry without a direct contribution to the risks.
   Now draw up the notes for a speech of rebuttal by the head of a large corporation.
2. Select two leaders in the American labor movement and explain the differences in their philosophy and their methods.
3. Draw a cartoon showing the weapons of labor arrayed against those of management. In a second panel illustrate the same idea, adding the role of government as the third party.
4. What are the arguments against compulsory arbitration
   (a) by unions?
   (b) by management?

Present the argument of the public in support of compulsory arbitration of major labor disputes.

5. Bring the following ideas into a discussion of automation:
    (a) We must create two and a half million new jobs each year to keep our labor force employed.
    (b) Fifty percent of the jobs of 1975 have not as yet been created.
    (c) We must learn to use leisure time intelligently or automation will be a curse, not a boon.
    (d) Today's education must be technical and must emphasize skills.
    (e) Automation may create a temporary unemployment problem, but in the long run it will increase the number of jobs.

6 Natural Resources, Capital, and Management: Their Uses and Rewards

Preview

Although labor is extremely important in producing the goods and services we want, there would be no products without the other three factors: natural resources, capital, and management. We are concerned here with what contribution each of these factors makes in the production process, how business enterprise acquires the right amount of each, and what rewards are received for the part which each factor plays. Having a limited supply of all factors of production, we find that the question of how we allocate these resources to produce what the consumers want is still our central problem. As with labor, the rewards must be based on what each unit of a factor contributes to the total value of the product. We will have to return to our classical model of pure competition in order to determine resource allocation, as well as to study conditions which deviate from it.

Overview

What considerations are most important in determining the value of property?

What considerations determine the vast differences in interest rates?

What is meant by a "fair profit"?

104

Part A   *Production and Distribution Characteristics of the Factors of Production*

Selecting the best combination of factors

We have already indicated that production involves the combining of certain amounts of four ingredients—natural resources (such as land), labor, capital, and management—to make the goods and supply the services we want. The businessman goes to the market for the factors of production knowing that he wants to produce certain kinds of goods in certain amounts and that, in order to do so, he will have to buy certain quantities of each of the factors of production. He should have some idea of the value of the products he will make when he offers them for sale in the consumer market. Actually he cannot be sure of this value, since prices may change, but he tries to make a logical estimate. He will

The successful business adds factors of production so long as the marginal revenue product (the value in dollars that the last factor adds) is as large as or larger than the marginal cost (the cost in dollars for employing the last factor added).

then buy the best combination of the factors of production to produce the goods. Determining how many units of each factor to use so that his costs will be lowest and his revenue highest is the key to his success in business. It is also the answer to our basic question of allocating our limited resources to yield the greatest return in satisfaction to the consumer. This principle can be seen in the following example, Table 6–1, where

---

Table 6–1   Input-Output Analysis of Factors of Production

	Units	
Natural Resources	6	
Labor	60	**YIELDS** 100,000
Capital	8	units of
Management	26	production
	100	

	Units	
Natural Resources	6	
Labor	58	**YIELDS** 110,000
Capital	12	units of
Management	24	production
	100	

Altering the composition of the factors of production can increase our efficiency. The problem for the businessman is to add units of each factor only so long as the cost for each unit (the marginal cost) is less than the value which that unit can add (the marginal revenue product).

---

changing the combinations of the units that we put into production will yield a different value for the output (same cost but more revenue). We are assuming that each input unit, regardless of which factor of production is considered, costs the same. In the example we increase our output by reducing our labor and management inputs and increasing our capital inputs.

Each additional unit of production creates additional value, known as the marginal product. As long as the costs of additional units that we add (inputs) are no more than the value of the additional value created (output), we can continue to add factors to expand our production. As we noted in Chapter 3, the businessman will expand his production, requiring additional factors of production, to the point where his marginal cost is equal to his marginal revenue. Since each factor of production reaches the point of diminishing returns at a different level, we will have to decide which factors will be the most profitable to add. Using the technical information that shows the amount of output capable of being produced by specific inputs is known as the *production function.*

Dividing return among the factors

Many people think of distribution as the movement of goods from the initial pro-ducer to the final consumer. The economist has a special meaning for distribution relating primarily to the problem of *For Whom. Distribution* – or, more accurately, *functional distribution* – is concerned with who, or what groups, will get what portion of the value or income created. Another way of stating this question is: How do we divide the "pie"? The size of the portion which each factor receives is the reward for the value each has contributed. Stated in an oversimplified way, the value that each factor contributes is determined by the supply and demand for each of the factors in the market.

Although we measure the value that each factor receives in dollars, we call the reward that each receives by a different name. Labor receives wages; natural resources, rent; capital, interest; and management, profits. Figure 6–1 shows the portion received by each factor in 1929 and

THE MARGINALISTS AND NEOCLASSICAL ANALYSIS

The Industrial Revolution brought with it a host of social and economic problems that caused great discontent in Europe during the nineteenth century. Not satisfied with the answers provided by the classical economists, people turned to new methods, such as socialism, trade unionism, and government intervention, to find solutions.

Some economists were unwilling to accept either the popular alternatives to laissez-faire or certain aspects of classical economic thinking. These men, including W. Stanley Jevons and Alfred Marshall of England; Karl Menger, Friedrich von Wieser, and Eugen Böhm-Bawerk of Austria; John Bates Clark of the United States; Herman Heinrich Gossen of Germany; and Léon Walras of France, developed a new approach — the marginalist or neoclassical school.

Marginalism focuses on the problem of resource allocation. Given a certain quantity of the factors of production, how can these factors

be used to satisfy the most needs? Like the classical economists, these men set their theories within a laissez-faire environment and oppose interference with the free market. They concentrate on microeconomics — the analysis of the single firm, the individual producer and consumer, and the formation of price for a single good. Their early theory starts with the concept of marginal utility as it relates to demand, and later spreads to cover marginal cost on the supply side. The marginalist sets forth the use of marginal productivity to account for the payment to each of the factors of production and to assist the businessman in maximizing his profits. Emphasis is on the yield from each unit added, since this return influences the decision to buy or sell more.

The concept of marginalism is still important, although its use has been modified by more recent theories. Of these the most significant is the macroeconomic approach of Keynes.

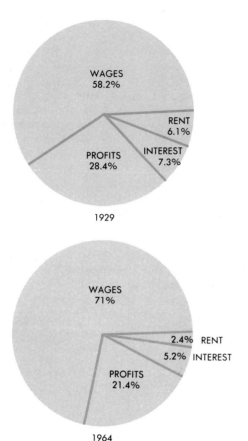

Figure 6-1   Distribution of National
Income Among the Factors
of Production

SOURCE: U.S. Department of Commerce

in 1964. Remember that the "pie" that was
divided in 1964 was far larger than that in
1929, thereby allowing all factors to receive
more.

Marginal productivity applied to the factors

In Chapter 4 we learned that the theory
of marginal productivity is based on the law
of diminishing returns. You will recall that
as we add more workers beyond a certain
point, each additional worker will add to the
total value of our production a lesser amount

than the preceding worker. This means that
it is profitable for us to keep adding workers
only until the marginal product, the value
created by the last worker, is equal to the
marginal cost.

This same theory is applied to the other
factors of production. Adding either land or
capital will show the same pattern of decreasing yields as units are added. When
the last additional unit costs more than the
value created by that unit, profits are bound
to be less. The producer should stop adding
factors of production before this, when the
marginal cost for resources and the marginal product—the added value obtained from
the resources—equal each other.

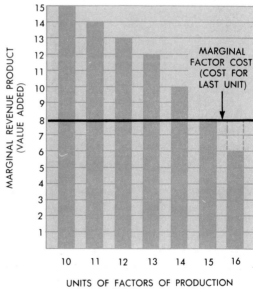

Figure 6-2   Most Efficient Production

It will pay the businessman to continue adding
units of factors of production as long as the value
created by the last unit (the marginal revenue
product) is not less than the cost for hiring the last
unit (the marginal factor cost). The use of the
sixteenth unit in this case would result in a loss.
Where should the producer stop adding units of
factors of production if the cost goes up to 10?

To make our understanding of the theory of marginal productivity more accurate, we must differentiate between marginal physical product and marginal revenue product. The former refers to the physical units added by the last additional factor whereas the latter refers to the dollar value added. Because businessmen and owners of the factors of production are interested in making the most dollars and because of certain technical aspects that need not concern us, we will use marginal revenue product.

Importance of the right combination of factors

In conditions approaching pure competition, the incentive for businessmen to seek new combinations of the factors of production to reduce costs and increase profits insures that the economy, and ultimately society, will progress. The development of new machinery costing less than the workers it replaces frees the displaced workers to seek jobs where their marginal productivity might be higher. This, of course, assumes that there are jobs for the displaced workers and that they are willing to move to another place for work. As we have seen, there is reason to question whether these assumptions about job opportunities and labor mobility are correct.

Firms that operate under conditions of imperfect competition must also consider their costs. However, because such firms have some control over supply and thereby can keep their prices higher than they would be under pure competition, they can afford to be less efficient. The poorly managed business operating under conditions of partial monopoly is able to conceal its wasteful use of limited resources under the cover of higher prices. The consumer must pay the difference.

Part B   Natural Resources and Rent

Natural resources (land, for example) are the ingredients that nature provides for use in production. Resources are distinguished from the other factors of production primarily because their supply is fixed. Our nation is very fortunate in the abundance and variety of its resources.

The nature of rent

When we use the term "rent," we are most likely to think of a tenant paying a certain amount of money per month for the use of property owned by a landlord. It may be a family "renting" an apartment, a businessman "renting" a store, or a salesman "renting" a car. When used in this way, *rent* means the price that is paid for the use of some durable good such as land, or buildings, or equipment, or even all three. Economists have a more exact term, *economic rent* (see p. 110), to distinguish this use from "renting" as applied above. *Land rent* is the price paid for land or other natural resources. It is the price paid for any factor of production that cannot be reproduced. It is subject to the same laws of supply and demand as are all other factors of production; but because the supply of natural resources is fixed, the supply curve is perfectly inelastic. This means that the price of rent is determined by demand. In our discussion we will use land in its common usage, recognizing that all natural resources may be treated in a similar manner.

Why do we pay rent?

Some of you may wonder why rent should be paid when nature, rather than man, has provided us with our natural resources. Why should anyone receive payment for something given to all of us? The answer is to be found in returning to our basic question of allocating limited resources to meet unlimited wants. With the supply of land and other natural resources inelastic, many businessmen and consumers will seek to own or use this fixed supply for their own benefit. But who should rightfully get it? Obviously, this should be the person who needs it most. How do we tell who has the greatest need? The classical economist would answer that it should be offered to the person who is willing to pay the most. This is because we determine value in our economic system by prices. Let us illustrate this idea by using the case of our "Build-a-City" business. After considering the advantages of several possible locations, we shall examine in detail the merits of the last location for three possible customers.

THE RIGHT LOCATION

We would like to find a location for our "Build-a-City" plant that is reasonably close to our source of supply for labor, for wood, and for inexpensive transportation to our consumer markets. The rent for land in the heart of the metropolitan area is very costly. Retail stores that depend on the gathering of thousands of consumers are all bidding to get the choice locations in the downtown area. With the supply of land so limited and the demand so great, the rent (the price for the use of the land) will be very high. Since we do not need thousands of customers to come to our plant, paying the high rent for this location would be a waste of money.

We cannot locate our plant in the residential section of the city because of zoning laws and "economic laws." It would make little sense for us to pay the cost charged to those seeking to rent or build apartments or homes in this residential area. Besides, the smoke and noise from our factory would create ill will toward our company.

Five miles outside the city on a major highway there is a piece of land for sale. It is large enough for our plant and for parking spaces for our employees. Very few residential dwellings are located there. Most of the surrounding area is now being used for farming. Public transportation for employees is available, since a bus from the city goes by the site every half hour. Our supply trucks can avoid costly delays in city traffic, and there is a railroad feeder line less than two miles away. Those competing with us for the land are farmers and land speculators who anticipate the expansion of suburbs, perhaps ten years from now. Our productivity per acre is far greater than that of the farmer, and the land speculator cannot afford to pay money out for ten years without any income merely in the hope that he may get a high price at some time in the future. We can afford to rent the land at a price slightly higher than either the farmer or the land speculator, because we can get the highest return from it. Our limited resources of land are thus finding their greatest value to society. Figure 6–3 shows this relationship graphically.

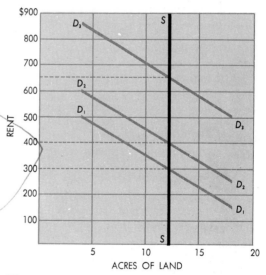

Figure 6–3 Price Determination of Land

Because the marginal revenue product of our business (D_3) is higher than that of the farmer (D_1) and of the speculator (D_2), we will be able to rent the land. Explain why we will not have to pay our full marginal revenue product for rent ($650) in the example shown here.

SAVOY PLAZA TO BE REPLACED BY 40-STORY GM TOWER

NEW YORK — A 40-story office building whose biggest tenant will be the General Motors Corporation will replace the famed Savoy Plaza Hotel on Fifth Avenue.

A representative for the hotel indicated that although the Savoy was now fully occupied, he did not consider the future as bright for the hotel industry in New York City.

A spokesman for General Motors confirmed the report, saying that an agreement between the two parties had been reached. The present 33-story building will be torn down to make room for the modern structure. At present GM has a lease on the 25-story structure at 1775 Broadway.

Land resources in mid-Manhattan are so limited that even the extravagant use of other resources may be required to make sure that the land will reach its marginal productivity.

In the example we have used, the land would not reach its full marginal revenue product. This is because in bidding for the land, the land speculator, who was the second-highest bidder, believed that his potential marginal productivity was a great deal less than ours. Since he was the only other person to bid against us, we were able to secure the land for slightly more than $400. If another manufacturer had been bidding against us, we might have had to go up to our full marginal revenue product of $650.

Economic rent

David Ricardo, one of the great classical economists (see p. 321), explained rent as the return arising from differences in the productivity of land. It can be figured as the difference between the income derived from using the land and the cost of producing that income. If the cost to a farmer for producing $5,000 worth of wheat is $4,000, including payment to himself for his labor

and his initiative and enterprise, then the economic rent would be $1,000. The farmer must pay himself for his labor and the capital he uses at the same rate as if he were working and using his capital for someone else. If he used more productive land so that the yield per acre was greater and his wheat was worth $6,000 while his costs remained the same, then the economic rent would be $2,000.

Even before you began to study economics, you may have heard the terms *marginal,* *submarginal,* and *supramarginal* applied to land. Actually these terms have a very specific meaning in economics. *Marginal land* refers to land in which the cost of producing income from it is equal to that income. With no surplus, it is no-rent land. *Submarginal land* describes land in which the cost of producing income from it is greater than the value of the income. This is wasteful use of our resources. *Supramarginal land* is land in which the cost of producing income from the land is less than the value of that income. Land that might be submarginal at one time may become marginal or even supramarginal when the demand for the products produced from it increases, causing prices to rise and income to go up. During World War II, when the demand for food increased, land that was submarginal and hence not used previously was brought under cultivation. The higher prices for food increased the income that could be derived from this land beyond the cost of production. Several years after the war, when war-ravaged countries were able to satisfy their own food requirements, the demand for our food declined. This brought prices down and caused much of this poor land to be withdrawn from use.

Relation of slums to rent

One of the major problems facing urban centers today is the existence of large slum areas. These neighborhoods not only provide substandard housing, but they also are costly to society in that the environment rarely offers residents the opportunities necessary to develop their full potential. In addition, crime rates are higher and health standards lower in slums than in other areas.

The reason most frequently advanced and usually accepted for the existence of slums is that the people living there cannot afford to pay a sufficiently high rent to make it worthwhile for the owners to improve present structures or to replace existing ones with better housing. The marginal cost for inputs (improving these homes) will not yield sufficient output, or marginal revenue (higher rent). If the owners do improve or replace their substandard housing, they usually raise their rent. Low-income families are then faced with trying to find new housing that they can afford. Since the chance of making money on good low-rent housing seems slight, few businessmen are willing to make the necessary investment.

Many Americans do not believe that the classical model has provided an adequate solution to the problem of low-cost housing. As a result, the federal government, acting through city and state governments, has aided in the development of low-cost housing. Public housing, started in 1934, has produced nearly 500,000 dwelling units. Many other Americans have objected to this approach, since it is considered an interference with the free-enterprise system. A more recent kind of aid has been the urban renewal and slum clearance program under way since 1949. Under this plan the federal government gives funds to cities for clearing land of existing substandard dwellings. Once the land is cleared, it is sold at a low price for redevelopment, including housing, by private builders. An objection

to this method is that it fails to provide enough low-cost housing, being designed more often for middle-income groups.

Recent investigations of rents in slum areas in New York City have caused many to question whether rents are really low and whether landlords could not improve their dwellings without raising rents any higher.

Does the government have a responsibility to interfere with private enterprise to upgrade housing conditions?

Part C   Capital and Interest

Competition for use of loanable funds

In Chapter 1 we defined capital as man-made instruments of production. We should expect interest to be the payment or reward to the owners of capital for the part their money plays in obtaining the means of production. When we think of interest, however, we are more likely to think of it as payment to those who lend money from those who borrow money.

In our economy, business, consumers, and the various levels of government all borrow money, and of course pay for its use. In borrowing, they compete with one another for the use of loanable funds.

BUSINESS PAYS FOR THE USE OF CAPITAL

When we consider the productive process from the viewpoint of management, we must first decide what to produce and then determine what natural resources and labor are needed to make these goods. If production is to be increased, it can most frequently be done by putting tools (machinery) into the hands of the worker to make him more productive. How will he be able to get these tools?

Let us first explain in a very simple way how the tools may be obtained, assuming that this is the only business in our society. Under our present system of production we produce $1,000 worth of goods per day. We now take 20 percent of our workers and shift their efforts into the manufacture of tools of production. This reduces the value of the items we are producing for consumption to $800 a day. After ten days we have sacrificed $2,000, but we have also completed the machines that we need to produce more goods. These machines represent added capital and were obtained by the company by sacrificing present output of goods. Is it worth it? Only if the value of our production has increased sufficiently to pay back the $2,000 we have lost plus some value in addition. If additional value is achieved, it is the result of the increased capital (tools) we added to the production process. This capital, like the other factors of production, must be paid for.

In our complex society today we define interest as the price paid for the use of money or loanable funds. The businessman who wishes to increase the size of his store—adding capital—or to buy machinery for his factory (also capital) borrows money.

He expects to be able to increase his business enough to pay back the principal (the amount of money borrowed) and the interest (the price for borrowing the funds) and still have money left over. The money he has borrowed has come from those who have saved some of their income instead of spending it all on consumer items. This in turn has freed workers who might have been producing consumer goods to engage in the production of capital goods. Furthermore those people who have money saved are now able to lend it for the production of capital goods and thus to receive interest as their reward for sacrificing their present desires to consume. We can now see the relationship between interest as payment for loanable funds and payment for capital.

CONSUMERS PAY FOR THE USE OF LOANABLE FUNDS

Consumers as well as businessmen borrow money. At the present time consumers owe more than $200 billion, which is not much less than the amount owed by businessmen. The reasons for consumer borrowing are many, but in each case the borrower induces the lender to forgo the use of his funds by offering interest. Some loans may be looked upon as an investment, as in the case of money borrowed for a college education. Some may be used to take care of an unexpected crisis. Some loans are for the purchase of goods that are costly but that are used for many years (durable goods). Demand for loanable funds by consumers competes with the demand for loanable funds by businessmen. In each case the borrower pays interest for the use of the lender's capital.

GOVERNMENT PAYS FOR THE USE OF LOANABLE FUNDS

The federal, state, and local governments also need to borrow money. Sometimes this money is borrowed to pay for major capital improvements, such as road construction; sometimes to meet an unforeseen emergency, such as a flood; and, in the case of the federal government, to finance a planned deficit to help overcome a depression. State and local governments often compete with others seeking to borrow, thus causing interest rates to rise. The federal government helps the smaller units of government to borrow funds by allowing the interest on their bonds to be tax-free.

Determining interest rates

Interest is stated as a rate of return for money borrowed, whether for business, for consumer spending, or for government use. The rate of interest specifies how many dollars the borrower has to pay for every $100 he borrows for one year. For the lender it is how many dollars he will receive for each $100 that he lends per year. A business that borrows $5,000 from a bank at five percent must pay back $5,250 at the end of one year. When interest is paid in advance, the borrower receiving principal minus interest, it is called *discounting*.

Stating interest as a rate rather than using absolute figures ($250 in the above example) allows the borrower to make a comparison with others borrowing different amounts. A business borrowing $10,000 for one year with $400 of interest is thus paying more dollars in interest than in our example above, but is paying a lower interest rate (four percent).

The examples used above assume that the borrower has the use of the entire principal for the full year. If payments are made on the principal before the end of the full term of the loan (many small loans are paid monthly), the interest is higher. This is because interest is being paid on the full amount ($5,000) when some of the principal has already been repaid.

There are many reasons why interest rates may vary:
1. The difference in the risk of repayment
2. The duration (long-term loans generally command higher interest rates)

3. The cost of administering the loan (short-term loans are far more costly when figured as a percentage of the loan)
4. The ability to shop around for the best "buy"

PURE INTEREST

Economists frequently speak of "the" interest rates as though the factors just mentioned did not exist and every borrower paid the same rate. They are referring to "pure" interest, which is the rate paid for the use of money without the factors mentioned above being taken into consideration. The rate of interest for long-term United States government bonds is usually cited as the closest approximation of pure interest, because the factors mentioned previously are almost eliminated.

The demand for loanable funds

Demand for loanable funds refers to the amount of dollars that people will borrow at different rates of interest for a given time. These demands come most often from the money requirements of businessmen, consumers, and governments. If we defined interest as the price paid for loanable funds, we could rightfully anticipate the reappearance of our familiar model of demand and supply.

DEMAND OF BUSINESS

What determines the shape of a demand curve for loanable funds? Once again the law of diminishing returns appears, with the result that the marginal revenue product of money causes our demand curve to slope downward. The first $1,000 that we borrow to improve the looks of a store or add to the productive capacity of a factory will generally yield a bigger return than the next $1,000. The second $1,000 will usually yield a bigger return than the third $1,000, and so on. The businessman must try to determine how much above the additional cost of adding units of capital he can earn and compare it to the cost of the interest he pays. He can afford to borrow up to that point where the interest for the last amount he borrowed (his marginal cost for loanable funds) is equal to the amount he can earn above his costs on the last unit he bought with the money he borrowed (his marginal revenue product). Thus if he borrows an additional $10,000 and must pay $600 for its use for a year, it will not pay him to borrow these funds unless he can anticipate earning more than this amount from the use of this money. Here, as with wage rates and rent, we see the theory of the marginal revenue product determining the demand. Because the money is usually spent on items that last many years, the businessman is forced to estimate what the yield will be on each unit of capital he buys.

DEMAND OF THE CONSUMER

Most of the money borrowed by consumers will not be used in the production process. However, it will probably be used for satisfying the needs of the borrower. It will, therefore, be subject to the law of diminishing marginal utility. This will produce a demand curve quite similar to the one applicable for the businessman; that is, it is downward sloping. Demand for meeting emergencies is very inelastic; for durable consumer goods such as automobiles, more elastic; and for luxury items, most elastic.

DEMAND OF GOVERNMENT

The federal government's demand curve for most loanable funds is inelastic. The reason is that most of the national government's debt came about during such emergencies as wars and depressions, when it was impractical to cover all expenditures through taxes. The demand curve of state and local governments tends to be more elastic.

INELASTIC TENDENCY

Because interest represents a relatively small part of the cost for capital expenditures or the buying of durable goods, demand for loanable funds is probably a good deal less sensitive to interest rates than the classical economists believed. Also, low interest rates usually have little effect in encouraging investment by firms when business conditions are declining. It is for this reason that the demand curve tends to be somewhat inelastic, particularly during depressions or recessions.

The supply of loanable funds

The supply of loanable funds refers to the amount of dollars that lenders will offer at different rates of interest for a given time. The sources of loanable funds are personal savings, business savings, and lending by commercial banks.

Most savings by individuals come from those who are in the middle and upper income groups. Over half of personal savings comes from families whose income is in the highest five percent in the nation. These people are more likely to save because they can buy the things they need and still have money left over. Much of our saving is for a particular purpose, such as a college education, a house, or protection in case of loss of income.

Most business saving finds its way back into business to support its growth. Particularly since World War II, companies have shown a tendency to use money from profits to support expansion rather than paying out all in dividends or borrowing money on the open market. Although such businesses are not contributing to the market for loanable funds, they keep existing supplies of loanable funds at a higher level by satisfying or reducing their own needs. When not using their savings, they sometimes make these funds available to other businesses.

When commercial banks make loans available to borrowers, they are extending credit. This provides a major source of loanable funds needed by businesses as well as by consumers. These functions will be explained more fully when we discuss banking in Chapter 13.

Not all savings are available as loanable funds. Some individuals and businesses may decide that they would prefer to keep their savings in a form that would not make their money available to borrowers. Their decision as to whether to hold their money or make it available is determined by their *liquidity preference,* the desire to keep savings in the form of ready cash.

AMOUNT OF LOANABLE FUNDS

What determines the amount of loanable funds? While economists are not in complete agreement, most recognize that higher interest rates will cause some savers to transfer some of their money from a highly liquid condition (cash) to loanable funds (interest-bearing securities). Modern economic theory places greater emphasis on the relationship of savings to the general economic well-being of the nation (national income). People save more as income rises.

Greater savings will provide more money for loanable funds. We can conclude that the supply curve of loanable funds slopes upward, opposite to the direction of demand for loanable funds, and like most of the supply curves we have been discussing.

Interaction of demand and supply of loanable funds

Interest rates, like the other factors of production, are determined by the interaction of demand and supply. With a given demand for loanable funds and a given supply, interest rates will be at the point where the supply and demand curves meet. By studying the horizontal axis in Figure 6–4, we can determine the amount of loanable funds that will be borrowed.

According to classical theory, interest in the free marketplace exercises a major

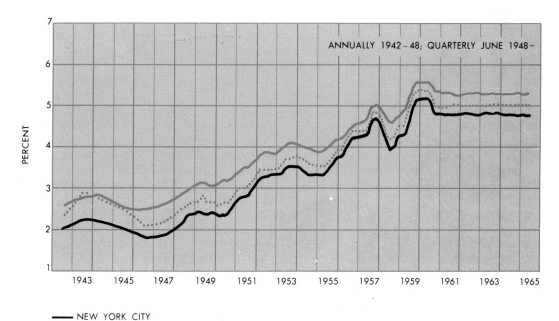

ANNUALLY 1942–48; QUARTERLY JUNE 1948–

PERCENT

——— NEW YORK CITY
······ OTHER NORTHERN AND EASTERN CITIES
——— SOUTHERN AND WESTERN CITIES

Figure 6–4   Bank Rates on Short-Term Business Loans

Why are interest rates lower in New York City than elsewhere? SOURCE: Federal Reserve System, *Historical Chart Book*

influence in regulating the economy. In answer to the question of how to allocate our resources, loanable funds will be steered into those businesses which can afford to pay the highest interest rates. These are the same businesses which have the highest marginal revenue product and are producing the things that the consumer wants most. High consumer demand, supply remaining equal, means high prices. High prices will induce businessmen to expand their capital facilities, even if they must borrow at high interest rates. This results in increasing the production of goods consumers want. It will usually bring higher profits as well.

Another regulatory role that interest is supposed to play is that of keeping savings and investment in balance. When business conditions are poor, there will be more loanable funds available (supply) than businessmen and consumers want (demand). Interest rates will go down to a point where many businessmen will find it profitable to borrow. This will help stimulate the economy. If business conditions are rising so fast as to create a threat of inflation and a shortage of loanable funds, interest rates should rise enough to discourage marginal producers from expanding. This subject will be discussed further in Chapter 11.

How sensitive the demand and supply of loanable funds are to interest rates is a matter of controversy. The recent flow of loanable funds to higher-paying markets outside this country, together with the present tight money situation, has caused some economists, who have previously minimized the influence of interest as a factor in the distribution of loanable funds, to reevaluate their answers.

How free is the market for loanable funds?

Until the 1930's the price for loanable funds was largely determined by demand and supply in a free market. As the government has become increasingly involved with the total economy, the lending market has become much less free. The government, by borrowing large sums of money—more than business and consumers during World War II—influences the interest rates set by the Federal Reserve Bank. Government support for certain kinds of loans—to housing, small business, and the farmer—and its powers of taxing and spending also affect a very large portion of the market. Because of this government influence most economists refer to the price for loanable funds as an *administered price,* subject to modification by individuals. Some economists believe that the government has gone too far in trying to control the money market. Others think that it is the duty of the government to control the money market in order to help keep the economy prosperous.

Part D   Management and Profits

What is profit?

Management, or enterprise, is directly responsible for initiating production. The businessman (entrepreneur) takes his cue from consumers, deciding what they want or, in the case of a new product, what he thinks they might want. If he believes that he can organize a business by assembling the other three factors of production into an efficient producing unit and selling his product so that his revenue will be greater than his cost, he will go ahead. It is the expectation of making a profit that is his incentive.

Profit means different things to different people. According to some public opinion polls, many people are not sure what it is, but they are sure it is too large and represents too much of the consumer's dollar. The worker may look at profit as an unfairly large payment to management that deprives him of a higher wage. The businessman thinks of profit as being the differ-

DOLLARS DRAWN TO MEXICO BY HIGH INTEREST RATES

LOS ANGELES — Interest rates ranging from eight to ten percent on short-term loans to Mexican industrial firms are attracting dollars that have been searching for high returns. Some Europeans are also lending money to take advantage of the high returns.

Several months ago rates reached a high of about ten percent. However, as funds flowed in, some of the interest advantage declined. Rates are still attractive enough to draw funds from sophisticated investors in other countries.

Loanable funds will flow where they will receive highest interest rates.

ence between his total revenue and total cost. Let us now see if we can develop a more exact definition of what constitutes profit.

Gross profit is the difference between what a businessman sells his product for and what it costs him. The merchant buys $100,000 worth of merchandise during the year and sells it for $135,000. His gross profit is $35,000. The percentage difference between his cost and selling price is 35 percent, and he calls this his "markup."

Net profit is what the businessman has left after he has paid his expenses—rent, wages, and interest—and has set aside money to allow for the loss due to depreciation (wearing out) of his capital. Our merchant has to subtract his payment of rent ($3,000), wages ($10,000), interest on money borrowed ($500), repairs and upkeep ($500), taxes ($500), electricity and other expenses ($500). His expenses for operating his business come to $15,000. His gross profit is $35,000 and his net profit is $20,000.

Economists have a narrower definition of what constitutes profit. They are con-

cerned with payment to all the resources that have gone into production, whether they come from outside the business, like those listed above, or from inside the business. Costs that come from the outside are called *explicit costs*. Those costs within the firm are called *implicit costs*. Economists point out that our merchant has not paid himself a wage (some prefer the term "salary") or interest on his own capital that he has invested in his business. If he worked for someone else for the same hours and with the same skill, he would be paid a going market wage for his effort. Likewise, if he took his money out of the business and placed it in securities involving similar risks, he would receive dividends. Since economists are concerned with the allocation of resources and their efficient use, they must think in terms of *alternative costs* (sometimes called *opportunity costs*)—the value that could be produced if these implicit factors were used in the production of other things. If the merchant could get a job paying him $12,000 a year and earn five percent, or $1,000, on his investment of $20,000 of capital, economists would insist that he subtract an additional $13,000 from his net profit. *Economic* (or *pure*) *profit* is what is left after all explicit and implicit costs for wages, rent, and interest are paid. Of course, it is possible to have a loss instead of a profit. What is the economic, or pure, profit of our merchant?

Why should there be profits?

Since our merchant has been paid for his labor and for interest on his capital, why should he receive profits as well? Probably the most important justification for profits is that the expectation of profits acts as a motivating force to get people to:

1. start businesses to produce goods and services that consumers want

2. think up new or better products to attract customers (innovation) and assume the risks of production

3. improve the efficiency of production, resulting in the use of fewer resources at lower cost

4. provide funds for improvement and expansion of the firm

To see how the expectation of profits might influence business decisions, let us return to our own business venture, "Build-a-City." Why did we wish to start a business at all? We all had jobs that gave us a living wage. In addition, statistics were available to us showing that an average of three hundred businesses fail throughout the nation each week. Why look for trouble? Probably we took the chance because we felt that we could be one of the small number of firms which succeed in making large profits, more than we could earn in our present jobs. It may have been the profit motive which caused us to think about a new product that consumers would want, or it may be that we thought about the new product first and then decided that the idea could be put into action, thus providing us with a profit. In either event society benefits by the motivation that profits give to producing new and better products. The economist Joseph Schumpeter (see p. 61) believed that much of society's progress could be attributed to the influence of the profit motive on new ideas in business.

With our business operating successfully, we now look for ways to improve it. We experiment with new forms and different kinds of wood, and we work to achieve more efficient production. By obtaining new machines, buying raw materials from different sources, and hiring more workers rather than paying overtime, we are able to cut our costs. These reduced costs may lead to additional profits. In a less favorable situation, where competing producers of toys have lowered costs and taken away some of our business, we may have to find methods of reducing our costs to make any profit at all. In either event the motivation of profits has benefited us as well as society.

If our business is doing well enough so that we are thinking of expanding our productive capacity, we will have to obtain additional funds. We can borrow the money by selling bonds or going to the bank. However, if interest rates are high, we may want to finance it ourselves. Rather than taking our profits out of the business and enjoying a higher standard of living now, we use these profits to pay for expansion. Because of implicit costs we must decide whether our money, resulting from profits, will yield more by being invested in our own business or by being invested in something else. We may consider the element of reducing our risks by diversifying. This can be done by putting our profits in other kinds of enterprises. What influences will determine the course we will follow?

What are the sources of economic profit?

If we lived in a society which had pure competition and a static economy where no changes ever took place in products, efficiency, consumer preferences, and sources of supply, we would have no economic profit. With all knowledge complete, all factors would receive their marginal revenue product and the market price would leave no surplus for economic profit.

The real world we live in is not static. It is changing constantly—and in many different directions. Our economy rarely sees pure competition at work. Therefore, economic profit does exist. When it exists because of innovations or inventions or efficiency—all of which allow a firm to have a temporary advantage—profit may be looked upon as a just reward. Sometimes profit results from pure chance, such as a major change in supply or demand, or both, that makes existing inventories more valuable. Sometimes profits are made by not paying the factors of production their full marginal revenue product. These sources of economic profit stem primarily from dynamic aspects in society and cannot be easily avoided. What is more, they are usually associated with progress and will hurt the economy only rarely, and then only temporarily.

Effect of competition on profit

Profit, in the long run, can easily result from differing degrees of imperfect competition. Under strong competitive conditions an industry that is making high profits will attract additional firms into the field, causing prices to decline. If, however, barriers such as patents are placed in the way of new firms entering the field, profits may continue to be high. If a business concern is able to restrict supplies (shift the supply curve to the left), prices will be artificially high and yield higher profits. A study of the profits of various industries in the United States showed that those which were most competitive—textiles and clothing—had the smallest profits, whereas those that were most like monopolies and oligopolies—automobiles and electrical equipment—had the largest profits.

PATENTS AND COPYRIGHTS

There are two special cases that we should recognize in which government action endorses monopoly and thereby interferes with a competitive market in determining price. In order to encourage inventions and new ideas, the government issues *patents* to inventors. Upon approval from the United States Patent Office, the inventors will have a monopoly on their inventions for 17 years. *Copyrights* on the publication of literary productions are issued to authors for 28 years and may be renewed. The monopoly prices allow for higher profits, but these profits are the rewards for furthering progress.

FRANCHISES

A *franchise* is a license granted by some governmental authority to a business, giving it the exclusive monopoly to perform a particular service in a given area. A franchise is usually granted to a natural monopoly because it is in the interest of society to

prevent duplication of service. Under the franchise prices are regulated by government and profit is considered a major factor in determining those prices. Public utilities are perhaps the best example of this practice. In such cases, the franchise grants an exclusive monopoly to perform a particular service. Prices are regulated, usually in relation to profit.

How large should profits be?

The debate on the size of profits seems to be a never-ending one. Although our classical model calls for no economic (pure) profits in the long run, it does allow for temporary profits. Such profits help to allocate resources where society thinks they are needed most, and the profits also motivate business to operate efficiently and provide new and better products. Actually it is the expectation of making profits that causes businessmen to take risks, to innovate, and to increase their efficiency. However, if businesses did not make profits, there would be no expectation, and thus no motivation to produce.

Since perfect competition is rare, the amount of profits is partially determined by the varying degrees of imperfect competition. Monopolistic practices may yield excessively high profits, causing consumers to pay more for the product than they would under competitive conditions. These higher prices may also protect inefficient operation and interfere with the allocation of resources. Very high profits in an industry have frequently brought governmental investigations by Congress, the Justice Department, and various regulatory agencies.

Businesses that involve great risk will have to offer opportunities for substantial rewards to provide incentive. Those businesses that are quite stable can attract firms without having to offer such high rewards. When the conditions of supply and demand that are characteristic of pure competition are too distorted by interference with a relatively free market or by

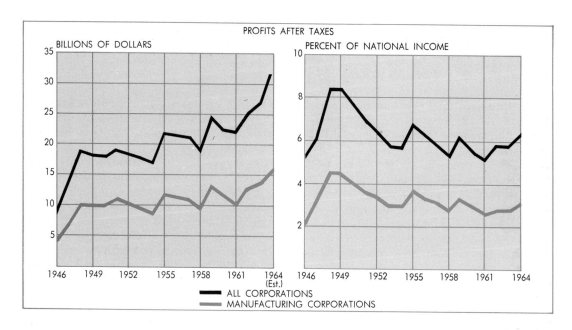

A Look at Corporate Profits

Figure 6–5

Corporate profits after taxes reached $31.5 billion in 1964, according to preliminary findings of the Department of Commerce. The rise for that year was the third consecutive one in corporate profits, an achievement not matched in other postwar years.

Dollar profits, like any other share of income, must be placed in the context of the general expansion of the economy. In this three-year period, 1961–64, corporate profits as a percent of national income advanced from 5.1 percent to 6.2 percent. Their share was thus enlarged but is still below the general level between 1947 and 1955. The behavior of profits of all corporations is due

mainly to corporations in manufacturing, since they account for approximately half of all corporate profits. Manufacturing profits also attained a record level in 1964, though the growth rate was less than that of all corporations since 1961.

The 1964 performance of corporate profits requires a word of caution. Because of variations in accounting techniques, recent changes in tax laws, greater complexity of business operations, and the inadequacy of depreciation charges in periods of rising prices, comparisons of profits are becoming more and more questionable, especially over long periods of time. SOURCE: N.I.C.B., *Road Maps of Industry* No. 1521

special circumstances such as war, some government action is called for. A tax beyond the normal corporation profits tax, known as the *excess profits tax*, was in operation during World War II. It is an example of government action to protect the consumer.

Profits after taxes for all business corporations have tended to fluctuate rather closely with general business conditions.

The variation in profit from industry to industry shows how competition can act in limiting profits.

Perhaps the only answer that we can safely give to the question of what size profits should be is: They should be as large as necessary to attract enough businesses to provide an adequate supply of the goods and services that consumers want at prices they are willing to pay.

Part E *The Problem: Should We Rely on the Classical Model to Distribute Income Fairly to the Factors of Production?*

In Chapter 4 and again in this chapter we have shown how the various factors of production are paid. Our model calls for each factor to be used to that point where its marginal factor cost and the marginal revenue product are equal. Each businessman, when he enters the market for the factors of production, tries to follow the marginal product theory, although he may not be familiar with the technical aspects of it. He certainly will not buy an additional factor of production unless he thinks it will give him greater value than what he has to pay for it. According to the classical model, if all businesses operate in this way, the businessman will realize his greatest possible profit and society will benefit from the most efficient allocation of its limited resources.

There are many critics of this theory. Most of the opposition has focused on the concern that one factor of production might receive too large a portion of the "pie" at the expense of other factors. Some critics have suggested eliminating the use of the classical model entirely on the grounds that the assumptions it makes are no longer applicable. Others have suggested altering it in such a way that it will be more in keeping with the world that is. In our discussion of the problem, you will find samples of both kinds of reasoning, with comments and questions. You will be shown a broad spectrum of ideas. Consider all the alternatives before reaching a tentative conclusion. Keep in mind the total productive process as well as the role of functional distribution to the factors of production.

Critics who oppose the model

The best-known critic of capitalism and the chief architect of scientific socialism (communism) was Karl Marx (see p. 354). A more detailed analysis of Marxist thinking will appear in the consideration of comparative economic systems in Chapter 16. However, his theory of the value of labor is pertinent to our present discussion of the fair distribution of income to the factors of production.

MARX'S THEORY OF THE VALUE OF LABOR

All wealth, said Marx, is the result of the labor that is put into its creation. Natural resources have no value unless man uses them. Capital is a product of man's labor. The income that landowners and investors receive is unearned because they are contributing nothing to the value of the product. What the capitalist receives in the form of rent, interest, and profit is surplus value that rightfully belongs to the worker. The worker is exploited and the capitalist is the exploiter, dividing society into two hostile groups. The capitalist accumulates more and more capital, but the worker does not have the purchasing power to buy back the goods he produces. This leads to declining demand and periodic depressions. Eventually a revolution will take place, and labor will then receive the full value for its product.

According to Marxian theory the United States, with its predominantly private-enterprise economy, should see labor receiving a progressively smaller and smaller share of the national income and landlords, investors, and management receiving an increasingly larger share. However, Figure 6–1 shows that, in fact, wages have been the only reward that has increased as a percentage of the national income. Marx further indicated that, with capital accumulating faster than it is needed, interest rates should be constantly falling. However, although this may be true in the long run, the opportunities for capital investment have usually kept pace with the supply.

If the market with its pricing mechanism does not determine answers to the allocation of resources—the *How, What,* and *For Whom*—what will? Is a central planning board, as in the case of communism, in a better position to make decisions than the market, where the consumer is the decision-maker? While it is true that the market economy of the United States may have some weaknesses, has the Soviet Union, claiming to follow the Marxian model as a guide, done any better?

HENRY GEORGE AND THE SINGLE TAX MOVEMENT

Another critic, although of only a portion of our model, was an American writer named Henry George. In his famous book *Progress and Poverty,* published in 1879, George advocated a plan that caused such interest that it resulted in the sale of over a million copies of his book. He even came close to winning the election for mayor in New York City.

Henry George reasoned that, although the supply of land in the world is fixed, the number of people using it increases. With the increase in its use, the value of the land increases. Thus, land on the edge of a city will increase in value as the population of the city spills over into the suburbs. The owner of the land is now able to collect a higher rent than before, even though he didn't earn it. Since he did not make the land or improve the land, what he receives in rent is unearned increment.

Henry George believed that the receipt by landlords of pure, or economic, rent was the cause of all poverty. If this rent were taxed at 100 percent, all society would share in the value which nature and the movement of population made possible. He said that the income from such a tax would be sufficient to finance all government activity and permit the abolition of all other taxes.

Because of this, it was called the Single Tax Plan. The money saved by eliminating other taxes could then be used in the production process.

A most obvious shortcoming of the single tax proposal today is that rent is estimated to be less than three percent of the national income whereas government expenditures are over 20 percent. Another practical difficulty lies in determining how much economic rent is derived from a particular income payment. These criticisms, however, are not applicable to the justice of taxing economic rent; they apply only to the single-tax proposal and its implementation.

A more valid problem, although one still concerned with implementation, is how to make the last owner of land that has changed hands many times pay when his cost for the land reflects the "profits" made by previous owners. While the government might overcome this objection by paying the present owners with long-term bonds, the interest shown by the public and most economists is too small to expect any such action in this country. Some underdeveloped countries are considering such a proposal.

Critics who accept the model with modifications

Throughout our study of economics we have made reference to the world that "is" and the world that "ought to be." So far, the "ought-to-be" world has largely been our classical model operating under market conditions of pure competition. In Unit III we will introduce a new model (Keynesian) that is playing an increasingly important part in the American economy. However, among those who accept most of the classical model, there are those who feel that the world that "is" has so distorted the original theory that new methods should be applied to the functional distribution of income. These new methods would either revive the intent of the classical economist who sought an efficient and fair method of distribution or recognize the importance of other values in our Western heritage. Several brief examples will illustrate this point.

THE NEED TO CONSERVE NATURAL RESOURCES

The unique feature about natural resources in comparison with other factors of production is their relatively fixed supply. This results in an inelastic supply curve and means that demand is the cause of changes in price (rent). When the demand for natural resources increases rapidly, owners of natural resources are anxious to take advantage of the high prices.

Because the supply of resources is limited, critics question whether price alone should be allowed to determine use. If it is, farmland may be overworked to produce crops selling for high prices, with no regard for renewing the fertility of the soil. Timber may be cut without replacing cut-down trees with young seedlings. Because oil belongs to the owner of the property on which it comes to the surface, even though most of it may be under the ground of neighboring properties, wasteful drilling procedures are encouraged. Resources are often used today for immediate gain, with little thought for the needs of future generations.

Until the beginning of the twentieth century the thought prevailed that our country had an unlimited supply of natural resources. Wasteful practices were allowed because new sources of supply were constantly being discovered. Finally, men such as Theodore Roosevelt and Gifford Pinchot, Chairman of the National Conservation Commission; Frederick Haynes Newell, Chief Engineer of the Reclamation Service; and others made great efforts to have the government step in to conserve our resources so that future generations would not suffer because past and present generations were selfishly concerned only with their immediate satisfaction. While most of our conservation program has been designed to encourage individuals to practice conservation (rewards for crop rotation, for example), the government has at times been forced to abandon the policy of laissez-faire. Withdrawing from use substantial tracts of public land has won public support, although it has been criticized by some private interests as interference with our private-enterprise system and the market mechanism for the allocation of resources.

THE NEED TO LIMIT UNEARNED INTEREST

We have justified the payment of interest as a reward for saving instead of consuming and as a necessary condition if the economy is to have sufficient funds to buy the capital needed for its growth. We cannot expect people to make funds available without some reward. Actually, interest rates in this country have on the whole been quite low, due in part to the availability of loans to businessmen, farmers, veterans, and others through agencies of the government. Criticism of our present system of distribution of rewards for loanable funds is concentrated on those receiving interest from inherited wealth.

The right to hand down property—including loanable funds—is part of our entire concept of private property. Very few people in our country would question the right of anyone to bequeath to his heirs enough for them to live decently and to have the means to get a good start in life. However, many have questioned the fairness of allowing heirs to live on accumulated fortunes without earning anything themselves. To prevent what may be called "unearned interest" and the perpetuation of a "moneyed class," states have passed *inheritance taxes* (on those receiving) and the federal government has imposed *estate* and *gift taxes* (on the estate or giver). These taxes have been aimed primarily at estates above $60,000. Since there are various "loopholes" in the inheritance laws, few people have protested.

Some economic historians claim that it was through the accumulation of huge fortunes that we were able to have enough loanable funds in this country to support our economic growth. With high taxes on accumulated wealth we may dry up our sources of loanable funds and the government will have to step in to supply what is needed for our capital expansion.

Critics ask whether it is justifiable for unearned income to furnish the capital for economic growth. Since the overwhelming majority of our population does not have enough funds to furnish businessmen with capital, would we be better off if the government made decisions as to where loanable funds should go?

THE NEED TO LIMIT UNEARNED PROFITS

Profits have been justified as necessary to reward management and owners for risks, efficiency, innovation, and invention. When profits are made because of monopolistic practices, they hurt society rather than benefiting it. Most economists in our country would recommend more vigorous competition to eliminate unearned profits resulting from imperfect competition. However, many have doubted whether any government policy can produce sufficient competition. To prevent profits from going above the amount they might be expected to reach under pure or near-pure competition, taxes may be imposed on the amount above a "fair" profit. This was done during World War II and again during the Korean conflict, but most people accepted it as only an emergency measure. Why cannot such an excess profits tax be used at all times? Will it diminish or destroy incentive? Will it penalize our most efficient? Does the society really benefit when it permits monopolistic practices, even if it taxes excess profits?

Considering an answer

How free do we want our economy to be? Do the economically strong receive greater rewards than are received by the weaker factors involved in production? To what extent should rewards be based on the degree of service to society? What problems can a planned economy have in distributing its shares to the factors of production? Some of these questions will be asked again later when we compare economic systems. As you read further, tentative answers to these questions may appear. Have you made any judgments so far?

REVIEW — the highlights of the chapter

1. Dividing the income received from production among the factors of production is called functional distribution.

2. The interaction of supply and demand will determine the price for each factor of production.

3. Additional units of factors of production will be added up to the point where the marginal revenue product and the marginal factor cost are equal.

4. Getting the right combination of factors can improve the efficiency of production.

5. Rent is most commonly defined as the price for the use of some durable good. Land rent is the price for the use of natural resources. Economic rent is the price paid for any factor that cannot be increased or decreased in response to price changes.

6. Unlike other factors, the supply of land (and of most other natural resources) is fixed and is shown by an inelastic supply curve.

7. Although some critics question the justification of paying rent, such payment helps allocate natural resources efficiently.

8. Interest is the price paid for the use of loanable funds. This is like saying that it is payment for the use of capital because of the use that is made of this money.

9. Businessmen, consumers, and governments borrow money and pay interest.

10. Interest is stated as a rate of return. Rates vary because of risk, time, administrative costs, and competition in the market.

11. Demand for loanable funds is subject to the influence of the marginal revenue product for businessmen and diminishing marginal utility for consumers; it is inelastic for the federal government.

12. Supply of loanable funds comes primarily from individuals in the highest income group and from business itself. Higher interest rates will tend to decrease the liquidity preference of people.

13. Since 1930 the price of loanable funds has been determined less and less by the free market as government has increased its borrowing and its control over interest rates.

14. Profit means something different to the public, the businessman, and the economist. The economist, who is interested in payments to all factors of production, must consider both explicit and implicit costs before figuring economic profits – what is left over after all other factors have been paid.

15. Profit serves our economy well when it is used as incentive for management to make products wanted by the consumer, to increase business efficiency, and to stimulate progress. Economic profits are eliminated in a static economy with pure competition. Profit from imperfect competition represents inefficient use.

IN CONCLUSION: *some aids to understanding*

Terms for review

functional distribution	interest
marginal cost	principal
marginal revenue product	discounting
land rent	gross profit
economic rent	economic profit
submarginal land	net profit
single tax	explicit costs
copyright	implicit costs
franchise	alternative costs
liquidity preference	patent
administered price	"fair price"
production function	excess profits tax
loanable funds	surplus value

Questions for review

1. Allocating the various factors of production and distributing rewards to them are basic problems of business enterprise.
    (a) Explain by using an example how the income you received from the sale of an item would be divided among the various factors of production.
    (b) Under what circumstances would the cost of the various factors change?

2. Why might it be said that the most successful entrepreneur is the one who combines the factors of production most efficiently?

3. Explain how rent is determined exclusively by demand.

4. Using the classical view of rent, explain why payments of rent for land differ with varying degrees of productivity.

5. Interest, like rent, represents payment for use — in this case, use of loanable funds.
    (a) Explain how paying interest for the use of money can be justified.
    (b) What factors determine the rate charged?
    (c) How has the role of the federal government influenced the rates of interest?

6. Interest differs in some respects from the payments made to other factors of production.
    (a) Explain the reasons for variation in the demand for loanable funds which influence the individual consumer, the businessman, the federal and local governments.
    (b) How may changes in interest rates help regulate the economy?
    (c) When and why is the demand curve for interest inelastic?

7. Interpretations of the word "profit" differ according to the individual's point of view. Explain the meaning of the term "profit" to the businessman, the public, and the economist.

8. What value does economic profit have for the economy in the short run?

Additional questions and problems

1. Henry George was among those suggesting modification of the classical model of capitalism.
    (a) Explain the basic ideas of the single tax as advocated by Henry George.
    (b) What effect would the application of his theory have on land development today?
    (c) What are the major objections to his theory?

2. The meaning of "fair profit" is different to producer and consumer, and varies from one industry to another.
   (a) Study the information available on some of the cases in the drug industry and present the arguments of the producer and the government concerning prices and profits.
   (b) Study some of the requests of public utilities (railroad, telephone, electricity) for rate changes and indicate the factors used by these utilities to determine the base they use.
3. Explain the statement "Profits are the lifeblood of the American capitalist system."
4. As a major factor of production, labor is entitled to a proper reward.
   (a) Why has labor demanded a greater share of the profits of industry?
   (b) Criticize or defend the contention that labor is entitled to a greater share of profits.
5. Division of profits among the factors of production is a continuing problem.
   (a) Present the arguments for and against a ceiling imposed on profits of industry.
   (b) Defend the philosophy of the excess profits tax.
6. What are the major conclusions to be drawn from Figure 6-1 on page 107?
7. Explain in detail why the addition of units of capital, land, and labor by businessmen will not necessarily bring greater returns.
8. Make a graphic presentation illustrating the concept that the increase of the factors in the previous question is significant only to the point where they reach the marginal revenue product.

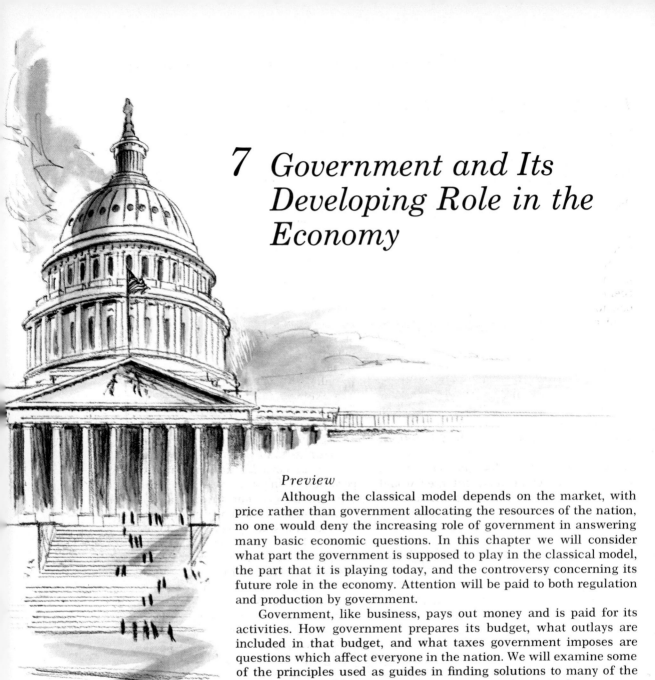

7 Government and Its Developing Role in the Economy

Preview

Although the classical model depends on the market, with price rather than government allocating the resources of the nation, no one would deny the increasing role of government in answering many basic economic questions. In this chapter we will consider what part the government is supposed to play in the classical model, the part that it is playing today, and the controversy concerning its future role in the economy. Attention will be paid to both regulation and production by government.

Government, like business, pays out money and is paid for its activities. How government prepares its budget, what outlays are included in that budget, and what taxes government imposes are questions which affect everyone in the nation. We will examine some of the principles used as guides in finding solutions to many of the controversial problems concerning government's role in the economy.

Overview

What responsibilities should government have in the economy?

Why are government expenditures mounting?

How can the fairness of a tax be evaluated?

Is our public debt dangerous to our economy or to our society?

128

Part A   The Nature of Government's Role in the Economy

Government's role in the classical model

The classical model is frequently referred to as the private- or free-enterprise system because it places its emphasis on the decisions of the consumer and the decisions of the businessman arrived at individually without interference by the government. What is produced is determined by the consumer—registering his demand in the market—and by the businessman—seeking to make profits—catering to the consumer's wishes. According to the classical tradition the individual is in a better position to know what he wants and what is good for him than is the government. Any interference by the government would alter the free flow of goods and services as ordered by the consumer.

Quite a different condition exists when the government makes all the decisions on the allocation of resources—the *What, How,* and *For Whom.* Those advocating such a system would admit that the individual's wants might not be met, but they would hasten to point out that those who control the government are in a better position to decide what is good for the entire society.

We pointed out in Chapter 1 that no nation practices either of the previously described conditions in pure form. However, the first point of view plays a major role in the economic planning of the United States, whereas the second philosophy guides the Soviet Union in its economic programs.

Although the classical economist wants a minimum of government interference, he still recognizes the importance of maintaining an environment in which the market economy can flourish. If capitalism is to function, certain conditions must exist and be preserved.

PILLARS OF CAPITALISM

Private property, the right of the individual to exercise reasonable control over the things he owns, provides a major incentive for producing. Related to this is *freedom of contract,* allowing individuals to enter into agreements resulting in production and distribution of goods and services. *Economic freedom*—guaranteeing the individual the right to move within the economy to the job he wants, to buy or sell property as he sees fit, and to start a business if he wishes to—permits the economy to change. *Competition* assures efficiency of production and safeguards the consumer.

The four conditions just described are the pillars of the classical model and must be present if the system is to function smoothly. It is government's role in the classical model to see to it that these conditions exist, that the nation is protected internally (the police and fire departments) and externally (the armed forces), that the life, the liberty, and the property of all within its boundaries are safeguarded.

CAPITALISM, GOVERNMENT, AND OUR BUSINESS

Let us consider for a moment the importance of the requisites of capitalism in connection with our theoretical business, "Build-a-City." When we incorporated, we went to the state government to obtain a charter. Having a charter gave us status as a separate entity before the law. Economic freedom allowed us to enter into this business, and gave us the assurance that what we earned was ours (taxes excluded). If our property were not protected from thieves, fire, and foreign invasion, we would have little incentive to work hard, save, and build a larger plant. If we could not be sure of the enforcement of contracts, we would be gambling every time we filled a big order for a customer. Refusal on the part of the customer to meet his contractual obligations could mean our ruin. In each of these instances we depend on government not to perform the economic functions but to assure an environment where economic functions can be carried out.

Historical role of government in the American economy

Although our "ought-to-be" world places great restraint on government action, a brief look at the roles government has played shows how far we have moved from the classical theory. Let us examine some of the beliefs developed and practices followed concerning the changing role of government's activity in our economy.

GOVERNMENT AS A HELP TO BUSINESS

Since business is responsible for organizing our factors of production and producing our wealth, anything that government can do to aid business will help the entire economy. Alexander Hamilton in his "Report on Manufactures," supporting tariffs as a protection to industry, and Henry Clay with his American System, favoring protective tariffs and a "home market" for American products, believed that the country would benefit if business thrived. The development of protective tariffs, land grants to railroads, strong patent laws, and guarantees on certain business loans are examples of government intervention on behalf of business.

GOVERNMENT INTERVENTION TO ENFORCE COMPETITION

The passage of antitrust laws—the Sherman and Clayton acts—was received with mixed feelings by classical economists. Some claimed that it was proper for the government to maintain competition to insure the survival of capitalism. Others argued that such laws represented needless government interference. They said that to break up trusts was to penalize the most efficient and would only reduce incentive.

GOVERNMENT AS A HELP TO WEAKER ECONOMIC GROUPS

Because business was strong and had advantages at the market for buying the

Under what circumstances should government set up its own enterprise?

factors of production, many thought that government should step in and help weaker groups. This idea resulted in the exemption of labor from the antitrust laws and in such aids to labor as minimum wage and maximum hour laws. Price supports for agricultural products are also an interference with the free-market price, but they represent a further attempt to aid weaker economic groups.

GOVERNMENT AS A PRODUCER IN THE ABSENCE OF BUSINESS VENTURE

Although most consumer needs are met by business, some needs have not been fulfilled. When this condition exists, it is usually because business produces to make a profit and only indirectly seeks to fill needs. Originally there was no profit to be made in producing electric power in the Tennessee Valley; under these conditions private enterprise had no incentive to risk capital that appeared to have little chance of returning a profit. The federal government, which has no need to show a profit but is obliged to consider the needs of its citizens, moved in to fill the void. In the case of atomic energy, private enterprise did not have the resources to develop so costly an industry. Utilities at the local level and Social Security at the national level are other areas in which the government is a direct producer.

How deeply should the government be involved in the economy?

One of the major controversies today concerns the degree of government involvement in the economy. Although you as students do not yet have all the necessary tools to analyze this question (we return to it in later chapters), it is important for you to give it preliminary consideration in order to understand the purposes and thinking behind the controversy.

Most Americans, accepting the free-enterprise system, would agree that govern-

THE INSTITUTIONALISTS AND REFORM

One of the outstanding contributions of the United States to economic thinking was the development of the institutionalist approach to economics. Thorstein B. Veblen (1857–1929), John R. Commons (1862–1944), and Wesley C. Mitchell (1874–1948) were the three dominant figures of this school.

Unhappy with the many social and economic ills of the early 1900's, these men were not satisfied with the laissez-faire approach of the classical and neoclassical economists. Studying the environment, they disclosed the existence of widespread poverty, depressions, growing monopoly, and government favoritism towards business. In such circumstances they were unwilling to trust society to the "magic" of economic laws that were supposed to correct all imbalances and bring about a "harmony of interests."

In place of the theorizing of the orthodox economists, the institutionalists substituted the study of the environment and its institutions as an approach to the "real" world. Finding socialism unacceptable because of its militancy and its conflict with the established order, they sought social reform through greater participation of the government in the economy. Let the government act as an umpire between competing economic groups and interfere when extreme imbalances in the distribution of income develop! Let the government provide social security, reform credit institutions, and enforce protection for the weaker economic groups!

Many of the reforms advocated by the institutionalists have become an integral part of our social and economic system. With the accomplishment of these changes, which include some of the New Deal legislation, and with some of their thinking expressed in later theories, such as the Keynesian, the institutionalists today have only a small following. Few, however, could deny the important role they played in developing our present economic institutions.

ment should take whatever steps are necessary to preserve the pillars of capitalism. Protecting property, insuring the enforcement of contracts, and assuring economic freedom require government involvement. Enforcing competition is far more controversial, though most citizens agree that the government must have the right to protect the consumer from monopolistic power. Sharp differences of opinion exist concerning the desirability of government regulation of the market; even greater differences exist relative to what government should produce. Many political campaigns have been, and undoubtedly will continue to be, waged over this issue. A closer look at the issue reveals that there is a broader area of agreement than disagreement among the American people, although campaign oratory sometimes might seem to indicate otherwise.

PRINCIPLES GUIDING GOVERNMENT'S ROLE IN THE ECONOMY

Both tradition and theory have provided us with the following principles, which many economists believe will help to guide us in deciding how deeply the government should become involved in the economy:

1. Government should remain outside the economy so long as the people's needs are being met by private enterprise. When these needs are not met and there appears to be little chance of their being met by business, government must step in. Almost everyone agrees that the post office should be handled by government, since business has neither the resources nor the desire to enter this field. In launching Telstar and Syncom, government went into partnership with business, doing what private enterprise alone could not do. Controversy has long existed concerning the adequacy of private enterprise to meet the health needs of all citizens. Despite the passage of the Medicare bill of 1965, debate still continues on the role of government in this field.

2. When government does furnish a service or product, it should do so through existing facilities and capacities of business. The government uses military equipment, but business builds much of this on contract with the government. There is no controversy when the government orders private enterprise to build the equipment necessary for sending a man to the moon or for supplying our armed forces. In contrast, controversy does exist over the ownership of atomic-energy power plants which supply power for communities. In this case the government has already spent a tremendous amount of money for research; in addition, facilities must be built and paid for. Controversy also extends to public facilities sold to business.

3. If government must furnish a service, it is more acceptable if it is done at the lo-

Government expenditures are largely made through private industry.

To what extent is government regulation of private enterprise justified? What criteria would you suggest for regulation?

cal and state levels. There is little controversy over local support of public schools, but there has been much controversy over federal aid to education.

4. Services that do not lend themselves to a market economy but are generally agreed by citizens to be necessary for the society as a whole are handled by government. All of us recognize the need for national defense, but what price should each citizen pay for it? In this connection the fact that the state has the power of compulsion is important. Those who do not feel the need for national defense must still share in the cost. Government support of the arts is a subject of controversy because not all citizens agree that it is a necessity and because generous contributions by families and foundations have made the problem noncritical.

DIFFERING INFLUENCES OF CITIZENS AND CONSUMERS ON THE ECONOMY

Although people are usually both citizens and consumers, the influence of these groups on the economy is not equal. A look at the differences in their influence gives us added bases for comparing the decision-making process of private and public sectors of the economy.

1. A citizen is able to influence the public sector of the economy by casting his one vote. Theoretically, each citizen's vote counts the same as every other citizen's, although it must be recognized that money can affect this voting. A consumer, by spending his dollars in certain ways, helps to determine what will be produced in the private sector. The rich man, by spending many more dollars, has a far greater influence, although this is balanced to a certain extent by the fact that there are many more people of modest means than people of wealth.

2. A citizen has little influence on the specific expenditures in the public sector, since his representatives cannot run on a platform listing how all public revenues will be spent. Special elections for specific projects, such as school bond issues, are the exception. The consumer can carefully consider each purchase, weighing the satisfaction he may receive from it against all other possibilities.

3. Citizens frequently organize themselves into political groups in order to increase their influence over the public economy. Only rarely have consumers organized to effect a change in the private sector.

In considering whether some aspect of the economy is better suited for the public or the private sector, the student should weigh his influence as a citizen and as a consumer. Abraham Lincoln's words might be used as a guide: "The legitimate object of government is to do for the community of people whatever they need to have done, but cannot do at all or cannot do so well for themselves in their separate individual capacities."

The growth of public expenditures

One of the most striking facts about the American economy is the tremendous increase in expenditures by all levels of government in the last thirty-five years. Governments today are spending over eighteen times as much as they did in 1930. Whereas one out of every nine dollars of our national income was spent by government then, about one out of every four dollars is spent in the public sector today. Figure 7–1 shows this increase in actual dollars spent.

APPRAISAL OF INCREASE

Those who are in greatest sympathy with the tradition of the classical model are deeply concerned about this trend, and on occasion have used increased government spending as evidence of what they call "creeping socialism." Although there can be no denying the increase in the size and activities of the public sector, Figure 7–1 greatly distorts this increase in several ways:

1. Prices today are about twice as high as they were in 1930, requiring the government, as well as businessmen and consumers, to pay twice as much to receive equal goods or services.

2. Our gross national product, the total value of all our production, is about three and one-half times as large today as in 1930, so that the *percentage* of our total income going into the public sector has increased far less than Figure 7–1 might suggest.

3. In 1930 our country had a minimum of international military commitments, whereas today we consider ourselves the leader of the free world. Greater responsibility has resulted in a tremendous increase in government expenditures. In recent years the cost of our multibillion-dollar space program has added to the increase in government spending.

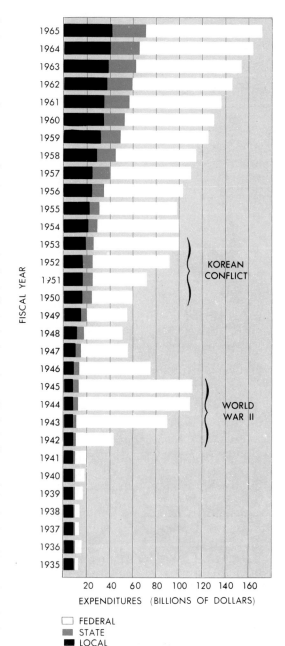

Figure 7–1   Growth of Public Expenditures, 1935–1965

SOURCE: Bureau of the Census

Since few people would deny that national defense is a legitimate function of government, the inclusion of the costs of World War II and recent military expenditures along with other government expenditures cannot be used as proof of "creeping socialism."

The change in government expenditures as a percentage of gross national product may be seen in Figure 7-2. This

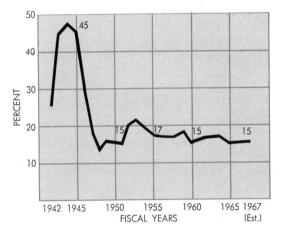

Figure 7-2 Federal Budget Expenditures as a Percentage of the Gross National Product, 1942-1967

SOURCE: Bureau of the Budget

gives a more accurate picture of the increase of government's functions in the economy in terms of the total economy, although it does not detail these changes, such as the increase in military and space expenditures. Federal spending as a percentage of gross national product has actually declined since 1953, whereas total government expenditures measured in the same way have remained fairly constant. From 1940 to 1960 social welfare expenditures as a percentage of gross national product increased less than two percent, from 8.4 percent to 10.3 percent. When we compare government receipts as a percentage of GNP in rich industrialized countries

with the same figures in underdeveloped countries, we find that the former have about 20 percent going to government, while the latter have substantially less.

INCREASE IN PUBLIC SERVICES

The facts just stated seem to indicate that government's role in the economy, except for the huge increase in military expenditures, has not increased. This is *not* so. Such government services as medical aid and loans to the business community have increased considerably, and it appears that they will continue to increase. However, these additional services have merely kept pace with the general increase in our total wealth and standard of living. Just as more people are able to buy more and better goods and services in the private sector, so

One form of government service that has increased significantly is that of relief to disaster areas. Federal aid is granted only on the specific request of a governor or of the President and is given only after state and local aid has been exhausted or is clearly inadequate.

our government has been able to provide additional services from the "bigger pie" in which everyone shares.

Besides additional services by government, the growth of regulatory agencies and the existence of laws regulating the private sector have greatly increased the role of government in the economy. Antitrust legislation, labor legislation, banking legislation, and the creation of the Federal Trade Commission, the Interstate Commerce Commission, the Securities and Exchange Commission, and the Federal Communications Commission illustrate how far we have departed from one aspect

of the classical model, in which government remained outside the economy even though this departure strengthens other aspects. Although historians, with their advantage of hindsight, may be able to evaluate whether we have gone too far, we are obliged as citizens to come to some tentative decisions now about the economic course on which we should steer our ship of state. And although you might wish to come to a conclusion at this time, you should probably make it a tentative one. Many other important economic concepts are yet to be considered, and you may wish to change your mind.

Part B   The Nature of Government Expenditures

Planning for spending:
the mechanics of preparing a budget

Although differences exist in budget procedures at different levels of government and for different state and local governments, the mechanics of budget making usually follow a certain pattern. The procedure described suggests the desirability of a balanced budget. Exceptions to this general rule will be noted in Unit III.

ADMINISTRATION
INITIATES BUDGETS

The chief executive (President, governor, mayor) calls upon his administrative heads to prepare estimates of their departments' needs as much as eighteen months in advance of actual expenditures. The administrative heads consult their staffs, their past budgets, and the demand for new or expanded activities within their departments. They submit an estimate of their needs, sometimes higher than they expect to receive, since they know it will be easier for them to cut down than it will be to obtain additional appropriations. The chief executive consults with his budget director and recognizes that his expenditures add up to a sum far beyond what he can expect

government revenues to be. This means that, unless he reduces his budget, he will have to ask for additional taxes—not always a popular request with the electorate. Since administrative heads are responsible for the operation of their departments, the chief executive usually allows them to make the necessary adjustments. After the chief executive receives the revised estimates, he either accepts them, or, if the total request still seems too high, he, together with his budget-maker and close associates, will make the final reductions.

LEGISLATURE APPROVES BUDGETS

The federal budget, usually a thick document resembling the telephone directory of a large city, is submitted to the legislative branch, which must give final approval. Once there, the budget goes to various committees, which scrutinize sections of it. Because of the complexity of such a document, experts must be called in and hearings must be held. Some interests will be seeking special privileges; others are concerned with keeping taxes low. The House Ways and Means Committee and the Senate Finance Committee (or a joint committee) make final recommendations be-

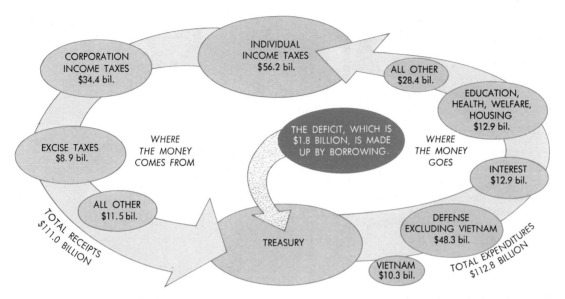

Figure 7–3   The Federal Budget: Four Aspects of Its Relation to the Economy

SOURCE: Bureau of the Budget

fore submitting it to the entire legislature. Rarely does the chief executive get all he asks for. The budget which finally emerges is usually a compromise of many forces. A similar but less complex procedure is generally followed at other levels of government.

TYPES OF BUDGETS

Governments usually have more than one budget. The one which we are likely to hear discussed is the *administrative budget,* which is the administration's request for funds. The *cash budget* includes in addition the money collected and spent in government trust funds, such as Social Security and unemployment insurance (note "Restricted Receipts" in Table 7–1 on p. 138). The latter budget has a greater influence on the total economy than the former.

What governments spend for

As you have seen, almost all spending is carried on at the three major levels of government—federal, state, and local. Some similarities exist in the nature and

procedures of spending at all levels. However, the three levels of government differ significantly in the things for which they spend their money.

FEDERAL EXPENDITURES

In analyzing federal expenditures, one fact stands out above all others: the major portion of outlays is either for national defense or for expenses resulting from international conflicts in the past. Table 7–1 shows approximately two thirds of the budget going for national defense, interest on the national debt (primarily due to military expenditures), veterans' services and benefits, international affairs and finance, and space research; all other government operations share the remaining one third. It would be easy to conclude from this example that federal expenditures have risen almost exclusively because of our international commitments. This is *not* so. We spend about twice as much today on labor and welfare as we did for all federal expenditures for the average year in the

Table 7–1   Summary of Federal Budget Receipts and Expenditures
(billions of dollars)

	Actual 1965	Estimate 1966	Estimate 1967
RECEIPTS FROM THE PUBLIC			
Unrestricted Receipts			
Individual Income Taxes	48.8	51.4	56.2
Corporation Income Taxes	25.5	29.7	34.4
Excise Taxes	14.6	13.0	13.3
Estate and Gift Taxes	2.7	2.9	3.3
Customs	1.4	1.7	1.8
Other Receipts	6.3	7.2	8.8
Restricted Receipts			
Employment Taxes	16.9	18.8	24.3
Unemployment Tax Deposits by States	3.1	2.9	2.9
Veterans Life Insurance Premiums	.5	.5	.5
Total Receipts from the Public	119.7	128.2	145.5
PAYMENTS TO THE PUBLIC			
National Defense	50.8	57.4	61.4
International Affairs and Finance	4.6	4.1	4.4
Space Research and Technology	5.1	5.6	5.3
Agriculture and Agricultural Resources	5.4	4.6	3.6
Natural Resources	2.8	2.9	3.0
Commerce and Transportation	7.4	7.0	6.6
Housing and Community Development	.9	2.0	1.2
Health, Labor, and Welfare	28.3	34.1	39.3
Education	1.5	2.3	2.8
Veterans Benefits and Services	6.1	5.6	6.4
Interest	8.6	9.3	10.2
General Government	2.3	2.4	2.5
Allowance for Contingencies	−.2	−.2	*
Deposit Funds (net) (see Restricted Receipts above)		.1	.4
Other Undistributed Adjustments (see Restricted Receipts above)			
Agency Payments for Employee Retirement	−1.0	−1.1	−1.1
Deduction from Employees' Salaries for Retirement	−1.0	−1.1	−1.1
Increase (−) or Decrease in Outstanding Checks, etc.	.9	−.1	.1
Total Payments to the Public	122.4	135.0	145.0
Excess of Receipts from (+) or Payments to (−) the Public	−2.7	−6.9	+.5

*Less than $50 million
SOURCES: Executive Office of the President; Bureau of the Budget

1920's. More money was spent on agriculture by the federal government in 1964 than for all federal expenditures in 1933. Although changes in price levels account for some of these dramatic differences, and defense outlays continue, the fact is that government involvement in other areas of the economy has increased significantly.

STATE EXPENDITURES

Total state expenditures and total expenditures of local governments are about the same size—each about one fifth of all government expenditures. However, the last fifteen years have seen state budgets growing at a faster rate than the federal budget, more than doubling during the

1950's. Most of this increase has been due to the expansion in highways and education, the two accounting for about half of all state expenditures. Public welfare, hospitals, and health are the largest remaining areas of expenditures.

LOCAL EXPENDITURES

Local government expenditures are concentrated primarily on those things which local residents feel most directly and over which they believe they should have the most direct control. Education accounts for nearly half of the expenditures; following far behind are highways, police and fire protection, public welfare, health and hospitals, and government control. With the cost of education increasing so rapidly, and local governments being so restricted in their taxing powers, local units have been forced to turn more and more to the states for financial aid. How much federal aid to

local communities will be needed to supplement state aid is now a major controversy.

Before World War I local governments accounted for over half of all government expenditures. When the federal government moved into the field of welfare in the 1930's and increased its military expenditures in the 1940's, local government expenditures fell to about one eighth of the total. However, this trend has been reversed. Like state government expenditures, local outlays have been increasing faster than expenditures of the federal government. Most students of public finance are of the opinion that unless local units of government are given additional powers of taxation, they will have to turn more and more to the state and federal governments either for funds or for the direct furnishing of services. Figure 7–4 shows how all state and local governments spent their money in 1963.

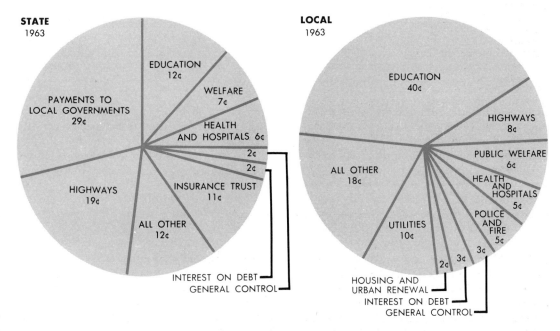

Figure 7–4 Combined State Expenditures and Combined Local Expenditures

SOURCE: U.S. Department of Commerce, Bureau of the Census

Part C   The Nature of Government Revenues

Sources of government income

Governments finance their expenditures from a variety of sources, including taxes, receipts from other levels of government, earnings from government enterprises, fines, and fees. While taxes are, by far, the major source of government income, receipts from other levels of government are important. The federal government gives grants to states on a matching basis for welfare and health, and most recently to local governments for fighting poverty. State governments give funds to local governments, frequently on a per capita basis. New York State distributes over half of its revenue to local units of government in this way.

Money collected from public agencies, often called "authorities," is a more important source of revenue at the local and state levels. The same is true for fees, licenses, and fines. Taxes, however, remain the single most important source of revenue, particularly at the federal level.

Why must governments tax?

With all levels of government in our country spending about one fifth of our gross national product and employing about one out of every six workers (including members of the armed forces), it is quite clear that these governments represent the largest buyers in both the market for goods and services and the market for factors of production. If governments hire about eighteen percent of all workers, they are taking these workers away from possible jobs they might have in the private sector. These workers are producing something (usually services) that the society, acting as citizens rather than consumers, has decided it needs. This production is considered more valuable to the nation, as determined by our elected government, than if these workers were employed in the private sector. We get the factors of production to work for government rather than private enterprise by offering sufficient dollars. Where does the government get the money to pay these dollars? The easiest and most obvious way to answer this is to refer to the sources of government revenue previously listed. However, such an answer ignores the problem of the relationship of government activity to the total economy.

Before we consider this problem further, we should observe that the federal government alone in our nation may legally print money to pay its bills. The greenbacks printed during the Civil War were money of this kind. A few changes in existing laws would allow the federal government to do the same thing today. If it did so, it could eliminate taxes and people would have more money to spend in the private sector for the many things they wish but could not previously afford. This sounds wonderful but, as you probably suspect, there is a major flaw. The weakness here comes because we are likely to think of wealth in terms of money rather than in terms of goods and services.

Returning once again to the relationship of government to the total economy, you may recall that our basic economic problem is limited resources to fill unlimited wants, forcing us to make choices. If we utilize all our factors of production most efficiently and this production adds up to 100 units, all within the private sector, there will be no resources left to produce units of production in the government sector. If we decide that we need 20 units of production that government produces, we can get it only by increasing our resources (which in this instance we cannot do) or by taking factors of production away from the private sector. By printing money to pay for its production, the government increases the dollar demand without increasing the supply of production. This results in price increases, as you may readily see by consulting the graph for supply and demand on page 29.

In contrast, the government, by taxing, takes money that people might spend in the private sector away from them. This reduces the demand for units of production in the private sector, freeing the units of production that are now unemployed, and allows for a transfer of the factors of production from the private to the public sector. If payments by government and private enterprise are the same, taxes of 20 percent reduce the demand of people by 20 percent in the private sector market. Units of production in the economy can now be divided, 80 units produced by private enterprise and 20 units produced by government. By taxing, government has diverted the factors of production from the private sector to the public sector without threatening stable prices.

What determines a fair tax?

Few people think of taxes as payment for certain services received by government. The major reason for not thinking in these terms is that it is difficult for us to put a price tag on the specific benefits which we receive from government. Supply and demand may determine the price of consumer goods, such as clothing, and they may even suggest the proper allocation of resources between education and defense. However, they do not answer the question of how much you, as a taxpayer, should pay for such services as fire or police protection, which is another matter entirely. This in turn raises the question of what principles should be used to determine tax assessment.

BENEFITS RECEIVED

The oldest principle applied to the determination of a fair tax is that of *benefits received*. Differing little from purchases made in the private sector, this principle asks the taxpayer to pay the government according to the benefits he derives from government. While it is logical to tax gasoline to pay for roads used by cars, buses, or trucks, we could hardly expect people on welfare to pay the tax that will be used to support them. A much more complex problem is the determination of the benefits derived by each citizen from a collective service such as defense, or police or fire protection.

ABILITY TO PAY

Most people in our society believe that those who have the greatest wealth or the highest income should pay the most taxes, regardless of the benefits they get from government. The reasoning behind this principle is that as a taxpayer's wealth or income increases, his ability to pay taxes increases even faster. Using the theory of diminishing marginal utility explained in Chapter 2, the payment of the last dollar of $20,000 of income will involve far less sacrifice than the parting with the last dollar of a $10,000 income. While very few people would suggest that all taxpayers should make equal sacrifices, the practical needs of raising revenue without causing an undue hardship make this principle acceptable without testifying to its absolute fairness.

Determining the fairest principle to use for a just tax is a question of values rather than of economic science, and is determined in the political process. Nevertheless, the American people have apparently accepted to a certain extent the principle of *ability to pay*, and our American tax system reflects this acceptance.

Other factors in evaluating taxes

Many other factors, in addition to fairness, must be considered before levying a tax. From the government's standpoint, the total revenue that a tax yields is a primary consideration. Local and state governments must find taxes that provide a fairly predictable and steady income. The federal government needs a tax program that is flexible enough to help the economy during changes in business activity, as we will see in Chapter 11. Consideration must be given to the cost of collecting a tax, since high costs incurred in administering it, both for the taxpayer and for the government, may make it uneconomical.

EFFECT ON PRODUCTION

Another major consideration is the effect that the tax has on production. One of the most frequently used arguments against a high income tax is that it destroys the incentive of businessmen and employees to work harder and more efficiently. The favorable results for the economy from the federal income tax reduction in 1964 (see p. 150) have given weight to this point of view. Although evidence can be found both to prove and disprove that taxes affect initiative, few economists would deny that a point can be reached at which such an effect could take place. It must, therefore, be kept in mind in the preparation of new taxes or the raising of rates.

EFFECT ON SPECIFIC GOODS

Taxes can have significant influences on the sale of specific goods or services sold. A tax on oleomargarine affects not only its sale but also that of similar products, such as butter. A cabaret tax may force the proprietor of a restaurant to eliminate entertainment. A tax on electricity may lead to increased buying of gas appliances. Using your knowledge of demand and supply curves, tell what happens to the quantity purchased when a tax forces the price up. Does it matter whether the demand is elastic or inelastic? For an illustration of the effect of an excise tax on the sale of fur coats, turn to pages 4 and 5 of the classical model insert that follows page 44.

REFLECTION OF VALUES

Some taxes reflect our society's moral values. It is far easier for lawmakers to place a tax on tobacco and liquor than on almost any other commodity. It is easy to get the impression that society is saying, "If you smoke and drink, you will have to pay for your indulgence in more ways than one." Those who believe that high taxes can discourage people from buying cigarettes or liquor underestimate how inelastic the demand for these products is.

CONVENIENCE

No taxpayer finds a tax convenient to pay, but those who write our tax laws must consider the time and manner of collection that will cause the least hardship. Before World War II, when the federal income tax was relatively low, payments were generally made by income taxpayers once a year. Most families would find such an arrangement today almost catastrophic. The burden of paying taxes becomes more tolerable through the withholding of a predetermined amount from each paycheck or by making payments four times a year. Simplicity of directions for payment is also important.

SHIFTING THE BURDEN

A factor which those who make our tax laws must carefully consider is, Who will bear the ultimate burden of the tax? Frequently a tax placed on one person or group can be *shifted* to someone else. A manufacturer may shift the tax placed on him to the retailer. The retailer, in turn, may shift the tax to the ultimate consumer. It is important to determine the *incidence* of the tax, that is, where it finally comes to rest and where shifting can no longer take place. Taxes can be shifted backward to the initial producer as well as forward to the consumer. The effects of shifting can be more far-reaching than merely asking the consumer to pay more. The increase in price can cause sales to decline, eventually resulting in the loss of jobs. A good tax should place the incidence where the tax-makers intended it to be.

Evaluating ability to pay

In seeking to evaluate a tax for fairness according to the ability-to-pay principle, economists have frequently used one particular criterion: that taxes should be judged on the relationship of the tax rate to the tax base. A *tax rate* is the percentage that is taxed. The *tax base* is the subject on which the tax is levied. If the tax rate increases as the tax base increases, the tax is *progressive*. If the tax rate remains the same, regardless of the tax base, the tax is *proportional*. If the tax rate decreases as the tax base increases, the tax is *regressive*. Figure 7–5 shows the differences graphically.

Using an income tax as an example, a regressive tax would be one in which the first $1,000 of income might be taxed at ten percent, the next $1,000 of income at eight percent, the next $1,000 at six percent, the next $1,000 at four percent, the next $1,000 at two percent, and one percent for all additional income. With this tax rate a man with a taxable income of $5,000 would pay $300, or six percent of his income, while a man with a taxable income of $10,000 would pay $350, or 3.5 percent of his income. A proportional tax would call for a uniform rate, say five percent, so that our man with the lower income would pay $250 while our wealthier man would pay $500.

A progressive income tax might call for one percent on the first $1,000 of taxable income, two percent on the next $1,000, three percent on the next, continuing with an increase of one percent in the tax rate on each additional $1,000 of income up to $90,000. In this case the first man would pay $150, or 1.5 percent, and our second taxpayer $550, or 5.5 percent.

The regressive tax places the greatest burden on lower income groups, whereas the progressive tax falls most heavily on people with higher incomes. Few taxes are enacted that are deliberately designed to be regressive. This would be bad politics and would run counter to our sense of justice. However, any tax in which every taxpayer pays the same number of dollars, regardless of his income or tax base, is very regressive. The poll tax is an example. A retail sales tax that is placed on all purchases appears to be proportional, say three percent, but is, in effect, regressive. This is because the lower income groups spend a greater proportion of their income (frequently all of it)

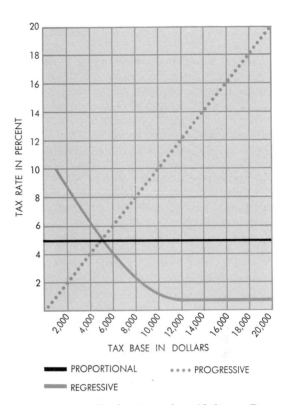

Figure 7–5 Evaluating the Ability-to-Pay Principle

In evaluating taxes according to the ability-to-pay principle, they may be classified as progressive, proportional, or regressive, depending upon the relationship of the tax rate to the tax base.

than the upper income groups; the spending of those with high incomes is relatively less affected by the sales tax. Many economists believe that, in determining ability to pay, income is probably a better tax base than amount spent.

As we continue our study of taxation and government spending in Chapter 8, additional problems of evaluating taxes will appear. Each tax must be examined in the light of our total tax structure. Also to be considered are the implications of government spending in excess of income, to be discussed at length in Chapters 11 and 14 and related to spending policy.

REVIEW: the highlights of the chapter

1. The classical model calls for a minimum of government interference in the economy so as to allow the allocation of resources to be according to consumer preferences. It is the responsibility of government to provide an environment favorable for the market economy by preserving the pillars of capitalism: private property, freedom of contract, economic freedom, and competition.

2. Government's role in the American economy has become more active as it seeks to satisfy the needs of the people. How deeply involved government should be in the economy is controversial, although tradition and theory have provided principles to guide our answers.

3. Citizens and consumers may be the same people, but their influence on the economy is different.

4. Public expenditures of the federal, state, and local governments have increased enormously in the last thirty years, although inflationary prices and military expenditures account for a substantial part of this increase. An additional factor has been our demand for more and better services, particularly in education and welfare.

5. Government budgets are prepared by chief executives and their administrative staffs, but they require legislative approval. Political considerations play a part in their preparation and passage.

6. The major source of government revenue is taxes. Government imposes taxes to move resources from the private to the public sector without jeopardizing prices.

7. Taxes may be evaluated according to the principles of benefits received or ability to pay, their revenue yield, their effect on production and the allocation of resources, their convenience to the taxpayer, and the shifting of their incidence. A tax may be judged progressive, proportional, or regressive, depending on the relationship of the tax rate to the tax base.

IN CONCLUSION: some aids to understanding

Terms for review

pillars of capitalism	benefits-received principle
administrative budget	progressive tax
cash budget	proportional tax
tax shifting	regressive tax
incidence of the tax	ability-to-pay principle
regulatory agency	tax rate
Clay's American System	tax base

Questions for review

1. The classical model of capitalism forms the basis of the American economic system.
   (a) Describe the four basic pillars of the capitalist system.
   (b) What role must the government play to insure an environment favorable for the proper functioning of the capitalist system, even though this role is contrary to the original system?

2. Throughout our nation's history the federal government has aided business development in many ways.
   (a) Describe the various methods that the government has used to help business.
   (b) What role did Alexander Hamilton and Henry Clay play in helping business?

3. As the economic strength of part of the business sector increased, the role of government in relation to business changed.
   (a) Describe the steps which were taken to insure competition.
   (b) How did the government help weaker sectors of the economy?
   (c) How did the government take over some of the functions of the business community?

4. Write two brief paragraphs giving the arguments for and against the involvement of the government in regulating the market and in entering the field of production.

5. Every individual may have an impact on the national economy. Briefly describe the two roles in which the individual can use his influence. What is the effect of each role on the public sector and the private sector of the economy?

6. Increased government spending has a significant influence on the economy as a whole.
   (a) Using the charts in Figures 7–1 and 7–2, list the arguments to refute the charge that the expenditures of the federal government reflect a "creeping socialism."
   (b) Indicate how the changing role of government is reflected in the increase of government spending.

7. With minor changes in the law the federal government can pay its bills merely by printing the required amount of money. Explain why the government usually turns to taxation for its revenues rather than using what appears to be the more painless method of printing more money.

8. In levying taxes, one important consideration is the "fairness" of a particular tax or of an entire tax system.
   (a) Distinguish between a progressive and a regressive tax.
   (b) What is meant by a proportional tax?
   (c) What danger does the "soak the rich" idea present?

Additional questions and problems

1. In describing the role of the various factors of production, some economists suggest that the government must be included. Defend this idea by indicating the role government plays.

2. "Democratic capitalism has provided a middle road between complete laissez-faire and complete government control." Criticize and defend this statement.

3. List four major headings you would use in preparing the affirmative in a debate. *"Resolved*: The United States government must remain completely outside the economy."

4. United States citizens have a dual role, both as voters and as consumers, in exerting their influence on our economy.
   (a) Give three examples of each role that the citizen plays.
   (b) Describe two conditions in which his two roles may cause him to have opposite points of view on the same matter.

5. The trend toward increased government spending may be interpreted in a variety of ways.
   (a) Using the graphs in Figures 7–1 and 7–2, describe the reasons why both are needed to give a full and true picture of the government's increase in expenditures.
   (b) List two arguments which could be used by those who say that we are on the road to "creeping socialism" and two answers in rebuttal.
   (c) In a brief paragraph explain how added government services have increased the cost of government.

6. In the course of our nation's history, government has played an evolving role in the economy.
   (a) Make a time line of the economic development of the United States, listing the highlights of the opposing forces, aids to business, and controls over business.
   (b) How is the philosophy of the role of government on the economic scene reflected in these actions?
   (c) Does the added activity of the government indicate a possible weakening of our capitalist system?

8 Government and Public Finance

Now that we know why government taxes us, and since we have some of the tools for evaluating taxes, we shall examine several of the more important kinds of taxes. This should be far more than an academic lesson. With the cost of government rising almost yearly, the need for choosing between alternatives in both spending and taxing arises. How will each of these taxes affect you as a consumer, as a producer, and as a citizen? You may escape payment in one of these roles but be hurt in the other roles you play.

An alternative to raising money through taxes is borrowing. Frequent government borrowing has resulted in our having a huge public debt. Is such a debt harmful? Does it differ from a private debt? Can we pay it off? If we did, how would it affect the economy? In this chapter we will examine these questions and perhaps arrive at some tentative answers.

Part A   The Federal Tax System

Tax revenues: progressive or regressive?

As we have observed in Table 7–1 (see p. 138), our federal government secures its revenue from a wide variety of sources. It is obvious that *individual* and *corporation income taxes* are the largest source of revenue. Apart from *employment taxes,* such as Social Security payments which go into the federal trust fund, approximately seventy percent of all federal revenue comes from income taxes. A very small portion of our total revenue comes from estate and gift taxes and from customs collections, which were a major source of revenue in the nineteenth century. A larger share comes from federal *excise taxes,* which are sales taxes often placed on specific goods and services, such as alcohol, tobacco, gasoline, motor vehicles, jewelry, and admissions to places of entertainment. These taxes are frequently the result of the treasury's constant efforts to raise new revenue without causing too much political backlash.

Other than income taxes and estate and gift taxes, federal taxes are regressive. Taxes on commodities and services are not based on the buyer's income. Although people with higher incomes are more likely to spend the greater amount for jewelry, furs, and admissions to expensive places of entertainment, this is more than compensated for by the percentage of income spent by the people in lower income groups for such needs as gasoline, automobiles, and appliances. The latter have also been most affected by the raising of federal excise taxes. Social Security payments may seem to be proportional to income. However, since they are based on a maximum tax base of $6,600, people earning more than this amount have that portion free from this tax. Part of the regressive feature of Social Security taxes is lessened when benefits are considered.

Taxes on the transfer of estates and on sizeable gifts have been collected by the federal government since 1916. The great majority of people never need concern themselves with estate taxes, since the tax base does not start until deductions above $60,000 are reached. However, above this amount the rates are highly progressive, reflecting the strong sentiment against an aristocracy of wealth. Taxes on large gifts are used to discourage the evasion of estate taxes by transfers made before death.

Income taxes: major source of revenue

Among those who favor the ability-to-pay principle of taxation, net income of individuals or businesses is usually considered the fairest tax base. Although there is broad support for taxing net income at a progressive rate, there is considerable controversy over what to consider as net income, what deductions to allow, and to what extent corporations should be taxed. A few examples will illustrate the problem of trying to find an answer to what is fair for all and yet will provide adequate income.

"First dollar I ever earned—after taxes."

WHAT CONSTITUTES INCOME?

Should food grown by a farmer to feed his own family be counted as income? Should payment in kind, such as commodities given to a lawyer by a client, be counted as income? Should fringe benefits, generous with some companies and meager with others, go untaxed? Why should a homeowner be allowed to deduct his real-estate taxes from his income whereas the tenant who pays these taxes to the landlord in rent is allowed no such deduction? Is the standard $600 exemption fair for an infant as well as for an adult? Should a person such as a baseball player or an actor, who earns a high income during a short productive period of his life, be asked to pay the same rates as a person whose income is more evenly earned throughout his working life? Should income made by the sale of property that has increased in value be taxed as income earned "on the job"? Should a tax be imposed on a corporation's profit as well as on the dividends received by the stockholders? Should profits reinvested in a business be taxed in the same way that distributed dividends are?

Our federal income tax laws have to provide answers to all these questions. None of the answers can satisfy all of those affected. The correct answers of today may not be satisfactory tomorrow. As you encounter these problems in preparing a tax return, injustices will probably be obvious to you. The problems facing our lawmakers in trying to meet each individual citizen's needs and standard of values are very great. Remember that our tax laws do attempt to reconcile these differences.

PREPARING A PERSONAL INCOME TAX REPORT

The tax base for income taxes is called *taxable income*. Taxable income is what remains after subtracting allowable deductions and exemptions from gross income. Most wage earners can figure their federal income tax by adding together the sum of their wages from all employers, their interest from savings, their dividends from stock in excess of a certain allowable amount, and any other unrecorded income. The total thus arrived at represents gross income. From the total they then either subtract the *standard allowable deduction* – ten percent of gross income up to a maximum amount of $1,000 – or they itemize their deductions if their total will exceed the standard deduction, and then subtract these deductions from gross income. It usually pays to itemize deductions only when expenses for some accident or illness are high; when interest payments, usually for mortgages on homes, and taxes are significant; or when some loss from theft or casualty adds up to a substantial portion of what the standard deduction would be. Contributions to charitable organizations and certain expenses related to the earning of income are also deductible. Exemptions or credits are then subtracted from this sum. An exemption is a specified amount on which the taxpayer does not pay any tax. The federal government allows $600 for the taxpayer and $600 for each dependent who receives more than half his support from the taxpayer. Additional exemptions are allowed for the blind and for people over 65.

When all deductions and exemptions have been subtracted from the gross income, the amount remaining is the taxable income. Once that has been determined, the taxpayer turns to the appropriate tax rate schedule to determine what his tax is. It is generally better for married couples to file a joint return. Table 8–1 shows the rates for 1965 for married taxpayers filing a joint return.

EVALUATING THE PERSONAL INCOME TAX

A brief study of the table on tax rates shows how progressive our federal income tax is. Rates start at 14 percent on the first $500 of income for individuals or $1,000 for married couples, and go to 70 percent on all

Table 8–1   Tax Rate Schedule for Personal Income Tax for Married Taxpayers
Filing Joint Returns and Certain Widows and Orphans
(taxable years beginning after December 31, 1964)

TAXABLE INCOME	TAX
Not over $1,000	14% of the taxable income.
$ 1,000 to $ 2,000	$ 140 plus 15% of excess over $ 1,000
2,000 to 3,000	290 plus 16% of excess over 2,000
3,000 to 4,000	450 plus 17% of excess over 3,000
4,000 to 8,000	620 plus 19% of excess over 4,000
8,000 to 12,000	1,380 plus 22% of excess over 8,000
12,000 to 16,000	2,260 plus 25% of excess over 12,000
16,000 to 20,000	3,260 plus 28% of excess over 16,000
20,000 to 24,000	4,380 plus 32% of excess over 20,000
24,000 to 28,000	5,660 plus 36% of excess over 24,000
28,000 to 32,000	7,100 plus 39% of excess over 28,000
32,000 to 36,000	8,660 plus 42% of excess over 32,000
36,000 to 40,000	10,340 plus 45% of excess over 36,000
40,000 to 44,000	12,140 plus 48% of excess over 40,000
44,000 to 52,000	14,060 plus 50% of excess over 44,000
52,000 to 64,000	18,060 plus 53% of excess over 52,000
64,000 to 76,000	24,420 plus 55% of excess over 64,000
76,000 to 88,000	31,020 plus 58% of excess over 76,000
88,000 to 100,000	37,980 plus 60% of excess over 88,000
100,000 to 120,000	45,180 plus 62% of excess over 100,000
120,000 to 140,000	57,580 plus 64% of excess over 120,000
140,000 to 160,000	70,380 plus 66% of excess over 140,000
160,000 to 180,000	83,580 plus 68% of excess over 160,000
180,000 to 200,000	97,180 plus 69% of excess over 180,000
Over $200,000	110,980 plus 70% of excess over 200,000

The personal income tax is designed to be progressive. Can you think of ways in which people with high incomes can avoid its progressive intent? SOURCE: U.S. Treasury Department, Internal Revenue Service

income above $100,000 for individuals and $200,000 for married couples. The rates above 14 percent do not apply to the entire income. Each portion of the income is taxed at a different rate. Although a wealthy married man who has a taxable income of $200,000 has reached the 70 percent bracket, his tax on his entire taxable income amounts to slightly more than 55 percent. Before the Revenue Act of 1964 the tax rate reached 91 percent on incomes above $200,000 for individuals. How would you evaluate such a tax rate?

It is difficult to shift the incidence of the personal income tax. However, there are ways of avoiding taxes by finding "loopholes" in the laws and even by criminal evasion. *Avoidance* is a legal way to reduce tax payment, whereas *evasion* refers to illegal means. Both have the effect of reducing the government's revenue from personal income taxes.

The personal income tax supplies a large proportion of the federal government's revenue. It tends to reduce the inequality of income existing before taxes. Thus, the taxpayer who earns $6,000 before paying income tax may retain $5,500, whereas the $60,000-a-year man may be left with $42,000. Both benefit about equally from government expenditures, but the low-income taxpayer has paid 8 percent of his income in federal personal income taxes while the high-income taxpayer has paid

30 percent. The other more regressive taxes we have mentioned reduce some of this difference.

The fact that there are high rates on high incomes does not mean that people in higher income groups pay most of the taxes. The United States Treasury Department reported that in 1961, 52 percent of all federal income tax money came from the lowest tax bracket, which at that time was set at 20 percent withholding, and only 6 percent came from the tax bracket of over 50 percent. Of course, a far higher percentage of our population is in the lowest tax bracket than in the higher ones.

CORPORATION INCOME TAX

Business corporations, like individuals, must also pay taxes on their income. In fiscal 1965 the federal government collected over $26 billion from corporation income taxes. This amounted to approximately half of what the federal government collected in personal income taxes and over 20 percent of the federal government's total revenues.

A corporation income tax is based on a corporation's annual income after it has paid its expenses. Dividends to stockholders are not included as expenses. Unlike the personal income tax, there are only two rates, 22 percent on earnings up to $25,000 a year and 48 percent on all other earnings. This follows the principle of ability to pay, but it is far less progressive than the personal income tax. The incidence tends to fall on the stockholders in highly competitive businesses because shifting it to the consumer will raise prices but cut down on sales. In oligopolies, where prices can be largely determined by the producers, the customers frequently must bear the burden.

EVALUATING THE CORPORATION INCOME TAX

The corporation income tax is often criticized as an example of double taxation. Not only must the company pay taxes on its profits, but also individual shareholders must pay personal income taxes on dividends paid by the company. The principle of ability to pay is ignored in taxing dividend income. The small stockholder has been given some relief by the provision allowing taxpayers to deduct the first $100 they receive in dividends from their personal income ($200 for married couples filing joint returns). In addition, money that is gained from the increase in the value of stock sold at least six months after its purchase is considered a capital gain. The law allows the seller of such stock to pay at a lower rate on the capital gain. However, gains from stock owned for less than six months are taxed at the rate of regular income.

Many businessmen have complained — probably with some justification — that high corporate taxes interfere with their opportunities to reinvest their profits in their business. Such interference can hinder the growth and modernization of businesses. Some industrial nations that have expanded rapidly in the last fifteen years have far lower taxes on corporations than we do, and many economists believe that low corporation taxes have been a help in this business expansion. The lower tax rates on corporate income put into effect with the Revenue Act of 1964 may give us more information about this problem. The future may see even greater changes in the corporation income tax. However, it is doubtful that the government will be willing to give up such a lucrative source of revenue.

Part B   State and Local Tax Revenues

Sources of revenue

State and local governments, like the federal government, depend on a number of taxes for their income. Figure 8–1 shows a composite of all state and local governments' tax revenue by type. In addition to the revenue received from taxes, the state governments received in 1963 about $7.8

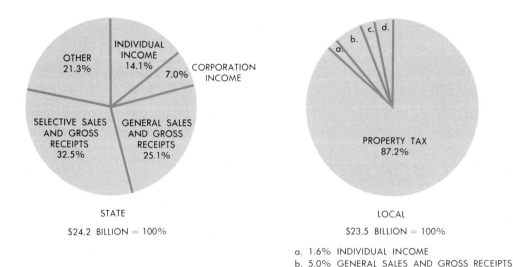

STATE

$24.2 BILLION = 100%

LOCAL

$23.5 BILLION = 100%

a. 1.6% INDIVIDUAL INCOME
b. 5.0% GENERAL SALES AND GROSS RECEIPTS
c. 2.7% SELECTED SALES AND GROSS RECEIPTS
d. 3.5% OTHER

Figure 8–1   Sources of State and Local Government Revenue, Fiscal 1964

The tax structure for states, although not as progressive as for the federal government, more closely follows the ability-to-pay principle as the individual income tax becomes a greater source of state revenue. Local governments have regressive tax structures because of their reliance on the property tax as their major source of tax revenue. The use of new kinds of taxes may make local taxes less regressive. Figure 7–4 shows the expenditures of state and local governments. Federal government expenditures and sources of tax revenue are shown in Table 7–1. SOURCES: N.I.C.B., *Road Maps of Industry* No. 1521; Tax Foundation, Inc.; Bureau of the Census

billion from the federal government and over $11 billion in fees and other sources. Local governments received in 1963 slightly less than $1 billion from the federal government, over $11.8 billion from state governments, and close to $12.4 billion in fees and from other sources. Income from state taxes accounted for 55 percent of state revenue, while income from local taxes amounted to slightly less than 50 percent of local revenue. The trends of the states' dependence on the federal government for aid and of the local governments' dependence on the states have been upward each year.

State tax systems

The largest single source of state tax revenue is the general retail *sales tax*. Most states having such a tax impose it on all

purchases, although there is a growing tendency to exempt food and medicine to ease the burden such a tax imposes on people with low incomes. Some items carry state excise taxes in addition to general sales taxes, federal excise taxes, and, on occasion, local taxes. If we remove all taxes from cigarettes the price becomes almost unrecognizable. Excise taxes are popular with legislators because they are easily hidden and less likely to antagonize voters. Collection of excises is relatively simple, involving either periodic sales reports or the sale to the manufacturer or distributor of a revenue stamp. In highly competitive industries the incidence must fall on the consumer because the producer does not have enough economic profit to absorb the ad-

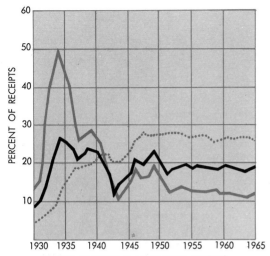

EXCISES AS PERCENT OF FEDERAL RECEIPTS

SALES TAXES AS PERCENT OF STATE AND LOCAL RECEIPTS (EXCLUDING GRANTS-IN-AID)

COMBINED TOTAL AS PERCENT OF TOTAL RECEIPTS

Figure 8–2   Excise and Sales Taxes as Percent of Government Receipts

As federal revenue from excise taxes has declined, state and local dependence on receipts from sales taxes has increased. SOURCE: U.S. Department of Commerce, Office of Business Economics

ditional cost. In less competitive areas the burden is either shared or shifted to the consumer, so that the tax will not cut too heavily into profits.

The general retail sales tax places the incidence directly on the consumer, but it would not be accurate to assume that the producer is unaffected. Higher prices to the consumer result in fewer sales, thereby affecting everyone. Although it is easy to collect, and the burden is seemingly light because the consumer (taxpayer) pays only a small amount at a time, the tax is very regressive and evasion is not difficult. The family with an income below $5,000 will probably spend all of it. With the exception of rent, their entire income may be subject to this tax. The family with an income of $50,000 will probably spend only part of it. That part which they do not spend is not affected by the sales tax.

EVALUATING THE SALES TAX

With three fourths of all states collecting general sales taxes and many local governments turning to it to help solve their problem of raising enough revenue, attempts have been made to lessen the regressive features of this tax. A number of states have exempted food. If medicine, fuel, and utilities are also exempted, the general sales tax becomes slightly progressive at low-income levels, proportional at middle-income levels, and regressive only at upper-income levels. Families with low incomes spend the largest portion of their income on rent and food. As income rises, a larger percentage of income is spent for other items, thereby increasing the percentage of income taxed. Actually, the percentage of income that can be saved in the higher income brackets increases so rapidly that the regressive features of this tax remain, even with the exemptions mentioned.

An increasing number of economists have suggested that all necessities should be exempted from excise and general retail sales taxes and that the same taxes on luxuries should be raised substantially. To follow this suggestion would allow these taxes to conform to the ability-to-pay principle. The difficulty with such a procedure lies in determining what constitutes necessities and luxuries. People with lower incomes spend a greater percentage of their income on tobacco, for instance, than do people in the upper levels of income. What is the difficulty in exempting clothing? Although there may be some items that everyone considers luxuries, such as expensive jewelry, furs, and limousines, the amount of revenue yielded by a tax on them would be too small to meet the needs of government. For a further discussion of the question of

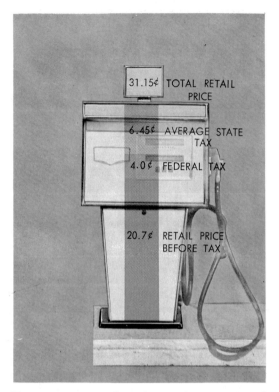

31.15¢ TOTAL RETAIL PRICE

6.45¢ AVERAGE STATE TAX

4.0¢ FEDERAL TAX

20.7¢ RETAIL PRICE BEFORE TAX

Taxes on some goods make up a large portion of the total cost.

individual values related to standard of living, turn back to the problem at the end of Chapter 2.

OTHER STATE TAXES

Gasoline taxes and fees collected for drivers' licenses and automobile registration are good examples of the benefits-received principle. Some states earmark all such revenues for road construction to reassure those who use the highways that they will get what they pay for. Since drivers also benefit from other state services, it is doubtful whether putting receipts in the general revenue fund makes much of a difference in benefits received.

More than two thirds of the states have income taxes that follow the pattern set by the federal government. The rates are, however, far lower, generally running from one to eight percent, with rates in only a few states going higher. State income taxes are far less progressive than the federal income tax but more progressive than most other state taxes.

Tax receipts from corporate income, inheritance and gift taxes, and property taxes make up the remainder of state tax revenue. The first two are progressive, while the vanishing state property tax is regressive. Inheritance taxes differ from the federal estate taxes by being placed on the receiver rather than on what is given.

Local tax systems

Property taxes are the oldest and, among local governments, the most widely used source of revenue. They account for 80 percent of all tax revenues raised at the local level and about 50 percent of all revenue received by local governments, including payments from state and national government sources. Property taxes are divided into two categories—real estate taxes on land, and personal property taxes on such things as securities, furniture, and automobiles.

One of the major reasons that property taxes have remained an important source of revenue is that it is a relatively simple matter to have them yield the revenue needed by the government. If a school district needs to raise $2 million to finance its annual operation and the property that it can tax is *assessed* at $100 million, officials set the tax rate at two percent of assessed valuation. If expenses go up the following year to $2.5 million, then the tax rate is merely raised to 2.5 percent.

EVALUATING PROPERTY TAXES

Administration of property taxes has often been so inefficient and unfair that some people doubt that this tax should be allowed to persist. Appraising the true value of property, particularly personal property, even when it is done by experts, is very difficult, and assessors are not necessarily chosen or elected because they are experts. Not all people report all their property, and there is a strong tendency to undervalue that which is reported. The assessor cannot be expected to be an expert appraiser of all things and a detective to determine whether property is hidden, and still manage to remain on speaking terms with other members of the community. Since it is common practice to underestimate the value of property, the honest citizen is severely penalized.

Determining the value of real estate is not quite so difficult as appraising personal property, but it is doubtful that many communities achieve great accuracy in their assessments. Real estate values have climbed faster than assessments, and changes in neighborhoods have brought about changes in the value of properties. When property is sold, the value can be determined; but little real property is sold often enough to keep pace with changing values. Local governments find it easier to obtain the extra revenue they need by raising tax rates rather than risk antagonizing voters by reassessing properties in order to increase the tax base.

At one time ownership of property was a fairly good criterion of ability to pay. As our nation has become more industrialized, salaries and profits have become more important factors on which to judge a taxpayer's ability to pay. A small family does not need as big a house as a large family. Assuming that each family has the same income and builds a house of similar quality, the bigger house of the larger family will be assessed for more, although the smaller family probably has a greater ability to pay. Cheaper property tends to be overassessed in comparison with high-priced property. Wealthier people are more likely to have influence with assessors or to threaten court action because of overassessment. Tenants usually have property taxes shifted to them as part of their rent.

JERSEY FACED WITH RAISING ADDITIONAL REVENUES

Sales or Income Tax Needed to Meet Growing Expenditures

TRENTON, N.J. — One of the major problems the Governor and the State Legislature will face after the forthcoming election is what new taxes to impose on the people of this state in order to meet growing expenditures.

New Jersey is one of the few states without a statewide sales tax or an income tax, the two most important and widely used sources of state tax revenues. Most observers believe that no matter which party wins control, one of these two taxes or a combination of both will be needed to meet the accelerating costs of education, highways, and health and welfare.

In 1964 New Jersey had the lowest per capita state revenue in the nation, $124. Mississippi, the poorest state in terms of average individual income, had a per capita revenue of $174, while New York had $203. Alaska had the highest per capita revenue, $595, but most of its money came from the federal government.

With state government expenditures increasing at a faster rate than federal, it becomes increasingly difficult to find new sources of revenue.

Several characteristics of the property tax which have emerged from our discussion are that it is (1) regressive to a considerable degree, (2) capable of being shifted to tenants and, in the case of factories, to consumers, (3) easily evaded, and (4) almost impossible to administer efficiently. Although this tax reflects the benefit principle with regard to police and fire protection and certain other services furnished by local governments, it is frequently used to support such general services as education. And although the federal government is prohibited from using it and state governments are turning to other sources of revenue, the property tax probably will remain the major source of revenue for local governments.

OTHER LOCAL REVENUES

Sales taxes are becoming more popular with local governments, which are finding the need for more revenue but at the same time are meeting greater resistance to raising the property tax. Additional revenue is obtained by fees, permits, receipts from parking meters, and municipal businesses. A relatively new but increasingly important tax now used by several cities is a tax on wages and salaries of all persons working within the city. While this *payroll* tax ignores income from interest and profits, it does force those who work in and use the facilities of the city but live in the suburbs to share in the costs of operating the city. Who would be likely to favor such a tax?

Part C   Evaluating the American Tax System

Appraising current practices

A good tax system should encourage the efficient and full utilization of a nation's productive capacities without hindering the allocation of resources according to the wishes of consumers. It should yield the revenue needed to finance whatever government operations its citizens decide on without disturbing economic growth and stability. The tax burden should fall according to a principle or principles which society accepts as fair to all.

Although few would disagree in theory with using these criteria for evaluation, there is strong disagreement when our specific taxes are measured against them. There is general agreement that the ability-to-pay principle, tempered by benefits received, should determine how the tax burden should be distributed. There is less agreement as to what tax base should be used in determining ability to pay. Avoiding the use of "good" or "bad," since they involve value judgments rather than economic conclusions, let us see what generalizations we can come to about the American tax system:

1. The final incidence of many taxes at all levels of government is not where lawmakers intended.

2. Excise and business taxes ultimately do affect the allocation of resources according to the wishes of consumers. This happens because people act differently as citizens voting for services in the public sector from the way they act as consumers shopping in the private sector.

3. Business taxes affect the economic growth of some businesses, particularly small businesses, in which capital may be hard to obtain.

4. Many taxes are ill conceived and are merely politically expedient devices to raise additional revenue with a minimum of voter protest.

5. Tradition, the high yield of revenue, government needs, and inertia are responsible for the continued existence of certain taxes, even though such taxes may fail to meet most of the criteria for a good tax. One example of this statement is the property tax.

6. Federal taxes, due to the importance of the personal income tax, are mildly progressive.

7. State and local taxes, due to general retail sales and property taxes, are slightly regressive.

8. Most economists agree that taxes as a whole are mildly progressive among all families except the poorest and the wealthiest. The poorest families pay

regressively whereas the wealthiest pay more progressively.

9. Federal taxes are considered to be not merely producers of revenue but also an important instrument for economic growth and stability. This use of taxes will be discussed in Unit III.

10. Many economists think that the American tax structure, while better than that of most other industrial countries, is too much of a hodgepodge resulting from considerations of political expediency, and could be improved considerably by being simplified and reorganized.

Taxes at the present time will reduce your purchases in the private sector of the economy by over 25 percent. It is doubtful that this percentage will decrease and, if the trend continues, it will likely be higher. As both a consumer and a citizen, you should be concerned about an equitable tax structure. Since our tax laws are changed frequently, you should become aware of directions in which changes might be made.

Part D   Public Borrowing and the Public Debt

Reasons for borrowing

It might seem that the most direct way of meeting governmental financial obligations would be by taxing to the extent necessary to obtain the required revenue. However, there are times when such a procedure is not possible. When governments are unable to meet their financial obligations out of their current revenues, they can make up the difference by borrowing. This borrowing creates a public debt, the size of which is the subject of much controversy. Public borrowing and public debt are frequently compared to the borrowing and debt of businesses and families. Although these kinds of debt do have certain features in common, there are also very significant differences. Failure to recognize these differences has led to much misunderstanding of the nature and significance of our public debt.

There are four main reasons why governments borrow:

1. Short-term adjustments have to be made to correct the imbalance of revenues and expenditures. Because expenditures may be somewhat greater than expected, or tax collections slower or smaller than expected, governments make short-term loans. Expenditures tend to be spread throughout the year, whereas tax collections are frequently made only annually or semiannually. Short-term loans are easy to finance, and the interest rates on them are very low.

2. Financing major public works that will be used over many years usually requires borrowing. To wait until the government had the money would deprive people of essential services. It is sound financial policy to pay for such projects over no longer a period of time than the years during which the project will furnish services to the people. Some public projects, such as the Tennessee Valley Authority, state turnpikes, and municipal transportation systems, yield revenue from which the loans can be paid back.

3. Emergencies that cannot be anticipated cannot be expected to be paid for out of current revenues. Wars and natural disasters have added greatly to our public debt.

4. Deliberate spending in excess of current income has been done by the federal government as a means of stimulating the economy. The use of such action will be considered in Unit III.

The size of the public debt

If someone had predicted thirty years ago that the gross debt of the federal government would reach $300 billion by the

1960's, those listening would probably have said that we would be on the verge of bankruptcy and would have runaway inflation. The facts that our gross federal debt is over $300 billion and that prices have increased about two and a half times, but also that our government's credit is excellent and that our economy has been steadily expanding, are evidence of the difficulty of making long-range predictions.

When the term *federal debt* is used, it commonly refers to the gross debt, which includes all outstanding obligations of the federal government. Most economists consider the net debt, which includes only the federal obligations held by the public, more significant. This is because payments from one government agency to another have a relatively small effect on the economy. The figures cited in Figure 8–3 refer to the net

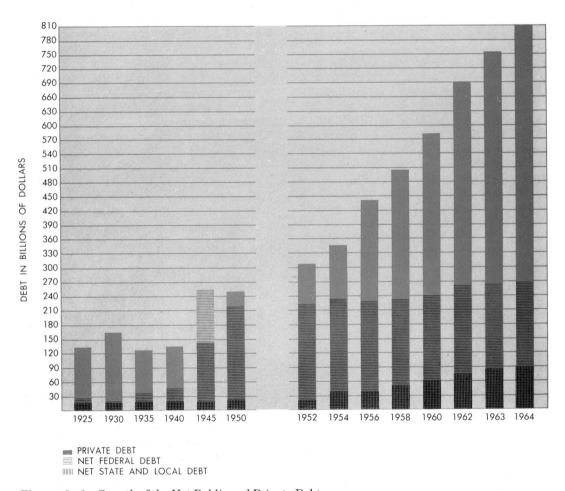

Figure 8–3 Growth of the Net Public and Private Debt

Although the net public debt has risen sharply, notably since World War II, private debt has risen even faster. SOURCES: Federal Reserve System, U.S. Treasury Department, U.S. Department of Commerce

amount, but those used elsewhere are for the gross amount.

Figure 8-3 shows the growth of the net public debt of the federal, state, and local governments and the growth of private debt. Although increased prices greatly distort the size of the increase, the rapid growth is evident. What is also obvious, but not widely recognized, is that since 1945, the end of World War II, the percentage of the net federal debt to the total debt has *decreased* significantly while the private debt has *increased* very sharply. There has also been an increase in the percentage of the debt owed by state and local governments. Those who suggest that the federal government should learn to live within its budget as families and businesses do, are not acquainted with all the facts.

The size of any debt must be considered in relation to the size of income. A family with an income of $50,000 a year can afford to carry a debt of $5,000 better than a family with a $5,000 income can carry a $500 debt. In 1935 our gross federal debt was

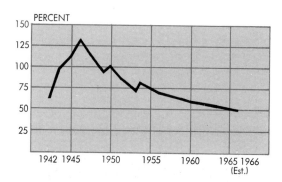

Figure 8-4   Public Debt as Percent of the Gross National Product

During World War II federal expenditures rose much faster than revenues, causing the public debt to skyrocket above the gross national product. The chart shows that the gross federal debt is declining in relationship to the growth of the economy (gross national product). SOURCE: U.S. Department of Commerce

only $34.4 billion, and national income was $56.5 billion. In March, 1965, our gross federal debt rose to $318.4 billion, but our national income went up to an annual rate of $534.3 billion. The percentage of our federal debt in relation to our national income had, therefore, declined.

A similar change is demonstrated in Figure 8-4, which shows the gross federal debt as a percent of GNP. When did the greatest increase in the debt take place? Does this correspond to the information in Figure 8-3? We can conclude that the primary cause of the present large size of the federal debt is the financing of military expenditures during World War II and the defense budget necessitated by the cold war. Only a small portion of the debt can be attributed to government budgets purposely designed to create a debt as a means of stimulating the economy.

Ownership of the federal debt

Our public debt, unlike that of many other countries, is held internally. This means that the American people owe this money to themselves. Table 8-2 shows who holds the federal government securities. An internal debt is paid when the government takes some of its revenue, paid by Americans, and meets its obligations on bonds and notes held by other Americans, or, in some instances, the same Americans. This procedure has frequently been characterized as taking money out of one pocket and putting it into another pocket. This interpretation must be qualified by pointing out that frequently the pockets do not belong to the same people. In other words, paying off an internally held debt does not mean a reduction in the total wealth, but it frequently results in a redistribution of the wealth.

An externally held debt is one that is owed to a foreign country. In this case the people of one country must take out of their pockets money that will go into the pockets of people in a different country. In this case, payment causes a real reduction in the

Table 8–2   Ownership of United States Government Securities, May, 1965

	Billions of dollars	Per cent of total
United States Government Agencies and Trust Funds	60.7	19
Federal Reserve Banks	37.6	12
Commercial Banks	60.	19
Mutual Savings Banks	6.	2
Insurance Companies	11.1	3
Corporations*	20.0	6
State and Local Governments	23.2	7
Individuals	69.1	22
Miscellaneous Purchasers†	30.9	10
Total	318.4	100

* Other than commercial banks, mutual savings banks, and insurance companies. † Savings and loan associations, dealers and brokers, foreign accounts, corporate pension funds, and nonprofit institutions.

SOURCE: *Federal Reserve Bulletin*, May 1965, p. 720

wealth of the country paying the debt. A large part of the British debt has been held externally, and paying this debt off means a real sacrifice in the standard of living of the British people. Externally held debts are similar to private debts in terms of the real sacrifices involved in repayment.

The consequences of a public debt

The existence of a federal debt is always a matter for general concern. However, the average citizen is probably more concerned about the national debt than is the average economist. Let us consider some of the fears associated with our growing debt to see whether, according to the criteria of economists, they are justified.

CAN WE GO BANKRUPT?

Many economists believe that, since the federal government has the power to tax or print money, it need never go bankrupt. The ratio of our debt to our national income has declined. The credit of the United States government is probably better than that of any other government or institution in the world. The interest rates the government pays reflect this fact. Table 7–1 shows the amount of interest currently paid by our government.

Although some governments have gone bankrupt, their financial failure was due to

declining national income in relation to public debt. This unfavorable ratio caused a lack of confidence in the government's ability to meet its financial obligations in money that had reasonably stable purchasing power.

WILL FUTURE GENERATIONS BEAR
THE BURDEN OF THE PRESENT DEBT?

Wars, which are chiefly responsible for the large size of the debt, imposed most of their burdens on those who were living at the time. The real economic sacrifice came when productive factors were turned to making armaments instead of making the goods and services that people of that generation would have wanted and produced had there been peace. These goods and services that might have been produced can never be realized. Why? Because the resources that would have made them were making other things, primarily armaments. Future generations bear the burden of using their productive resources to repair what has been destroyed. They are also handicapped by not inheriting the additional supply of capital goods that each generation adds to help each succeeding generation. In weighing these costs, however, we must consider whether this is too high a price to pay for the preservation of freedom.

Is the interest on the national debt a burden?

Although many people are of the opinion that paying the interest on the national debt is only the transfer of money from one pocket to another, there *can* be harm to some people. To the extent that taxpayers and interest receivers are different people, so will the burdens and benefits be shifted. Those who pay high taxes tend also to receive high interest; because of this, there is doubt whether the effect of redistribution is great.

Do government securities use up savings that private enterprise needs for expansion?

Government's problem has been to stimulate businessmen to invest, not to compete for funds. It is in part because business has not invested that government has had to stimulate the economy.

Can increasing the debt be inflationary?

If the government sought to pay its obligations by printing money, inflation would be the consequence. More money would be competing for the same amount of goods, causing prices to rise. Large-scale government borrowing at a time when all our productive resources are being used is also highly inflationary. However, government officials realize these dangers and are unlikely to take such inflationary steps. We will consider this question again in Chapter 11.

Public debt: some added considerations

Most of the answers to the questions previously raised would seem to indicate that we have little to fear from the growing public debt. Most economists believe that if the debt is closely observed and used rather than abused, it presents no great dangers. However, a policy of easy borrowing can encourage waste and stimulate inflation, especially if done at inappropriate times. It can also result in an unfavorable redistribution of income and psychologically disturb business investment. By being aware of these problems, we can be the masters of our debt rather than slaves to it, and thus derive benefits rather than harm from it.

Part E The Problem: To What Extent Should We Have Public Development of Our Power Resources?

The problem to be considered here is closely related to the question discussed in Chapter 7, "How deeply should government be involved in the economy?" However, Chapters 7 and 8 are both essential to an understanding of the role of government as a producer in the economy and to finding a tentative solution to our problem.

Some parts of our economy have been traditionally operated by government with little question of whether such involvement is desirable. For example, the post office and the public schools are traditionally part of the public sector. On the other hand there are a few people, primarily socialists, in our country who question the desirability of having most of our production stem from the private sector. Private ownership for most of our economy seems secure. There is, however, an area that is neither black nor white, and is capable of stirring as heated a debate as anything in politics. Most of this gray area is occupied by utilities that are natural monopolies in which competition means waste.

In many industrialized countries power and transportation facilities are government enterprises. In our own country some municipalities own their transportation systems and power utilities. Until 1933 the federal government avoided ownership of power utilities, but since the development of the Tennessee Valley Authority as a government-owned enterprise the debate on

The question of how wide the range of government's activities should be, exists in many forms and at all levels of government. In how many ways is government involved in supplying water? Which of these activities do you consider essential? Which could be omitted or done by other means?

the expansion of public ownership of power projects has become intense. We will focus our attention on the arguments for and against public ownership and development of power resources. Although the tools you have learned to use will help you to understand the problem better, the answer you finally arrive at will depend largely on the values you hold.

The case for government ownership

The federal government became involved in power development rather late in our history and did so only reluctantly. It eventually did become involved because private utility companies, motivated only by the desire to make a profit, neglected the needs of too many Americans. The vast river basins of this country can be a source of great wealth or the means of destroying wealth. The federal government, using the multipurpose approach of developing flood control, irrigation, land reclamation, navigation, and power, can truly best serve the interests of the American people. This is shown clearly by the broad benefits the Tennessee Valley Authority has brought to the people in the area it serves. Success in this area has led to the setting up of other federal projects in the Columbia River basin, Missouri River basin, and a number of other areas.

Our country's resources are a priceless heritage that should not be exploited for private gain. Through the facilities of the federal government—far greater than those of private corporations—planning for long-range gains in many different kinds of activities can bring about the most effective results. The total development of an area which, to begin with, seems too poor to attract capital because profit expectations are discouraging, results in increasing incomes and economic opportunities, thereby benefiting all the people of the area. Businesses are attracted to the region because of inexpensive power, causing land to increase in value. In time the whole country will profit by the taxes that high incomes and rising land values yield. Only after the government has made the investment of developing an area and profits seem assured does private enterprise show its interest. Why should the people collectively pay to start a project and then, when the benefits start accruing, turn them over to the few?

The low power rates charged by TVA, far lower than had been charged by private utilities, not only attracted industry to that area, but also acted as an economic "yardstick" to show that the demand for electric energy is far more elastic than was believed previously. Many private companies lowered their prices for industrial users and found their profits the same as or larger than before. The public industry showed the private industry what was possible in terms of development.

Our country's needs for more power are expanding at such an increasing rate that public development is essential. Private utilities have not been able to meet the needs of our national defense efforts and the expanding needs of private enterprise. It was fortunate that the government had expanded facilities to meet the needs imposed by World War II. We must not risk stifling our economy or neglecting the needs of all our people by waiting for private enterprise to take the initiative for developing facilities only when profit expectations are high. Furthermore, we have no moral right to turn our government-built or -financed facilities over to private utilities so that the few may profit at the expense of all.

The case against
government ownership

This country is traditionally committed to the private-enterprise system, not merely because of sentiment but also because it is the system that most efficiently provides us with the goods and services the consumers want. Private enterprise, encouraged by the profit motive, is able to develop the resources we require and to do this at the necessary rate. Government operation interferes with the allocation of our resources according to the price or market system, depriving the consumers of the right to make choices.

Government operations may well be less efficient because top management is more likely to be appointed out of political considerations than according to the wishes of stockholders who want profits. Losses may go unnoticed for years, since they can easily be made up out of the public treasury.

Building extravagant or even unneeded facilities may result from the insistence of small but politically powerful groups rather than from real economic needs. The meeting of a legitimate need in one area may require supporting an unneeded project in another area in order to get the necessary political support.

Lower prices from public power plants are the result of government's favorable borrowing and tax position. Private utilities have to pay their full share into the public treasury, thus helping people throughout the country, whereas tax-exempt public enterprises benefit only the area being served. The purchaser of public power is being subsidized by all the taxpayers.

The position that water resources belong to all the people and therefore should be developed publicly is no more valid than claiming the same for land and minerals. There is no great public support for government ownership of land and minerals. Why, then, should there be so much concern about private development of water and power resources?

The argument that the federal government must supply power because private enterprise is not doing the job seems weak when we see how frequently private enterprise has been prevented by government from entering new areas for power development. When public utilities tried to develop the hydroelectric potential at Hells Canyon on the Snake River, the proponents of public power stood in their way. While flood control is admittedly a job for government, private companies should be allowed to share in developing power resources and to participate in distributing them.

The argument of using public power as an economic yardstick to measure a fair price is unacceptable, since measurements must be made with yardsticks of equal length. Measuring a tax-exempt, federally subsidized project against one which has no subsidy and must pay taxes is unfair.

If the federal government is allowed to own our electric utilities, what is to prevent it from moving into other areas of private enterprise? The American economy has been primarily an economy of free enterprise and has given us the highest standard of living in the world. Chipping away at its foundation can weaken confidence in our traditional American system.

Considering an answer

The positions both for and against government development of power resources are appealing when read separately. Reading the arguments of each side may present the person seeking an answer with a difficult choice. Citizens, to be effective, must be prepared to make such decisions and to express their ideas through voting or letter writing or some other form of political activity. Following is a list of questions which you should consider in the course of finding a solution to our problem:

1. Which system is likely to be more efficient in the long run?

2. Which system may be expected to serve the public interest better?

3. Is there a conflict between efficiency and public interest? If so, which of these considerations should prevail?

4. Does public power development weaken the free-enterprise system? Does it provide added opportunities for business?

5. Is there room for both public and private ownership? If so, what criteria do you suggest for determining which to use?

REVIEW: the highlights of the chapter

1. The largest portion of federal revenues comes from income taxes, both personal and corporation.

2. State revenue is obtained mainly from sales taxes, gasoline taxes, income taxes, business taxes, fees, and grants from the federal government.

3. Property taxes and state grants are the major sources of revenue for local governments.

4. Federal taxes are mildly progressive, whereas state and local taxes are mildly regressive. Much can be done to improve our tax system.

5. The public debt stems from government borrowing to make up the difference between its revenues and expenditures. The tremendous increase in the size of the debt has been a source of concern and controversy.

6. The major portion of the federal debt is the result of international conflicts.

7. The private debt has expanded faster than the public debt.

8. While a large public debt can have adverse consequences, so long as its growth is accompanied by increases in the national income and it is managed carefully, it need not cause great concern.

9. Controversy exists over government ownership of public power.

IN CONCLUSION: *some aids to understanding*

Terms for review

taxable income	public debt
personal property tax	internal debt
taxpayer's exemption	excise tax
double taxation	estate tax
standard allowable deduction	federal debt
sales tax	avoidance
evasion	employment tax

Questions for review

1. What is meant by the statement "The personal income tax is the great equalizer in American society"? Do you agree or disagree?

2. Explain why local governments may need financial help from the state or federal governments or new taxes for sources of revenue to maintain services for the citizen.

3. From your reading you undoubtedly recognize the need of the various levels of government for taxes.
   (a) What are the major sources of taxes for the federal government, state governments, and local governments?
   (b) What are the main advantages and disadvantages of each tax?

4. According to the criteria you have learned for evaluating taxes, what are the major weaknesses in the American tax system?

5. Under what circumstances do governments tend to borrow money? When the government is in need of additional funds, why does it borrow money rather than printing it?

6. What changes have taken place in the size of the net public and private debt since 1945? How do the changes in federal spending compare with changes in the GNP over the same period? What conclusions may be drawn from this information?

7. Why are most economists not alarmed at the sharp increase in our public debt?

Additional questions and problems

1. Indicate the arguments you would use to a legislative committee to secure special tax privileges for athletes, performers, and authors. In your discussion it might be helpful to consider the tax laws on depletion allowances to producers of oil and gas.

2. Since you will eventually be concerned with paying income taxes, it is important that you become familiar with procedures of payment.
    (a) Bring to class a federal personal income tax form.
    (b) Using this form, prepare a return for a family of four with a gross income of $8,000 per year. You may either itemize typical deductions or take the standard deduction.

3. Draw up a list of arguments based on the benefit theory and the ability-to-pay theory against each of the following taxes: (a) high corporation taxes, (b) estate taxes, (c) sales taxes.

4. If your state government needed additional revenue, what recommendations would you make? Explain the reasons for your choice.

5. Public and private debt have certain similarities, but they also have very basic differences.
    (a) Differentiate clearly between the borrowing done by the public sector and that done by the private sector.
    (b) Why could it be said that borrowing by the public sector cannot be judged without specific references to the nation's GNP?

6. Develop a list of criteria for use in determining the need for public ownership. According to your criteria,
    (a) which areas should the government move out of or into?
    (b) what circumstances might cause you to alter your decisions?

7. Using the basic tools which you now have for analyzing taxes, prepare a recommendation for changes in the tax structure of your local unit of government.

9 The Consumer and His Role in the American Economy

Preview

The purpose of production is primarily to satisfy consumer wants. In theory, it is the consumer who provides answers to the questions of what to produce and how to allocate the resources needed for production. However, consumers' choices are limited in a number of ways — by their individual incomes, by imperfect competition, and by psychological and social pressures that influence their demands. The needs of consumers in poor countries are quite different from those in rich countries like our own.

In this chapter we will see what role the consumer is supposed to play in the classical model and what forces in our society have placed limits on his power. We will then consider whether the consumer needs protection and, if so, what kind of protection. Particular attention will be given to inequality of income, demand creation, and consumer credit.

Overview

How influential are consumers in deciding the *What* of production?
What effect has our growing affluence had on consumer sovereignty?
Do consumers need to organize to protect their interests?

Part A   *The Consumer and His Sovereignty*

The consumer's role in the classical model

Adam Smith, the chief architect of the classical model, used the principle of *consumer sovereignty* as the foundation of his entire system. He wrote, "Consumption is the sole end and purpose of all production," and he had no sympathy with systems that favored the producers. Consumers go to the market to buy the goods and services they want. Business listens and sets production according to consumer preferences. The question of *What?* is answered by the consumer. In answering the *What?* the consumer is also influencing the allocation of resources.

Because consumers, individually and collectively, have limited resources (incomes) and unlimited wants, they will have to make choices. In making choices they seek to maximize their total satisfaction. Because each consumer knows best what will provide him with the greatest satisfaction of his wants, there should be no restraints on having him register his demands except where he may harm others. The idea that the individual, rather than the society collectively, should determine the *What* is fundamental to the classical tradition. The reasoning is that if each individual can maximize his own satisfactions, then the entire society will do the same.

Many economists believe that time and experience have made clear a flaw in this last argument, called the "fallacy of composition." They believe that what is true for the individual is *not* necessarily true for all society. Conversely, what is true for the society as a whole is not necessarily true for every individual within it.

DEFINING NEEDS

If consumers are to determine individually the *What,* they do so by deciding what their needs or wants are. The individual consumer's identification of his own needs, if done without any qualifications, can present problems. Some people have little experience and poor judgment in shopping. Money is sometimes spent on gambling, drinking, and lavish entertainment at the expense of providing necessities for oneself and family. In an affluent society like ours, wants are sometimes created as businesses seek to boost sales. Frequent style changes create quick obsolescence, and advertising influences wants that are in no way related to survival or, in many instances, to physical comfort.

Some people believe that in a society where needs go far beyond physical survival, consumers should have protection from themselves and others. Others think that consumers identify only their selfish, short-run needs and give little thought to the collective good of the society. They point to the failure to approve school bond issues at a time when purchases of luxuries are increasing.

Before doing away with consumer sovereignty, it might be wise to consider whom you will allow to decide the *What.* Undoubtedly consumers make errors, but they also learn from their mistakes. What group would you trust more?

LIMITATIONS ON CONSUMER SOVEREIGNTY

In a mature, predominantly private-enterprise economy like our own, three factors limit the sovereignty of the consumer and the possibility of satisfying his needs completely. These factors are: (1) the distribution of personal income, (2) demand creation by business, and (3) imperfect competition. These conditions all have the effect of placing limits on the consumer. Each deserves our careful consideration.

The distribution of personal income

A family's consumption is dependent on its income, its savings, and its credit. Of the three, income is the most important and is the major factor in determining what the other two will be. Since spending is usually adjusted to current income and expectations of future income, we need to know the characteristics of personal income to understand the consumer better.

Critics of capitalism usually concede that total wealth and total income in the United States are high. They concede that average income is high, but they say this is not a true picture of how people are actually living because the great concentration of wealth among a few distorts the average. How true is this statement?

DISTRIBUTION OF FAMILY INCOME

Table 9–1 shows the changes which have taken place in the distribution of family income in selected years from 1929 to 1963. Compare the number of consumer units for each level of income in 1929 with that of the corresponding income level in 1963. What changes do you find in the number of units and the percentage at the various levels? The fact that vast inequalities of income remain, in spite of the trends just observed, is evident in that more than 34 percent of the units had incomes under $4,000 a year, whereas almost 16 percent were over $10,000.

Table 9–1   Average Family Personal Income and Distribution of Consumer Units by Family Income Class in 1954 Dollars[a]

FAMILY PERSONAL INCOME IN 1954 DOLLARS (a) (BEFORE INCOME TAX)	1929	1935-36	1944	1950	1959	1961	1962	1963
Average (mean) Family Personal Income	$3,791	$3,343	$5,268	$4,943	$6,097	$6,243	$6,490	$6,613
NUMBER OF CONSUMER UNITS(b) (MILLIONS)								
Under $2,000	12.9	16.3	7.1	9.7	8.3	8.5	8.0	7.9
$2,000 - 2,999	8.4	7.8	5.8	7.2	6.0	6.0	5.8 }	12.1
3,000 - 3,999	5.6	5.2	6.0	7.7	6.8	6.7	6.5 }	
4,000 - 4,999	3.0	3.4	5.7	7.2	6.8	6.8	6.7 }	13.1
5,000 - 5,999	1.9	2.0	4.9	5.4	6.4	6.4	6.4 }	
6.000 - 7,499	1.6	1.5	4.4	4.8	7.4	7.8	8.1	8.3
7,500 - 9,999	1.2	1.0	3.7	3.7	6.6	7.1	7.5	8.0
10,000 and over	1.5	1.2	3.3	3.2	7.0	8.0	8.9	9.3
Total	36.1	38.4	40.9	48.9	55.3	57.3	57.9	58.7
PERCENTAGE DISTRIBUTION								
Under $2,000	35.8	42.2	17.4	19.8	15.1	14.8	13.9	13.5
$2,000- 2,999	23.4	20.4	14.2	14.7	10.8	10.5	10.0 }	20.6
3,000 - 3,999	15.5	13.4	14.7	15.8	12.3	11.8	11.2 }	
4,000 - 4,999	8.3	8.9	14.0	14.7	12.2	11.8	11.5 }	22.4
5,000 - 5,999	5.2	5.3	12.0	11.0	11.5	11.2	11.1 }	
6,000 - 7,499	4.3	4.0	10.6	9.8	13.5	13.7	14.0	14.2
7,500 - 9,999	3.3	2.6	9.0	7.6	11.9	12.3	13.0	13.5
10,000 and over	4.2	3.2	8.1	6.6	12.7	13.9	15.3	15.8
Total	100.0	100.0	100.0	100.0	100.0	100.0	100.0	100.0

(a) In 1963 the consumer price index was 14.0 percent higher than in 1954. Thus 1954 dollars can be converted to 1963 dollars by multiplying by 1.14.
(b) Families and unattached individuals.

SOURCE: U.S. Department of Commerce, Office of Business Economics

However, a closer analysis of Table 9–1 shows the distribution of income to be somewhat less uneven than these figures imply. Of the 58.7 million family units reported, more than 11 million consisted of individuals living alone. Although reported as family units, they were mainly young people at the beginning of their earning careers; older people who had their incomes supplemented by pensions, savings, or contributions from government or family; and the handicapped, who frequently received aid from sources similar to those that supplied the old. The median income of this group was $2,700, while that for all families was $6,500.

Differences in income are lessened in still another way—by the federal personal income tax. In Chapter 8 we saw how progressive this tax is. Being graduated, it tends to reduce the extremes of difference in income shown in Table 9–1.

Several favorable trends in family income may be found in the reports of the Department of Commerce, which showed that from 1956 to 1962 income per family had increased $1,130. Although taxes and higher prices took away some of the effect of this increase, purchasing power per family still increased substantially. In addition, the percentage of families with incomes under $4,000 has been decreasing and of those with incomes above $10,000 has been increasing.

LORENZ CURVE

One method of determining inequality of income distribution is by using the *Lorenz curve*. On the horizontal axis of Figure 9–1 we find the percentage of family units, and on the vertical axis the percentage of total personal income. If income were distributed with absolute equality, 20 percent of the family units would have 20 percent of the income, 40 percent of the family units would have 40 percent of the income, and we would eventually have a diagonal line.

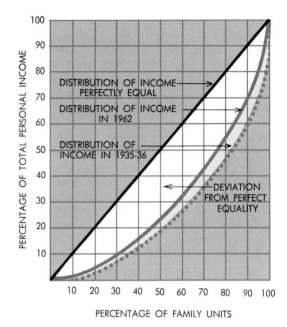

Figure 9–1   Lorenz Curve

The 45° line shows what perfect equality of distribution would look like. The Lorenz curve shows the degree of inequality in the distribution of personal income. SOURCE: U.S. Department of Commerce, Office of Business Economics

However, since our lowest 20 percent of family units receive only 4.6 percent of the income, the next 20 percent only 11 percent, and so on, we find the income curve dropping below the diagonal. Figure 9–1 shows the distribution of personal income in the United States using the Lorenz curve for 1935–36 and for 1962. The fact that the distribution curve is closer to the diagonal line of perfect equality indicates the trend toward more equal distribution. Although too little evidence is available for us to draw firm conclusions, it appears that industrialized countries with more mixed economies than ours—such as Sweden, Israel, and Australia—have a more equal distribution of personal income, while greater inequality seems to prevail in less-developed countries.

DIVIDING PERSONAL INCOME

The question of the distribution of personal income is a matter of individual values that the citizens of each country must decide for themselves. Socialists in Western Europe and in this country have advocated government ownership of basic industries and greater services by government as a means of creating a more nearly equal standard of living. However, the general rise in personal income, with even the lowest incomes more nearly adequate than in former years, has greatly reduced the appeal of the socialist argument in our country.

Income differences and the existence of poverty

Even though there has been a trend toward equalization of income, inequality still exists. The fact that there has been a reduction in the number of families living at a *subsistence* level, barely able to acquire the physical necessities for survival, is encouraging. However, the fact that so many remain, at a time when we are witnessing one of the greatest economic booms in our nation's history, is deplorable. President Johnson has declared a "War on Poverty," with programs designed to raise incomes and to increase benefits at the lowest levels. Having this hard core of families suffering from poverty in our midst not only bothers our conscience but also hurts the economy.

GEOGRAPHIC DIFFERENCES

The existence of important differences in personal income among the various regions of our country can be seen on the map,

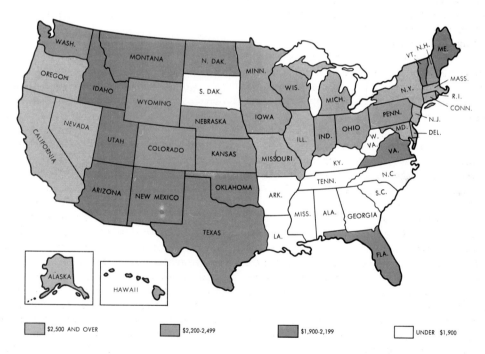

Per Capita Personal Income in the United States, 1963

There are significant regional differences in per capita income in the United States. SOURCE: U. S. Department of Commerce

which shows the average personal income in the Southeast to be $1,819 for 1963, whereas it was $2,886 in the same year for the Far West. Per capita income in one of our poorest states was only $1,379, whereas that same year it was $3,372 in another state. Not one of the twenty-two states in the Southeast, the Southwest, or the Rocky Mountain region had a per capita income as high as the national average of $2,443. Fortunately, most of the poorest states have shown a greater increase in per capita income in the last ten years than has the national average. In part this is attributed to the industrialization of the South and to the general decrease in unemployment.

DIFFERENCES AMONG OCCUPATIONS

There are significant differences in the median income among occupations. The median income of agricultural workers is less than $1,700 a year, while it is over $6,200 for railroad employees. The average salary of teachers is less than 40 percent of that of dentists and about 25 percent of that of physicians. Those working in the wholesale trade receive over 40 percent more than those in retail trade. Those working in the radio and television industry receive on the average twice as much as those working in all the service industries. Some jobs offer little opportunity to escape from the very lowest income bracket.

DIFFERENCES WITHIN OCCUPATIONS

Differences between the lowest and highest paid groups within an occupation are often greater than among occupations. The Lorenz curve would bend deeply away from the equality-of-income line for businessmen and lawyers, while the curve would be far less steep for schoolteachers and workers in organized industries.

DIFFERENCES IN INDIVIDUAL ABILITIES

Differences of ability undoubtedly account for differences in income. Intelligence, physical fitness, appearance, and temperament are all important factors in

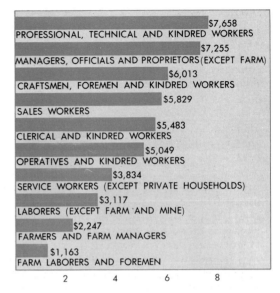

ANNUAL INCOME IN THOUSANDS OF DOLLARS

Figure 9-2   Median Money Income of Males by Occupation

Differences in the median income of different occupations are partially explained by the educational requirements of higher paying jobs. SOURCE: U.S. Department of Commerce, Bureau of the Census, *Current Population Reports,* Series P-60

determining what income we can earn. However, it is probable that income is distributed less equally than the distribution of these characteristics. This raises an ethical question as to whether those born with limited ability to earn decent incomes should be forced to have a lower standard of living.

DIFFERENCES IN RELATION TO MINORITY GROUPS

There are significant differences in the median income of minority groups compared with the population as a whole. Women have a far lower median income than men, even in states where the law requires "equal pay for equal work." The same is true for Negroes, Puerto Ricans,

Mexicans, Indians, Chinese, the handicapped, and the elderly. These groups are frequently discriminated against by not having access to better-paying jobs. A man is more apt to be chosen for an administrative job than a woman, even as principal of an elementary school. Negroes often have difficulty getting jobs in retail sales except in predominantly Negro neighborhoods or areas where wages are too low to attract other sales help. Some unions have kept Negroes and Puerto Ricans out, claiming they did not apply or lacked sufficient skills to qualify for membership. There is evidence to indicate that racial discrimination has been an important factor in admittance to membership in labor unions.

Discrimination in job opportunities frequently stems from beliefs widely held by

JOBLESS RATE OVER 25 PERCENT FOR NEGRO YOUTHS

WASHINGTON — According to unpublished government statistics, the jobless rate for Negro teen-aged boys has climbed above 25 percent. This is almost twice as high as for their white counterparts and over four times as high as the jobless rate for the nation as a whole.

The big increase in this group of jobless started in 1953 and has been above 21 percent since 1958. White teen-aged males have also experienced a major increase in the rate of unemployment, but at a lower rate.

Officials in many major cities are hoping that programs started under the Economic Opportunities Act will reverse the trend.

Unemployment is a far greater problem for some groups of our population than for others.

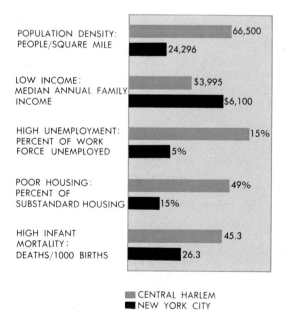

POPULATION DENSITY: PEOPLE/SQUARE MILE
66,500
24,296

LOW INCOME: MEDIAN ANNUAL FAMILY INCOME
$3,995
$6,100

HIGH UNEMPLOYMENT: PERCENT OF WORK FORCE UNEMPLOYED
15%
5%

POOR HOUSING: PERCENT OF SUBSTANDARD HOUSING
49%
15%

HIGH INFANT MORTALITY: DEATHS/1000 BIRTHS
45.3
26.3

■ CENTRAL HARLEM
■ NEW YORK CITY

Figure 9–3   Harlem—Five Factors Behind the Negro Discontent

Negroes have far less opportunity to earn and enjoy wealth than do most other Americans. SOURCE: New York *Times*, August 2, 1964

employers in all sections of the country, in industries as well as professions, that some groups of people are lazy or inferior. Evidence showing these beliefs to be false and legislation outlawing job discrimination have not fully solved the problem. With high unemployment rates and low median wage incomes, members of racial minorities, the young, the handicapped, and the elderly have cause for concern.

Unfortunately these discriminatory practices, resulting in low income, create conditions that can kill ambition and aggravate the problem still further. Many states, recognizing that discrimination is not only morally indefensible but economically unsound, are now beginning to give this problem the attention it deserves. On the national scene the legislation in the civil rights field and the executive orders barring discriminatory practices in federal employment contracts mark a shift from the previous pattern of discrimination against minority groups. We are only now beginning to give this problem some of the attention it deserves.

EDUCATIONAL DIFFERENCES

Many studies have been made that show a direct relationship between years of education and median income. The annual median income of high school graduates is between $1,500 and $2,000 higher than that of people who have only an elementary school education. College graduates show an even greater difference in their median income over high school graduates. The evidence clearly shows that education pays in dollars and cents as well as in other benefits. This is true even if one considers the loss of income while attending school or college and paying interest on money borrowed to attend college. The high school dropout has little chance of achieving even the median income for the nation, and his chances of unemployment are twice as great as for those who complete high school.

SIGNIFICANCE OF POVERTY

The problem of extreme inequality in income distribution is partly regional. It has been accentuated by businesses' moving to new areas, such as textile firms moving out of New England; and by basic changes in production, materials, and technology, such as seen on the farms and in the coal fields of Appalachia. The growth of seasonal industries and employment has accentuated the problem. The lowest income groups contain a large proportion of people with little preparation for earning a living in today's world. Often coming from very unfavorable surroundings, these people may face great emotional problems in adjusting to a better environment. Those who live in city or rural slums for any length of time may easily become depressed; they thus limit their opportunities of going on to something better. Ambition and incentive are important, but maintaining them is difficult when the odds against success seem so great. The prob-

WIRTZ REVEALS PLAN TO CUT TEEN-AGE UNEMPLOYMENT

WASHINGTON — Secretary of Labor W. Willard Wirtz revealed the plans for a new program to reduce the hard core of unemployment of jobless teen-agers from 800,000 to 200,000.

Mr. Wirtz called the plan a human resources development program requiring the cooperative effort of all three levels of government as well as that of private organizations. The new program will require a case-by-case study of the causes behind unemployment.

Referring to the West European practice of subsidizing apprentices and vocational training through public revenues obtained from a payroll tax, Mr. Wirtz said it was "a public responsibility to aid every young person until he is equipped to be self-supporting." This will require greatly expanded efforts in vocational training, on-the-job training, and apprenticeships.

Mr. Wirtz said that the Department of Labor is now developing plans to provide counseling by the Employment Service to students in every high school in the country, starting with those in low-income neighborhoods.

When unemployment exists, our resources are not being fully utilized. Both public and private agencies are working to reduce unemployment.

lem of this group can be outlined in purely economic terms, such as not making full use of our human resources, limiting consumer satisfaction, and stifling the growth of the national income. However, the problem is far more than a purely economic one. It is rather a failure of society to provide enough opportunities for all our people so that they can enjoy human dignity and a fair share of the benefits that our resources have made available. The continuance of large groups of poor people in our society

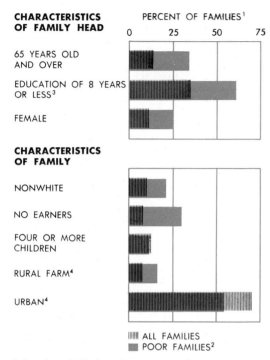

CHARACTERISTICS OF FAMILY HEAD

PERCENT OF FAMILIES[1]

65 YEARS OLD AND OVER

EDUCATION OF 8 YEARS OR LESS[3]

FEMALE

CHARACTERISTICS OF FAMILY

NONWHITE

NO EARNERS

FOUR OR MORE CHILDREN

RURAL FARM[4]

URBAN[4]

ALL FAMILIES
POOR FAMILIES[2]

1 Based on 1962 data (except as noted).
2 Families with income of $3,000 or less.
3 Based on 1961 income (1962 prices).
4 Based on 1959 data.

Figure 9–4 Characteristics of Poor Families Compared with All Other Families

Not all groups have equal opportunities or receive equal compensation for equal work. SOURCE: U.S. Department of Commerce

"I said you'd all get a share!"

has caused many of us to question very seriously the division of our resources. Do we want to have slum eradication or an all-out space program? Or can we have both?

Efforts to fight poverty

Public policy appears to be directed at increasing the size of the national income and guaranteeing that the smallest portion is adequate for individual survival. Our federal tax structure and expenditures reflect some tendency to reduce the inequality of income. Some redistribution of income takes place by the government's collecting taxes at a progressive rate and transferring some of this money through welfare activities to the lowest income group. A total of $51.9 billion was paid out in welfare by all levels of government in 1960. With the lowest income group receiving a very significant portion of this amount and the highest income group receiving very little, the effects of inequality are reduced somewhat.

PUBLIC ASSISTANCE

Public assistance to those who are unable to provide for themselves is now generally accepted as part of government's responsibility. Public housing, school lunch programs, and medical services – together with aid to the physically handicapped, to veterans, and to children from broken homes – provide for the minimum physical necessities of those who cannot provide for themselves. Although assistance may result in giving those receiving aid a standard of living higher than that of most people in the world, recipients of aid compare their lot only with that of other people in our own country. Giving aid, then, is not a solution.

SELF-HELP

An approach that is better from the point of view of human dignity as well as of the economy is to help those in the lowest income group learn the skills and find the opportunities necessary for supporting themselves. Much of the antipoverty legislation initiated by President Johnson and passed by Congress in 1964 was designed to do just this. Money is provided to help school dropouts resume their education, aid needy college students with part-time work, and offer jobless youths training programs. Projects have been set up to teach new skills for which there is a demand to those whose skills are no longer needed because of automation or changes in demand. Money is available, mostly for low-interest loans, to help farmers improve the efficiency of their operations. Some of the human resources needed for this project come from Volunteers in Service to America (VISTA), modeled after the now-famous Peace Corps.

In February, 1966, a Presidential commission agreed on the need for major social and economic changes. They recommended a guaranteed minimum annual income to replace much of our present welfare pro-

JOB TALENT CENTERS HELP SKILLED NEGROES AND PUERTO RICANS FIND JOBS

NEW YORK — The Mayor's Committee on Job Advancement said that through the efforts of its Job Talent Centers located in Manhattan and Brooklyn it has been able to place 3,500 qualified Negroes and Puerto Ricans in skilled professional and administrative positions.

Many companies have been seeking out skilled workers from these minority groups but with little success. On the other hand, many Negroes and Puerto Ricans did not know such opportunities were available. The Job Talent Centers have been successful in bringing companies and skilled workers together.

Information and communication are important if markets are to be effective.

gram, two years of free college for all, and vast federal works projects. Although some of this may be considered a dream today, increased productivity and economic growth may make it all a reality before the present decade ends.

Part B   The Relation of Demand Creation to Consumer Spending

How personal income is spent

In an economy as wealthy as our own, less than half of the consumer's dollar is spent on food, clothing, and shelter. While poor countries concern themselves with producing enough to provide the bare necessities of life for their people, business in our country devotes a great deal of its energy to stimulating consumer demand for things that the consumer could get along without, and in some instances would not

have thought about were no effort made to whet his appetite. We will consider how the American consumer spends his money and what is done to increase his demand.

There are countless individual variations in the ways families spend their money. Each family tries to maximize its satisfactions with the income it has available. Since needs and tastes differ, budgets also differ. Speaking generally, poor families spend most of their income on food,

Table 9–2   Personal Consumption Expenditures by Type of Product or Service
(millions of dollars)

PRODUCT OR SERVICE	1929	1939	1947	1958	1964	1964 % of total
Food and Tobacco	21,239	20,916	56,089	82,363	100,140	25.1
Clothing, Accessories, and Jewelry	11,193	8,406	22,760	31,911	40,018	10.0
Personal Care	1,116	1,004	2,225	5,031	6,778	1.7
Housing	11,530	9,139	15,665	41,127	59,461	14.9
Household Operation	10,735	9,624	23,989	42,275	57,980	14.6
Medical Care	2,937	2,848	6,897	16,472	25,211	6.3
Personal Business	4,158	3,313	5,426	12,768	19,761	5.0
Transportation	7,612	6,365	15,172	35,634	51,555	12.9
Recreation	4,331	3,452	9,249	15,817	23,824	6.0
Private Education and Research	664	620	1,243	3,140	5,304	1.3
Religious and Welfare Activities	1,196	938	1,984	4,178	5,791	1.5
Foreign Travel and Other (net)	511	209	5	1,824	2,884	0.7
Total Personal Consumption Expenditures	77,222	66,834	160,704	290,069	398,907	100.0

SOURCE: U.S. Department of Commerce, Office of Business Economics

housing, and medical care and very little on recreation. As income goes up, the expenditures for recreation, education, and household equipment increase more rapidly. Money spent for food, housing, and clothing must not be thought of as including only necessities. Eating in fine restaurants, having homes with central air conditioning, and owning clothes for formal affairs are a far cry from meeting the needs for survival. On the other hand we must be careful when we use the word "necessity." The clothing needed and purchased by a teacher is different from that of a factory worker, although their incomes may be the same. The junior executive may have a difficult time explaining to a $5,000-a-year employee that he cannot make ends meet even though he is earning $12,000 a year. However, to the executive, some things are necessities that to other people would be luxuries.

The United States Department of Commerce has analyzed the personal consumption expenditures of the American people for 1962. This analysis is shown in Figure 9–5. It should be pointed out that it is very

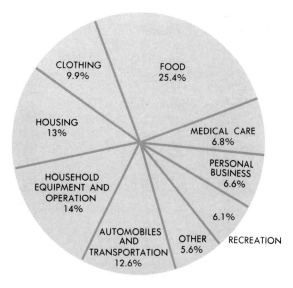

Figure 9–5   Personal Consumption Expenditures

As personal income increases, the percentage of income spent for food declines whereas the percentage of income spent for recreation increases.
SOURCE: U.S. Department of Commerce, Office of Business Economics

difficult to place certain expenditures in a simplified distribution like this. The cost of food includes charges for the processing of the food so that the housewife does less of the preparation. Beverages and tobacco are included as food costs. Many appliances are included in the cost of housing. Durable goods—those things that do not need to be replaced after each use and which last for a considerable time—make up an increasing percentage of our total budgets. Because consumers can make automobiles, appliances, and other durable goods last an extra year or more, the demand for these products fluctuates considerably. Those businesses connected with the production and sale of durable goods must create demand in the mind of the consumer, if none already exists.

Advertising: a key to demand creation

Thorstein Veblen, an economist and sociologist (see p. 131) at the University of Chicago at the beginning of the twentieth century, studied the spending habits of the American people. He observed that the rich tried to demonstrate their superiority by their extravagant purchases. He called buying expensive things for show *conspicuous consumption*. He observed that this practice occurred at all levels of income. Today we often refer to this practice, especially as it affects the average family, as "keeping up with the Joneses." Read the advertisements for luxury cars and note the appeal to social status. When an advertisement says "Move up to———," the implication is that you will enjoy more prestige. In some circles a mink coat means that the wearer "has arrived." Paintings, jewelry, and even collections of books are bought because the "best" people have these things. The assumption is that purchasing these prestige items will make you one of the "best" people.

BUILT-IN OBSOLESCENCE

Automobile and appliance manufacturers may work hard to improve their product, but they know that style changes, along with new gadgets, will make the consumer consider his present model obsolete. This built-in obsolescence puts pressure, primarily of a social nature, on the consumer to trade in a product still in good condition for a new one. The entire structure of the market in several fields is based on "trade-ins" and "moving up." The greatest appeal of this technique is to the middle class and to a newly rich group, both characterized by social and economic mobility, to whom "status symbols" are visible evidence of their progress. People at the lowest economic level cannot afford to play this "game," while those long established at the upper economic level do not have to play it.

THE CASE FOR ADVERTISING

Changes in hair styling and clothing, colors for decorating, and even new packaging give the "new look." The consumer is bombarded by all the media of mass communication—by $14 billion worth of advertising in 1964—about three times the amount spent in 1947. Advertising agencies, using the information that psychologists have provided on the suggestibility of man, have used advertising to limit consumer sovereignty; they have thereby placed a powerful weapon in the hands of the producer. This change has somewhat altered the consumer's position from what is called for in the classical model, but this is not necessarily a disadvantage. As we will learn in Chapter 11, a mature capitalistic economy must at various times stimulate consumer demand in order to avoid a depression. This stimulus to consumer demand can come from government; it can also come from business. Advertising is business' way of stimulating consumer demand. If that demand is allowed to decline, production will fall off and so will jobs, because the income that consumers need in order to make their purchases will no longer be available.

PUT A TIGER IN YOUR TANK!

Reprinted by permission of Humble Oil & Refining Company ©
1965

Among the objectives of advertising are product
identification and popular acceptance of a product.

As a means of providing information to
the consumer, advertising can be looked
upon both favorably and unfavorably. Proponents point out the need for advertising
to acquaint the public with the existence of
new products and improvements in older
products. How does the businessman let the
public know that he has something special
to sell? If we want to sell our "Build-a-City"
sets, we can send salesmen to retailers and
leave to them the initiative for selling our
sets. However, let us suppose that retailers
are not advertising or that they hesitate to
take on a new and untried product. By advertising we go directly to the consumer to
inform him of our toy and create a demand.
Consumers can then request that retailers
have "Build-a-City" sets in stock.

THE CASE AGAINST ADVERTISING

Critics of advertising point out that the
great expense of advertising can be met
only by large, established firms. Introducing
a new product requires more money than a
small producer can afford. Big advertising
campaigns, aimed at *product differentiation*, lead the public to think that only the

Some protest the consumer's choices. They find he has been wasteful, shortsighted, and preoccupied
with glittering baubles. Should someone else do the choosing for him?

"name brands" can be trusted, since they are the only ones that have "zing" in them. This belief leads to imperfect competition, limiting consumer choices.

Other criticisms of advertising include the waste of money, since no real value is added to the product; distortion of values through television and radio; and creation of consumer demand for such things as tobacco, beer, and patent medicines. Testimony taken before a Senate investigating committee revealed that the drug industry spends more on advertising than it does on research. Critics also question the real value to the consumer of the information he is given in advertisements.

ADVERTISING AS A PART OF OUR ECONOMY

Many of the criticisms of advertising are undoubtedly true for particular cases, but they need not be so for advertising in general. There is a need for the advertising industry, as for many other segments of our economy, to take stock of its code of ethics. The government has already taken steps to control certain kinds of advertisements through the Food and Drug Administration. Self-policing by business will avoid additional government controls.

In an economy where more than half of consumer purchases are for things not necessary for survival, creation of demand through advertising may be an important means of keeping business on an even level. There is little likelihood of a decline in its importance.

The relation of imperfect competition to demand creation

Consumers' choices are limited and impeded by having markets with less than pure competition. When new firms find it difficult to introduce their products into the market either by not being allowed to enter the market or by not being able to let the consumer know about their product, progress is stifled and the consumer must take what the few large firms have to offer.

"FAIR-TRADE" LAWS

In the 1930's a new method of pricing was introduced as a means of helping the small businessman. This practice, known as *retail price maintenance*, allowed the manufacturer to set the retail price at which his products would be sold. It prevented retailers from cutting prices on established products. During the Depression, several states passed legislation, known as "fair-trade" laws, to enforce the practice of retail price maintenance. These laws were a benefit to manufacturers, who feared that price-cutting might cheapen a product in the eyes of the consumer.

More important politically was the fact that such legislation protected the small businessman from possible price-cutting by chain stores and large department stores. Large companies could afford to sell items at a lower price because of their more efficient operation. When fair-trade laws were first passed, small business was a larger employer than it is today. Unemployment was a greater source of wasting our resources than was the poor allocation of our resources because of artificially maintained prices. Because chain stores were prohibited from price-cutting, more consumers would patronize small businesses. Increased sales kept small business active and maintained employment at a higher level.

It is hard for consumers to see anything fair in legislation that compels them to pay higher prices. On items covered by the law, prices are generally far lower in states without fair-trade laws than in those with them. There is no convincing evidence that small businesses do appreciably better in states with these laws than in states without them.

The Miller-Tydings Act in 1937 and the McGuire Act in 1952 gave the support of the federal government to fair-trade laws. Pressure by several manufacturing groups won approval for this legislation in spite of the disapproval of the federal administrative agencies most directly concerned and of labor, farm, and consumer groups. What these groups could not do is now being done by the spread of discount stores throughout the country. Some economists believe that where these stores appear, retail competition is approaching what the classical model envisioned, and the consumer is once again placed on his throne. In rural areas, mail-order businesses have increased competition and helped to reduce prices.

Part C   Consumer Credit—A Factor in Demand

Consumer savings

Personal savings and *consumer credit* have an important effect on consumption. Since saving is the opposite of consumption, an increase in one will, for a given income, bring about a decrease in the other. Consumer credit allows the consumer to expand his consumption without gearing his buying strictly to his savings or income. In a mature economy like our own, demand creation is important. It is doubtful, though, whether demand could be expanded without consumer credit.

WHAT DETERMINES SAVINGS

Consumer saving usually varies according to income. Families are able to increase the percentage of income saved as income rises. Savings for all families in our country also fluctuate with the national income, increasing as income increases. During the Depression of the thirties savings dropped so low that in 1932 and 1933 people actually spent more than their incomes, resulting in dissavings. During World War II, when incomes went up but consumer goods were in short supply, savings amounted to over twenty percent of take-home pay. Since 1951 the proportion of consumers' savings to their disposable personal income has been quite consistent, about seven percent.

WHAT CONSTITUTES SAVINGS

By savings we do not mean merely the money deposited in a savings bank, stored in a vault, or hidden under a mattress. Money paid on a life insurance policy or invested in stocks or bonds, or even mortgage payments which go beyond interest and depreciation are considered in the same category. Most families like to have a reserve of some kind. It provides a buffer for emergencies, and it gives the family additional security.

HOW SAVINGS ARE HELD

In considering where to put savings, the consumer should consider *safety*, how quickly and easily they can be converted to cash (*liquidity*), the *rate of interest*, and how they will *fluctuate* with prices. Usually, no one form of savings can be strong in all these characteristics. Deposits in savings accounts provide safety and liquidity, but they usually yield a relatively low return and they do not give protection against sharp price rises. Stocks are not so safe, particularly if the owner does not have a long period of time to convert them into cash. However, they are more likely to yield a higher rate of return and give better protection against inflation than other forms of savings. Most consumer economists recommend diversifying savings so that changing conditions will never place the family in too difficult a position. However, each family has to determine how its own best interests will be served.

CHANGES IN HABITS OF SAVING

In recent years, savings have become less of an immediate factor in altering consumer decisions. This has come about because of the tremendous availability of consumer credit. At one time families usually delayed purchases until they had the entire purchase price put aside. Some consumers feel that it is immoral to "buy on time" or to use credit because it is spending money that does not belong to them. It was not until the twentieth century, and primarily in the United States, that large-scale consumer credit became an acceptable and integral part of consumer behavior.

Growth of consumer credit

Consumer credit, not including mortgages, has increased from $5.6 billion in 1945 to $76 billion in 1965. This almost fourteenfold increase has expanded much faster than the increase in incomes. In 1945 consumer credit amounted to only 3.8 percent of disposable income, whereas in 1965 it had increased to 17 percent. The largest portion of this increase was in *installment credit,* which differs from other consumer credit in allowing the seller to repossess the article purchased if the buyer defaults on payment. This practice involves greater risks for repayment because the article purchased loses value as it is used. More than a third of installment credit is granted for automobile purchases. Noninstallment credit is made up of charge accounts, service credit, and single-payment loans. All of these have increased from three to five times in the last twenty years. Installment credit makes up about three fourths of consumer credit. About forty percent of installment credit is held by commercial banks, with sales finance companies, retail outlets, and other financial institutions making up the rest.

How credit affects the consumer

The availability of credit has led to new patterns of consumer spending. Credit has the appearance of extending the range of choices open to the consumer. However, many people question whether use of credit always permits the consumer to exercise choice most effectively.

ADVANTAGES

One of the great difficulties encountered by most young married couples is that their needs are greatest when their incomes are lowest. Furnishing an apartment, buying a car, and meeting the costs of raising young children when the breadwinner has

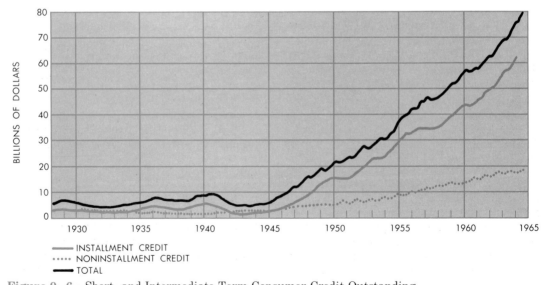

Figure 9–6   Short- and Intermediate-Term Consumer Credit Outstanding

Compare the changes shown here with those indicated in Figure 8–3. SOURCE: Federal Reserve System, *Historical Chart Book*

his first job present an overwhelming problem. A washing machine is needed more when children are young than when they grow up and leave home. Why wait and save for the washer when it can be paid for in regular installments while it is being used? Many families must purchase durable goods such as automobiles and appliances by means of installment buying or not at all.

Businessmen are as concerned about the availability of consumer credit as are consumers. They know that a drop in consumer credit can bring significant drops in consumer purchases. Credit frees the consumers from waiting until they have enough savings to allow them to make their purchases.

SOME DANGERS

There are serious disadvantages to credit. Buying on credit involves extra costs. Interest rates vary, but there have been enough cases reported of total interest costs being greater than the original price of the purchase to serve as a warning to those who borrow. Stores which grant credit are hard pressed to compete in price with those that demand immediate payment for merchandise.

Another danger is that credit lures people into buying things they may not need. Many people are tempted to exceed their financial means when they look only at the amount of the down payment and the size of each month's payment. "No money down and three years to pay" and "For pennies a day you can own a new———" are catch phrases that get too many American families into debt "over their heads." Consumers can help themselves by

1. determining what the cost of the credit will be in addition to the original cash price
2. deciding whether their income is sufficient to carry the payments without too many other sacrifices
3. shopping for credit as they would for other purchases
4. reading all the print in credit contracts

Part D   Protecting the Consumer

As we sketched the design of the classical model, we learned that all the people playing a part in it—businessmen, labor, owners of other factors of production, and the consumer—were expected to act independently. Since the system is organized to provide benefits to the consumer, competition rather than cooperation between those within each group was considered essential. We have already pointed out how each of the interest groups has sought collective action to protect itself from others. While labor and management have organized to guard their special interests, the interests of the individual consumer have frequently been neglected. Consumer cooperatives, private consumer agencies, and government have all been used to provide some measure of protection for the consumer.

The question remains whether the interests of the consumer are adequately protected within the limits of present practices. Before answering, we must consider

1. why the consumer needs protection
2. what protection is now available to him
3. what people believe about the adequacy of protection

Why does the consumer need protection?

Before the big impact of the Industrial Revolution, the consumer had a relatively simple task of making choices and judging quality. Little of the merchandise offered for sale was packaged, so he could see what he was buying; and it was reasonably easy to judge the quality of the few simple items offered for sale. In some instances, if the consumer did not like what he saw, he went home and made the article himself.

Today the consumer finds himself surrounded by hordes of products, packaged in multicolored wrappings in every conceivable shape and size and all claiming to do the best job. The technical considerations necessary to determine quality are well beyond the knowledge of the average consumer. Claims and counterclaims, giveaways, coupons, packaging, and trademarks add confusion to chaos. Determining what is the best appliance, the best fabric, or even the best canned food frequently turns out to be a "hit-and-miss" choice. Making errors on quality and performance may be costly. In most instances the cost is money, performance, or satisfaction; but in some instances it might be health and safety. A poorly wired electrical appliance or a dangerous drug could produce a disaster for the consumer.

Freedom of consumer choices is frequently limited by manufacturers. We have mentioned demand creation and advertising as methods of reducing consumer sovereignty and transferring it to the producer. This tendency has gone so far that some marketing specialists have changed their attitude of giving the consumer what he wants to making the consumer want what they have to offer him. Misleading advertising, imperfect competition, buying by habit, the use of only brand names, and the unorganized position of the consumer in contrast to other groups in our economy have made the need for some kind of consumer protection vital.

What protection does the consumer now have?

Although the original objective in the classical model was to benefit the consumer, later influences have interfered with the realizing of that aim. We have seen that some groups concerned with the factors of production, such as labor and management, organized to protect their interests. Organizing for protection became important for consumers, too, especially as created demand and "easy credit" added to the need for protection.

CONSUMER COOPERATIVES

Today consumers get protection from both private and public sources. Perhaps the most important outcome of consumers' attempts to organize themselves in order to protect their interests has been the development of *consumer cooperative* stores. Organized by consumers for the purpose of getting good merchandise at reasonable prices rather than for making profits, these stores have spread throughout the country. Their appeal has been primarily in rural areas, although labor unions have sometimes encouraged their development in cities. Membership is slightly above 3.5 million people.

PRIVATE RESEARCH ORGANIZATIONS

Two nationally famous private organizations dedicated to protecting the consumer are *Consumers' Research* and *Consumers Union*. Both organizations test and rate products in their laboratories, considering safety, quality, and price. Ratings are given to various brands on the basis of these criteria. Their publications accept no advertising, in contrast to most other periodicals. Attempts have been made to demonstrate that these organizations show favoritism, but these charges have never been proved. While budget limitations, limited samplings, and errors can creep in, these groups provide information valuable in guiding the consumer. *Good Housekeeping* and *Parents' Magazine* put seals of approval on products which guarantee the authenticity of advertising claims, but no attempts are made to compare the value of competing products.

BUSINESS

Some retail stores and some producers of particular products set up standards and endorse these products with their name or seal of approval as having met these standards. Giant distributors of merchandise, such as Sears, Roebuck & Company and Macy's department store, have their buyers test products before they acquire merchandise that will carry their name on it. Producers of electrical equipment usually seek to have their products tested to get the seal of the Underwriters Laboratories placed on their product, indicating that safety requirements have been met. Producers and reliable retail stores will usually stand behind the products they sell, frequently with money-back guarantees. The Better Business Bureaus and chambers of commerce help consumers by searching for frauds which cheat the public. None of these sources help the consumer determine which products are best, but they do eliminate some dangers to consumers.

LOCAL AND STATE GOVERNMENTS

Local, state, and federal governments provide the consumer with protection. Local governments protect water purity, sanitation of all places handling food, and safety of buildings through inspections and building codes. State and local governments check scales for accuracy, license many types of workers who perform services, and set up controls over insurance companies, banks, private educational institutions, utility rates, and credit agencies. Some states have an agency to aid consumer protection. Variations between states and units of local government in the protection offered remain so great that some federal action has been called for.

FEDERAL GOVERNMENT

The federal government has passed many laws and set up many agencies designed to aid and protect consumers. The Food and Drug Administration has set up standards to protect the consumer from the introduction of harmful drugs, adulterated foods, faulty labeling, and misleading packaging. The Federal Trade Commission looks to see if unfair trade practices will hurt the consumer. The Federal Communications Commission and the Interstate Commerce Commission have some regulatory controls over rates. The Bureau of Standards and the Department of Agriculture are also concerned with protecting the consumer.

The unequal protection given to consumers because of differences in the way state and local governments treat this problem and the diffusion of responsibility within the federal government as to which agency is primarily responsible for protecting the consumer caused President Kennedy to send a special message to Congress asking for additional protection for the consumer. In 1964 a Consumer Advisory Council was established to assist the Council of Economic Advisers.

Part E   The Problem: Does the Consumer Need More Protection?

The case for more protection

Although a great deal of progress has been made in protecting the consumer, much remains to be done. Among the reasons for increasing consumer protection are (1) insufficient competition, (2) misleading advertising, (3) artificial demand for unnecessary or even harmful products, (4) deceit in packaging, and (5) introduction of new products not sufficiently tested to be safe beyond question.

What specific safeguards does the consumer need in order to protect his interests? When he buys on the installment plan, he should know in dollars and cents how much the interest carrying charges will be. He should know that the medicines he buys have been adequately tested; he should be able to buy drugs by their generic name rather than brand name, so as to be able to get them at the lowest price. His food products that are concealed in packaging or are difficult to evaluate should be graded in standardized terms. All food products, whether shipped in interstate or intrastate commerce, should be similarly graded. Heavy penalties should be imposed on all businesses shown to use not only false but also misleading advertising. All plants producing goods that could prove potentially dangerous to the consumer should be subject to regular inspection.

Although some of the above conditions are being regulated and improved under existing law, inadequate funds appropriated to the enforcing agencies have not allowed for proper enforcement. Overlapping supervisory authority has caused confusion. A proposal has been made to create within the federal administration a Department of the Consumer having influence equal to that of the departments of Agriculture, Commerce, and Labor. Such a proposal would allow for centralizing all activities — research, education, legal recommendations, and enforcement. This may be the only way the consumer will get the protection he needs in this fast-changing and complex world.

The case against more protection

The real and ultimate responsibility for protecting the consumer must rest with the consumer himself. Our political and economic systems assume that the individual in our society is rational and capable of making correct decisions. Given the opportunity for an education, the citizen-consumer is in a reasonable position to know what it is he wants and how he can express his wants. There are ample safeguards furnished by all levels of government, by businesses themselves, and by private agencies. If fraud, negligence, or harmful goods or services hurt the consumer, he has recourse to these agencies as well as to legal action. The individual, both as citizen and as consumer, has means of protecting his interests. However, just as the citizen will get the government that he deserves, so the consumer will get the products he deserves.

The alternative to our present system would be a highly regimented society which would pay scant attention to the individual consumer's choices and would have little respect for his ability to determine what he wants. In the planned economy of the Soviet Union, where the *What* is largely determined by an economic planning committee, goods and services do not meet the quality of American standards. The more restrictions we place on the freedom of business to determine what and how it can produce, the less variety we will have in our choice of products.

Allowing business to share in demand creation with the consumer has advantages for everyone. In an affluent society like our own, demand creation is necessary to keep production at a high enough level to provide employment for our work force. Without it, production might very well decline to a serious degree. In addition, business invests great sums of money in the development of new products. Progress does not come exclusively from consumers. It may also be initiated by business, but it is clearly in the interest of all.

The conscientious consumer who shops carefully and makes full use of existing facilities to protect his interests is helping not only himself but the entire economy. By demanding better goods for lower prices he assures the efficient use of our limited resources as well as the introduction of new and better products. These benefits occur because honest and capable businessmen are rewarded, whereas inefficient and wasteful ones are punished. Consumers can be kings in a prosperous society, but this is possible only if they are willing to make choices and to exercise judgment.

Considering an answer

Just as we have faced other problems, we must also be prepared to answer the question of how much freedom of choice we want. With freedom goes the responsibility of judging, and we must have knowledge if we are to exercise our choices wisely. Can the individual consumer be expected to have sufficient knowledge, in some instances of a technical nature, to make wise decisions? If government takes the first step to aid the consumer by making knowledge available, should it take a second step in advising the consumer on what decisions he should make, and a third step in taking action where the knowledge it has may be to the consumer's advantage? What responsibility has government to protect the consumer who ignores whatever knowledge is available?

In considering answers, we must recognize that a paternalistic government may provide maximum security, but possibly at the expense of individual freedom. However, the price of complete freedom may be the loss of our security. Can you find a plan which would permit a maximum of freedom without endangering our security as consumers and citizens?

REVIEW: *the highlights of the chapter*

1. The classical model assumes that the objective of production is consumption. It is the consumer who determines what the production shall be as he registers his wants in the market.

2. Needs of consumers differ. In wealthy nations, a great deal of production is for goods and services not needed for survival.

3. Consumer sovereignty is limited by the distribution of personal income, the creation of demand by business, and imperfect competition.

4. A family's consumption is dependent on income, savings, and credit. The first is the most important. The Lorenz curve, used for measuring distribution of income, shows family unit incomes to be quite unequal. However, incomes tend to be more nearly equal today than they were in the 1930's.

5. Differences in income exist among regions, occupations, people of different abilities and education, and minority groups.

6. The largest portion of the lowest income group is made up of people who have little preparation for earning a living. Among this group may be found widows, the elderly, members of minority groups, people with little education, those from broken homes, and people with physical or mental disabilities. Many programs are aimed at helping these people to increase their earning power as well as to supplement their present incomes.

7. In our economy efforts are made, largely through advertising, to create demand among consumers. Some controversy exists as to the benefits of demand creation, particularly for products which critics say are not necessities.

8. Imperfect competition, including legally sanctioned fair-trade laws, limits consumer choices and efficient use of resources.

9. Consumer savings, amounting to approximately seven percent of disposable personal income, may be kept in a variety of ways, each having particular advantages or disadvantages in safety, liquidity, interest, and stability of value.

10. Consumer credit, which has increased almost fourteenfold in the last twenty years, allows consumers to use products while they pay for them. Credit can help consumers and business if used wisely.

11. Controversy exists as to how far the government should go in attempting to protect the consumer and to supervise business.

IN CONCLUSION: some aids to understanding

Terms for review

fair-trade laws   consumer cooperatives
Lorenz curve   public assistance
durable goods   conspicuous consumption
personal income   built-in obsolescence
installment credit   subsistence

Names to know

VISTA   Thorstein Veblen
War on Poverty   Miller-Tydings Act

Questions for review

1. The system of classical capitalism is meant to operate for the benefit of the consumer.
   (a) What is meant by the phrase "The consumer is sovereign"?
   (b) In what ways is this sovereignty limited?

2. Measured against the values of political equality, the great inequalities of an economic system based on unlimited competition for profit have appeared inconsistent.
   (a) What is the essential difference between equality of opportunity and equality of income?
   (b) What is the economic philosophy of the "War on Poverty"?

3. There has been a tendency to blame the poor economic status of minority groups exclusively on discriminatory practices and on unequal abilities and opportunities. Today we recognize that while discrimination still exists, other factors such as geography, education, automation, and relocation of business all contribute to the vast pockets of unemployment.
   (a) Describe the problems faced by minority groups in seeking to improve their economic status.
   (b) How are these problems sometimes self-perpetuating?
   (c) What efforts have been made by government to help erase these problems?

(d) What recommendations can you make to solve the problems caused by geography and relocating of businesses?

(e) In what manner will changing educational goals help to ease the burden of minority groups?

4. What is meant by the statement "Income and need determine what is necessity and what is luxury"?

5. Explain the following statements and evaluate their truth:

(a) Advertising is the lifeblood of producing for consumption through demand creation.

(b) Advertising may lead to improper waste and excessive cost.

6. List the arguments for and against federal and state laws on fair-trade practices.

7. Describe the role of savings and credit in consumer spending.

8. What are the major factors the consumer should consider in determining the form of his savings?

9. Make a balance sheet listing the advantages and the disadvantages of credit buying for the consumer and the producer.

10. Consumers have found it necessary to protect their interests.

(a) Explain the reasons for the development of laws for consumer protection.

(b) Defend the continued use of laws to protect the consumer.

(c) What steps have consumers taken to help themselves?

(d) What public and private agencies are available for help?

Additional questions and problems

1. Consumer protection takes many forms and involves the consideration of many kinds of values.

(a) Present the arguments for and the arguments against labeling cigarettes as a cause of cancer.

(b) What effect might such labeling have on the multibillion-dollar tobacco industry?

(c) Investigate and report on the basic changes in advertising appeal for cigarettes before and after the Surgeon General's report in 1964 on cigarette smoking.

2. "The ever-expanding role of government in extending fair-trade laws, curbing advertising, controlling credit, and policing by more and more government agencies presents a threat to the democratic capitalist system." Do you agree? Defend your decision.

3. Explain the meaning of the phrase *caveat emptor*. To what extent does it express correctly the philosophy of present marketing and consumption? What recent legislation has been designed to increase consumer protection?

UNIT III
The American Economy as a Whole

Chapter 10.
*Measuring the Nation's
Economy*

Chapter 11.
*National Income Analysis—
A New Model*

Chapter 12.
*Money and Prices and
Their Relation to the Economy*

Chapter 13.
*Banking and the Creation
of Money*

Chapter 14.
*Formulating Modern
Economic Policy*

RAD IN
RED ROP
STRUTH
S&P
TALLEY
TEC M
TEL COM
WA SHO
WATER
WEST LD
KY
WERNER
WHSHLD
WS BG
WORLD
Stock

10 *Measuring the Nation's Economy*

Preview

This chapter is designed to introduce you to the study of modern macroeconomics, the study of the economy as a whole. Here you will learn what tools the economist uses in evaluating the basic state of the economy. Just as the physician measures the health of a patient by checking many factors, so the economist must look at many indicators to judge whether the economic machine is working properly. When the reports are in, the economist, like the physician, can diagnose and prescribe. Foremost among these tools is a new model to explain the working of our economic system.

The new model we are to examine in Unit III is known by many names—"the new economics," "the new capitalism," "the Keynesian model," and other intriguing titles. Whatever you call it, you should recognize that it is consistent with what we have described as a mixed capitalistic system. It differs from the classical model by approaching the economy from the aggregate, or national, standpoint rather than from the viewpoint of the individual firm or institution, and it modifies and adds to rather than replaces the classical tradition. It is not a different economic system in the sense that socialism or feudalism differs from capitalism. Many economists like to think of it as an extension of classical capitalism designed to meet the problems and conditions of today's world.

Overview

What measurements would be needed to diagnose the condition of the national economy?

Once these measurements had been made, what difficulties might be encountered in evaluating the data?

What evidence of changing business activity can you point to in your own community within the last four years?

Part A National Income Accounting

The national economy

Frequently, when businessmen and people interested in matters of business gather, conversation turns to a discussion of economic conditions. Although attention may be focused primarily on purely local conditions, broader questions will be raised concerning such topics as unemployment, prices, inventories, the stock market, steel production, and automobile and department store sales. Although such conversation may help to clarify some issues, evaluating overall economic conditions for a country as large and complex as ours is not really a simple task. One segment of our economy may be growing at a time when another segment may be declining. Some producers may be more prosperous than ever at a time when most businessmen are complaining of losses. You may be surprised to learn that a very few businesses did quite well during the Great Depression of the 1930's. Conversely, during its most prosperous times our nation has had more than two hundred business failures a week. However, businessmen know that no matter how well they may be doing at present, they will, in all probability, eventually feel the general trend of the economy. In order to make wise decisions about their own businesses,

Table 10-1 Major Economic Indicators

	Latest	Year Ago	Change
UNEMPLOYMENT (issued monthly in per cent of labor force)	3.7	4.8	down 1.1%
INDUSTRIAL PRODUCTION (monthly, base of 1957-59 = 100)	152.9	140.7	up 9%
GROSS NATIONAL PRODUCT (quarterly, in billions)	$714.1	$657.6	up 9%
WHOLESALE PRICE INDEX (monthly, base of 1957-59 = 100)	105.5	101.3	up 4.1%
CONSUMER PRICE INDEX (monthly, base of 1957-59 = 100)	112.0	109.0	up 3%
PERSONAL INCOME (monthly, in billions)	$561.0	$517.8	up 8%
RETAIL SALES (monthly, in billions)	$25.6	$22.9	up 12%
INSTALLMENT DEBT (monthly, in billions)	$68.8	$60.9	up 13%
STANDARD & POOR'S STOCK INDEX (weekly)	87.84	89.85	down 2.2%
MANUFACTURERS' ORDERS (monthly, in billions)	$45.5	$40.7	up 12%
MANUFACTURERS' INVENTORIES (monthly, in billions)	$69.7	$63.7	up 10%
CORPORATE PROFITS (quarterly, in billions, after taxes)	$45.9	$37.8	up 21%
CAPITAL SPENDING (quarterly, in billions)	$58.9	$50.4	up 17%

A variety of measurements are used in studying economic development and predicting the direction of trends. SOURCE: *Newsweek*, May 16, 1966

Although the growing number and accuracy of measurements provide the economist with more workable data for forecasting, the evaluation and interpretation of such data are often the subject of controversy.

they must have some knowledge of the economy as a whole. By what means can we determine the direction of economic trends and evaluate their movement?

KEEPING OUR RECORDS

In order to study economic development, many kinds of information are necessary. It is as essential for a nation to keep records of its economy for evaluation of the past and projection of future progress, as it is for a physician to keep careful records of his patients. It was not until 1929 that the United States departments of Commerce and Labor started to keep accurate measurements of the nation's economy.

Economists know that measuring particular segments of the economy is comparatively easy. However, for detailed analysis, certain kinds of information are of special value—those concerned with the overall view. We do not want to see only the trees; we want to see the forest, too. In economics, when we examine the economy as a whole, we call the study *macroeconom-*

ics. This approach differs from that of Unit II, where we made a detailed study of individual factors of the economy; study in that perspective is known as *microeconomics.*

Gross national product: the basic measure

In reading reports of the nation's economic condition in a newspaper or magazine, you would very likely encounter the term *gross national product,* or simply GNP. It is the measure most often used to determine how well the economy is faring; it is used by government and business alike in order to determine their future policies and plans. What does GNP include? If the retail prices of all the goods and services produced during the year were added up, the figure arrived at would be the gross national product for that year.

METHODS OF FIGURING GNP

There are three different approaches to determining gross national product. All three will yield the same answer, since each is trying to do the same thing—to measure the total value of goods and services produced in the nation during the year. The first view has already been described: GNP represents the final market price or retail value of all production. This view is easy to understand because it is exactly what GNP says it is—the value of the nation's production, or product, before subtracting anything from the total. Shortly we will be subtracting items from GNP, and the word "gross" will be replaced.

The expenditure approach to GNP

It is also possible to look at GNP from the point of view of goods and services bought rather than produced. This method is called the expenditures approach; it records who is buying the goods and services in the marketplace. There are four categories of buyers: (1) individuals buying as households, (2) government, (3) businesses, and (4) foreign purchasers, which we shall call "foreign investment."

About two thirds of all expenditures in the marketplace are for consumer goods and services and are made by families buying to satisfy their needs. These items include durable goods such as washing machines and cars, nondurable goods such as food and gasoline, and services such as entertainment and medical expenses. Economists call these household purchases *personal consumption expenditures.*

The second largest buyer is government. This includes all levels of government and accounts for almost one fifth of total expenditures. Most items of all government budgets—federal, state, and local—are included. The major exceptions are those publicly owned businesses that sell to the people—for example, the post office and some transportation systems and utilities. These are included under personal consumption expenditures.

Investment expenditures made by business account for most of the remaining purchases. Under this category are included all purchases of capital goods (such as machinery and equipment), all construc-

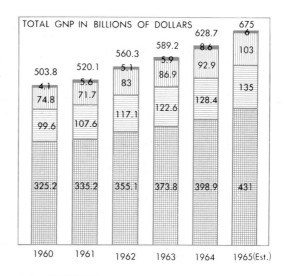

NET EXPORTS
PRIVATE INVESTMENT
GOVERNMENT PURCHASES
PERSONAL CONSUMPTION

Figure 10-1   Gross National Product and Its Components

Government purchases climbed about a third in the 5-year period since 1960, but so did the total GNP. Slightly less was the increase in personal consumption of a little over 30 percent. Private investment jumped more—nearly 40 percent. And net exports, after more than doubling by 1964, dipped in 1965. SOURCE: *Christian Science Monitor*, January 11, 1966

tion (including homes), and the differences between inventories at the beginning of the year and the end of the year. If total inventories were to decline during a particular year, it would mean that we used more goods than we produced and the difference would have to be subtracted. If inventories are higher, the additional value of goods must be added.

The final and smallest item in the expenditure approach is net foreign investment. It is calculated by adding together all the expenditures made by foreign countries in the United States and subtracting from that amount the total of all the purchases we made abroad. In 1961 this difference amounted to $4 billion. It is possible to arrive at a negative figure, as occurred in 1959, when net foreign investment in our country was −$0.8 billion. Because foreign investment is so much smaller than the other categories, we shall ignore it in our analysis. However, the subject will be considered further in Chapter 15.

Although the logic of the expenditure approach is clear, the question may arise of how the total value of production and the total value of expenditures can be the same when some of the product is not sold. It is true that some of the production is not sold to the ultimate consumer; but if we regard it as part of the inventory bought by other producers, then there is no difficulty in seeing that the totals of the expenditure approach and the production approach are equal.

The income approach to GNP

The third method of determining GNP is through analysis of income. Since the factors of production are responsible for the making of goods and services, it is possible to add up all the payments made to those involved in this production. The sum of all wages, salaries, interest, rent, and profits, plus indirect business taxes and capital consumption, must be indicated. The resulting total represents the payments, or income, side of the goods and services produced, and is most frequently referred to as *gross national income*, since it is dealing with income rather than production. However, the gross national income should be equal to the gross national product. Whether the production, the expenditure, or the income approach is used, the same total is reached—the gross value of what the nation produced for the year. Remember that product refers to the value of production, whether produced or bought, and income to the payment for that production. Figure 10–2 shows the expenditure and income approaches.

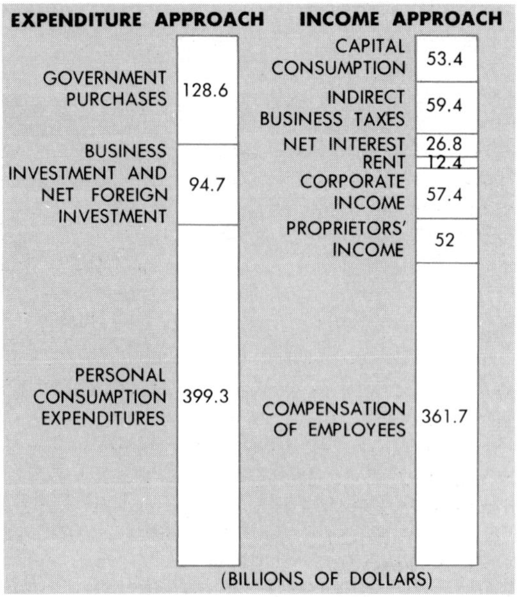

Figure 10–2   Two Views of the GNP, 1964
SOURCE: U.S. Department of Commerce

Common errors in computing GNP

When statisticians figure GNP, they may easily make two types of errors: (1) double counting and (2) adding transfer payments when measuring value created. Unless corrected, these mistakes give a distorted picture of economic conditions, preventing an accurate accounting and evaluation of actual production.

DOUBLE COUNTING

One of the problems in determining GNP, using the production method, is how to avoid double counting. You will remember that in our first definition of GNP we were careful to refer to value as the final market price or retail price. An example, illustrated in Table 10–2, will make the reason for this distinction obvious.

When a farmer sells his cattle to a slaughterhouse, he receives payment for his product. The slaughterhouse sells the meat at a higher price to a wholesale dis-

Table 10-2   An Illustration of Double
             Counting

	CORRECT METHOD		DOUBLE COUNTING
	Price Received	Value Added	
Farmer	$1,000	$1,000	$1,000
Slaughterer	1,200	200	1,200
Distributor	1,500	300	1,500
Retailer	2,000	500	2,000
		$2,000	$5,700

tributor. The wholesale distributor sells the meat at a higher price to retail stores, which in turn sell the meat to consumers at a still higher price. Each of the above—the farmer, the slaughterer, the distributor, and the retailer—has contributed value to the final product. We must add the value that each has contributed. However, we must *not* add the total price received by each. If we do so, we will have added the farmer's contribution four times, the slaughterer's three times, and the wholesale distributor's twice. Doing so would be *double counting*. We must remember to figure only the value added in each step of production but never the total value paid by each of those involved in the various stages of production.

As you can see from Table 10-2, the correct value of the product added to society's wealth is $2,000, not $5,700. The value created in each stage of the production must be added only once.

INCLUDING TRANSFER PAYMENTS

Another kind of double counting may take place when figuring GNP on the income side. Should the money that Uncle Henry gave you for a graduation gift be added to your income when figuring GNP? If you do add it, you will be double counting. You did not create value; Uncle Henry did. Therefore, Uncle Henry will have to include in his income the gift he gave you. What you received is called a *transfer payment*, since the value was not created by you.

Another type of transfer payment is the receipt of Social Security benefits. Value is created during working years, and during those years it counts as income for GNP. However, the value created to pay for Social Security is not received until payment is made during retirement. It is a transfer payment, since value created by you in the past and added to the GNP at that time is now given to you to use.

OTHER WEAKNESSES

There are other weaknesses also inherent in the determining of gross national product. Economics tends to be a rather cold, unemotional, and frequently undiscriminating discipline. When GNP is computed, we consider value only in terms of dollars and cents. In the present context only when the product or service is actually offered for sale on the market does it have value. This means that one of the most valuable contributors in our society, the housewife and mother, is not given credit for contributing to GNP. If she does the same work for someone else and is paid for it, the amount of her paycheck can be included. The same may be said of that great American institution known as "do it yourself." Steps built by someone in your family, or even by a neighbor, do not count unless some payment is made. Volunteer work done by millions of Americans is never considered as part of GNP because these people are not paid for their labor.

Another problem in the GNP approach—one that some experts consider a major weakness—is the failure to distinguish between the billions of dollars spent on luxuries and the billions of dollars spent on education, steel mills, and other goods and services associated with the strength and productivity of a nation. These critics may have a valid argument if GNP is used for comparing the military potential of nations, for example, of the United States and the Soviet Union. However, this criticism does not actually apply to the GNP as a measuring device, but rather to its use in measuring something it was never meant to measure, such as military strength. In a democratic society based predominantly on free enterprise it is the consumer who decides what goods and services he wants and, therefore, what goods and services will be produced. A system such as we have places confidence in the many rather than in the few to determine what is in their best interest.

GNP as a basis for comparison

Since gross national product is a measure of the real wealth of a nation—the value of all its goods and services—we may wish to consider how our country's annual GNP has grown and how it compares with that of other nations of the world. Any time that these evaluations are made, a standard measuring device must be used. Therefore, when we compare the GNP of our country at different times, we must be sure that the dollars we are measuring with are constant dollars, that is, that they purchase equal amounts of goods and services. When we compare our GNP with that of another country, we must equate its unit of currency—such as an English pound, a French franc, or an Italian lira—with our dollar. The attempt in both cases is to keep the measuring device equivalent.

FLUCTUATIONS IN GNP

Tracing the growth of our nation's GNP is complicated by the fact that until 1929 the United States departments of Commerce and Labor did not keep records of the gross national product and other similar measurements. However, studies made by the National Bureau of Economic Research give a fairly accurate picture and show something of the patterns of growth of the GNP. Our annual production of wealth (GNP) increased over six and a half times from 1900 to 1964, and our population rose somewhat less than two and a half times during this same period. This means that

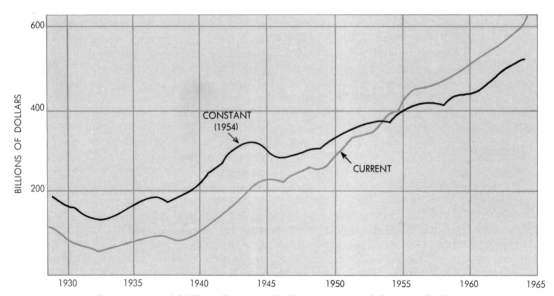

Figure 10-3   Comparison of GNP in Constant Dollars (1954) and Current Dollars

Why is GNP in constant dollars (1954) higher than GNP in current dollars up to 1954 and lower than in current dollars thereafter? SOURCE: U.S. Department of Commerce

the production of real wealth per person during this period increased more than two and a half times. Figure 10–3 shows our economic growth from 1929 to 1963. Although a general upward pattern is evident, major fluctuations also appear. The decline for the 1930's indicates the seriousness of the "Great Depression." Although numbers are emotionless, a brief discussion with someone who remembers the thirties, or reference to books about that period, will give you some idea of the hardship associated with those years.

With the beginning of World War II a remarkable acceleration of growth appeared. The GNP rose 75 percent from 1939 (when the war began in Europe) to 1944 (the last full year of the war). The end of the war brought about a decline, with only a moderate rise in 1948 and no increase at all in 1949. Then a sharp increase occurred because of American involvement in the Korean conflict. The drop in 1954 is consistent with the declines which occurred after our involvement in the two world wars. Apart from a decline in 1958 the rise from 1954 to the present has been consistent.

OUR GNP COMPARED WITH THAT OF OTHER COUNTRIES

When we compare the gross national product of the United States with that of other countries of the world, it is obvious why a famous economist referred to ours as the "affluent" society. Table 10–3 shows the relative position of several selected countries in terms of GNP. Note that these statistics place Russia in second position, far behind the United States in total value of goods and services. All the other nations listed produce collectively only about two thirds of what we do. Figure 18–4 on page 411 contains information on GNP in additional foreign nations.

If the GNP of each of these countries is divided by the total population of each, the resulting amount represents *per capita output*, which provides a measure of the total value per person created in each of the countries listed. Table 10–4 gives this information. Occasionally these figures are

Table 10–3   Gross National Product for Selected Countries

(billions of dollars)

COUNTRY	GNP
United States	522
U.S.S.R.	210
Great Britain	72
West Germany	63
France	55
Communist China	52
Japan	40
Canada	38
Italy	31
India	30
Greece	3
Peru	2

The figures given represent rough estimates of GNP for the early 1960's, with values converted to 1961 U.S. dollars. SOURCE: United Nations publications

Table 10–4   Per Capita Output for Selected Countries

(dollars)

COUNTRY	AMOUNT
United States	2,820
Canada	2,050
Sweden	1,560
Great Britain	1,400
France	1,290
West Germany	1,270
U.S.S.R.	950
Italy	630
Japan	400
Peru	180
India	75
Communist China	70

Per capita output measures the value created per person per year. These figures are rough estimates for the early 1960's, converted to 1961 U.S. dollars. SOURCE: United Nations publications

used to interpret the relative standard of living of people in particular countries. Such conclusions are not very reliable, since they fail to take into consideration the vast inequality of wealth within a country. However, we can note that the output per American worker is almost three times that of the Soviet worker, seven times that of the Japanese worker, and about forty times that of the Indian or Communist Chinese worker. These statistics emphasize how remarkably productive our economy is.

Other measurements

Although gross national product is the most frequently used measurement of our national economy, there are a number of other measurements closely related to GNP that are very important. As we move from GNP through four additional measurements, we should understand better the production, expenditure, and income approaches. You may find it helpful to remember that "product" emphasizes the value of what is produced, and "income" the payment to those producing.

NET NATIONAL PRODUCT

One weakness of using GNP for measuring total output is that it fails to take into account the loss in value of capital goods that takes place in the course of producing the total output. Because machinery depreciates as it is used, part of the production of society must be devoted to merely replacing the value of the capital goods used up in the production process during the year. For example, a farmer has a tractor that he estimates is capable of ten years' operation in helping to produce his crops. He recognizes that each year he must set aside a portion of the money received from the crops to pay for the value used up in his tractor in the production process. If he does not, he will be fooling himself on how much real value he has created. When the tractor breaks down completely ten years after its first use, the farmer is confronted with the total cost of replacement.

GNP gives an exaggerated picture of output, just as the farmer received a distorted view of his income. In both instances, failure to take into consideration the fact that capital was consumed (depreciated) in the process of producing accounted for the error. This error can be corrected by finding the GNP and subtracting from it *capital consumption,* the part of the capital goods depreciated in the production process. The remainder gives a more accurate picture of the actual value of output for the year. That truer value is called *net national product* or *NNP.* It is usually about one eleventh smaller than GNP. Thus, a GNP of $675 billion in 1965 means that our NNP was $614 billion for the same year.

NATIONAL INCOME

Although we have explained GNP from the output, the expenditure, and the income approaches, GNP and NNP traditionally show the output approach. The word "product" used in the previous measurements suggests this. *National income,* on the other hand, measures the income side and is defined as the total earned income of all the factors of production, namely, profits, interest, rent, wages, and other compensation for labor. It does not equal GNP because the factors of production are not paid two items—(1) capital consumption allowances and (2) indirect business taxes—both of which are in-

Table 10–5   National Income for 1964
(billions of dollars)

Compensation of Employees	391.9
Proprietors' Income	54.5
Rental Income	18.6
Corporate Profits and Inventory Valuation Adjustments	73.1
Net Interest	16.8
	$554.6

SOURCE: U.S. Department of Commerce

cluded in GNP. Indirect taxes are such things as sales taxes, property taxes, and excises that are paid by businesses directly to the government and consequently reduce the income left to pay for the factors of production. The money put aside for capital consumption is for replacement and is not counted as income. Table 10–5 shows that over two thirds of national income goes for wages, salaries, and other forms of compensation.

PERSONAL INCOME

Whereas national income shows the income earned by the factors of production, *personal income* measures the income received by individuals or households. Corporation profits are included in national income because they are earned. Out of these profits, however, corporation profit taxes must be paid to government, and some money must be put into the business for expansion. Only that part of profits distributed as dividends goes to the individual;

therefore, out of corporation profits, only dividends count as personal income. The factors of production earn money for Social Security and unemployment insurance contributions; but this money goes to government (which is not a factor of production), not to individuals. It is, therefore, part of national income but not part of personal income.

On the other hand, money received by individuals when they collect Social Security or unemployment compensation is not money earned, but it *is* money received. Interest received on government bonds is also considered in this category because so much of the money received from the sale of bonds went to pay for war production, which no longer furnishes a service to the economy.

DISPOSABLE PERSONAL INCOME

The money that people receive as personal income may be either spent or saved.

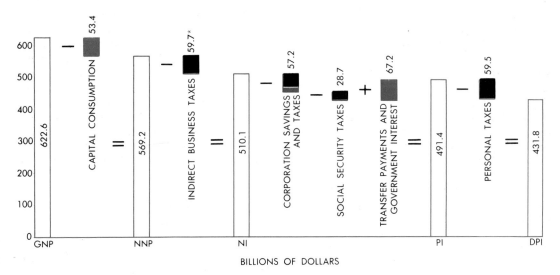

Figure 10–4 Measurements of the Nation's Income

SOURCE: U.S. Department of Commerce

However, not all spending is completely voluntary. A significant portion of our income goes to pay personal taxes. Most workers never receive the money they pay in personal taxes, since it is withheld from their paychecks. The money that individuals are left with after they have met their obligations in regard to taxes is *disposable personal income.* Our disposable income can be divided between personal consumption expenditures and personal savings.

It is important to remember that personal saving is what is left after spending. It is quite possible to have a minus savings, or a dissaving. How can this occur?

Figure 10–4 shows how each of the five measurements of the economy discussed here is arrived at. With this information we can summarize the various measures of our national income as follows:

1. *Gross national product (GNP)* is the retail price of goods and services produced during a given period, usually a year.
2. *Net national product (NNP)* is the gross national product minus the capital consumed in producing GNP.
3. *National income (NI)* is NNP minus indirect business taxes (not considered payment for production), or the total payments earned by factors of production.
4. *Personal income (PI)* is NI minus corporation savings and taxes and Social Security payments (taxes) plus transfer payments and government interest, or it is the income received by individuals.
5. *Disposable personal income (DPI)* is PI minus personal taxes, or it is the addition of personal consumption expenditures and personal savings.

Part B   Measuring Business Activity

In our economic system it is business that has the primary responsibility for production. In the measurements already studied, government has occupied a very significant place, receiving income (usually from taxes) and spending money. However, even when government receives and spends, a significant portion of this is done through business. In Chapter 11 we will be concerned with the relationship between government and business in terms of the general trend of the economy. We know that business activity is vital to the nation's economy, and we will here discuss some of the ways used to measure it.

Every businessman is interested in knowing both how his particular business is faring in comparison with other businesses and what the general business climate is. On the basis of this information he can make plans for his own business. There are two broad categories of *business indicators* that he can turn to for information: representative indicators and general indicators.

Representative indicators

Although the American economy is very complex and made up of many facets, some parts of the economy are so important that they not only give us an indication of how well that part of the economy is doing but they also show a high degree of consistency with other parts. The reason for the high correlation is usually that these *representative indicators* actually are involved in or reflect many other businesses. There are three types of representative indicators: leading, coincident, and lagging.

LEADING INDICATORS

Measurement of our country's iron and steel production has been used for many years by businessmen to evaluate the condition and health of the economy. Iron and steel are basic metals and are used in the production of automobiles, appliances, buildings, machinery, and even such nondurable goods as toys. By watching the production of iron and steel, businessmen can usually gain some idea of what will be happening shortly in businesses that use this basic metal. Because the output of the iron and steel industry is used in the production of so many other goods and precedes the general level of business activity, it is not only a representative indicator but also a *leading indicator.*

COINCIDENT INDICATORS

Freight carloadings are important because most of the goods we produce must be transported, and railroads account for a large portion of our transportation. Although railroads transport primarily heavy goods, they have been a far more reliable measurement than other forms of transportation. Unlike iron and steel production, carloadings run parallel with business activity and are called *coincident indicators.*

LAGGING INDICATORS

A third example of a representative indicator is retail sales. A sampling of retail store sales is taken in representative cities. The sales include a wide range of the production going to the final consumers, and therefore constitute a good indication of business activity. However, the measurement for retail sales is a *lagging indicator,* following the general business trends.

Because each indicator has weaknesses, we must be careful not to trust too much to any one of them. Since the end of World War II a number of substitutes, such as aluminum and plastics, have been used to replace steel in many industries. The introduction and partial success of the compact car has reduced the amount of steel needed in the automobile industry. Increased truck and airplane transportation has cut into the railroad business. Nevertheless, as shown in Figure 10-5, these representative indicators (with the GNP in constant dollars) are for the most part reliable and reassure us of the general value of these measurements.

Look in the financial section of your Sunday newspaper to see if you can find other examples of representative indicators.

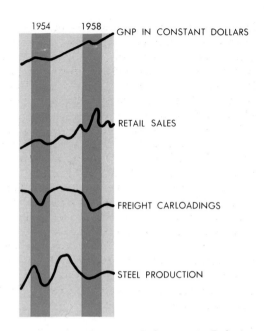

Figure 10-5   Business Indicators in Relation to GNP

Business indicators help economists evaluate the state of the economy. Which of the indicators shown reflects the trends of the business cycle most accurately?

Which of these do you think are leading indicators? Which are lagging? Why?

General business indicators

Rather than rely on the measurement of one segment of the economy, even if that single indicator is representative, economists have put several different phases of our business activity together into a general, or composite, indicator. Perhaps the most widely used is that put out by the Cleveland Trust Company. It seeks to show the fluctuation of business activity back to 1790. It must rely on several different measurements for the earlier years, since data for some of our modern measurements are not available or are unsuitable. Figure 10-6 shows the changes in American business activity from 1899 until 1963, and indicates the key reasons for these changes.

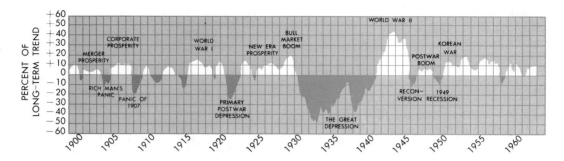

Figure 10–6   Fluctuations in the American Economy

The pattern of general business activity can be determined by combining several indicators into a composite. SOURCE: The Cleveland Trust Company, Cleveland, Ohio

Changes in business activity

A word of caution must be given in interpreting measurements of our nation's economy. There are three types of changes in business activity: seasonal, trend, and cyclical. In the evaluating and forecasting of business activity, the effect of these changes—particularly of business cycles—must be considered.

SEASONAL FLUCTUATIONS

Some seasonal variations are caused by nature, which provides a more favorable environment for certain kinds of production, such as construction, at one time of the year than at others. Some variations are caused by man; in these, tradition often plays a part, as with gift-giving at Christmastime. Economists make allowances for these differences. A chart may indicate an upturn in retail sales in January, although dollar sales were actually higher in the preceding month.

TRENDS

Trend changes refer to extended periods of time and indicate the long-range direction of the economy. Figure 10–6 shows more business activity in 1923 than in 1946. This does not mean that more business was done or more goods produced in 1923 than in 1946. During those twenty-three years our capacity to do business and to produce increased tremendously. However, our business activity in 1923 in relation to our potential in that year was greater than our business activity when compared with our potential in 1946. Figure 10–7 shows how trend is taken into consideration. Let us now turn to cyclical changes.

Business cycles

The fluctuations that we have seen in all the measurements of our economy have been observed and studied by economists for many years. These ups and downs of the many phases of business activity deviate

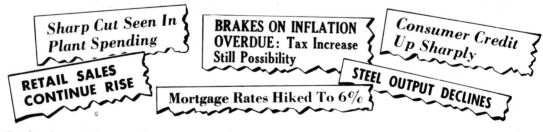

Do the changes shown in these news items add up to expansion or contraction of the economy?

PHASES OF THE BUSINESS CYCLE

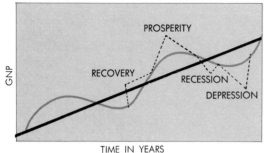

IN MEASURING BUSINESS ACTIVITY, NORMAL GROWTH RATE MUST BE TAKEN INTO CONSIDERATION. PHASES OF A SINGLE BUSINESS CYCLE ARE INDICATED.

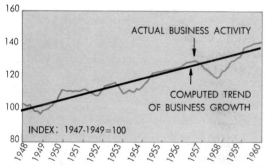

THE INDEX OF BUSINESS ACTIVITY MAY BE MEASURED AGAINST THE TREND OF BUSINESS GROWTH.

Figure 10–7 Measuring Business Activity

Trend is a factor that must be considered in measuring business activity. SOURCE: Morgan Guaranty Survey

from what we might expect the normal increase in our economy to be; and although they do not show a perfect rhythm, it is easy to discern a pattern. These rather regular fluctuations are called *business cycles*.

Economists have noted four phases in a business cycle. The upswing is usually referred to as *expansion* or *recovery*, the uppermost point as the *peak* or *prosperity*, the downswing as *contraction* or *recession*, and the low point as *depression*. The first graph in Figure 10–7 shows these four phases labeled with the terms we shall use: recovery, prosperity, recession, and depression.

Recovery is associated with increases in demand, which are reflected in production, employment, prices, and payments to the factors of production. All measurements of business activity will not rise at the same rate. Prices will tend to rise more slowly than production, and interest rates and retail sales may not increase at all in the early phase of the recovery. However, the general tendency will be upward for the great majority of indicators. When most indicators reach a high or a near-high, we are in the prosperity phase. Capital goods such as machinery will usually be on the decline by the time retail sales hit their peak, but the composite picture reflects optimism.

An examination of Figure 10–6 shows that prosperous periods do not continue indefinitely. In the recession phase some of the leading indicators—such as average hours worked, durable goods, construction, and steel—have been going down and such coincident indicators as employment, industrial production, and freight carloadings have also started to decline. When most of the indicators hit low points, a pessimistic outlook such as we associate with a depression becomes prevalent.

Studies reveal that the average length of a full cycle is slightly less than four years, that more time is spent in economic expansion than in contraction, and more time in prosperity and depression than in recession and recovery. However, the variations in the length of time and the severity of the cycles are so great that these statistics are not very useful when we try to analyze any one particular cycle.

Major theories regarding the causes of business cycles

If we were to make a systematic study of the theories concerning the causes of business cycles, we would soon find ourselves overwhelmed. The number of theories seems to be almost as great as the number of students studying the problem. However, since most of the differences are in emphasis, we can arrange these theories in categories. The most common way to classify them is according to whether the causes are external or internal.

External causes of cycles

Theories based on external causes attribute fluctuations to forces that exist and operate outside the economic system. The best known are those that relate to weather, war, population growth, innovation, and political events. We will consider a few examples of the reasoning which underlies these theories.

SUNSPOTS AND BUSINESS

One of the earliest economists to develop a theory explaining business cycles was an Englishman, W. Stanley Jevons. Writing in 1875, he pointed out a high degree of correlation between sunspots and business conditions. At first glance it might appear ridiculous to connect two such seemingly unrelated factors, but on deeper reflection the logic becomes evident. Sunspots influence the weather, and the weather in turn affects agricultural production. An increase in agricultural output will bring about greater demand for farm equipment, transportation, and credit. This increase will in turn lead to a rise in business activity. Poor weather caused by sunspots will bring about a reversal in the pattern, explaining the downswing in the economy.

This theory, and other similar meteorological theories, proved to be very significant fifty years ago. Today these theories are less important because agriculture plays a smaller part in the economy of industrialized nations. Farm production, although still affected, is somewhat less dependent upon favorable weather.

INNOVATIONS

One of the most widely discussed theories—one that lends itself to a modern industrial society—is the *innovation theory*, developed principally by the late Harvard professor Joseph Schumpeter (see p. 61). According to Schumpeter new ideas and processes, whether they be new methods of doing business (supermarkets), new machines (computers), new products (television), or the opening up of new sources of raw materials (gold rush), are introduced in clusters. Although these inventions and discoveries may be made during a period of contraction of the economy, it is not until a few daring innovators put money into developing them that a wave of investments is made. This leads to an expansion of the economy, stimulating production and income. However, the wave will finally run its course, leading in time to recession and depression. During the slowdown new ideas and processes will be developed, but they will have to wait for enterprising men or firms to introduce them.

Some inventions, such as the steam engine and the automobile, have led to numerous other inventions and have resulted in tremendous investments in these areas. Other innovations have resulted only in minor investments. This is particularly true of fads, such as miniature golf and hula hoops. What other innovations affecting business activity can you think of?

Internal causes of cycles

Theories based on internal causes relate fluctuation to factors within the economy itself. As the economy expands, forces are generated that will, at a certain level, work to bring about a contraction. Likewise, as a recession reaches the point of a depression, forces within the economy will reverse the cycle. Examples of internal causes are underconsumption, overinvestment, psychological factors, and monetary causes. Let us explore the logic related to the last two of these theories.

PSYCHOLOGICAL FACTORS

Those who prefer the theory of psychological causation (for example, the late English economist A. C. Pigou) criticize the innovation theory, claiming that it is not basic, since new ideas are always to be found. What is more basic is the optimistic outlook of businessmen who sense an improvement in the economic climate. They become receptive to inventions that have yet to be tried. When other businessmen learn that more investments are being made, they are anxious to "get in" at the beginning of the expansion. An upswing, particularly in the more basic industries, increases employment and personal income. This, in turn, encourages consumers to go out and spend. An increase in consumer spending encourages retailers to build up their inventories before prices rise. New firms may be encouraged to enter the marketplace, further increasing investment and employment. Their entry will also lead to increased competition.

Just before the revival has reached its height and becomes a full-fledged prosperity, there will be some business leaders, cautious and pessimistic, who will begin to offset the trends, fearing that expansion has reached its limit. They will start to curtail operations, eliminating overtime work for their employees, reducing the size of their inventories, and discontinuing planned expansion. Other businessmen, hearing of these contraction activities, may become frightened. Workers may sense the uncertainty and fear a reduction in their earnings. This will affect their buying habits and will contribute to a recession.

The psychological theory, like the others examined, is criticized primarily because it is not basic; that is, it depends on other considerations. Business leaders and consumers are optimistic or pessimistic because of some other factor. President Hoover's suggestion during the depression of the early thirties that "prosperity is just around the corner" was of little value in reversing the contraction then occurring.

MONETARY THEORY

Another example of an internal cause is the monetary theory of the cycle, primarily developed by the English economist R. G. Hawtrey. The amount of money that banks have available for investment varies considerably. At the beginning of a revival, banks have plenty of money available and interest rates are low. The low interest rates and the ease in getting loans from the bank encourage businessmen to borrow and to expand their operations. As more and more do so, the availability of money declines and the interest rate increases. Prosperity is soon reached, but by the time it is, the banks no longer have money to lend out and interest rates are prohibitive for all but a few. Investments then decline, reducing spending and employment. Soon signs of a recession are visible. The decline will continue, finally reaching a depression. However, as the decline progresses, the supply of money that banks have available for credit starts to increase, causing interest rates to drop. Soon the easy access to low-cost loans will make investment opportunities too attractive for businessmen to pass up. Expansion will once again take place.

There is no doubt that the monetary theory explains a great deal about business fluctuations and, as we shall see in Chapter 13, proper action can do much to counter the direction of the cycle. However, there have been times when bank credit was available and interest rates were low but businessmen did not respond. Likewise, a shortage of money, with businessmen bidding interest rates up, has frequently failed to dampen enthusiasm in a period of expansion.

The importance of interacting factors

Most economists believe that business cycles are caused by a number of interacting factors, and that no single formula is sufficient to explain the complex set of reactions that actually takes place. Furthermore, analysts stress the differences between one business cycle and another and usually consider the primary causes to be different for each cycle. The labels of the composite index in Figure 10–6 show the causes of the major fluctuations in the American economy in the twentieth century.

Do they indicate any consistent pattern of causes for the various cycles?

The greatest fluctuations tend to occur in investment or in capital goods, which react to such external causes as wars, technological changes, and increases in population. Any additional investment due to external causes will set in motion a series of internal factors which will tend to magnify the results. Additional machinery means more jobs. More jobs will lead to bigger paychecks. Bigger paychecks increase the demand for goods and services. However, even with optimism running high the amount of capital goods will reach a saturation point and investment will begin to decline, leading to a shift in the cycle.

Although investment appears basic, it can be changed by external factors or it can be dependent on the level of income or production. Those who believe investment takes place in response to the growth of income and production, rather than the reverse, adhere to the *acceleration principle*. According to this view a high level of income is not enough to keep the economy moving upward, since the machinery in operation and the amount of merchandise in stores have been pushed to a high level, equal to what is needed. If no additional growth takes place, the only new machines

and merchandise required are for the purpose of replacing those which become worn out or are sold. Therefore, an increase in the demand for automobiles will cause the automobile producer to buy new machines to manufacture the automobiles; however, once he has enough machines for this high level of automobile production, the only new machines he needs are to replace those that are worn out. The producer of the machinery needed to make automobiles can maintain his high level of production only when there is a growing demand for automobiles, not a sustained high demand. Table 10–6 shows how a recession can start when sales merely level off rather than taking a definite turn downward.

Anticipating fluctuation

If businessmen are to operate successfully, they must anticipate the fluctuations of the business cycle and gear their production accordingly. In order to do this they frequently employ economists to determine the direction in which the economy seems to be moving. The government also employs a large staff of economists who track the business cycle and try to predict its direction. Using evidence from their studies, these specialists make recommendations in an effort to reduce the extremes of the cycle and to maintain stability in the economy.

Table 10–6 Business Fluctuation Explained by the Acceleration Principle

	OUTPUT OF "BUILD-A-CITY" SETS	MACHINES USED IN PRODUCTION	NEW MACHINES PURCHASED		
			REPLACEMENT	EXPANSION	TOTAL
1962	100,000	5	1	0	1
1963	120,000	6	1	1	2
1964	140,000	7	1	1	2
1965	160,000	8	1	1	2
1966	160,000	8	1	0	1

Merely sustaining consumer production at a high level, as shown above for 1966, is not enough to keep the producer of capital goods at the same level of production. The producer of machinery depends on a growing market at the consumer level if he is to avoid a contraction of his business. The same principle holds true for the wholesaler supplying the retailer with merchandise.

ECONOMISTS PREDICT CONTINUED EXPANSION IN U.S. ECONOMY FOR YEAR

SAN FRANCISCO — A survey of economists in government, business, and the academic world reveals the overwhelming majority to be optimistic about the year ahead. Most think that the current expansion, now in its fifth year, will continue at about the same rate, with a moderate tapering off at the end of the year.

They predict that the gross national product will rise about 6 percent, or about $40 billion, that prices will remain quite stable, and that unemployment will fluctuate between 3.8 and 4.2 percent of the labor force. They also predict record profits and personal income.

A few of the economists surveyed are less optimistic. They fear that strikes in several major industries may check the present expansion. They also foresee that any major wage increases above 4 percent, higher than the estimate for increased productivity per worker, will be inflationary and may discourage new business investment.

Both businesses and government are dependent on economists' forecasts in planning for the future. As in weather forecasting, errors will occur due to the use of imperfect tools and unpredictable variables.

FORECASTING CYCLES

Many students of economic theory, such as Joseph Schumpeter (see p. 61), have turned their attention to the problem of business cycles. Recently many economists have stressed the need to identify cyclical patterns and, if possible, to counter their severe effects.

It is important that fluctuations in business activity be predicted and corrective action prescribed. What success do economists have in forecasting business activity? There is little difficulty in predicting seasonal changes. So long as no major unexpected external cause occurs, long-range economic trends can be forecast with some accuracy. However, attempts to predict the ups and downs of the business cycle have too often been unsuccessful. Leading indicators—such as industrial stock prices, residential construction, steel production, and new orders for durable goods—have been of some help, but they have also been misleading at times. Just as jokes are made about errors in predicting the daily weather, so the economist is criticized when his carefully planned projection fails. Despite occasional mistakes, the weatherman keeps trying, and so does the economist. Each is employing new methods which will lead eventually to more accurate forecasting. We still rely heavily on the weatherman, since we know that he is right far more often than is our friend who predicts weather on the basis of the aches in his joints. In the same way business firms and government are far better off depending on the economic forecasts of the professional analyst.

In this chapter we have seen a variety of means for measuring the national economy. We have also observed the wide range of fluctuation occurring in the economy. This instability has been the major problem facing economists in the twentieth century. Recessions and depressions have meant unemployment, lower wages, reduced or vanished profits, losses and bankruptcy for business firms, smaller revenue for government, and a stifling of vitality and growth for the economy. In Chapter 11 we will examine methods of stabilizing the economy through the use of a new model of capitalism developed about thirty years ago. Before we turn our attention to solutions for the problem of economic instability, however, let us consider one aspect of it that is of particular significance to the immediate discussion.

Part C   The Problem: Is Economic Instability an Integral Part of the American Economy?

The problem defined here, unlike those previously dealt with, is not intended to be answered immediately. Rather, it is designed to help introduce you to some of the controversial thinking associated with the ideas presented in this unit. The tools needed to arrive at even a tentative conclusion will be discussed in the next four chapters, in addition to those already described here. Chapter 16, "Economic Systems Other Than Capitalism," will provide additional information and analysis, particularly with respect to communist criticism of capitalism and, in turn, the flaws inherent in this criticism.

Read the arguments that follow, keeping in mind that modern economic analysis and policy as developed since the mid-1930's and used since the end of World War II may provide some answers to the problem of economic instability. Whether these answers are sufficient or correct is a matter that you should consider very carefully as you continue with this unit.

A negative evaluation

Many economists and political leaders have looked upon our economic system— that of capitalism—with mixed feelings because of the weaknesses related to its cyclical behavior. Karl Marx, the major theoretician of scientific socialism, or communism (see p. 354), regarded capitalism as an important and essential part of the evolution of society and thought that it made significant contributions to man's attempt to find answers to the major questions of economics. He considered it far superior to the feudal system, which it replaced, in organizing society to produce the goods and services needed. By encouraging the accumulation of capital, the instruments for production could increase, thereby making greater production possible.

Marx believed, however, that the increased production would be of little benefit to the worker, whom he considered primarily responsible for production, as explained in the surplus value theory (see p. 121). The capitalist—the owner of the instruments of production—by denying the worker the full value for his production, prevented him from buying back the goods he produced. With a surplus of goods in the marketplace, competition would increase, with the stronger businesses absorbing the weaker. This narrowing of ownership would lead to a concentration of wealth among a few great capitalists, who gained their profits from unearned increment—that portion of wages that the workers rightfully earned but were not paid. An economic system thus organized would inevitably experience major business fluctuations.

Lenin, a disciple of Marx, took these ideas a step further, applying them to the world economic situation. Because workers lacked sufficient income to buy back the goods they produced, the capitalists would have to seek foreign markets for their surplus. They also needed a place to invest their capital. With an overexpansion of investment at home because of insufficient purchasing power to obtain the goods already on the market, interest rates at home would be lower than in backward nations. In order to secure these markets and investments, it would be necessary to have friendly governments or to control the governments in the foreign countries concerned. If these two methods did not work, it would become necessary to assume political control over the country. This theory is what the communists are referring to when they speak about "capitalistic imperialism."

According to Lenin, when capitalists throughout the world reach a saturation point in seeking markets and investing in backward countries, they must then turn either to wars or to wartime economies to bring an end to depressions. Huge government expenditures for armaments would stimulate production, leading to a business revival. Lenin concluded that only in an economy whose production is based purely on need rather than on profits and whose workers receive full value for their efforts can business cycles, with the misery that accompanies the depression phase, finally be eliminated.

Doubts about our economy's ability to eliminate major fluctuations in the business cycle are not confined to communists. A brief look at the actual record of business cycles—the occurrence of depressions accompanied by widespread human suffering—would cause most people to pause and wonder whether instability in business activity might not be an inherent disadvantage of our economic system. A frequent subject of controversy among responsible citizens is whether our economy could stand the effects of disarmament.

Do such doubts mean that Marx and Lenin were correct in their prophecy? Must we have war, cold or hot, in order to keep our machines humming and our workers employed? Must we choose between living in a world on the brink of a nuclear holocaust and living in a nation with millions of workers periodically unemployed and never being secure about their income? If we wish to eliminate this dilemma, must we turn to communism? None of these alternatives would be acceptable to the overwhelming majority of Americans, but there remain some irritating facts that cannot be ignored.

A brief review of any of the indicators in this chapter shows that business cycles do exist. The statistics show further that the years preceding the wars in this century were periods of depression and that wars brought recovery. After the wars primary

postwar depressions set in, only to be followed by the boom of prosperity. However, without the assist brought by a war economy, the wheels of our economy slowed down and recessions started.

A closer look at the period since World War II illustrates the pattern described above. After the boom of the war and a short period of recession and reconversion to a peacetime economy, the combination of stored-up demand for civilian goods and accumulation of savings by workers ushered in a period of great prosperity. Late in 1948 the economy started to contract, leading to a recession in 1949. The next boom came with the Korean conflict, which lasted until 1953. During this time military expenditures tripled, with a corresponding expansion of production. With the end of the war came a contraction of the economy. This was short-lived, for another expansion took place and lasted four years. Recession in 1957–58 and again in 1960–61 interrupted generally good times. The recovery that followed can be attributed to our large military expenditures, our missile program, and our near-$100 billion federal budget.

Although no serious depression has occurred since the 1930's and no total war since 1945, the amount of money we have spent for armaments to maintain national defense in the past several decades has certainly been a major factor in keeping a large portion of our economy working. Our defense program accounts for approximately ten percent of our employed labor force and about the same percentage of the value of our goods and services. Certain industries and regions are almost completely dependent on defense contracts. Is the fifty billion dollars a year we spend on defense the factor that insulates us against a serious depression?

A positive evaluation

In 1962 a committee of economists was brought together to study the economic consequences of disarmament for the

United States Arms Control and Disarmament Agency. The conclusions of the committee indicate that disarmament should almost certainly be taken by degrees and that important readjustments would have to be made to absorb the surplus capacity in defense industry if defense expenditures were reduced. However, the committee suggested that the same kind of planning we now use to take care of declining industries, such as coal, might be employed to cope with the decline in spending for the military. They suggested a plan for meeting this problem which would involve more government action, including such specific suggestions as (1) large retraining programs, (2) strengthening unemployment compensation, (3) granting more liberal benefits to workers who are released, and (4) planning for more consumer-oriented research and for diversification by shifting defense contractors to production of civilian goods. They concluded that if the government is willing to plan ahead and lead in fostering an optimistic program, there is no need for a contraction of the economy to occur as a result of disarmament.

One of the leading students of business cycles, in answer to a question about the amount of progress we have made in creating economic stability, said that although business cycles are still characteristic of our economy, their impact on individuals has been appreciably reduced in the last twenty-five years. The last serious depression occurred in the 1930's; by comparison the last four recessions have been extremely mild, with the longest one lasting only thirteen months. Changes in the structure of the American economy and the action taken by both industry and government in response to changes in business activity have not only made our recessions shorter and less severe but they have also changed the nature of the decline. While many of the factors making up the composite picture of our business cycle continue to fluctuate con-

siderably, personal income and consumption have been relatively stable. In addition, businessmen, knowing that the government is not going to stand idly by while unemployment mounts, no longer allow their inventories to drop quite so far. Such action on the part of business has served as a stabilizing element in maintaining production. The great progress that has been made in the last generation in reducing economic instability can be continued if coordinated action between government, business, and labor can be used with courage and vision to offset cyclical tendencies.

Although four recessions have taken place since 1948, not once did disposable personal income or consumer expenditures decline. These recessions have lasted only half as long as the average of pre-World War II recessions. The end of the conflict in Korea brought about a decline of $14.3 billion in government spending. In addition, business concerns canceled $12.9 billion in contemplated new plant equipment and inventories. Even with such reductions, the GNP declined only about $2 billion.

Karl Marx said that depressions were the result of the workers' not receiving full value for their labor and consequently not being able to buy back the goods they produced. However, from 1948 to 1962 the total financial compensation to American employees of corporations more than doubled while corporate profits before taxes increased only about 60%. With consumer spending rising even during periods of minor contractions in business activity and with the poor getting richer (the number of families whose income was below $4,000 a year was reduced by half from 1950 to 1964), it would appear that the prophecy of Marx was less than accurate.

Considering an answer

Now that you have read two distinct points of view, each persuasive when considered by itself, you are in a position to investigate the problem further. Although no one denies that economic fluctuations exist, there is great controversy about how serious they are to our economy and to our society. We need to examine these variations further to see if significant progress in controlling them has been made, whether a depression like that of the thirties could happen again, and whether disarmament is possible without a serious depression.

In Chapter 11 we will go on to discuss the theory of income determination, which will give you some insight into the forces that affect our level of income. The three following chapters will discuss other conditions and issues relating to the problem introduced here. Will your answer after reading them be the same as your tentative conclusion now?

REVIEW: *the highlights of the chapter*

1. The study of the economy as a whole is called macroeconomics, in contrast to microeconomics, the study of individual units.
2. Gross national product (GNP) is the total retail value of all the goods and services produced during a year.
3. There are three methods used to determine gross national product: the product (or output) approach, the expenditure approach, and the income approach.
4. The product approach uses as its base the sum of goods and services produced. The expenditure approach determines GNP by totaling spending in the marketplace. The buyers are divided into four categories—individuals buying as households, government, businesses, and foreign purchasers. The income approach arrives at gross national income (GNI) and refers to total payments made to those involved in production in addition to capital consumption and indirect business taxes. The gross national income is equal to gross national production.
5. In determining GNP, only that value produced for the market is counted. As a result, labor that is not rewarded by wages or payment cannot be considered part of GNP.
6. Net national product (NNP) measures the value of goods and services added to the nation and is determined by subtracting from GNP the value of the capital consumed in producing it.
7. National income (NI) measures income rather than product and is the total earned income of all the factors of production. It is NNP minus indirect business taxes.
8. Personal income (PI) is the income received by individuals before they pay their personal taxes. It is determined by subtracting Social Security payments and corporation savings and taxes from national income and adding transfer payments and government interest.
9. Disposable personal income (DPI) refers to the total value of personal consumption expenditures and personal savings. It is determined by subtracting personal taxes from personal income.

10. There are three kinds of variation in business activity: seasonal, trend, and cyclical.

11. There are four phases to a business cycle: recovery, prosperity, recession, and depression.

12. The average length of a full business cycle is slightly less than four years. More time is spent in expanding than in contracting, and more time in prosperity and depression than in recession and recovery.

13. External causes of business cycles refer to forces outside the economic system. The ones most frequently referred to are those that relate to weather, war, population growth, innovation, and political events.

14. Internal causes of business cycles refer to factors within the economic system. These include overinvestment, psychological factors, and monetary causes.

15. Although investment (capital goods) shows the greatest fluctuation, most economists think that business cycles are caused by many interacting factors, with no simple formula sufficient to explain all reactions.

16. It is important for the health of the economy to be able to interpret trends, predict business activity, and prescribe policy in order to reduce the extremes of the business cycle.

IN CONCLUSION: some aids to understanding

Terms for review

GNP (gross national product)	macroeconomics
NNP (net national product)	microeconomics
NI (national income)	double counting
PI (personal income)	transfer payments
DPI (disposable personal income)	business cycle
	unearned increment
Great Depression	representative indicators
capital consumption	leading indicators
external and internal theories	coincident indicators
acceleration principle	lagging indicators

Names to know

W. Stanley Jevons	Joseph Schumpeter
A. C. Pigou	R. G. Hawtrey

Questions for review

1. What is the essential difference between the macro and the micro approach in the study of economics?

2. One of the tools used to compare the economic strength of nations is the GNP of each nation.
   (a) What methods may be used to arrive at GNP?
   (b) What are the errors that may occur in computing GNP?
   (c) Why are "constant dollars" needed for a true picture of GNP?
3. What other methods and measures are available to judge the strength of the national economy?
4. Draw up a series of equations to demonstrate the meaning of each of the following: GNP, NNP, NI, PI, DPI.
5. The state of health of the business community may be judged by various indicators. How may this evaluation be made over a long period? What dangers are there in forecasting?
6. Cyclical variations are a constant threat to economic stability.
   (a) What is meant by the business cycle?
   (b) What are its various component phases?
   (c) Describe the external and internal forces which are responsible for fluctuation in business activities.
   (d) Why is it important for the businessman to make a successful prediction of business trends?

Additional questions and problems

1. Psychological factors and monetary causes are the bases of internal theories regarding fluctuation in business that are discussed in this chapter. Select one of these and use it to trace the various phases of the business cycle shown in Figure 10–6.
2. Explain your reaction to the statement that economists are generally successful in predicting business activities.
3. Compare the theories of W. Stanley Jevons and Joseph Schumpeter regarding business cycles. Using specific examples to support your viewpoint, try to decide which of the two theories you consider more pertinent today.
4. Assume that a depression or recession occurred in your community. Discuss with other members of your class the effect it might have on each of the following: (a) your family's income, (b) your own income (if you were employed), (c) retail stores and restaurants, and (d) industries. Is it possible for anyone to benefit from the unfavorable economic conditions?
5. Explain why it would not be valid to say that the national income and the gross national product are equal.
6. Using the *Economic Almanac*, prepare a series of graphs showing
   (a) GNP
   (b) personal income
   (c) disposable personal income
   (d) national income
   for the years 1929, 1933, 1939, 1945, 1949, 1954, 1957, 1962, and 1966. What conclusions can be drawn from your material?

7. The occurrence of business cycles has led to criticism of the capitalistic system.
   (a) Present the basic ideas of Karl Marx in his surplus value theory.
   (b) What addition to communist theory did Lenin introduce?
   (c) How has the economic growth of the United States in the last twenty-five years been a refutation of these theories?

8. Business cycles have had a significant influence on our country's economic development.
   (a) Make a chart of the business cycles which have occurred in the United States from 1800 to the present.
   (b) Explain the causes of the major variations before 1933.
   (c) In your opinion should the federal government exercise more controls? Give reasons to support your answer.

11 National Income Analysis—A New Model

Preview

In the United States we have the resources and the science and technology which ensure enough production to meet our basic needs for survival, with many luxuries in addition. Unfortunately, our system has frequently operated far below its potential level of output. When workers are unemployed and resources are not utilized, our economic system is falling short of optimum performance.

Economists set up models of economic systems in the hope that these will guide us in making full and efficient use of our productive resources. Most economists set as a goal the operation of our economy at a full-employment level without inflation. In this chapter we will examine a new model that will show how the level of our national income is determined and how this income can be changed to sustain full employment without inflation. We will compare the classical model and the Keynesian model, both operating within the framework of our mixed capitalist system, to see how each is designed to achieve the goal of full employment without inflation.

Overview

Explain the relationship between a nation's income and employment level.

What are the major components that determine the size of gross national product?

How important is it for a nation as wealthy as ours to utilize its resources fully?

Should a country try to operate its economy in the same manner as a family? Give reasons for your answer.

Part A   Full Employment Without Inflation—
The Classical Answer

Identifying our goals

In Unit II we mentioned that economists develop theories and prepare models to show how an economic system should work in answering the major questions of allocation. We showed how, in our market economy, the price system allocates resources; we also found that some of our resources, such as labor, may not always be fully utilized. People in our country are increasingly agreed on the desirability of setting as a goal for our economy a level of production that would provide jobs for everyone who wants to work. When production is at a level below this, our economy faces a decrease in demand and a general contraction of the economy. On the other hand, if production goals are set at a level beyond what our resources can achieve, the result is inflation, not additional production. For example, employers collectively do not obtain additional labor by bidding against each other for the services of workers.

Most economists believe that a *full-employment economy* (one in which everyone in the working force who wants to work can find a job) without inflation is a goal for all countries. Maintaining this condition involves smoothing out the peaks and troughs of the business cycle so that stability and economic growth are consistent with the increase in resources for production. The problem may be stated in this way: How can our system yield a GNP large enough to sustain a full-employment economy without causing inflation?

GNP AND FULL EMPLOYMENT

When economists refer to a "full-employment GNP," they mean that the economy is producing enough goods and services (GNP) to employ all those in the labor force who wish to work. If some of the working force remains unemployed when the GNP is at $700 billion, additional pro-

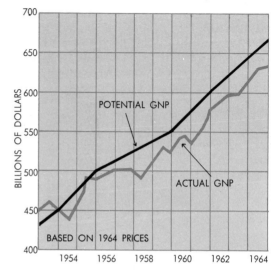

Figure 11-1   GNP: Potential and Actual Performance

The difference between our economy's actual level of production and its potential level is sufficient to eliminate most of our nation's poverty.

duction of goods and services would be required to raise the level of employment. Increasing the GNP to $750 billion might provide the jobs necessary to reduce unemployment. It is important to recognize that a small percentage of unemployment is accepted as normal. Because there are always some people in the process of moving into or out of the labor force or perhaps moving from one job to another, unemployment below four percent of the labor force is usually considered full employment. With eighty million people in the labor force, unemployment below 3.2 million would be considered full employment.

Determining GNP:
the classical viewpoint

Although considerable agreement exists on the desirability of a full-employment economy, differences remain regarding the methods by which this condition can and should be achieved.

The classical, or laissez-faire, economist accepts the general principle that the economy should operate without interference with the laws of supply and demand and that government should be involved in the economy as little as possible. Under these conditions, flexibility of prices, wages, and interest rates will keep our economy producing at a level high enough to sustain full employment without inflation. Although there might be times when external causes would bring about production above or below a level of full employment without inflation, such deviations would be temporary. A closer look at the classical

economist's position, using tools from the previous chapter on national income measurement, will help clarify how gross national product is determined.

Figure 11–2 is designed to assist in explaining how the gross national product is determined. It will be most helpful to you if you will refer to it in proceeding from step to step in the explanation that follows. Figure 11–2 is divided into four parts, (a) to (d), and will be explained as we move from the left side, (a), to the right side, (d).

FULL-EMPLOYMENT LEVEL (a)

We have defined full employment as the amount of goods and services we would have to produce in order to employ at least 96 percent of our labor force (at or below the four percent unemployment rate). This

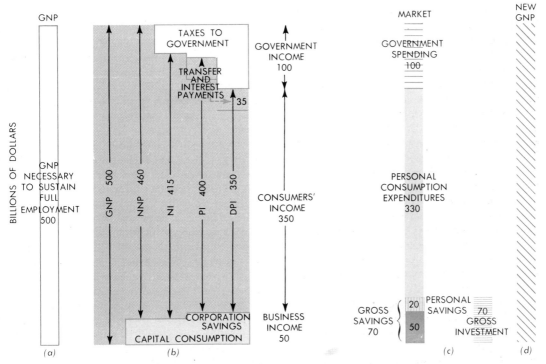

Figure 11–2 Determination of GNP

Gross national product will remain at the full-employment level if government spending equals government revenue and business invests all the money saved.

amount increases each year as productive capacity grows. As the labor force becomes larger and more skilled, and as the use of equipment and other resources becomes more efficient, an ever-increasing gross national product will be required to sustain full employment.

Economists can estimate the size of GNP that is needed to achieve a full-employment level (as in Figure 11–2) without inflation. In Figure 11–2, we use the figure $500 billion because it is easier to work with. In reality it would be between $720 and $800 billion, depending on the growth of our productive resources and on the year being considered.

GROSS NATIONAL INCOME (GNI) (b)

You will recall that gross national income is the same figure as gross national product. The former measures the dollars received for producing whereas the latter measures the retail value of the product. In (b) we see how the $500 billion of GNI is distributed. As we move from left to right, from gross national income to disposable personal income, income is divided among three groups: business, government, and consumers.

As shown at the top of the chart, $135 billion goes to government, mainly in the form of taxes. However, of this amount, $35 billion is returned to individuals in the form of transfer and interest payments. This leaves government with $100 billion. At the bottom, $50 billion is put aside by all businesses for capital consumption and by corporations for savings. Individuals retain $350 billion in disposable personal income (including the $35 billion from transfer and interest payments which is indicated by the arrow on the graph). The right-hand side of (b) is what the economy looks like before consumers go to the market to spend. Our $500 billion gross national income is now divided into $100 billion for government, $50 billion for business, and $350 billion for consumers.

EXPENDITURES IN THE MARKET (c)

In (c) we see the GNP (the product side) and the expenditures which are made for goods and services by those now in possession of the dollars (GNI). Keep in mind that the two sides are equal. If all the GNI ($500 billion) is spent, all the goods and services ($500 billion) will be sold.

To clarify the explanation, let us visualize production as taking place throughout a single year but expenditures as taking place only at the end of the year, when annual production is complete. Imagine for that occasion a giant market with the entire $500 billion GNP for sale and with government, consumers, and business there to buy.

In (c) we observe that government is spending exactly the same amount as it has received (excluding the money it has taken in and returned for transfer and interest payments). It has taken $100 billion from businesses and individuals in the form of taxes and has then spent that $100 billion in the market. This would be that rare occurrence when government balanced the budget—a situation that our classical economist would doubtless approve of!

Next, consumers go to the market. Consumers have $350 billion to spend—their take-home pay (DPI). However, we see that their personal consumption expenditures amount to only $330 billion, $20 billion being placed in personal savings. If this $20 billion is not spent by someone, $20 billion worth of production will remain unsold.

Now it is businesses' turn to buy. They find it necessary to replace used equipment and inventories for the production of goods and services for the next year. When businesses go to the marketplace to buy, they do not make purchases to satisfy their needs as consumers. Instead, they buy to produce or distribute goods and services to other producers, to distributors, or to the consumer. Thus, instead of calling their purchases "consumption expenditures," we call them *investments* (that which is used to further production).

In (*b*) we can see that businessmen put aside a total of $50 billion—$42 billion for capital consumption and $8 billion in corporation savings. In (*c*) we have added to this $50 billion the $20 billion that consumers have saved to give us $70 billion, a figure that we call *gross savings*. The $70 billion in gross savings means there must be $70 billion worth of production left unsold in the market. It is crucial to know what will happen to the gross savings.

If businessmen invest the total amount of gross savings ($70 billion), they will use up the remainder of GNP. Note in (*c*) of Figure 11–2 that gross savings and gross investment are the same. That part of income that had not previously been spent (gross savings) has now been used to buy up the remaining production through investment. This means that in the example all the goods and services on the market have been purchased, since all government income has already been spent, as well as most of the income received by the various factors of production which has been spent as personal consumption expenditures. As our imaginary year ends, all the gross national income has been used to purchase all the gross national product. What do you think will be the size of next year's GNP?

THE NEW GNP (*d*)

Business, which provides the bulk of the GNP, has in the past year produced and sold an output worth $500 billion. It is not likely that businesses would try to reduce their production. Since everything produced has been sold, why should business consider producing less? Lower production would mean that the price tags for all production would add up to less than $500 billion. It would also mean that less than $500 billion would be paid in income (GNI).

Why wouldn't companies try to produce more than in the past year? They might try, but if they did so they would immediately

encounter problems, such as a shortage of workers. (At present we are assuming that no additional workers or other productive resources are added to the working force.) You will remember that GNP has been set at a full-employment level. If businesses seek to get more workers by raising wages, these workers will have to come from some other industry. The additional production in one industry will be offset by a decline in the production in another. As businessmen compete with one another for scarce workers and resources, wages will rise. However, since total production would be no greater, we would have a demand greater than supply. Prices would rise. The new GNP would *look* bigger because the prices of goods and services would be higher, and income would be greater because workers would be getting more wages. (Other factors of production would also have larger income.) This new GNP would be higher in dollars, but it would be the same as the old GNP in goods and services. In other words, if we try to move the GNP higher when production is already at a full-employment level and when capacity to produce is not being increased, the result is inflation. The exception to this situation would be an increase in capacity to produce, made possible by using more workers and more efficient machines.

We can conclude that if the economy is operating at a full-employment level and businesses invest the same amount as that which is saved, GNP will continue at the same high and desirable level.

Investment and saving

What if investment is not equal to savings? Certainly business cannot always be expected to invest the same amount as gross savings. Since saving (the opposite of spending) and investment seem to be the keys to determining the new GNP, let us see what happens when they are not equal. Figure 11–3 shows gross investment when (*a*) less than and (*b*) more than gross savings.

SAVINGS LARGER THAN INVESTMENT

Let us suppose that businessmen have a gloomy outlook for the next year. Some production remains, even after both government and consumers have been in the market. Businessmen, looking at the remainder, sense that there has been less buying than they hoped for (more savings), or they think that people, having bought so much in the previous year, might cut back on their spending in the next year. Under either of these circumstances businesses will be less likely to invest very much money for next year's production. They may buy fewer machines or let inventories in their stores decline. If enough businesses do this, total investment will add up to less than total savings and there will be goods and services left in the market. Companies will then cut back their production because the supply of production is greater than the demand. They will employ fewer resources. Some workers will have to be let go, some machinery will be idle, and marginal firms will be forced out of business. As a result of these changes, the new GNP will be lower. The decline in production will cause a drop in employment—below the level of full employment. It would appear from this illustration that when savings exceed investment, a lower GNP will result. This condition is illustrated in Figure 11-3(a).

INVESTMENT LARGER THAN SAVINGS

What would happen if businessmen invested more than the amount saved? Let us suppose that they come to the market expecting that purchases in the new year will be larger than in the past year. As they start buying the remaining production, they soon realize that there is a greater demand

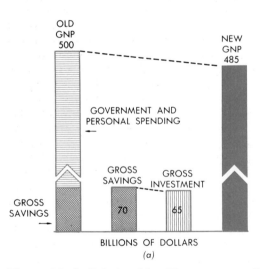
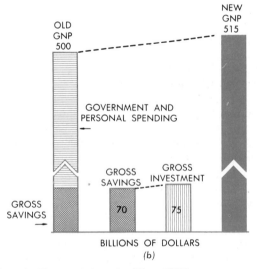

Figure 11-3 Relationship of Investment to Savings in Determining the New GNP

When GNP has been at full employment and gross investment is less than gross savings, the new GNP will fall. The new GNP will be less than the old GNP by some multiple of the difference between savings and investment ($70B − $65 = $5B. $500B − $485B = $15B. $15B ÷ $5B = 3 (the multiplier).

When GNP has been at full employment and gross investment is more than gross savings, the new GNP will rise by some multiple of the difference between them (3 × $5B = $15B greater GNP). The new GNP will be no larger in goods and services but will appear greater because of inflation.

for production than there is supply of production. You might reasonably ask how this is possible when the income side and the production side are supposed to be the same. The answer is that the money businesses use for investment comes from savings, but not necessarily from savings confined to last year. Besides, as you will learn in Chapter 13, banks can extend the credit necessary to provide money to businesses, with the result that current investment can exceed current savings.

If investment does become greater than savings, and if *aggregate demand* (the expenditures of government, consumers, and business) exceeds the aggregate supply of current production, the GNP will increase. However, since we are already operating at a full-employment level, as shown in Figure 11–2, the increase of investment over savings will lead to inflation. This occurs because the demand for production exceeds the capacity to produce. Figure 11–3(*b*) shows what happens to GNP when investment is larger than savings in a full-employment economy.

Changing interest rates

According to classical theory, the two conditions pictured in Figure 11–3 would be only temporary. Two factors would act to correct these situations: interest rates and wage-price flexibility. Let us see what effect these factors might have.

If businessmen invested less than savings (Figure 11–3*a*), the GNP would fall below the level of full employment. This economic decline would result in a decline in the interest rates on savings as well as lower rates for those who wished to borrow money for investment. With more money available from savings than investors wish to borrow, the laws of supply and demand would bring about a reduction in interest. The new low rates of interest would soon provide the necessary corrections in the economy. Since interest is an inducement for savings, the lower interest would pro-

duce more spending and less saving. Previously, the high interest rates may have discouraged businessmen from investing. Now lower rates for loans would encourage them to borrow in order to increase their inventory or buy new machines. With lower interest rates stimulating consumer spending and business investment, savings and investment would soon be in balance and the GNP would once again be at the full-employment level.

Wage-price flexibility

What if the changing interest rates did not produce all the results desired? If this were the case, the classical theorist would expect flexibility in wages and prices to do the rest of the job. With GNP still below the full-employment level the surplus labor resulting from this decline would bring about a reduction in wages. The lowering of wages would cut down the cost of production, allowing businessmen to reduce prices on their goods. These lower prices would lead to increased sales, requiring employers to hire additional workers. On the income side the factors of production would receive less in dollars (lower wages, lower profits) because prices have declined. However, costs on the product side would also amount to less because of the lower prices there. The number of dollars of GNP might be lower and the sum of the price tags might be lower, *but the all-important sum of goods and services would be at the level of a full-employment economy.* When prices and income both decline the same amount, the real GNP (that is, the goods and services produced and consumed) will not be reduced. A little time to allow wages and prices to adjust downward will bring a new dollar figure (perhaps $480 billion) for the full-employment GNP.

According to classical theory, interest rates and wage-price flexibility also exert a corrective influence when investment is greater than savings. What might the stages of this self-regulating process be?

Are there errors in the classical theory?

The classical economist described the capitalistic system as a successfully self-regulating system that would always come to rest—that is, reach a state of equilibrium—at the full-employment level without inflation. According to classical theory this result occurs because of flexibility in the interest rate for savings and investment and because of flexibility in wages and prices.

In opposition to classical beliefs, however, many economists contend that events have shown that the theoretical readjustment does not always take place. Small rises and declines in the business cycle could be explained as temporary maladjustments that correct themselves; some of the larger peaks and troughs could be explained by external causes such as wars. The major economic occurrence which cannot be explained so easily is the Great Depression of the 1930's. During those years many of the economists who followed the classical tradition, as well as some of the political leaders and businessmen who accepted their theories, generally believed that "prosperity was just around the corner." They said that if we would just wait a little longer, the natural self-regulating factors that make the market economy an excellent system would correct the terrible imbalances that were producing a shrinking GNP and contributing to even greater unemployment.

Although these people were willing to wait for the corrective effect to occur, a majority of the American people apparently

were not. With the growing readiness to find other solutions, the time was ripe for the introduction of a new economic model, or at least some modification of the old one. There was increasing need to explain why self-regulation was not doing the job required and to recommend action for relief.

Before unemployment insurance, expanded government welfare, and assistance under the antipoverty program became available, the unemployed often suffered great hardship. Conditions became acute during periods of recession and depression.

Part B   A New Model (Government Excluded)

John Maynard Keynes and the "new economics"

Politically, the change in our economic policy is associated with the New Deal and Franklin D. Roosevelt; in economics it is

associated with an English economist, John Maynard Keynes (pronounced *kānz*). As the originator of a new model, Keynes was responsible for bringing about a major revolution in economic thinking. In the course

JOHN MAYNARD KEYNES AND THE "NEW ECONOMICS"

John Maynard Keynes (1883–1946), more than any other economist in the twentieth century, is responsible for modifying classical thinking among the industrial nations of the West. During the 1930's the United States and the nations of western Europe were mired in the Great Depression. As the inoperativeness of the self-correcting mechanism of classical economics became more apparent, the need for new solutions to the problem became even more acute. However, the microeconomic approach of the marginalist school provided no satisfactory answer. Many economists realized that new concepts must be introduced if capitalism was to survive.

The first significant contribution to a solution of the problem came from the Swedish economists, particularly Professor Gunnar Myrdal, using the aggregate or macroeconomic approach. Their analysis of the relationship between savings, investment, and income was very similar to the conclusion of Keynes in his monumental work, *The General Theory of Employment, Interest, and Money*, published in 1936. Keynes emphasized the correlation between national income and employment. He showed that income was determined by consumption, investment, and government spending. Consumption changes with income (as do savings), but income is mainly influenced by the amount of investment. Because investment is the least stable of the three items determining income and because it may not be adequate to maintain national income sufficient to achieve full employment, the government should intervene to promote full employment. This it is able to do through the use of appropriate monetary and fiscal policies.

Economists today recognize that Keynes' approach had certain weaknesses. It was oriented for the short run and the model was static, without significant attention to economic growth. Furthermore, he did not recognize that in the long run people's spending habits change, adapting to the higher levels of income. Nevertheless, Keynes' ideas, together with related theories of economic growth, form the basis for the "new economics," the theory most widely accepted by economists in the nations of the Western industrial world.

of it many economists turned from classical theory to the "new economics," based largely on Keynes's theories. According to the new ideas, a mature capitalist economy is not always able to maintain itself at a full-employment level without the onset of inflation. Inflation occurs because the two key items for self-regulation — changing interest rates and wage-price flexibility — are not sufficiently effective in preventing it.

DOES INTEREST REGULATE SAVINGS AND INVESTMENT?

The classical economist reasons that consumers will deprive themselves of some goods and services if they have sufficient incentive. To understand the flaws in this reasoning, ask yourself these questions: Would you take your savings out of a bank and spend them if interest rates declined? Is high interest the incentive that makes you save? Although a surplus of savings is going to lower the interest rate and allow businessmen to borrow at lower rates of interest, would you, if you were in business, increase your investment when people are spending less, even if you could borrow at lower rates?

Now let us consider some further questions. Suppose that the economy was already at a full-employment GNP and that businesses were investing in excess of savings (an inflationary situation). With a shortage of savings, interest rates rise, thus encouraging people to save and discouraging business from investing. Would you, as a businessman, refuse to invest because of higher interest rates at a time when people are buying more and prices seem to be rising, particularly when you know that rising prices will make it easier for you, a debtor, to pay back your loan?

If your answer to each of these questions is *yes*, you have a tendency to agree with the classical theorists. Before you arrive at a final answer, however, read on and study additional information that might influence your decision. In a later chapter we will see that interest rates do play a part in encouraging and discouraging business investment, but not necessarily in the self-regulating manner identified above.

Challenges to the classical theory

Some of the answers which you have given to the preceding questions may conflict with the classical interpretation of the function of interest. But if interest rates are not the key in determining savings and investment, what is? Modern economists have discovered that saving and investing are seldom, if ever, carried on by the same people. In reality much of existing savings comes from families that may be motivated to put money aside for anticipated spending or for financial security. Studies reveal that savings are closely tied to the level of national income. The higher the national income, the greater the amount of savings. As for investment, the most significant factor in its determination is the amount of profit that businessmen *anticipate* making. Although interest rates can be and sometimes are factors in determining profits, businessmen will more probably react to rising or falling sales expectations. Few businesses would increase their inventories or plant equipment when the economy is contracting, even though interest rates may be low.

The theory of self-correction through wage-price flexibility is also subject to strong criticism. In this case the flaws are probably due to major differences between the classical model and the actual func-

tioning of the economy. A downswing in the economy will undoubtedly cause some decline in wages and prices, but that downward movement is very limited. The cost of labor is actually prevented from declining significantly. This inflexibility of wages is due primarily to two factors: minimum wage laws and the power of organized labor in maintaining wage levels.

The movement of prices is equally "sticky." Many of the products we buy come from industries in which prices are administered. Other prices may also be influenced by price-fixing or by regulation by government or business. As a result recessions do not usually bring any significant decline in prices. Certainly there is not enough decline to result in any significant increase in purchasing power because of the lower prices. Therefore, instead of a downswing resulting in a lowering of wages and prices, we find fewer workers employed and prices declining so slightly that increased buying is unlikely. As a result little self-correction takes place.

Consumption, savings, and income

If traditional capitalism, contrary to theory, does not have a feature of self-correction, what can be done to provide a full-employment economy without inflation? As you have already learned, the GNP level is dependent on the relationship between savings and investment. Having explored the criticisms of the classical interpretation of these key factors, let us see what Keynes and other modern economists learned about them that might be useful in developing a new model for our economy — one that would remain within the broad framework of capitalism.

As we saw previously (p. 181), when we speak of savings, we are also speaking about consumption. This is true because of their complementary nature: What we do not save we spend and, of course, what we do not spend we save. Therefore, our discussion of savings is equally a discussion of consumption. We must also point out that for the present a consideration of government is omitted because we are assuming that government income and expenditure will be exactly equal. In Figure 11–2 we used the figure of $500 billion to represent a full-employment GNP without inflation. Since government income and expenditure amounted to $100 billion, the full-employment noninflationary GNP for the private sector (including both consumers and business) would be $400 billion.

When we examine national income statistics, we find a very strong and direct relationship between consumption and GNP. As any of the five major national income measurements go up, the amount of consumption also increases. Figure 11–4 shows consumption and disposable personal income for a thirty-six-year period. Note that consumption increased by almost the same percentage as did disposable personal income except for the years of World War II. During those years the availability of goods

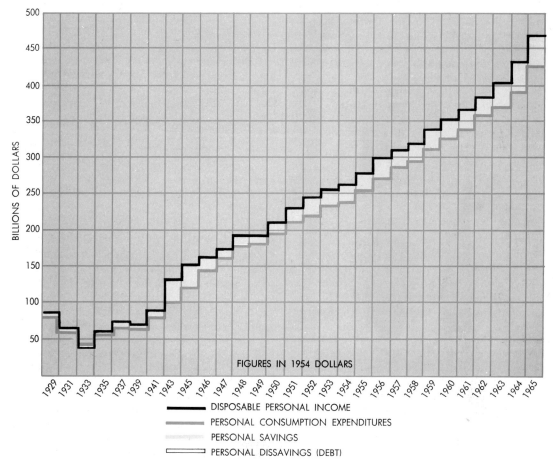

DISPOSABLE PERSONAL INCOME
PERSONAL CONSUMPTION EXPENDITURES
PERSONAL SAVINGS
PERSONAL DISSAVINGS (DEBT)

FIGURES IN 1954 DOLLARS

Figure 11–4   Disposable Personal Income Influences the Level of Consumption

As disposable personal income increases, so does consumption. Compare savings in the last ten years with those of 1933 and the World War II years. SOURCE: U.S. Department of Commerce estimates

for private consumption was too small to be considered typical. However, during a recent decade, consumption has been approximately 92 to 95 percent of DPI.

In 1960, DPI was $350 billion and consumption was $339 billion. Where was the $11 billion that was not spent? It must have been personal savings—that part of the DPI that was not consumed. If we measured savings for the last ten years, we would find that, like consumption, they too have been remarkably constant.

Figure 11–4 also tells something about personal savings, shown on that graph by the light shading, for those years when DPI is greater than personal expenditures. In most years since the Depression, substantial personal savings are indicated.

Looking at the year 1933 we see something quite different. What does this change mean? If the spaces (light shading) below the black line and above the green line indicate savings, then the space (shown in white) below the green line and above the black line must indicate dissavings, or spending more than was received. How can we spend more than we earn? As we have seen (p. 181), we do it by borrowing, by using savings accumulated in earlier years, or by buying on credit.

At very low levels of income people will spend more than they earn. As income increases, consumption and income will come into balance. Soon income will surpass consumption and savings will grow. The greater the aggregate income (DPI), the greater the consumption, but also the greater the savings.

A new economic tool: the 45° line

For a better understanding of the relationship between income, savings, and consumption, we should become familiar with a new economic tool, shown in Figure 11–5. On the graph the horizontal axis measures income and the vertical axis measures consumption. Line Y is a diagonal, 45°. Any point along the 45° line is

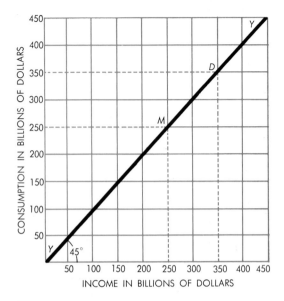

Figure 11–5   A New Tool: the 45° Line

Using the 45° line approach, a new tool, we can better understand the theory of income analysis. Points M and D on the line Y show consumption equal to income.

equally distant from the horizontal (income) axis and the vertical (consumption) axis. Point M on the 45° line in Figure 11–5 shows income and consumption to be the same. It tells us that we are spending *all* our income, regardless of the size of that income.

But do we spend all we earn? Look back at Figure 11–4. Although that graph shows consumption as increasing with income, it never shows them to be the same. Only when income was very low was consumption more than income. This means that the 45° line, Y, shows the range of incomes, but it is not an accurate picture of consumption at each level of income.

Now let us turn to Figure 11–6. Here consumption for each level of income is plotted. The consumption line (C) is lower than the income line (45° line, or Y). The light shaded area between consumption

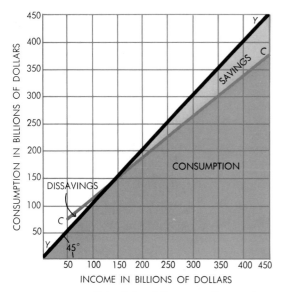

Figure 11–6   Schedule of Consumption and Savings

The 45° line (Y) measures levels of income. The consumption line (C) measures what spending is likely to be at different levels of income. The difference between income (Y) and consumption (C) is savings (S).

and income is savings. As we continue to learn about the new model, the usefulness of this new tool, national income determination, will become evident.

Propensity to consume and save

Although prices, consumer credit, availability of goods, and fluctuations in purchases of durable goods are all considered factors in determining consumption, most modern economists agree that income is the single most important factor. Figure 11–7 uses the 45° line to analyze income. In Figure 11–2, $500 billion represented the GNP needed for full employment without inflation, with $400 billion of this in the private sector. With that same amount for the private sector, Figure 11–7 shows that $330 billion of gross private income will be spent by individuals in the market and $70 billion will be gross savings. Why

will gross private income be spent in this way? Economists have discovered that people tend to spend and to save certain proportions at particular levels of income. This tendency to spend certain amounts at certain levels of income is called the *propensity to consume.* The tendency to save a certain amount at a certain level of income is called the *propensity to save.* With an aggregate private income of $400 billion the propensity to consume will be $330 billion and the propensity to save, $70 billion.

If we are to sustain a $400 billion gross private income with gross savings at $70 billion, how much gross investment is needed? You will recall that if the new GNP or, in this case, the new gross private income is to equal the old gross private income, gross investment must equal gross savings. A gross investment of less than $70 billion will mean less production and therefore less employment and a lowering

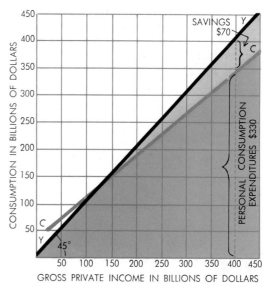

Figure   11–7   Schedule of Propensity to Consume

The propensity to consume and the propensity to save increase as income increases.

of our gross private income. A gross investment greater than $70 billion can only cause inflation, since we are already producing at full employment.

Determination of income

Figure 11–8 shows what will happen if gross private investment is only $50 billion (b), $20 billion less than gross savings. Then, at the market (c), with $330 billion of personal consumption expenditures and $50 billion in investment, there would be $20 billion of goods and services left over (or not produced). The new gross private income will be insufficient to sustain full employment. However, instead of the gross private income dropping to $380 billion, our diagram shows it dropping to $350 billion (e). This is due to the *multiplier effect*, which in this case is 2½. Briefly, the multiplier effect refers to the

fact that any change in spending or investment, either public or private, brings about a greater change in income. This is shown in (d). In our example $20 billion additional investment by business will increase income by $50 billion. Thus, the multiplier is 2½. What would happen in the example above if all things remained the same except that there was a gross investment of $60 billion? More will be said about the multiplier on page 238.

Using the 45° line to determine income

Let us now consider the example previously explained in Figure 11–8, but this time let us see how it looks using the diagram with the 45° line. This combination is shown in Figure 11–9. You will recall that the 45° line indicates income and that line C is the actual consumption line, or the propensity to consume (the tendency to

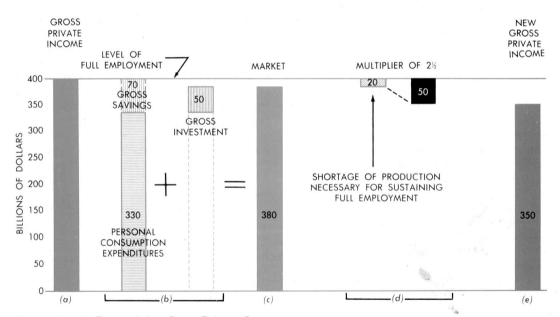

Figure 11–8 Determining Gross Private Income

When gross private investment is less than gross private savings ($20 billion less), new gross private income will decline by an amount ($50 billion) greater than this difference because of the multiplier effect.

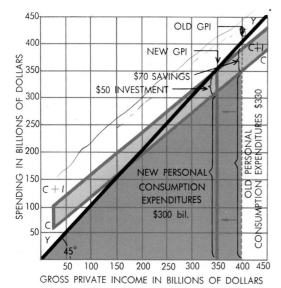

Figure 11–9 Determining Gross Private Income Using the 45° Line

Here we see the same example as in Figure 11–8, but this time we use the 45° line as a tool for analysis.

spend certain amounts at various levels of income). Move to the right along the horizontal axis, which measures gross private income, until $400 billion is reached. The broken vertical line shows what the propensity to consume will be and what the propensity to save will be at the gross private income level of $400 billion. You can see that it is the same as that found in Figure 11–7.

Let us see what happens to the gross private income when only $50 billion is invested while $70 billion is saved. The C line shows the consumer in the market. The businessman also goes to the market, so his "purchases" (investment, I) must be added to the personal consumption expenditures (C). This is done by adding $50 billion, his investment, to personal consumption expenditures, as shown in C + I (consumption plus investment). Line C rises because consumption increases with income. Line

C + I is parallel to line C because investment has been fixed at $50 billion, regardless of income. We can now find the new gross private income. Locate the point where the C + I line crosses the 45° line (our income line). It is shown by the arrow labeled "New GPI" and points to $350 billion, the new gross private income.

NEW INCOME MEANS NEW CONSUMPTION

In Figure 11–9 you can see that the new GPI is lower. Personal consumption expenditures have dropped to $300 billion. This occurs because consumption is determined mainly by income. What happens to savings when income has been reduced to $350 billion? Since personal consumption expenditures are now $300 billion and since what is not spent is saved, we know that savings will drop to $50 billion. The level of spending and the level of saving have both decreased as income has fallen.

WHEN INVESTMENT IS LARGER THAN SAVINGS

Using the 45° line diagram, we can determine what gross private income would be when investment is increased to $75 billion. We would raise the C + I line $75 billion above the C line instead of $50 billion above. The new GPI would be at the point where the new C + I line crosses the 45° line, Y. What would personal consumption expenditures be? How much would savings be? Would this new gross private income be good for the economy?

By now you should recognize that if we know the nation's propensity to consume (that is, the consumption or C line) and we know what gross investment is, we can determine what gross private income will be. Once again we are able to see the importance of the relationship of consumption, as well as investment, to savings.

Let us leave our diagrams and statistics for a moment and consider in a very general way what these illustrations mean. A contracting economy (reducing GPI from

$400 billion to $350 billion) results when retail stores do not fill up with merchandise and manufacturers do not increase production or invest sufficiently to use up the savings available. Since fewer workers are needed, income declines. When that happens, consumption also drops, and so does the ability to save. The diagrams and statistics shown here tell an unemotional story. For a more personal view of how a contracting economy may hurt people, talk with someone whose income has been lowered or who has been removed from his job because of a decline in business activity.

Fluctuating investment and income

We have seen the economic reactions which take place when gross private income dropped to $350 billion, $50 billion below the level needed for full employment. Now let us consider what can be done to expand income back to the $400 billion level. We cannot afford to wait for the possible readjustment that may occur (due to a drop in the wage-price level or to changing interest rates on savings and investment) to bring about the necessary expansion. What other means are available for achieving it? Might consumers be persuaded to spend more at the market? During the 1957–58 recession President Eisenhower urged the American public to buy more in an effort to stimulate business. Advertising and sales by retailers were also used extensively to increase business. Certainly an increase in consumption by the public would motivate businesses to increase investment. Greater personal consumption expenditures, C, plus greater investment, I, would certainly bring about a greater gross private income. Although it is true that both personal consumption expenditures and gross investment determine aggregate income, the variation in investment is far greater than that in consumption, as shown in Table 11–1. Note, too, that the decline in investment is accompanied by an actual decline, or a slowdown, in the increase of the GNP.

Table 11–1   Fluctuation of Investments and Personal Consumption Expenditures
(billions of dollars)

	Personal Consumption Expenditures	Gross Investment	Gross National Product
1947	165.4	31.5	234.3
1948	178.3	43.1	259.4
1949	181.2	33.0	258.1
1950	195.0	50.0	284.6
1951	209.8	56.3	329.0
1952	219.8	49.9	347.0
1953	232.6	50.3	365.4
1954	238.0	48.9	363.1
1955	256.9	63.8	397.5
1956	269.9	67.4	419.2
1957	285.2	66.1	442.8
1958	293.0	56.6	444.5
1959	313.5	72.7	482.7
1960	328.2	71.8	502.6
1961	337.3	68.8	518.7
1962	356.8	79.1	556.2
1963	375.0	82.0	583.9
1964	399.3	87.7	622.3

Gross investment fluctuated far more than personal consumption expenditures. Compare the rise and fall of investment with GNP. Lines are drawn under recession years. SOURCE: U.S. Department of Commerce, Office of Business Economics

Although not all economists agree, most of them would list the amount of business investment as a greater factor in determining aggregate income than the more stable consumption by householders. Therefore, in order to raise aggregate income so as to attain full employment, it is more important to get businessmen to increase their investments. In terms of the diagram with the 45° line we may say that the problem is to raise the C + I line so that it will intersect the 45° line at $400 billion or whatever the full-employment level may be. Before we attempt to solve the problem of how to increase investment, let us return to the market to consider the actions of another important buyer – government.

Part C   *A New Model (Government Included)*

Until now we have been able to omit government from consideration because we were proceeding on the assumption that the government was balancing its budget, keeping expenditures equal to revenues. Actually, we know that this has rarely happened in recent times, particularly at the federal level. Since 1930 most of our federal budgets have shown deficits, with greater expenditures than revenues. In the years since 1930, budget surpluses have occurred only six times. What have been the effects of the unbalanced budget on the economy?

The unbalanced budget

In Chapter 8 you learned that the federal government is less restricted than families, businesses, or local and state governments in keeping its budget balanced. The United States government may not only borrow money, but it can actually print money to pay its bills, as it did during the Civil War. However, such a great power, if not used wisely, might well destroy the nation's economy. The German government after World War I tried such a way out of its difficulties, with devastating inflation as the result. The Republic of China during and immediately after World War II followed the German example, with similar results. Our own government has, in general, avoided such extremes and the hardships of uncontrolled inflation resulting from the indiscriminate printing of money. The discussion that follows is concerned with the effects of an unbalanced budget as it increases the national debt.

As we have previously seen in Figure 11–2, when government goes to the marketplace, it purchases more than $100 billion worth of goods and services, slightly less than one fifth of all goods and services bought, and usually more than the total bought by businesses through gross private investment. This sizable purchase requires

Severe inflations disrupt the entire economy, causing people to lose confidence in money transactions and to revert to barter. In 1923 German marks were baled as waste, worth no more than the paper they were printed on.

the employment of a large portion of our work force. In order to pay for these goods and services, the government collects revenue, chiefly in the form of taxes, from almost everyone. Paying taxes to the government limits people's spending for tangibles such as automobiles and for intangibles such as vacations. However, it does supply them with collective benefits such as schools, roads, and defense against foreign invasion. As you know, we have in our economy a long tradition of free enterprise, preferring to have individual households make independent decisions on what and how much they want of the goods and services available. However, as our society has

234 THE AMERICAN ECONOMY AS A WHOLE

become more complex and as people have become more interdependent, the demands and expenses of government have increased.

Growing federal expenditures

In Chapters 7 and 8 we observed the pattern of increasing federal spending. We found that many factors contributed to this rise. Of particular importance recently have been the growing costs of national defense. When our nation became the leader of the free world, its defense costs rose sharply. We accept defense as a legitimate sphere of government activity; in addition, most of us admit that taking on the responsibility of leadership in the free world involves a greater cost for defense. However, few of us like the fact that these new obligations cut directly into our personal income, depriving us of additional goods and services.

Federal spending has increased in other areas besides defense. Demands for such benefits as better educational facilities, roads, and welfare have increased the share of government purchases from slightly more than a twelfth of the national income before World War I to about a fifth at present. Instead of making almost all our decisions at the market, we now make some of our choices regarding goods and services at the polling booths, where we vote for the party which we think will make the best decisions regarding our collective wants.

We know that government's role in the economy has increased by greater purchasing in the market and by the collecting of more revenues. Government powers also have increased through such changes as the employing (both directly and indirect-

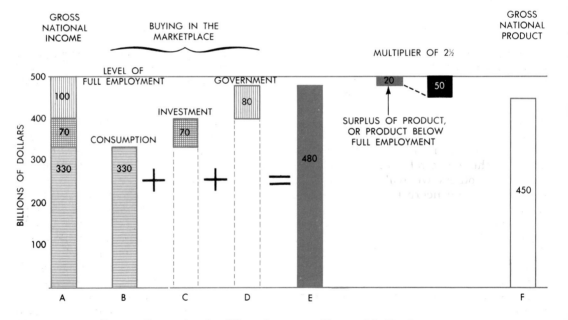

Figure 11–10 Income Determination When Aggregate Demand Is Too Low

If the private sector of the economy is sufficient to sustain full employment but the government collects more in revenue than it spends, the GNP will decline by a multiple of the difference between government income and government expenditures. The new aggregate income is not sufficient to maintain the economy at a level of full employment.

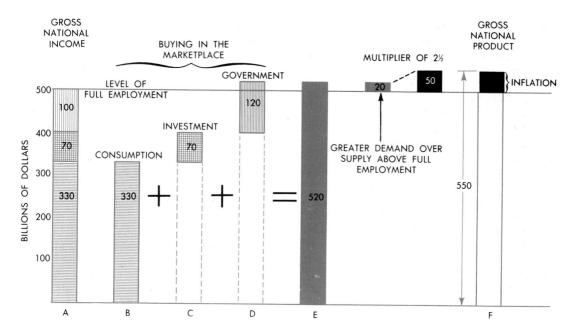

Figure 11-11 Income Determination When Aggregate Demand Is Too High

If the private sector of the economy is sufficient to sustain full employment but government spends more than it collects, the GNP will rise by a multiple of the difference between government income and government expenditures. The aggregate demand (total spending) is greater than the capacity of the economy to produce, resulting in an inflation.

ly) of more workers; by greater control over business, labor unions, farmers, and professional people; and by various subsidies. Some of these controls we have already dealt with; others we will consider later. Our immediate concern is the significance to the economy of increased government expenditure and control when the government's budget is not balanced. How does this governmental activity affect the national economy under differing employment conditions?

Determining income with government included

INCOME BELOW FULL EMPLOYMENT

Let us assume, as we did in Figure 11-2, that $500 billion of GNP is required to achieve a full-employment economy. Let us further assume that private consumption

and investment add up to $400 billion, with $100 billion still awaiting collection by the government. What would happen if government collected this $100 billion but spent only $80 billion? Figure 11-10 provides an answer. Instead of the economy's falling only $20 billion below the $500 billion full-employment GNP level, it has declined $50 billion, due again to the multiplier effect. By spending less than was collected, the government has left goods and services unpurchased in the marketplace. As unsold stocks of their merchandise accumulate, businessmen will probably plan to reduce production below the previous year's level, since this surplus may lead to reduced prices and profits. Curtailing production will reduce the GNP below the level of full employment.

INCOME ABOVE FULL EMPLOYMENT

In contrast with the preceding example, let us assume that the private sector of the economy begins as in that case, but that this time government takes in $100 billion and spends $120 billion. Adding together private consumption, investment, and government spending brings the aggregate demand for goods and services to $520 billion, which is above the full-employment product of $500 billion. With the demand for goods and services above the supply and the economy already operating at the full-employment level, inflation would be the outcome. Figure 11–11 demonstrates this situation, with the multiplier compounding the effect by two and a half times. The new GNP is $550 billion, $50 billion above full employment and therefore inflationary.

Income determination with the 45° line

Let us see how the information on income determination shown in Figures 11–10 and 11–11 looks when combined with the diagram of the 45° line.

INCOME BELOW FULL EMPLOYMENT

Figure 11–12 shows aggregate income falling $50 billion below the full-employment income of $500 billion, just as it did in Figure 11–10. Our aggregate income, Y, is determined by adding consumption, C, plus investment, I, plus government spending, G, together; it is found at the point where the C + I + G line crosses the 45° line (Y line), which is at $450 billion. Income will be below the full-employment level because $20 billion worth of goods and services have *not* been purchased by consumers, businessmen, or government or by any combination of them. Because of this surplus, businessmen in general will reduce production, realizing an income of $50 billion less (the multiplier effect) than $500 billion, the full-employment level. An increase in C + I + G of $20 billion, represented by the striped area (A) above the C + I + G line, would provide the demand for goods and services needed for full employment.

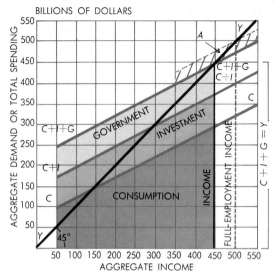

Figure 11–12   Income Determination Using the 45° Line— Underemployment

Aggregate income is determined at the point where aggregate demand, consumption plus investment plus government spending, intersects the 45° line. C + I + G needs to be increased by $20 billion (A) in order to attain a full-employment income.

INCOME ABOVE FULL EMPLOYMENT

Figure 11–13 shows what happens when aggregate demand, the C + I + G, is greater than full-employment income (note Figure 11–11 also). The C + I + G line crosses the Y line at $550 billion, $50 billion above full-employment income. Under these circumstances the demand for goods and services is greater than can be supplied with the existing labor force. Businessmen, in their desire to fill the greater demand, bid against one another to obtain workers and other resources, causing prices to rise. Production will be at the $500 billion level, or full employment; however, because of rising prices, the goods and services will carry a total market price of $550 billion. This full-employment level is not desirable because it is inflationary. If the C + I + G

KEYNESIAN MODEL

This is an exercise in the functioning of the Keynesian model. Its purpose is to show you how our aggregate income is determined and how our policy decisions can bring about changes in that income.

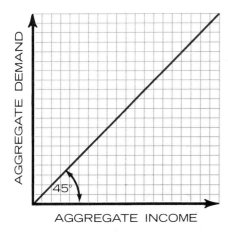

On our graph the vertical axis measures aggregate demand (spending). The horizontal axis measures our aggregate income. A diagonal line, 45°, shows total spending of income.

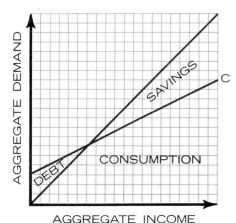

We know that consumers do not spend all their income, but will save as their income increases. Line C shows consumers spending more as their income rises. What they do not spend, they save. The area between the 45° line and the consumption line represents savings (or debt).

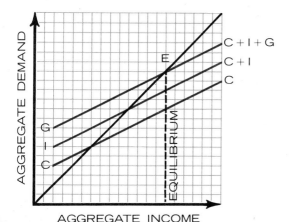

In addition to consumer spending, we have business investment (I) and government spending (G). Total spending, or aggregate demand, is shown by consumption (C), investment (I), and government spending (G). Aggregate income, or equilibrium, can be determined where the C + I + G line crosses the 45° line. This relates to the formula for income determination: C + I + G = Y (income).

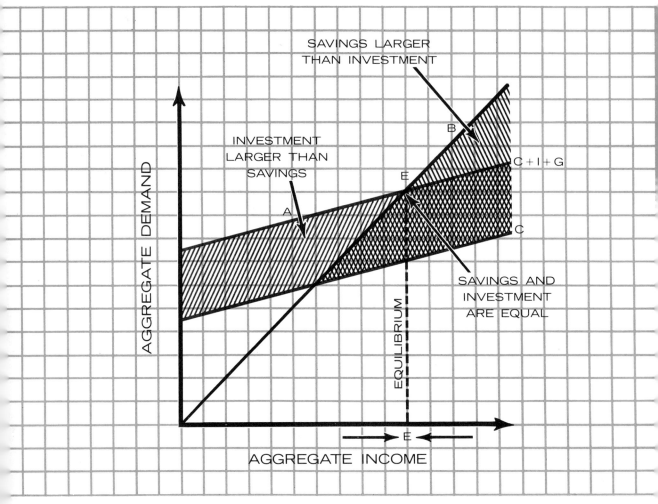

Aggregate income will be in equilibrium where investment [public (G) and private (I)] equals savings. At A, investment is larger than savings (demand greater than supply encourages expansion) and aggregate income will rise. At B, savings are larger than investment (supply is larger than demand) and aggregate income will decline. At E, investment and savings equal each other (equilibrium) and aggregate income will remain unchanged.

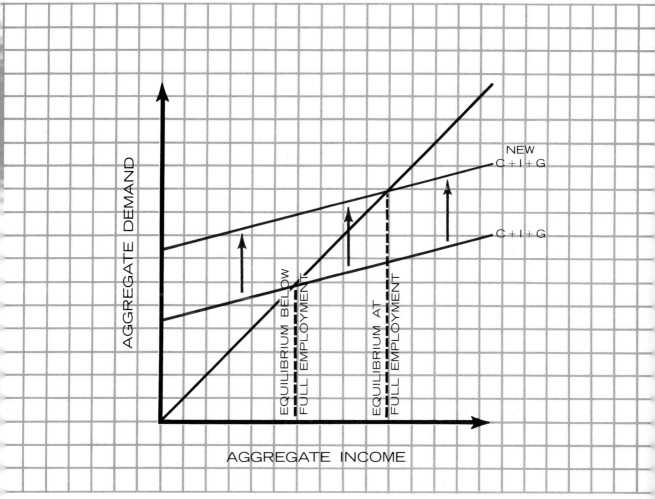

Keynesian economics, or what some call the new capitalism, calls for economic policy to bring the equilibrium point up to full employment without inflation. Graphically, this is represented by raising the original C + I + G line (total spending), which crossed the 45° line below full employment, to the new C + I + G line. The new aggregate demand is now sufficient to sustain full employment without inflation.

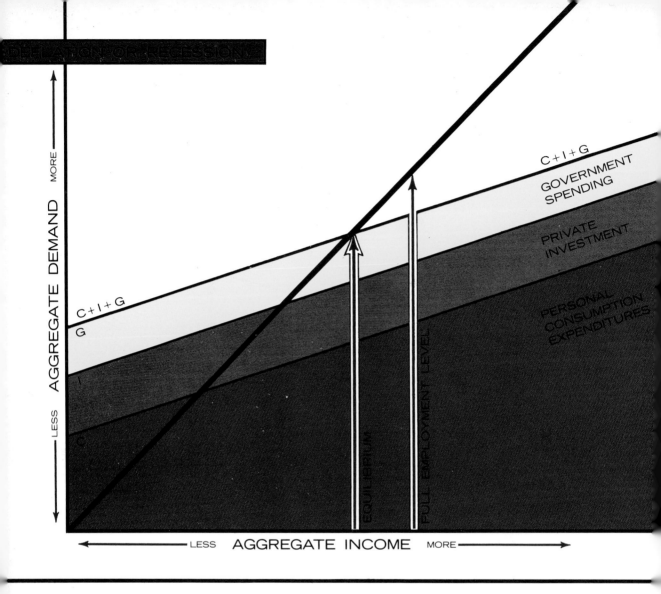

AGGREGATE DEMAND

MORE

LESS

C + I + G

GOVERNMENT SPENDING

PRIVATE INVESTMENT

PERSONAL CONSUMPTION EXPENDITURES

C + I + G

G

I

C

EQUILIBRIUM

FULL EMPLOYMENT LEVEL

LESS — AGGREGATE INCOME — MORE

You see here a graphic representation of the economy in equilibrium below the full employment level. Personal consumption (C) [black], business investment (I) [dark], and government spending (G) [light] add up to total spending, or aggregate demand. The C + I + G line crosses the 45° line at equilibrium below full employment. Savings and investment are equal at this point. The economy is not making full use of its resources. It is producing below its capacity because aggregate demand is not sufficient to support full employment.

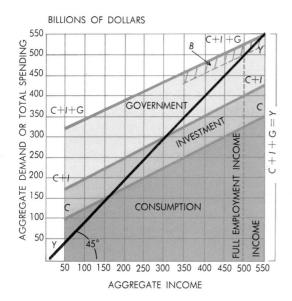

Figure 11-13 Income Determination Using the 45° Line—Inflation

Aggregate demand is greater than what a full-employment income can supply, thereby causing an inflation. $C + I + G$ must be reduced by $20 billion (B) in order to reduce aggregate income to the full-employment level.

(the aggregate demand) can be reduced by $20 billion, supply and demand will reach an equilibrium level at full-employment income, $500 billion. In Figure 11-13 the $C + I + G$ line must be lowered by the amount shown in the striped area (B), $20 billion, so that it crosses the Y line at $500 billion, the full-employment income level.

Equilibrium

By now it is clear that the relation between savings and investment is critical in the question of maintaining GNP at full employment. Let us look further at the interaction between these factors.

Think of savings as all production not bought by consumers, C. On our 45° line diagram it is the space between the C line and the 45° line. Think of investment as made up of private I (business) and public

G (government). It is the space between the C line and the $C + I + G$ line. These areas are shown in Figure 11-14. With these revised definitions it is evident that if savings are greater than investment (government and business not buying all the production remaining after consumer purchasing), the aggregate income will fall. Savings larger than public and private investment produces a declining aggregate income ($S > I =$ declining Y). By contrast, if investment is larger than savings (government and business demand more production than that which consumers leave at the market), income will rise ($I > S =$ rising Y). Under these conditions, aggregate income will be at the point where savings and investment are exactly the same. That is the *equilibrium point*, shown in Figure 11-14 at E. It

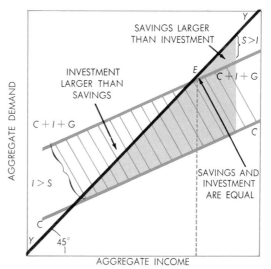

Figure 11-14 Determining Aggregate Income Using Savings and Investment

Aggregate income is at that point where investment (private and public) and savings (gross savings and taxes) equal each other. This is shown at point E, equilibrium (where the $C + I + G$ line crosses the Y line). When $I > S$, income will rise. When $S > I$, income will decline.

is also the point where our $C + I + G$ line crosses the 45° line because at that point $S = I$.

You will recall that a major disagreement exists between the classical economist and the Keynesian economist over the question of where equilibrium will be achieved. The classical economist maintains that if the economy is free from any restraints in the operation of the market (supply and demand operating under pure competition), equilibrium will be at the full-employment level without inflation. The new model indicates that equilibrium can be and frequently is at a point below full employment. This is so when investment is smaller than savings.

Achieving full employment without inflation

As we have noted earlier, many economists believe that one of our major goals is that of achieving a full-employment econ-

"Reminds me of that crazy idea of Henry Ford's that you can make more selling at lower prices."

—from *Straight Herblock*, Simon & Schuster, 1964

omy without inflation. Using our new tools for analysis, we would phrase it as having the $C + I + G$ line intersect the Y line at an income level high enough to support full employment but not so high as to cause inflation. It is possible to implement the goal of full employment without inflation by means of government policy. Chapter 14 will present a further consideration of the policies mentioned here.

When $C + I + G$ is too low (below $500 billion), a policy providing for corrective measures to increase it should be put into effect if full employment is to be maintained. For example, a tax cut like the one enacted in 1964 gives consumers more money to spend, thus raising consumption, C. If investment, I, and government spending, G, stay the same, $C + I + G$ will increase. An increase in I might be brought about by a cut in the corporation income tax, as happened in the same year. Likewise, G can be increased by additional government expenditures, whether for schools, the space program, or a new river project. There is much disagreement about which policy is best, but any of these—and many others as well—can be used to raise aggregate demand, $C + I + G$, to full-employment income.

When aggregate demand is above the full-employment income level, a policy for lowering it is needed if inflation is to be prevented. Such a measure would be the opposite of those previously used. Raising taxes, cutting government expenditures, or discouraging business investment would all help to lower the $C + I + G$ line, making it possible to achieve the goal of full employment without inflation.

The multiplier effect

At several places in this chapter we have noted the importance of the multiplier effect in magnifying changes. To understand better its causes and effects, we must consider it in more detail. To do this we will begin by returning to Figure 11–12. The

$C + I + G$ line crosses the 45° line at $450 billion. If we add $20 billion of government purchases, the $C + I + G$ line moves upward so that it crosses the 45° line at $500 billion, a gain of $50 billion. Additional purchases of $20 billion bring about an increase of $50 billion of aggregate income, showing graphically the multiplier effect. The same effect can be brought about by consumers' spending more or businesses' investing more, since an increase by any one purchaser or combination of purchasers in the marketplace results in raising the $C + I + G$ line and raising aggregate income by some multiple of the additional purchase.

WHY THE MULTIPLIER EFFECT?

You are probably wondering why there is a multiplier effect. To find an answer, let us suppose that government spent an additional $20 billion more than it collected or that business increased its investment by that amount. We will assume that prices will remain constant and that we are operating our economy at a level below full employment. Thus, the injection of this new investment or government spending will not create a demand for goods and services in excess of our ability to produce them. The bulk of the $20 billion would probably be received by suppliers of goods. They would spend part of it and save part of it. The part they spent would be received by workers and other suppliers — in general by people who would in turn spend part of it and save a part. Employees receiving additional wages and businessmen receiving additional profits would take part of their money to the market to spend and would save the rest. The effect of the additional $20 billion of spending on the nation's economy as a whole would far exceed that basic figure because it would continue to be spent, though in an ever-decreasing amount. Since part of the $20 billion is spent many times, the total effect is far greater than the original amount only.

DETERMINING THE MULTIPLIER

Since we must allow for the multiplier, we need to know in advance what the amount of it will be, if we are to make accurate predictions of change. Earlier, we explained people's spending habits as a propensity to consume — the tendency to spend a certain amount of their income at a particular level of income. When income and spending increased, so did the ability to save and the amount saved. If we add $20 billion of income to the economy by way of investment or additional government spending, what portion of this amount received initially will be spent? If 60 percent, or $12 billion, is spent, we can say that three fifths of the *additional* income is the new propensity to consume. You recall that we refer to the last unit as "marginal." Since we are not speaking about what fraction of total income is spent but only the fraction of the additional unit, we refer to this three fifths as *marginal propensity to consume.* Eight billion dollars of the $20 billion of additional income is saved. That means that two fifths of this additional income is saved. The *marginal propensity to save* is two fifths. Marginal propensity to consume — three fifths (or $12 billion) — plus marginal propensity to save — two fifths (or $8 billion) — will equal one, or the total new income added. If you know the marginal propensity to save, you can easily figure out the marginal propensity to consume $(1 - \frac{2}{5} = \frac{3}{5})$. To find the multiplier, merely invert the marginal propensity to save, which gives $\frac{5}{2}$ (or $2\frac{1}{2}$). If you know the marginal propensity to consume, you can calculate the marginal propensity to save by subtracting it from 1 and then inverting to give you the multiplier $(1 - \frac{3}{5} = \frac{2}{5}$; invert to $\frac{5}{2}$, or $2\frac{1}{2})$. What would the multiplier be if the marginal propensity to consume were three fourths? What would be the increase in aggregate income if businessmen invested $10 billion more and the marginal propensity to consume were five sixths?

SOME NEEDED CORRECTIONS

In explaining how to determine aggregate income, we have taken some liberties by oversimplifying. This can lead to a distortion if we fail to make the proper corrections. You will recall our assumption that, though production takes place throughout the year, payment for that production and the spending of income received took place only once during the year — at the end. Our diagrams may be accurate for the past but not in determining income for the future. Although government and businesses draw up budgets for the year, and many consumers also plan their expenditures, we know that both income and expenditures are subject to an almost infinite number of changes. If consumers become excited about a product, as they did with automobiles in 1964 and 1965, they will increase their purchases. This in turn may increase investment in the middle of the year. More profits and wages increase income and the revenue that government receives from income taxes.

Economists analyze accumulated data; from this information they project plans and make forecasts. They sometimes make mistakes, since economics is not an exact science. For example, government economists underestimated income for 1963 by a considerable margin. Too many variables either cannot be controlled or are not measured with sufficient accuracy. Man tends to be fickle on the production line and in the marketplace. This does not mean that analysis, projection, and planning are a waste; we are far better off making educated guesses and trying to control conditions than gambling on the unknown. With the development of more and more measurements of the economy like those described in Chapter 10, and with data available at more frequent intervals, it is expected that economic analysis will become more exact.

The economist and the economy

We have now discussed some of the major tools that modern economists use in attempting to analyze the economy and to frame economic policy. The economist working for a large corporation knows that personal income will be a major factor in determining personal consumption expenditures. This is one of his major considerations when he prepares his report to management advising them on conditions affecting production goals.

Government economists are responsible for advising the executive and legislative branches on tax programs, expenditures, tariffs, and subsidies. In attempting to keep the economy operating at or near the full-employment level without inflation, they work constantly with the various measurements of aggregate income. They need estimates of personal consumption expenditures and business investment in order to determine the consequences of government spending. They seek to determine what the multiplier effect will be if the government

When private investment is not sufficient to stimulate a full employment level of spending, government may provide the needed help. Can government supply too much stimulation to the economy?

decides on a policy of *deficit spending* (spending more than it takes in). Will such a policy bring the economy up to full employment or will it exceed the full employment mark and create an inflation? The tools we have learned to use are designed to help determine aggregate income so that sensible policies can be developed to cope with the fluctuations in the economy.

Before proceeding, let us look again at the two models described—the classical analysis and the new Keynesian approach. Some economists, many businessmen, and perhaps the majority of the public have a greater respect for the classical approach. Speeches in Congress are often more in tune with what Adam Smith called the "invisible hand," or the market system. Since most economists do not accept either model completely and since most government planning is set up somewhere between the two approaches, the argument continues.

Part D   The Problem: Which Model?

In the beginning of our study of economics we identified the basic problem: How do we allocate our limited resources to meet our unlimited wants most efficiently? Finding an answer involves the setting up of a model or economic system that will utilize fully the resources at our disposal. Bringing the four factors of production together in the right proportion at the right time to produce the right quantity of goods and services that the society has decided it wants is the goal of all economists. This must be done while achieving full employment without inflation. Anything less would be wasting our resources. There is a great deal of disagreement about how to achieve these objectives.

The following discussion presents the case for both the classical approach and the Keynesian approach. After reading these two positions, consider a typical comment made by an economist reflecting this controversy: "There are no classical economists, there are no Keynesian economists. The thinking of all economists combines elements of both theories, but for everyone, the combination is different." As you read, try to decide what place there is for each of the two positions in our total economy.

The case for the classical model

The classical economist believes that the market economy can best achieve the desired goal only if the natural laws of supply and demand are allowed to operate. He would willingly admit that our economy has not yielded all it should. However, he would give as the reason for its failure our unwillingness to follow the model, not the inadequacy of the model. Our recessions, and even the Great Depression, caused the hardships they did because of interference with the mobility of the factors of production and the goods and services produced. Minimum wage laws and labor unions, administered prices and monopolistic competition, government subsidies and "confiscatory" taxes, all of which interfere with incentive and discriminate against certain industries and persons, have prevented the self-correcting mechanism of the market economy from working. Blaming the model for not achieving our economic goals is avoiding the truth, since the prescription of the model was not followed.

In order to achieve our desired goals, the classical economist thinks that we must not change the model, but rather return to a real use of the classical model. Specifically, this would involve vigorous enforcement of our antitrust laws, elimination of the union shop, and doing away with all wage and price controls. It would also require eliminating all subsidies (with the possible exception of those to new industries), reducing government involvement (by either ownership or control) in the economy, and developing a tax structure that would act as a real incentive for capital investment. It is granted that loud cries of protest would go up against such a program. However, after a short period of readjustment the economy would experience a vigorous increase as new incentives motivated the forces for production.

With wages and prices far more flexible, the goods and services that people really want would be reflected in the marketplace; that is, supply and demand would come into balance. Efficiency in production and the quality of goods and services available would all improve as competition became a more significant factor. Those whose incomes are high would work harder to increase their earnings because they would retain most of their money rather than turning much of it over to the government in the form of taxes. Those who were unemployed would have a better chance of finding work, since employers would be allowed to offer much lower wages than at present. This would motivate them to hire more workers. Price flexibility would allow the lower wages paid during periods of moderate downturns to buy more because a slackening of demand would result in a lowering of prices. Resources would be directed where they were needed most because market prices would direct their flow. A society which is dedicated to freedom and the individual deserves the efficiency and freedom of a market economy.

The case for the new model

The Keynesian economist denies that a mature capitalist society can have the mobility of resources that the classical economist assumes. He also denies the possibility of the extreme flexibility of prices and wages that is needed to bring supply and demand into balance at the full-employment level. If the economy fails to respond to changes in demand and to changes in costs brought about by technological changes, and to risk capital needed to start new enterprises, it will become sluggish. When investment drops below savings, as it has frequently done, some additional spending, whether private or public, is needed to provide the stimulus necessary to the economy in order to bring it back to the full-employment level. Since few people would accept enforced spending by the public or investment by businessmen as a solution, it would seem most logical to charge the government with the responsibility of developing policy to stimulate the economy to the desired full-employment level. Since the market has not provided the stimulus by making private spending and investment attractive enough, it is necessary that government become involved through *monetary policies* (involving interest and the availability of credit) and *fiscal policies* (budgeting by the government to create a surplus or deficit). Such additional spending will raise the $C + I + G$ high enough so that it will cross the 45° line at the full-employment level.

If the economy is overstimulated, government action to lower the $C + I + G$ line will reduce the inflationary trend. It would be inconsistent with our political principles to prevent people from spending or investing. However, government policy that would discourage inflationary action could be approved or disapproved at the polls.

Even if price, wage, and interest flexibility did provide some help in lessening unemployment, our society is largely committed to minimum wages and "fair" prices, with the result that the flexibility would be of only a limited nature. Any government that merely stands by waiting for the natural laws of the market to act while millions of people are unemployed would undoubtedly find itself out of office after the next election. Why should an economy – and more important, why should people – suffer when we have in our possession the economic know-how to provide a full-employment economy without inflation?

Considering an answer

The two points of view given here represent differences not only in analysis and interpretation but also in personal values. Identify the conflict in value judgments expressed in the two positions. Which set of values do you tend to agree with? Has your opinion changed in any way in the course of our study?

Do you believe that we can change the present direction of our economy and move toward a more market-oriented society? What groups in our society would be helped most by such a change? What groups would be hurt most? Would the advantages and disadvantages deriving from the change be temporary or permanent? In what ways does the "new economics" change our traditional consumer-oriented society? Is freedom for the individual (consumer and citizen) seriously jeopardized?

In arriving at an answer, try to decide how the principles and reasoning presented here, as well as your new tools for analysis, apply to the basic economic problems and goals we have identified.

REVIEW: *the highlights of the chapter*

1. The classical model expects a full-employment economy without inflation to be achieved merely by allowing the natural laws of supply and demand to operate and by keeping government out of the economy as much as possible.

2. According to the classical model temporary dislocations in the economy are corrected by changes in interest rates and fluctuations in wages and prices.

3. Major business fluctuations, particularly the long-lasting major depression of the 1930's, led to the acceptance of a new economic model.

4. John Maynard Keynes, an English economist, developed a new model well within the capitalistic system. He thought that insufficient attention was being paid to providing a demand adequate to maintain a full-employment economy. Since interest and wage-and-price flexibility did not stimulate demand sufficiently, the government became responsible for setting policies that would accomplish this purpose.

5. The aggregate income of the nation is determined by adding personal consumption expenditures to business investment to government spending ($C + I + G = $ income).

6. According to the new model, when consumption plus investment plus government expenditures does not add up to enough production of goods and services to employ everyone in the working force who wishes to work, policies must be set up to increase spending. This can be accomplished by increasing government expenditures over government income (deficit spending), by encouraging businessmen to invest more, or by using other economic policies. Personal consumption expenditures change primarily with income and are not altered so easily.

7. When consumption plus investment plus government spending adds up to an amount that exceeds what we are capable of producing, inflation will occur. Policy to discourage personal consumption expenditures, business investment, or government spending will be needed.

8. People tend to spend particular amounts of their income at different income levels. This tendency in spending is known as the propensity to consume. The tendency to save certain amounts of income at certain income levels is known as the propensity to save.

9. The amount of *additional* income that people tend to spend is known as the marginal propensity to consume. The amount of *additional* income that people tend to save is known as the marginal propensity to save. The marginal propensity to consume and the marginal propensity to save add up to one.

10. In the planning of economic policy the multiplier effect makes it unnecessary to increase or decrease aggregate spending ($C + I + G$) by the full amount to bring that spending up to or down to the level of full employment without inflation. The multiplier effect causes a greater increase in aggregate income than the amount of additional spending added or subtracted by the amount which is the reciprocal of the marginal propensity to save.

11. Most current economic policy combines elements of the classical model and the new model. Enforcement of antitrust laws and planning for a temporary budget deficit by means of a tax cut are examples of economic policies that utilize both the old and the new models.

IN CONCLUSION: *some aids to understanding*

Terms for review

gross national income	propensity to consume
gross savings	45° line
full-employment economy	deficit spending
balanced budget	fiscal policies
multiplier effect	marginal propensity
$C + I + G = Y$	to consume
propensity to save	Keynesian model

Questions for review

1. How does the classical economist answer the following questions? (a) How will full employment without inflation be achieved? (b) What accounts for our failure to achieve the level of full employment without inflation?

2. The theories of John Maynard Keynes have had a major impact on economic thinking. In what ways did he disagree with the classical economists?

3. What do the new economists consider to be the major factor in determining investment? Explain, using the 45° line diagram, why aggregate income will be at both the intersection of the $C + I + G$ line with the 45° line and the point where savings and investment (both public and private) are equal.

4. If investment is larger than savings, what will probably happen to income? Why does this take place? Under what conditions is it likely to be harmful to the economy?

5. If the full-employment level without inflation is estimated to be $700 billion and if aggregate demand $(C + I + G)$ is equal to only $670 billion, what amount of additional spending is needed? Assume the multiplier to be 3.

6. Arrange the following people in order, from high to low, according to their probable marginal propensity to consume:
(a) a farmer whose income is $3,000 per year
(b) an executive whose income is $50,000 per year
(c) a teacher whose income is $8,500 per year
Explain the reasons for the order you have used.

7. If most Americans suddenly accepted Benjamin Franklin's philosophy of "a penny saved is a penny earned" and significantly increased their savings, how might this change affect the national economy (a) immediately and (b) after a year's time?

8. Why is economic forecasting so difficult? What justification exists for its continued use?

Additional questions and problems

1. Figure 11 – 1 records the GNP for the United States from 1954 to 1964. Although there are fluctuations, the trend is primarily upward.
(a) What are the major reasons for this rise?
(b) What government policies were employed to avoid major inflationary and deflationary periods?
(c) Can there be any serious dangers associated with the continuous increase?
(d) What role does the constantly increasing federal debt play in this picture?

2. Discuss the advantages and disadvantages of stimulating the economy by means of
(a) increased personal consumption expenditures
(b) increased business investment
(c) increased government expenditures

3. Talk to a businessman, a worker, and a professional person about their solutions to the problem of stimulating the economy. Do their opinions differ? If so, why and in what way?

4. Using a newspaper or popular weekly news publication, indicate news items about government policies that will affect the GNP. If you were a congressman, would you support these policies?

5. If a new industry entered your community, what effect might it have on other businesses? Do you think the citizens of the community should help finance the bringing of new industry to town? Explain the reasons for your answers.

12 Money and Prices and Their Relation to the Economy

Preview

The purpose of economic activity is to produce, distribute, and consume the goods and services wanted by society. In economies with specialization of production, where exchange is necessary, money plays an important role. It can be used to stimulate or discourage production, to facilitate distribution and exchange of goods and services, and to measure values. Because money is so enmeshed in people's lives, it has frequently been looked upon as an end in itself rather than as a means to accomplishing the economic purposes indicated above.

Although money is used and sought by virtually everyone, many people are uninformed or mistaken concerning its real nature and its role in serving the economy. In this chapter we will consider these aspects of money, as well as the relationship between prices and money.

Overview

What is money?

What gives money its value?

In what ways may the use of money affect the economy?

How are money and prices related?

247

Part A   Money—Its Functions and Characteristics

Have you ever examined closely the money which you like to acquire and spend? Look at a $5, $10, or $20 bill on which "Federal Reserve Note" is marked over the portrait. In the upper left portion above the seal a statement written in fine print tells that the note is *legal tender* and that it "is redeemable in lawful money at the United States Treasury, or at any Federal Reserve bank." Does this mean that your bill is *not* lawful? At the bottom center the same note says, "Will pay to the bearer on demand X dollars." Does this mean that your X-dollar bill is *not* X dollars?

Much confusion exists about the real nature of money. Many people are under the impression that it has no value unless it is backed by gold or silver. They think that the Federal Reserve note is only a symbol for money, and that real money is the precious metal behind it. Some people look upon money as wealth, and believe that it must therefore have *intrinsic* value.

If we were to study the history of money, we would find that in different places and at different times a variety of things have been used as money. Cattle, shells, beads, tobacco leaves, and various metals—including iron, zinc, bronze, and copper—have all been used as a basis for exchange. The precious metals, particularly silver and gold, have proved most satisfactory for this purpose and have been most commonly used in modern times.

Although the United States backs its Federal Reserve notes with at least twenty-five percent gold, its citizens are not allowed to use gold as money or to convert dollars to gold. This leads us to the conclusion that *it is not what money is but what it does* that is important.

The functions of money

Under simple economic conditions, where most goods and services were produced by the family, necessary exchanges were usually accomplished by bartering goods for goods. Hunters might exchange furs and meat for grain and ammunition. Although the variety of things that our early ancestors produced was remarkable, total production was small because they did not specialize. As specialization developed, it not only increased production but also made the barter system very nearly impossible. Although it might be possible for you to pay a doctor or a lawyer with the goods and services he wants, what would a giant corporation like General Motors do to pay its employees? What could it accept in payment for its cars? How would it decide what stockholders should receive? Any economy with specialization of production needs a *medium of exchange*. This is the chief function of money.

MEDIUM OF EXCHANGE

Returning once again to the basic model of our economy at work, we can see

MONEY IS A MEDIUM OF EXCHANGE

clearly how money serves as a medium of exchange. When businesses sell their goods to consumers, they receive payment in the form of money. This money is then used to pay those who created the goods and services. Since consumers are also the owners of the factors of production that created the value, they receive payment in the form of money. Money itself does not satisfy wants, but it is very convenient for helping us to exchange the many different forms of value in our society. The owner of the factors of production is exchanging for money the value he creates by using his labor, land, or capital. He prefers to receive payment in money rather than by direct payment of goods because the business that is using his services may not have the goods he wants. By giving money to the supplier of factors of production, he can go to the market for goods and services and, now acting as a consumer, buy goods and services there. In this way money becomes the single item that can be used by consumers and businesses for exchanging values.

MEASURE OF VALUE

A second function of money is its use as a measure of value. How do we compare the value of a shirt with that of a seat at a concert? What is the value created by a carpenter who builds a bookcase, or by a cobbler who puts new heels on a pair of shoes? Just as we need measurements for distances, weights, and energy, so we need measurements for the value of things offered at the market. In a barter economy we can speak of a shirt as being worth a seat at a concert, but in a money economy we use a *unit of account*. In the United States the dollar is our *measure of value*. Thus, the shirt is worth $5 and the seat at the concert is worth $5. All things having value at the market may be measured with the common unit of account, the dollar. The use of such a unit aids the exchange of goods.

STORE OF VALUE

A third function of money is its use as a store of value. You may seek to accumulate your wealth, or the purchasing power that you have earned, rather than spending it immediately. Money is the form in which savings are accumulated.

MONEY IS A MEASURE OF VALUES

MONEY IS A STORE OF VALUE

MONEY IS A STANDARD OF DEFERRED PAYMENTS

STANDARD OF DEFERRED PAYMENTS

The last function of money is its use as a standard of deferred payments. When you buy something but do not pay for it immediately, your payment is expressed in terms of money to be paid in the future. With the increase in installment buying this function has become increasingly important.

Characteristics of money

In order for money to perform the functions indicated, it should possess a number of special characteristics that augment its use as legal tender:

1. It should be *durable* so that it will not wear out too quickly; or, failing this, it should be replaceable at a low cost.

2. It should be *portable* so that carrying it will not be burdensome.

3. It should be *divisible* so that the value of items that are fractions of the unit of account (for example, cents) can be calculated and handled easily.

4. It should be easily *recognizable* so that all will know what it is and what its value is.

5. It must be *homogeneous* so that all similar units have equal value.

6. It should have a high degree of *stability of value*, or people may hoard it, waiting for its value to increase, or spend it immediately for fear of its losing value.

7. Most important of all, it must be *acceptable*. Only when it is accepted as purchasing power in the broadest market can it truly serve as a medium of exchange.

From commodity to paper money

As we have seen, commodities have often been used in simple economies as a basis for exchange. If a commodity becomes standardized as money, it will usually lose much of its commodity form and take on instead the aspect of money. When gold and silver were used as money, they became scarcer as ornaments. As economies became more complex and transactions increased, paper money representing units of gold or silver was used. This convertible paper money could be redeemed for the gold or silver that it represented. It is much easier to pay several thousand dollars in paper money than to do so with gold or silver. So long as people recognized that they could convert this paper money to gold or silver, they gladly accepted it.

INFLEXIBILITY OF THE GOLD SUPPLY

One of the major difficulties in using gold, silver, and other precious metals as the basis for a money system is that as an economy continues to develop and greater value is produced, the amount of money in circulation, serving as a medium of exchange, needs to increase also. However, the supply of precious metals depends more on unpredictable discoveries than on the need for it. If no new gold is discovered and if no equally acceptable money is added to the money supply, prices will probably decline. This reduction, together with the shortage of money, will have an adverse effect on business.

By reducing the amount of gold or silver that stands in back of convertible paper money or by printing money which cannot be converted, the government can expand the amount of money available to meet the economic needs of the society. By freeing the money supply from the limitations of chance gold discoveries, these methods give the government some flexibility in managing the supply in circulation.

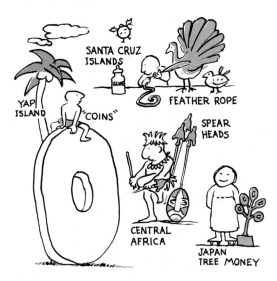

Many commodities have been used as money. Why is commodity money less acceptable in a mature economy?

DANGERS INHERENT IN COMMODITY MONEY

There are, however, several dangers in allowing government to change the backing of money or to print inconvertible paper money. If government allows some money to be converted and other money not to be converted, or if it has two kinds of money (as we once did), one of which is backed by a higher-valued amount of metal, the effect known as *Gresham's law* will set in. This law states that when two types of money are in circulation and have equal stated values but are not equal in demand (the backing of one is worth more than the backing of the other), the less desirable type will drive the other out of circulation. This means that the government must either allow all money to be redeemable with the same metal or allow no money to be redeemable. In 1933 all gold and *gold certificates* were ordered to be turned over to the United States Treasury in exchange for other kinds of money, largely because some people, fearing that other kinds of money would decline in value, had begun to hoard these certificates and coins.

Another danger in a government's printing inconvertible paper money is the irresponsibility with which it may be done. *Fiat money*, which is money that circulates by order of the government, is usually resorted to in order to meet emergencies. Our greenbacks issued during the Civil War had behind them only the promise of the government to pay. If money is issued faster than the output of goods increases, prices will rise rapidly and the value of money will fall correspondingly, as we saw in Chapter 11 (see p. 233). Many economists believe that the metallic backing of money will be less significant to the economy as governments grow wiser in understanding the true role of money and as they learn to regulate the supply of it with responsibility.

Our present money supply

There are many kinds of money in use in the United States today. Some, such as

Table 12-1 Money in Circulation in the
United States, December, 1965

(millions of dollars)

Fractional Currency	3,546
Federal Reserve Notes	36,973
Silver Certificates	651
Other Currency	886
	42,056
Demand Deposits	131,200
Total Money Supply	173,256

SOURCE: U.S. Treasury Department; Federal Reserve System

gold and silver bullion and gold certificates, are held by the government or Federal Reserve banks and are used for backing of other currency. Treasury notes of 1890 and national bank notes make up too small a portion of our total money to be of significance. The three major kinds of money in use may be classified as *fractional currency, paper currency,* and *bank money.*

FRACTIONAL CURRENCY

A very useful but relatively small portion of our money supply is in the form of coins. This so-called "fractional currency" — pennies, nickels, dimes, quarters, and half-dollars — is extremely convenient for the very large number of small purchases we make. With the increasing use of vending machines and with the growing popularity of coin collecting as a hobby, a temporary shortage of coins recently developed. In a newspaper advertisement during the shortage one bank offered to pay people $1.02 for a dollar's worth of change on a particular day. The demand for "change" in that area was greater than the supply.

Coins make up about two percent of our total currency. Fractional currency is sometimes referred to as *token money* because the value of the metal it is made of is considerably less than its face value. A rise in the market value of the metal above the face value of the coins could cause some people to melt down their coins.

PAPER MONEY

About one fifth of our money supply is made up of various kinds of paper money, sometimes known as currency. The bulk of this money is issued by the Federal Reserve banks and is known as Federal Reserve notes. Silver certificates, which now constitute slightly more than one percent of our total money supply, were issued by the United States Treasury from 1878 to 1963. Legislation in 1890, largely in response to the demand of Western silver and agrarian interests, required that the Treasury buy silver bullion to back currency and coinage. Because the need for silver as a commodity has greatly increased, legislation was passed in 1963 dropping the requirement that part of our currency be in silver certificates, and $1 Federal Reserve notes were then printed for the first time. The remainder of the paper currency is made up of United States notes, national bank notes, and Treasury notes of 1890, all of which are in the process of being retired in order to create a more uniform currency.

BANK MONEY

Almost four fifths of our total money supply is made up of bank money, or *demand deposits.* Most people know this kind of money as deposits in commercial banks or as money in their checking accounts. Technically, it is the deposit account that is the money rather than the check itself, since insufficient funds in the account would make the check about as valuable as a counterfeit bill.

Because writing checks is convenient and so much safer than carrying large amounts of "cash," about ninety percent of all transactions are made by check. Checks are the means of transferring ownership of demand deposits. As long as they are accepted as a medium of exchange, they may properly be called bank money or demand deposit money.

Near-monies

In addition to the three kinds of actual money considered, *near-monies* are also used commonly in our economy. Families and businesses hold large amounts of *liquid assets* that come close to being money. The most important categories of near-money are deposits in savings banks and in savings and loan associations, savings deposits in commercial banks, and United States government bonds held by families and businesses (excluding banks and insurance companies). We cannot call these highly liquid assets money because even though they can be very easily converted to currency or demand deposits, they do not circulate as a medium of exchange. You cannot write a check on money in savings accounts (the savings bank may issue you its check) and you cannot pay for merchandise with a government bond.

Although near-monies do not circulate in the same way that currency and checks do, they are of some importance in evaluating people's spending habits and analyzing the price level.

Part B   The Relationship Between Money and Prices

Price levels and price indexes

Although some disagreement exists concerning what effect the supply of money has on the economy, economists generally recognize that a change in the supply can influence business activity and the price level. The relationship between money, prices, and business activity is explained by the quantity theory of money, or the *equation of exchange* (see p. 257). Before we can understand this relationship, however, we must first consider what is meant by the price level and how it is measured.

PRICE LEVELS

If you were to look at a newspaper printed in 1933, you would be surprised at the prices prevailing at that time. You might feel envious as you read about the five-cent bus fare, the loaf of bread or quart of milk for less than fifteen cents, and the dinner at a good restaurant for one dollar. This kind of information about costs provides an indication of *price levels* – the average prices for things purchased during a given period of time. Price levels are extremely important because, taken together with income, they determine the standard of living.

Price levels are also important from a slightly different point of view. If prices are low, money will have greater value, since a given amount of money will buy more goods. In contrast, high prices have the effect of reducing the value of money, since the same amount of money will buy less.

INDEX NUMBERS

Price levels are usually measured by the use of index numbers. A *price index* is a device for measuring the changing value of money over a given period of time. It can also be a measurement of the average price of a number of selected commodities at a given time, such as the index designed to measure the cost of living. Since the prices of the things you buy determine the real value of your money, both definitions of index numbers are appropriate.

HOW INDEX NUMBERS ARE CONSTRUCTED

Economists make use of a number of different price indexes. Each one is designed to measure the price level of a particular market. The two most widely used are the Wholesale Price Index and the Consumer Price Index, both compiled and issued by the Bureau of Labor Statistics of the United States Department of Labor. Industrial production and farm prices are other commonly used indexes. We will use a simplified example of the Consumer Price Index to illustrate the method involved in constructing an index.

We begin by selecting a *base period*, usually three years, in which no war or major depression took place (a "normal" period). We then select a number of common goods and services frequently bought by consumers and assign a relative weight to each item. This weight is determined by economists according to the relationship of purchases among the various items. For example, more weight must be assigned to coffee than to shoes because so much more of the former is bought. Next we add up the sum of the prices times the weighted quantity for all items for each of the years selected. We then add up the sums for the three years and divide by the number of years (3) to get the average price for these items during the base period. We give that figure an index of 100.

Let us suppose that the sum of prices times a weighted quantity for selected items bought in 1957 equals $2,400, in 1958 it equals $2,500, and in 1959 it equals $2,600. The average of these amounts ($7,500 ÷ 3) equals $2,500, which becomes our index of 100 for the base period. Once the index for the base is established, the change in prices for any subsequent year can be computed in relation to the base.

Let $2,500 equal the index 100 for the base period 1957–1959. In 1965 we find that the average price times the weighted quantity for the same items priced earlier now equals $2,750. We then use the following formula:

$$\frac{\text{sum of the prices times weighted quantity for 1957–59}}{\text{sum of the prices times weighted quantity for 1965}} = \frac{100}{X}$$

$$\text{or} \quad \frac{2,500}{2,750} = \frac{100}{X} = 110$$

We find that, from the base period to 1965, prices have *increased* 10 percent; therefore, the value (or purchasing power) of money has *decreased* 10 percent.

Because the things that consumers buy change both in kind and in number, the men who figure the price index must from time to time make substitutions of items selected and weights assigned. Changes must be made with great skill and care so that there will be no distortion of the measurement that gives us the price level or the cost of living index. However, we must remember that the results can be interpreted only as an approximation of actual prices or of the cost of living at a given time.

Figure 12–1 shows the changes in consumer and wholesale prices from 1929 to

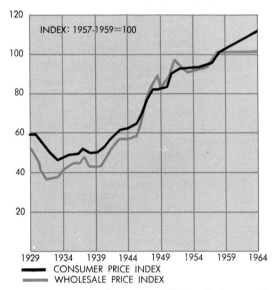

CONSUMER PRICE INDEX
WHOLESALE PRICE INDEX

Figure 12–1   Consumer Price Index and Wholesale Price Index, 1929–March 1965

Prices increased most rapidly from the beginning of World War II until 1960. SOURCE: Bureau of Labor Statistics

1964, with the period 1957–1959 selected as the base period. According to the indexes prices more than doubled from the 1930's to the 1960's. If we add the increase in federal income tax and Social Security taxes and also consider the decrease in the value of money as is shown in Figure 12–2, we can

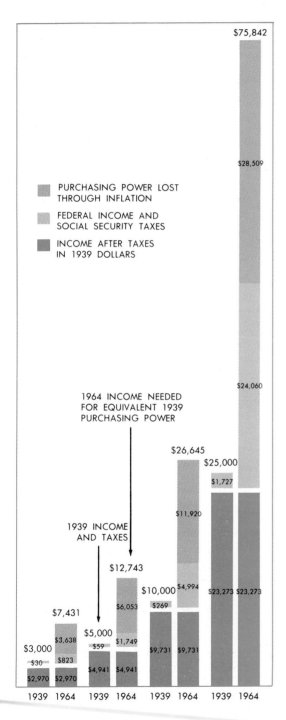

$75,842

$28,509

PURCHASING POWER LOST
THROUGH INFLATION

FEDERAL INCOME AND
SOCIAL SECURITY TAXES

INCOME AFTER TAXES
IN 1939 DOLLARS

1964 INCOME NEEDED
FOR EQUIVALENT 1939
PURCHASING POWER

$24,060

$26,645

$25,000

$1,727

$11,920

1939 INCOME
AND TAXES

$12,743

$26,645

$10,000 $4,994

$23,273 $23,273

$7,431

$6,053

$269

$3,000

$3,638

$5,000

$1,749

$9,731 $9,731

$30

$823

$59

$2,970 $2,970

$4,941 $4,941

1939 1964   1939 1964   1939 1964   1939 1964

understand the need for additional income to maintain the same standard of living in 1964 as in 1939. Actually, incomes have increased faster than both prices and taxes, so that the standard of living is higher today than it was earlier in the period.

Why are stable prices important?

In recent chapters we have observed the relation of inflation and deflation to GNP and to other measurements of the economy as well as to the goal of full employment. Now we are prepared to consider them in a different context—in relation to money supply and prices. *Inflation* may be defined as an increase in the general price level or a decrease in the value of money. *Deflation* is a decrease in the general price level or an increase in the value of money. Economists generally agree that stable prices are desirable and that inflation or deflation has a harmful effect on the economy. There are a number of reasons that support this conclusion. Let us see how changes in price levels affect various segments of the economy.

BORROWING

One economic activity that closely follows changes in price levels is the borrowing of money. A change in the price level from the time money is borrowed to the time it is paid back means that, in effect, the original agreement is changed. The

Figure 12–2   The Two-Way "Squeeze"

The federal income and Social Security taxes shown are for a married couple with two children. The average deductions for each bracket were based on data reported by taxpayers to the Internal Revenue Service, and the taxes were computed in accordance with the new rates and provisions for 1964. No allowance is made for other taxes—federal, state, or local. The purchasing power lost through inflation is based on the change in the Consumer Price Index of the Bureau of Labor Statistics. SOURCES: U.S. Treasury Department; Bureau of Labor Statistics; The Conference Board; N.I.C.B., *Road Maps of Industry* No. 1475

Table 12–2   Major Trends in the Purchasing Power of the Dollar
(changes of 25 cents or more)

DECLINES	NUMBER OF YEARS	PERCENT DECLINE	RANGE OF DECLINE	AMOUNT OF DECLINE	AVERAGE DECLINE PER YEAR
1808– 1814	6	39	$ .87–.53	$ .34	$.057
1834– 1836	2	22	1.24–.97	.27	.135
1860– 1865	5	54	1.34–.62	.72	.144
1897– 1920	23	70	1.75–.53	1.22	.053
1932– 1958	26	64	1.26–.44	.82	.032

RISES	NUMBER OF YEARS	PERCENT RISE	RANGE OF RISE	AMOUNT OF RISE	AVERAGE RISE PER YEAR
1814– 1830	16	134	$.53– 1.24	$ .71	$.044
1839– 1843	4	36	.97– 1.32	.35	.088
1865– 1896	31	182	.62– 1.75	1.13	.036
1920– 1932	12	138	.53– 1.26	.73	.061

SOURCE: *Banking, Journal of the American Bankers Association*, December, 1964

borrower will repay the lender an amount of purchasing power different from that which he originally borrowed. If the price level has risen ten percent, the borrower is paying back dollars that will buy ten percent less in goods and services than this same amount of dollars would have bought originally. Such a change benefits the borrower or debtor and harms the lender or creditor. Deflation also affects both debtor and creditor. How will its impact differ from that of inflation?

FIXED INCOMES

Stable prices are very important to people living on fixed incomes. For them an inflation may result in a lower standard of living. A teacher who retired on a pension of $150 a month in 1950 might have expected to live out the rest of her life in modest comfort and independence. Today, being quite old, she probably requires part-time help in caring for herself and her household. This added expense and the fact that her $150 a month will now buy goods and services worth only $110 at 1950 prices may very well have reduced her to a condition of poverty.

Other kinds of fixed income are similarly affected by inflation. A life insurance policy taken out in 1940 paying the benefi-ciary $12,000 may have seemed adequate at that time. Today its real value is less than half the original face value. Rent and wages set in fixed dollars and covering long periods of time, as well as interest on bonds, are subject to the same loss of purchasing power when the price level moves up.

In contrast with inflation, deflation would increase the purchasing power of the incomes described here. However, the trend in recent years has not been in the direction of deflation. The years since 1940 have witnessed an almost steady increase in prices, and the purchasing power of people on fixed incomes has steadily decreased.

INVESTMENTS

As you learned in Chapter 11, rising prices encourage businessmen to invest. If the investing is done when the economy is producing less than its full-employment capacity, the effect on prices will be slight because the increased dollars will result in increased production. Additional investment made when the economy is operating at or close to production capacity would accelerate the inflationary pressure, since little or no additional production can follow. Deflation, on the other hand, tends to slow down investment and thereby to increase unemployment.

The value of common stock will generally rise as fast as or faster than rising prices, reflecting the increased dollar value of businesses and the tendency for businesses to earn greater profits. A deflation will bring about a decline in the value of common stock. Preferred stock will change in value more closely with the price level, rising less in an inflation and falling less in a deflation because the dividends it pays are frequently set at a fixed percentage.

Because the amount of interest on bonds is fixed, the dollar value of bonds tends to remain stable, regardless of the price level. Consequently, to a bondholder an inflation will mean a reduction in purchasing power, whereas a deflation will give him increased buying power.

The relationship between money and price level

The relationship between money and price level is of great significance in our economy. For a better understanding of how they interact, let us use as an example a simple economic situation, eliminating all costs but labor. There are twenty people in our example, and all are employed at a bakery whose only product is bread. Each day twenty loaves of bread are produced. Everyone in the economy works and receives $1 a day. At the end of the working day all are paid $1, and they go directly to the market, which has twenty loaves of bread for sale. What will the price of a loaf of bread be? If it sold for more than $1, there would be loaves of bread left over and no one to buy them. Supply would be greater than demand and the price would have to come down. If the price were less than $1, the consumers would soon bid the price up, because demand would be greater than supply. At $1 per loaf the market is cleared.

What would happen if one person of the twenty decides that the workers are being exploited and are entitled to a raise? The proprietor might perhaps agree to pay everyone $2 a day rather than undergo a work stoppage. In order to pay the higher wages he must have twenty additional dollars made available to him, giving a total of $40. However, there are still only twenty loaves of bread available per day. The day the raise comes through, workers rush to buy bread. With $40 of money and twenty loaves of bread, what will happen to the price? In a short time the increased money (demand) will drive up the price to the equilibrium level, where the market will be cleared. What would happen to the price of a loaf of bread if the proprietor reduced wages to 50 cents a day?

Let us suppose that the amount of money in the economy remained the same but that production increased to forty loaves a day. What would happen to the price of a loaf of bread? If prices were to be stable, the money supply would have to be increased as production increased. Our example shows in a very simplified way how price level is determined by the quantity of money and the units of production offered for sale.

VELOCITY OF CIRCULATION

Our example may appear unrealistic, since people usually are not paid every day and do not spend immediately exactly what they earn. The fact remains, however, that as people earn, they also spend. Money circulates in the economy from consumers to producers and back to consumers several times during a year. The process by which money changes hands in this way is called the *velocity of circulation* or simply *velocity*. A $1 bill that circulates three times, or that has a velocity of 3, has the same economic effect as $3 that circulates once. If we produced 3,000 loaves of bread a year, the price level would react in the same way whether there was a payment of $3,000 with a velocity of 1 or $1,000 with a velocity of 3.

THE EQUATION OF EXCHANGE

As we noted earlier (see p. 253), economists use an equation, called the equation of exchange, to express the relationship between money, prices, and business trans-

$$M \times V = P \times T \\ (NNP)$$

Price level is influenced by the effective money supply.

actions. This equation may be written as $MV = PT$ and is explained as follows:

M is the money supply (currency + demand deposits).

V is the velocity of circulation.

P is the general price level (index number).

T is the total business transactions in the economy.

The left-hand side of the equation, MV, represents the total effective money supply or total spending for the year. The right-hand side, PT, is the total business for the year. Using our previous example, if money supply is \$1,000 and its velocity is 3, and if we produce and sell 3,000 loaves of bread, the price level can easily be determined. $MV = PT$ is easily converted to

$$P = \frac{MV}{T}, \text{ or } P = \frac{\$1,000 \times 3}{3,000} = \frac{\$3,000}{3,000} = \$1$$

If we double the money supply (M) and keep velocity (V) and transactions (T) the same, we will have doubled the price level, causing an inflation. If we double the number of transactions (T) but keep M and V constant, we will have cut the price level in half, causing a deflation. It would now appear possible to draw the conclusion that if we want the economy to grow (have a higher GNP) and yet want to maintain sta-

ble prices, we must balance an increase in actual production (T) with an increase in spending, or MV.

A case taken from actual history will demonstrate this conclusion. From your studies in American history you may recall the variable economic circumstances of the farmer in the period from shortly after the Civil War until the turn of the century. During the Civil War our nation's money supply, M, had increased with the introduction of greenbacks. Although production increases during wars, the supply of civilian goods does not increase but may even be reduced. With money supply high and transactions in the civilian market limited, inflation results. Prices for farm products are high. Many farmers borrowed money after the Civil War for newly introduced equipment and for the development of new lands. They did so at a time when the price level was high. Although production increased rapidly after the war, the money supply did not (that is, business transactions, T, grew but money supply times velocity, MV, did not). This brought about a decline in the price level, particularly for agricultural products. As a result farmers had to pay back more in terms of purchasing power than they had borrowed.

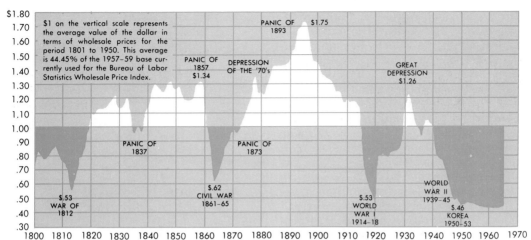

Figure 12–3   Purchasing Power of the Dollar in Wholesale Markets, 1800–1964

In computing the series on purchasing power of the dollar, an average of the index over the 150-year period 1801–1950 was used as the base. A base thus obtained represents the entire period rather than any single year. SOURCE: *Banking, Journal of the American Bankers Association*, December, 1964

Farmers sought a variety of answers to the problem of deflation. One solution was to increase M in order to generate an inflation. Higher prices would mean that fewer bushels would be needed to pay back what was owed. One early suggestion was to increase M by issuing more greenbacks. Later the free and unlimited coinage of silver was urged for the same reason. Although neither of these solutions was adopted, M did eventually increase as a result of changes such as the Sherman Silver Purchase Act (repealed three years after its passage), the discovery of gold in Alaska, and the development of the cyanide process for the more efficient extraction of gold from ore.

CHANGES IN VELOCITY

Our explanation of the equation of exchange and the example of prices of farm products after the Civil War would seem to indicate that the amount of money in circulation *causes* a change in the price level. Until recently most economists believed that velocity remained almost constant. Studies have shown, however, that this is not always true, particularly over short pe-

riods of time. An increase in the amount of money may be followed by a decline in the velocity, as happened during World War II.

LBJ discovers perpetual motion?

In the period since World War II the quantity of money has grown at a slower rate than production, but velocity has increased. Still, in the long run, money velocity has been relatively stable. Although declining during the two world wars and the depression of the thirties, and increasing during the prosperous twenties, fifties, and sixties, it has nevertheless confined its fluctuations to between 2 and 4 and has been close to 3½ during most of this period.

The equation of exchange is still regarded by economists as important in showing the relationship of money to prices and business transactions. A great deal of economic policy is concerned with the control of *M* as one way of keeping a stable price level and influencing business activity.

Effect of changes in the money supply

The actual effect resulting from a change in the money supply depends to a large extent on whether the economy is operating at a full-employment level. From the end of the 1930's until 1942 there was a sharp increase in our nation's money supply, with a corresponding increase in production. During the beginning of this period over nine million people were unemployed and a large part of plant capacity was idle. The additional money stimulated production to a full-employment level. Notice that this change took place without any significant corresponding increase in the price level (about three points). The increased amount of money was matched by an almost equal increase in goods and services, with only a moderate increase in prices. A different effect took place after the war. About one year after the war ended, the price level rose sharply, by twenty-five percent in three years. Although doing away with price controls was a factor, a more basic cause of the increase in prices was the accumulation of money and near-money that could be easily converted into cash and spent for goods. Since our econ-

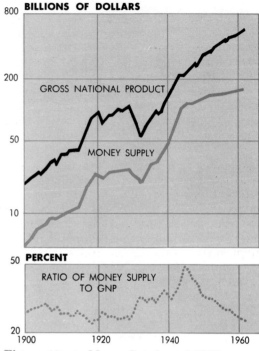

Figure 12–4   Money Supply and GNP

Although the money supply does not have a constant relationship to the GNP, it does fluctuate in the same direction. SOURCE: Federal Reserve System, *Historical Chart Book*

omy was already operating at full capacity, we could not produce all the goods and services demanded by consumers and businesses. By bidding against one another they forced prices to rise.

During the 1950's and 1960's our money supply increased far more slowly than did production, as shown in Figure 12–4. The increase in velocity offset some of the effects of the slow growth of *M*. The price level increased very slowly between 1952 and 1956 and after 1959.

DEMAND-PULL INFLATION

The classical explanation for inflation is called *demand-pull*. This label is used because it explains inflation as we have just done – too much money pursuing too few goods. Figure 12–5 illustrates four conditions in relation to price levels – two of a stable price level and one each of inflation and deflation – resulting from the relationship of money to production.

Although the demand-pull theory sounds reasonable as an explanation for much of our inflation, there are times when it seems to explain nothing. One such time was the period from 1956 to 1960, when the price index rose more than ten points. During these years our economy was operating below full-employment capacity. Though it is true that M was increasing at a slower rate than production and some economists thought that we had more to fear from unemployment than from inflation, other economists offered a different explanation (mentioned previously in Chapter 5, p. 97) for the slowdown in business activity at a time when prices were rising.

COST-PUSH INFLATION

These economists suggest that there is a new kind of inflation that originates on the supply, or cost, side rather than from an excess of demand. The year 1956 was a good year for business, and many of the big labor unions negotiated three-year contracts containing very favorable terms. Profits were very high, and business expected that increased efficiency in production and, if necessary, some of the anticipated additional profits could absorb costs without raising prices. When a recession struck in 1958, the previously negotiated wage increases put great pressure on business to pass these increased costs on to the consumer. Economists call this kind of inflation *cost-push*.

In our economy, with its big labor unions and giant businesses, both of these groups are able to exert some pressure on

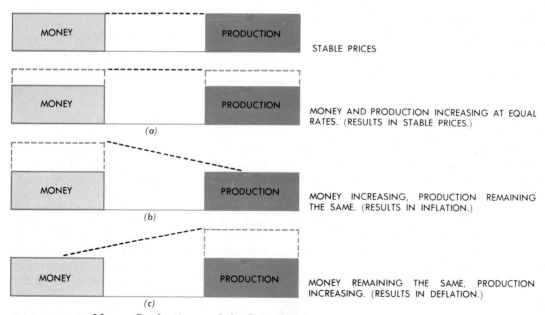

STABLE PRICES

MONEY AND PRODUCTION INCREASING AT EQUAL RATES. (RESULTS IN STABLE PRICES.)

(a)

MONEY INCREASING, PRODUCTION REMAINING THE SAME. (RESULTS IN INFLATION.)

(b)

MONEY REMAINING THE SAME, PRODUCTION INCREASING. (RESULTS IN DEFLATION.)

(c)

Figure 12–5   Money, Production, and the Price Level

The amount of money available for spending in relation to the goods and services available in the market determines whether prices will tend to be *(a)* stable, *(b)* inflationary, or *(c)* deflationary. These examples assume velocity to be constant.

ECONOMIC GUIDEPOSTS

Wage-price guideposts, or guidelines, are a yardstick used to measure the extent of the cost-push type of inflation. These guideposts were first utilized by President Kennedy in the 1962 negotiations with the steel industry over price increases; later they were applied even more extensively by President Johnson. The Council of Economic Advisers prepared for the President an estimate of what they considered to be the average national increase in output per man-hour (3.2 percent is the figure that has been used). Using this estimate as a guide in measuring the normal increase in productivity, the President has asked labor leaders to keep within it in making requests for wage increases. Any wage settlement above the Council's estimate is considered inflationary. Since the cost of limited increase could be absorbed by the rise in productivity, management has in turn been asked not to raise prices on its products. If productivity for a particular industry increases beyond the estimated amount, that industry is expected to reduce the prices for its goods.

To persuade the steel companies to rescind their announced price increases, President Kennedy employed a variety of pressures, including the prestige of his office, a direct appeal to the public, the threat of antitrust action (which was later carried out), and government purchasing from companies that did not raise prices. President Johnson used the huge stores of aluminum and copper held by the government for use in emergencies as a means to keep those industries from raising prices. Knowing that the government would actually be able to reduce market prices by releasing some of its own supplies for sale, the companies concerned decided to abide by the price guide.

Neither labor nor management has been happy with the government's efforts to enforce conformity to the guideposts, claiming that such restrictions interfere with free collective bargaining. Wages have increased somewhat more than the 3.2 percent suggested and prices have tended to increase at an accelerated rate since the last few months of 1965. However, many economists believe that the increases in both prices and wages during 1966 were in fact a reflection of the demand-pull type of inflation as the economy reached the full-employment level.

the market. Although wages and prices seem to be flexible in their upward motion, the facts that unions can exert some control over wages and that businesses exert some control over prices have almost canceled out downward pressures. Business blames labor for what it calls the "wage-price" spiral, saying that higher wages mean higher costs, which it cannot absorb without a price increase. Labor points out the considerable power of business in controlling prices, frequently pushing prices beyond the point of paying for increased wages. These higher prices reduce the purchasing power of increased wages and cause workers to seek added gains. Management can afford to pay increases because of higher profits and increased productivity.

It is probably true that both the demand-pull and the cost-push theories of inflation have a place in explaining rising price levels. Historically, the most severe inflations have been caused by demand-pull. "Creeping inflation," or inflation that takes place slowly over a period of several years, when it occurs during periods of less than full employment can frequently be explained by cost-push. Some economists have suggested that inflationary pressures come from only certain segments of the economy rather than from total demand or overall costs. Economists have learned a great deal about inflation. With this knowledge they have been able to help in formulating policies that have been useful in preventing excessive price spirals. On the other hand, it would be a mistake to think that they "know all the answers."

In our next chapter we will consider our nation's banking system, its effect on M, and its means of influencing business activity and the price level.

Part C   The Problem: How Dangerous Is a Creeping Inflation?

A view of the American economy from 1952 to 1965 shows a slow but steady increase in prices. Only twice during this time, from 1956 to 1957 and from 1957 to 1958, did the Consumer Price Index jump more than two points. Nevertheless, prices during this period have increased more than fifteen percent and have done so at a time when the unemployment rate was, more frequently than not, above five percent. Controversy exists among economists as well as among businessmen and government policy makers concerning the seriousness of a so-called "creeping inflation" and its effect on the economy. Here you will encounter two very different points of view on this problem. Most opinion probably would fall somewhere between these extreme positions.

The focus of disagreement is the question of whether it is possible to have a desirable rate of economic growth without a creeping inflation. If a nation's population is increasing, some economic growth is necessary merely to maintain the present standard of living. If people's standard of living is to increase, the growth rate must surpass the increase in population. Greater productivity of machinery (capital) is important for economic growth, but so is the full use of the labor force. Is a creeping inflation necessary if our economy is to operate at or close to the full-employment level and if it is to have sufficient growth to raise our standard of living? Or are stable prices a better stimulus to economic growth and maintaining full employment?

The case against creeping inflation

Some economists believe that there is no basic conflict between economic growth and stable prices. In fact, stable prices encourage economic growth, as shown in the 1920's and more recently in 1963 and 1964. It is even possible to find prices rising when little growth is taking place. For example, from 1956 to 1958, when economic growth slowed down and the unemployment rate reached 6.8 percent (in 1958), prices on the Consumer Price Index rose six points.

Three major factors are primarily responsible for economic growth in the United States: the increasing size of the labor force, the development of a more skilled labor force, and the addition of more capital per worker. Investment in new machinery depends, at least in part, on the level of savings. Since creeping inflation discourages savings, from which the investment for new machinery comes, it acts to discourage economic growth.

Creeping inflation can, and frequently does, provide a temporary stimulus to business. Inventories are sometimes built up to guard against a rising price level, and capital equipment may be bought for the same reason. This buildup, however, can bring on a serious recession when inventories start to pile up and new machinery has been purchased at a faster rate than might be expected if prices were stable. As merchants try to sell off some of their large stocks of merchandise, they cut back on their orders to middlemen and producers. Producers have no need to order new machinery from producers of capital equipment. The recessions of 1953–54 and 1957–58 are frequently attributed to the desire of businessmen to reduce their inventories, which were too large in relation to the current demand.

Rising prices are a cause of hardship to many people in our society, particularly those who live on fixed or relatively fixed incomes. Older people who live on pensions and unskilled workers who may not have union protection are hurt as they see their purchasing power declining year by year. For more than ten years after World War II the salaries of people with relatively fixed incomes declined in purchasing power as prices rose faster than salaries. This situation occurred most often where there were no strong unions to protect workers against the price rise.

If wage increases could be kept in proportion to increases in output per man-hour, we could progress toward price stability without sacrificing economic growth. Labor leaders, however, are expected to obtain maximum gains for their workers. Nevertheless, those opposed to creeping inflation believe that unless some restrictions are put on the collective bargaining power of unions, there can be little hope of curbing the cost-push inflation. Any restraint on unions would be vigorously resisted. Nevertheless, the benefits derived from stable prices would far exceed any short-term gains made by those now having advantages of income or influence.

Having accepted the use of government policy to promote an economy with high-level employment, we must be equally committed to having government take whatever action is necessary for maintaining stable prices.

The case for creeping inflation

Although, as we have noted, some economists are opposed to creeping inflation, others favor such a policy. They point out that the inflationary tendencies in almost all industrial countries in the 1950's and 1960's have been caused by a combination of strong aggregate demand and production costs rising faster than output per man-hour (cost-push). With strong unions demanding wage increases greater than the increase in workers' productivity, prices have had to rise also. The only way to avoid such increases is to tighten the money supply enough to increase unemployment and thereby discourage wages from rising. An unemployment rate above five percent of our civilian labor force can keep prices quite stable, as was shown in the period from 1960 to 1964.

Although such a policy would put an end to price increases, it also would mean that the potential growth of our economy was not being realized. Is it worthwhile for us to forgo the production of an additional one million workers in order to keep price increases confined to one percent per year instead of about two percent? If our economy fails to grow at its maximum rate, not only do we suffer from the burdens of an immediate unemployment problem but the future growth rate will be affected. Production (consisting in part of capital goods) lost by unemployed workers today can never be made up.

If prices increase at a steady two percent per year, businessmen are encouraged to keep their inventories high and to replace them quickly. Stable prices or falling prices cause businessmen to delay their investments in new merchandise or replacements, since holding off may mean buying at a lower price. Although it is true that sharp price increases may cause businessmen to overload their inventories, making the risk of a recession severe when business starts to level off or decline, the antirecession measures taken in 1961 show that we can reduce the effect and length of these adverse trends.

Some people who fear the effects of creeping inflation suggest reducing the bargaining power of unions. Even if this solution were desirable — and a great many would say it is not — its use is very unlikely. Big unions, with their strong collective bargaining powers, are here to stay. President Johnson's appeal to union negotiators to confine wage demands to the increase in output per man-hour did not stop the United Automobile Workers from asking for and getting an increase above this amount in 1964. Some recent wage increases have been even higher.

The argument that the United States will price itself out of the world market with creeping inflation is not valid. Most industrial nations have seen their wages and prices rise even faster than ours, and there are indications that our own competitive position will be strengthened.

The evidence points to a conflict between maximum economic growth on the one side and stable prices on the other. We have more to fear from stifling growth and having sizable numbers of our work force unemployed than from the effects of creeping inflation. Any ill effects of a slowly increasing price level can be largely offset by such means as encouraging efficient methods of management, putting clauses in insurance and pension plans to allow for increasing price levels, establishing wage contracts that reflect the price level, and setting up investment programs that are based on purchasing power rather than on fixed dollars.

Considering an answer

It is the economist's dream to see his country maintain full employment and rapid economic growth without any increase in the general price level. From 1963 to 1965, as the economy of the United States grew rapidly and approached the level of full employment, prices were remarkably stable and few economists worried about inflation. However, in 1966, when the economy approached full employment, wholesale prices started to rise sharply. Disagreement over policies for meeting this new situation became intense. The arguments cited in our present problem were widely used in the debate on this critical issue of economic policy.

So long as the economy is below full employment, or is "overheated" by aggregate demand in excess of the capacity to produce, little disagreement occurs. It is when the economy appears to be moving from one situation into another that controversy is most intense. At this point the values held by decision makers become as important as the tools available for arriving at answers. Is it more important to prevent a creeping inflation by sacrificing some of the program of the "Great Society" or to assume the risks of inflation in the hope of providing our people with more opportunities and a higher standard of living? Economic history is filled with examples of nations which suffered from uncontrolled inflations as well as nations which managed to keep prices stable but experienced a severe reduction in growth. What are the consequences to the economy if the decisions of policy makers are wrong?

REVIEW: *the highlights of the chapter*

1. Many myths about money still exist in popular thinking. One of the most common is that money must have intrinsic value, as gold does, in order to function as money.
2. An economy which has specialization of production needs money as a medium of exchange.
3. Money also functions as a measure of value, a store of value, and a standard of deferred payment.
4. If money is to perform its functions well, it must be durable,

portable, divisible, recognizable, homogeneous, stable in value, and (most important) acceptable to the public.

5. As an economy grows and becomes more complex, commodity money will give way to convertible paper money. Eventually, inconvertible paper money may become standard, as it has in our economy.

6. Unifying the rules on redeeming or not redeeming all money in the domestic market can avoid the effects of Gresham's law. As governments become more responsible in controlling money, the need for backing of currency becomes less important.

7. The three major kinds of money in use today are fractional currency, paper currency, and bank money or demand deposits. The last kind constitutes nearly four fifths of our money supply.

8. Near-monies are liquid assets that can be easily converted into money. Deposits in savings institutions and U.S. government bonds are the two most important categories of near-monies.

9. Price levels are the average prices paid for goods and services for a given period. Changes in price levels can be measured by comparing the index numbers corresponding to various prices.

10. Inflation is an increase in the general price level or a decrease in the value of money. Deflation is a decrease in the general price level or an increase in the value of money.

11. Stable prices are important in protecting the debtor, the creditor, the investor, and people living on fixed incomes.

12. There is a relationship between money, the price level, and business transactions that can be expressed in the equation of exchange: $MV = PT$.

13. Although studies have shown that velocity of money varies, it has been sufficiently stable in the long run to be regarded as significant in showing the relationship of money to prices and business activity.

14. The effects of increasing or decreasing the money supply when the economy is operating at full employment will be different from the effects at a lower level of employment.

15. Demand-pull inflation occurs when too much money pursues too few goods. The excess demand results in rising prices.

16. Cost-push inflation is caused by price rises due to increasing costs. This situation can develop when wages increase faster than output per man-hour or when prices rise faster than wages, forcing workers to seek higher wages.

IN CONCLUSION: *some aids to understanding*

Terms for review

medium of exchange	base period
Gresham's law	deferred payments
Federal Reserve notes	Treasury notes
greenbacks	fractional currency
silver certificates	near-money
currency	fiat money
commodity money	equation of exchange
liquid assets	index numbers
price level	deflation
inflation	demand-pull inflation
velocity of circulation	cost-push inflation
intrinsic value	guideposts
wage-price spiral	creeping inflation

Questions for review

1. Money serves many purposes in a nation's economy. List and explain the major functions of money.
2. What are the specific characteristics of money?
3. Government policies in regard to money supply and price levels make it possible to reduce the more extreme effects of inflation and deflation.
   (a) What are some actions that the government can take to influence price levels and the supply of money?
   (b) What are the potential dangers of each of these actions?
4. Explain the meaning of the following statements:
   (a) "In a complex economic world money is anything that most people accept freely."
   (b) "Money is the most common denominator for all production."
5. Explain the effects of deflation and the effects of inflation on the following: (a) a pensioner, (b) a lender of money, (c) an owner of common stock, (d) an owner of fixed-rent property, (e) a union wage policy committee, and (f) a civil service employee.
6. Explain the statement "The business and consumer segments of our economy can plan most effectively if assured of price stability over a period of time."
7. What is meant by the following ideas?
   (a) "Full employment without inflation is the underlying strength of our economy."
   (b) "Wage increases need not be inflationary."
   (c) "Industry is responsible for resisting price increases."

Additional questions and problems

1. Indicate the areas of the United States where the following commodities were once used as money: (a) tobacco, (b) furs, (c) jugs of whiskey, (d) wooden coins, (e) nails. Explain the circumstances of using the commodity as money in each case.

2. Explain these statements:
   (a) "At times in our nation's history the pressure of special interests and particular segments of the economy has resulted in laws affecting our money supply."
   (b) "The election of 1896 might well be called the 'Battle of the Standards.' "

3. Associate particular historic events and national legislation with the major changes shown in Figure 12-1.

4. Select fifteen commodities and five services available to the consumer both in 1925 and at present.
   (a) Assign an appropriate cost to every item for each date. Make a total of the costs for each date.
   (b) Create index numbers for each item, using 1925 as a base of 100. When your lists are complete, compare the prices for each item at the different dates. What conclusions can you draw?
   (c) Explain some of the reasons for the use of the index numbers.
   (d) What weaknesses are inherent in the use of index numbers?

5. In this chapter you have been introduced to new ways of interpreting changes in our economy.
   (a) Using the chart in Figure 12-4, explain the fluctuations in GNP and money supply from 1930 to 1932 and from 1940 to 1946.
   (b) What factors of our economy made the period 1950 to 1964 one of gradual change rather than of radical upheaval?

6. Because of the delicate balance between inflation and deflation in our economy, a change in wage rates is of particular significance.
   (a) Select any of the major national labor contracts negotiated in the last two years and explain how the balance between the demands of labor and the concessions of management represents a potential inflation of the demand-pull and cost-push categories.
   (b) Assume you are the representative of the public in a labor dispute. What arguments would you use to make both union and management negotiators realize that a purely selfish approach would hurt both?

13 Banking and the Creation of Money

Preview

In the previous chapter we considered the importance of money to the national economy. Here we are concerned with financial institutions that deal with money and credit. Through these institutions the money that people save is made available to those who need it for investment or purchases. Like all resources, money must be carefully allocated in the right amounts, to the right places, and at the right times in order to further the production of the goods and services that consumers want.

Controlling the supply of money as a means of influencing business activity and price levels is important for the well-being of the entire economy. The role of our nation's banking system as an intermediary in the flow of money and as a factor influencing the amount of that flow is the major concern of this chapter.

Overview

What are the major functions of banks?

How does a commercial bank create money?

What controls over banking do you consider necessary?

How does our banking system serve the government as well as business and the consumer?

Part A   Kinds of Financial Institutions

Banks and their functions

To many people the term "financial institution" refers to a bank, which they may think of primarily as a convenient place to deposit their valuables, particularly money, for protection against the hazards of theft and fire. Actually, there are many different kinds of businesses that may be called banks or financial institutions. Although each of these may serve a particular purpose, they all have one activity in common—collecting money from a source that does not need it immediately and channeling it to others that do have an immediate use for it. Thus, these various financial institutions serve as intermediaries in the flow of money throughout the economy. In addition to this general activity, they carry on a number of more specialized functions.

DEPOSITORIES

The earliest banks were mere depositories for the safekeeping of valuables. Centuries ago many people deposited their gold in the vaults of goldsmith shops and withdrew it as needed. In order for such a bank to meet its expenses, depositors paid a fee to have their money stored. Later, as these banks issued notes payable in gold, bookkeeping and the balance sheet became important tools for keeping accurate records.

LENDING

With many businesses and individuals wanting to borrow money and with funds lying idle in their vaults, banks naturally turned to the business of lending money. Depositors were told that if they would permit the banks to use their money for lending, they would not have to pay a storage fee. Under certain conditions they could even receive payment (interest) for the use of their money. The banks could afford these arrangements because they loaned the money out at a rate of interest higher than they paid to the depositors. In our own economy this lending function, by which the money of depositors is channeled to various categories of borrowers, is performed by *savings banks*.

MONEY CREATION

In the course of lending money, bankers discovered that the total amount of money they had on deposit fluctuated very little. Although individuals might alter the size of their accounts considerably from day to day, the total of all deposits in a particular bank remained fairly constant because withdrawals by some people were usually balanced by the deposits of others. This discovery allowed bankers to use most of the money on deposit for loans with little fear of a shortage of funds, even when depositors wished to withdraw their money.

Using this knowledge, *commercial banks* today are in effect able to create money by using funds from *demand deposits* as the basis for additional deposits, in the form of loans extended to borrowers. This function is of great importance to individual banks and to the whole economy. Let us see how banks create money, though we recognize that our example holds true for the banking system as a whole rather than for any single commercial bank.

A bank with $1 million on deposit can keep $100,000 in reserve, in case withdrawals temporarily exceed deposits, and lend out the remaining $900,000. Loans are made merely by placing the amount of money borrowed in an account under the name of the borrower. The borrower can then issue a check on his account. These checks form a medium of exchange and can be considered money. The bank now has $1 million in demand deposits from original deposits and an additional $900,000 created by the borrowing and the use of money credited to demand deposit accounts. Both the original depositor and the borrower are entitled to write checks on their accounts.

Other financial institutions and their functions

In addition to commercial banks, many other kinds of financial institutions exist in our economy. They are designed to meet the different requirements which people have for their savings. Each of these institutions tends to have a particular function and to serve a certain kind of depositor.

SAVINGS INSTITUTIONS

There are three major forms of savings institutions: *mutual savings banks*, *savings and loan* (or building and loan) associations, and *savings departments* in commercial banks. These institutions take the money for which people have no immediate need and place it in personal savings deposits. Although they do not often do so, savings institutions may request depositors to give a notice of intent to withdraw funds. Because of this requirement, savings accounts are called *time deposits*, in contrast to the demand deposits (checking accounts) of commercial banks, from which money may be withdrawn at the depositors' will.

Most of the savings in these institutions come from people of modest income who expect to receive interest on their money but are unwilling to take much risk. Mutual savings banks invest their deposits in real estate mortgages, government bonds, and securities that yield a return in interest higher than that paid to depositors. Savings and loan associations concentrate primarily on home mortgages. Savings banks are usually restricted by law to investments in securities that have little risk. This requirement protects those whose savings are based on modest incomes and to whom loss of these savings might be economically disastrous.

PERSONAL TRUSTS

Trust companies and the trust departments of commercial banks invest the funds of people with financial security who want to provide income for their families. The money deposited in these institutions is invested in many different types of securi-ties, usually not speculative in nature but providing an assured return. These personal trusts must not be confused with the industrial trusts mentioned in Chapter 3.

INSURANCE COMPANIES

The purpose of *insurance companies* is to allow people to pool their resources in order to minimize the risk associated with accident, sickness, death, and other unpredictable circumstances. In 1964 life insurance companies in the United States had assets of over $145 billion. Although the money they collect must be paid out at some time, they control huge sums of money, most of which are placed in long-term investments. The largest portion is put into bonds and mortgages, although significant investments, strictly regulated, are made in real estate and stocks.

CONSUMER CREDIT INSTITUTIONS

In Chapter 9 we discussed the tremendous increase in consumer credit which has taken place in recent years. Consumers borrow from small finance companies, credit unions, sales finance companies, and the small-loan departments of commercial banks. Most finance companies do not obtain their loanable funds from the public. Instead they frequently turn to other financial institutions, from which they borrow at rates lower than those at which their clients can borrow. For example, Ford and General Motors have set up finance companies as an aid to their dealers in selling cars. *Credit unions* are set up on a cooperative basis and are organized for a particular group, such as civil service employees, workers in a large company, or people who live in a housing development. Members of a credit union may put their savings into the credit union and receive shares for these deposits. Each share earns interest for the contributor. Members may borrow at comparatively low rates of interest.

OTHER FINANCIAL INTERMEDIARIES

Large businesses frequently require money for long-term capital investment beyond the resources of most commercial

Banks are becoming less and less specialized in their operations as they add new functions to increase their market for customers.

banks. Such firms may decide to raise the money through the issuance of bonds or stocks. Investment banks or, less often, brokerage houses may be asked to manage the sale of these new securities (see p. 48).

The federal government, too, has become a major source of loans in a number of fields. Through a variety of agencies it assists farmers, home owners, small busi-

nesses, and smaller units of government. In many instances the government does not lend the money itself, but merely insures the payment of the loan to the private banker up to a certain percentage of the loan. This practice has made borrowing possible for many families and businesses to which loans might otherwise not be available.

Part B　Commercial Banks and the Creation of Money

Organizing and operating a bank

As we have seen, commercial banks are unique among financial institutions because of their ability to create money. Demand deposits (checking accounts) make up about four fifths of our money supply. The ability of these banks to maintain and create demand deposits by means of loans and investments influences the supply of money, *M*, in our economy. Because other financial institutions do not have demand deposits and no checks may be written on their accounts, they do not exercise control over the amount of money in circulation.

In Chapter 3 we set up an imaginary business in order to explain business organization and some of its problems. Let us do the same with a commercial bank, having as our objective an understanding of the part played by these banks in our economy.

ORGANIZING A BANK

Banking is a business in which the product offered for sale is money. As with other businesses the incentive is to earn profits. We can best accomplish this aim by offering to the public what it wants and by operating our business as efficiently as possible. In this way we are serving ourselves and society at the same time.

We begin by calling a meeting of people who would be interested in using their money to organize a commercial bank. At this meeting we must decide how much capital will be needed and whether we wish to function as a state bank or a national

bank. Both the state and federal levels of government have laws regulating the operation of the banks under their authority. Having agreed that we will raise $200,000 in capital, enough for us to qualify as a national bank in a city of our size (40,000), we decide to petition the United States Comptroller of the Currency to issue us a charter. Having become a legal corporation under the name The Felix National Bank, we can begin to sell stock in our company. We appoint a board of directors, which in turn appoints a president and other officers. In the meantime a building has been selected and renovated to meet a bank's needs, and a staff has been hired.

As we begin our operations, we set up a balance sheet—a statement showing *assets*, *liabilities*, and *net worth*. Assets are items that the bank owns or has claims to. Liabilities are claims made by others against the bank. The difference between the two is the net worth, made up of payments by stockholders and profits earned but not paid to the owners. It is called a *balance sheet* because assets always equal (or balance) liabilities and net worth.

THE FELIX NATIONAL BANK
BALANCE SHEET
September 1, 1966

ASSETS
Cash $200,000

LIABILITIES AND NET WORTH
Capital stock $200,000

As a national bank we must become a member of the Federal Reserve System (of which some state banks also are members). We deposit our money with the Federal Reserve Bank (see p. 279) in our region, which deposits it in our *reserve account.* Our bank is now considered a member bank. We ask the Federal Reserve Bank to return $50,000, which is entered on our books as "cash in vault," in order to take care of our immediate business needs. This withdrawal reduces our reserve account to $150,000.

At the end of one week of business, in which we have concentrated our efforts on persuading people to make demand deposits, we have $300,000 in new accounts. We deposit this money, some in currency and some in checks, with the Federal Reserve Bank in our reserve account. Our balance sheet now reads:

ASSETS

Cash in vault	$ 50,000
Reserve account	450,000
Total assets	$500,000

LIABILITIES AND NET WORTH

Deposits	$300,000
Capital stock	200,000
Total liabilities and net worth	$500,000

Until now we have not mentioned the matter of expenses incurred in running the bank, and we have made no effort to earn money. Obviously, we cannot continue in business this way very long; we must begin to use our "merchandise," money. To do this, we set up a loan department, which makes loans totaling $50,000. They are made by crediting to the account of the borrower the amount of his loan; that is, our bank, when it makes a loan, places in a demand deposit account belonging to the borrower the amount he has borrowed. In return, the borrower gives us a *promissory note.* Our balance sheet now reads:

ASSETS

Cash in vault	$ 50,000
Reserve account	450,000
Loans	50,000
Total assets	$550,000

LIABILITIES AND NET WORTH

Deposits	$350,000
Capital stock	200,000
Total liabilities and net worth	$550,000

As we saw previously, lending money results in the creation of new demand deposits. By this action the supply of money in circulation is increased. We will, of course, earn money by collecting interest on the money loaned, but that is not considered a part of the process of money creation.

We would be very poor bankers if we continued to utilize less than 10 percent of our assets. As bankers we have as our objectives to: (1) make money for our stockholders, (2) have enough cash and highly liquid assets on hand so that our depositors know that they will be paid whenever they wish to withdraw money (write checks on their accounts), and (3) help the businessmen in the community with short-term credit to take care of their needs for loanable funds. All we have done so far is to protect our depositors. In order to achieve our other objectives we shall have to put more of our money to work. We can do this by granting additional loans, some to local businessmen, and by placing a portion of our money in safe interest-bearing securities that can easily be converted into cash for meeting withdrawals. Thus, our other objectives are met, either directly or indirectly.

With increases in both demand deposits and loans, our bank begins to operate more efficiently. We will assume that, after we have been in business for two years, our bank has doubled in size. Our balance sheet might now look like this:

ASSETS

Cash in vault	$ 50,000
Reserve account	250,000
Loans	400,000
Securities	350,000
Fixtures	50,000
Total assets	$1,100,000

LIABILITIES AND NET WORTH

Deposits	$ 800,000
Surplus	50,000
Undivided profits	50,000
Capital stock	200,000
Total liabilities and net worth	$1,100,000

Let us analyze the various items on the balance sheet to see why our money is distributed as shown there. First we will consider the items listed as assets.

CASH IN VAULT

Our bank needs cash on hand to take care of its day-to-day business. Because withdrawals are usually matched by deposits, a bank rarely needs more than about two percent of its demand deposits in cash. Since this money earns no interest for us, it would be foolish to keep a large amount on hand. We have been on the cautious side, making sure an adequate supply of currency is always available.

RESERVE ACCOUNT

As a member bank of the Federal Reserve System we are required to keep a certain percentage of our demand deposits on account with the Federal Reserve Bank in our district. The Federal Reserve Board of Governors sets the *reserve ratio*, the amount that must be retained in the reserve account in relation to total demand deposits. For a bank in our city the reserve requirement is 12 percent. The balance sheet shows that we are cautious in this respect.

LOANS

We know that we can earn the most money and serve the community best through loans, provided that these are made to borrowers who offer little risk. Businessmen often need cash to carry them from one business season to another. Helping businessmen to start or expand operations can result in more business for the community and, eventually, more demand deposits and more loans for our bank.

For loans involving somewhat more risks than we would like, we ask the borrower for *collateral*: stocks, bonds, or other property of value to make the loan more secure. Interest rates are usually highest for consumers who borrow in our small-loan department. The fixed cost for processing a loan accounts for part of the higher rate.

SECURITIES

Rather than take a chance on additional loans with high risks, we use most of our remaining money to buy various securities, mostly United States government short-term securities. Although these Treasury bills and certificates generally pay between three and five percent interest rather than the five to six and a half percent paid on business loans, they involve no risk and can easily be converted to cash if needed to meet withdrawals. Since no payment of interest is allowed on demand deposits, this smaller return is better than it might at first appear. These securities are often referred to as *secondary reserves*.

FIXTURES

The term "fixtures" refers to the material items of value in the building we rent. Since our company owns them, we can consider them as part of our total assets.

DEPOSITS

We will next consider the items listed under the heading "Liabilities and Net Worth." As you know, the value of total liabilities and net worth is equal to the value of total assets.

The deposits referred to on our balance sheet under the heading of "Liabilities and

Net Worth" are the demand deposits previously referred to. They are made up of *primary deposits*, those made by people depositing money in the bank, and *derivative deposits*, those that come into being by borrowing from the bank.

SURPLUS, UNDIVIDED PROFITS, AND CAPITAL STOCK

Taken together, these three items make up our net worth. Surplus and undivided profits come from the money we have earned through loans and investments (profits) but not paid out to the owners. Capital stock is held by the people who own shares in our business.

We cannot expect derivative deposits to remain in our bank very long, inasmuch as those who borrowed the money did so because they needed it to meet their expenses. When in turn they pay their creditors, the checks reduce deposits in our bank as the amount of each check is added to the account of the creditor in his bank. Thus, although the loan may not have increased the demand deposits in our bank for more than several days, the loan has, in the course of being spent, increased the total demand deposits in the banking system as a whole. Most demand deposits in our country originate from bank loans.

Limits to credit creation

Since our highest earnings come from lending money to businessmen and others, why do we limit this activity? If profit is really our objective, why don't we continue to lend as much as possible so long as we have customers who involve little risk to us? Although it is true that we need only a small percentage of cash on hand in relation to the total amount of our demand deposits, there is always the danger of a period of heavy withdrawals in which current deposits are not sufficient to balance the withdrawals. As bankers we recognize that a balance must be maintained between the cash we have available and the credit (loans) we have extended.

In 1933 the number of bank failures increased sharply. Rumor was often sufficient to cause a run on a bank, making failure more likely. Establishment of the Federal Deposit Insurance Corporation has almost completely eliminated this cause of failure.

FEDERAL DEPOSIT INSURANCE CORPORATION

Before 1933, and particularly during the period from 1929 to 1933, bank failures were not uncommon. If a bank overextended itself in creating credit or if several of its important loans could not be repaid, depositors in the bank would frequently become panicky and begin to make large withdrawals—to make a run on the bank. Since the bank had only a fraction of its deposits backed by currency (fractional reserves as opposed to 100 percent reserves), the bank would soon be unable to meet withdrawals and most depositors would lose their money. If the bank could borrow money from another bank to pay those withdrawing money, people's confidence would return and they would probably redeposit their money. Frequently a bank merely needed time to improve its cash position by calling in some of its loans and not making additional ones. In 1933 the number of bank failures reached a peak, forcing the federal government to intervene and close the banks temporarily. To help restore the public's confidence and strengthen the banking community, Congress passed legislation setting up the Federal Deposit Insurance Corporation. This corporation, an agency of the federal government, now insures over ninety percent of all bank deposits up to $15,000 per deposit. The FDIC has built up its insurance fund by charging one twelfth of one percent on the total deposits of member banks.

As a result of the protection provided by the FDIC and other kinds of supervision, bank failures have been reduced to a few isolated instances, due mainly to embezzlement. Since people know that their deposits are insured, they no longer rush to withdraw their money if they become concerned about the financial condition of their bank. The delay gives banks the time needed to adjust their cash credit balance, thereby reducing the possibility of bankruptcy.

LEGAL RESERVES

Since the creation of the FDIC, less need exists for keeping a bank's cash-to-credit ratio high because it is unlikely that a run on the bank will occur. In addition, *legal reserves* are set by the Federal Reserve System for member banks and by the state for nonmember banks. These requirements set an upper limit on the amount of credit a bank can create. If the reserve requirements are set at 20 percent, the bank can have demand deposits equal to five times its reserves. A bank with $1 million of demand deposits must have $200,000 on reserve (cash in vault is included as reserve). If its actual reserves are

$300,000, it has $100,000 of *excess reserves*.

What use can the bank make of this $100,000, which exceeds the requirement of 20 percent? It may lend up to four fifths of it, or $80,000, and retain $20,000 in reserves. This may at first appear to you to be a four-to-one ratio, $1 of reserves to $4 of loans. However, you will recall that the reserve must be included in your demand deposits, and the ratio is *reserves* to *demand deposits*, not *reserves* to *loans*. Loans plus reserves equal demand deposits ($80,000 + $20,000 = $100,000), or a 5-to-1 ratio to reserves ($20,000). If the legal reserves were increased to 25 percent, how much excess reserves would the bank have?

Although the legal reserves do serve to provide safety in regard to a bank's cash-credit balance, their major purpose is to limit the extent of credit creation. *By limiting credit creation, we also limit the size of the major portion of our money supply, demand deposits.*

LOSING RESERVES TO OTHER BANKS

When depositors in our bank write checks to people with accounts in other banks, our bank must pay cash to the other banks. This payment reduces our reserves and increases the reserves of the other banks. Normally, the checks written by our customers and deposited in other banks are offset by the deposits our customers make with checks from other banks. We would not expect our reserve to change much as checks *against* our reserves are balanced with checks *for* our reserve.

However, if we lend money to the limit of our legal reserve, we risk having an adverse clearing balance (an overdraft) in our account with the Federal Reserve Bank. Since people with derivative deposits usually write checks almost immediately on their borrowed funds, far more so than those with primary deposits, we would probably find that our reserves had declined below the legal requirements as checks drawn on our bank are presented for payment from our account with the Federal Reserve Bank. When this happens, we must pay a penalty to the Federal Reserve Bank.

Creation of money by the entire banking system

The fear of having an adverse clearing balance limits a single bank in using its excess reserves. However, if the banking system is considered in its entirety, we can see that adverse clearing balances for some banks must be matched by favorable clearing balances of other banks. If more money is drawn on our account than we gain from checks deposited with us from other banks, we lose reserves. To understand what happens when the banking system creates money by expansion of demand deposits, let us follow an example through all the steps of the process.

CREATING MONEY BY DEPOSITS

Mr. Smith, our imaginary customer, arrives at the First Bank with $1,000 in cash, which he deposits in his checking account. The First Bank, with demands for loans exceeding its ability to grant them, now has additional money to work with. We will assume that the Federal Reserve has set the legal reserves at twenty percent. The First Bank lends $800 to Mr. A and puts $200 in its reserve account with the Federal Reserve Bank in its district. Mr. A immediately writes a check on his derivative deposit to Mr. B. First Bank officials are not worried, since they have already anticipated that Mr. A would withdraw his money from the loan and have put the $200 aside to take care of legal reserve requirements.

Mr. B deposits Mr. A's check in his own account in the Second Bank. With $800 in a new deposit the Second Bank lends $640 to Mr. C and puts $160 (20 percent of $800) in reserves. Mr. C now pays Mr. D the amount of $640, which Mr. D deposits in his account. The Third Bank loans $512 to Mr. E and puts $128 in its reserve account. Mr. E pays the $512 to Mr. F.

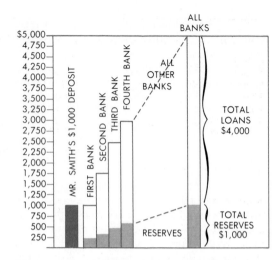

Figure 13–1   Expansion Process of the Banking System

Mr. Smith's new $1,000 deposit eventually serves as the support for $5,000 of deposits ($4,000 loans and $1,000 reserves) with a 20 percent reserve requirement.

Mr. F deposits Mr. E's check in his account. With the new deposit of $512 the Fourth Bank loans $409.60 and protects its twenty percent legal reserve requirement by putting $102.40 in its reserve account.

This expansion process continues on through the banking system until all of Mr. Smith's $1,000 of currency ends up in the reserves of the banks involved. Through the banking system's process of granting loans, Mr. Smith's $1,000 has been expanded to $5,000 of deposits.

We can see in Table 13–1 that, with a 20 percent legal reserve requirement, one dollar of reserves can support five dollars of deposits or four dollars of loans. Reserve dollars are frequently called "high-powered" dollars because adding or subtracting reserve dollars has the ultimate effect of increasing or decreasing deposits by many times the reserve dollars themselves.

By now you may wonder why the First Bank could not take Mr. Smith's $1,000

Table 13–1 An Illustration of the Creation of Money by Deposits

BANKS	DEPOSITS	RESERVES	LOANS
First	$1,000.00	$ 200.00	$ 800.00
Second	800.00	160.00	640.00
Third	640.00	128.00	512.00
Fourth	512.00	102.40	409.60
All Other Banks Together	2,048.00	409.60	1,638.40
Total	$5,000.00	$1,000.00	$4,000.00

deposit and add it to its reserve account. In this way the First Bank could expand its loans to $5,000. This would be acceptable if those who borrowed the money left all of it in their accounts or if the First Bank were the only bank in existence. However, people who borrow money use it; when their checks are deposited in other banks, the First Bank would not have the reserves or cash to make payment to the other bank.

You may also wonder how the First Bank (and subsequently every other bank) is able to meet its reserve requirements when the Federal Reserve Bank subtracts from its reserve account the $800 drawn on it when Mr. B deposits his check in the Second Bank. Remember that the First Bank has put only $200 of the original $1,000 in its

reserve. The answer is that the First Bank, like other banks, will tend to have check clearances against its reserves offset by check clearances added to its reserve account. Because of this the $200 put in the First Bank's reserve account is enough to meet the reserve requirement.

It is important to recognize that the individual banks *cannot* expand their deposits five times: each bank that lends money no longer has use of the funds. The bank's balance sheet would show that its loans and investments would be no larger than four times its reserves or four fifths of its deposits. *It is the banking system as a whole that expands our money supply, M, through the use of demand deposits, as shown by the total in Table 13–1.*

Part C   The Federal Reserve System

With the exception of the First Bank of the United States (1791) and the Second Bank of the United States (1816), our federal government concerned itself less with banking operations than did the governments of other industrial nations during the nineteenth century. This period of inaction ended in 1913, when Congress passed the Federal Reserve Act. This legislation, later expanded, created the Federal Reserve System to serve as the central banking institution of the United States, providing currency, regulating the total amount of money in the economy according to need,

and furnishing other financial services needed by both public and private sectors of the economy. Our Federal Reserve System differs from the centralized banking systems of most other industrial nations by being a relatively new institution, by being more decentralized, and by not being government-owned. Our nation's monetary policy is in the hands of a small group of appointed specialists who are responsible for serving the interests of the general public rather than the stockholders of any single bank or group of banks and who must at times act on behalf of the government.

Organization of the Federal Reserve System

By the Federal Reserve Act our country is divided into twelve districts, each with a Federal Reserve bank located in one of the major cities in the district. Ten of the districts have at least one additional branch bank. The boundaries of each district, the location of the Federal Reserve banks, and the location of the branch banks are shown on the map.

FEDERAL RESERVE BANKS

Each Federal Reserve bank is owned by its member banks, which are required to buy stock in it. Member banks receive dividends, but it must be emphasized that the Federal Reserve banks do not operate for profit. Each bank has a board of nine directors, six chosen by the member banks and three appointed by the Board of Governors. Only three of the nine members may be bankers; thus the board of directors is designed to operate in the public's interest. Although the policy of each Federal Reserve bank must conform to the general policy set by the Board of Governors, many decisions are made in the best interests of the district, including what rate of interest should be charged to member banks. These decisions, however, must have the approval of the Board of Governors.

BOARD OF GOVERNORS

The final responsibility for the functioning and policy making of the Federal Reserve System is with the seven-man Board of Governors, which oversees the entire system. Members of this Board are appointed by the President and are con-

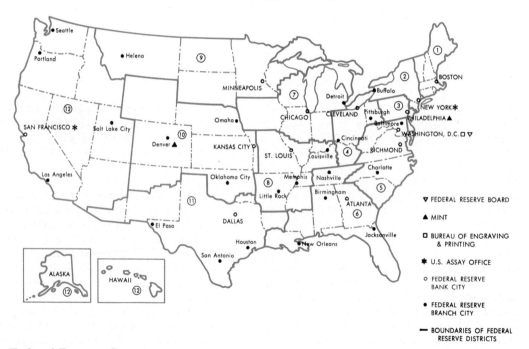

The Federal Reserve System

The Federal Reserve System is the federal government's chief means for implementing banking and monetary policies. Shown in addition are the Treasury Department's mints, assay offices, and Bureau of Engraving and Printing. SOURCE: Federal Reserve System, *Federal Reserve Bulletin*

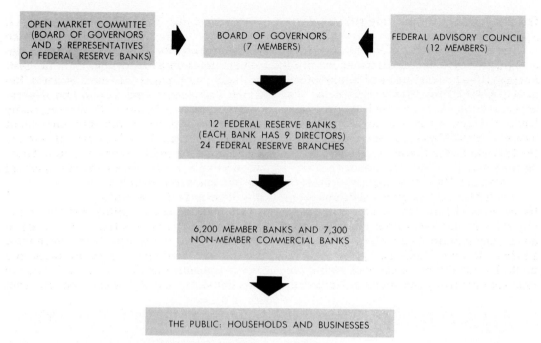

Figure 13–2   Organization of the Federal Reserve System

SOURCE: Federal Reserve System, Board of Governors

firmed by the Senate for 14-year terms. These terms are arranged so that a new appointment is made every two years, a provision which minimizes the influence of pressure groups. Originally organized to coordinate the functions of the Federal Reserve banks, the Board has gradually increased its influence on the entire system.

FEDERAL OPEN MARKET COMMITTEE

One of the most important functions of the Federal Reserve System is the purchase and sale of government securities. These activities are carried on by the twelve-member Federal Open Market Committee. Seven of its members are the members of the Board of Governors, and the other five are presidents of Federal Reserve banks, always including the president of the New York Bank.

This committee meets frequently to determine policy on open-market opera-

tions, which influence our money supply. It gives specific instructions to its agent, the Federal Reserve Bank of New York, regarding the purchases and sales of government securities (see p. 285).

FEDERAL ADVISORY COUNCIL

Each Federal Reserve bank annually selects from its district a prominent commercial banker to serve on the Federal Advisory Council. This Council, which meets in Washington at least four times a year, is designed to present the views of bankers to the Board of Governors. Its powers are purely advisory.

MEMBER AND NONMEMBER BANKS

About 6,000 of the almost 14,000 commercial banks in the United States are members of the Federal Reserve System. All national banks must be members, and some state banks are also. These member banks hold about eighty-five percent of all demand deposits and include all the large banks. They are required to comply with the numerous regulations of the Federal Reserve System, including periodic examinations by the Federal Reserve bank inspectors. The Federal Reserve System also exerts a strong influence over nonmember banks, which have working agreements with member banks and use certain services of the Federal Reserve System.

Services of the Federal Reserve

The Federal Reserve System provides a wide range of services to banks throughout the country. Through these services its influence extends from the highest levels of government down to the local community. We will examine the activities of the Federal Reserve before going on to analyze its role in determining and carrying out particular policies.

HOLDING RESERVES OF MEMBER BANKS

As you have seen, the Federal Reserve Bank in each district holds on deposit the legal reserves of its member banks. Cash in the member banks' vaults may also be counted toward these reserves. Any amount held on deposit above the legal reserves (that is, excess reserves, described previously on p. 277) may be drawn upon by the member banks. Member banks try to keep a balance between having sufficient reserves to avoid falling below legal reserve requirements and having too large excess reserves which earn no interest. Banks frequently borrow from one another to maintain this delicate balance.

PROVIDING CURRENCY FOR CIRCULATION

Currency in our country comes either from the United States Treasury or from the Federal Reserve banks. As we saw in Chapter 12, Federal Reserve notes make up eighty-five percent of our currency. The Federal Reserve banks issue this currency to member banks as they need it by the simple means of subtracting it from their reserve accounts. Although there is always a need for new currency to replace that which wears out, public demand for currency increases sharply at certain times of the year, such as the Christmas season. The Federal Reserve banks keep a large supply of currency on hand so that member banks can draw on their accounts as the new money is needed.

During February, when business activity normally declines and there is less need for currency, the member banks frequently find themselves with too much cash available. They simply redeposit the surplus of currency with the Federal Reserve bank, just as their customers have done with them. This cash is then credited to their reserve accounts.

PROVIDING A CLEARING HOUSE FOR CHECKS

With more business being handled by check than by cash transactions, the process of clearing checks is almost staggering in its complexity. Figure 13–3 shows the steps involved from the time a check is written in payment for merchandise until the time it is subtracted from the checking account of the buyer.

Although many large cities have clearing houses where representatives of each of the commercial banks can meet to settle their accounts with other banks in the city, checks from out of the city are turned over to the Federal Reserve Bank for collection and crediting to reserve accounts of member banks. The Federal Reserve System handles about five billion checks a year. This total also includes checks of nonmember banks that may use the check-clearing services of the Federal Reserve.

SERVING AS FISCAL AGENT FOR THE FEDERAL GOVERNMENT

Because the United States Treasury has no bank of its own, the Federal Reserve serves as its fiscal agent. This activity involves keeping most of the government's accounts. Receipts from taxes, the sale of

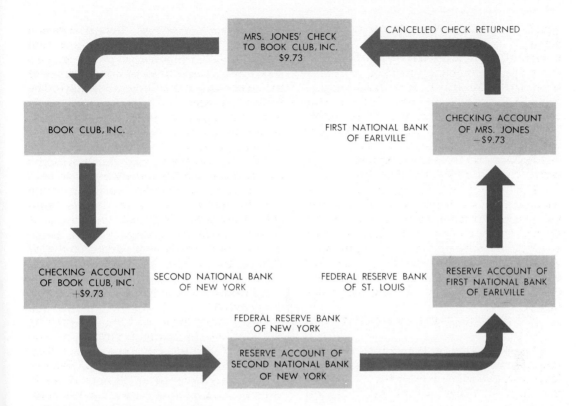

Figure 13-3   The Route of a Check

One of the services furnished to banks by the Federal Reserve System is the clearing of checks.

securities, and other collections as well as payment for salaries, the redeeming of securities, and other expenses are handled through the Federal Reserve System.

SUPERVISING OF MEMBER BANKS

The authorities of the Federal Reserve banks exercise wide supervision over member banks by such means as detailed reports on the management, investments, loans, and other activities of the banks. Periodic inspections, together with those made by the Federal Deposit Insurance Corporation and by the Comptroller of the Currency for national banks or inspectors for state banks, help to protect the public, improve banking practices, and maintain the standards of nonmember banks.

The role of the Federal Reserve in controlling the supply of money

In preceding chapters we have seen that the nation's economy is subject to fluctuations and that such fluctuations are accompanied by changes in the price level. We found that there is a relationship between the supply of money, M, the price level, P, and business activity, T. As our nation's central bank, the Federal Reserve System exercises considerable influence over the size of M. Through its control over discount rates, open-market operations, and the reserve ratio it can help to provide a full-employment noninflationary economy. Let us see how it can use these three major tools to attain this objective.

RESERVE BANK OFFICIALS HINT AT POSSIBILITY OF TIGHTER MONEY POLICY

WASHINGTON – Presidents of two Federal Reserve banks have indicated the possibility of a change in monetary policy by the Federal Reserve Board.

Alfred E. Hayes, president of the New York Bank, and W. Braddock Hickman, head of the Cleveland Bank, said in separate talks that the trend may very well be toward inflation after the unprecedentedly long period of economic expansion. Mr. Hayes warned that the present supply of money might be too generous and that the possibility of a tighter money policy was being considered by the Board.

The Reserve Board carries out its monetary policies by influencing the lending activities of member commercial banks. It does this on a day-to-day basis through the sale and purchase of Government securities, which add to or subtract from the member banks' reserves. It also influences reserves through changes in the discount rate – the interest rate charged to member banks for borrowing reserves – and in the ratio of reserves that banks must keep on hand.

Officials of the Federal Reserve banks must keep a close check on changing price levels as well as on other economic indicators with a view to using monetary policy as a stabilizer.

DISCOUNT RATE

We know that the Federal Reserve banks provide a banking system for private commercial banks. Banks use this system in two main ways – for depositing funds and for borrowing. When businessmen face a shortage of funds, they go to commercial banks to borrow. When these member banks are short of reserves, they may borrow from the Federal Reserve bank. They can do this by using the promissory notes from their own customers as collateral.

The rate of interest that the Federal Reserve bank charges member banks for loans is called the *discount rate*. The Reserve bank can raise or lower that rate with the approval of the Board of Governors. Raising the discount rate to member banks will in turn cause them to raise interest rates to their own customers. Lowering the discount rate will allow member banks to offer lower interest rates to their customers.

Discount rates of member banks are set at levels similar to those on secondary reserves, such as short-term United States securities. Banks will usually sell these securities to increase their reserves before borrowing from the Federal Reserve banks. Although discount rates have a strong influence on all interest rates, they are relatively less effective when banks have large excess reserves or a great many liquid assets.

OPEN-MARKET OPERATIONS

The Federal Reserve System, acting as the fiscal agent for the federal government as well as the chief instrument for controlling the supply of money, buys and sells short-term government securities through *open-market operations*. These purchases and sales are made through dealers who represent investors interested primarily in Treasury bills (three- to six-month loans). We have seen that commercial banks often hold such securities as secondary assets and frequently buy and sell them to adjust their own reserve positions.

When the Federal Open Market Committee orders the Federal Reserve Bank of New York, as the agent for the System, to sell securities, this action has the effect of reducing the reserves of commercial banks, thereby reducing their ability to lend money. Let us see how this result takes place.

The Federal Reserve Bank contacts a dealer in Treasury bills and sells him $1 million worth of these securities. He buys these bills for Company A, which has surplus cash that it does not plan to use for three months. Company A wants to earn interest on this surplus money rather than let it lie idle. To pay the dealer, Company A draws checks on the several banks with which it has accounts. This withdrawal reduces the excess reserves of these banks and consequently their ability to grant additional loans. Deposits and reserves have both been reduced. Since each reserve dollar supports several times as many deposit dollars, banks will be forced to restrict their credit expansion by several times the amount of the loss in reserves. When a bank buys Treasury bills, its reserves are reduced. Because its excess reserves are used up even faster, credit expansion is restricted to an even greater degree.

Suppose that the situation is reversed and that the Reserve Bank is ordered to buy

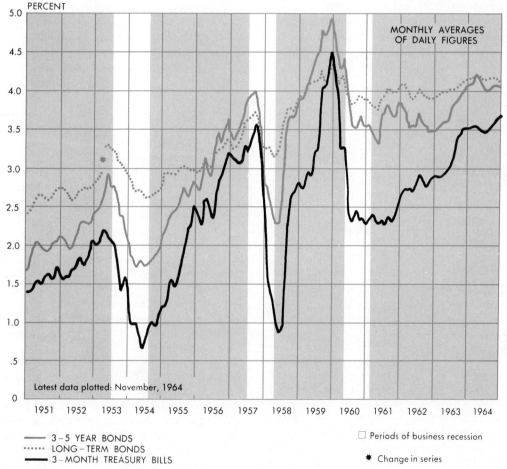

PERCENT

MONTHLY AVERAGES OF DAILY FIGURES

Latest data plotted: November, 1964

——— 3–5 YEAR BONDS
········· LONG–TERM BONDS
▬▬▬ 3–MONTH TREASURY BILLS

☐ Periods of business recession

✳ Change in series

Figure 13–4   Interest Rates in Relation to Business Cycles

The changing of interest rates helps control the business cycle by regulating the volume of money. Note how interest rates decline during business recessions. How do lower interest rates affect the supply of money? SOURCE: Federal Reserve Bank of St. Louis, December, 1964

securities. Company B has Treasury bills which it wishes to sell. When its dealer sells these bills to the Federal Reserve Bank, Company B receives payment through a check drawn on the Federal Reserve Bank. Company B then deposits this check in its accounts at several banks. These banks then forward their checks to the Reserve Bank for credit to their reserve accounts. Deposits and reserves have been increased equally, and since one reserve dollar can support several deposit dollars, the banks now have excess reserves to use for loans. Each dollar added to the reserves allows commercial banks to loan several dollars, creating new demand deposits.

In order to stimulate purchases and sales of securities, interest rates may have to be changed. If there are too few buyers, the interest these securities pay may have to be increased. This will affect the interest rates in all other markets.

Open-market operations are the *most important* tool of the Federal Reserve System for expanding and contracting the money supply. Unlike the other tools, this one is used on a day-to-day basis.

RESERVE REQUIREMENTS

As we have pointed out previously, the Board of Governors of the Federal Reserve has the power to raise or lower the reserve requirements of member banks within cer-

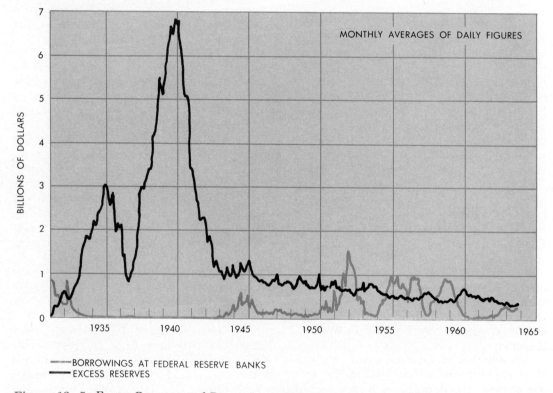

Figure 13–5 Excess Reserves and Borrowing in Relation to Business Cycles

During the Great Depression of the 1930's the demand for loans was small and banks had large excess reserves. Member banks had almost no need to borrow from Federal Reserve banks. SOURCE: Federal Reserve System, Board of Governors

tain limits. For central reserve cities (New York and Chicago) and other reserve cities the minimum reserve requirement for demand deposits of member banks is 10 percent; the maximum is 22 percent. For all other banks (known as country banks) the reserve requirements for demand deposits may range from seven to fourteen percent. The reserve requirements for time deposits may vary between three and six percent.

Changing the reserve requirements is the single *most powerful* tool of the Federal Reserve for expanding and contracting the supply of money; as such, it is used sparingly. If the legal reserve requirement is ten percent, it means that $1 of reserves can support $10 of demand deposits. A twenty percent reserve reduces the number of dollars of demand deposits a reserve dollar will support to a ratio of 1:5. Banks which have plenty of excess reserves can readily adjust as the ratio is raised. Those member banks whose reserves are low will be forced to borrow or sell securities, or do both, to meet the new requirements. If this action is taken when the discount rate is high and when the Reserve banks are not interested in purchasing securities in the open market (providing a source of cash to banks), the member banks may face an economic crisis. These banks will have to curtail their lending operations; this effect is, of course, exactly what the Federal Reserve intends to achieve when it raises the reserve requirements. Reducing reserve requirements creates additional excess reserves, allowing member banks to make additional loans. This should result in increasing the money supply.

Other controls used by the Federal Reserve

In addition to its three major methods of controlling credit, the Federal Reserve has several minor methods which it exercises from time to time. The major methods are aimed at the control of the entire supply of money, whereas the minor methods are aimed at particular markets.

MARGIN REQUIREMENTS

When people buy stock through their broker, they may pay a part of the purchase price and borrow the rest, using the stock as collateral. The percentage of the total price that must be paid at the time of purchase is called the *margin*. The Board of Governors of the Federal Reserve has the power to determine what the margin will be. When the margin requirement is set at fifty percent, the buyer must pay for half the amount of his stock purchase and may borrow the remainder. If the Board decides that there is danger of inflation due to excessive speculation on the exchanges, it may raise the margin requirement. Such a case occurred in 1958, when margin requirements were raised to ninety percent. In 1962 the margin was dropped to fifty percent. Why might these changes have been made?

MORAL PERSUASION

The officers of the Federal Reserve banks have frequently tried to persuade bankers to follow policy recommendations by such means as face-to-face talks, letters, and releases to the press. The purpose of this moral persuasion is to induce member banks to be selective in increasing or decreasing credit when it appears that granting credit for certain types of loans might be harmful, although credit for other loans might not be. This technique for regulating credit has had only moderate success, and almost no success when banking has been very competitive.

TEMPORARY POWERS

During periods when inflationary pressures seemed particularly strong, as during World War II and the Korean conflict, Congress has given the Federal Reserve additional powers over credit in selective fields. Because durable goods, such as automobiles and appliances, were in extremely short supply during the war years, the Board of Governors was able to regulate the down payment and limit the period for payment on such purchases. By increasing down payments and reducing the time for payment, demand for these goods was reduced and the inflationary pressures lessened. As supply of these goods caught up with demand, the regulations were allowed to lapse. A similar regulation in the early 1950's accomplished the same purpose for real estate. Such selective controls might again be used if Congress thinks they are needed to fight inflation.

The Federal Reserve and the use of monetary policy

The most important purpose of the Federal Reserve System is to control the supply of money that the nation needs in order to maintain an expanding economy with stable prices. Through the functions of the Federal Reserve, *monetary policies* can be adjusted to allow for the expansion or contraction of demand deposits according to the needs of the economy. Thus, an infla-

tion may be met by (1) increasing the discount rate, (2) the Federal Reserve's selling securities in the open market, and (3) raising the reserve requirements on demand deposits. When particular parts of the economy are severely affected, selective controls may be used. A deflation in the economy would call for the opposite type of monetary policy. The major controls over the supply of money involve regulation of the excess reserves of its member banks by the Federal Reserve.

The monetary policies of the Federal Reserve System are a help in controlling business cycles and in promoting the objective of a full-employment economy without inflation. In Chapter 14 we will consider the use of both monetary policy and fiscal policy as instruments for maintaining a healthy economy.

A "tight money" policy can do much to curb investment and thereby lessen the aggregate demand. While such a monetary policy is helpful in dealing with the classical demand-pull inflation, it provides little help in checking a cost-push inflation.

Part D   The Problem: How Effective Is Monetary Policy in Achieving Our Economic Goals?

In 1961 the Commission on Money and Credit, an independent research and policy group supported by several private foundations, issued a report on our nation's financial institutions. As you might expect, there was no agreement on how well our government's monetary policy works. Nevertheless a consensus was reached on some issues. The report also produced some suggestions for improving our system and some new thinking about what monetary policy can and cannot do.

In presenting some of the arguments for and against the effectiveness of monetary policies we are not looking for "exact answers," since we do not have absolute standards for evaluating these policies. We recognize that what may be the best answer in one case may not be in another. What we do hope to achieve by looking at both points of view is a better understanding of our entire monetary policy and its strengths and weaknesses.

Several qualifications must be made before presenting the two positions. We have ignored the role of monetary policy on the international scene, particularly in regard to the problem of balance of payments. There is frequently a conflict between what is good monetary policy domestically and what is good monetary policy internationally (see p. 343). We are also leaving the effect of *fiscal policy* (changing business activity by regulating expenditures) for consideration in the next chapter. Since monetary and fiscal policy are very closely related, it is difficult to distinguish the effects of each one separately. If you will keep in mind that our objective here is limited to evaluating monetary policy, these limitations should not interfere with our partial analysis. You will find the arguments related to ideas discussed earlier in this unit.

Monetary policy is effective

Many economists agree that economic policy should be aimed at a full-employment economy without inflation and with a rate of growth that will provide an increasing standard of living for all. Since money plays an active role in influencing price levels and business activity, monetary policy contributes substantially to the achievement of these goals through control over the supply of money.

Monetary policy is a highly effective way of stabilizing prices. By carefully watching and evaluating business conditions and price trends, the Federal Reserve can restrain inflationary and deflationary tendencies before they pose too serious a problem. Although the supply of money will change through the action of individuals— spending, saving, and borrowing—these actions in turn are greatly influenced by limits placed on the availability of money and the interest rates.

When the economy seems to be expanding too fast and too many dollars are pursuing too few goods, the Federal Reserve can limit the growth of M by raising the reserve requirements. The result of such action is that demand for loanable funds will be greater than supply, thereby increasing interest rates and forcing some prospective borrowers to postpone their plans for investing or buying. As the amount of demand deposits created through loans is reduced, inflationary pressures can be relieved.

If the economy appears to be entering a recession, more money can be made available by the Federal Reserve's purchase of securities in the open market or reduction of reserve requirements. This increase in the supply of money will result in lower interest rates, thus encouraging the marginal borrower to carry out plans for investment or purchase. By encouraging the creation of additional demand deposits through the availability of money for loans and through the reduction of interest rates, monetary policy can help to reverse the deflationary tendency that may have developed.

If we remember the equation of exchange ($MV = PT$) and assume little change in velocity (V), we can see how changing the supply of money can affect both the price level and business transactions. Only if T increases at the same rate as M will P remain unchanged.

Such policies as making money available to businessmen and reducing interest rates will not in themselves make businessmen borrow. Nevertheless an "easy money" policy creates an environment that encourages expansion. The lowering of the discount rate during the recessions of 1954, 1958, and 1960 was intended to counteract the slowing down of business activity. In contrast with this action, a policy of "tight money" was used during the upswings from 1955 to 1957 and in 1959 to moderate the tendency of business to expand too rapidly. Using monetary policy to dampen business booms and to offset declines by stimulating business expansion helps us to achieve the economic objectives of full employment without inflation and adequate economic growth.

Finally, monetary policy has an advantage over fiscal policy in that it is much more flexible. When the Board of Governors of the Federal Reserve discovers a trend in the economy, it can act quickly to meet the changing conditions. It does not have to wait for long Congressional debates, as happens in applying fiscal policy. Monetary policy can be altered quickly according to changing requirements and can be a significant factor in creating economic stability.

Monetary policy is not effective

Some economists believe that the monetary policies in current use by our government will not achieve the goals of our economy because they place too many restrictions on business. In our economy total demand is made up of consumers, government, and business. It is this aggregate demand that will determine the level of income of our nation. Of these three groups it is business at which monetary policy is primarily directed. Consumer spending and savings, except for real estate, are determined mainly by income and are little affected by interest rates. This is particularly true of installment buying. Government spending is likewise only rarely curtailed because of changing interest rates; moreover, such curtailments have occurred only in the case of state and local governments. Therefore, we can conclude that monetary policy is effective only in controlling business investment.

The "easy money" policy used to offset a recession is weak because businessmen do not borrow merely because money is available and interest rates are low. They borrow when they believe that they can earn money as a result of business expansion. During a recession, when even existing facilities of a business are not being fully used, it is unrealistic to think that the businessman will add new facilities. The period of the Great Depression pointed out this weakness in monetary policy.

Although a "tight money" policy can be more effective in combating an inflation than an "easy money" policy can be in dealing with a recession because it can actually "dry up" excess reserves, it too has serious weaknesses. These weaknesses are (1) the use of internal financing by large firms in noncompetitive enterprises, (2) the conflict of interest between the Federal Reserve and the Treasury, and (3) the inability to influence a cost-push inflation.

1. Since World War II, big businesses that are not in price-competitive industries have built up large surpluses of cash by not distributing the bulk of their profits

in dividends. They have been able to finance much of their modernization and expansion programs out of these funds without having to turn to the banks. In this way interest rates or the availability of excess reserves has almost no influence on curtailing their plans. Even when they do have to borrow, monopolistic firms can pass the higher interest charges on to their customers. Small businesses in competitive industries are hard hit by tight money, and such a policy discriminates against them.

2. Although the Federal Reserve is interested primarily in controlling the supply of money and will therefore effect an increase in interest rates to deal with an inflation, the United States Treasury, which uses the Federal Reserve as its fiscal agent, is interested in borrowing money at a low rate of interest. Although this conflict of interest is not very serious now, it was during World War II and in the years immediately following. It could become a serious problem again at some future time.

3. Monetary policy is designed to curb a demand-pull inflation by restraining spending. Because a cost-push inflation arises from the supply side, reducing the excess reserves can actually aggravate the condition. This was illustrated in 1958, which was a year of recession as well as one in which the Consumer Price Index climbed 2.7 points. "Tight money" discouraged investment and economic expansion at a time when unemployment was growing. Monetary policy is not able to cope with such circumstances or to bring about the changes needed.

Considering an answer

The debate on the effectiveness of monetary policy still goes on among both students and experts in economics. It is unlikely that it will ever be resolved, but in the process of searching for answers we learn more about the kinds of policies which should be used to realize our economic goals.

At this point you, the student, might well ask, "If the experts disagree, how can I expect to provide an answer?" Actually, since experts disagree over most important controversies, the final decision must be made by others — the citizens — through their support of programs and policies. Such indications of broad popular support will generally influence government action and policy.

Consider, for example, the importance of a demand-pull inflation and the problem it continues to pose for the economy. Does making money more easily available and at lower interest rates encourage investment? Does monetary policy play favorites and, if so, is this bad for the economy as a whole? These are a few of the questions that you should consider in arriving at an answer.

REVIEW: the highlights of the chapter

1. There are many kinds of financial institutions. All are concerned with collecting money from sources that do not need it immediately and channeling it to those that do.

2. Savings institutions, personal trust companies, insurance companies, consumer credit agencies, investment banks, and commercial banks all serve a particular purpose in channeling funds. The government's influence over the process of lending has become increasingly important.

3. Banks serve as depositories for valuables and as agencies for lending money. Commercial banks create money through loans.

4. The creation of demand deposits by commercial banks is the most important source of money in our economy. Some of their money must be kept in reserve to meet customer withdrawals and the reserve requirements of the Federal Reserve for its members. Although banks invest some of their money in short-term securities – mainly United States Treasury bills – at low interest rates, they usually lend most of their money to businesses and individuals. The latter type of loan provides them with the highest interest rates.

5. The Federal Deposit Insurance Corporation was created in 1933 to insure depositors against loss of their money in case of bank failures.

6. Although a single bank is limited in its ability to create demand deposits, the banking system as a whole can lend several times its reserves, the amount depending on the reserve requirements. A 20 percent reserve requirement (1:5) will allow demand deposits to expand to five times the size of bank reserves.

7. The Federal Reserve System acts as the central bank for the United States. It is decentralized into twelve districts, each with a Federal Reserve bank (located in a major city) and its own board of directors. The entire system is coordinated by the seven-man Board of Governors.

8. The chief function of the Federal Reserve is to regulate the supply of money according to the needs of the economy.

9. The major tools for controlling the volume of money are:
   (a) Discount rate – the rate of interest member banks must pay when they borrow from the Federal Reserve bank.
   (b) Open-market operations – the purchase and sale of securities, primarily short-term government notes, by the Federal Reserve bank.
   (c) Reserve requirements – the amount of money member banks must keep in reserve in relation to their demand deposits.

10. The Federal Reserve has also been given selective controls over specific markets, such as the purchase of stocks on margin.

11. Monetary policy is the adjustment of the money supply to help in achieving our economic goals of full employment, stable prices, and economic growth.

12. Inflationary tendencies may be offset by reducing the supply of money through such measures as raising the discount rate, selling securities in the open market, and/or raising the reserve ratio. Recession may be offset by actions opposite to these.

13. There is considerable controversy over the effectiveness of monetary policy in helping to achieve our economic goals.

IN CONCLUSION: *some aids to understanding*

Terms for review

savings bank

credit union

collateral

secondary reserves

legal reserve

discount rate

margin requirement

personal trusts

commercial bank

time deposit

reserve ratio

balance sheet

derivative deposits

member bank

reserve requirement

clearing house

Names to know

Federal Reserve System

Board of Governors

FDIC

Open Market Committee

Questions for review

1. What is meant by the statement "The banking system performs the role of intermediary in regulating the flow of money"?

2. A major share of the banking in our country is carried on by commercial banks and savings banks.
   (a) What differences exist between these two kinds of banks?
   (b) How does each strengthen the economy of a community?

3. Explain how a commercial bank "creates money."

4. Why could a district Federal Reserve bank be called the bankers' bank?

5. Explain why banks are required to hold reserves.

6. Why is our money supply expanded by the entire banking system rather than by the operations of a single commercial bank?

7. The Federal Reserve has a strong influence on our money supply.
   (a) Why are open-market operations called the most important tool of the Federal Reserve System?
   (b) Why are reserve requirements called the most powerful tool of the Federal Reserve System?
   (c) What are the weaknesses of the discount rate as a means of controlling our money supply?

8. Explain why the establishment of the FDIC has created confidence in our banking system among depositors.

9. In what ways does the Federal Reserve System act as the fiscal agent of the United States?

Additional questions and problems

1. Find in a local newspaper, or obtain from the bank at which you do business, a copy of its balance sheet. Evaluate its financial condition, using specific references to liquidity, reserves, loans, types of securities, and reserve ratio. In what ways does this bank benefit the community?

2. Explain the statement "Seven men may determine the expansion and contraction of the entire credit system of the United States."

3. Why is the Federal Reserve Bank of New York more important than any other Federal Reserve bank? Give at least three reasons.

4. Explain the roles of Alexander Hamilton, Andrew Jackson, Woodrow Wilson, and Franklin D. Roosevelt in the development of the banking system of the United States.

5. Draw a chart illustrating the increase and decrease of cash and reserve deposits in your local bank and its Federal Reserve Bank when the reserve ratio goes from 10 percent to 20 percent. Use the amount of $100,000 as total deposits, with one coin as a symbol for $1,000.

6. Explain the steps by which a check made out by you to a firm in Portland, Oregon, would be cleared.

14 Formulating Modern Economic Policy

Preview

In Unit I and in Unit II we became acquainted with the classical approach to economics. We learned what many of the tools of this system are, how they work in the marketplace, and how they answer the basic questions of economics. In Unit III we have been introduced to a new model, the Keynesian. We have learned to use tools for both fiscal and monetary analysis so that we can not only understand our economy better, but also try to formulate policy to serve our economic goals. In the present chapter we will see how fiscal and monetary tools can be used together in an effort to achieve full employment, keep a sufficient rate of economic growth, maintain price stability, and minimize cyclical fluctuations. One of the tasks of the modern economist is to assist in the formulation of policies that will help to achieve these goals.

In previous chapters we have stressed the differences between the old and the new models. Few economists today are exclusively classical or exclusively Keynesian in their approach. They recognize the importance of a free-enterprise system and the key role of the market in allocating our resources. However, they believe that the automatic adjustment mechanism that supply and demand is supposed to make will not always promote our economic objectives. In these instances monetary and fiscal tools may be utilized to give the economy the assistance necessary. Modern economic policy is a synthesis of the old and the new models.

Overview

List in order of importance the economic goals you think our country should have. Explain the reasons for your preferences.

How can the classical and Keynesian models be used to work toward the same goals in our economy?

Explain how a conflict in values can lead to a conflict in defining and implementing economic policy.

Part A   Our Nation's Economic Goals

Full employment

Before the crisis of the 1930's, economists paid little attention to the problem of unemployment. Until that time economic theory had assumed that unemployment was self-correcting and that any tampering with the automatic mechanism of the free market would do more harm than good. J. B. Say (see p. 12), a French economist who was an advocate of the laissez-faire school, formulated an economic theory stating that equilibrium would be achieved at the full-employment level because supply would create its own demand. His reasoning was seldom questioned. Any rise of unemployment was looked upon as only a temporary condition. Past experience tended to support this theory, so there was little reason to question it. The turning point in the attitude toward unemployment came during the Great Depression of the 1930's, when unemployment rose from about three percent in 1929 to more than 24 percent in 1933.

THE 1930's: UNEMPLOYMENT AND THE KEYNESIAN THEORY

Although progress was made in reducing unemployment by means of the New Deal measures of President Franklin D. Roosevelt, the problem of mass unemployment was a major concern until the start

Excerpt of an open letter from John Maynard Keynes to President Franklin D. Roosevelt, published in the New York *Times* on December 31, 1933:

As the prime mover in the first stage of the technique of recovery, I lay overwhelming emphasis on the increase of national purchasing power resulting from governmental expenditure which is financed by loans and is not merely a transfer through taxation of existing income. Nothing else counts in comparison to this . . . .

As early as 1933 the famous English economist recommended to President Roosevelt increasing government spending to stimulate the economy.

of a wartime economy following our entry into World War II. As economists began to lose confidence in the self-correcting mechanism of the market, they began to seek new solutions to the problem of unemployment. In 1936 John Maynard Keynes published his theory on employment. His ideas, which became the basis for the new model that we examined in Chapter 11, attracted attention immediately. Encouraged by the new ideas, economists began a reevaluation of our entire economic system that eventually led to major modifications and to the development of new policies.

THE EMPLOYMENT ACT OF 1946

When World War II ended, the hopes of the American people for the future were high. Once again the economy was operating at a full-employment level. With the memory of the economic hardships of the thirties still deeply implanted in their minds, the majority of the people were not willing to trust a policy of laissez-faire exclusively to determine the performance of the economy. Sharing this point of view, Congress passed the Employment Act of 1946, which stated in part:

The Congress declares that it is the continuing policy and responsibility of the Federal Government to use all practicable means consistent with its needs and obligations and other essential considerations of national policy, with the assistance and cooperation of industry, agriculture, labor, and State and local governments, to coordinate and utilize all its plans, functions, and resources for the purpose of creating and maintaining, in a manner calculated to foster and promote free competitive enterprise and the general welfare, conditions under which there will be afforded useful employment opportunities, including self-employment, for those able, willing, and seeking work, and to promote the maximum employment, production, and purchasing power.

Although the Act does not go so far as to commit the federal government to a full-employment economy, it does charge the government with the responsibility of taking steps to create an environment that will promote maximum employment. In addition, it provides for the Council of Economic Advisers, which is directly responsible to the President. The Council prepares an annual report on the health of the nation's economy and suggests methods to improve it. President Kennedy, who was not only well versed in economics but also recognized the significance of its role in the functioning of government, relied heavily on Dr. Walter Heller, Chairman of the Council, to help formulate an economic program. President Johnson has also worked closely with his economic advisers.

SHOWING FULL EMPLOYMENT WITH OUR MODELS

If our economy operates at less than full employment, it is failing to make use of all our resources. We will be without the production that the unemployed are capable of producing. If as many as one fifth of our people live at the poverty level when we have resources that are not being used, such a situation represents a weakness in economic policy.

In Chapter 11 we saw full employment represented in models using a vertical bar graph and the 45° line. Since we shall be using these models in this chapter, let us review them briefly, using the two models in Figure 14–1 as our basic examples.

Economic growth

We have seen in Tables 10–3 and 10–4 how the value of our nation's goods and services has grown and how high it is compared with that of other nations in both total and per capita wealth. A measure of this value increase can be seen in our growth rate—the percentage increase in our GNP in constant dollars from one year to the next. It had been about three percent per year from 1870 to World War II. Since World War II it has increased to about five percent; however, the growth has been uneven. Although no nation of the world comes close to challenging our primacy in overall wealth and though we increase the absolute value of our production more than other nations, our recent *economic growth rate* has not been as rapid as that of several

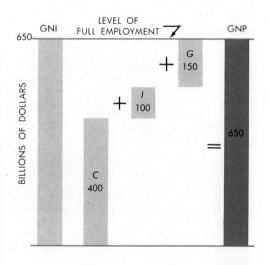
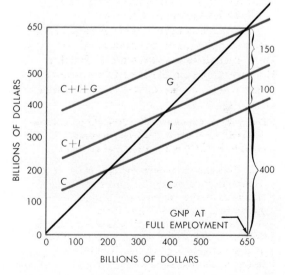

Figure 14–1   Models of Full Employment

These models show full employment at $650 billion. Personal consumption expenditures (C) + business investment (I) + government expenditures (G) = aggregate income (gross national product).

other countries, notably West Germany, Japan, and – in most years of the last two decades – the U.S.S.R. Whether the Soviet Union will ever overtake the United States in total wealth is questionable, but its economic rise has tremendous international consequences.

THE IMPORTANCE OF ECONOMIC GROWTH

Figure 14–1 repeats, using a higher GNP, the simplified analysis of national income of Figure 11–2, with a full-employment economy in a stationary condition. However, the situation is in reality more complex. With our population growing every year, output of goods and services must be increased just to keep per capita income at the same level. If we wish to improve our standard of living, we must increase production faster than population. India is an example of a nation whose output is increasing, but no more rapidly than population. This situation has resulted in a lack of improvement in the standard of living of India's people.

With our labor force growing larger every year, economic growth can be accomplished by putting the additional human resources to work. If we combine our first two objectives, full employment and economic growth, it means that our full-employment GNP must grow each year. Although a $650 billion GNP might put a labor force of 75 million to work, a larger GNP will be required to have full employment with 78 million. When we add to this the increased output per worker resulting from new inventions, from increased skill of workers, and from more capital invested per worker, our full-employment GNP must rise even faster. Figure 14–2 shows our models in an expanding economy based on full employment and economic growth.

Our knowledge of economic growth and the forces that determine it is far from complete. We know that it depends on a variety of factors, including the capital goods we put into the hands of workers, the skill and education of workers, technological advances, and the quality and quantity of our

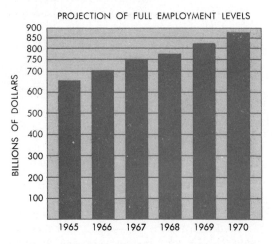

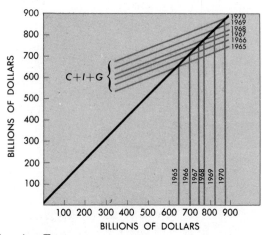

Figure 14–2 Models of Full Employment in a Growing Economy

Full employment models must take into consideration the growing potential of a dynamic economy. The increases in our labor force, in our capital, and in our knowledge provide the potential for economic growth for the nation. The increase in our capacity to produce means an increasing GNP, which in turn helps to achieve a full-employment level.

natural and human resources. We will discuss this subject further in Chapter 18 when we consider the economic growth of underdeveloped countries.

Price stability

We have already noted in Chapter 12 the many problems that an unstable price level can pose to the nation as a whole as well as to segments within the economy. Although the Employment Act of 1946 does not mention price stability as a goal, the attention paid to prices by the President's Council of Economic Advisers and by the Joint Economic Committee (which advises Congress on economic matters), together with the concern shown for it by every President since World War II, establishes it as an important economic goal.

In Figure 14–3 the model is used to show how the economy can maintain stable prices should it attain full employment with adequate economic growth. Under these circumstances, controlling the money supply so that it stimulates production to

the full-employment level without causing an inflation becomes the goal of monetary policy.

Economic stability

If we can achieve full employment with adequate growth and at the same time maintain price stability, there will be no extreme fluctuations in the performance of the economy. The extreme peaks and troughs shown in our business cycles, particularly the contrasts between the 1930's and 1940's, should be eliminated and replaced by slight undulations caused by the somewhat uneven investment opportunities, technological advances, and slight variations in the number of people joining and leaving the working force. Figure 14–4 shows how the business cycle as illustrated in Chapter 10 (p. 205) would be modified if we were able to achieve economic stability.

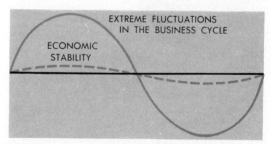

Figure 14–4 Dampening the Business Cycle

By achieving full employment, adequate economic growth, and stable prices we avoid extreme fluctuations in the business cycle.

Other goals

In addition to the broad overall objectives that we have noted involving macroeconomics, we identified in relation to microeconomics in Unit II a number of goals that many people consider equally important. One of the most important of these goals is the most efficient use of limited resources by business to produce the goods society wants (low prices and high-quality products for the consumer).

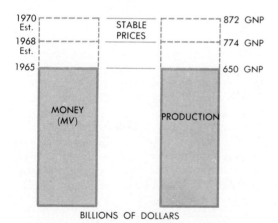

BILLIONS OF DOLLARS

Figure 14–3 Growth, Money Supply, and Price Stability

GNP is at full employment without inflation for 1965 ($650 billion). With a growth rate of 6 percent our supply of money will have to increase in order to avoid deflation. If it increases faster than production, we are likely to have inflation.

A highly competitive market protects the consumer and rewards the efficient producer, assuring a dynamic economy.

Another important goal is the fair distribution of income. Just as it is important to have the national economy—the "pie"—grow bigger, it is also important that whatever the size of the "pie," it be divided in a way that the society approves.

Many people would include as an objective a highly decentralized market. Others might emphasize the protection of weaker economic groups, such as small business and the farmer. Maximizing the freedom of both consumer and producer would be placed high on many lists. Providing equal economic opportunities for everyone has become an important goal for many

people, particularly as the civil rights movement has gained strength. In the next chapter we will discuss free trade among nations, which many economists, including Adam Smith, have urged.

The goals of economics are decided not by the economist but by the society as a whole. Inasmuch as economic goals involve value judgments and different goals may have conflicting values, it is the responsibility of the citizens and the government in a democratic nation to determine what goals to pursue and what priority these objectives should have. When citizens, through their elected representatives, decide what goals to pursue, the economist can suggest the tools to use in order to achieve these objectives.

Part B   *The New Model's Approach to Economic Policy*

Having examined the broad objectives of our economy and having observed some of the tools that are used to carry out fiscal and monetary policy, we are now ready to put these tools to work in order to achieve our economic objectives. Specifically, we want to know how we can utilize the tools developed by modern economics in order to formulate a fiscal and monetary policy that will provide full employment, satisfactory economic growth, and price stability without major fluctuation in the business cycle. At times in this survey reference to the Keynesian model insert may be helpful.

Discretionary and automatic stabilizers

The tools that we have identified with monetary and fiscal policy are used to stabilize the economy; that is, they are designed to reverse the direction of the business cycle when the economy appears to be expanding or contracting too rapidly. Thus, modern macroeconomic policy is used to reduce the severity of the fluctuations in the business cycle by *countercyclical* (reversing the direction of the cycle) action.

The tools by which this is accomplished are known as *stabilizers*.

DISCRETIONARY STABILIZERS

Any economic tool utilized for countercyclical action on the decision of designated officials is known as a *discretionary stabilizer*. When several tools are used to compensate for the economic fluctuations and are brought into action by some governmental authority or authorities, the program proposed is called *discretionary policy*. At present all our monetary tools, such as the discount rate and open-market operations, are discretionary because action must be initiated by the Board of Governors or the Open Market Committee. A tax cut is an example of fiscal policy that is discretionary.

AUTOMATIC STABILIZERS

Discretionary policy, if it is to work efficiently, is dependent on accurate forecasting. Predicting a drop in business activity and taking appropriate countercyclical action can be harmful if the forecast turns out to be wrong. Consider what would happen in a home without modern heating controls if, after a warm spell was predicted and all the fires were banked, a severe cold spell suddenly arrived instead. In economics, to guard against the difficulties of forecasting, automatic stabilizers are used. *Automatic stabilizers* are tools which work against the cycle of their own accord without any action being required by a public official, just as the thermostat of the modern heating unit in our home will automatically maintain the temperature inside at the required level, regardless of changes in the temperature outside. One example of an automatic stabilizer is the federal income tax. When income rises, not only does the payment in dollars to the government go up but the proportion of payment to income rises also. When income declines, tax payments are reduced in proportion even faster. This result occurs because the progressive feature of the income tax arranges personal incomes according to level, or bracket, each of which has its own tax rate. An upswing in business would cause people to pay higher taxes and curb some of their purchasing power. A downswing would result in smaller tax payments, leaving people with proportionately more money to spend. In a similar manner unemployment insurance acts as an automatic stabilizer.

Fiscal policies and their effects

Modern fiscal policy calls for the use of public spending and public taxation to help achieve the economic goals of full employment, economic growth, price stability, and little cyclical fluctuation. Countercyclical action calls for inflations to be dealt with by the preparation of budgets that will produce a government surplus, whereas recession would be treated by means of budgetary deficits. Government, as the largest single revenue receiver and spender in the nation, is thus in a strategic position to raise or lower aggregate demand in the economy. It can do this either by altering tax rates or by changing its spending program, or by a combination of both methods. Figure 14–5 uses

several models to show our economy in an inflationary boom. Let us see what fiscal policy can do to reverse the cyclical trend.

Using taxes as a tool

When the government taxes the people, it decreases their disposable personal income and thereby also reduces personal consumption expenditures (C). By increasing taxes the government can reduce C even further. By decreasing taxes, it can increase C.

In Figure 14–5 we see that the aggregate demand – consumption plus investment plus government spending ($C + I + G$) – is greater than what the economy can produce, resulting in an inflation. Modern fiscal policy calls for reducing aggregate demand to eliminate the inflationary forces. By increasing taxes and making sure that there is no corresponding increase in investment or government spending, aggregate demand can be decreased. On our models this is shown by reducing C and keeping I and G the same, so that $C + I + G$ is equal to full employment without inflation.

Discretionary tax policy

When the government economists sense a strong inflationary trend, they may suggest that legislation be passed to increase taxes. Excise taxes may be raised on a large number of goods and services, or they may be specifically directed at those goods and services which are likely to be most in demand but short in supply. The personal income tax can be increased generally or selectively. If inflationary forces are very strong, as they were during World War II, the rate increases might be placed on the lowest income group, since those people tend to spend all their income. People in the upper income groups save a substantial portion of their income; raising taxes for them would probably reduce their savings more than their expenditures. A recession calls for policies opposite to those just described in order to increase C. We

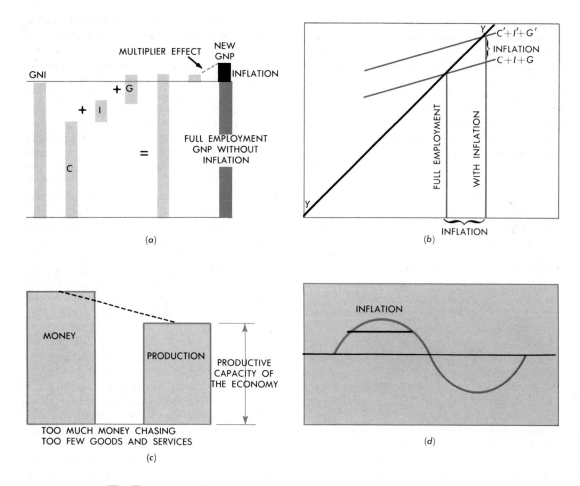

Figure 14-5 The Economy in Inflation

Several views of the economy in an inflation are shown here. In (a) and (b) the models for income analysis (C + I + G = Y) show an aggregate demand greater than the full-employment capacity of the economy. In (c) too much money is chasing too few goods and services. In (d) the business cycle is shown at an inflationary peak.

must recognize that in either situation good economics may have to give way to good politics in selecting a course of action.

Taxes can also be altered to change the size of business investment. Rarely (primarily during a war period) would attempts be made to discourage investment, since an increase in *I* usually results in increasing the productive capacity of the economy as well as the demand side. Stimulating *I* can

be done by allowing businesses to deduct their new investments from their gross profits (depreciation allowance) faster than previously. A reduction in the corporation income tax will also stimulate *I*.

TAXES AS STABILIZERS

Probably our most important automatic tax stabilizers are our progressive personal income tax and our corporation income tax. We have already seen that an increase in the national income would bring a proportionately larger increase in tax receipts without any action on the part of Congress or the President. This would have the effect of slowing down the increase in C and, consequently, decreasing aggregate demand. Similarly, a reduction in national income would bring about a proportionate reduction in tax receipts, with a smaller reduction in disposable personal income.

Some of our other tax programs also have a stabilizing effect. For example, during periods of low unemployment the taxes that support our unemployment compensation program flow into the reserve fund much faster than money is paid out. If the business cycle should reverse itself and unemployment increase, payments would be made faster than money would flow into the fund, thus providing a countercyclical effect. The same results occur in the case of Social Security payments.

GOVERNMENT SPENDING

Unless the taxing tool is used in conjunction with government spending, fiscal policy cannot be planned effectively. Raising C through a tax cut can be offset by reducing government spending, G. Likewise, a reduction in C by a tax increase can reduce aggregate demand in the private sector. However, a corresponding increase in government spending will increase the public sector and neutralize the effect. Although the illustrations cited will bring about a change in the allocation of resources between the public and private sectors, it is only through the creation of budgetary deficits and surpluses that we actually change the aggregate demand. Assuming that government revenue remains constant or nearly constant, let us see how government spending changes aggregate demand and modifies the business cycle.

GOVERNMENT PURCHASES

In Chapter 7 we learned that a very significant portion of government expenditures is used for the purchase of goods and services. Defense spending, support for our space program, and a variety of public works projects involving the construction of highways, dams, and public parks are extremely important for meeting specific needs. They also are important in accounting for a significant portion of aggregate demand.

Just as it is traditional to expect a government to prepare a budget listing the things it wishes to furnish its citizens, it is also characteristic of those who advocate the new economics to think of government expenditures as a tool to regulate the aggregate demand in order to achieve full employment without inflation. During an inflation, modern fiscal policy might try to reduce the G. Under such circumstances only the most important government projects would be approved, and an attempt would be made to cut all unnecessary spending out of the budget. A recession would call for increasing G. Those projects that were delayed under an inflationary condition would now be started. Older projects already under way might be expanded. The purpose of the additional expenditures is not merely to secure additional goods and services for the nation but also to increase the G element with the intention of stimulating the economy.

Government spending (G) is somewhat slower in affecting the aggregate demand than changes in taxes because time is required for starting projects. Once they are under way, it is difficult to stop them, even if the economy has moved out of recession and toward an inflation. They do have an advantage over a tax cut, however, because they guarantee that the funds will be spent at least once. This tends to increase the multiplier effect (see p. 238). They also provide for direct employment and usually help the durable goods industries, which are often hardest hit by recessions.

TRANSFER PAYMENTS

In addition to the automatic stabilizers financed by specific taxes for certain transfer payments, such as Social Security

"Annual income Twenty pounds, annual expenditure Nineteen Nineteen six, result happiness. Annual income Twenty pounds, annual expenditure Twenty pounds ought and six, result misery."
— Mr. Micawber's advice to David Copperfield

Mr. Micawber's advice may still be appropriate for the family, but many would doubt its applicability to government. What is good sense for the family may not be good for the economy as a whole because savings, when not invested, can be a drag on the economy. If private enterprise does not invest these funds, then government may develop policy that will put them to work. What policy is best for any particular time may be highly controversial.

and unemployment insurance, the government frequently provides money out of general tax funds for direct payments to groups that are hardest hit by a recession. Money is given to states to permit them, whenever their jobless rate remains high for an extended period, to increase the length of time during which unemployment compensation is paid. By the parity system farmers receive payment from the government if they have huge crop surpluses (see p. 381). Giving grants and loans to students provides opportunities for increasing the skills of the working force as well as reducing the number of potentially unemployed workers that join the labor force each year.

Evaluation of fiscal policy

There are many citizens in our country who believe that the federal budget should be balanced annually. They think that it is just as important for the nation to live within its income as it is for the family, and they believe that to do otherwise, as in deficit spending, is immoral.

THE UNBALANCED BUDGET

However, many other people think that such an attitude is at variance with modern economic theory. In fact, most contemporary economists believe that a balanced federal budget may under certain conditions work directly against the economic interests of the country. During a recession a declining national income reduces government revenues. If the budget is to be balanced, government expenditures must be sharply curtailed and taxes may have to be raised. Both actions would result in a decline in aggregate demand (C and G would fall), hastening the decline. An inflationary boom would result in increased revenue, allowing the government to increase its expenditures when resources are already being used to capacity. Higher revenues and increased spending would intensify the fluctuations in the business cycle.

COUNTERCYCLICAL BUDGETS

Preparing federal budgets with a view to countering the movement of the business cycle has gained a great deal of support among economists since the end of World War II. The prolonged period of the upswing and the sharp increase in our economic growth rate following the tax cut of 1964 won over many people whose previous

ARE RECESSIONS GONE FOREVER?

WASHINGTON — A question that would not have been considered seriously only a few years ago is being discussed regularly by economists and political leaders today. With the economy continuing to move ahead in an unprecedented manner and for an unusually long period of time, the question is being asked whether the ups and downs associated with business cycles and recurrent in the American economy are still inescapable.

While politicians and economists disagree on the answer, it cannot be disputed that almost all indicators show the economy to be healthy and expanding. Gross national production, personal income, investment, and employment all show continued growth with almost no interruption and very little leveling off. This has been accomplished with a price level that has been amazingly stable. Unemployment, which formerly presented a problem, has now declined below the 4 percent level, due in part to recent programs of the Great Society.

For a time, much of the credit for the happy state of the American economy was given to the tax cut on incomes in 1964 and the cut in excise taxes in 1965. More recently, defense expenditures have become increasingly important, with the chance that anti-inflationary measures will be used if the upward trend in the economy becomes too steep.

The success of the "new economics" in moving the economy toward the national economic goals of full employment, economic growth, and stable prices has been impressive during the first half of the 1960's. Some economists remain skeptical about its effectiveness in curbing the inflation which became a problem in 1966.

main concern was balancing the budget. The argument used to support passage of this tax cut was partially aimed at critics of this type of fiscal policy. Its adherents pointed out that only by increasing the tax base could we really hope to balance the budget. Reducing taxes would increase the national income sufficiently so that the drop in the tax rate would be more than offset by the bigger incomes that would be taxed. Most economists agree that the tax cut accomplished what it was designed to do. The economic upswing was prolonged, the economic growth rate was bettered, government revenues were increased, and prices were kept reasonably stable. The unemployment rate was reduced to 3.7 percent by early 1966. With increased government spending for the Vietnam conflict, the problem concerning tax policy was reversed. The question now became: "Should we increase taxes to reduce aggregate demand in order to avoid an inflation?"

PROBLEMS IN FISCAL POLICY

In order to achieve a desired effect, correct timing of fiscal policy is extremely important. Applying our tools too soon may convert a newly begun upswing into a recession. Applying our tools very late, which is more likely to happen, reduces some of the effectiveness of the policy and may cause an inflation.

It is very difficult to take the appropriate action at precisely the right time. In Chapter 10 we saw how difficult it is to predict the course of business activity. Since the various parts of our economy do not move in the same direction simultaneously, determining the best leading indicator (see p. 202) is extremely difficult.

Political considerations play a major part in slowing down the initiation of appropriate fiscal policy. If taxes are to be raised, what taxes should be selected for change? A congressman must consider which of his constituents will raise the greatest objection, as well as which tax will be best for his constituents and for the economy. If an increase in expenditures is called for, which state or congressional district will be most favored with appropriations? Historically, Congress has tended to act very slowly in response to economic changes; when it has finally acted, the action has frequently been too late or too little to be really effective. The Joint Economic Committee, in an evaluation of the use of discretionary fiscal policy in 1960, pointed out our reluctance to increase taxes to curb inflation and our unwillingness to increase government expenditures during a recession. Recently, a greater willingness to utilize these policies has become apparent. A reduction in excise taxes was enacted quickly in 1965; in 1966 some of these taxes were restored because of changes in economic conditions.

Fiscal activities of state and local governments tend to reinforce the trend of the business cycle. When the cycle moves upward, their incomes increase and so do their expenditures. Falling incomes reduce their revenues and they respond by cutting their budgets. Raising taxes during recessions and lowering them during inflation is quite common and only serves to aggravate the unfavorable condition. Constitutional and statutory requirements sometimes require governments to act in this way, although a more common reason for this action may be the widespread belief that an annually balanced budget is desirable.

Appropriations for defense constitute, directly and indirectly, over half of our federal budget. Unfortunately for the economy our defense requirements do not run countercyclical to our business activity. With our national security having first priority on considerations of spending, efforts to avoid economic fluctuations may be hampered.

Inflationary forces of the cost-push type result from the efforts of pressure groups trying, rightly or wrongly, to improve their relative economic position. Such forces are largely immune from the stabilizers we have mentioned. Pressures from the President or from public opinion have provided some restraint in the past, but we have no assurance that this informal method will be successful in the future. Having the

Council of Economic Advisers announce what the increased productivity for the previous year has been and using this change as a guide for wage negotiations may lessen the effect of the cost-push type of inflation — if, that is, their advice is followed.

Monetary policies and their effects

Modern economic policy calls for the use of monetary policy as well as fiscal policy to achieve our economic goals. Through control of the supply of money and of interest rates, the aggregate demand can be influenced to move upwards or downwards in order to create greater economic stability. In Figure 14–5, (a) and (b), the $C + I + G$ must be reduced, and in (c) the supply of money contracted. Monetary policy works primarily on investment (I), and our discussion will be concerned mainly with policy that influences the size of I.

In Chapter 13 we saw that the Federal Reserve could increase or decrease the supply of money (M) by its open-market operations and by changing discount rates and reserve requirements. In Chapter 6 we saw that interest rates are determined by the supply and demand for loanable funds. By the combined use of these tools, monetary policy can be used to influence the size of I.

REDUCING INVESTMENT

If the economy appears to be entering on an inflationary spiral, the Board of Governors of the Federal Reserve will decide to take appropriate action. They will call together the Open Market Committee and give instructions to the Federal Reserve Bank in New York to sell government securities in order to reduce the excess reserves of the member banks. This action will limit the money that member banks have for the granting of loans. The Board may also decide to raise the discount rate to discourage member banks from borrowing from the Federal Reserve Banks. They probably will delay changing the reserve requirements, hoping that the course of action already outlined will be enough to tighten credit

How independent should the "Fed" be? President Johnson confers with William McChesney Martin, Chairman of the Board of Governors, following a difference of opinion over raising the discount rate.

and stop the increase in prices. Their action shows that monetary policy is discretionary rather than automatic, since they had to initiate action.

As the supply of M is reduced, the supply curve shifts to the left, increasing the interest rate. The increasing of the discount rate will also raise interest rates. Since businessmen will borrow only when they think they can earn more money on what they have borrowed than what they must pay in interest, those with a low marginal productivity for loanable funds (who expect to make little on what they borrow) will postpone borrowing. Figure 14–6 shows how higher interest will reduce I.

To combat a recession, an opposite course of action would be employed. The discount rate might be lowered, the Federal

Reserve Bank might buy securities, and the reserve requirements might be lowered. The increased supply of M would lower interest rates, and investments would as a result increase from (a) to (b) in the model shown in Figure 14–6.

The example that we have used here pictures investment as being generally responsive to interest rates. Most of the "new" economists do not accept this principle for low interest rates when the economy is functioning in low gear. Their objections to this theory were presented in Chapter 11 (see p. 225).

Evaluation of monetary policy

We have already evaluated monetary policy in Chapter 13, but a review of our

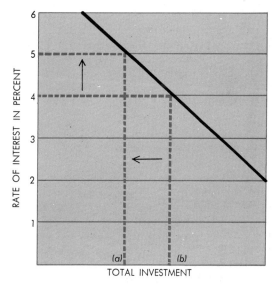

Figure 14–6 Controlling Business Fluctuations Through Changing Interest Rates

Increasing the interest rate (↑) reduces investment (←) from (b) to (a), lowering aggregate demand and reducing inflationary tendencies. Lowering interest rates can be used to increase investment and fight recessions, although this practice is considered more controversial than the practice of increasing interest rates.

findings in the larger context of the present chapter may be helpful. Monetary policy is more effective in controlling booms than recessions for the reason that demand-pull inflations can be curbed by restricting the supply of loanable funds. In a recession the supply of M may be increased and interest rates lowered, but there is no way of forcing businessmen to make investments. The old cliché, "You can lead a horse to water but you can't make him drink," describes this problem in monetary policy when the economy is contracting.

Monetary policy is far more flexible than discretionary fiscal policy and can be changed more quickly, although there is usually a time lag for the new credit policy to take effect. People who look with the most favor on monetary policy as an instrument for control point out that it is neutral in that it does not discriminate against any particular borrower. Critics disagree with this argument. They point out that the large, well-established corporations supply the funds for their own financing by using their undistributed profits, whereas small and expanding companies that must finance expansion by bank loans are hardest hit when credit controls are tightened.

"Living at the foot of a volcano"

Jacob Burck, © Chicago Sun-Times

'Gee, Frank, don't you just love living in a period of extended economic boom?'

Drawing by William Hamilton: © 1966, The New Yorker Magazine, Inc.

Another argument criticizing the use of policies affecting the long-term growth rate of the economy is that by the tightening of credit, investment in capital goods may be discouraged. Increasing capital goods should increase the productive capacity of the economy. Although it may be temporarily desirable to reduce inflationary pressures by reducing M, we may also be slowing down the long-range growth potential of the other side, production. Such an effect would be undesirable.

Part C   The Classical Approach to Economic Policy

In our economy many forces interact to help in stabilizing economic conditions. For example, individual businesses can by their own action do much to compensate for fluctuations in the business cycle. The classical approach, through the automatic stabilization provided by the laws of supply and demand, is geared to reducing the harmful consequences of economic fluctuation. This result is best achieved, however, in a free competitive market.

When the economy is expanding and demand is greater than supply, a number of changes are set in motion. Prices will rise, thereby acting as a curb on demand. Wages will rise, discouraging employers from hiring additional labor. Loanable funds will become scarce, causing interest rates to rise and discourage additional borrowing. In those parts of the economy where demand is greatest and supply least, profits are likely to be high and to attract new capital. The expectation of profit may also lead to the transfer of capital from less profitable ventures to more profitable ones. These reactions to an expansion of the economy may eventually curb the business boom. As the economy contracts, prices will fall, increasing demand; wages will fall, encouraging employers to hire; and interest rates will fall, stimulating investment. These reactions would eventually have the effect of expanding the economy again.

In the competitive market the individual firm reacts within the framework just described. In the expanding market the businessman is less worried about price competition, since his company may already be operating at the fullest possible capacity. The buyer who is uncertain about making a purchase is discouraged by high prices and may delay action, hoping for prices to decline. The high interest rates being paid on his savings reward him for postponing his purchase. The businessman wants to expand operations, but wages are too high and the workers available are relatively less productive. Since high interest rates prohibit him from buying new equipment, he will probably decide to wait.

In a recession the businessman must be very conscious of price competition. He can hold a sale of merchandise in order to stimulate business. He can hire good workers at low wages because the supply of workers in relation to demand has increased. Maintenance, repair, or even replacement of equipment and fixtures may now be taken care of with a low-interest loan. These and other actions taken by the individual firm can help to stimulate the economy.

PROBLEMS OF THE CLASSICAL APPROACH

As you have seen several times previously, the classical approach assumes the existence of pure competition or a close approximation to that condition. Prices and wages must be flexible in order to move resources to the places where they are needed most. Many economists believe that the lack of pure competition prevents the market mechanism from doing the job anticipated by the classical economic theorist. Prices and wages are flexible primarily in an upward direction, and tend to move downward very slowly or not at all.

Some economists think that economic stability can best be achieved by a return to the framework of the classical model. Measures such as vigorous enforcement of anti-trust laws and a reduction in the bargaining power of labor unions will allow us to achieve all our economic objectives with a minimum of government interference. However, such a return to earlier conditions would be very difficult to carry out at this period in our history, particularly in view of the possible political consequences.

A synthesis of economic theories

Few economists today are either strictly classical or strictly Keynesian in their approach. They are aware of the fallacy of composition—the false notion that what is true for the individual is also necessarily true for society. Both microeconomics, with its emphasis on the efficiency of the firm, and macroeconomics, with its emphasis on the economy as a whole, are taken into consideration in determining economic policy. The automatic mechanism existing in a market economy is extremely important in the allocation of our resources, in answering the *What, How,* and *For Whom.* Many economists believe, however, that a policy of laissez-faire will not satisfy our economic objectives adequately, and that its assumptions about a free market cannot always be accepted. It is at this point that they turn to the Keynesian approach for assistance. They believe that the government, with powers far exceeding those of any individual or firm, can and should use fiscal and monetary tools to guide the economy toward its chosen objectives.

We now have an economy based on mixed enterprise, with the greatest emphasis on the private sector. It is as consumers and producers that we make most of our economic decisions; however, we also make decisions, although indirectly, as citizens. Most of the property of our country is owned privately, but our demands for schools, roads, national defense, and many services make government's role in our economy extremely important. Thus, the economic system we have today is in practice a synthesis of the old and new models. Modern economic policy has not eliminated the classical tools; it has merely combined and modified them to fit into our changing world so that we can best achieve full employment, adequate economic growth, and price stability without the harmful effects of major cyclical fluctuations.

Part D   Some Controversial Policy Suggestions

We will now proceed to consider four suggestions concerning economic policy. These policies are well known and are frequently discussed by economists, politicians, businessmen, labor leaders, and the well-informed public. One of the four has not yet been tried; the other three are in very early stages and may still be considered experimental. Each suggestion is designed to achieve at least one of our economic goals—but often at the expense of another goal.

In evaluating these policies, you will wish to consider what effect each one will have on the economy in regard to the attainment of the economic goals we have discussed. When you have weighed the relative benefits and disadvantages in fulfilling one goal at the possible expense of others, explain why you favor or reject the proposal and identify the values that guided you in making your decision.

Automatic stabilizers

Some economists have dreamed of the day when there would be available built-in stabilizers sufficiently sensitive to respond directly to changes in business activity and successful enough to maintain smooth functioning of the economy so that we might merely sit and observe the operation.

Of course, there might be an occasional need for half a turn of the economic wrench here and a full turn of the political screwdriver there, but for the most part the automatic stabilizers would do the job. Such an idea differs little from that of the classical economists, except that in this instance man would have to create the machinery and put it into action. We shall survey some recent proposals for carrying out at least a part of this suggestion.

AUTOMATIC TAX RATE CHANGES IN CORPORATION AND PERSONAL INCOME TAXES

Although the present income taxes are already important automatic stabilizers in our economy, they are admittedly not effective enough to do away with discretionary policy in regard to tax changes. Legislation which would change the tax rate automatically without further legislation by Congress could act as a strong economic stabilizer of the economy. Every six months the GNP, the Consumer Price Index, the Industrial Production Index, and the unemployment rate would be compared with the same figures in the previous six-month report. If the combination of these measurements (combined to give a composite index number) indicated that the economy was moving ahead too rapidly for our productive capacity and that inflation seemed imminent, the tax rate could automatically increase by two percent (or a variable percentage depending on how sharp the economic expansion is). A decline in the composite index number, indicating a recession, would automatically reduce the tax rate.

The automatic changing of the tax rate with the change in the direction of the economy would minimize the occurrence of economic fluctuations. It would eliminate the time lag that occurs when Congress must debate each proposal separately. It would also be neutral in its geographic effects so that each representative in Congress would not have to fear discrimination against his area. As the plan became refined, automatic rate changes might be reduced to three-month intervals, and greater rate changes might automatically be set for higher income groups in order to increase investment when economic growth seemed the slowest, or to give greater rate changes to the lowest income groups when the unemployment rate was growing fastest and there was a need to increase C.

WEAKNESSES IN AUTOMATIC TAX RATE CHANGES

Criticism of such a plan would be most intense in Congress. Using a system based on automatic rate changes would mean surrendering one of Congress' most important powers. It is highly doubtful, even if the plan were good in all other respects, that our legislature would approve.

Taxing is only one half of fiscal policy. A change in government revenues influences our national income only in relation to our government expenditures. Such a policy would greatly restrict the flexibility of the government's spending program, and meeting specific needs might become a consideration secondary to economic stabilization in making government policy.

GUARANTEED ANNUAL WAGE AS AN AUTOMATIC STABILIZER

Industries which are subject to major seasonal fluctuations find great variations in their payrolls and the number of workers they employ in a given year. Unions have recognized that workers in such industries have little security; moreover, the unions are under a severe handicap in budgeting their expenditures. Although unemployment insurance provides some stabilization of income, a vast difference remains between bringing home $110 in a pay envelope and receiving $42 in unemployment compensation. Salaried executives receive an annual income that usually continues whether business conditions are bad or good. Annual salaries provide stability of income to the individual and help in stabilizing the income of the community. If some kind of *guaranteed annual wage* (GAW) were provided for workers in enough industries, it could act as an automatic stabilizer for the nation.

In the mid-1950's the automobile manufacturers, the steel companies, and several other large companies signed contracts with unions offering modified guaranteed annual wages. The most widely used plan provided for workers with some company seniority to receive supplementary unemployment benefits from the company during periods of seasonal unemployment. The temporarily unemployed worker might have his $42 unemployment check from the state supplemented by an additional $28 (usually up to 65 percent of his regular pay) from the company. Although such a plan does not provide a guaranteed annual wage, it is a step in that direction. It not only eases the hardship of unemployment for the individual worker, but it also eases the reduction in consumption that would hurt those who depend on the worker's expenditures.

The guaranteed annual wage, and even the modified supplementary unemployment benefit plan, force the producer to schedule his output on a yearly basis and thus result in real economies in the use of capital. The money to support these plans is put into funds which can be drawn on when needed. Such funds tend to reduce the effects of the business cycle by being built up during periods of expansion and reduced during periods of contraction.

WEAKNESSES IN THE GUARANTEED ANNUAL WAGE PLAN

Many industries do not lend themselves to plans such as the guaranteed annual wage or supplementary benefits. In addition, the plans may increase fixed costs unduly and discourage investment. New industries and those that are declining would be particularly hard pressed to commit themselves to such costs. Such plans also reduce the mobility of labor, thereby preventing business from adapting to changes in consumer preferences. They also make expanding industries think twice about hiring additional labor because of the long-term commitments that follow. In addition, a portion of the money in the fund is restricted in its use. Since the employer would rather see steady growth than periodic fluctuations, the only change that such a plan could bring is to pass on to the consumer the added costs that may be incurred in its operation.

Qualitative measures

Some economists have pointed out that fiscal and monetary policy might be used to push up aggregate demand to a GNP level that would support full employment without actually achieving full employment. Our economy today needs not just *any* labor; it needs *skilled* labor to meet our increasingly automated economy. The unemployed today are primarily of two groups: (1) those who are unskilled and lack either the physical, mental, or emotional requirements to find and hold jobs and (2) workers living in specific regions that have chronically high unemployment rates. Unless we direct our spending to help these two groups, our aggregate demand will have to move well into the inflationary area to reach full employment. The added dollars may increase the demand for more goods and services, but if businesses do not have workers available who have the skills to produce the goods and services, inflation, not full employment, will result. Let us see what programs exist for helping the people in these two groups.

AREA REDEVELOPMENT

After many years of effort, legislation has now been passed allowing the federal government to assist areas with high chronic rates of unemployment in meeting their problem. "Distressed areas," those whose unemployment rate is considerably above the national average and has been

UPHILL STRUGGLE IN APPALACHIA

HOPE IS OFFERED POVERTY AREA

CHARLESTON, W. VA. — Although the eleven-state region known as Appalachia lags behind the rest of the country in development, it contains great economic contrasts. Statistically, Appalachia compares unfavorably with other areas of the nation in unemployment, housing, education, and many other measurements of economic health. Yet it also includes great industrial cities, rich suburban areas, resorts, and famous universities.

Automation and changing consumer needs have hurt this area particularly hard. Coal miners have become unemployed because of mechanization, and the lumber business has declined as forests have been cut down. Factors such as frequent floods, poor roads, and unharnessed waterpower have discouraged the introduction of new industries.

The federal government has set up a coordinated program to rehabilitate the area. Over a billion dollars has been appropriated for controlling floods and water pollution, improving soil and reclaiming mined-out lands, constructing highways and access roads, and developing programs for vocational education. These projects, together with other federal anti-poverty programs, offer new hope to an area that has a long uphill struggle before it.

The existence of areas of poverty in the midst of plenty may be caused by a change in demand, a lack of mobility of labor and capital, or an absence of required skills among workers. Increasing aggregate demand does not eliminate structural unemployment.

so for at least a year, become eligible to receive loans and grants to be used for attracting new industry, for retraining workers for new skills, and for making improvements in public buildings.

The general economy of West Virginia and Pennsylvania has been severely affected by the decline in the coal industry. Unemployment rates have been high, and displaced coal miners have been slow to move out of the area to seek other employment. Attracting new industry through tax inducements and plant subsidies, and retraining programs to give the coal miners new skills, can reduce unemployment considerably without the necessity of applying inflationary pressures to the rest of the country through generally increasing aggregate spending.

So far the program has had only moderate success, but the amount of money that has been appropriated has been so meager in comparison to the needs that no fair evaluation can be made. Utilizing area redevelopment as a major program to achieve full employment without causing inflationary pressure will require a far greater financial commitment than has been made so far.

WEAKNESSES IN THE REDEVELOPMENT PLAN

Critics of this program point out that state and local governments are the logical governments to administer these activities. They reason, too, that the area which benefits should be the area to pay for it. In addition, such programs reduce the tendency of labor to move where it is needed most. Inducing industries to come into these areas with the aid of government funds gives these areas a competitive advantage. Some industries might even move from an area which has natural advantages for efficient operation merely to take advantage of the government subsidy. This would be an inefficient use of our resources.

TRAINING THE UNEMPLOYABLE

A very large percentage of our unemployed have little chance for employment, no matter how high the aggregate demand is, because they have no marketable skill. As one part of the government's war on poverty, the Office of Economic Opportunity was set up to develop, approve, and administer job-training centers. At these centers trainees receive vocational training in such areas as office work, equipment maintenance, cooking, sales, metal work, and health services. They also receive general education because so many are school dropouts and are seriously limited in basic skills such as reading. Hundreds of Job Corps centers have been set up throughout the country, operated by businesses and educational institutions. At some of these centers trainees live on a selected site, such as Camp Kilmer, New Jersey, and receive room and board plus $30 a month. Other Job Corps projects use the neighborhood approach and try to furnish trainees with part-time jobs while they are in training.

As with area redevelopment the funds appropriated have been meager. If these programs are to be really successful, the country must commit itself to the expenditure of billions of dollars, as we have done in subsidizing the farmer and in committing ourselves to the space program.

WEAKNESSES IN
TRAINING PROGRAMS

Critics of these retraining programs have pointed out that such projects increase the public sector of the economy at the expense of the private sector. Even though private enterprise is involved in the training program, the money to finance such programs and approval of them must come from the federal government, and that inevitably means government control. Increasing the offerings of present school programs can accomplish the same thing at less cost and with no increase in government control. The free market, not only for the purchase of goods and services but for the businessman's purchase of his labor needs, is still the best method of directing people to the positions that they want and that our society needs.

Post-Keynesian thinking: an added consideration

Many economists have suggested that we are now living in a post-Keynesian world. The classical tradition emphasized efficiency and the Keynesian tradition stressed stability. Today, however, concern is focused primarily on maintaining continued economic growth. Achieving this objective depends to some extent on the use of ideas from both traditions. Let us see how such a synthesis is possible.

These economists point out that the quantitative approach, which income determination ($C + I + G = Y$) emphasizes, has not done the job of achieving a full-employment economy, although it has certainly helped. The fact that one fifth of our nation still lives in poverty has motivated the federal government to employ the qualitative approach as well as the quantitative approach in the Great Society. The war on poverty includes a wide array of programs aimed at raising the economic position of those who have received few benefits from our affluent society. The new federal programs to help finance education and research—two of the most important ingredients for economic growth—are reflections of this new thinking. Most unemployment today is *structural;* that is, it is caused by such factors as the lack of skills, the change in consumer preferences, and the immobility of labor. Investment in human resources (education) and in pure research and technology appears to be the direction of the future.

Considering our basic problem of limited resources and unlimited wants, do you think that the solutions we have discussed are adequate? If not, what alternatives exist? Is it possible that our affluent society no longer has the basic problem of scarcity? What new problems can you foresee? As citizens and consumers you will share in the continuing search for solutions.

REVIEW: the highlights of the chapter

1. Our economic goals include full employment, adequate economic growth, price stability, and a minimum of economic fluctuation. By the Employment Act of 1946 the federal government accepted far more responsibility for establishing a favorable economic climate to make possible the achievement of our economic goals than the classical economist might have wished.

2. Other economic goals include efficient use of resources, fair distribution of income, freedom for the consumer and producer, equal opportunities for all, and freer trade.

3. The tools of fiscal and monetary policy can be used to help achieve our economic goals. They are designed to raise or lower aggregate demand in order to produce a countercyclical action.

4. Automatic stabilizers, such as the personal income tax and unemployment insurance, lessen the effects of the business cycle without the need for direct action by any agency of government.

5. Discretionary policy requires deliberate action. Government spending and altering taxes to produce budgetary surpluses and deficits are examples of discretionary fiscal policy.

6. Altering taxes works more quickly in compensating for the expansion and contraction of the economy, but government spending is more likely to result in a greater multiplier effect.

7. Monetary policy is more flexible than fiscal policy. By altering the supply of *M* and changing interest rates, investment may be changed. Monetary policy is more effective in fighting an inflation than a recession.

8. The classical model depends upon the automatic mechanism of a free market economy to achieve our economic goals. The lack of wage and price flexibility and the low mobility of our resources limit the market's effectiveness.

9. Since World War II, recessions have been shorter, less frequent, and less severe. Periods of expansion have been longer and less sharp.

10. Most economists today are neither exclusively classical nor exclusively Keynesian in their approach. They recognize the need for using elements of both approaches.

11. Controversial policy suggestions are introduced, discussed, and evaluated to see if they can be of help in achieving our objectives. The achievement of one goal may mean the sacrifice of another.

12. Post-Keynesian thinking emphasizes economic growth and qualitative methods for dealing with structural unemployment.

IN CONCLUSION: some aids to understanding

Terms for review

structural unemployment	price stability
economic growth	countercyclical policy
automatic mechanism	growth rate
automatic stabilizers	unbalanced budget
area redevelopment	guaranteed annual wage

Names to know

Council of Economic Advisers	Office of Economic Opportunity
Employment Act of 1946	Job Corps

Questions for review

1. The ideas of Keynes led to the adoption of new economic policies for our nation.
   (a) Explain the reasons for the Employment Act of 1946.
   (b) Why may this law be considered a major change in the theory underlying our nation's economic system?
2. Considering that we are the wealthiest nation in the world, why is our continued economic growth important?
3. Economists tend to agree on our broad economic goals, although they may differ on the means of achieving them.
   (a) What are the major economic goals of the United States?
   (b) How are our economic goals determined?
4. Several tools are available for influencing the pattern of business cycles.
   (a) Explain the difference between automatic and discretionary stabilizers.
   (b) Give several examples to illustrate each stabilizer.
   (c) What are the dangers in using hasty discretionary action to bring about countercyclical activity?
5. Explain why an annually balanced budget is at variance with modern economic theory.
6. How may political considerations interfere with appropriate fiscal policy?
7. Explain the following statements:
   (a) "Monetary policy is more flexible than fiscal policy."
   (b) "Monetary policy is more effective against inflation than against recession."

8. Why is it appropriate to call the present economic policies of our government a "synthesis"? Use examples to illustrate your answer.

9. What are the weaknesses associated with using the guaranteed annual wage as an automatic stabilizer?

10. Explain what is meant by a "qualitative approach" in contrast to a "quantitative approach." What advantages and disadvantages are there in each approach?

Additional questions and problems

1. Actions and policies of the federal government are basic in effecting economic changes.
   (a) Contrast the policies of the Roosevelt–Truman years with those of the Eisenhower administration.
   (b) Compare the policies of the Kennedy-Johnson years with those of the two previous administrations.
   (c) Make a chronological list of the agencies of the federal government that have been created to help in stabilizing our economy. What does each agency do?

2. As a project in research, look up the statistics on GNP, employment, unemployment, and national tax structures for 1961, and then find the same figures for 1965.
   (a) Prepare a table comparing the two sets of figures.
   (b) Explain the effect of the tax-reduction legislation passed by the 88th Congress on the national economy.

3. Explain the statement "Political leaders on the state and local levels will often vote for measures contrary to what might be good economic policy on the national level."

4. If you were granted full power to make economic changes,
   (a) what variations would you make, using the classical approach, to bring about a larger "pie"?
   (b) what variations would you make, using the new model, to bring about a more equitable distribution of income?
   Would you consider the two preceding approaches necessarily in conflict?

5. The term "welfare state" is often used to describe our economy.
   (a) What is meant by the term "welfare state"?
   (b) How might the existence of a welfare state interfere with the patterns of the classical model?
   (c) In what specific ways is the welfare state compatible with the new model?

UNIT IV
The American Economy and the World

15 *International Trade and Finance*

Preview

In the first three units our main study has been the American economic system and its basic theories and practices. We have paid little attention to the economy of our country in relation to the world scene. In this chapter we shall consider the importance of international trade and the mechanics of international finance.

The subject of free trade is debated by economists just as the question of a freely operating market is. There is apparent logic in specialization and the law of comparative advantage; at the same time international trade has often been hampered by special interest groups that have used tariffs and other restraints for selfish motives.

An added factor in determining the extent of international trade is the method that nations use in paying one another. International finance is itself complex; in addition, its patterns often reflect political motives. International monetary policy can be a help to the movement of trade; however, it can also be used to hinder trade.

In recognition of the importance of trade and finance to world economic development, institutions such as the International Monetary Fund and GATT (General Agreement on Tariffs and Trade) have been designed and developed to encourage world trade. The degree of their success in solving age-old problems will have significance for the standard of living of most of the people of the world. Regional institutions have also been developed. We shall see the growth of one of these, the European Economic Community (the Common Market), and consider whether it poses a threat to our own economy and to our participation in world trade.

Overview

Of what value is foreign trade to the United States?

How can nations pay each other when their currencies differ?

What effect may regional trade associations such as the Common Market have on the American economy?

320

Part A   Why Should a Nation Trade?

The basis for trade

The classical point of view toward trade is set forth by the English economist David Ricardo in his book *On the Principles of Political Economy and Taxation:*

Under a system of perfectly free commerce, each country naturally devotes its capital and labour to such employments as are most beneficial to each. This pursuit of individual advantage is admirably connected with the universal good of the whole. By stimulating industry, by rewarding ingenuity, and by using most efficaciously the peculiar powers bestowed by nature, it distributes labour most effectively and most economically; while, by increasing the general mass of productions, it diffuses general benefit, and binds together by one common tie of interest and intercourse, the universal society of nations throughout the civilized world. It is this principle which determines that wine shall be made in France and Portugal, that corn shall be grown in America and Poland, and that hardware and other goods shall be manufactured in England.

Ricardo's ideas formed the basis for a new concept of trade for Britain and, later, for many other nations. Many of Ricardo's arguments in favor of *free trade* continue to be valid, although political and economic conditions have changed greatly since his time. Let us consider some of the ideas and influences that contributed to other theories of trade.

ADVANTAGES AND PROBLEMS OF SPECIALIZATION

In Chapter 1 we saw that as society has grown more complex, man as a producer has had to become more specialized, exchanging the goods and services produced in order to satisfy more wants. And, as we also discovered, specialization increases production. Geographic regions of our country may specialize by taking advantage of their particular climatic conditions or their

DAVID RICARDO AND HIS CONTRIBUTIONS

David Ricardo (1772–1823) was, with Adam Smith and Thomas R. Malthus, one of the three great English economists who started the classical school. As an individual he defied the stereotype of the theoretician who is unable to understand or cope with the real world. Trained by his father as a stockbroker but disinherited because of family disapproval of his marriage, he amassed a considerable fortune through investments before reaching the age of thirty. The leisure thus acquired gave him time to follow intellectual pursuits — first science and then economics — after reading Smith's *The Wealth of Nations.* He wrote books on a variety of economic subjects. For a time, he served as a member of Parliament, where he was influential in reshaping Britain's policies regarding trade.

Smith and Ricardo were both deductive thinkers, framing possible answers to explain economic behavior and using logic to support their theories. However, they differed in that Smith emphasized problems of production whereas Ricardo concentrated on those of distribution. Smith was the optimist, with his hopeful analysis of economic growth and possible betterment of man's living conditions. Ricardo, in contrast, helped to earn for economics the label "gloomy science," which has since clung to this discipline. He reasoned that, because the amount of land is fixed, the constant increase in world population will make man's survival more and more precarious.

Ricardo is primarily known for his labor theory of value, his theory of rent, and the law of comparative advantage in trade. He viewed the exchange value of a commodity in terms of the labor time involved in making it. Later Marx used this theory in developing his own rationale. In explaining rent, Ricardo applied the law of diminishing returns, but did not give sufficient credit to improved technology as a means of greatly increasing the yields from land. His theory of comparative advantage, often referred to as comparative cost, was ideally suited to the new policy of free trade.

skilled labor supply or their natural resources. In the same way nations of the world have an unequal distribution of economic factors with varying conditions and advantages. These inequalities become the basis of specialization.

Along with its obvious advantages, specialization brings problems. Nations realize that too great dependence on foreign trade can be a weakness. Many industrial nations have believed that, to be strong, they must try to be self-sufficient and meet their own needs as fully as possible. However, self-sufficiency for a nation is usually relative. In analyzing the economic potential of nations, we find that some nations are far closer to self-sufficiency than others. Even the United States and the Soviet Union, with their vast territory and abundant resources, are not completely self-sufficient. They must supplement their own products and resources; moreover they can obtain many things more cheaply by importing them than by attempting to produce them domestically. In 1965 United States trade amounted to about $20.9 billion in imports and about $25.5 billion in exports. These amounts have been increasing yearly; even so, they do not reveal the true importance of our foreign trade. For example, they do not indicate how important many of our imports are to the rest of our economy,

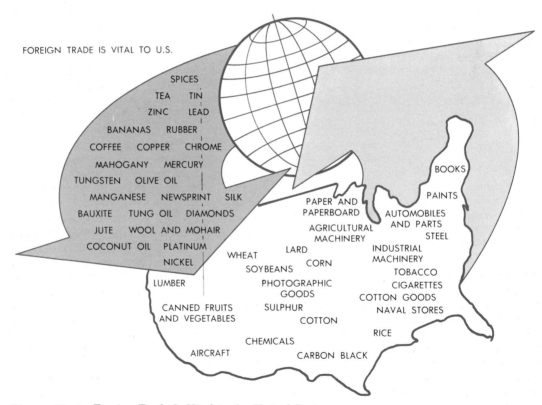

Figure 15–1 Foreign Trade Is Vital to the United States

Many of the items we import are necessary to maintain our high standard of living. SOURCE: "ABC's of Foreign Trade," *U.S. Trade Policy in Brief,* Department of State Publication 7713, 1964

nor do they reflect the importance of our exports to the economies of other nations.

IMPORTANCE OF FOREIGN TRADE
TO THE UNITED STATES

To supplement its own natural resources, our country imports most of its uranium, rubber, manganese, nickel, tungsten, and cobalt—all so vital to our industrial machine and to national defense. Most of our supply of these comes from foreign countries. More iron ore and copper are being obtained abroad as our own supplies grow smaller or more costly to use. As a reflection of our rising standard of living, we also import many quality manufactured items that foreign nations specialize in, such as perfume, lace, china, cameras, and pieces of art. Another category of imports is foods which our country cannot produce. Almost all of our coffee, tea, and tropical fruits are brought from abroad.

Although our nation might try to become self-sufficient in some of these imports, to do so would create new problems:

1. It would become necessary to find substitutes for some products we now want and enjoy.
2. More money would have to be spent to produce things that could be imported at less cost.
3. The economy of other countries which depend on our trade would be hurt. In time our exports to those nations would be correspondingly reduced.

The law of comparative advantage

Most people can readily accept the idea that countries should manufacture and raise those things that they can produce more cheaply than others and import those things that other countries can supply at a lower cost. This principle, or law, is known as *absolute advantage*. It is somewhat more difficult for people and nations to recognize that they can profit by concentrating their efforts on producing those things in which they have the least disadvantage. Ricardo, the economist quoted earlier,

pointed out that all nations would be better off if they devoted their labor and other resources of production to those things in which they have the greatest *comparative advantage* over other nations. This would reduce the relative costs of production and result in greater total production throughout the world. We call this principle the law of comparative advantage.

A simple example may help to clarify this concept. Bricklayers usually earn about $5 an hour, well above the minimum wage anywhere in our country. People who mow lawns rarely earn above the minimum wage. Suppose that you are a bricklayer with more work available than you can accomplish, but that you are also quite expert in mowing lawns. You can cut your own grass in 45 minutes, whereas it takes those who mow lawns in your neighborhood one hour to do the same job. Even though you can mow your own lawn more efficiently than others can, it is to everyone's advantage for you to specialize in bricklaying and for someone else to mow your lawn. The value you create laying bricks in 45 minutes (the time it takes you to mow your lawn) is greater than the value created by the person mowing your lawn in an hour—at least $4 as opposed to $1.50. Your comparative advantage in bricklaying is far greater than that in mowing your lawn.

Reasons for interfering with free trade

If we consider free trade only in terms of the theoretical economic arguments involved, there can be little objection to it. However, we must recognize that in reality absolute free trade seldom exists, and that those who oppose it are not without their reasons. Let us examine the arguments for and against free trade, recognizing that neither position is generally followed completely. We have for the most part followed moderate positions somewhere between the two extremes.

MERCANTILISM

From the sixteenth century to the eighteenth a popular viewpoint held by many economists, statesmen, and merchants was that a nation should direct its policy in such a way that it would accumulate gold and silver in its treasury. Those who held this idea considered these precious metals to be the principal form of wealth. They sought to accomplish their goals by strict regulation of trade so that the total value of the exports of the nation would be greater than the total value of its imports. The difference in value between the shipments made by each of the nations would in turn be compensated by payment in gold by the nation that showed the deficit. *Mercantilism*, as this system of thought was called, tried to gain a "favorable balance of trade" by following policies that would encourage exports and discourage imports. Much of the reasoning behind mercantilism stemmed from the falsely held belief that a nation, like a business, must sell more than it buys in order to prosper. This viewpoint served as a guide for the British in governing their American colonies.

The classical economists pointed out several obvious fallacies in mercantilist theory. Besides the advantages of specialization, the simple fact remains that nations must import in order to export. Precious metals cannot always flow in one direction. Also, when a nation keeps exporting its products and importing gold, the prices of its goods and services are going to rise and it may price itself out of the international market. In the sixteenth century mercantilist Spain found that many of the benefits of importing huge quantities of gold were dissipated by the inflation that followed. We know too that real wealth is the goods and services that people want, not the instrument for buying.

Although some of the old mercantilist theories can still be heard, most of the current objections to free trade are based on political, military, and economic considerations which differ from the earlier rationale. Those who wish to restrict internation-al trade are known as *protectionists*. They generally favor high tariffs and other restrictions on goods imported into the country so that domestic products will not have to compete with foreign goods in their own markets.

NATIONAL DEFENSE

Protectionists often argue in favor of national self-sufficiency for reasons of defense, since wars can cut off goods that are essential to a nation's survival. Therefore, even though it might be more costly to produce synthetics, such as rubber, at home, the importance of protecting the nation must come first. Protecting home industries involved in the nation's defense by restricting the importation of such goods must take priority over economic efficiency and cost.

Critics of this position argue that such a policy encourages extreme nationalism, which is one of the causes of wars. If nations were more interdependent, not only would they understand each other better but they would be less capable of making war.

INFANT INDUSTRIES

Another argument advanced by protectionists is that the growth of a nation's industry must be encouraged. An industry in its early growth is at an economic disadvantage when competing with a well-established industry. For example, manufacturing was much more highly developed in England than in our country when we became independent. Our new industries could not compete with those of England. By giving these industries protection, we helped them to get started. Our country might never have become the industrial giant that it is today had we not given such protection.

Protection actually benefits not only the industry itself but also the consumer. The sacrifices that the consumer makes in the form of paying higher prices are more than offset by the additional productivity of the country, the new jobs created, and the gradual lowering of prices as competition attracts more businesses into the field and efficiency increases.

The objection to this theory is that it is rarely the infant industry that asks for protection. On the contrary, Congress is besieged by the lobbies of well-established industries. Because such industries have failed to become efficient, they look for extra protection from foreign competition. At what point should developing industries no longer need protection?

PROTECTING THE WAGES OF LABOR

It is frequently pointed out by labor, and agreed to by management, that the high standard of living of the American worker requires management to pay high wages. By contrast, foreign firms pay far lower wages, keeping the cost of production down and allowing these firms to sell at prices below those charged by American firms. A large number of American workers might be thrown out of work because they cannot compete with poorly paid foreign labor.

Such an argument would be valid if the output per man-hour were the same in our country as it is in other countries. However, under these circumstances it is doubtful that we would be engaged in such production at all. The reason we have been able to have a favorable balance of trade for so many years is that our costs have not been higher than those of comparable foreign goods. This favorable relationship can exist because the real cost of labor is measured in output per man-hour. The American laborer, with the highest skills and the best capital equipment available, is able to produce so much more in a given period of time that the cost of labor for a given commodity is often lower than it is when that same item is produced in another country. American firms can justify production only when that production is efficient. Our increasing exports should give us confidence in our efficiency.

PROTECTING THE JOBS OF LABOR

As we learned from the problem concerning automation in Chapter 5, any threat to employment is a serious matter to both labor and business. In spite of the high average productivity of American business and labor, the threat of foreign competition is ever present. Although in a competitive market the closing of inefficient plants may become necessary, doing so creates a difficult situation not only for the owners and workers of the firm affected but also for the community in which the business is located. Representatives from areas that are particularly hard hit by foreign competition band together frequently to lobby in Congress for the protection of the American worker. It is difficult to explain to those so affected that other industries are thriving and that other workers have jobs because foreign nations have been able to increase their imports of our products by earning dollars through their sales to us. Many economists point out that it is wiser and better for all concerned to help communities hurt by foreign imports by means of retraining programs and the locating of more efficient industry in their areas than by fighting the never-ending battle against foreign competition.

Barriers to trade

In the course of establishing policies to guide their economic development, nations have often turned to practices which interfere with the free flow of international trade. Protectionists have used the methods described here to accomplish their purposes, whereas people advocating free trade have tried to remove or modify the practices of protectionism.

TARIFFS

The device most commonly used to restrict imports is the *tariff*. A tariff is a tax placed on goods that move into or out of a country. Such a tax is sometimes called a *duty*. Most countries, including the United States, place duties only on imports. Duties are *specific* when the sum to be paid for each commodity is a specified amount; they are *ad valorem* when the amount to be paid varies with the value of the product. An ad valorem tariff of 25 percent on cameras would mean that a $25 duty is paid on a $100 camera and a $50 duty on a $200 camera. *Revenue tariffs*, usually placed on items not produced extensively in a country, are designed for the income they yield; *protective tariffs* are designed for the protection of home industries. The higher rates of the protective tariff usually have the effect of reducing revenues because they may restrict the importation of goods.

QUOTA RESTRICTIONS

An *import quota* establishes the maximum amount of a particular item that can be brought into a country during a given period. It is usually even more restrictive than a tariff. One nation might willingly accept a high tariff in order to sell goods to another, but a quota set by the latter nation would place an absolute limit on the import of restricted items, regardless of the duty.

OTHER HINDRANCES

In addition to tariffs and quotas, other less direct devices have been developed to discourage trade. A country may limit the amount of foreign exchange it will give to importers. Uncertainty about how an imported item is to be classified and, consequently, what duty will be placed on it, can also inhibit trade. Some items may be labeled as unhealthful when the real reason for the exclusion might be that a domestic firm is seeking protection. If a government wishes to discourage trade, it can find a variety of ways for doing so.

The development of United States trade policies

Recognizing the need for income, the first Congress to meet under the new Constitution passed a modest revenue tariff on July 4, 1789. Essentially an agricultural nation, we hoped to exchange our products and raw materials for Europe's manufac-

tured goods. Soon the protectionist sentiment of Alexander Hamilton found many adherents of the ideas expressed in his "Report on Manufactures." Later Henry Clay, in his American System (see p. 130), continued the idea of encouraging American industry by tariffs, while providing a market for agricultural products.

Although the nation depended heavily on the revenue it received from the tariff, protectionist rates tended to increase. An exception to this trend was the interlude of lower rates, from 1833 to the Civil War, during which time the agrarian South and West dominated Congress. The rate increases resumed again once the Civil War started, and continued until 1934, when the Trade Agreements Act was passed. Some attempts were made to lower the tariff during Cleveland's administration, and a degree of success was achieved in the lower rates of the Underwood Tariff Act during Wilson's first term. However, these attempts were in turn canceled out by even larger increases in the rates of the tariffs that followed. The climax was reached with the passage of the Hawley-Smoot Tariff Act in 1930, establishing the highest tariff rate in our history—52.8 percent on the value of all goods imported.

DIFFICULTIES IN LOWERING
THE TARIFF

You might wonder at this point why Congress passed such high tariffs although it recognized that such an economic policy might do more harm than good to the country as a whole. The answer is to be found in the way tariffs are made. Some Congresses have started out with the intention of lowering rates and yet have passed a tariff with duties even higher than those in effect when they started. How can such an about-face occur?

There are a number of ways to resolve this contradiction. Individually, a congressman may be interested in a general lowering of the tariff—except, perhaps, for the industries in his own district. In order to get the protection he seeks for those industries, he must agree to support the protection of industries in which other congressmen are interested. The result may be Congressional "logrolling" and a higher tariff, which may actually be contrary to the interest of the general public. Another source of pressure for protective legislation is the lobbies maintained in Washington by groups with special economic interests.

A NEW APPROACH: TARIFF NEGOTIATION

Faced with a serious depression and declining foreign trade, President Franklin D. Roosevelt decided to try a new technique for lowering the tariff. Instead of asking Congress for a new tariff law, he asked it for authority to alter duty rates, up to 50 percent of existing rates. This power would allow the administration to negotiate trade agreements within a broadly defined area, and to enter into trade agreements with other nations without submitting these agreements for Senate approval. Each agreement made would be applicable not only to the country it was made with but to others also ("most-favored nation" clause).

Congress responded by passing the Trade Agreements Act of 1934, which gave the administration authority to negotiate reciprocal trade agreements. But Congress did not surrender to the President all its power to regulate tariffs. It sharply limited the duration of the law so that the President had to come to Congress regularly to ask for its renewal. Several times there was a strong movement against renewal. After World War II, amendments were passed which greatly restricted the President's power to negotiate tariff agreements.

PERIL POINT AND ESCAPE CLAUSE

Two of the amendments limiting the President in trade negotiations have been the peril point provisions and the escape clause. The *peril point* is the lowest duty that can be charged on imports without

threatening the existence of a domestic industry. A committee is set up to investigate the arguments for and against tariff reductions and to decide what the peril point is before a trade agreement is negotiated. If a domestic industry finds itself hurt by a new trade agreement, it may appeal to the United States Tariff Commission for an investigation. If the Commission thinks that the complaint is justified, it may recommend to the President that he cancel the duty reduction under the *escape clause*. These two amendments completely ignore the law of comparative advantage, and they threaten any goodwill that might come from the signing of a trade agreement.

THE TRADE EXPANSION ACT

With realization growing that our nation had more to gain than to lose by the expansion of world trade, President Kennedy secured bipartisan legislation which took an approach somewhat different from that of President Roosevelt. The Trade Expansion Act of 1962 gave the President the power to raise and lower duties by at least 50 percent; in addition it allowed rates to be reduced by as much as 100 percent on duties of less than six percent, on articles whose export from our nation and the European Economic Community makes up 80 percent or more of free world exports, and on tropical farm and forest products.

The President was also authorized to negotiate for entire categories of products, such as textiles, and to bargain with the Common Market nations as a single unit. To soften the effect on industries hard hit by tariff reductions, the Act provided for retraining programs and resettlement allowances for workers displaced through foreign competition.

EVALUATION OF RECENT TARIFF POLICY

The results of our nation's policy to increase its foreign trade have been mixed. Overall, rates have been reduced considerably from what they were under the Hawley-

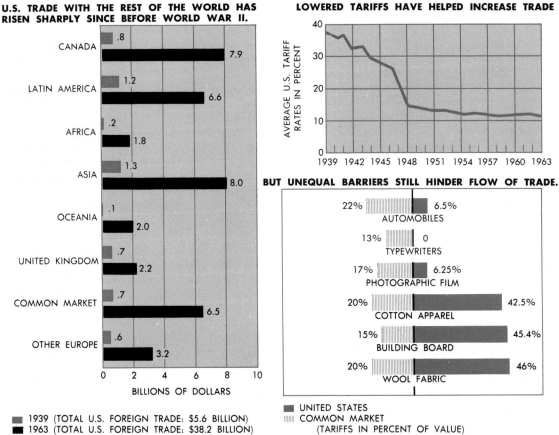

U.S. TRADE WITH THE REST OF THE WORLD HAS RISEN SHARPLY SINCE BEFORE WORLD WAR II.

CANADA .8 / 7.9
LATIN AMERICA 1.2 / 6.6
AFRICA .2 / 1.8
ASIA 1.3 / 8.0
OCEANIA .1 / 2.0
UNITED KINGDOM .7 / 2.2
COMMON MARKET .7 / 6.5
OTHER EUROPE .6 / 3.2

0   2   4   6   8   10
BILLIONS OF DOLLARS

■ 1939 (TOTAL U.S. FOREIGN TRADE: $5.6 BILLION)
■ 1963 (TOTAL U.S. FOREIGN TRADE: $38.2 BILLION)

LOWERED TARIFFS HAVE HELPED INCREASE TRADE

AVERAGE U.S. TARIFF RATES IN PERCENT

40 / 30 / 20 / 10 / 0

1939 1942 1945 1948 1951 1954 1957 1960 1963

BUT UNEQUAL BARRIERS STILL HINDER FLOW OF TRADE.

22% / AUTOMOBILES / 6.5%
13% / TYPEWRITERS / 0
17% / PHOTOGRAPHIC FILM / 6.25%
20% / COTTON APPAREL / 42.5%
15% / BUILDING BOARD / 45.4%
20% / WOOL FABRIC / 46%

■ UNITED STATES
▥ COMMON MARKET
(TARIFFS IN PERCENT OF VALUE)

Figure 15-2   United States Trade and Some Barriers Now Under Review

SOURCE: New York *Times*, May 10, 1964

Smoot tariff of 1930. Today more than 85 percent of all our tariff rates are under 26 percent, and more than 50 percent of our imports (by dollar value) have rates of five percent or less. Those who favor free trade (or freer trade) have much to be cheerful about.

In spite of the progress in rate reduction, many restrictions in the law remain for protectionists to use. A number of commodities still have very high duties, in some instances amounting to over 40 percent of the value of the imported product.

In the years since World War II the trends in international commerce have seemed to favor an expansion of trade and the use of fewer restrictions. The United States can take a major portion of the credit for setting this trend. The reciprocal trade agreements and President Kennedy's Trade Expansion Act both contributed to a new atmosphere in foreign trade. Recognition was growing, in our own country and abroad, of the ideas that almost all nations have a vested interest in trade and that trade agreements bring mutual benefits.

Part B   International Cooperation to Expand Trade

Many social scientists have long held that one of the basic causes of war—if not *the* basic cause—is the selfish, unlimited pursuit of economic gain by nations acting independently of one another. The struggle between "haves" and "have-nots" is not confined within the borders of a country; it frequently expresses itself between competing countries. If nations would recognize that the best assurance for their own economic well-being is helping to increase the size of the world's "pie," some of the tensions between nations might be significantly reduced.

World War II marked a turning point for many nations in the development of trade policies. From the horror and ravages of World War II there emerged a determination never to allow such destruction to happen again. Motivated by this spirit, the United States and some European countries took giant steps to make, at first the entire world, and failing this, the free world, more of a united economic community.

The United States takes the initiative

One of the innovations of the Trade Agreements Act of 1934 was the use of tariff negotiations as an instrument of government political policy in international affairs. Shortly, the close relation of economic interests and political concerns was to be further emphasized. Even before the United States entered World War II, many Americans recognized the stake that we had in a world that was subject to aggression. Congress, therefore, modified our strict neutrality laws to allow an arrangement known as lend-lease. This trade agreement provided to Great Britain and her allies supplies desperately needed to carry on the war, and it left details of payment for a later date.

When we entered the war we increased our aid, so that by the end of the war we had handed over $50 billion to our allies. These countries, in turn, supplied us with $7.8 billion worth of goods during the same period of time. Most of the $42.2 billion balance was canceled after the war because we recognized that we had been fighting a common enemy and that repayment by these war-torn countries would impose on them tremendous sacrifices that might undermine what the aid had been able to accomplish.

AID AND LOAN PROGRAMS
AFTER THE WAR

When the war ended, the only major nation in the world whose production facilities were intact was the United States. For the rest of the world, shortages of consumer goods presented a problem of immediate survival. Almost as pressing a problem was the lack of capital equipment, which threatened to make it difficult for the war-torn nations to solve their problems of scarcity and reconstruction for many years.

The American people rose to the occasion by showing a degree of altruism toward the rest of the world that no other nation has matched in peacetime. From 1945 to 1950, when our own domestic economy was in a period of scarcity (our aggregate demand was greater than our productive capacity), we gave to the world over $28 billion in grants and long-term loans. Most of the immediate needs we met through our contributions to the United Nations Relief and Rehabilitation Administration (UNRRA). That total reached more than $11 billion, of which the major share went to western Europe.

Early in 1948 we appropriated money under the European Recovery Program to help Europe help itself. The idea was initiated by our Secretary of State, George Marshall, and was popularly referred to as the Marshall Plan. ERP became known as

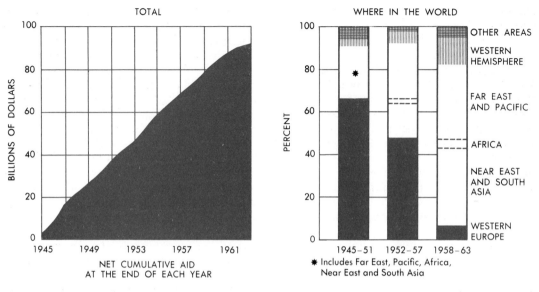

Figure 15 – 3   United States Foreign Aid, July 1, 1945, to June 30, 1963

While American aid continues to increase, the percentage of aid going to different regions of the world has changed. SOURCE: N.I.C.B., *Road Maps of Industry* No. 1482

the Organization for European Economic Cooperation (OEEC), and later the Organization for Economic Cooperation and Development (OECD). Much of the thinking behind the plan was to prevent the spread of communism because of the appeal communism has for people living in great economic uncertainty. However, there was also the recognition that a strong, economically healthy Europe could eventually become important for our own progress through increased trade.

Many billions of dollars of aid and loans have been granted under other programs. Military expenditures under our alliance system have strengthened the defenses of the free world and have frequently provided dollars to bolster the economies of the recipient nations. Our aid for economic development for underdeveloped areas has shown how conscious we are of the importance of solving world economic problems to the mutual benefit of our own and

other nations. One program that has cost little but has accomplished much in increasing living standards abroad is the "Point Four" program suggested by President Truman in 1949. It, like the more recent Peace Corps, offers technical know-how to countries whose workers lack such skills.

Today we can see how farsighted our aid policy was. Through rehabilitation and development of their productive capacities most European nations are wealthier now than they have ever been. Their prosperity and goodwill constitute a bulwark against the advance of communism. In addition we now export far more than we did before World War II (see Figure 15–2).

Not all aid has been carried out by our government alone. Besides the more than $96 billion given in foreign aid by our government from 1945 to 1964, American businesses had invested abroad nearly $41 billion by the end of 1963. Figure 15–4 shows how these investments were distributed by area and by industry.

GENERAL AGREEMENT ON TARIFFS AND TRADE

Following the close of hostilities after World War II the United States took the initiative in expanding international trade. In 1947 we, along with twenty-two other nations, signed the General Agreement on Tariffs and Trade. Under the Agreement, representatives of member nations meet at regular intervals to review mutual tariff policies and to set duties on certain goods. The Agreement has provided a useful framework for discussing multilateral trade agreements.

GATT, as the agreement has come to be called, is based on the ideas of (1) reducing tariffs through negotiations, (2) eliminating import quotas, and (3) applying the most-favored nation treatment so that there will be no discrimination against any nation. By 1964 over 70 nations had agreed to adhere to at least part of GATT. This number included all the major Western countries, many of the underdeveloped nations, and some of the communist countries. The advantage of the GATT approach over the reciprocal approach is that liberalization of trade is done collectively. The Trade Expansion Act of 1962 was designed to overcome disadvantages of the earlier approach and to supplement the policy for negotiations under GATT.

In November of 1964 the world's major trading nations met in Geneva to begin what has come to be called the Kennedy Round of tariff talks. At this meeting each country submitted a list of its "sensitive" products that it wished excluded from negotiations. The remaining products constituted a substantial portion of what is included in world trade. GATT has been successful in cutting the tariffs on them to a considerable extent.

Protectionist sentiment continues to be strong among many groups in this country as well as in other major trading nations. Lower tariffs on agricultural products have been particularly difficult to negotiate, although the agreement by Common Market countries on an external tariff in this area

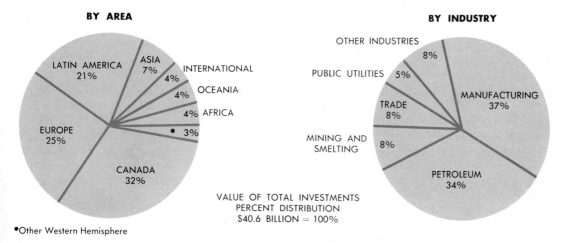

BY AREA

LATIN AMERICA 21%
ASIA 7%
INTERNATIONAL 4%
OCEANIA 4%
AFRICA 4%
* 3%
EUROPE 25%
CANADA 32%

VALUE OF TOTAL INVESTMENTS
PERCENT DISTRIBUTION
$40.6 BILLION = 100%

BY INDUSTRY

OTHER INDUSTRIES 8%
PUBLIC UTILITIES 5%
TRADE 8%
MINING AND SMELTING 8%
MANUFACTURING 37%
PETROLEUM 34%

*Other Western Hemisphere

Figure 15–4   Direct Investments Abroad by U.S. Business, 1963

Direct government loans and grants have been supplemented by investment by American businesses. Compare the areas of private investment with those of foreign aid, as shown in Figure 15–3. SOURCE: N.I.C.B., *Road Maps of Industry* No. 1499; U.S. Department of Commerce

"Tariff talks."

is considered a "breakthrough." In the decades since World War II, progress has been made in furthering our international trade and in reducing barriers to trade. But some observers think that it has been minor in comparison with what remains to be done.

Developments in Europe

In the aftermath of World War II the nations of western Europe also decided to reappraise their economic circumstances and trade policies. They realized that if they were ever to improve their economic position, they would have to forget their past jealousies and move toward some form of economic integration. The threat of Soviet expansion on one side and the encouragement by the United States on the other brought about a spirit of cooperation among previously feuding powers that even idealists had not dared hope for. The progress of these nations under the European Recovery Program strengthened their resolve for new directions of development, based on mutual benefit. What has emerged is a testimonial to the advantages of nations working together in contrast to the narrow policies of self-sufficiency pursued before the war.

FIRST AGREEMENTS

The first significant agreement on economic integration to emerge in Europe was the economic union in 1947 of Belgium, the Netherlands, and Luxembourg called *Benelux*. Common tariff schedules for imports from other countries were set, tariffs between the three nations were reduced significantly, and plans were made for full economic integration for the future. The advantages of such an arrangement were soon evident to other powers.

In 1950, under the leadership of the French economist Jean Monnet, sometimes referred to as "Mr. Europe," France, West Germany, and Italy joined the Benelux nations and agreed to unify their coal and steel business in the European Coal and Steel Community. The success of this venture and the resolving of anticipated difficulties encouraged the six nations to move toward even greater integration.

THE EUROPEAN COMMON MARKET

The next important step in economic integration came with the signing of the Treaty of Rome in 1957, which launched the beginning of the European Economic Community (the Common Market, or "Inner Six"). The nations of the Coal and Steel Community agreed to eliminate all tariff and other trade barriers between them and to erect a common tariff for outside nations over a period of twelve to fifteen years. Furthermore, they agreed to coordinate other economic policies such as the free flow of capital and labor within the market and a common antitrust policy in order to encourage competition. These agreements were strongly supported by United States foreign policy.

The trade program began on January 1, 1958, with a 10 percent tariff reduction and a 20 percent increase in the import quotas on nonagricultural products for the six members within the Common Market.

Table 15–1 Some Comparisons: The United States, OECD, EEC, and EFTA

(1963 figures, unless otherwise noted)

	U.S.	OECD[1]	EEC[2]	EFTA[3]
Area (thousand square miles)	3,615	1,552	450	494
Population (millions)	189.4	340	175	92
Labor Force (millions) 1962	75	149	75	43
Crude Steel Production (million metric tons)	99	106	73	30
Coal Production (million metric tons)[4]	426	482	257	205
Electricity Production (billion kilowatt-hours)	1,008	656	338	283
Automobile Production (thousands of cars and commercial vehicles)	9,100	7,855	5,578	2,178
Gross National Product (billion dollars)	585.1	404	243.4	132.6
Milk Production (million metric tons)	57	105	66	30
Imports (billion dollars)	17.0	71.5	[5] 24.9	26.4
Exports (billion dollars)	22.9	62.0	[5] 21.9	22.2

[1] OECD member countries in Europe: Austria, Belgium, Denmark, France, Germany, Greece, Iceland, Ireland, Italy, Luxembourg, Netherlands, Norway, Portugal, Spain, Sweden, Switzerland, Turkey, and United Kingdom. Canada, Japan, and the United States are also members of the OECD.
[2] EEC member countries: Belgium, France, Germany, Italy, Luxembourg, and Netherlands.
[3] EFTA member countries: Austria, Denmark, Norway, Portugal, Sweden, Switzerland, and United Kingdom.
[4] Hard coal and lignite in terms of hard coal equivalents.
[5] Excludes intra-community trade.

SOURCES: OECD, AID, FAO, Council of Economic Advisers, and U.S. Department of Agriculture

Since integration has moved ahead so rapidly, the projected time for the complete elimination of all internal tariffs and adoption of a common external tariff has been moved ahead to 1967. The great prosperity and economic growth rate of the participating nations has been impressive, and this has become the second-largest free-trade area in the world. Much of the future will depend on France and her attitude toward relinquishing national sovereignty.

The signing of the Treaty of Rome represents a significant milestone in the integrating of economies by the signatory nations.

A setback in the integration of the economies of the Common Market nations took place late in 1965, when France, following the policies of her president, Charles de Gaulle, boycotted the meetings of Common Market representatives. Conflict over the degree of integration, over the question of subsidies for farm products, and over the level of the external tariff has had a discouraging effect. However, France's resumption of participation in meetings, in January of 1966, and her acceptance of the reduction of internal tariffs to 20 percent of their 1957 level have shown that she does not really wish to end the organization. In spite of threats to its cohesion the Common Market will probably survive.

The initial high hopes and goodwill that the Common Market engendered among its members have been helpful in the establishment of other mutual undertakings. The creation of the European Atomic Energy Community (Euratom) for the peaceful development and use of atomic energy, the Court of Justice, the Council of Ministers,

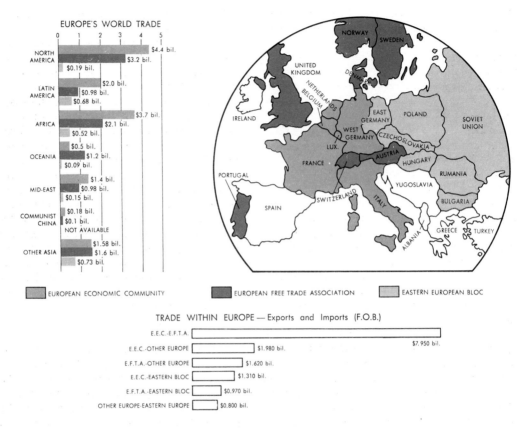

EUROPE'S WORLD TRADE

NORTH AMERICA	$4.4 bil.; $3.2 bil.; $0.19 bil.
LATIN AMERICA	$2.0 bil.; $0.98 bil.; $0.68 bil.
AFRICA	$3.7 bil.; $2.1 bil.; $0.52 bil.
OCEANIA	$0.5 bil.; $1.2 bil.; $0.09 bil.
MID-EAST	$1.4 bil.; $0.98 bil.; $0.15 bil.
COMMUNIST CHINA	$0.18 bil.; $0.1 bil.; NOT AVAILABLE
OTHER ASIA	$1.58 bil.; $1.6 bil.; $0.73 bil.

▪ EUROPEAN ECONOMIC COMMUNITY   ▪ EUROPEAN FREE TRADE ASSOCIATION   ▪ EASTERN EUROPEAN BLOC

TRADE WITHIN EUROPE — Exports and Imports (F.O.B.)

E.E.C.-E.F.T.A.	$7.950 bil.
E.E.C.-OTHER EUROPE	$1.980 bil.
E.F.T.A.-OTHER EUROPE	$1.620 bil.
E.E.C.-EASTERN BLOC	$1.310 bil.
E.F.T.A.-EASTERN BLOC	$0.970 bil.
OTHER EUROPE-EASTERN EUROPE	$0.800 bil.

European Trade Blocs

The movement of the nations of Europe into regional trading blocs has led to a decline in tariff barriers, an easement in payment problems, and, as a consequence, the expansion of trade within each of the blocs. SOURCE: New York *Times*, January 21, 1966

and a Parliamentary Assembly have all given hope to those who look forward to the establishment of a European federation based on economic integration.

EUROPEAN FREE TRADE ASSOCIATION

One unfortunate aspect of the Common Market is that its existence poses problems and a possible economic threat to other European nations that are not members. Great Britain did not originally want to become part of the Common Market because of her long-standing preferential trade and monetary arrangements with the Common-

wealth nations. Britain imports large quantities of food and raw materials and puts very low tariff duties on these products in exchange for low rates on the products that she exports to the Commonwealth nations. If Britain were to join the Common Market with its common external tariff, she would have to forfeit the Commonwealth benefits. Until 1961 she did not consider this sacrifice worthwhile.

In 1960 another economic unit appeared in Europe when Britain joined with six other European nations—Austria, Denmark, Norway, Portugal, Sweden, and

Switzerland—to form the European Free Trade Association (EFTA, or "Outer Seven"). These nations became a unit apart from the Common Market. They agreed to lower their own tariff barriers to Association members, but they made no agreements to set up a common external tariff or to integrate their economies in other ways. Although the EFTA nations have made progress in lowering their tariffs and increasing their trade, they have not had as high a rate of economic growth as the Common Market nations have had. In addition, the growth of internal trade within the Common Market has been so great that there is concern that nations lying outside the Market may have their exports to Market nations displaced.

In 1961 Britain reached the decision that the Common Market offered her greater opportunities for economic development and trade expansion than she had under her existing arrangements, and she applied for membership. Other EFTA nations followed suit. Until now, negotiations for admission of these other nations to the Common Market have not been successful. (Greece was admitted as an associate member in 1962, and Turkey in 1964.) Some of the difficulties that stand in the way of the admission of new members may be eased when EEC is more fully integrated.

LATIN AMERICAN FREE TRADE ASSOCIATION

Latin-American nations watched with interest the economic changes taking place in Europe after the war. The success of the EEC led seven nations—Argentina, Brazil, Chile, Mexico, Paraguay, Peru, and Uruguay—to sign a treaty creating the Latin American Free Trade Association in 1961. By 1967 all South American countries, with the exception of Bolivia and Guyana (but including Mexico), had joined. Although tariffs have been cut or abolished on over 8,000 items and trade within the Association has increased considerably, the fact that benefits have not been equal for all participating countries has hampered negotiations.

Progress within the Latin American Association has been slow for other reasons, too. The resources and conditions for growth there are scarcely comparable to those of western Europe. Nevertheless, opportunities for economic expansion and increased trade do exist. Here, as in Europe, our nation's economic policy supported the new development. In 1961 the "Alliance for Progress" was signed between the United States and Latin-American nations. Created to encourage economic development, the Alliance encouraged investment and technical assistance to promote development of industry, transportation, and trade. Some economic improvement in this underdeveloped area is already apparent. However, continuing efforts, together with political stability, are essential.

OTHER REGIONAL TRADE ASSOCIATIONS

Regional associations are also appearing among underdeveloped nations in Africa and Asia. These groups vary greatly in resources and potential for trade and economic development. How successful these associations can be without a *customs union*, a common external tariff similar to that of the Common Market, is open to question.

The communist nations have also developed associations for trade, although these differ from others because of government ownership and economic control within each country. In part, these associations are a mechanism for self-defense; these nations have resented the expansion of trade in other areas of the world, especially in the Common Market. They also think that they could improve their own trading position with the West if no regional agreements such as EEC and EFTA existed.

A democratic alliance

United States policy since World War II has been aimed at building a stronger free world. It is designed to protect our country and its allies against the possibilities of communist aggression and to encourage sound economic growth and closer ties among these nations. Our greatest efforts were centered on western Europe, and the results have been dramatic. Now that the economies of those nations have been re-established, we are directing more of our efforts toward meeting the needs of the underdeveloped nations. In the course of both these undertakings we have widened our own market and increased our own trade.

There is some apprehension that in assisting other nations we have created a potential threat to our own economic well-being. Will the Common Market prove to be a competitor so strong that it will cut into our trade, hurt our workers, and interfere with our economic objectives? On the other hand, is it possible for us to join together with EEC and other regional trade associations in the formation of a giant trade area, an economic association of democratic nations that could realize the potential benefits that should be obtainable through international trade? We will discuss this problem after we learn about another major barrier to trade, international payments.

Part C   International Finance — The Mechanics of Trade

Since the founding of our company that produces "Build-a-City" sets, the business has grown rapidly. Through expansion and skillful management we have been able to meet the domestic demand for our product. A recent survey of overseas markets has convinced us that demand for our product exists there also. Consequently, we have expanded production, with the intention of selling "Build-a-City" sets abroad.

It does not take us long to discover that exporting brings new problems to our business. Among these one of the most difficult is arranging foreign payment for our merchandise. In exporting our "Build-a-City" sets, we naturally want to be paid in our own currency — dollars. But how can other countries with different monetary systems pay us in dollars?

Companies which do business abroad receive payment in their own currency. French exporters would expect to be paid in French francs, English exporters in British pounds, and Japanese exporters in yen. This means that the French importer who is buying our merchandise must find some means of obtaining dollars in order to pay us. If he cannot obtain dollars, he cannot buy our sets, and our sales overseas will be reduced. In turn, trade between the United States and France will be reduced. International payment barriers between nations, like tariffs, can thwart trade. Let us see what methods and institutions have been developed to aid in selling goods in the world market.

How foreign transactions are financed

Importers and exporters in most countries need to obtain foreign currency in order to carry on their business. If you wish to import French perfume, you will need to obtain some form of payment that will satisfy the French firm. Let us suppose that a French perfume company fills your order for 100,000 francs' worth of perfume. You could go to a large city bank, or your own local bank might carry out the transaction by dealing with a bank that handles foreign exchange. You would pay the bank $20,000 plus a small commission to obtain a special check called a *bill of exchange*, which you would send to the French firm. This check is a claim on foreign currency (*foreign exchange*). It may be exchanged for other currency, five francs to one dollar (1 franc = $.20). The French firm will take your foreign exchange check and cash it in a French bank in order to receive its payment of 100,000 francs. The French bank will present the foreign exchange check to

Economists disagree on the seriousness of our international payments problem, especially when its solutions interfere with our domestic economy.

a branch of the American bank in France and receive payment. When we sell our "Build-a-City" merchandise to a French firm, the procedure is reversed.

EXCHANGE RATE UNDER
THE GOLD STANDARD

For many years gold served, at least indirectly, as the major means of international payment. The countries of western Europe, the United States, and many other trading nations were on the *gold standard*.

Their monetary unit—e.g., the dollar, the franc, the pound—was convertible to gold of a certain fineness. If the dollar was convertible to five times as much gold as the franc and both governments were willing to convert their currency to gold on request, the *exchange rate* was 5 to 1 (five francs to one dollar). This resembles the exchange of fractional currency to the dollar, such as twenty nickels for one dollar. Such a system is called the *gold-par rate of exchange*.

FLUCTUATIONS OF THE
EXCHANGE RATE

Currency, like all scarce goods, is subject to the action of supply and demand. When a nation offers attractive goods for sale at reasonable prices, other nations will want to purchase these goods. As a result the demand for that nation's currency will be great; if it were to circulate in a free exchange market for currency, its value would go up in relation to currencies that were not in such great demand. Under the gold-par rate of exchange, the value of currencies did not fluctuate much. If the demand for dollars were to go up in relation to francs, the French would merely convert their francs to gold and pay Americans in gold. There would, of course, be a shipping charge for sending the gold to this country; and it was this shipping charge, known as gold points, that determined how much the exchange rates could fluctuate. Because exchange rates were quite stable under the gold standard, international traders knew what foreign currencies would be worth. Stable conditions of exchange helped facilitate trade between nations.

DEVALUATION OF CURRENCY

In the 1930's, as world-wide depression set off a chain reaction of declining demand, many nations tried to stimulate their international trade by devaluation of their currency. To *devalue currency* is to change the rate of exchange by reducing its value in relation to the value of other currencies. When nations are on the gold standard, they accomplish this by lowering the gold content (value of their monetary unit in gold) of their currency.

If France devalued the franc from $.20 to $.10, it would mean that each American dollar could buy ten francs instead of five. In the case of our purchase of French perfume we could buy twice the amount of perfume for the $20,000 that we spent, provided the French price of the perfume remained the same. We could offer it to the American consumers for half the price. This would increase the sale of French perfume on the American market and increase French exports, thereby stimulating the French economy.

The effect of devaluation on trade depends on several factors. If other nations devalue their currency by the same amount, all the nations doing so stand in the same relative position as they did before devaluation took place. The first nation to devalue might have a temporary advantage, but it would make little difference in the long run. A second consideration is whether prices of the goods exported will also rise on the domestic market because of shortages created by greater exports. Past experience indicates that such prices do rise and cancel out some of the gains from the devaluation. A third factor is whether exporters raise their prices on goods so that the consumers of the nation importing the goods can buy at a significantly lower cost.

RESERVE CURRENCIES

In today's world the devaluation of the dollar or the British pound would have special meaning. Because the United States agrees to buy or sell gold from other countries at $35 an ounce, our dollar is literally as good as gold. Britain, although not guaranteeing the conversion of the pound to gold, agrees to convert pounds to dollars. This, in effect, backs the pound with gold. Because these currencies can be converted to gold directly or indirectly and because they are so widely used in trade, many nations use the dollar and the pound as reserve currencies to back their own currency. As a result, if either the pound or the dollar should be devalued, it would affect not only these currencies but all currencies which have dollar or pound backing.

Great Britain went off the gold standard in 1931 because prices in her economy were declining as a result of the depression. In order to keep up with other countries in her exports, her prices would have to continue to fall in order to compete on the international market. Adhering to the gold standard would require depressing prices at home as well as abroad, and this would aggravate the depression. If, however, Britain devalued her currency, she could try to keep her domestic prices up, but at the same time lower the prices of things she exported. The lower prices on her exports would result in other countries' buying more British pounds with their gold or currency.

This change in policy, however, helped the British very little because other countries soon followed her example. Preoccupied with their own national economic problems and following a policy of economic nationalism, most nations abandoned the gold standard. They were no longer willing to adhere to the fixed exchange rates that the system required, nor were they willing to buy or sell gold at a fixed price and in unlimited quantities.

EXCHANGE RATES TODAY

Although supply and demand for particular currencies play an important part in determining exchange rates, and in the long run may be decisive in determining values, there are today virtually no instances of a completely free market where currency is permitted to fluctuate without interference. Most of the major trading nations have moved to a modified gold standard called the *gold-exchange standard*. This system prohibits the circulation of gold within a country but continues government settlement of its international obligations by payment of gold. Nations usually put an official exchange rate on their currency so that its value in relation to that of other currencies can be determined. However, this fixed exchange rate can be maintained only by governments acting to keep the market price for money and the official price close to each other. In the absence of any gold standard many techniques have been developed to stabilize the exchange rates, but stabilization remains a problem.

Toward the end of 1964, after a long period during which the value of her imports exceeded that of her exports, Britain found the value of her pound sterling sinking and, as a result, the demand for it declining. The official rate of the pound in dollars was $2.80. When it dropped below $2.79, the British government went to the world's money markets and started buying pounds with her dollar reserves. By buying enough pounds she hoped that the supply of her currency could be reduced sufficiently to raise its value. Ordinarily, a country can regulate its currency close to the official rate by buying and selling its currency in the money market. In this instance an offer by the United States to buy up additional pounds with dollars was required to raise the price of the pound.

The balance of payments

When nations have financial dealings with one another, it is very unlikely that the total value of goods purchased by one nation will equal precisely the total value purchased by the other. The nation that has made the greater purchases must make up the difference in payment. In order to determine whether a nation must pay or be paid by other nations, a statement, called a *balance of payments*, listing all transactions that a nation and its people have with all other nations, is prepared each year. On one side of the balance sheet are listed receipts (credits) and on the other side payments (debits). The total of receipts always balances with the total payments because the difference is always made up by the flow of money and credits into or out of a country.

WHAT THE BALANCE OF PAYMENTS INCLUDES

Figure 15–5 shows a simplified picture of the United States' balance of payments. The largest single item on both the receipts and payments sides is the exchange of goods. Such goods are called visible items, since they represent tangible merchandise.

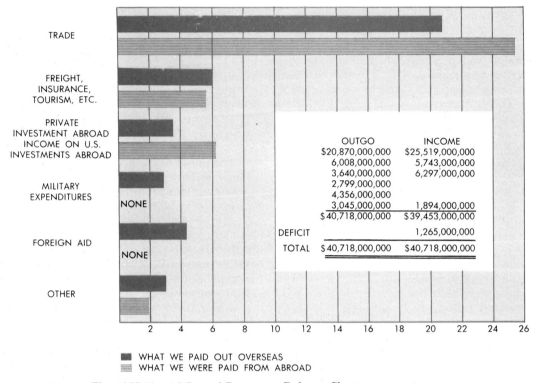

	OUTGO	INCOME
	$20,870,000,000	$25,519,000,000
	6,008,000,000	5,743,000,000
	3,640,000,000	6,297,000,000
	2,799,000,000	
	4,356,000,000	
	3,045,000,000	1,894,000,000
	$40,718,000,000	$39,453,000,000
DEFICIT		1,265,000,000
TOTAL	$40,718,000,000	$40,718,000,000

■ WHAT WE PAID OUT OVERSEAS
☰ WHAT WE WERE PAID FROM ABROAD

Figure 15–5   The 1965 United States' Payments Balance Sheet

The United States' balance of payments shows a deficit. This accounts for the outflow of gold from the United States. SOURCE: New York *Times*, January 17, 1966

Comparison shows that we exported more than we imported by a considerable margin, and, if this were the only item on our balance sheet, we could expect dollars and gold to flow into our country. In terms of goods alone, we have had and continue to have what many economists call a *favorable balance of trade.* Actually, because of our heavy spending of other kinds abroad, the flow is in the other direction—a condition called an *unfavorable balance.*

The word "favorable" is used because of the assumption that it is to our advantage to sell more than we buy. Many people, like the mercantilists of old, think of wealth in terms of gold instead of goods and services. If the gold were to remain idle, this

so-called favorable balance of trade would lower our standard of living because we would have fewer goods and services. You recall that production, not money, is the true measure of a standard of living.

Other items on the balance sheet in addition to goods exchanged are, for the most part, invisible items, representing payment for intangibles. Payments of this kind which we must make to others include services to Americans abroad, investments by foreigners in our country that earn income for them, loans to foreign businesses and governments, and our military expenditures abroad. These payments may be made in dollars or gold (the dollars that foreigners earn may be exchanged for gold). Payments are made to us from other nations for services to foreigners, travel by foreigners in the United States, income that Americans receive from their investments abroad, investments and loans to our country, and military transfers under our aid program. These items earn for us foreign currency or gold with which to make our payments to others.

CHANGES IN THE UNITED STATES' BALANCE OF PAYMENTS

For many years after World War I the United States was a *creditor nation;* that is, foreign nations owed us more than we owed them. As our gold reserves and foreign currency holdings grew, we often had

How can we achieve a balance of payments?

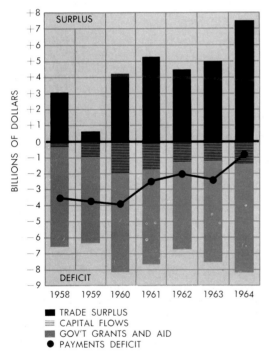

Figure 15-6 Source of United States' Payments Deficits

Because our foreign aid program, both military and economic, adds to our unfavorable balance of payments, it is increasingly controversial. SOURCE: New York *Times*, January 11, 1965

to lend money to nations with *dollar shortages* to enable them to go on trading with us. After World War II our various aid programs allowed foreign nations to continue to buy from us, and until 1949 we continued to have a surplus in our balance of payments. Our gold stocks in that year reached a peak, $24 billion, about two thirds of the estimated world total of gold.

From 1950 to 1965, with the exception of a single year, the United States has had a deficit in its balance of payments, in spite of our favorable balance of trade. Our nation's foreign aid program of economic and military assistance, together with most of the invisible items listed on the balance sheet, have more than used up the credits gained from the greater value of our exports over our imports. The resulting deficit in payments has compelled us to use our reserves of foreign currency and gold to pay our obligations abroad. By the end of 1965 our gold supply had dropped below $14 billion, about 35 percent of the world's estimated supply. Of even greater consequence than the loss of our gold is that a very large portion of our deficit in balance of payments was made by giving foreign nations our short-term IOU's. If they should "cash these in" (demand payment in gold), our gold reserves would fall much lower than they have up to the present time. Becoming a *debtor nation* has made us change many of our policies on trade and finance.

What does the deficit in our balance of payments mean? We were not seriously concerned about our deficit in payments until 1958, when foreign claims on our gold became almost equal to our gold holdings. We had previously built up such huge gold reserves that the possible problem of a deficit in our balance of payments never occurred to us. Today these foreign claims are even greater. If all these claims were to be made at the same time, we would not have sufficient gold to make payment.

There is little chance that all our creditors will make a claim on our gold holdings. So long as other nations want to buy our goods—and the yearly increases in our export trade indicate that they do—there is little danger. However, American economic policy must now take our balance of payments into consideration.

OVERCOMING OUR DEFICIT

The government has already taken a number of steps to ease the payment deficit. Military expenditure in Europe has been decreased by asking our allies to assume more of the burden of defense and by having our military personnel buy American goods whenever possible. We are encouraging overseas visitors to our country and discouraging Americans from traveling and buying abroad. To discourage American investors from turning to the higher interest markets in other countries, interest rates within our country have been increased, and a tax has been placed on earnings from abroad. At the same time our surplus of exports over imports has continued to be substantial. These measures have not eliminated the deficit, but they have helped to reduce it.

Because international trade is by far the most important item in the balance of international payments, it is essential that, until invisible items can be balanced, we

PRESIDENT MOVES TO STOP GOLD DRAIN

ASKS CONGRESS FOR LEGISLATION TO END $3 BILLION BALANCE-OF-PAYMENTS DEFICIT

WASHINGTON — President Johnson has called on bankers, businessmen, and tourists to work together in an effort to halt the $3 billion U.S. balance-of-payments deficit.

In a message sent to Congress the President urged legislation to cut the duty-free exemption for tourists returning with goods to $50 in retail value. In addition he urged a two-year extension of the penalty tax on the purchase of foreign securities. He asked that this tax be extended to include U.S. bank loans and long-term private credit.

The President asked the American tourist to "see the U.S.A." first, indicating that it was the patriotic thing to do. Last year American tourists spent $3 billion abroad.

Mr. Johnson said that the dollar is strong and that we are making progress toward solving our international payments problem, but he added that progress has been too slow.

Most observers believe that the heart of the President's program is its voluntary features. The success of this move will depend on the cooperation of bankers, businessmen, and tourists.

How serious the problem of the present unfavorable balance of payments is and whether we can solve it without rigid government regulation are matters of controversy among economists and leaders in government.

earn a substantial trade surplus. In order to do this we must be sure that our products for sale abroad are high in quality and low in price. Moreover, inflation can no longer be considered merely a domestic problem. If prices of our products rise, foreign nations will look to other countries for less expensive goods. Making sure that our output per man-hour increases and our prices remain stable is an important way to insure the growth of our trade.

The deficit problem is a consequence of our nation's having become a mature creditor nation and having assumed a role of leadership in world politics and trade. With power and riches go responsibilities. If we believe in freedom and want other nations to share in the benefits that come with individual liberty and economic progress, we must be willing to pay a price. Winning the minds of the people of the newly emerging nations is difficult and expensive, but in the long run it is to our own advantage.

International financial institutions

Before World War II, two important financial institutions were organized in order to facilitate international trade and payments. The Bank for International Settlement, primarily a European institution, made it possible for the leaders of central banks to work together in arranging temporary loans in order to stabilize currencies and in considering other problems of importance to international finance. The Export-Import Bank, an agency of the United States government, was set up in 1934. Borrowing funds from the Treasury Department, it makes loans to help finance trade between our country and other nations. It has also stimulated private loans by guaranteeing their repayment. By 1965 it had disbursed approximately $8 billion.

Other international financial agencies were organized in the postwar years. Even before the war ended, representatives of forty-four nations met at Bretton Woods, New Hampshire, and signed an agreement that created the International Bank for Reconstruction and Development, known as the World Bank, and the International Monetary Fund. The purposes of these institutions were to (1) help restore the war-ravaged nations, (2) aid underdeveloped nations, (3) assist in stabilizing exchange rates, and (4) facilitate trade by allowing nations to borrow currencies needed to pay for imports.

WORLD BANK

The World Bank now has over one hundred nations as members, with a subscribed capital of about $21 billion, over $2 billion of which is paid in. The latter sum can be used for loans, while the former is a guarantee fund to assure creditors. Funds come from subscriptions by members. By 1964 the Bank had made 424 loans totaling $8.7 billion in 77 countries and territories. Most of the early loans were for reconstruction, but these were soon outweighed by loans for the development of such things as roads, ports, power plants, pipelines, railroads, and industry.

These development loans are for a period of fifty years, with no repayment due for the first ten years but with regular repayment thereafter. In many instances the Bank guarantees a loan that is actually made by a private bank. It is run on a sound financial basis and may in no way be considered a give-away organization. Each loan application is investigated. Already a vast number of projects that have helped the economies of emerging nations are completed, with repayment made.

INTERNATIONAL MONETARY FUND

The International Monetary Fund serves a different purpose. It provides the largest source of international credit for short-term borrowing to facilitate trade. As with the Bank the borrowing nation must show how it expects to pay back its obligations. By 1964, 102 nations had contributed gold, pounds, dollars, and other national currencies to the International Monetary Fund in accordance with a quota agreement assigned on the basis of ability-to-pay. Fifty-eight member countries had borrowed over $11.5 billion by September 1965, compared with about $2.5 billion by 1961.

The short-term credit available from the Fund is an aid in balancing payments between nations. If Italy were short of dollars, for instance, she could go to the Fund and buy the dollars she needs with her own currency. When her balance-of-payments position improved she would buy back the Italian lire with dollars or gold.

The Fund has served an additional useful function by obliging its members to make no change in the exchange rates of their currency that is greater than 10 percent of its original par value (value of a currency expressed in ounces of gold or dollars). Ordinarily, a 10 percent depreciation in the par value of its currency can help a nation overcome a deficit in its balance of payments. The lower prices of its export goods to foreign nations stimulate its international sales. If this adjustment does not help, the Fund may permit additional depreciation of the nation's currency.

During its first ten years the Fund's operation was somewhat of a disappointment. Its resources were not sufficient to meet the needs of postwar readjustments, and there were occasions when nations disregarded their obligations concerning depreciation of their currency. Since the middle of the 1950's, however, the Fund has gained prestige as a stabilizing factor in monetary exchange. Even the United States has made use of its facilities to improve its international financial position.

Part D   The Problem: Is the Common Market (EEC) a Threat to the United States?

During the 1950's the economic supremacy of the United States seemed secure, and only the Soviet economic system existed as a challenge to that supremacy. A combination of favorable conditions, including geography, a hard-working dynamic population, and a political and economic structure favorable for growth, made it possible for less than one sixteenth of the world's people to produce over forty percent of the world's goods and services.

By the early 1960's some of the conditions supporting our nation's economic supremacy had begun to change. The remarkable success of the European Common Market—due in part to our support of it—resulted in a reorienting of the patterns of international trade and finance.

As the economic structure of Europe has become more integrated, the gap between our own productivity and that of the Common Market has steadily decreased. Trade within the Common Market has increased to such a degree that a first glance at the goods in a large European department store might cause the shopper to wonder which of the Common Market countries he was in. In addition to its increased productivity the Market's common external tariff could create a problem for nations that have always exported much of their merchandise to this area. Does the emergence of this new giant economic power represent a threat to our nation's trade and economic position, or is it an added bulwark to a strong new international system whose economic benefits will be shared by all, including our own country?

The Common Market is a threat

Many of the economic advantages that the United States has enjoyed in the past, giving it strength in the competitive world market, now appear to be diminishing. As the competitive position of the Common Market has improved, the competitive capability of the United States has been correspondingly reduced.

The growing worldwide demand for goods—including products from the Common Market—has encouraged European businesses to develop the mass production techniques that have been basic to the success of our own industry. By adopting standardization of parts and large-scale production, they now compete with our own industry in many goods, such as television sets and cars. Mergers have greatly increased the size and efficiency of many firms.

The growing depletion of some of our richest resources has reduced our advantage of abundant raw materials for industry. As we turn to the world market for new sources of these materials, we enjoy no advantage over other nations in our buying position. Reduced costs for shipping of raw materials have also lessened the advantage of having domestic supplies.

The comparative advantage that the United States has had in the possession and use of capital has also diminished greatly. Capital is accumulating at a faster rate in the Common Market than in our own economy. Over $18 billion of private long-term American capital moved to Europe for investment from 1955 to 1965, a period when our nation was having a problem with its balance of payments.

Many large American firms have set up plants in Europe to take advantage of the expanded market and the lower costs of production there. With no investment of Common Market capital they bring with them the benefits of the costly research done in our own country to improve the quality of products. It is questionable whether the profits from these businesses that are remitted to the United States compensate for plants not built and workers not hired in this country. With the United States government and industry supplying technological know-how and modern machinery, we have built up competition that is hurting our own economy.

American agriculture, which has competed successfully in the European market in the past, has been finding it increasingly difficult to climb over the barriers of the external tariff set by the Common Market. The so-called "chicken war" of 1964 (in which a high tariff on certain American poultry products greatly reduced their purchase within the Market) and the attempt to block American wheat have not only hurt our agricultural exports but have cost the European consumer money. If the Market's external tariffs are expanded in an attempt to aid special interest groups and nations within the Market, we can expect trade between that region and the United States to decline in the future.

The Common Market offers great benefits

When, in 1962, President Kennedy asked for and got from Congress the Trade Expansion Act, it was with the view that the economic integration of Europe could benefit the United States, and indeed all the free world. Strengthened by the power to negotiate with the Common Market and following the basic principles of GATT, the United States sat down at the conference table in Geneva, Switzerland, late in 1964, with most of the world's major trading nations. This meeting opened what is known as the Kennedy Round of tariff negotiations. Its major objective was the expansion of world trade. From this meeting and subsequent negotiations have emerged hopes for a new era in international trade—one that would promise long-range benefits for all participating nations.

The economic integration of Europe has been a great boon to American trade. Instead of reducing American exports to Europe, the demand created by industrial development within the Common Market has more than doubled our exports to that region since 1952. Shipments of American goods to the Common Market increased eighty percent in the first six years of EEC history. This contrasts with an expansion in American imports from EEC countries of only fifty-four percent. The new affluence in Europe, especially within the Common

Market, has significantly increased foreign purchasing from the United States.

Although firms in the Common Market have increased their efficiency and can compete with our industrial products on some items, they are still many years behind American companies in the production of most durable consumer goods. With American industries investing billions of dollars in modernized factories and automatic equipment, our advantage is likely to continue into the foreseeable future.

The declining advantage of our nation in natural resources has been partially offset by such gains as our development of synthetic materials and electronic devices. Our leadership in the technology of finding substitutes for scarce raw materials actually consitutes a growing advantage.

The Common Market community, the largest trader in the world, cannot afford to stifle trade with any nation, least of all the United States. Trade accounts for twenty-four percent of the EEC gross product, but accounts for only seven percent of our own GNP. The Common Market has more to lose by stifling trade than does the United States.

Several signs point to a common interest between the United States and the Common Market nations concerning trade. For example, most rates of the Common Market external tariffs and of American tariffs correspond closely. The active participation of Common Market nations with other GATT members in the Kennedy Round of tariff talks also shows their concern with reducing the barriers to trade. EEC has more at stake than does the United States in increasing world trade. Debates within the Common Market by most of its members indicate their desire to work closely with the United States. Such cooperation is in her own self-interest as well as that of her largest single customer, the United States.

Considering an answer

It would be wrong to assume that only the future will determine which of the positions presented here is correct. You have the tools to arrive at a conclusion and the power as citizens living in a democracy and consumers in a free market to try to influence policy. The interested citizen-consumer can put pressure on the government to alter our international trade policy, just as vested-interest groups do. The letters you write to your representative in Congress, the way you vote, and the products you buy are important in determining whether we pursue a policy of economic nationalism or a policy of free trade, or take a position somewhere between these two extremes.

REVIEW: the highlights of the chapter

1. Foreign trade is important because no nation is completely self-sufficient. Specialization in output by different countries offers the same advantages as it does within a single country. Most nations must rely to some extent on foreign trade for materials and products which they lack entirely or cannot produce profitably.

2. The law of comparative advantage shows how total production is maximized when each nation specializes in making those things in which it has the greatest relative advantage over other nations.

3. Among the reasons given by protectionists for interfering with the free flow of trade are need for a "favorable balance of trade,"

requirements of national defense, protection of infant industries, and protection of labor's wages and jobs.

4. The major barriers to trade are tariffs and quotas, although other devices are also used.

5. United States tariffs were protectionist in nature, with but few exceptions, until the passage of the reciprocal Trade Agreements Act of 1934. Shifting power to the President to negotiate trade agreements has allowed us to lower our tariffs more easily, although Congress retains power to allow exceptions. The Trade Expansion Act of 1962 gave the President additional power to negotiate trade agreements.

6. After World War II the United States took the initiative in helping to rebuild war-torn economies. It provided immediate relief with supplies of consumer goods as well as aid for long-range economic development. Technical knowledge and help to underdeveloped nations were supplied through "Point Four" grants and the Peace Corps.

7. European nations have responded well to the initiative of the United States by moving toward economic integration. This integration has led to the development of the Common Market (EEC) and the European Free Trade Association (EFTA). Other regional associations have been set up in Latin America, Africa, and Asia, but none has developed as fast and as completely and with such dramatic results as the Common Market.

8. International trade requires the exchange of currencies in the settlement of accounts. An importer must make payment to an exporter in the latter's national currency. If the importer's country lacks such currency, or does not have the means to buy it, trade may be hampered.

9. The rate of exchange is the value that one currency has compared to other currencies. For many years, when nations were on the gold standard, the rate of exchange was stable. Devaluation and the abandonment of the gold standard created greater fluctuations in the exchange rate.

10. Exchange rates today are stabilized in several ways, including the gold-exchange standard, the buying and selling of currencies by nations in order to keep their exchange rate in the money market close to their official exchange rate, and agreements under provisions of the International Monetary Fund not to make valuation changes greater than ten percent.

11. A balance of payments is a statement listing all transactions that a nation and its people have with all other nations during a year. When payments are greater than receipts, a nation has a deficit, which results in a flow of gold out of the country. In 1950 the United States moved from a surplus to a deficit in its balance of

payments. This continuing deficit became serious enough to necessitate changes in our economic policy in 1958.

12. Several international financial institutions exist to aid nations in economic development and foreign trade. Two of the most important agencies are the World Bank and the International Monetary Fund.

13. Controversy exists as to whether the Common Market represents a threat as a strong competitor to the United States' economy and trade or whether the growth of EEC may be the beginning of a more prosperous era for both the United States and the western European community of nations.

IN CONCLUSION: some aids to understanding

Terms for review

mercantilism	law of comparative advantage
infant industries	favorable balance of trade
ad valorem duty	free trade
peril point	tariff
lend-lease	quota restriction
Point Four	most-favored nation
Inner Six	escape clause
Alliance for Progress	Outer Seven
exchange rate	foreign exchange
currency devaluation	gold standard
balance of payments	negotiated tariff

Names to know

Benelux	International Monetary Fund
EEC	GATT
Common Market	Export-Import Bank
EFTA	World Bank
David Ricardo	Trade Agreements Act

Questions for review

1. The quotation "No man is an island" may well be applied to nations and their trade. Explain how this idea might be applied specifically to the imports and exports of the United States.

2. Foreign trade is a significant factor in the American economy.
   (a) Why can it be said that the standard of living in the United States is partially dependent on foreign trade?
   (b) Evaluate the statement "Although foreign trade represents only

about seven percent of our total economic activity, its impact is felt in every section of the United States."

3. Explain the following apparently contradictory ideas:
   (a) Nations should concentrate on producing those things which they can produce most cheaply.
   (b) It is often advisable to import some things that can be produced at home in order to help the total economy.

4. Assume that you are delivering a speech advocating a high tariff policy.
   (a) Explain the arguments you would use on behalf of (1) labor, (2) new industries, and (3) national defense advocates.
   (b) What arguments would be used to answer your contentions?

5. Differences of opinion exist regarding the effect of tariffs on trade.
   (a) Make a list of possible barriers to the smooth flow of international trade and explain how each works to hinder trade.
   (b) Show in what ways low tariffs might increase our nation's export trade.

6. Explain these statements:
   (a) The huge sums spent after World War II by the United States in foreign aid were necessary for Europe's salvation and our nation's own economic health.
   (b) The cost of foreign aid might well be a small investment for a large return in friendship and world peace.
   (c) American efforts at building European economic cooperation may, in the long run, result in a serious curtailment of United States trade.
   (d) GATT represents collective action, whereas reciprocal trade is bilateral.
   (e) The success of the United States' economic help to Europe resulted in defensive economic measures by the Soviet Union behind the iron curtain.
   (f) Latin America has joined with the United States in mutual economic cooperation.

7. Discuss the following statements, presenting the facts involved and evaluating the general truth of each assertion.
   (a) Exports and imports are only the visible items in the balance of payments.
   (b) The invisible items may be just as important as the visible to a favorable balance of trade.
   (c) The United States has been forced to reexamine its economic policies because of a continuing deficit and gold outflow.

8. Explain:
   (a) How both the World Bank and the International Monetary Fund operate
   (b) What the major differences are between the two agencies
   (c) How these agencies contribute to keeping world peace

Additional questions and problems

1. On an outline map of the United States indicate in red those areas and their products which depend on exports of goods and in black those areas and industries whose existence depends on continued imports of raw materials. What conclusions can you draw from the information on the map?

2. Prepare a list of arguments to support each of these positions:
   (a) Favoring the policies of classical mercantilism
   (b) Favoring completely free trade

3. Compare the Alexander Hamilton–Henry Clay ideas on tariff policy with the Franklin D. Roosevelt–Cordell Hull policy in the following categories:
   (a) The United States' economic conditions
   (b) Influence on the American scene
   (c) Influence on the international scene
   (d) Resulting economic growth and change

4. Jean Monnet is considered the major architect of the EEC.
   (a) Write a brief summary of Monnet's work in the establishment of European economic cooperation.
   (b) Evaluate this effort as a prelude to the establishment of a United States of Europe.

5. It has been said that a nation's economic growth can be traced in its tariff policies.
   (a) Draw a line graph depicting the average rates of United States tariffs from 1789 to 1965.
   (b) Explain the reasons for the tariff policy during the period from 1833 to 1862 and for the almost steady rise from 1862 to 1934.
   (c) How does the developing role of the United States as a world power become apparent in this graph?
   (d) Explain the meaning of these statements: "Congress still holds the tariff reins" and "Congressmen often think locally rather than nationally when it comes to tariff policy."

6. Using the financial pages of your newspaper, make a chart showing ten foreign currencies and their equivalents in United States currency.

7. Assume that you bought $10,000 worth of goods in each of the ten countries selected in the preceding question.
   (a) How would you pay for these goods?
   (b) To whom would the advantage accrue if the exporting country devalued its currency by fifty percent?

16 Economic Systems Other Than Capitalism

Preview

Throughout our study of economics we have made constant reference to the classical model of capitalism, to the Keynesian model, and to variations of these forms. Our focus has been primarily on the mixed capitalistic system in both its theory and its practice. The modifications that we have observed were still within the basic framework of capitalism, with little attention paid to other clearly defined economic systems.

In addition to capitalism there are three major economic systems—socialism, communism, and fascism. Each of these has its own model, explaining why it offers man the greatest hope for the future; each has had sufficient appeal to win millions of followers. In these systems, as in capitalism, there is a difference between the theory (the "ought-to-be") and the practice (the "is"). Each model has critics who oppose certain of its aspects but choose to keep its framework, preferring to modify the system rather than change to another.

Before we can analyze these systems, we must separate them from their accompanying political structures and the emotional overtones often generated by isms. Once this is done, the basic differences among the systems become apparent. These differences form a spectrum with one extreme labeled individualism and the free market and the other labeled collectivism and centralized control.

Overview

Explain the difference between political and economic systems.

What differences in values do you think exist between the adherents of capitalism, of socialism, of communism, and of fascism?

What criteria might you use for measuring the effectiveness of an economic system?

Part A   What Economic System? The Theory

In our present-day world there are three major economic systems competing with capitalism—*socialism, communism,* and *fascism.* Each of these has developed a model explaining the logic of its own system. Each must, like capitalism, concern itself with the problem of scarcity and the allocation of resources. Answers must be furnished for the *What, How,* and *For Whom.* Production and distribution are as important to the socialist, communist, and fascist economies as they are to the capitalist economy. We shall consider each of these systems from the point of view of its differences from capitalism or other systems, the model it follows, variations suggested for the model, and weaknesses inherent in each form.

Socialism

Socialism is found today in Norway, Sweden, Denmark, and Israel; it has existed in some degree at various times in Great Britain, Australia, New Zealand, the Netherlands, and Belgium. Most western European nations have strong socialist parties that have held political power often enough to influence the economic system strongly. To most Europeans socialism has a more favorable connotation than does capitalism, and several political parties oriented toward capitalism use the word "social" or "socialist" to make their cause more appealing to the people.

A number of underdeveloped nations, including India, have chosen socialism as their preferred system. The Socialist party in the United States has never been very successful at the polls, but it is interesting to note that many of the particular programs it has advocated have eventually become law.

DISSATISFACTION WITH CAPITALISM

Modern socialist thinking has developed largely as a protest against the misery that accompanied the Industrial Revolution. Instead of looking upon the factory system as a way to improve the lot of the poor, early socialists considered it responsible for crowded slums and low wages. Most objectionable of all was the idea that laissez-faire policies would best serve the public interest. Specifically, the socialists objected to these aspects of capitalism:

1. Private ownership of the tools of production—that is, of capital—leads to increasing inequality of wealth. Having a great advantage over the worker in bargaining, the capitalist receives a larger portion of the "pie" than he deserves.

2. Profit rather than need is the motivation for production. Because of this, scarce resources may be wasted on goods and services that serve no useful purpose, whereas other goods and services that do have real utility, especially to poorer people, are in short supply.

3. Competition is often wasteful. Duplication of effort, built-in obsolescence, advertising, and shortsighted exploitation of natural resources to make a quick profit are characteristic of capitalism's wasteful methods.

4. Planning by businesses on an individual basis leads to overproduction, causing business cycles. Cycles, in turn, lead to frequent depressions, which add to the waste of resources and the feeling of insecurity among workers.

5. The concentration of capitalistic wealth brings with it a concentration of political power. Greater concern is shown for property rights than for human rights.

6. Capitalism tends to lead to imperialism as businessmen seek raw materials, markets, and places to invest their surplus capital. When their investments abroad are threatened, they call on their government to provide protection. Such involvements may lead to war.

THE SOCIALIST MODEL

In a socialist economy the basic problems of scarcity and allocation of limited resources are solved by producing for use or need rather than producing for profit. By having most of the means of production owned and controlled collectively, usually by government, production can be planned and distribution organized to assure fairness for all. Socialist theory believes that instead of the market's determining what shall be produced, how it shall be produced, and for whom the production is meant, the government should provide the answers. Plans are carefully drawn so as to avoid waste, and production is aimed at improving living standards. Inequalities of income are reduced because distribution does not allow the strong to take advantage of the weak. Overproduction, duplication of effort, and depressions are avoided as competition is replaced by cooperation and planning.

Socialists believe in moving toward their goal of government ownership and control by gradual means and through democratic processes. The freedom of choice of the consumer and the producer may be curbed as the society moves from capitalism to socialism, but the decisions that citizens make as they go to the polls affect the economy even more than under capitalism. When property is *nationalized*—taken over by the government—the owners are to be compensated. Socialists claim that only by doing away with private ownership of capital and the power derived from that ownership can the state be economically and politically democratic.

VARIATIONS OF THE MODEL

Major differences exist among socialists as to how extensive government ownership and control should be. These differences are reflected in the many forms of socialism, all varying in organization, method, or emphasis.

The oldest and most idealistic form of socialism is known as "utopian socialism."

It is based on the belief that men can live together best in an environment which stresses cooperation rather than competition. Utopian socialists sought to set up communities where men would work together in harmony with little or no direction by government. Robert Owen (1771–1858), of Wales, and the followers of Charles Fourier (1772–1837), of France, set up experimental communities in the United States, hoping to show by example the superiority of their system so that other people might wish to live in the same way. The failure of these experiments and the lack of any strong formal organization, at a time when industrial organization was bringing about great changes, ruined any chances they may have had for success.

After the defeat of radical movements in Germany and England in the middle of the nineteenth century, a new attempt at social reform was made. Based on certain teachings of the Bible and directed primarily at workers, this movement was known as "Christian socialism." According to its teachings society should be organized on the principles of concern for humanity and belief in the brotherhood of man. Repudiating violence and class struggle, the Christian socialists advocated use of the private property of the rich for the benefit of all. They supported a broad program of reform designed to lessen the sufferings of the poor.

You have already become acquainted with another form of socialism—that of Karl Marx. Marx referred to his socialism as "scientific," claiming that his analysis was based on scientific reasoning. In his two famous works, *The Communist Manifesto*, written in collaboration with Friedrich Engels, and *Das Kapital*, Marx explained his criticism of capitalism and predicted its eventual destruction and its replacement by socialism. Much of the thinking of present-day communism is based on these writings.

KARL MARX, THE REVOLUTIONARY

Karl Heinrich Marx (1818–1883) was born in Trier, in the German Rhineland, the son of a middle-class Jewish family. At the age of seventeen, he began his college education at the University of Bonn where, following his father's wish, he began the study of law. However, he soon changed to history and philosophy at the universities of Berlin and Jena, receiving his doctor's degree.

Marx had hoped to pursue an academic career; but when this became impossible because of his radical ideas, he turned to journalism instead. His political views soon led to the suppression of his newspaper by the government, whereupon Marx moved to Paris. There he studied political economy, particularly the writings of French utopian socialists. Although their theories interested him, his own views were more extreme. While in Paris he met Friedrich Engels, who shared his opinions and who later collaborated with him to produce the famous *Communist Manifesto*. Exiled from France at the request of the Prussian government, Marx moved to Brussels. He returned to Germany during the Revolution of 1848. Expelled again, he settled in London. There he became active in workers' organizations and continued to develop his own theories.

In his later years Marx spent most of his time in the British Museum, where he read and wrote, earning a meager living by preparing articles for the New York *Tribune*. He and his family suffered from poverty and poor health, but these circumstances did not deter him from writing his famous book, *Das Kapital,* and organizing and leading the International Workingmen's Association, later known as the First International. The second and third volumes of *Das Kapital* were edited by Engels and published after Marx's death.

The influence of Marx on the noncommunist world has been more in the fields of business cycles, stages of economic development, and interpretation of history than in the advancing of economic theory. However, the vast importance of his thinking to the development of the communist world gives his work a significance beyond its contributions to economics alone.

Marx saw history not as a meaningless succession of events but as social change resulting from the struggle of classes. With the transition from agricultural to industrial production, a change in the dominant economic class was taking place. Under capitalism economic power would become so concentrated that society would be divided between the few capitalists owning all the means of production and the masses of workers owning nothing.

Marx explained the concentration of wealth in industry by the doctrine of *surplus value*. All wealth, he argued, is produced by labor, with the other factors of production being either passive or also the result of labor. Because the worker is not paid the full value of what he produces, the capitalist is able to accumulate this reservoir of surplus value – the difference between what the worker produces and what he earns. As this process continues, the middle class disappears and the society becomes divided between the capitalist (the exploiter) and the worker (the exploited).

Since workers lack the means to buy back the goods they produce, overproduction soon leads to depressions. As this condition develops, the position of the workers becomes even more intolerable. Eventually, the workers will unite and throw off capitalist domination by a revolution. With the capitalists gone, the means of production will be owned and operated by the workers. Since all people will be workers, there will be only one class. The struggle between classes will cease because the separation between owners of the means of production and workers will no longer exist. In effect, the new society will be "classless."

Toward the end of the nineteenth century a new direction in socialist thought appeared. Led by Eduard Bernstein in Germany and by Sidney and Beatrice Webb, George Bernard Shaw, H. G. Wells, and the Fabian Society in England, the new movement rejected Marx's class struggle and sudden revolution. In its place the "revisionists," as they came to be called, favored a gradual evolution to socialism. Progress for society through education and political control gained at the polls is preferred to class struggle. In extending its ownership of productive facilities, the government must proceed slowly; in some cases, such as public utilities, municipal ownership is favored over national ownership. The policies of the present British Labor party have been greatly influenced by the thinking of the Fabian Society, which incorporated many revisionist ideas. However, much of Britain's production remains in private control and her government is democratic.

Socialist ideas were sometimes incorporated into political and economic movements, such as anarchism, syndicalism, and guild socialism, whose main emphasis was on ideas other than socialism. Each sought to eliminate private property, and each had strong objection to the existing organization of government. The anarchist looked at the state as the source of all evil and wished to substitute for it self-governing groups living in voluntary associations. The syndicalists wanted to organize workers into one big union which would carry out a general strike and overthrow capitalism. Each industry would then be run by workers in autonomous units, which would be federated for overall direction. Guild socialism recognized the need for government, but it wanted to organize the society into producers and consumers, each with a national association. Industry was to be run by employees organized into guilds. Though significant in their time, these groups have little influence and importance today.

WEAKNESSES IN THE SOCIALIST POSITION

Just as the socialist can find fault with capitalism, so the capitalist can point to weaknesses in socialist thought. In particular, the supporters of capitalism criticize these aspects of socialist theory:

1. Socialism lacks incentives for increasing effort, whereas under capitalism, private ownership of wealth, including capital, is a motivating force. Under collective ownership unproductive members of society are subsidized by their more productive fellows, reducing incentive for both. In the system of private enterprise the individual businessman can see in a most direct way the rewards for his energy and ability.

2. Substituting production for need in place of production for profit may sound very altruistic, but who determines what need is? Even if that question could be solved to everyone's satisfaction, the fact remains that profits are as great in industries producing necessities as in those producing luxuries. In either case, profits will be made when individual consumers indicate their needs by buying what they wish. And isn't the will of the people expressed more clearly and directly by the individual vote in the marketplace than by the collective vote, even of a democratically elected government?

3. Although competition does produce some duplication and waste, it more than compensates for this by eliminating the inefficient producer and motivating those who stay in business to improve their products and reduce their costs. The cost of advertising is more than compensated by the increased market for goods resulting from the economies of large-scale production, which in turn results from the larger market.

Competition also yields an indirect benefit by offsetting political decisions.

People frequently exercise more care in spending their own money than in evaluating the consequences of their choices in voting.

4. Overproduction and economic fluctuations can and do occur in socialist countries as well as in capitalistic countries. Modern capitalistic economic policy has greatly reduced the length and severity of recessions. Moreover capitalism, with its millions of producers, has more flexibility to adapt to changing demand.

5. Concentration of wealth has not taken place in capitalist economies as the socialists have predicted. Instead, the ownership of our giant corporations is increasingly widespread. Today millions of our workers are themselves capitalists.

6. Capitalism shows no greater tendency toward imperialism at present than does socialism. Many socialist countries have actually sought out private capital as an aid to development. Competition for raw materials and markets is more closely related to capital accumulation and trade than to the type of economic structure involved.

7. Although socialists strongly support freedom and democracy and reject communism because it ignores civil rights, the amount of regulation and central planning necessary in socialism reduces consumer sovereignty and limits the decisions of workers.

Freedom is more closely tied to the political traditions of a country than to the economic system it chooses. In such socialist countries as New Zealand, Denmark, and Israel there is great respect for civil liberties. Likewise, the socialist charge that in capitalism there can be no real freedom because economic concentration leads to political concentration seems absurd when one looks at the number of elected officials, including American presidents, who were opposed by "big business" interests.

Communism

On the surface the theories of present-day socialism and communism seem more marked by similarities than by differences. Both systems make the same criticisms of capitalism. Both received impetus from the writings of Karl Marx. Perhaps the problem of distinguishing between the two systems is one of semantics, concerning the meaning and use of the term "socialism." Both the Soviet Union and some western European nations refer to their systems as socialist states, but the informed observer knows that the socialism of western Europe and that of the communist world are two different and incompatible systems.

ANALYSIS OF THE STAGES OF COMMUNISM

Unlike most socialists, who believed in progress by peaceful evolution, Marx believed the transition from capitalism to communism would follow a particular pattern and would be accompanied by a violent revolution. Communist theoreticians have classified this process in four stages.

The first stage is marked by the overthrow of capitalism by the workers, and is followed by their seizure of the government.

The second stage is characterized by the establishment of a *dictatorship of the proletariat*. A centralized authority is necessary because the majority of workers are not capable of ruling, and direction by a small, intelligent leadership—the Communist party—is required. Under the dictatorship the destruction of the capitalist class is completed, and society is reorganized along socialist lines, with private ownership and profit abolished. The state now owns and operates the means of production.

In the third stage the dictatorship of the proletariat is replaced by the establishment of a "socialist" society. The political state will still exist and, because there may still be opposition, will have considerable power; economic production is to be controlled by the workers. Because production would still be limited, output and payment would be "from each according to his ability, to each according to his work."

The fourth and highest stage is that of the true "communistic" society. Production will be in such abundance that work and payment will be made "from each according to his ability, to each according to his need." The political state will no longer be necessary because there will no longer be any antagonism between classes. Administrators will be needed, however, to supervise industrial complexes.

The communists of the U.S.S.R. claim that they have now reached the third stage—that of socialism—and they hope to have enough production to attain actual communism by the middle of the 1970's.

DIFFERENCES BETWEEN SOCIALISM AND COMMUNISM

As we have seen, the communists seek to end capitalism by revolution, whereas the socialists wish to do it through the ballot box, adhering to constitutional procedures. In socialism, education and persuasion are substituted for the militant class struggle advocated by the communists. For the most part, socialists believe in an orderly transfer of the means of production from private to public ownership. This changeover can be accomplished by gradually increasing the size of the public sector, thereby allowing capitalism and socialism to live side by side during the period of transition.

One of the important differences between socialism and communism may be seen in their treatment of nationalized property. Under socialism, fair payment is to be made to the owners. Since communists look with disdain upon the capitalist, considering the property he owns as stolen from the people, they expropriate private property without any compensation. Furthermore, they do not accept a mixed economy (although they did in practice in Russia between the years 1921 and 1927) and believe in total nationalization.

Finally, socialism has a high regard for the political freedom of the individual. It does not seek to control the total way of life of the people; instead, it is responsive to popular will expressed through elections. Communism, on the other hand, is totalitarian, seeking to subject not merely economic affairs but all individual thought and activity to the good of the state.

WEAKNESSES OF COMMUNISM

In our analysis of socialism we have already identified many of the weaknesses of communism. To these, other criticisms must be added:

1. With his materialistic interpretation of history, Marx focused attention on the role of economic forces in determining the course of history. Those people who owned wealth or the means of acquiring wealth—land in an agricultural society, boats in a maritime state, machinery in an industrial nation—also controlled the forces of government and determined their policies and direction.

   There is little doubt that Marx made a substantial contribution to the understanding of history, since too little attention had been given to economic forces before his time. At the same time he committed the error common to all those who seek a single answer—oversimplification. No single factor can possibly explain all historical development. Events occur because of multiple causes, with no one factor predominant throughout history.

2. Marx predicted that the proletarian revolution to overthrow capitalism could come only in advanced capitalistic nations. If this were true, the United States, Britain, and western Europe should have been the first to experience such revolutions. Instead, communism has developed most frequently in nations that are just beginning to emerge from feudalism into the capitalist stage.

3. Marx predicted that the polarization of classes would grow to the point where almost all people would be industrial workers and the rest would be capitalists. Writing a hundred years ago, he did not anticipate the growth of the "salariat," or white-collar workers, who identify with the middle and upper classes. Today, the salariat constitute the largest percentage of workers. To them, the class struggle as envisioned by Marx is almost meaningless.

4. Marx anticipated the decline of interest rates as the accumulation of more and more capital would eventually lead to a shortage of new areas for investment. In contrast to Marx's expectations, good opportunities for investment continue to exist today, and interest rates tend to fluctuate in the same way and for the same reasons that they always have.

5. Marx predicted that only through revolution could there be any reforms for the workers. He failed to foresee the economic gains and humanitarian reforms that have been carried out by democratic capitalistic nations without resort to force.

6. Marx and other communist theoreticians looked upon capitalist theory as a rigid doctrine incapable of solving the basic problems of a dynamic society. The capitalism of today, in theory as well as in practice, is not the same as the capitalism that Marx observed or prophesied about in the nineteenth century. Current communist theoreticians commit the same error as their predecessors, although it is more likely that they do so for propaganda purposes rather than out of sincere conviction.

Fascism

Fascism is the term associated with the economic and political system of Italy, Germany, and Japan before and during World War II. Variations of this system survive today in the governments of Spain, Portugal, and several Latin-American countries. Except in these countries, fascist parties are today small and relatively lacking in power. However, the ideas of fascism are still very much alive and assume a variety of guises. Given the right stimulus, they could prove a real danger to the institutions of democracy.

Unlike capitalism, socialism, and communism, fascism does not have a clear-cut model or even a major literary work that clearly defines what it is or how it functions. Its political and economic aspects are so intertwined that separating them, as we have done with the other systems, is difficult. However, we can determine some of the major ideas and principles that set fascism apart.

ECONOMIC ASPECTS OF FASCISM

Fascism combines capitalism's private ownership of the means of production with communism's state planning. Industry, although privately owned and profit-seeking, is organized into corporations or estates under the strict regulation of the government. Membership of corporate leaders in the fascist party and participation by them in planning insures close government control of the business community. Labor unions are also severely regulated, and workers who challenge their leaders' authority suffer severe penalties. Central planning replaces the market mechanism as the means of controlling production and allocating resources.

Fascism is traditionally oriented toward a war economy. For example, when Italy, Germany, and Japan were unable to solve their serious economic problems, they turned to giant rearmament programs. Projects such as these provided swift relief for depression and unemployment. It is doubtful whether economies thus oriented could survive for long without a war.

After the outbreak of World War II the resources of conquered countries were used to support the economies of the fascist nations. Slave labor produced food for the conquerors and war materials for new conquests. Only defeat could halt the war-directed economic development of traditional fascism.

POLITICAL ASPECTS OF FASCISM

Under traditional fascism, individualism is replaced by the most extreme form of nationalism. Social and economic considerations are subordinated to the purposes of the state. For example, to expedite rearmament, the power of labor unions in fascist countries was curbed through the combined efforts of powerful industrialists and fascist political leaders. Leadership pyramids to the top so that the dictator, "Il Duce" or the "Führer," holds total authority. When Hitler was introduced to people at a Nazi demonstration with the words "Hitler is Germany, Germany is Hitler," it meant that he was the embodiment of all the glory of the German nation and that everything must give way to his will.

Unlike many other dictatorships, fascism seeks mass support for its activities and programs. Support is also won from the traditional centers of leadership—the industrialists, landowners, and especially the military leaders—who may be frightened by the prospect of labor discontent. A third source of support is the salariat, who are inclined to fear the rise of the working class and may even be jealous of higher wages paid to industrial workers. A policy of "divide and rule" enables the centralized authority to maintain control.

As a totalitarian system dominating all aspects of life, fascism employs science, literature, and the arts as instruments of political power. Emphasis on nationalism has in some cases led to belief in national and racial superiority. This supposed superiority becomes a justification for conquest of other peoples, cultures, and nations.

As we have seen, a few neofascist nations still exist. Since they are lesser powers, lacking the economic resources for political expansion, they are less threatening to other political and economic systems than the earlier, more powerful fascist nations were. Yet even in these countries the size of the armed forces and the influence of military elements are far greater than in other countries with comparable resources.

COMPARISON OF COMMUNISM AND FASCISM

Communism and fascism are both totalitarian systems that have emerged in the twentieth century. But whereas communism has grown and flourished in poor and underdeveloped countries, fascism has taken hold in capitalistic and more highly industrialized nations. The major pre-World War II fascist states—Italy, Germany, Japan, and later Argentina under Perón—were capitalist states with limited experience in democratic institutions. Distrusting democracy and seemingly unable to solve their problems through existing means, they turned to fascism as an alternative. China and Russia, by contrast, were emerging from feudalism and never really developed democratic institutions. To them communism became a means of industrializing and advancing their total economic development.

WEAKNESSES OF FASCISM

The course and outcome of World War II betrayed the economic weaknesses of the fascist nations. Their dependence on a war-oriented economy, their financial instability in time of crisis, and their economic collapse at the end of the war cast serious doubts on any possible economic merits of fascism. The performance of the present fascist nations in meeting the needs of their people suffers in comparison with that of other systems. Probably the greatest weakness of fascism, at least in the long run, is its political system and the values on which it is based. Its substitution of emotion for reason, the state for the individual, might for right, violence for peace, and government by the few for government by the many conflicts with the values held by most people and most nations in the twentieth century. The record of violence and brutality built up by fascist leaders during the Second World War is too well known and too repugnant to win universal support.

The fact that fascism does not now exist in any powerful nation or that only small fascist organizations are found in major countries does not mean that fascism is no longer a danger. Fascism, intolerance, disregard for law and order, and the love of militarism did not disappear with the defeat of the Axis countries in World War II. Our best protection against any totalitarianism—communist or fascist—is the free marketplace of ideas as well as of products.

Private ownership of the means of production in no way assures a free market economy. The economic control exercised by these Axis leaders almost equaled their political control.

Part B   What Economic System? The Reality

Having examined the models of the three major competitors of capitalism, we are now ready to analyze the basic principles of these systems. When we speak to an adherent of any one of these systems, he will tend to exaggerate the differences among them. If, however, we can remove ourselves from the emotional involvement often associated with a discussion of isms, we can more clearly identify the real issues.

The political and economic spectra

Every scientific discipline seeks to organize knowledge in such a way that it can be handled easily. Criteria are drawn up so that groups of ideas, bodies of knowledge, and systems may be categorized. When the political scientist classifies a country's political system as a democracy or an oligarchy, he has taken a number of characteristics into consideration and sees which of

COMPLETE FREEDOM

COMPLETE CONTROL

Figure 16–1 The Political Spectrum

Anarchy offers the individual citizen complete freedom with no government coercion. Totalitarianism subordinates the individual completely to the good of the state.

these categories comes closest to describing the political state he is examining. The economist does the same thing in trying to classify a nation's economic system. Actually, no nation's system, political or economic, conforms exactly to the model.

The basic issue, both politically and economically, is the degree of freedom allowed to the individual. In Figure 16-1 we can see the complete political spectrum as it moves from left to right. At the extreme left we see the complete freedom of the individual with the absence of any government coercion. Such a condition, the absence of government, is called "anarchism." At the extreme right the citizen has surren-

decides the answers to the basic economic questions of *What? How?* and *For Whom?* On the right side of the spectrum the consumer is king. His decisions, expressed by his purchases, and the response of private enterprise, expressed by supply, determine the use of our resources. It is the market mechanism at work. Laissez-faire, or classical capitalism, keeps the government out of decision making as much as possible.

Mixed capitalism, sometimes called *welfare capitalism*, favors decisions by the consumers but allows for some central planning. As we move toward the left from mixed socialism to socialism to communism, central planning increases and the

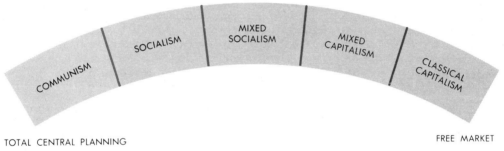

TOTAL CENTRAL PLANNING

FREE MARKET

Figure 16-2 The Economic Spectrum

Classical capitalism makes the consumer king and the regulator of the entire market. Communism (before the state withers away) calls for the greatest amount of central planning, with very little consumer sovereignty.

dered all his freedom to a government which has total control over every aspect of his life—totalitarianism. Absolute monarchy is listed on the extreme right because it refers to rule by one person. Constitutional monarchy, as in Britain, can be just as liberal as other democracies because the constitution guarantees the rights of the people. In an oligarchy the few would rule, whereas in a democracy rule is by the many. The political spectrum defines the extent of personal freedom the citizen has in relationship to government authority.

In Figure 16-2 we see the economic spectrum. Here the difference lies in who

reliance on the market mechanism declines. At the extreme left we see total central planning, where government makes almost all the decisions and consumer choices are given little attention.

Our economic spectrum is not complete unless we include the ownership of wealth. In Figure 16-3 we see complete private ownership on one side and complete collective ownership on the other. Although no countries have either of these extremes, classical capitalism calls for a maximum of private ownership and communism calls for a maximum of collective ownership, particularly of capital goods. Again we see

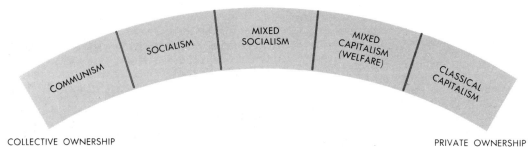

COLLECTIVE OWNERSHIP   PRIVATE OWNERSHIP

Figure 16–3 The Economic Spectrum of the Ownership of Wealth

Classical capitalism calls for a maximum of private ownership, whereas communism calls for a maximum of collective ownership.

the different degrees of stress on ownership of wealth given by mixed capitalism, mixed socialism, and socialism.

TYING THE POLITICAL AND ECONOMIC SPECTRA TOGETHER

When we try to determine where to place a particular nation on the two spectra with freedom as one of the criteria, we must consider both its political and economic systems. Although the British Labor party places great emphasis on central planning and believes in nationalizing some of its nation's basic industries, it can do these things only with the approval of the British electorate and with just compensation to owners whose private property is lost to collective ownership. No such limits are placed on the Soviet government.

Either democracy or totalitarianism as a political system can exist with either private or collective ownership. The Fascists in Italy and the Nazis in Germany allowed private ownership of even the basic industries, but there was little freedom, even for the owners of business. Conversely, democracy can be practiced in nations, such as our own, that rely primarily on the market mechanism for the allocation of resources, or in nations that have a great deal of central planning, such as Sweden.

Mixed economic systems

No major country today has wholly private ownership or collective ownership of

property. No economy relies entirely on the market mechanism or on central planning for deciding the *What, How,* and *For Whom.* We may classify nations as capitalist, socialist, communist, or fascist, but even within each category there are substantial differences. The "mixture" in Israel is different from the "mixture" in New Zealand; the "mixture" in Yugoslavia differs from that in the U.S.S.R.

Instead of analyzing a nation's economic system in terms of isms, we might more appropriately inquire what part of the economy is governed by a free market and what part by central planning. When the problem is viewed in this way, we recognize that important differences exist not merely between countries but within countries. In the last thirty-five years one of the major differences between our Republican and Democratic parties has been the extent to which each advocated central planning by the federal government. The Republican party has generally resisted the increase in central planning and has favored reliance on the market mechanism. It has also resisted increasing collective ownership. The Democrats have gone far in supporting central planning and government ownership of some projects such as the TVA.

Economic systems evolve

Advocates of a particular economic system may preach and work to have their

The contrasting productivity of privately and collectively owned land seems to indicate a difference in incentive. What inference might be drawn from the situation shown here?

system take the place of what exists, but the chances of installing a completely new economic system are remote. Economic systems grow slowly, and only occasionally are changes speeded up. Under Roosevelt's New Deal policies and Labor party policies between 1945 and 1951 in Britain, significant changes occurred. In both instances the amount of central planning was accelerated. However, when opposition parties came to power, there were no great withdrawals from the major changes that had taken place. Modifications were on emphasis and degree rather than on kind.

When the Communists took control in Russia in November of 1917, they tried to replace the existing system with pure communism. Their attempt was not successful. Realizing the need for compromise, Lenin in 1921 launched the New Economic Policy (NEP), which combined elements of both communism and capitalism. For the next seven years limited private ownership and the profit motive were allowed to exist side by side with collective ownership. Gradually, central planning and collective ownership were increased, and by 1928 Stalin restored solely communist principles.

The Central Peasants' Market in Moscow, where peasants sell privately raised produce, is an example of Soviet use of capitalist techniques.

Recent changes

Each of the political-economic systems we have considered has changed from the model as originally conceived. The reality of the present may represent a major departure from past theory. In each system recent changes have indicated new directions of development.

TREND OF THE AMERICAN ECONOMY

Our nation's economy today is a far cry from what the classical economists envisioned. In Chapters 7 and 8 we saw the changes in size and influence of our various levels of government. Today approximately one fourth of our GNP is spent by our local, state, and national governments. Additional services, particularly in health, welfare, education, and the broad field of research, are being added regularly. Other government services of long standing are being expanded rapidly. Government influence over economic groups—including labor, business, and professional groups—is being extended. Economic decisions are being made less often by individual consumers than previously, and central planning is increasing at all levels of government.

Are we losing our freedom and becoming totalitarian? Most social scientists would answer with a resounding *no!* They believe that what we have done is to transfer some of our decision making as consumers to decision making as citizens. Increased specialization and interdependence have forced us, sometimes reluctantly, to give up our individual sovereignty for the common good. So long as we have a free marketplace to learn the facts and evaluate ideas, and so long as we have the power through elections to reverse the trend, we need not fear the future.

In spite of the trend toward central planning, the private sector of our economy is still almost three times as large as the public sector. Most of our economic decisions are still made by individual consumers and producers, and we continue to rely on the market mechanism to allocate most of our scarce resources. We may properly call our nation's economic system one of mixed capitalism.

TREND OF THE SOVIET ECONOMY

Since Stalin's death in 1953, trends in the Soviet Union have indicated a decrease in centralized planning. Each year the State Planning Commission, known as the "Gosplan," makes the basic economic decisions. However, greater attention is paid today to the setting of quotas and to the suggestions of regional councils and even plant managers. Although the consumer appears to have relative freedom in deciding his own purchases, most consumer prices are determined not by supply and demand but by the state. If more overcoats

Something capitalistic is happening to Russian communism. After decades of rigid control by Moscow, Soviet production is increasingly geared to what the people want rather than to what central planners prescribe.

than jackets are made, and if consumers want more jackets, a tax is placed on the jackets to discourage their purchase. The state also permits the sale of certain food products—those grown by farmers on their own time and on specially designated land—in a free market, very similar to our own.

Most Soviet workers are free to work where they wish, although some of them are required to work on special projects. Little reliable information is available on the number of people held as forced labor, but such labor is thought to exist. Wide differences are found in the pay scale of Soviet workers, probably greater than in our own country. Scientists, plant managers, and skilled technicians have the highest incomes. The Soviet Union has adopted capitalistic incentive plans by paying *piece rates* (wages determined by output) and by offering various kinds of bonuses to managers who meet or exceed their production quotas.

A close check is maintained over the economy by the State Control Commission and the Gosbank, which handles all banking in the Soviet Union. The Gosbank works closely with the central planners, providing funds according to plan requirements. As you know, in our country the market mechanism determines the allocation of capital.

Since the removal of Premier Khrushchev in 1964, the Soviet Union has moved further toward the use of capitalist techniques. A Soviet professor of economics, Yevsei Liberman, recently recommended certain profit incentives in place of bureaucratic planning. He called for more market research, with increasing attention to the adjustment of prices according to supply and demand. In a number of selected industries, evaluation of economic performance is now being measured by means of profit on investment.

It is possible that as the Soviet economy matures and accumulates enough capital to

SOVIETS TRYING PROFIT SYSTEM

LEADING ECONOMIST PLEADS FOR MORE INITIATIVE

LONDON — One of the leading Soviet economists, Professor Yevsei G. Liberman, has advocated proposals for using the profit motive as an incentive for increasing initiative and efficiency. Originally mentioned two years ago, Professor Liberman's proposal to introduce management techniques long familiar to Western economies has now received strong support from other Soviet economists as well as from Soviet leaders.

Several industries have been selected to test "Libermanism." The theory behind the proposals is that profit should play a major role as an incentive to producing goods wanted by the consumer. Experiments in breaking the tight hold of central planners on production have already taken place in the clothing and shoe-manufacturing industries with excellent results. Others are now scheduled for several coal mines, a car-loader plant, and the manufacture of TV sets.

The post-Khrushchev rulers are committing themselves to such capitalistic devices as market research, price adjustments to reflect supply and demand, measuring the rate of profit on investment as a gauge of efficiency, and limited consideration of interest payment for the use of capital. Not many years ago such techniques would have been considered heresy by Soviet communist leaders.

Recent trends in the Soviet economy have been in the direction of market orientation rather than central planning.

provide a much higher standard of living for its citizens, the trend toward greater freedom may be accelerated. However, central planning and government ownership remain the key to that economic system.

Communism in China differs significantly from that in the Soviet Union. It would be unwise to attempt a comparison, since the Soviet Union is already an industrialized nation whereas China is only beginning to make the transition from an agricultural economy. Our discussion of communism is based on the present Soviet system. Although many features of that system would also pertain to China's communism, others would not.

TREND OF SOCIALISM

Because early socialists were discontented with great inequality of wealth, one of their major objectives was achieving greater equality in the distribution of returns from production. They hoped to accomplish this by nationalizing the means of production so that profits, the alleged cause of inequality, could be shared by everyone. They also sought to provide for all a minimum standard of living as a means to economic and social security.

As we have seen, these objectives are no longer the goals of socialists exclusively. Such goals have in fact become a reality, or close to a reality, in many of the more affluent nations. Mixed capitalism—the economic doctrine of many political parties in the Western world—has accepted many of these same objectives, but it has not considered it either desirable or necessary to do so by nationalizing industry. Social legislation providing for the poorest members of society has been passed by a Conservative government in Britain and by both Republican and Democratic administrations in the United States. Socialist nations have, like our own, used the progressive income tax and the inheritance tax to achieve greater economic equality. Greater emphasis on increasing productivity and raising the GNP so that even the smallest individual share will provide a decent living standard has replaced the desire to make the distribution of wealth more nearly equal.

Because of changes in socialism itself and in other systems, the old socialist slogans have lost some of their appeal. When the British Labor party came to power toward the end of 1964, its leader, Prime Minister Harold Wilson, sounded more like the late President Kennedy or President Johnson than the head of a party dedicated to socialism. Apart from advocating the nationalization of the steel industry, the only significant difference claimed by the Labor leaders was that they could govern better.

CONCLUSION

What conclusion does our study of economic systems lead us to? Economic models are important because they supply the guidelines for answering the big economic questions. They designate the direction in which a society and its people think they should be moving. However, as we have seen, there is a difference between the theory and the reality of economic systems. The basic difference between systems is largely a choice between using the market mechanism, with its emphasis on freedom and the individual, and using central planning, with its emphasis on collective decisions and collective ownership. Totalitarianism and democracy can exist with either private ownership or collective ownership.

Economic systems evolve over a period of time. Capitalistic systems are using more central planning, and communist countries are experimenting with the market mechanism. British socialism has varied according to political climate, elections, and changing economic circumstances.

What we as citizens of a democracy must remember is that we have the power and responsibility to guide our economic system in the direction we believe will best accomplish our individual and national goals. It would be unfortunate if we failed, either through ignorance or through irresponsibility, to realize the benefits of our democratic heritage.

Part C   The Problem: Progress or Weakness in the Soviet Economy?

There can be little doubt that the Soviet Union represents a distinct economic threat to the United States. Premier Khrushchev made an open challenge in 1957, calling it economic war. He claimed that the Soviet Union would soon surpass the United States in production and boasted that the Russians would "bury" us. Soviet achievements in science and technology have added substance to his claims. The underdeveloped countries of the world are aware of this challenge. Since many of them are not as yet committed to either system, they are watching the progress of the two competing systems.

In trying to evaluate Soviet economic progress, we must be aware of certain problems. We must not assume that the goals of our mixed capitalistic system are the same as those of the Soviet system. We must recognize that resources, both human and natural, are not the same. Lastly, we are not certain about the accuracy of Soviet figures. In some instances errors in comparison are made because methods and techniques in compiling statistics differ; in other instances no data are available.

The remarkable progress of the Soviet economy

In the last forty years the Soviet Union has been transformed from a largely preindustrial, feudally structured nation to the second largest industrial power in the world. It has introduced central economic planning on a scale never before attempted; its growth in production is unquestioned. Since recovering from the effects of World War II, the Soviet economic growth rate has been remarkable—more than a nine percent yearly average by Soviet estimates and about six percent by independent Western calculations. This compares to a growth rate of approximately three percent for the same period in the United States.

In spite of many claims that Soviet production is inefficient, most of her industrial expansion must be attributed to increases in output per worker, since the labor force has increased less rapidly than production.

Although most experts put the Soviet GNP at about one half of ours, this comparison is not a true measure of the relative economic strength of the two nations. In order for the nation to achieve such a high rate of growth, the Soviet citizen has had to forgo many consumer goods. The standard of living of the Russian people is improving, but it has gained at a slower rate than parts of the economy designated by Soviet leaders as essential. Although Soviet military power may not equal our own, it is strong enough to pose a real threat to the free world.

Any underdeveloped country wishing to become highly industrialized must sacrifice current consumption for capital investment. This is exactly what the Soviet leaders have done. Consumption as a percentage of GNP is lower in the Soviet Union than in the United States, but capital investment is far greater. It is from this additional capital investment that increased productive capacity is obtained.

Differences between the two systems in the productive capacity of heavy industry are far less than the differences in GNP would seem to indicate. In the production of new machine tools the U.S.S.R. is ahead of the United States. In steel, coal, and electricity the gap is being closed. The increase in the productive capacities of these basic industries may soon be reflected in higher living standards for the Russian people.

There is no doubt that borrowing from the advanced technology of Western nations has helped the Soviet Union to progress. However, she has developed a large number—and in some fields such as engineering, a greater number than our own—of highly trained specialists in the sciences, engineering, and managerial operations who provide new knowledge and techniques to sustain continuing development. In addition, the Soviet economy has been almost "depression-proof." Keeping the economy geared to full employment has eliminated the waste of resources that Western nations experience when, during a recession, they have idle labor and unused productive capacity.

Weaknesses in the Soviet economy

If the Soviet economy is to achieve its objective of overtaking that of the United States, its economic growth rate must be twice our own. In other words, since our GNP is about twice that of the Soviets, only if their growth rate is twice the size of our own rate can they increase their total GNP as much as we do. An increase of $30 billion of GNP in the Soviet Union represents about a nine percent gain, whereas an equal increase in our nation's GNP would be at the rate of less than five percent.

There is reason to believe that the greater growth rate of the U.S.S.R. as compared with that of the United States will not be maintained. The almost spectacular success of the American economy in the last few years has increased our growth rate to 5 percent in 1964 and 5.5 percent in 1965. The latter figure was the highest of any major industrial nation in the world and, according to one reliable source, was about 1.5 percent above the Soviet Union's rate for the same year. During these same years the Soviet Union has experienced a major failure in agriculture and has been forced to import huge quantities of wheat. There is good reason to believe that one of the major causes of Khrushchev's removal

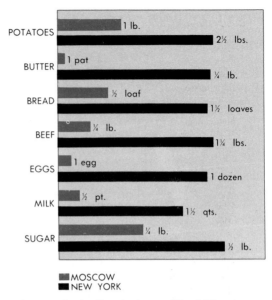

Figure 16-4 Comparison of Real Wages

This diagram compares real wages of the average worker in New York and Moscow. In each case all the basic foods shown can be purchased with an hour's pay. SOURCE: New York *Times,* April 25, 1965

was the great difficulties faced by the Soviet economy. The boast that the Soviet Union would catch up to the United States by 1970 was no longer being repeated. Instead, a slowdown in the growth rate seemed to be occurring.

The earlier spectacular growth rate of the U.S.S.R. was accomplished at such a great sacrifice to the Soviet people that their leaders now may be changing the emphasis of production. Consumer goods seem to be receiving a higher priority than previously, and greater concern for quality may reflect consumer resistance to inferior merchandise.

There is some evidence that the best and most accessible natural resources are being depleted and that in the future such resources will be difficult and costly to obtain. It is possible that the law of diminish-

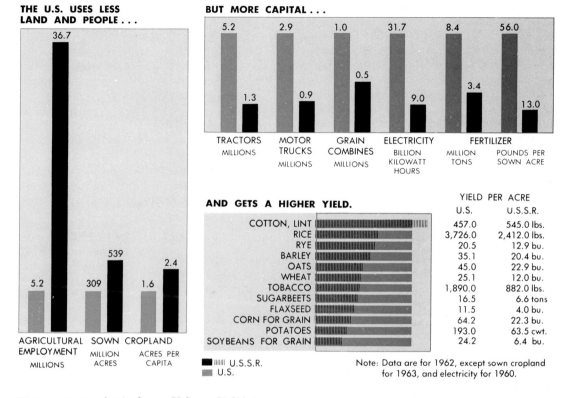

THE U.S. USES LESS LAND AND PEOPLE . . .

BUT MORE CAPITAL . . .

AND GETS A HIGHER YIELD.

	YIELD PER ACRE	
	U.S.	U.S.S.R.
COTTON, LINT	457.0	545.0 lbs.
RICE	3,726.0	2,412.0 lbs.
RYE	20.5	12.9 bu.
BARLEY	35.1	20.4 bu.
OATS	45.0	22.9 bu.
WHEAT	25.1	12.0 bu.
TOBACCO	1,890.0	882.0 lbs.
SUGARBEETS	16.5	6.6 tons
FLAXSEED	11.5	4.0 bu.
CORN FOR GRAIN	64.2	22.3 bu.
POTATOES	193.0	63.5 cwt.
SOYBEANS FOR GRAIN	24.2	6.4 bu.

U.S.S.R.
U.S.

Note: Data are for 1962, except sown cropland for 1963, and electricity for 1960.

Figure 16–5 Agriculture: U.S. vs. U.S.S.R.

Devoting relatively much less land and labor to agriculture than the Soviet Union, the United States achieves a greater output through the extensive use of tractors, combines, fertilizers, and other forms of capital. In fact, our nation's agriculture is so productive that it has a surplus, while the Soviet Union has struggled to meet basic food needs. SOURCES: Joint Economic Committee of the Congress of the United States; N.I.C.B., *Road Maps of Industry* No. 1478

ing returns will soon be setting in for both natural resources and technological improvements.

The modifications that have been and continue to be made in the Soviet economic system indicate that central planning may be less efficient in a maturing industrial society. Whereas high conformity of products and production methods may be satisfactory in a society that is forcing industrialization, it is less acceptable when people already have a subsistence level of living and look for something better.

Finally, the noneconomic consequences of forced industrialization and collectivization required the coercion and subjection of millions of people. Although Soviet leaders have justified such ruthlessness as a means to an end—that the Soviet Union has become the second industrial power in the world—it seems unlikely that such values would ever be acceptable to people living in political democracies.

Considering an answer

The comparison of a variety of economic systems helps to clarify the strengths

and weaknesses of each one. Points of like-
ness and difference among systems provide
a basis for evaluation and give us a more
objective basis for analyzing the working
of our own system. Distinguishing between
economic and political aspects of these
systems gives an added dimension to our
analysis. Finally, making such comparisons
increases our awareness of our own values
as individuals and as citizens.

The following questions will guide you
in evaluating Soviet economic progress:

1. What criteria are most important to you
as consumer, producer, and citizen in

evaluating an economy? How does Soviet
progress measure up to these criteria?
2. Are the factors responsible for economic
growth the same at all stages of development? What changes in these factors
have taken place in the course of development in the U.S.S.R.?
3. Are the recent changes in performance
trends of the Soviet and American economies likely to be temporary or permanent? Why?
4. How do your personal preferences and
your own sense of values influence your
evaluation and answers to the problem?

REVIEW: the highlights of the chapter

1. The three major economic systems competing with capitalism are
socialism, communism, and fascism. Each system has reasons for
rejecting the other models and for choosing its own way of answering the basic economic questions.
2. Socialism rejects production for profit and private ownership of
the means of production. In their place, it puts collective ownership and production for need. It prefers central planning to the
free market in economic decision making. Unlike communism it
can live side by side with capitalism and prefers to nationalize
industry gradually through education and the ballot box. There are
many forms of socialism.
3. Marx, the father of communism, believed that all history can be
explained as a series of class struggles between those who own
the means of production and those who seek power. Communists
believe that capitalism can be overcome only by revolution. They
envision society as moving into higher stages, eventually attaining
communism. When that occurs, production will be so great that
payment will be according to need. Much of what Marx predicted
has failed to materialize.
4. Fascism, as contrasted with communism, has developed in countries already industrialized but with limited experience in political
democracy. Like capitalism, it allows private ownership, but it
substitutes central planning for the free market. Like communism, it is a totalitarian system embracing every aspect of life; the
individual is completely subservient to the state. It advocates
emotionalism, racism, violence, and a regimented society.
5. No nation falls completely into any one of these three systems.
The political spectrum extends from complete freedom for the
individual citizen in his relation to the state to complete control by

government. The economic spectra extend from a free market to total central planning and from complete private ownership to total collective ownership.

6. Systems in most countries are mixed, with differences existing within countries as well as between them. Changes in these systems tend to evolve gradually.

7. The trend in the United States has been toward more central planning; in the Soviet Union, it has been toward limited experimentation in the use of the market; and in socialist countries, it has been toward less insistence on nationalization.

8. The economic growth of the Soviet Union has posed a real challenge to the American economy. Underdeveloped countries are watching with interest the progress of the rival systems.

IN CONCLUSION: some aids to understanding

Terms for review

socialism	utopian socialism
nationalization	Christian socialism
scientific socialism	anarchism
syndicalism	fascism
welfare capitalism	totalitarianism
social legislation	collective ownership
proletariat	communism
revisionism	surplus value

Names to know

Robert Owen	Fabian Society
Karl Marx	*Das Kapital*
Friedrich Engels	*Communist Manifesto*
Charles Fourier	Gosbank

Questions for review

1. In considering isms, we have found close parallels between economic and political philosophies.
   (a) Explain the idea "Although there are close ties between economic and political systems, the characteristics of the two kinds of systems are not necessarily the same."
   (b) What questions does each kind of system attempt to answer?
2. For some people the spectrum of economic systems is represented most clearly in graphic form.
   (a) Make a four-column chart. In column 1 list the four major economic systems. In column 2 place the names of several

countries which correspond to each category. In column 3 list the basic economic essentials of each system. In column 4 identify the political system that is associated with the countries in column 2.

(b) How do you account for the variations in political systems among the different economic groups?

(c) What factors might cause the wide variations in the standard of living of nations within a single category?

3. The old maxim "There's many a slip 'twixt the cup and the lip" might be rewritten for economic systems: "There is a vast difference between the theory and the actual practice."

(a) Why do these differences exist?

(b) Give an example of these differences in each of the systems.

4. Explain this thought: "The appeal of socialism found fertile soil among those who felt they did not share in the wealth they produced and feared that they could not get sympathy or help from government."

5. There are several variations of socialist economic philosophy. Identify four different versions and describe the ways in which they differ from one another.

6. Identify the major economic ideas set forth by Karl Marx.

(a) What are the four stages in the development of communism from capitalism?

(b) What proof exists that some of these stages have not fully materialized?

7. What are the essential differences in the methodology to be used by socialists and communists in achieving their goals?

8. Explain the meaning of the following statements about fascism and evaluate their general truth:

(a) Economically, fascism is the wedding of capitalist and communist planning.

(b) Individualism is almost totally lacking in both the political and the economic spheres.

(c) Previous failures of fascism may not prevent its recurrence in today's troubled world filled with hungry people.

(d) The role of morality and of human values is an unimportant consideration in fascist planning.

9. Explain the meaning of each of these statements:

(a) "Communist countries are using capitalist ideas, capitalist countries are using central planning, and socialists are marking time."

(b) "The particular conditions within each nation determine the degree of political and economic control exercised there."

(c) "In the United States, political parties differ on the role government should play in economic activity."

10. Explain the idea that the mathematics of growth rates based on the current GNP for each nation makes it very doubtful that the U.S.S.R. will bury the United States economically in the near future.

Additional questions and problems

1. Make a study of one of the communities established by the utopian socialists.
   (a) Describe the techniques used to implement the socialist theories on which that community was based.
   (b) Explain the major reasons for the failure of these methods.
2. Write a brief report explaining the reason for calling Sweden's economy "the middle way."
3. The Roosevelt New Deal has been called the "road to socialism" and the "savior of American capitalism." List and explain the arguments supporting each point of view.
4. Compare the ideas on the role of government expressed by F. A. Hayek in his *Road to Serfdom* with J. K. Galbraith's theories in *American Capitalism: The Concept of Countervailing Power.*
5. Discuss the statement "The political changeover in the U.S.S.R. in 1964 may have had its origin in the economic failure of the Khrushchev regime."
6. "Man does not live by bread alone" could be used as an indictment of both the classical economic system and the Marxian communist model. Explain the meaning of this statement and, using examples, show how you agree or disagree with it.
7. How are the ideas implied in the phrases "The struggle for the minds of men" and "One third of the earth's people are hungry" reflected in the contest between the capitalism of the United States and the communism of the Soviet Union?

UNIT V
Contemporary Problems of the American Economy

Chapter 17.

Problems Faced by Certain Segments of Our Economy

Chapter 18.

Problems Faced by Our Economy as a Whole

17 Problems Faced by Certain Segments of Our Economy

Preview

Having completed our study of the tools necessary for economic analysis, we are now ready to apply them to some of the unresolved problems confronting us. We have had some practice in using an economist's information and skills in analyzing the problems presented in previous chapters. Here we will concentrate on the special problems faced by three important segments within our economy—farmers, small businessmen, and the aged.

In each of these cases we will follow the same general procedure. Once we have identified the problem, we will consider its causes, its development, and its present status. Finally we will examine the proposed solutions and try to draw some conclusions of our own.

Keep in mind that these problems do not have a single "right" answer. You should look upon your solutions as tentative because as conditions change, as your understanding grows, and as your values and ideas are modified, you may wish to change your opinions. By this continuing search, you, the student and citizen, are acquiring the skills and knowledge necessary to arrive at the solutions which are best for you and your country.

Overview

To what extent does the fact that many people regard farming as "a way of life" complicate the solving of the farm problem?

Explain why you agree or disagree with the saying "Small business is the backbone of the American economy."

Identify the economic problems of people over 65 years of age that are not a major concern to other age groups.

Part A   The Farmer

Defining the problem

When we speak of a problem in the social sciences, we are referring to an unresolved controversy that can be defined and analyzed. We know that within the wide scope of such questions lesser related issues may also exist. One serious problem in our economy is that of "agriculture," or "the farmer." Usually when people speak of "the farm problem," they are referring to the relatively low income of the farmer in comparison with the income of other groups in the economy. Some people confuse the problem with its causes; they identify the problem as the relatively low prices which farmers receive for the products they sell in contrast to the high prices farmers pay for the products they buy.

In approaching the problem we face the question of what our farm policy should be. By keeping a wide perspective, we are recognizing that a large segment of our economy may not be sharing sufficiently in the nation's affluence and that changes in policy can improve the situation.

A century of change

In the last one hundred years American agriculture has, like industry, gone through major changes. Among the important differences are the number of people employed and the amount of food produced. Just before the Civil War about one half of our labor force was engaged in agriculture, with each farmer producing enough to feed approximately five people. Today about seven percent of our labor force works in agriculture, and each farmer feeds about thirty people. These changes have come about as a result of a technological revolution—the agricultural counterpart of the Industrial Revolution—that has increased worker output at an amazing rate. The use of machinery, improved methods, hybrid seeds, special fertilizers, and better insecticides has made it possible for fewer and

Figure 17–1   Relation of Farm Output to Number of Workers

The remarkable rise in farm output has been accompanied by an equally dramatic decline in the number of farm workers. SOURCE: U.S. Department of Agriculture

fewer farmers to supply more and more food.

These innovations have brought significant changes in the character of farming. One indication of change is the fact that farming "as a way of life" is disappearing and is being replaced by farming as a business. To be successful the modern farmer must deal with problems similar to those of the businessman. He needs large amounts of capital to invest in improvement. Like the single proprietor he must have knowledge of all aspects of the total operation, and be prepared to compete successfully.

Another important measure of change is the size of the farm unit. A steady reduction in the total number of small farms is in marked contrast to a corresponding increase in large operating units. Today less than ten percent of the nation's farms account for one half of the total sales of farm products. By contrast, about two million farms, 65 percent of the total, produce only 13 percent of our agricultural output. Although the importance of agriculture in the economy has declined relative to industry, it remains the largest single producer.

In the century which we are considering, one aspect of farming has not changed. Economists recognize that farm income tends to fluctuate far more widely than industrial income does. For example, during the two world wars prices rose faster for farm products than for industrial goods, and the farmer's income increased accordingly. These short periods of prosperity were more than offset by tumbling prices and income after the wars, particularly during the years of the Great Depression in the thirties. Overall, the income of farmers has lagged far behind that of other groups.

Causes of the farm problem

We have seen that farming, like other parts of the economy, has undergone vast changes in the past century. But these changes do not in themselves constitute a special problem warranting favored treatment. We must go on to consider whether other factors operate to make the farmer's problems different from those of other producers. Is there anything unique in his situation that should single him out for special consideration?

Of all the sectors of our economy farming comes closest to meeting the conditions necessary for pure competition. If we disregard the role the government has played, we find in agriculture all the criteria identified in Chapter 2 as necessary to have the market mechanism work. If this is so, why has government intervention become necessary?

INELASTIC DEMAND FOR FARM PRODUCTS

Perhaps the single most important factor behind the farm problem is the inelastic demand for agricultural products in general, and for the major farm products in particular. Although our increasing population and larger incomes create a need for more food, the demand for food rises more slowly than the demand for industrial prod-

ucts. After all, no matter how great our income, we can eat only so much! In addition, rising incomes bring about a change in demand for certain foods. Poor nations must feed their people with grains, such as rice and wheat, whereas richer nations use more meat. In the former, large segments of the population may be permanently undernourished; in the latter, people may be more concerned with reducing their calorie consumption than with increasing it.

Let us see how the American wheat farmer is affected by our increased national wealth. For a graphic analysis of this problem, let us turn back to page 4 of the classical model of supply and demand, following page 44. Note that the demand schedules are inelastic, more vertical than horizontal. This situation exists because the American people can afford to buy food products made from wheat with very little reduction in purchases as the price rises. On the other hand, if the price declines, they will not increase their purchases by large amounts.

According to the supply and demand graph, supply (S) intersects demand (D) so that the quantity exchanged is 1.4 billion bushels and the price is $2.12 per bushel. The wheat farmers will receive $2.968 billion. When we turn the transparent page, we see that the new supply and demand curves would intersect where Q^1 (quantity exchanged) is 1.6 billion bushels and P^1 (price) is $1.50 per bushel. The wheat farmers, producing more wheat than before, receive only $2.400 billion, or $.568 billion less than they did before. We might conclude that wheat farmers collectively make the greatest gain from growing less wheat rather than more.

At first glance it appears that the solution to the wheat farmers' problem is simple—let them all grow less wheat! Unfortunately, this solution is an example of the fallacy of composition. The same paradox found in thrift and savings exists also for the farmer—what is good for the individual is not necessarily good for the entire group. If you were a wheat farmer, even the largest wheat producer in the nation, you would know that the amount of wheat you grew was not large enough to influence the price of wheat. Under these circumstances the more wheat you grow individually, the greater your income will be. Let the other farmers cut down!

ADDED COSTS—THE "MIDDLEMAN"

You may frequently have heard complaints about the increased cost of food. If food prices are apparently so high, why do farmers complain about low prices for their products?

As producers, farmers receive only a small part of the final retail price of food products. Much of this price is made up of charges for services such as processing and distributing. Those who work in this intermediate area, between producer and consumer, are known collectively as the *middleman*. Their costs have risen steadily, and new costs, such as for special packaging or processing, may have been added, resulting in even higher retail prices. The price for a package of cereal is many times greater than the value of the grain that has gone into it. In terms of the final retail price the farmer's share may be relatively small.

TOO MANY FARMERS

In agriculture, like industry, significant increases in worker productivity have taken place. Because of this and also because of the relatively slow increase in the demand for food products, fewer and fewer farmers are needed to produce an adequate supply. Usually, readjustments occur according to the classical model. The surplus of producers causes income to drop and directs the marginal farmer into other areas of the economy that yield a better return. However, although it is true that the total number of farms and of farmers has declined, it has not done so at a fast enough rate.

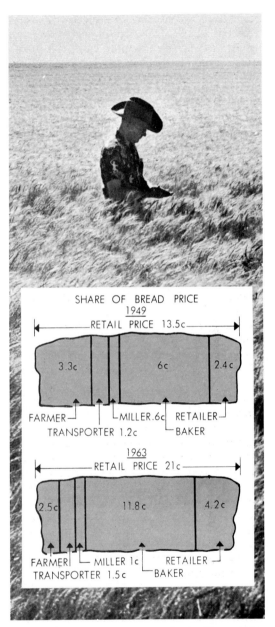

The cost of processing food has increased while the share that the farmer receives for food products has declined.

There are several reasons for this slow rate of change. We have seen that, for many Americans, farming is a way of life. The farmer is his own boss. He can bring up his children away from what he may consider to be the "evils of the city." The air he breathes and the food he eats, the space he has and the kind of work he does, bring rewards beyond merely earning a living. In spite of the hard work and financial limitations, the farmer is, by his own standards, leading the best kind of life.

The fact that there are more farmers than are needed creates a problem, further complicated by the fact that the birthrate in rural areas is higher than that in cities.

Although the mobility of young people in rural communities is high and many farmers are being absorbed into urban centers, there are still too many farmers in terms of our needs.

PRICES AND COMPETITION

The prices of agricultural products reflect the fact that farming is highly competitive. Were it not for government intervention, these prices would be determined in the free market. In contrast, the prices of products which the farmer buys are, for the most part, not subject to the same kind of competition. Many of the things he purchases come from industries with administered prices, where price decreases

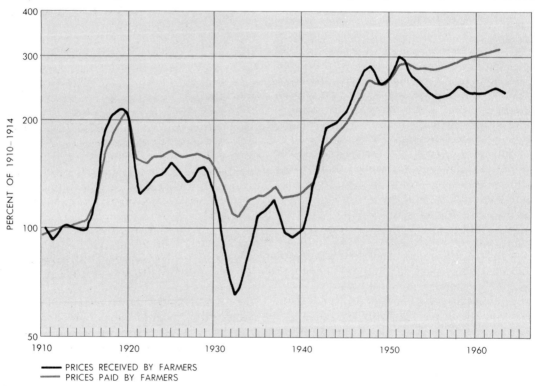

PERCENT OF 1910–1914

PRICES RECEIVED BY FARMERS
PRICES PAID BY FARMERS

Figure 17–2   Prices Received and Paid by Farmers

Prices received by farmers exceeded prices paid by farmers, when measured as a percent of 1910–1914 prices, only during the two world wars. The critical world food shortage has improved the farmer's position since 1965. SOURCE: U.S. Department of Agriculture, Economic Research Service

rarely occur. This difference in competition puts the farmer at a disadvantage in comparison with other producers in the economy.

When some people complain that agricultural products get special treatment, the farmer is quick to point out that many of our industries are able to keep their prices high because of tariff protection. He also accuses labor of causing higher prices because of the control that unions have over the supply of labor. Why should he be subject to a high degree of competition when others are not?

SPECIAL RISKS OF FARMING

Few sections of our economy are as much at the mercy of the weather as farming is. A severe storm or drought can seriously damage, or even wipe out, a farmer's crop. Insurance protection against certain disasters is available, but the cost of adequate protection is prohibitive. In any event, efforts to offset risks add to the cost of production and reduce possible profit.

The beginning of federal aid

The history of federal aid to the farmer goes back over one hundred years and embraces a wide variety of projects. The Morrill Act of 1862 provided for the establishment of land-grant colleges primarily designed for the education of the rural population and for promoting education in agriculture and the mechanical arts. In the 1920's more specialized assistance was made available. Government credit agencies were established to grant the farmer low-interest loans. A Federal Farm Board was created by President Hoover to encourage crop limitation and the formation of cooperatives on a voluntary basis. A half-billion dollars was supplied to help stabilize prices. The Rural Electrification Administration was created in the 1930's to help bring the benefits of electric power to sparsely populated areas where supply by privately owned utilities would have been uneconomical. The Agricultural Extension Service was created to do research and provide information on improving farming techniques. Crop insurance at a price below the cost to the government was started in 1938 to protect the farmer against losses caused by weather and insects.

In recent years the government has helped the farmer by means of the sale and distribution of food both at home and abroad. School lunch programs and donations of food for foreign disaster areas have helped to relieve surpluses. Farmers whose products are sold abroad have received help from *subsidies*, by which the government makes up the difference between the higher domestic price and the lower foreign market price. Efforts to lower tariffs on agricultural products in order to increase world trade have also been a help.

In spite of the number of such aid programs and their implementation from public funds, it is recognized that they have had only limited value. They have not provided basic, long-term solutions to the farm problem. Other approaches, however, have provided more effective help. These solutions have had two primary purposes: (1) raising the price received by the farmer relative to what he must pay for goods and (2) raising the farmer's income. It is usually assumed that incomes will rise if prices are increased.

Later programs for farm aid

The depression crisis of the 1930's led to new and broader measures to help the farmer. Most of these were designed to raise prices and to improve the farmers' income, although a few included other values as well. Each program has been initiated by federal legislation and has been modified by successive administrations.

PARITY AND PRICE SUPPORTS

The key idea behind most of the major solutions offered to solve the farm problem from the New Deal to the present is *parity*. Parity is an attempt to provide a basis for economic equality for the farmer in relation to other groups in the economy. Specifically, it is designed to keep the purchasing power of a unit of farm production (a bushel of wheat, for example) equal to the purchasing power of the units of production that the farmer buys.

Under the New Deal, parity was based on prices for the period from 1909 to 1914, considered to be "normal" years for the farmer's economic position in relation to that of other economic groups. If the price index of the goods the farmer bought during those years averaged 100 and the average price of a bushel of wheat during this same period was $2, the attempt would be made to keep approximately the same relationship in prices. If, in 1929, the price index of the products the farmer bought was 150, what price would the farmer receive for his bushel of wheat if he were to maintain the same purchasing power for his unit of production?

Let us set up an equation to express the price relationships involved here. The price per bushel of wheat during the base period (a) divided by the price index for products which farmers buy during the base period (b) equals the (parity) price per bushel of wheat in the current period (c) divided by the price index for products which farmers buy in the current period (d):

$$\frac{a}{b} = \frac{c}{d}$$

In our example $\frac{\$2.00}{100} = \frac{X}{150}$, or $3.00 per bushel of wheat. The $3.00 per bushel would give the wheat farmer the same purchasing power for the product he sells as the real cost of the things he buys.

Now that we have seen how parity prices are arrived at, let us see how, in actual practice, payment of the parity price is made to the farmer. Farm prices above the free market price are maintained largely through the operation of the Commodity Credit Corporation, a federal agency. If the support price is $2 a bushel and the market price is $1.80, the farmer puts his crop into

storage and receives a government loan amounting to $2 per bushel. If supply drops sufficiently to raise the market price above $2, he takes his crop out of storage, sells it, and repays the loan. If the price fails to go to $2, he merely keeps the $2 per bushel that the government has lent him and the government must take the loss. For the fiscal year ending in June, 1965, slightly more than $3 billion was extended for price supports by the Commodity Credit Corporation. This amount is smaller than in some previous years.

With few exceptions, farmers have accepted the parity formula as fair. Many other people, however, think that this system tends to favor the farmer at the expense of other groups in the economy. Critics of the parity price system point out that the period from 1909 to 1914 was an unusually good time for farmers in comparison with other producers. They also emphasize that output per worker and output per acre have increased very rapidly in agriculture; as a result, abiding by parity gives higher prices to farmers than to other producers in the economy. In addition, this program has not only cost the consumer more money in higher prices, but as a taxpayer he has to pay the high costs for storage.

Many changes have already been made to modify the original parity system. Some legislation has called for rigid price supports for specific crops, such as wheat, corn, cotton, tobacco, and rice. Other laws have established flexible price supports which allow the Secretary of Agriculture to alter the parity price as he sees fit. Congress has never permitted parity to be 100 percent; the parity price range has generally fluctuated between 70 and 90 percent. The base period for which parity is computed has been changed to more recent dates in some instances.

Further changes in the parity system may be expected. Because our legislatures have had a disproportionately large rural representation, farm legislation has been based mainly on the parity formula. However, the character of future legislatures may change, since the Supreme Court decisions in *Baker* v. *Carr* (1962) and in succeeding cases have established the need for redistricting to maintain the principle of "one man, one vote." As rural influence is reduced, the parity principle may not continue to be the basic formula for farm legislation in the future.

ACREAGE CONTROL AND SOIL CONSERVATION

Recognizing that low prices for farm products are the result of inelastic demand and too great a supply, the government has based some programs on efforts to restrict the supply. Under the New Deal a program was begun which tried to do this through *acreage control*, limiting the number of acres to be planted. The farmer was paid according to the number of acres withdrawn from cultivation as well as for the use of certain soil-conservation measures.

If yield per acre had remained constant, this plan might have been effective in reducing surplus. However, a reduction of supply did not occur. Farmers withdrew their poorest acres from cultivation, used more fertilizer and the best hybrid seeds, and produced even more than before.

In recent years other programs, similar in nature, have been used, and have proved only slightly more effective in reducing surpluses. The *soil bank* program of 1956 paid farmers to withdraw land from the cultivation of cash crops and to substitute the planting of timber or cover crops. It was based on the ideas of restricting output, giving the farmer an income subsidy, and conserving soil.

In general, the programs for limiting production through restricting the use of land have not been very successful. No real reduction in the supply of farm products has been accomplished through them, and in 1965 a record crop was harvested.

PRICE DIFFERENTIAL PLAN

Successive Democratic and Republican administrations have proposed plans to maintain guaranteed price supports to the farmer but at the same time to allow the consumer to pay the free market price. If crops were sold below the support price in the market, as would probably happen, the farmer would be paid *directly* the difference between the market price and the support price. In this way storage costs could be reduced and the consumer could benefit by lower prices. Whether the direct subsidy to the farmer to make up the difference between the two prices would cost the taxpayer as much as the savings made by consumers and by reduced storage charges is difficult to determine. Public opinion has never given strong support to this plan.

INCREASING DEMAND

Many programs have been proposed and a great deal of money has been spent to create new uses and develop new markets for our surplus crops. Except for increased sales abroad, both private enterprise and government have failed to find new ways to alter demand significantly.

DUMPING ON FOREIGN MARKETS

The suggestion – seemingly simple and obviously humanitarian – has been made that we sell our surpluses abroad, particularly to friendly nations, at very low prices. The loss might be considerable for a year or two, but this practice might win us friends, serve as a weapon in the cold war, and eliminate our surpluses.

It would indeed be nice if the problem were that simple. However, such a policy would antagonize those nations which need to sell agricultural products in order to import other goods. Argentina and Canada would be seriously harmed in the sale of their wheat, as Egypt would be in the sale of cotton. In addition, the practice of *dumping* (selling at prices well below normal market prices) can be met by retaliation, which could hurt our own trade.

RETRAINING PROGRAMS FOR FARMERS

We have seen that one cause of the farm problem is the fact that there are too many farmers. In reality, most of our farm programs have been designed to help the marginal farmer, who has difficulty subsisting even under the most favorable conditions. A major criticism of the programs based on price supports and income subsidization is that a large portion of the money spent on them goes to successful farmers who do not need such help. Many younger people from marginal farms would welcome the chance to move elsewhere if they had some other way to earn a living. Farming is the only occupation that many of these people know, and they feel uncertain about entering new fields.

The retraining programs recently set up (see p. 176) include opportunities for farmers as well as for unskilled urban workers. It is still too early to evaluate the success of these programs. However, indications are that the mobility of the farmer into other areas of the economy is too low to regard this as a major solution, especially for those farmers who are already over thirty-five years of age.

Should we return to a free market?

People who resent what they consider favored treatment for the farmer point out that the expenditure of many billions of dollars on agricultural programs has added to the existing prosperity of large-scale farmers but has done little to help provide the owners of small farms with more than a subsistence living. They suggest that we return to a free market for farm products; in time the marginal farmer will be eliminated and surpluses will be reduced. Such a change would be no more than we ask of the small businessman.

If we have any confidence in the market mechanism as an efficient means of allocating our economic resources, we should allow it to operate in agriculture.

That segment of our economy is obviously overexpanded. So long as the American people subsidize farm products so heavily, the mobility of the farmer out of agriculture will remain low.

Under the price support system, payments of more than $250,000 in a single year have been made to one farmer for not producing crops. This is a clear example of inefficient resource allocation. We should shift to other areas of the economy a part of the money now spent on agriculture. Although justification can be made for helping people whose incomes are very low, the question remains whether farmers in general should be singled out for special treatment.

The arguments favoring a free market for farm products are answered by pointing out that the market conditions of agriculture are unique. Other segments of the economy, such as industry and labor, create their own protective devices. Administrative prices set by industry and wages negotiated by labor unions accomplish the same purpose as price supports—prices which are higher than would usually exist in a free market. Government provides industry with subsidies through tariff protection, and it subsidizes labor through minimum wages. Unemployment insurance protects most workers in a way not anticipated by the classical economist. Since farming fits the model of perfect competition more closely than do other areas of the economy, it needs government help to achieve what other segments of the economy have taken for themselves.

LOOKING AHEAD

By now you are able to appreciate the complexity of the farm problem. It is compounded of questions of economics, ethics, and politics. To solve it will require not merely technical knowledge but a consideration of values.

In reality, the very nature of the farm problem may be changing, and future solutions must allow for new conditions, such as a decrease in surpluses. In 1964 the size of our surpluses in all grains began to decline, due to heavy shipments abroad. In 1966 some economists, worried that our supplies of certain agricultural products were too low in spite of record harvests, recommended reversing our crop-limitation program. Although supply and demand seem to be more evenly balanced, it is uncertain whether this condition will continue.

What should our farm policy be? Are any of the proposed solutions described in this chapter satisfactory? Should we combine several of them? What new conditions must be anticipated? If a solution is found, will it be adopted? These are the questions you must ask yourself as a responsible citizen. As a consumer, a producer (possibly a farmer), and as a citizen you will be very much affected by the decisions to be made concerning our farm program.

Part B   The Small Businessman

Defining the problem

In the late thirties Ben Chase was employed as a butcher in a grocery chain store. He knew his trade well, worked hard, saved whatever he could, and dreamed of starting a business of his own. His wife, Gertrude, also had a job and added her savings to her husband's. In 1940 they heard of a small slaughtering and meat-packing establishment that was for sale in a rural area. With their own savings, a loan from a relative, and a loan from a bank, they bought their own business.

Ben and Gertrude worked hard, sometimes more than sixty-five hours a week. They were good managers, and they knew how to deal with the farmers and the meat distributors. Their business grew. When the war started, they had made enough contacts with farmers to insure a continuing supply. They had no difficulty in selling everything they could produce. Now semi-retired, they own a business worth a million dollars. They have lived the American dream.

A DIFFERENT STORY

When George Morris returned from military service in 1945, he got a job in a men's clothing store. He worked for two years learning many aspects of the business. At the end of that time he made the decision to go into business for himself. For $15,000 he bought a rundown store in a rather poor business location. His own savings and a loan from his parents supplied $10,000 of the cost; he borrowed the additional $5,000 from a bank.

George knew that the price was low in part because much of the merchandise was out of style. However, he believed that as he sold these goods (he had no capital to buy new merchandise and he had not established a credit rating yet) he would be able to replace them with the stylish clothing that people wanted. He hoped that by marking down the prices on what he had, he could soon clear out his old stock. He also counted on patronage from his many friends.

Two months after George opened his store, a new men's clothing store, part of a chain, opened three blocks away. Now the stock of suits that had but a short time ago been in style could not be sold for even a third of their original cost. George did not take in even enough money to pay his rent and his note at the bank. Most of his merchandise was valueless. By the end of one year George Morris was bankrupt, his store just another among the statistics of business failures.

Every year thousands of people like those in our hypothetical cases try to attain success in business. What they fail to realize, or choose to ignore, is that the average life expectancy of a business is less than seven years, that about forty percent of all retail businesses last less than two years, and that many of those that do survive pay their owners less than they could earn by working for someone else. If we define small businesses as those firms employing fewer than fifty persons and with annual sales of less than $1 million, then ninety-eight percent of all businesses are small. Yet the importance of small business in the nation's economy, together with the uncertainty of operations of many small firms, raises the question whether small business will continue to play an important role in our economy.

Changes in business

Until the Civil War almost all business in our country was small by any definition. Big business appeared first in manufacturing, where high fixed costs made large-scale operations the only efficient method of producing. In transportation, too, the large initial investment and high fixed costs made large-scale operations more feasible.

INCREASE IN SIZE

One of the clearest examples of change is found in the field of merchandising. Since colonial days the country store, or general store, owned by a proprietor or by several partners, has been a symbol of business enterprise. By 1900, however, the pattern of ownership began to change as the department store and chain store appeared. Chain stores could buy in huge quantities and save on per-unit costs; if sales lagged in one store, merchandise could easily be transferred to another. Mail-order houses also cut into the trade of the general store. Soon automobiles made it possible for people to shop outside their own neighborhood. Advertising in mass media gave large stores the advantage of a big market. Today these businesses and, more recently, discount houses, pose a seemingly overwhelming threat to small business.

By 1960 more than thirty-five percent of all employees covered by Social Security were employed by huge businesses constituting only one percent of the total number of all businesses. On the other hand, only seven percent of the workers are employed by the smallest business firms that make up sixty percent of the nation's employers.

PROBLEMS OF SMALL BUSINESS

The Senate Select Committee on Small Business reported in 1964 that although the nation was prospering, small business was not getting its full share. In 1961 firms with fewer than 250 employees did more than half the nation's business. Of the $100 billion gain in business output made since then, these firms shared only 40 percent of it, and their profits were growing at only one half the rate of those of big business. By contrast, in 1965, General Motors, one of the giants, had sales of $20.7 billion, and the American Telephone and Telegraph Company was not far behind.

We have seen that small businesses like George Morris's carry a high risk of failure. Between 1945 and 1959 the average number of business failures per year was 4,000, involving liabilities of $169 million per year. In the period from 1960 to 1964, the most prosperous period in our nation's history, the average number of business failures annually had increased to 15,200, with $1.185 billion liabilities per year. If a major recession should set in, we can expect the rate of failures to increase appreciably.

ADVANTAGES OF SMALL BUSINESS

If those of you who look to small business as the opportunity for the fulfillment of the American dream are discouraged by the statistics given here, there are other figures that tell a different story. There are nearly five million small businesses in this country. More businesses are born each year than die, and their number is increasing at a faster rate than our population.

If small businesses can continue to grow in number and size, they must have some benefits to offset the many handicaps. Small companies do have an advantage in

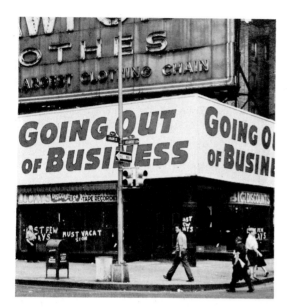

How is the economy both benefited and harmed by companies entering and leaving business?

certain kinds of business. Their scale of operations is particularly well suited to the making and retailing of highly specialized products, of articles that are subject to frequent and drastic style changes, and of items requiring craftsmanship as opposed to standardization. Professional and service establishments—such as barbershops, specialty stores, and shops producing special equipment or parts involving much hand labor—are also usually best organized as small firms. The supplying of components to big business by subcontractors is an established practice that is growing each year. New products are as likely to come from small firms as from large ones, particularly in cases where demand is uncertain and where no specialized machinery has been developed.

Although there may be more George Morrises than Ben Chases, the fact remains that the small businesses which both men represent constitute an extremely important and vital part of our economy.

Small firms are more mobile and can move in and out of business in response to fluctuations in the demand for their goods and services, with less effect on the economy. They can change their production or sales more easily, and they can perform functions in the economy that big business cannot and does not want to do. For these reasons small business not only needs to remain, but will remain.

Pros and cons of starting a business

The fact that the number of our business establishments is increasing indicates that, to many people, business constitutes opportunity. Though some, as we have seen, fail, others go on to become prosperous concerns. Some go on to become large companies with almost unlimited opportunities and rewards.

BENEFITS

In reality, hope for material gain is only one of the reasons why people go into business. Among other objectives and considerations are the following:

1. People think that self-employment will permit a greater degree of personal independence and freedom of action than is possible in large organizations.

2. They will have a greater opportunity to try out their own ideas, since the bureaucratic aspects of big business often make such ventures difficult or impossible within the framework of a larger organization.

3. They think that they can make the American dream come true. There are enough cases of success to make it a possibility, even if the risk is great.

4. The owner looks forward to reaping all the benefits from his own labors. He will not have to share with others what he himself has created and developed under a single proprietorship.

5. There is greater community recognition in being in business for oneself. This is true so long as one is successful.

DISADVANTAGES

Along with the potential benefits of going into business, there are certain definite disadvantages:

1. When one works for someone else, paychecks are regular, hours are usually shorter, and there is no financial risk of losing one's savings or of being unable to repay borrowed money.

2. The responsibilities of owning a business are considerable. Decisions have to be made frequently, and upon their outcome may rest the fate of the business.

3. The owner of a single proprietorship holds ultimate responsibility for all the problems of the business.

4. The regulations and restrictions made by all levels of government concerning business are usually irksome and sometimes costly.

5. Fringe benefits are frequently broader for employees than for employers.

6. Working for a very large business can sometimes offer greater income security than working for oneself.

7. There is an opportunity for advancement and reward in large business.

Why do businesses fail?

A number of studies have been made of why businesses in general, and small businesses in particular, fail. A very small number of failures, less than ten percent, were caused by such factors as poor health, fraud, disaster, neglect, and marital difficulties. The studies showed two main causes—poor management and insufficient capital—to be the most important.

Too many people go into business without sufficient training and knowledge to cope with the many demands of business. To the eager young man trying to make his mark in the world on his own, or to the retired couple who want to earn a few extra dollars to supplement a pension, it may seem simple to open up a filling station or a grocery store. Using these facilities as customers is quite a different matter from running them as successful business ventures.

Another important cause of failure is lack of capital. The typical small businessman starts out using all his own savings and borrowing as much as he can; he still probably has too little money to carry him through the first critical year, when sales are likely to be small. Banks are not eager to lend money to new and unproven firms. When they do, interest rates are likely to be high. Suppliers are seldom willing to advance much merchandise or raw materials until good credit ratings are built. With little capital, few new firms are able to take advantage of discounting their bills, a method of deducting a small percentage from the bill if paid within a specified period of time. They may not have the money or the credit to take advantage of bargains that they find. A business with sufficient capital, more frequently found among big corporations, has inherent advantages.

Lack of capital is frequently found to be responsible for other failures. When a downturn in the economy occurs and the pressure to continue operating increases, the big business with adequate capital available can more easily subsist until conditions improve. Inadequate capital can lead to poor accounting records because satisfactory employees cannot be hired. The absence of ready, accurate information on sales or inventory can lead to inefficient operation.

OTHER CAUSES OF FAILURE

Additional causes for failure include:

1. Too low a volume of business to cover fixed costs.

2. Overexpansion and overbuying during a business boom.

3. A general inability to control inventory.

4. Poor location, including competition from big business.

5. Lack of specialized knowledge. The small businessman is seldom an expert in all phases of business operation. He

has to perform so many different functions that he can seldom become the master of any of them. He may often wish that he had never gone into business "on his own."

The need for small business

Although we have at present a greater number of "births" than "deaths" in business, the large number of failures and the hardships and small return for time and effort may someday reverse this trend. Is small business important enough to our economy to justify our saving it?

Besides the figures cited previously on the contribution small business makes to increasing the size of our national output, there are many additional reasons for answering this question with a resounding *yes:*

1. Small business is the proving ground for ideas and resources, particularly human resources. Some businesses are started because their owners have new ideas of marketing, new methods of producing more efficiently, and new products to offer the consumer. Managers of small firms get experience and become managers of large firms.

2. Small business increases competition and keeps big business "on its toes." Although there are few drastic changes from one year to the next in the list of the 500 largest businesses in the country, the changes that do occur point up the fact that small business can grow to threaten the position of giants that may be less progressive.

3. Small business is more flexible and can adjust to changes more quickly. This allows it to perform certain services and to make certain products more efficiently than big business can. Specialized demands cannot always be met by big business. This is particularly true where demands are subject to erratic changes, as in women's clothing; highly specialized and limited markets, like specialized

bodies for certain kinds of motor vehicles; and markets, such as cement, that must be local in nature because of excessive transportation costs.

4. The economy needs the mobility of small firms within a particular market as well as between different markets. As the demand for goods and services changes, the need for more or fewer business firms and for special kinds of business operations also changes.

5. Finally, we associate small business and its opportunities with our system of democracy. It provides the chance for economic mobility in relation to social position, allowing people to move from one group to another. Small businesses also provide a significant number of leaders in community life. Look at the leadership of service clubs, parent-teachers' associations, and charity groups and you will find many men from small companies.

What can be done to help small business?

The evidence we have seen indicates an affirmative answer to our question "Does small business still have an important role to play in our economy?" It has also shown, however, that small businesses have many difficulties in surviving, and that many do not operate as efficiently as they might. Therefore, they may waste our limited resources.

We have seen that the two chief problems of small business, accounting for most of their failures, are managerial incompetence and insufficient capital. In both instances, the government has taken steps to provide assistance.

SMALL BUSINESS ADMINISTRATION

Although there are many agencies—private, local, and state—which help business, the largest and most important agency devoted exclusively to small business is the Small Business Administration. This agency, established by Congress in 1953, carries on the following activities:

1. It makes available to small businessmen information on management. Pamphlets on such subjects as factory construction, production techniques, and marketing are published periodically as aids to small manufacturers. For people in marketing there is material on sales training, location appraisal, personnel management, profit planning, and similar technical subjects.

2. It helps to provide access to capital and credit at reasonable rates. In addition to making its own loans, the SBA supervises small-business investment companies, which have been set up under special legislation for the purpose of furnishing capital to small business.

3. It helps obtain for small business a fair share of government contracts.

4. It provides loans to small businesses that have suffered from disaster such as fire, floods, and storms.

OTHER GOVERNMENT AID

The federal government gives added help to small business by setting lower rates in the corporation income tax for profits up to $25,000. Unincorporated businesses – and most small businesses are unincorporated – do not pay a corporation income tax. State and local governments often give small businesses an advantage in taxing, although this is frequently offset by special inducements made by communities to encourage big business to move into their location.

Local and state governments, and even geographic regions, have organized development and credit corporations to help business. State departments of commerce offer numerous services to businessmen. State universities frequently set up bureaus and research facilities which they make available to business.

SELF-HELP

Chambers of commerce, retail merchants' associations, and various other trade organizations offer many services to businessmen. Less publicized but just as important are the cooperatives that have been organized by small businessmen to give them the buying power of large companies. The National Retail Grocers Association is made up of regional cooperatives. Money put in by independent grocers is used to buy a warehouse and trucks, and to employ workers who will buy, store, and distribute merchandise to the individual stores. By banding together on their purchases, they have much the same buying power as huge chain stores do. This eliminates at least one advantage of big business over small firms.

Conclusion

Small business plays a very important role in our economy; but as in the case of the farmer the question remains whether it is receiving a fair share of the "pie." Much of small business is marginal business and, as such, seems to get only what is left over. Part of the problem of small business stems from the economics of size, but equally important are problems that can be solved through better management techniques. Some help has come from government and some from the efforts of businessmen themselves. There is evidence to indicate that additional help may be needed.

Part C   The Aged

Defining the problem

Another group for our special consideration is the elderly people of our nation. The conditions which affect them become of increasing concern as a growing percentage of our population is included in this category. The problem is further intensified by social changes (in family structure) and by economic changes (in enforced retirement and possibly limited income).

In a free agricultural society the position of older people is usually secure. As owner of the family farm, the head of the household—most frequently the father—retires from work when he feels ready and passes the operation of the farm on to his children. The children recognize that they will inherit the source of the family income; because of this they help to care for the farm and for their parents. The children are dependent on inheriting the farm, and the place of their elders is almost guaranteed. The farmhouse is frequently large enough to accommodate the entire family; if it is not, the children can build another house on the farm.

In an industrial urban society the place of the aged may be a precarious one. Because of the greater mobility of children, families tend to be more fragmented. Most housing is designed for two generations rather than three. More and more the state has assumed the responsibilities for the aged which were traditionally undertaken by the family. Because the family is no longer so cohesive a group, social problems of recognition, recreation, and companionship become more difficult of solution.

In an agrarian society the old are able to continue performing some productive economic functions. In an urban industrial society discrimination against older people starts at about 45 years of age and continues, so that 65 has become a mandatory retirement age in many businesses. In 1965 about one person out of five in the age group over 65 was working or looking for work. Those who were working were frequently in lower paying jobs with lower prestige (see pp. 172–173).

Figure 17–3 shows the income of people over 65 to be far below the national average. In 1963 one out of five of these people had an income of $1,000 a year or less, and one half had less than $3,000. These amounts are, of course, influenced by the limitations placed on earnings of people re-

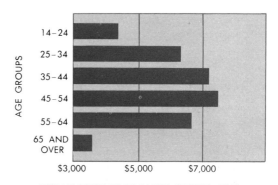

MEDIAN INCOMES OF FAMILY GROUPS, 1963

Figure 17–3 Earnings by Age Groups

Income decreases sharply beyond the age of 65.
SOURCE: New York *Times,* May 2, 1965

ceiving Social Security payments. Another fact to consider is that the average age of our population is increasing. In 1900 those over 65 made up only four percent of the population. Today they account for nine percent, or about 18 million people.

Medical science in the United States has increased our life expectancy from 47 years in 1900 to over 70 years in 1965. Should we allow the latter portion of these added years to be filled with poverty and despair for so many people? Do we have the resources to furnish a measure of economic security and to provide facilities for brightening the lives of the elderly? We can now pose the question of what should be done to create a more secure and happy life for the aged.

The effects of Social Security

Before the passage of the Social Security Act of 1935 the prevailing attitude was that each individual was responsible for providing for his own retirement. If this was not done, the question was asked, "Why should society have to take over the burden?" There was little recognition that an urban industrial society made people more interdependent and less able to control their own circumstances. This thinking,

Table 17–1   Percent Distribution of Population by Age, 1940–75

AGE	1940	1950	1960	1965	1970 (est.)	1975 (est.)
TOTAL POPULATION	100.0	100.0	100.0	100.0	100.0	100.0
Under 14 years	23.1	25.4	29.5	28.8	28.0	27.7
14–19 years	11.2	8.5	9.0	10.6	11.0	10.9
20–24 years	8.9	7.7	6.1	7.0	8.2	8.4
25–34 years	16.2	15.8	12.7	11.5	12.0	13.7
35–44 years	13.9	14.2	13.4	12.6	11.1	10.0
45–54 years	11.8	11.5	11.4	11.4	11.3	10.6
55–64 years	8.1	8.8	8.7	8.8	9.0	9.0
65 years and over	6.8	8.1	9.2	9.4	9.6	9.8

Projection of our population according to age categories shows an increase in the percent of people 65 years of age and over. SOURCE: U.S. Department of Commerce, Bureau of the Census

which might have been satisfactory when we were a nation of farm families, was carried over to a different kind of society.

In the absence of other provisions the poor and the aged were dependent on private charities and the meager provisions made by state and local governments. The Great Depression of the 1930's brought the problem into sharp focus and stimulated the passage of our major Social Security program, under the supervision of the federal government.

PHILOSOPHY BEHIND SOCIAL SECURITY

The importance of the Social Security Act of 1935 does not lie in its details. Its importance is to be found in its philosophy, which transfers responsibility for the aged from the individual and the family to the society. Individualism and the market economy were, in a limited sense, replaced by collective responsibility. Those who opposed this change were heard to cry "Socialism!" Each successive amendment for increasing benefits has been greeted in the same way.

Whether people choose to call the Social Security program socialistic or not is less important than the facts that

1. a public need existed that was not being met, and our Social Security program provided an answer

2. the financial basis on which the program is being run demands that payments be made by the individuals who will receive benefits

3. the United States was far behind such other industrial nations as Germany, France, and England in providing a security program for its people

After thirty years of operation our Social Security program is an integral part of the American economic system. The question is no longer whether to have Social Security or not; it is rather how far its coverage should be extended.

HOW SOCIAL SECURITY WORKS

The major operational principle behind Social Security is forced insurance. The individual must make payments to the government so that he may be protected when he can no longer provide for himself. The principle is the same as that used by private insurance companies. At present, protection includes a pension for old age, payments to survivors of breadwinners, unemployment insurance, and medical, hospital, and nursing-home care for the aged.

Since its inception the law has been broadened to include the vast majority of people in the labor force. For employees, payments are made by equal contributions from the employer and employee, except for unemployment insurance. The self-em-

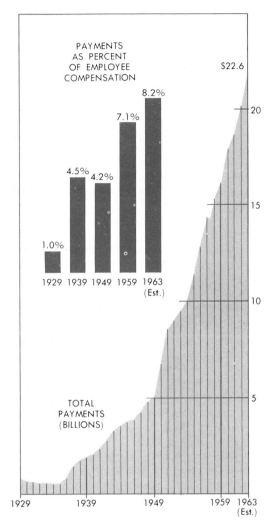

PAYMENTS
AS PERCENT
OF EMPLOYEE
COMPENSATION

$22.6

8.2%

7.1%

4.5% 4.2%

1.0%

1929 1939 1949 1959 1963
(Est.)

TOTAL
PAYMENTS
(BILLIONS)

1929   1939   1949   1959 1963
(Est.)

Figure 17–4 Employer Payments for
Employee Security in
Private Industry

Total wages and salaries of employees in private
industry increased by 20% since 1959, but employer payments for employee security rose 40%.
These payments climbed from 7.1% of total compensation in 1959 to 8.2% in 1963. Private pension and welfare funds make up 43.4% of the
total, unemployment insurance, 20.8%; old-age,
survivors and disability insurance, 28.8%; and
compensation for injuries, 7.1%. sources: Department of Commerce; The Conference Board;
N.I.C.B., *Road Maps of Industry* No. 1462

ployed pay one and a half times what employees pay. Both the rates and the tax base
have gone up during the years that Social
Security has been in effect. The rates are
scheduled to climb still higher in order to
keep the program self-sustaining.

The program of unemployment insurance is set up by the states within an approved framework designated by the federal government. Employers pay the entire
tax and the federal government provides
matching grants to states and pays part of
the administrative costs.

The Medicare program passed by Congress in 1965 is still too new for adequate
interpretation and evaluation. However,
there can be little doubt that it will be a
blessing to many older citizens who lack
the means to take care of their own health
needs.

Today application for a Social Security
number is often one of the first steps taken
by the student-citizen on becoming an active producing member of the economy.
Since the coverage under Social Security
laws changes frequently, it is advisable for
a worker to contact his local Social Security
office and obtain the latest information on
rates, benefits, and procedures.

Solutions to help the aged

The problems of the aged are many,
and although it is true that our Social Security system has been a great help, serious
problems remain. Many solutions have
been offered, and some have been tried on
a limited scale to help improve conditions
for our older citizens.

PRIVATE PENSION PLANS.

In 1964 the average payment made to
an individual collecting a retirement pension from Social Security was less than
$85 a month. Recognizing that payments
from Social Security were inadequate to
provide a decent standard of living for the
aged, unions have, since World War II, included pension plans for retired workers in
contract negotiations. These pension systems have grown at an accelerated rate,

The increase in people's average life span poses economic and social problems that long remained unrecognized. Today, "Golden Age" or "Senior Citizens" clubs provide social and creative activities.

so that today the assets of private funds are greater than those of public funds. It is too early to evaluate fully how extensively the benefits from these and other private pensions will reduce the economic distress of participants on retirement. There is no doubt, however, that such added retirement income will be of great help.

CHANGING SOCIAL SECURITY

There have been many criticisms of the way our Social Security laws operate. The two complaints heard most frequently concern the regressive nature of the Social Security tax and the failure to regulate payments on a cost-of-living basis. The tax is regressive because, given a fixed tax base ($6,600 in 1966) people with incomes over that amount pay a smaller percentage of their total income into the Social Security fund. If the Social Security tax were levied on a person's entire income, it would be proportional. The extra revenue derived

could permit additional benefits. Critics of this suggested change point out that benefits already tend to favor those who have contributed less, and that the present plan tends to redistribute income somewhat in favor of the lowest income group.

There is no doubt that an increase in the cost of living reduces the real income of benefits received. The proposal that payments be made according to the cost of living would provide guaranteed purchasing power. Opponents counter by pointing to the repeated increases that Congress has given and probably will continue to give. Any increases in existing benefits mean that present workers are subsidizing workers already retired. Deciding whether benefits should be increased is a problem of values to be solved by you as citizens, not by economists.

PREVENTING DISCRIMINATION IN EMPLOYMENT

Several states have passed laws prohibiting discrimination against older workers. However, legitimate differences in physical ability between older and younger workers limit the effectiveness of these laws. Somewhat more effective have been the special counseling and placement services set up by states to help older people find positions for which more mature workers are suited. A few private agencies have established businesses employing only older workers. They are hired at prevailing wages, and prices on the products must be competitive. It is too soon to evaluate the success of these programs.

HOUSING

Nearly two thirds of the people 65 and over own their own homes. This figure looks less encouraging when the condition of these homes and the problems of maintaining them are investigated. Many are in a state of disrepair, with the owners physically or financially unable to make improvements. Increases in property taxes have caused great hardship to the aged, since they usually live on fixed incomes. When younger people complain about the opposition of the elderly to school bond issues, they sometimes fail to recognize the hardship that older people face in paying the higher property taxes. Fixing property taxes at the amount in effect when people reach 65, or allowing some exemption for the aged as is done in the federal income tax (double exemption for those 65 and over), would help older people in planning for their retirement years.

Congress has passed special housing legislation making it easier for builders to invest in the construction of "communities for the elderly" and in other housing projects. Unfortunately, these projects are often too costly for those who are most in need.

LEISURE TIME

One of the most difficult adjustments that people have to make on retirement is filling the hours that were previously occupied with work. An additional problem is the feeling of depression that many older people have because they no longer con-

What share should the various groups of people of our nation have in the rising GNP?

sider themselves useful members of society. To meet these problems many communities have set up "golden age" and "senior citizen" clubs that offer opportunities for many kinds of activities, as well as opportunities for making social contacts. Both public and private agencies have set up programs, including adult education and recreation classes. Unfortunately, many of the elderly do not have the opportunity, the desire, or the knowledge of available facilities to take full advantage of them.

Conclusion

Like farmers and small businessmen, the aged have been faced with problems that seem a long way from solution. As a group they have not found the prosperity that would provide them with the means to make their retirement more than bearable.

Involved in finding answers to these problems is the basic question "How shall we allocate our resources?" Whether current producers (our present working force) should help support our past working force (those retired) is in part a question of social ethics. Economists point out that Social Security acts as an automatic stabilizer in compensating for the business cycle, and

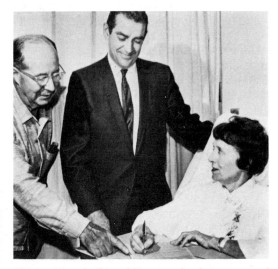

The increase in the public sector by the passage of the Medicare bill was in response to a popular demand for a solution to a major problem that the private sector had failed to meet successfully.

that it also helps in a very modest way to redistribute income.

Whether the individual should assume most of the responsibility of providing for his old age or whether there should be collective responsibility is a question of values. Economic analysis can help us to infer what the consequences of each course of action may be. The fact that you are born into a society with established values does not mean that you cannot or should not try to change them.

As one who is likely to be part of the working force within a short time, you will probably have to accept the idea that the society has assumed some responsibility for certain segments of the population, including the aged. However, you should, as a responsible citizen, decide whether you favor increasing or decreasing the collective responsibility. Do you want people of each generation to pay their own way individually or collectively in providing for their old age, or should our working force help to subsidize the older members of society when the resources they have set aside are inadequate to care for their needs? Do you want more benefits guaranteed when you retire? Do you want to control these benefits yourself or do you want Social Security to provide them? You may not always get your way, because as a citizen you agree to abide by the decisions that your democratically operated government makes. However, as a citizen you not only have a right, but also an obligation, to help make the decisions.

REVIEW: *the highlights of the chapter*

1. Three segments of our economy do not seem to be sharing equally in the prosperity of our times—farmers, small businessmen, and the aged.
2. The "farm problem" is generally associated with the low income received by farmers in contrast to others. This leads us to the question of what our farm policy should be.
3. The technological revolution on the farm has changed farming from a way of life to a business. Small farms are disappearing. Output per worker has increased so that seven percent of our working force provides more food than we now need. Ten percent of our nation's farms supply one half the sales of farm products.
4. The inelastic demand for farm products is largely responsible for the fact that farmers' incomes are not so stable as other workers' incomes and prices of agricultural products are less stable than those of other commodities. A small change in supply brings about a major change in price. Getting farmers to cut down on their individual production runs into the problem of the fallacy of composition.
5. Other causes of the farmer's economic problems stem from the increasing costs of the "middleman," the excessive number of farmers, the competitiveness of the market, and the weather.
6. The farmer has been offered many kinds of aid, but the major solutions have been aimed at raising farm prices as a means of raising his income. Most solutions have been based on the concept

of parity, equating the purchasing power of the farmer with that of others. Reducing supply in order to raise prices has been tried by controlling acreage and by soil conservation. Other solutions suggested are increasing the demand, the price differential plan, dumping on foreign markets, retraining farmers, and a return to the free market.

7. Evidence shows that the number of business failures has been increasing and that small business prospers less than big business. The major reasons for business failures are managerial incompetence and insufficient capital.

8. Small business has an important role to play in the economy. There are more businesses that start each year than fail. Small business is a proving ground for ideas and resources. It increases competition; it is more flexible and mobile, allowing it to adjust to changes and special demands; and it is associated with our democratic ideals.

9. To help small business solve its problems, Congress set up the Small Business Administration. This agency provides information on running a business, helps in financing, makes loans for disaster relief, and aids in obtaining government contracts.

10. Other aids to small business come in the form of lower tax rates; local, state, and regional development corporations; trade associations; and buying cooperatives.

11. The number and percentage of our total population over 65 has been increasing very rapidly, so that today one person out of every eleven is in this age category. Statistics show this group to be far below the national average in income and liquid assets.

12. Our nation's change from an agricultural society to an urban industrial society has created social, emotional, and financial problems for the elderly.

13. Our Social Security program has transferred financial responsibility for the elderly from the individual to the society as a whole. Protection is now provided through pensions, survivors' benefits, hospital and nursing care, and unemployment grants. Payments for most of these are made equally by employer and employee.

14. Some aids to the aged include private pension plans, aid in employment and housing, and development of leisure-time centers. Suggestions for improving our Social Security laws and property taxes offer additional hope for many.

15. In each of the segments of the society that have been considered here, you have been concerned with problems of values as well as problems of economics. As citizens who have the benefit of some understanding of economic analysis, you have a special obligation to arrive at answers and to work to see them adopted.

IN CONCLUSION: some aids to understanding

Terms for review

inelastic demand	subsidy
middleman costs	parity
flexible price support	acreage control
fixed costs	soil bank program
chamber of commerce	unemployment insurance
pensions	mandatory retirement

Names to know

Federal Farm Board	Morrill Act
Rural Electrification Administration	*Baker* v. *Carr*
Commodity Credit Corporation	Social Security Act
Small Business Administration	Medicare

Questions for review

1. Explain the meaning of the following statements:
   (a) "Modern technology and chemistry have changed agriculture from a way of life to a business."
   (b) "In the last hundred years the number of farmers has declined from fifty percent of our labor force to seven percent, but the total output of our farms has continued to accelerate."
   (c) "A small percentage of the nation's farms produce more than half the total output."
   (d) "For the American farmer the last hundred years have brought many periods of unstable prices and incomes."

2. One justification for giving special aid to the farmer is that many of his problems are unique.
   (a) Make a list of some of the causes of the problems of the farmer that are different from the causes of the problems of other producers.
   (b) Describe some of the solutions which have been tried to solve the farmer's problems.
   (c) Evaluate the merits of each of these measures.

3. Explain what is meant by the idea "The paradox for the farmer is that plenty may cause poverty."

4. Programs to help the farmer have focused on raising either income or the prices of farm products.
   (a) Describe the methods used by the government and the farmer to reduce production and to raise the price level.
   (b) Use any specific set of figures to demonstrate the working of parity payment.
   (c) Present the arguments for and against rigid price support.

5. One of the continuing debates of our economy concerns the relative merits of small business and big business.
   (a) What is the definition of "small business"?
   (b) If you were starting your own small business, what problems would you face?
   (c) What has the government done to help small business?
   (d) Why could it be said, "Managerial skill, research, and a strong bank balance might have prevented many failures"?
6. We may question whether small business is the backbone of our economy, but we cannot question the need for its services.
   (a) Draw up a balance sheet of the advantages and the disadvantages of both a small business and a large business.
   (b) Explain why a very small percentage of our business organizations employ the largest percentage of workers.
7. Using the information in Table 17–1, answer the following questions:
   (a) What is expected to be the net percentage change in the over-65 age group from 1960 to 1985?
   (b) Explain the reasons for the increasing percentage of people in this group.
   (c) Why is it essential that help be provided to meet the economic and social needs of this group?
8. In the past thirty years we have begun to develop a system based on collective responsibility for care of the aged.
   (a) What public plans are now in effect to care for the elderly?
   (b) Evaluate the merits of these plans, using criteria for social, economic, and ethical value judgments.
   (c) Why will this problem become increasingly important in the future?

Additional questions and problems

1. Identify and defend the viewpoint in the following statements:
   (a) "The United States government is aiding the marginal farmer in wasting our natural resources."
   (b) "Direct help to the farmer is justified so long as the government helps other segments of the economy."
2. Explain these statements:
   (a) "Government aid to the needy farmer results in major help to those farmers who least require it."
   (b) "Politics, ethics, and economics all help to determine our farm policy."
   (c) "Technology makes it possible for a very few to feed the many efficiently."
   (d) "The primary producer of food receives a very small share of the ultimate consumer's payment."

    (e) "Since the days of the New Deal the United States government has fought a losing battle on the farm surplus, but without the government the surplus might have 'buried' the vast majority of farmers."

3. Using the *U.S. Statistical Abstract, The World Almanac*, or the *Information Please Almanac*, make a graph for each of the following, using a separate line for each of the ten-year intervals (1900–1960):
    (a) Farm acreage in the United States
    (b) Number of farm families
    (c) Dollar value of production
    Then make a bar graph using the same intervals, showing:
    (d) Total farm income
    (e) Total industrial income
    (f) Individual farmers' income
    (g) Individual workers' income

4. Tell what is meant by each of these quotations:
    (a) "In the United States big business is the backbone of the total production, whereas small business supplies the specialization, the innovation, and the experimentation."
    (b) "Small businesses cast many ballots."
    (c) "Small business is the training ground for big business."

5. From what you know of the rise of big business in America, explain this theory: "The genius of American inventors, the wealth of natural resources, the presence of a benign government, and the availability of finance capital all combined to help big business develop in the United States after the Civil War."

6. Compare the treatment of big business by the author Ida Tarbell with that by the historian Allan Nevins.

7. Explain the following statements:
    (a) Our aged today represent nearly ten percent of the total population, and this percentage is increasing.
    (b) The change from a rural America to an urban America has diminished the importance of the aged in our society.
    (c) A partial solution to the problem of economic survival may be found in government Social Security programs, including Medicare.
    (d) The problem of the aged goes beyond mere subsistence; it is also social and emotional

8. Two widely differing attitudes toward the problem of the aged are represented here. Discuss the merits of each point of view.
    (a) "We must establish new goals and new values in attempting to solve the problems of the aged."
    (b) "The individual is coddled by not being forced to provide for his later years. The hard worker and the thrifty individual are thus forced to take on the burden."

18 Problems Faced by Our Economy as a Whole

Preview

Three problems that today occupy economists' attention to a greater degree than ever before are education, the economic development of emerging nations, and the controversy over increasing the private or public sector of our economy. In each of these fields changes have occurred since the end of World War II whose impact is being felt with greater intensity as each year passes. Each of these areas has raised problems that affect all of us; each has caused heated discussions among professional economists and responsible citizens, and has left many questions unresolved.

In this chapter we will examine these problem areas, define some of the issues, provide some of the facts and tools that are useful in analyzing the problems, and point out possible solutions. And again, you, the responsible citizen, using your own set of values and the facts and tools that economics provides for you, should try to arrive at your own conclusions.

Overview

Explain how investment in education pays big dividends to the individual and to society as a whole.

Why may it be necessary to lower living standards for the present in an underdeveloped nation in order to improve them later?

What factors need to be considered in determining whether the public sector should be increased?

401

Part A   Education—Investment in the Future

Changing demands in education

In 1900 about one out of ten children of high school age was enrolled in high school and one out of twenty-five of college age was enrolled in college. Today nine out of ten are enrolled in high school and almost one out of two is in college. In 1900 total expenditures for public schools below the college level were $215 million for a school-age population of 21 million. In the 1964–65 academic year these expenditures were $24.5 billion for 47 million children. As a nation, we spend more money on schools than on any other single enterprise except defense. Education can claim the honor of being the fastest growing major industry, with increases in annual expenditures running above seven percent for the last few years.

POPULATION CHANGE

There are four major reasons to account for the increasing expenditures in education. First, the national birthrate (number of births per 1,000 population) rose dramatically from 17.9 in 1940 to 23.6 in 1950. In the decade from 1950 to 1960 it was more than 23.3, but has declined somewhat since then. The effect of this increase on the number of pupils enrolled in public and private schools combined can be seen in Figure 18–1. The rapid gain in both elementary and secondary enrollment for the first decade is projected at a somewhat lower level for the second. However, the rate of college enrollment is expected to increase as indicated.

MORE YEARS OF EDUCATION

A second cause of increased expenditure is that the average number of years of schooling has increased even more dramatically than the increase in population. The number of students who graduated from high school in June, 1955, was 1.2 million. In June of 1965 it rose to 2.3 million, an increase of almost 93 percent. In 1955 only

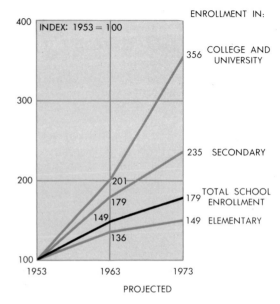

Figure 18–1   School Enrollment

The rapid increase in our population during the postwar years has had a tremendous impact on our educational system during the last decade, and the end is not yet in sight. Between 1953 and 1963, school enrollment, public and private combined, increased from 34.5 million to 51.4 million, and recent projections indicate that by 1973 there will be an additional 10.5 million enrolled in our schools. Although this addition is 6.4 million less than we had to absorb during the fifties, it still represents a faster rate of increase than projected population growth, both total and school age. SOURCES: U.S. Department of Health, Education, and Welfare; The Conference Board; N.I.C.B., *Road Maps of Industry* No. 1516

40 out of 1,000 enrolled in public schools (kindergarten through grade 12) were graduated. In 1965 approximately 54 out of 1,000 were graduated.

Part of the increase in the number being graduated from high school was due to population increase, but equally important were the strenuous efforts to prevent school dropouts and the demand for more advanced education to meet the needs of a far more complex society. In the early 1930's about one half of those who enrolled in high school dropped out before graduation. By the 1960's this fraction was reduced to about one third. The average school years completed by persons over 24 was 8.6 in 1940; today it is about 12 years. Part of this gain is due to the inclusion of vocational training in the curriculum.

The expansion in higher education has been even more dramatic. The number of high school graduates who enrolled in college in 1950 was close to 500,000; in 1964 it had increased to 1.2 million. College enrollment increased from 2.2 million in 1950 to 5.2 million in 1965. Projected enrollment for 1980 is over 10 million, about 60 percent of all 18-to-21-year-olds, compared to about 40 percent in 1960 and four percent in 1900.

Additional demands have been made on education as retraining programs and other adult education programs have become more important. It is too early to determine what the trend will be in these areas, but it seems likely that adult education will demand more and more of our resources.

CHANGES IN QUALITY

The third reason for the increase in cost of education is the improvements being made in the quality of education. Education has changed not merely in the size of enrollment and length of study but also in the character and quality of the education offered. The successful launching of the Soviet Union's first satellite, Sputnik I, caused American educators to reexamine their curriculums and to consider new teaching methods. Greater emphasis on mathematics and science—and more recently on foreign languages, economics, and sociology—has required new kinds of facilities, better teacher preparation, and new instructional materials. Laboratories for teaching of languages and swimming pools for physical education are becoming more common. Equipment that was once seen only in colleges is being brought into high school science laboratories. Specialists and consultants who were at one time considered an extravagance are now included as part of the educational staff without question as to their contribution. Few people doubt that the quality of our education today is better than it has been in the past. Continuing improvement, however, becomes an added expense.

REDIRECTING OUR RESOURCES

The fourth reason for the increasing costs of education relates to the market mechanism, illustrated by our satellite (see p. 8). In order to meet the growing costs, we have had to redirect our resources. Our giant satellite has had to send out signals to attract new resources and redirect old ones, particularly human resources, to meet our changing needs. Since 1950 we have had to replace more than 125,000 teachers annually in the public elementary and high schools, besides meeting an existing shortage of from 50,000 to 100,000 teachers. The need for college teachers—about 32,000 new ones each year—is even more acute.

The demand for these human resources is extremely difficult to meet. You will recall that the mobility of labor is greatest among unskilled workers, and that it is more difficult to increase the supply of workers who have greater skill and training. A minimum of four years beyond high school is required to train a teacher, and a fifth year is being demanded in many school systems, particularly at the secondary level. At the college teaching level, training is more likely to require seven to ten years beyond high school. With a somewhat inelastic supply curve and a greatly increased demand curve, how do we attract additional teachers? The teacher shortage becomes more understandable when we consider the number of overcrowded classrooms with overworked instructors who are paid salaries about equal to the average earnings of employees in all manufacturing industries, and less than workers in mining and transportation. Higher salaries will in time attract more teachers, but a time lag occurs because of the preparation period required.

The mobility of people qualified for college teaching is greater than that of public school teachers. With fewer than 14,000 Ph.D.'s granted yearly (a Ph.D. degree is required for teaching in many colleges and universities) and the demand for Ph.D.'s greater than 35,000 annually, there is intense competition among government, industry, and institutions of higher learning to obtain the services of these highly trained specialists. Higher salaries, federal loans, and subsidies during training have increased the number of people preparing for college teaching, but the supply will increase slowly because of the years of training and special qualifications required.

The need for additional classrooms and equipment has been almost as great as the need for human resources. Greater flexibility commonly exists for meeting these needs because the supply curve for construction and equipment is far more elastic than for human skills. It is easy to switch from the construction of office buildings to the construction of schools so long as the public is willing to pay.

In the years from 1957–59 to 1964–65 the national expenditures for public education have increased by 150 percent per pupil. Even more significant is the increase in the portion of our national income spent for education. From 1950 to 1964 expenditures for public schools rose from over three percent of national income to over five percent. The increase for all education, particularly higher education, was even greater. As a result we are now allocating more of our total resources for education than ever before. Figure 18–3 (see p. 406) shows how some of this money is being spent.

Why the need for more education?

The need for more years of education is a matter for both individual and national concern. From the individual's standpoint more education means, with few exceptions, higher income. From the national standpoint more education means meeting our shortage of human resources and increasing our economic growth.

DIFFERENCES IN INCOME AND THE DEMAND FOR LABOR

Statistics show that the average college graduate earns annually almost three times as much as the person who did not finish elementary school, and about 80 percent more than the one who finished high school. Unemployment rates for high school dropouts are far greater than for graduates, as Figure 18–2 shows.

The Department of Labor has warned young people that they will face increasing competition in the job market, and that education is one of the best ways to prepare for this. The projection for job opportunities to 1970 indicates the greatest need to be for new professional and technical workers, a somewhat lesser need for white-collar workers, an almost equal need for skilled blue-collar workers, very little need for new unskilled and semiskilled workers, and a declining need for farmers and farm laborers. Clearly, education, income, and demand for labor are all related.

EDUCATION AND ECONOMIC GROWTH

Many economists believe that the most important single factor for economic growth in a mature industrial economy like our own is education. The American worker is the most highly trained and best educated in the world, and he is also the most productive. Our business management is also foremost. The new knowledge and techniques of business should be developed and employed increasingly to benefit our entire nation. New production techniques can produce an abundance beyond man's high-

UNEMPLOYED AS PERCENT OF CIVILIAN LABOR FORCE

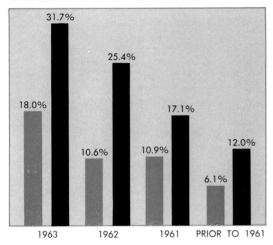

YEAR OF GRADUATION OR
YEAR LAST ATTENDED SCHOOL

■ GRADUATES
■ DROPOUTS

Figure 18–2   Unemployment Rate for High
School Dropouts

Education is becoming increasingly important
for employment. The unemployment rate among
dropouts is well above that of high school graduates. SOURCES: N.I.C.B., *Roaa Maps of Industry*
No. 1497; Bureau of Labor Statistics

est hopes. It may well be possible to eliminate poverty and satisfy the basic needs of
all our people in the not-so-distant future.

We have seen that all resources exist in
limited supply. However, the resource that
is scarcest of all is brainpower. To lose the
fruits of even one creative mind can cost
the nation dearly not only in terms of
money but also in terms of lives, suffering,
and failure to provide the inspiration of
happiness and beauty. To allow the talents
of a potential Albert Einstein, a Marian An-
derson, a William Faulkner, a Henry Ford, a
Pablo Casals, or a Jonas Salk to go undeveloped is to deprive all of us of a better
life. Can there be a better investment than
in "human capital"?

Footing the bill

With the cost of education rising at a
faster rate than our GNP and with our educational product well below the level of our
needs, the problem of obtaining the necessary revenue is a major one. It involves directing more of our resources into education, perhaps at the expense of some other
part of our economy, and making better use
of the resources we already have.

"Think this crop is worth saving?"
—from *The Herblock Book* (Beacon Press, 1952)

CHANGES IN TRADITIONAL
FINANCING METHODS

American education has traditionally
been financed by local government, largely
through the real property tax. Of the $2.1
billion received for public elementary and
secondary schools in 1930, $1.7 billion was
provided by local governments, $353 mil-
lion by state governments, and slightly
more than $7 million by the federal govern-
ment. By 1964–65 the pattern had changed
significantly. Of the $21.8 billion received
in revenue for public elementary and secondary schools, $12.2 billion came from

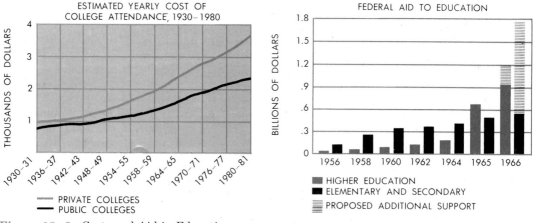

Figure 18-3 Costs and Aid in Education

As the costs of education rise, federal aid to students and to schools is increasing. SOURCE: U.S. Office of Education

local governments, $8.7 billion came from state governments, and $829 million came from the federal government. Although local governments continued to supply most of the revenue, the role of the state and federal governments has increased tremendously. State budgets and the federal budget for 1965–66 show that this trend is continuing at an accelerated rate. If it goes on, local financing will probably fall below 50 percent before 1970.

CAUSES OF THE CHANGE

Local school districts do not have the broad taxing power that the state and national governments have. Until recently almost all school revenue came from taxes on real estate. These taxes appear to be proportional, but they are, in reality, regressive. Many public administrators and public finance specialists are of the opinion that real estate taxes cannot be pushed much higher. In response to these opinions and to the pressure of real estate lobbies, state governments have been turning to the sales tax for additional revenue to use for educational purposes.

Even more significant has been the growing tendency of the states to increase their revenue by higher taxes – primarily income and sales taxes – and to return funds to the local school districts on a per student basis. The federal government, whose tax structure is the most progressive, appears to be following the lead of the states. Since our tax resources are greatest at the federal level, federal aid to education is expected to increase most rapidly.

FEDERAL AID TO EDUCATION

Tradition has placed control of our school system at the local level. Few people would deny the need for financial aid from the federal government, but they fear that with aid will come control. The preference for local control is based on the argument that those who are closest to a situation are in the best position to make decisions. It permits diversity, experimentation, and adjustment to particular needs. However, all school districts and all states obviously do not have equal ability to pay for good education. When President Johnson introduced his education bill, he pointed out that federal assistance was needed to bring the full benefit of education to regions where the return from state and local taxes cannot support an adequate system of education.

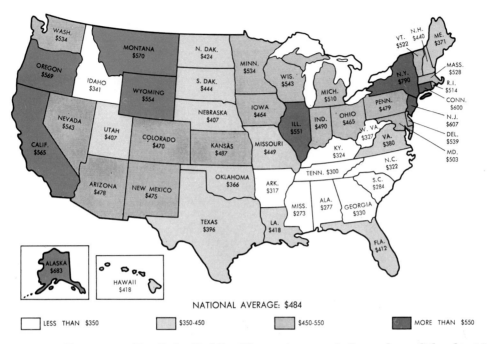

NATIONAL AVERAGE: $484

[ ] LESS THAN $350   [ ] $350-450   [ ] $450-550   [ ] MORE THAN $550

Current Expenditure per Pupil in Public Elementary and Secondary Schools, 1964

Federal aid to education can help reduce the range in the expenditures per pupil between states with very limited financial resources and those with greater financial resources. SOURCE: *Statistical Abstract*

In Mississippi 37 percent of families with school-age children had annual incomes below $2,000, whereas in Massachusetts and Connecticut only four percent were in this category. New York State spends almost three times as much per pupil as does Mississippi and with less effort because incomes are so much higher in New York. The Elementary and Secondary Education Act of 1965 tries to help correct this imbalance. Over half the money appropriated under this law goes to public school districts serving the economically needy.

By providing aid to economically depressed areas, grants for supplementary educational materials and centers of instruction, and scholarships to needy students, the federal education law bypasses the controversy over aid to local schools.

CONFLICT OVER AID TO PAROCHIAL SCHOOLS

On both the state and national levels there has been a continuing controversy over direct aid to parochial schools. The opponents of such aid declare that it would violate our constitutional provision for the separation of church and state. It might also encourage the development of additional private schools and result in a dual system of education. The proponents argue that parochial school students are entitled to the rights and privileges of citizens at government expense. They point out that in 1964, 20 percent of our student population below college, nearly 10.5 million students, attended parochial schools. If these parochial school pupils were to be enrolled in the public schools, the tax bill for education would be considerably higher. At present, certain educational materials are provided; in addition, some states are supplying transportation and lunches.

CHANGES IN HIGHER EDUCATION

The changing patterns of education are even more pronounced in higher education than at elementary and secondary levels. One significant trend is the increase of enrollment in public institutions. In 1950 more than one half of all college students attended private institutions. Today this enrollment is about 35 percent, and the projection for 1975 runs about 20 percent. This decline is matched by a corresponding increase in the number of students attending state and locally supported colleges and universities.

Increasing costs are another important trend in higher education. Figure 18–3 shows how the cost of such education has risen. In 1942 the estimated yearly costs for a student in a private college were about $1,150, and at a public college about $850. Today the private institution costs about $2,600 and the public institution approximately $1,700. The projections for 1975 raise the figure to above $3,000 for private and above $2,000 for public colleges. In addition, tuition pays for only a portion of the cost of higher education. With few exceptions college students are being subsidized by money received from all levels of government and from endowment funds provided by individuals and corporations.

There is ample evidence to show that the investment made in higher education pays excellent dividends. California, more than any other state, has committed itself to providing extensive opportunities for higher education for all its young people. Some people attribute much of its economic growth to this support. Today other states are following California's example. However, as in the support of elementary and secondary levels of education, the poorer states are at a disadvantage.

FEDERAL AID TO HIGHER EDUCATION

In 1960 federal aid to higher education was relatively insignificant, as shown in Figure 18–3. In contrast, proposed aid in 1966 is $1.2 billion. Unfortunately for the poorer states, this money is not used to equalize educational facilities. Indeed, a complaint against the existing program is that the allocation of funds is widening the gap of inequality. Critics protest that most of the money to support research is going to those schools that already have the best facilities. One answer to this objection is that the results of research and the continued betterment of already superior institutions benefit higher education throughout the nation.

HELP FOR THE INDIVIDUAL STUDENT

Aid for students attending private colleges and universities comes essentially from endowments and gifts. Some public help is available for students in both public and private colleges, but mainly in the former. There is a great variation among colleges in the percentage of the total cost that is paid by tuition. In many schools it is less than 20 percent, but the expense may still be prohibitive for many students.

There are three items of cost that the student must consider as part of the expense of attending college: (1) the tuition, (2) his living expenses, and (3) the money he could have earned if he were working rather than attending school (opportunity costs). This can mean a total potential expenditure of from $5,000 to $8,000 per year. If this expenditure is looked upon as an investment in human capital, the returns in the form of increased income for the individual and increased production for the society are well worth it. However, for the individual student and his family, the immediate actual expense, even though less than the potential, may present an insurmountable obstacle.

There are many sources that the individual student can turn to for financial assistance; in addition there are ways in which the student can reduce the cost. For the student of high ability there are scholarships offered by the school and by private donors. Some of these scholarships include living expenses as well as tuition, although rarely do they cover the entire cost. The number of scholarships available has been increasing at an accelerated rate. At the very best private institutions more than half the students are receiving some aid, and few students who do well academically are forced to leave for financial reasons.

Many state governments, as well as the federal government, have set up scholarship funds, and the number of these and the amount of money appropriated for them have increased each year. In addition, state and federal governments have set aside funds and given their own credit support to programs of student loans. These loans are long-term with low interest rates, and actually act as a subsidy for the student.

Several bills have been introduced into Congress to allow tax credits to people who are paying for higher education. This would allow the taxpayer to deduct a considerable amount of the cost of higher education from his personal income tax.

Most students earn some money during summer vacations; some work for several hours a week during the school term. Many colleges provide assistance to students in finding jobs. A number of students meet their expenses by working in the college library or laboratories. A few schools have developed programs that divide the academic year so that students work at jobs related to their area of study as a regular part of their training. The use of such programs is likely to be expanded.

More efficient use of our resources

Complaints are frequently heard about the inefficient use of existing educational resources. Agriculture and industry have increased their output per worker, but what has been done in education?

GREATER USE OF PLANT FACILITIES

Some schools operate their expensive plants on an all-year-round basis, claiming a saving of between 20 and 33 percent by this full utilization. The use of a trimester or quarter system and the addition of summer sessions are the most frequent methods. In addition to dollar savings, this system provides added opportunities and room for more students.

The year-round use of school facilities has disadvantages as well as benefits. An extension of the school year provides almost no saving on teacher salaries because the additional work load requires additional pay. Critics claim that such a program may reduce the quality of education because teachers frequently use their vacation time for advanced study, travel, and preparation for improving their classes. They also point out that a serious shortage of qualified teachers already exists, and that these plans would merely add more students without providing adequate instruction. The installation of air-conditioning equipment and the additional wear on the school plant may lower the expected savings. The increasing use of schools for adult education and as community centers has already reduced the number of hours that buildings are not in use. Critics add that many students cannot attend school on a year-round basis because they depend on summer earnings to continue their education.

Faced with increasing enrollment and mounting costs, schools must continue to search for ways to obtain the maximum use of their facilities. Experiments in utilizing school plants will undoubtedly continue. No conclusions on the quality of education or on the savings obtained from year-round use of facilities are yet available.

SAVINGS FROM IMPROVED TECHNOLOGY AND BETTER USE OF STAFF

In the last ten years, education has seen a host of innovations designed to improve the quality of learning and to increase teacher effectiveness. Teaching machines, team teaching, educational television, and audio-visual aids are used increasingly to enable teachers to work with more students and at the same time to carry on better individual instruction. In college introductory and survey courses, it is common practice for a major professor to lecture to a class of several hundred students. Once a week these large classes break up into smaller sections supervised by instructors and graduate students for discussions and quizzes. The same practice is now carried out on a larger scale by means of television.

Teachers' aides are being employed in increasing numbers to do many routine classroom tasks, freeing the teacher to concentrate on the highly skilled job of teaching. Although there is little doubt that these new techniques help relieve the shortage of teachers, controversy exists concerning their effect on the quality of education. The problems associated with increased enrollment must not be allowed to result in a loss of personal attention and guidance to the student. Meeting quantitative needs without sacrificing quality remains a major problem in our nation's educational system.

Part B   Economic Growth — The United States and the Emerging Nations

Nature of the new nations

In chapters 14 and 16 you have already been introduced to the concept of economic growth — the increase of production from year to year, or rate of increase of the real GNP. Since economic growth has reference to standard of living as well as to total production, we also measure it on a per capita basis — real GNP divided by total population. The first measurement tells us about the aggregate production of the economy, whereas the second measures how well the individual might satisfy his material wants.

The rate of economic growth is a significant measure of our nation's economic progress. It has also been a useful tool to economists in evaluating the development of countries that are economically less advanced. These nations — for the most part newly independent — need such information in planning for their economic development.

"HAVES" AND "HAVE-NOTS"

At one time the term "have" was used to describe a nation which held many colonial possessions whose resources and trade could supplement and add to the wealth of the parent nation. A "have-not" nation owned few if any such territories. Today we use these terms in a different sense. A "have" nation is one with relatively advanced economic development and a high GNP. A "have-not" nation is underdeveloped and its GNP is correspondingly low. Figure 18–4 illustrates this relationship between extent of development and level of GNP.

Although the economic development of the nations of the free world can be placed on a scale ranging from less than $100 per capita GNP to more than $3,000 per capita GNP, it is evident that the United States, Canada, and Europe, particularly western Europe, stand out sharply in contrast to the rest of the world. The United States and western Europe together account for 75 percent of the GNP of the free world. India, Pakistan, Nigeria, and Indonesia have per capita GNP's below $100 a year, compared to more than $3,000 a year for our own country.

Among the less-developed countries, average per capita income is substantially less than $200 a year. In these nations illiteracy rates are often over 50 percent. Many of them have infant mortality rates of over 100 per 1,000 infants born alive. Agriculture accounts for more than 30 percent of their GNP's, and in several instances more than

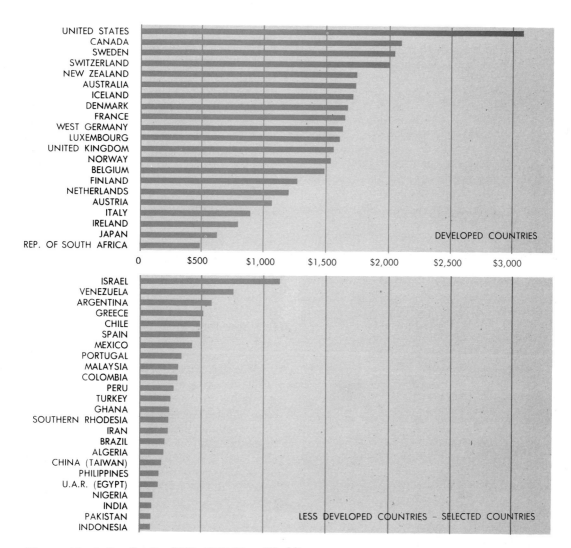

Figure 18–4 Per Capita GNP, 1963 (Free World)

In the developed countries of the free world per capita income averaged about 12 times that of the less-developed countries in 1963. Individual countries showed a considerable spread, however, and in some cases the per capita income of the less-developed countries actually exceeded that of some developed countries.

In making international comparisons, special considerations arise in interpreting the available data. The levels of GNP shown are at best rough estimates of the actual production within these countries. In some of the less-developed nations that have mainly agricultural or barter economies, estimates of GNP do not fully reflect available income. Also, since the national currencies were converted into U.S. dollar equivalents by use of official exchange rates (effective exchange rates were used where official rates were not applicable), the estimates used here do not reflect the substantial variations in the purchasing power of the dollar from country to country. SOURCES: N.I.C.B., *Road Maps of Industry* No. 1518; United Nations; Agency for International Development

50 percent. If we compare this with a typical west European nation with a per capita GNP of $1,500, illiteracy below four percent, infant mortality below 30 per 1,000, and agriculture making up about fifteen percent of GNP, we can better understand the contrast between "have" and "have-not" nations, with new nations usually among the latter.

THE NEW NATIONS — BACKWARD OR UNDERDEVELOPED?

At one time these nations were referred to as "backward" because in most respects their standard of living was below that of nations with more advanced technological development. Often there was contempt for the lack of progress among the people of these countries and belief that their poverty was a fact of life impossible to change. Since World War II, as these nations have

Noneconomic factors such as political stability and the prestige of employment in particular occupations are extremely important in determining economic growth. Nigeria's modest gains (high in comparison with those of most other African nations) reflect these conditions.

emerged from colonial status, their people have become restless and dissatisfied with their poor standard of living. Their leaders, brought into contact with a new world, wanted to improve the economic conditions of both people and nation. Governments which do not promise such changes have little chance of success.

In speaking of these nations the term "backward," with its stigma of inferiority, has given way to "underdeveloped" and "emerging." "Underdeveloped" refers to the fact that the potential for advancement is there but must be set in motion. "Emerging" gives a positive tone, indicating progress and hope. Technically, there is a difference between "underdeveloped" and "poor." Canada is underdeveloped and rich. Japan is highly developed but quite poor, at least in comparison with Canada. As used in popular literature, these terms describe nations that are both underdeveloped and poor.

THE NEW NATIONS — COMMUNIST OR DEMOCRATIC?

The awakening among these nations of a demand for better living and of a spirit of fierce nationalism is taking place in a world that is divided by a struggle for power. Communism, with its slogans of anti-imperialism and its promises of helping the underdog, has a propaganda advantage over the Western democracies, some of which were formerly colonial powers. The challenge to the United States as the leader of the free world to keep these nations from turning to communism is of major importance. We cannot permit ourselves to think of these nations as our "satellites" lest their intense nationalism drive them into the communist camp. We must walk a tightrope by offering aid and guidance without interfering with their newly won sovereignty. Moreover, we must make it clear that the communist world practices an imperialism of its own.

WHY WE SHOULD GIVE ASSISTANCE

With two thirds of the people in the free world living in the emerging nations and with the communist world doing all it can to win the people of these nations over to their system, it is important for our nation's security and well-being to offer a strong alternative to these people. Communism feeds on poverty, discontent, and violence. Our foreign policy has tried to provide assistance for peaceful development with free and stable governments.

What makes the success of our assistance program so difficult to achieve is the frustration and anxiety of the people who are eager to catch up with the developed countries immediately. When they fail to see quick results, they grow impatient. Some think that communism may offer them a faster way. On the other hand, statements are often made by their leaders that seem to indicate ingratitude for our aid, and it is difficult for the people of the United States to understand why these people are not grateful.

Economic growth in the emerging nations requires major changes on the part of the people. We can assist, but they must want to carry on development by themselves. Changing lifelong habits is not easy. If we try to tell these people what they must do, they will resent it. Truly, it is difficult to give and it is difficult to receive.

Stages of economic development

In analyzing a nation's economic progress, many economists have found it helpful to think of this as a sequential development. An important work in describing how economic development takes place was written by an economic historian and State Department advisor, W. W. Rostow. In his book *The Stages of Economic Growth: A Non-Communist Manifesto,*[1] the author describes five stages of economic growth, which follow an evolutionary pattern of development.

THE TRADITIONAL SOCIETY

The most important aspect of the traditional society is that its production possi-

[1] W. W. Rostow, *The Stages of Economic Growth: A Non-Communist Manifesto* (New York: Cambridge University Press), 1960.

bilities have a definite limit. This ceiling is the result of the society's not preparing in a systematic way for changes that could increase production. Although inventions and technological changes may take place, the society does not organize or plan for them.

The typical "traditional society" has about 75 percent of its labor force engaged in agriculture. Its production above consumption is usually wasted by the few who live well, and its capital is not invested for furthering production.

PRECONDITIONS FOR "TAKEOFF"

In order to move to the next stage, the traditional society must meet certain preconditions. Noneconomic changes include the following:

1. Changes in the attitude of the people toward the use of new production techniques and widening their markets
2. Creation of a middle class that has the freedom and is willing (driven by the profit motive) to bring about a change in organization
3. Existence of strong nationalism, with a government able to create an environment favorable to economic growth

In addition to these noneconomic changes, three technical factors are also preconditions for the "takeoff" stage:

1. Expansion of agriculture in order to feed the increased population resulting from a decrease in the mortality rate and the movement of people to the city.
2. Expansion of exports in order to pay for growing imports to be used in early stages of industrialization.
3. Expansion of investment in projects for public benefit, such as transportation and communication facilities, education, health, and sources of power.

"TAKEOFF"

When these preliminary conditions are met, the society may be ready for the "takeoff" stage. This stage is characterized by rapid growth in certain segments of the economy without corresponding growth in other segments. It differs from the previous stage in that its self-sustaining growth results from rising investment, particularly in capital goods. As economic growth accelerates and exceeds the rate of population growth, per capita GNP increases.

"THE DRIVE TO MATURITY"

Following the "takeoff" stage the society "drives to maturity" by applying "the range of modern technology to the bulk of its resources." Other segments of the economy start to grow, giving the economy more balance. The relative position of agriculture declines and the nature of the work force changes. The number of unskilled workers decreases and the number of semiskilled, skilled, and white-collar workers increases. Professional managers replace the "rugged individualist." Collective action by the working force makes itself felt in the marketplace. With industrialization the society becomes more urban.

THE MATURE NATION

When a nation reaches maturity, it can move in any one of three directions: (1) It can use its greater resources for more security and leisure, (2) it can use its greater resources for greater world power, or (3) it can move into the "age of high mass consumption," providing for its people more and more of the goods associated with a high living standard, such as automobiles, television sets, and automatic washers.

APPLICATION TO TODAY'S WORLD

Although not all economists agree with Professor Rostow as to the stages of economic development, most think that there is some value in recognizing that nations today do fit into particular stages. Using Rostow's explanation, Argentina, Brazil, India, and China are moving into the "takeoff" stage while most of the African nations are still in the traditional stage. It is

PARSON MALTHUS AND HIS THEORY OF POPULATION

Thomas Robert Malthus (1766–1834), professor of history and political economy, parish minister, and close friend of David Ricardo, is most noted for his book *An Essay on the Principle of Population*. Disagreeing with his father and with the utopian ideas that man could be perfected and was moving in that direction, Malthus predicted a dismal future for mankind.

Starting with Benjamin Franklin's observation that population in the New World tends to double approximately every 25 years, Malthus framed a theory of population. He said that there is a tendency for population to increase in a geometric progression (1, 2, 4, 8, 16, 32) whereas food supply tends to increase in an arithmetic progression (1, 2, 3, 4, 5, 6). This theory represents an application of the law of diminishing returns to the subject of population. The implications for man's future are clear. With a limited amount of land and an ever-increasing population, mankind is doomed to live in eternal misery. Increasing the output of food would be of little lasting benefit because it

would eventually result in a higher birth rate.

In the past, war and pestilence and famine held the population in check. However, with improvements in health and living conditions, these means could no longer be sufficient or acceptable. Ricardo recommended moral restraint as a primary solution, as well as late marriages, discontinuing aid to the poor, and keeping wages at a low level. Harsh though these remedies seemed, they were essential to keep population within limits for which food could be available.

Malthus did not foresee either the tremendous increase in productivity that would be brought about by the Industrial Revolution or the eventual reduction that would take place in the birth rate in highly industrialized countries. Nevertheless, when the present situation of rapid population expansion and slow rate of economic growth among the emerging nations is considered, many people wonder whether Malthus' conclusions may not be correct and his theory of population still relevant.

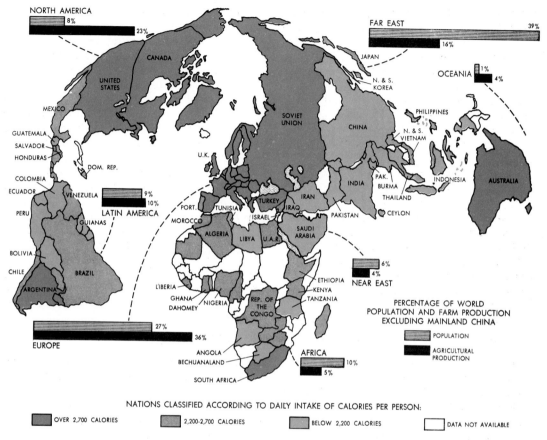

NORTH AMERICA
8%
23%

FAR EAST
39%
16%

OCEANIA
1%
4%

LATIN AMERICA
9%
10%

NEAR EAST
6%
4%

EUROPE
27%
36%

AFRICA
10%
5%

PERCENTAGE OF WORLD
POPULATION AND FARM PRODUCTION
EXCLUDING MAINLAND CHINA

POPULATION

AGRICULTURAL
PRODUCTION

NATIONS CLASSIFIED ACCORDING TO DAILY INTAKE OF CALORIES PER PERSON:

OVER 2,700 CALORIES   2,200-2,700 CALORIES   BELOW 2,200 CALORIES   DATA NOT AVAILABLE

World Problem: Population and Food

Statistics show food output lagging in precisely those regions that have the highest birthrate. Many solutions are suggested, but some involve a conflict of cultural values. SOURCES: New York *Times,* January 24, 1966; United Nations; Ford Foundation; FAO

dangerous, however, to assume that the emerging nations will follow the same pattern that developing nations have. Professor Rostow himself points out the risks in making such an assumption.

Being able to draw on technical knowledge and assistance in providing capital gives emerging nations a decided advantage in accelerating growth. However, the gains made through such growth may be offset by other changes. The application of modern medical knowledge may reduce the

death rate and increase the population so as to minimize the effect of a growing GNP. This problem becomes particularly acute if the population increase takes place when most good land is already in use.

Difficulties to overcome

When new nations achieve independence, they may suppose that with this step their problems are solved. In gaining self-government, however, they have assumed responsibility for their own growth and for a choice of political and economic

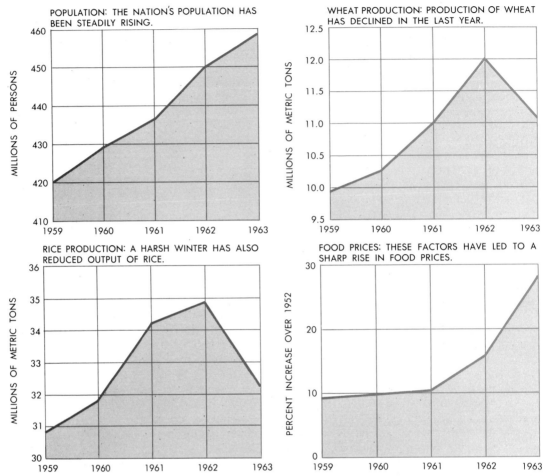

Figure 18-5   India's Problem—Population Up, Food Production Down

SOURCE: New York *Times*, September 27, 1964

systems. The latter decision is somewhat simplified because there are existing models to follow. However, special problems may exist that hinder the implementing of economic development, whatever the model.

POPULATION

Perhaps the most difficult problem facing the emerging nations is that of the population explosion. As we saw, the use of modern medicine reduces the death rate. With the previously high infant mortality rate cut and with people living longer, the size of the labor force in relation to the total population declines. It has often been necessary to devote the increased output per worker to the care of those who are too young or too old to work.

In most underdeveloped areas productivity has increased about three percent per year while population has increased about two percent. However, production of food has been erratic. From 1962 to 1963 India's population increased by eight million while her wheat and rice production, largely because of unfavorable weather conditions, declined about eight percent.

INSUFFICIENT CAPITAL

In the early stages of economic development, capital is relatively more important than it is in later stages. As you know, capital comes from savings. By not consuming all that is produced, that which remains (savings) can be used for investment (instruments of production). If output of consumer goods can be held down and the remaining factors of production used to produce machinery and other tools of production, economic growth can be not only increased but even speeded up.

Rich countries and totalitarian countries can regulate consumer spending, thereby increasing savings, with relative ease. Poor countries, on the other hand, find it very difficult to accumulate capital through saving. How can you expect to have much savings when per capita income is below $100 a year? The small wealthy class in such a country rarely invest their money in productive facilities as people of means do in highly developed countries. Many of them spend it on extravagant living; others, fearing the instability of their own currency and financial institutions, invest it abroad. Some savings are converted to things which keep their value, such as gold and jewelry, but which are static in terms of producing new wealth. These people are often criticized—sometimes unfairly—for not having confidence in their own country. Nevertheless, until sound financial institutions are developed and currency made stable, it is unlikely that internal capital in these nations will be sufficient to support growth.

OBTAINING FOREIGN CAPITAL

The emerging nations are hungry for capital, and they encourage businesses from abroad to invest. However, the people of these countries are often suspicious of foreign exploitation. Private investors have found themselves caught in the middle of internal feuding for power. Sometimes their property is expropriated with little or no compensation. Restrictions on whom they may hire and what they can do with their profits may make such investments unwise. Although the attitude of the emerging nations may be understandable, it is often not conducive to attracting new capital.

The amount of private United States capital being invested abroad has increased to such an extent that President Johnson has suggested methods of slowing it down in order to reduce our gold outflow. This money, however, goes to countries whose governments are stable and in which return on investment is high. It is not, for the most part, going to emerging nations, where the needs, but also the risks, are greatest.

HUMAN RESOURCES

There is rarely a shortage of people in the labor force in emerging nations. The problem is rather that human resources are undeveloped; there is an acute lack of people with skills and technical training. An urban industrial society requires literacy and skills far more than does a rural agrarian economy. A lack of teachers and of books and other educational facilities presents a serious problem that must be overcome if growth is to take place.

A shortage of people with managerial skills also stands in the way of progress in these countries. Too few people in management have the necessary training or the motivation to run efficient enterprises. Many in top management have their positions because of family standing rather than by reason of training or special abilities. If profits are low, it is usually the workers who suffer.

Patterns of development

There are many ways for underdeveloped nations to achieve economic growth. This problem is deeply entwined with the worldwide struggle for political power, and nations receiving aid should be aware that stronger and richer nations are seldom moved solely by generosity and goodwill in providing assistance. The objectives of the United States and the Soviet Union in aiding these countries go beyond merely providing assistance in economic growth. Military alliances and propaganda to win the minds of men often actually conflict with economic development.

As our foreign aid program shifts to the emerging nations, many of whom are uncommitted, the question of whether our aid should be primarily economic or military and political is argued more and more frequently in Congress and among interested citizens. Should we give aid to countries who admittedly are committed to socialism or to even more leftist views? What demands, if any, can we place on countries receiving our aid? What strings, if any, shall we put on our aid? Should we make long-term economic commitments to politically unstable countries? To what extent should emerging nations rely on foreign capital, and to what extent should they be responsible for themselves? These are the questions which we face in trying to develop a policy that will serve our own interests and those of the emerging nations.

COMMITMENTS

In spite of political and economic persuasion, some of the emerging nations remain unaligned. They refuse to become embroiled in a world power struggle, from which they have little to gain. Many nations, such as Egypt and India, have taken aid from both the Soviet Union and the United States. To some, it looks as if these nations are playing the big powers against each other in order to get as much aid as possible. To the realist who considers the emerging nations' needs, such a policy is understandable; to the moralist, it might be unacceptable. This is a question of values as well as of economics.

If we set as our objective the fostering of independent developing nations who will be free to choose their own system, and if we trust in their ability to make a choice, we cannot expect them to commit themselves. If, on the other hand, we believe that we should help only those who are willing to pay the price of alignment and accept the responsibility of commitment to a particular ideology, demanding such a commitment may seem reasonable.

CHOOSING THE "MIXTURE"

The emerging nations have several alternatives to choose from in deciding the balance between public and private sectors. However, in many instances their choice is limited either because they do not have enough people with adequate capital to meet development needs or because the people who do have the capital are unwilling to invest it. This limitation can be overcome, at least in part, by encouraging investment by private foreign capital. Such investment may be difficult to obtain because many of the governments of these countries are not stable. There is fear on the part of the investor that he will lose his investment through revolution or expropriation, and there is fear on the part of the people that such investment from abroad is a new kind of imperialism.

Some Americans, seeing that the "mixture" of our economic system has produced a very high standard of living and that our political democracy has provided us with freedom, insist that other nations should model themselves after us. Our success is so obvious that these Americans cannot see why anyone should not want to follow our example. We must beware the temptation to apply our own standards of democracy and freedom of the market to other nations in which conditions may be quite different. What some people fail to consider is that emerging nations may have completely different environments and unique problems. To many of these people, freedom, self-government, and democracy are abstractions of which they have little understanding. Getting enough to eat may be their primary objective, and to achieve it they may turn to whatever system or party promises them the most.

"Hey, fellas, which one should I put the basket under?"

CENTRALIZATION AND PLANNING

It would be entirely unrealistic for the emerging nations to rely on the market mechanism to obtain sufficient savings and investment for development. They simply do not have the financial institutions to provide this function. To initiate and carry

on development, such intensive effort is needed that planning for efficient resource allocation is essential.

All underdeveloped nations have formulated plans outlining their present and future development. Some of these are like blueprints, setting forth elaborate plans for the present expansion of the economy and for future growth, under tight government control. Some of these plans are in great detail and resemble those of the Soviet Union. Others are more general, merely suggesting a priority for growth and general direction for development. They may recommend that capital should be funneled to those things which will yield the greatest economic growth. However, in the absence of close supervision consumers are likely to make decisions that satisfy their immediate needs in preference to future national development. If the nation has little freedom, the government may act as it thinks best (and no one can be sure what is "best"), but there is no assurance that its decisions will be wise. Where freedom does exist and governments are elected by the people, capital may have to be spread thinly throughout the country so that everyone may share in the benefits from change. In such a situation economic efficiency may have to give way to political expediency. Making the right decisions can be complicated by lack of information and the desire to gain political advantage, as well as by conflicting ideologies and opposition to centralized planning.

CONSUMPTION OR CAPITAL GOODS?

Each of the emerging nations must face the difficult decision of what portion of its production it will devote to consumer goods and what portion it will devote to capital goods. All nations face this question to some degree. The choice is made more difficult for poor countries because they are so lacking in consumer goods. Placing greater emphasis on capital goods will bring greater growth and a higher standard of living for future generations, but this emphasis does little to relieve the miserable conditions of the present generation. Communist China has developed nuclear weapons, but at what cost to the standard of living of her present generation?

CONFLICTS FACED BY EMERGING NATIONS

Choosing the best course to follow presents numerous conflicts to the emerging nations. The choice involves decisions on how far to commit themselves in the cold war, what the proper balance between the public and the private sectors shall be, how much control and how much freedom are best politically as well as economically, and how much present sacrifice should be made for future gain. Sympathetic help, guidance, and understanding by the developed nations can go far in providing answers.

ISSUES INVOLVED IN FOREIGN AID PROGRAMS

Foreign aid programs must be considered not only from the standpoint of the recipients but also in terms of the interests and capabilities of the donors. Although aid may in part be used as a political instrument, its continued existence depends basically on the economic strength of contributing nations. Decisions on granting foreign aid cannot be separated from decisions concerning a nation's domestic economy.

In Chapter 15 we studied some aspects of the United States' foreign aid program. It may be helpful for you to review the kind and size of our commitment at this time. You should also consider, in the light of your understanding of the problems faced by the emerging nations, whether our com-

IRAN PRESSES FOR AUSTERITY DRIVE
PREMIER SAYS NECESSARY FOR ECONOMIC GROWTH

TEHERAN, IRAN — Premier Hassan Ali Mansur of Iran has asked the people of his country to begin an austerity drive as a means of increasing their economic development.

"We must tighten our belts, reduce personal and national expenditures, and use the money thus saved to increase production and the national wealth so that we can all benefit in the future," he said.

The austerity program includes reducing government expenditures by 15 percent in nonessential goods and services, imposing new taxes on consumer goods and on the wealthy, and levying a tax equivalent to $140 on each single-journey exit permit out of the country. It is estimated that the new program will bring in about $100 million in additional revenue the first year, with increases in subsequent years.

Underdeveloped nations must frequently lower their present living standards in order to direct their resources into the production of capital goods. Such austerity means extreme hardship for people whose per capita income is already very low.

mitments should be short-term or long-term and to what degree we should direct the use of our aid. How important is it to you to help these nations? Do you think such aid is worth the cost to our own economy?

Part C   The Private Versus the Public Sector—What Should the Balance Be?

Economic implications of the problem

In the course of studying our nation's economy, we have frequently made reference to the balance between its private and public sectors (see p. 161). We have shown how the public sector has grown in absolute terms, as a percentage of GNP, and in constant as well as actual dollars. We have also pointed out that if national defense expenditures are eliminated from both public expenditures and GNP, the rate of increase of the public sector in relation to GNP has been very small and at times has declined.

The question of what the right balance between the two sectors should be has sometimes been called the "Great Debate." The growing affluence of our society in the fifties and sixties has posed the question of what we should do with our newfound wealth. Shall it be distributed in the same proportion as it has in the past, or are we reaching a new stage of development that calls for a different distribution? Although values also play an important part in arriving at an answer, there is no doubt that this is basically an economic problem.

There are three major economic questions involved in this problem of balance: (1) the allocation of resources, (2) economic stability, and (3) economic growth. As we consider these questions, we will review the arguments over particular policies.

We must allocate our resources between the public and the private sectors and, in the process, maximize our satisfactions. Under certain conditions, people's interests as consumers may conflict with their interests as citizens. What might some of these conditions be?

ALLOCATION OF RESOURCES

Every society must make a decision on how it wishes to allocate its resources. In a totalitarian state the decision is made by the central government, with some attention paid to what the rulers think the people want. In a democratic state the people, directly or through their representatives, decide on the distribution of resources between the public and private sectors. The people, acting as citizens rather than as consumers, decide whether the marginal utility of their money will be greater when spent in the public sector or in the private

The people who think that we in the United States now have an imbalance and that we could gain more by diverting added resources into the public sector point out the abundance of our private goods—automobiles, TV sets, and electric appliances—as contrasted with the inadequate condition of the public sector—schools, roads, and public recreational facilities. They point out that as the society's total production increases, the percentage of total resources that must go to satisfying the basic needs of food, shelter, and clothing declines and more is left over to satisfy other needs. With increased specialization, industrialization, and urbanization the need for public facilities grows. Our greater interdependence makes it necessary to solve many of our problems collectively. The furnishing of water and sewer facilities may be done individually in a rural environment, but not in an urban environment. An industrial nation requires a more highly educated work force than an agricultural nation does. Government regulation increases as man becomes more dependent on and lives closer to his fellow man. For these reasons many people believe that we must increase the proportion of our resources going to the public sector.

Those who believe that the present balance is satisfactory or is too heavily weighted in favor of the public sector point out that about 20 percent of the family units in the United States live in poverty (below $3,000 per family and $1,500 per individual annual money income before taxes). The abundance in the private sector is a myth for a very large number of our people, and to divert resources away from them will cause them personal hardship. Moreover, the emphasis on cars laden with chrome and on color TV sets is out of proportion to actual consumer spending on these low-utility items. Less than 15 percent of personal consumption is spent on durable goods; in addition, many of these have high utility for the people buying them. Most consumers need all they now have to take care of their individual needs.

ECONOMIC STABILITY

You will recall that in order to maintain economic stability our aggregate demand must be sufficiently high to sustain full employment but not so great as to cause inflation. In Chapter 14 we found that modern fiscal policy suggests that if the economy is operating below capacity, aggregate income can be increased by tax cuts, which will increase spending in the private sector, or by greater government spending, which will increase the public sector, or by a combination of both methods.

Those who favor increasing the public sector point out that the marginal utility for consumer goods is already low and growing lower. They explain this by showing the great dependence we now have on advertising to *create* consumer demand. Advertising, for which we now spend some $12 billion a year, and built-in obsolescence of automobiles and appliances are required to raise consumer spending for goods consumers may not otherwise want. On the other hand, public wants are not manufactured nor are they even induced by the profit motive. In addition, people in the lower income levels tend to benefit more by the additional spending in the public sector. Advocates also point out that although no one can pre-

dict with any certainty how people will spend and save with the additional income from tax cuts, they can be more certain about public expenditures. The multiplier will be higher for spending in the public sector than in the private sector.

Those who oppose increasing the public sector point out that the marginal utility for extra dollars in government spending is also declining and that there is no reason to assume that it is higher than in consumer spending. The additional dollars can be spent on such superfluous frills as elaborate stadia, monuments with little meaning, research that has almost no utility, and roads and bridges whose costs bear little relation to their use. Are public extravagances more useful than private extravagances?

These critics also insist that many of the services being increasingly provided by government may be just as efficiently, or even more efficiently, provided by private enterprise. Research by private colleges and industry can yield as much per dollar as research by public institutions, and may well yield more.

ECONOMIC GROWTH

The major factors responsible for economic growth are increases in the labor force, better education, additional research, and more capital goods. Accelerating the growth rate in a mature economy like our own involves only minor sacrifices by the present generation. How may the balance between spending in the public sector and in the private sector affect long-term growth?

Those who favor increasing the public sector point out that the factors that are most responsible for growth are areas in which the government has the greatest responsibility. Better and longer periods of education provide our population with additional skills to increase output per worker. Retraining programs give skills and higher earning power to those who are unemployed or have low incomes. Basic research, which private enterprise rarely risks be-

cause such research is concerned with un-
covering truth rather than with making
profits, provides us with new ideas and
eventually new technology. It can also result in better health for a more productive
population. Preventive medicine, which is
mainly a public service, has reduced our
death rate, thereby increasing our labor
force. In contrast, our increased personal
consumption expenditures have sometimes
proved to be a detriment. Our health problems more frequently stem from overnour-
ishment than from undernourishment,
and from lack of exertion than from too
much strenuous physical activity.

Those who oppose increasing the public
sector point out that the period of the
greatest economic growth in the United
States (excluding the 1960's) came in the
periods 1871–1889 and 1896–1905, when
the public sector was very small. Inventions, capital accumulation, and better
health have in the past largely been the
contribution of the private sector. Although
there can be no doubt that increased spending by the government has been useful in
increasing growth, the question remains
whether the marginal productivity of dollars spent in the public sector is any greater
than, or even as great as, that of dollars
spent in the private sector.

Factors influencing the balance

The decision on what the balance between the public and the private sectors
should be is influenced by a number of factors, many involving values. The clash of
political forces is frequently centered
around the role of government in the economic field. Recent bipartisan support for
such legislation as Social Security extension does not mean an absence of difference of opinion on other similar issues.

FACTORS FAVORING
THE PUBLIC SECTOR

As the federal and state governments
have become more involved in furnishing
services for the people, there is less recog-

nition by the people of the cost of these
services. A community that needs a new
school may vote down a bond issue when
the local school district has to pay either all
or most of the cost. If the state or federal
government provides a sizeable part of the
cost, the chances that the bond issue will be
voted favorably improve appreciably. People often do not recognize that these additional costs must be met through taxes at
the state and national levels.

Our progressive tax structure leads indirectly to increases in the public sector.
The benefits received by people whose income level is below the mean are greater
than the cost to them. Since this group includes a majority of the voters, government
services—and the size of the public sector—may be expected to grow steadily in
size and scope.

In studying tariffs, we saw that logrolling among members of Congress can at
times result in legislation different from
what was intended. A similar situation may
occur with legislation for public projects.
The accommodating of interests, with or
without personal political gain, may result
in expansion of the public sector without
thorough study of the real issues involved.

FACTORS LIMITING
THE PUBLIC SECTOR

The traditional concept of capitalism,
the classical model, favors the private sector. Government's role in the economic life
of the society is a restricted one and the
consumer is sovereign. Although this is
hardly an accurate portrayal of our present
economy, it nevertheless places any suggestion of increasing the public sector on
the defensive. Private goods are furnished
at the demand of the consumer and no explanation is required. On the other hand
government must justify its requests for
additional spending.

Adherents of this viewpoint often
assume that the public sector can be increased only at the expense of the private

sector, even with the economy below full employment. The individual consumer is likely to look upon this as an infringement of his rights, since he will have less direct control over the money he earns. The general feeling persists that government is a necessary evil and that the less there is of it, the better. As government activity increases, individual freedom decreases.

One belief widely held among those who would limit the public sector is that government enterprise is less efficient than private enterprise. Public projects are not motivated by the desire for profit; they have no competition that compels them to improve efficiency and reduce expenses. Government "bureaucrats" may be accused of being not only less efficient than private managers but also of being interested solely in perpetuating themselves in power regardless of expense.

Resolving the controversy

The "Great Debate" will probably never be resolved, because we live in a dynamic society in which our resources and needs are changing and in which people have different values. At different stages of our national development, different needs have predominated. In the sixties we have seen a sharp acceleration of spending in the public sector. Expenditures for education, research, and highways have increased faster than the GNP. Expenditures for urban renewal and aid to depressed areas were very small at the beginning of the decade but have shown the sharpest increase. With increased urban representation in state and federal legislatures, resulting from recent court rulings (see p. 383), these trends may be expected to continue.

If there is an imbalance, our greatest hope for correcting it might be a reduction in defense spending that would allow us to transfer these resources to other kinds of goods and services associated with welfare and a better way of life. However, only time can tell whether such a reduction is possible. Increasing our growth rate so that additional resources can be poured into the public sector without sacrificing the private sector is another possible way to adjust an imbalance.

The decisions you must make as a consumer, a producer, and a citizen are truly awesome. Your teacher, the authors, and society as a whole hope that your understanding of economics will help you make better choices and decisions.

REVIEW: *the highlights of the chapter*

1. The increased costs of education are due to a population increase, a demand for more years of education, and changes in the quality of education. To meet them, we must prepare to redirect some of our resources.

2. Meeting the demand for teachers is difficult because of the somewhat inelastic supply and the greatly increased need. Material requirements can be fulfilled more easily because the supply curve for them is more elastic.

3. People with more education have better opportunities for getting jobs and keeping them, and they tend to earn higher incomes.

4. Education is one of the most important factors in economic growth, particularly in a mature economy.

5. In the past, education has been financed primarily by local governments through real estate taxes. State and federal fi-

nancing are playing an ever-increasing role because these governments have broader taxing powers.

6. Federal aid to education helps equalize educational opportunities. Controversy over federal aid arises because control of education is traditionally local and because aid to parochial schools raises the question of separation of church and state.

7. The cost of higher education to the individual and to the nation has increased faster than that of elementary and secondary education. There are many ways in which college students can obtain aid in meeting higher costs.

8. Attempts to increase efficiency in education have resulted in greater use of the school plant and the use of new teaching equipment and new methods of instruction.

9. Since World War II the poor and underdeveloped nations have been trying to catch up quickly with the more highly developed nations. Their progress has been complicated by the power struggle between the free and communist worlds.

10. W. W. Rostow has identified five stages of economic development: (a) the traditional society, (b) the preconditions for takeoff, (c) the takeoff, (d) the drive for maturity, and (e) the mature society.

11. Difficulties that must be overcome in emerging nations in order to have adequate economic growth include the population explosion, insufficient capital, lack of foreign investment, and poorly developed human resources.

12. The emerging nations may choose from among several alternative patterns of development. The question remains whether a mature nation should attempt to extend its influence along with its aid to less-developed countries.

13. Emerging nations have conflicts over what economic system to follow, what foreign commitments to make, and what the present generation should sacrifice to benefit future generations.

14. The United States' foreign aid program has shifted primarily to assisting emerging nations. Greater emphasis is being given to economic rather than military aid.

15. The "Great Debate" centers on whether the balance between the public and private sectors of our economy is a good one.

16. The major economic questions involved in this controversy center around the issues of allocation of resources, economic stability, and economic growth.

17. People who favor increasing the public sector point to the factors of greater affluence in the private sector, increasing needs in the public sector, low marginal utility of consumer dollars, greater benefits received by lower income groups from public spending, and the greater opportunities for economic growth made possible by increasing public expenditures.

18. People opposed to such an increase point out that a large number of family units live in poverty, that extravagant purchases account for only a small part of consumer spending, that the marginal utility of extra public spending can also be low, that many public services can be performed more efficiently in the private sector, and that economic growth can be as fast with investment in the private as in the public sector.

19. Forces exist in the environment and in the minds of people that act both for and against expanding the public sector. Changes in the balance will undoubtedly continue to occur.

IN CONCLUSION: *some aids to understanding*

Terms for review

emerging nations	the public sector
the private sector	school dropout
"human capital"	aid to education
trimester system	unaligned nations
population explosion	"takeoff" stage
the "Great Debate"	"traditional society"

Questions for review

1. Identify the many factors which have led to the great increase in educational costs in the last twenty-five years and explain the significance of each.

2. Explain in detail why the supply of teachers has not kept pace with the demand.

3. Development of human resources is of benefit to both the individual and the nation.
   (a) What are the practical advantages to the individual which come from increased education?
   (b) Why could it be said that the nation is richer when its population is well educated?
   (c) What sources of revenue are available to you as a student for continuing your education?

4. Changing circumstances make necessary a frequent review of government policies on foreign aid.
   (a) Indicate some of the advantages which would accrue to the United States by expansion of our foreign aid program.
   (b) What are the disadvantages and potential problems which might result?
   (c) In light of present international conflicts and the attacks on the United States' policies, should we reevaluate our plans? What alternatives are possible?

5. Establishing a framework for development can be a help in evaluating the progress of emerging nations.
   (a) Identify W. W. Rostow's five stages of economic development.
   (b) Select one nation to correspond to each stage and explain why each particular example is appropriate to that stage.
6. Prepare a balance sheet for the choices of an emerging nation in choosing between (a) a free capitalistic economic system and (b) a totalitarian state economy.
7. One continuing issue in American politics is what constitutes a proper balance between public and private areas of the economy.
   (a) Give the arguments of the "Great Debate" in favor of the extension of the public sector.
   (b) List some of the answers which the advocates of increasing the private sector would present.

Additional questions and problems

1. Assume that you are a school superintendent faced with the responsibility of meeting the educational needs of your community.
   (a) What plans can you propose for better use and more efficient operation of the school plant?
   (b) What would be the advantages and disadvantages of each plan to the taxpayers, the students, and the faculty?
2. Prepare a debate on the subject "*Resolved*, That public funds should be used to support parochial schools."
3. Explain the meaning of the following statements, using specific examples wherever possible.
   (a) "Use of our tax dollars for helping underdeveloped nations may be more important than similar expenditures for armaments."
   (b) "Recipients of American aid often display little thanks and much greed."
   (c) "National sovereignty and pride may clash with economic necessity."
4. The American people are becoming increasingly aware of the correlation between quality and cost of education.
   (a) Make a bar graph showing the per capita expenditures of ten states for public education. Include the states that spend the most and the least, as shown on the map on page 407.
   (b) In a second color, indicate the illiteracy rate of these ten states.
   (c) What correlation can you draw between the two graphs?
   (d) What general policy and specific recommendations would you make to close the gap in expenditures? Defend your thesis and your recommendations.
5. How is it possible for a nation to be underdeveloped yet rich, whereas, conversely, a nation might be highly developed yet poor?

6. What recommendations would you make to an emerging country with a per capita income below $200 to aid it in increasing its savings and investment in proportion to its GNP?

7. Explain how noneconomic factors may be as important as economic factors in the development of emerging nations.

8. Explain why the Supreme Court decision in *Baker* v. *Carr,* in 1962, may possibly change the balance between the public and private sectors of our economy.

9. Make a list of your community's most important needs and estimate their probable cost. Would the people in your community benefit more by spending this money in the private sector or in the public sector? Explain your answer.

Bibliography

SUGGESTIONS FOR GENERAL READING AND RESEARCH

Basic texts

Bach, George L. *Economics: An Introduction to Analysis and Policy,* 5th ed. Englewood Cliffs, N.J.: Prentice-Hall, Inc., 1966.

McConnell, Campbell R. *Economics: Principles, Problems, and Policies,* 3rd ed. New York: McGraw-Hill Book Co., 1966.

Reynolds, Lloyd G. *Economics: A General Introduction,* rev. ed. Homewood, Ill.: Richard D. Irwin, Inc., 1966.

Samuelson, Paul A. *Economics: An Introductory Analysis,* 6th ed. New York: McGraw-Hill Book Co., 1964.

Ulmer, Melville J. *Economics: Theory and Practice,* 2nd ed. Boston: Houghton Mifflin Co., 1965.

General sources of information

The Economic Almanac and *Glossary of Economic Terms.* New York: National Industrial Conference Board, Inc. (Revised annually)

Economic Report of the President. Council of Economic Advisers. Washington, D.C.: U.S. Government Printing Office. (Published in January of each year)

Information Please Almanac: Atlas and Yearbook. New York: Simon and Schuster. (Revised annually)

Oxford Economic Atlas of the World. New York: Oxford University Press, 1959.

Statistical Abstract of the United States. Washington, D.C.: Bureau of the Census, U.S. Department of Commerce. (Issued annually)

The World Almanac and Book of Facts. New York: The New York World-Telegram and The Sun. (Revised annually)

Newspapers and periodicals

Atlantic Monthly
Business Week
Challenge
Forbes
Fortune
Harper's
Newsweek
New York *Times*
    (particularly the Sunday edition)
Time
U.S. News and World Report
Wall Street Journal

SELECTED READINGS FOR INDIVIDUAL CHAPTERS

Chapter 1   Economics—What It Is and What It Tries to Do

Boulding, Kenneth E. *The Skills of the Economist.* Cleveland: Howard Allen, Inc., 1958.

Heilbroner, Robert L. *The Worldly Philosophers*, rev. ed. New York: Simon and Schuster, 1961. (Also available in paperback edition from the same publisher)

Hicks, J. R., and Albert G. Hart. *The Social Framework of the American Economy: An Introduction to Economics*, 2nd ed. New York: Oxford University Press, 1955.

Leamer, Laurence E., and Dorothy L. Thomson. *American Capitalism: An Introduction.* New York: Council for Advancement of Secondary Education, 1961.

Lewis, Ben W. *Economic Understanding: Why and What.* New York: Joint Council on Economic Education, 1957.

Robinson, Marshall A., and others. *An Introduction to Economic Reasoning*, rev. ed. Washington, D.C.: The Brookings Institution, 1962.

Chapter 2   Demand and Supply—An Answer to Resource Allocation

Bain, Joe S. *Price Theory.* New York: Holt, Rinehart & Winston, Inc., 1952.

Dorfman, Robert. *The Price System.* Englewood Cliffs, N.J.: Prentice-Hall, Inc., 1964.

Haveman, Robert H., and Kenyon A. Knopf. *The Market System.* New York: John Wiley and Sons, 1966.

Leftwich, Richard H. *The Price System and Resource Allocation,* 3rd ed. New York: Holt, Rinehart & Winston, Inc., 1966.

Liebhafsky, H. H. *The Nature of Price Theory.* Homewood, Ill.: Dorsey Press, 1962.

Stigler, George J. *The Theory of Price.* New York: The Macmillan Co., 1952.

Chapter 3   Business Enterprise

Adams, Walter, ed. *The Structure of American Industry: Some Case Studies,* 3rd ed. New York: The Macmillan Co., 1961.

Caves, Richard. *American Industry: Structure, Conduct, Performance.* Englewood Cliffs, N.J.: Prentice-Hall, Inc., 1964.

Cochran, Thomas C. *The American Business System: A Historical Perspective, 1900–1955.* New York: Harper and Row, 1962.

Mansfield, Edwin, ed. *Monopoly Power and Economic Performance.* New York: W. W. Norton & Co., Inc., 1964. (Also available in paperback edition from the same publisher)

Wilcox, Clair. *Public Policies Toward Business,* rev. ed. Homewood, Ill.: Richard D. Irwin, Inc., 1960.

Chapter 4   Labor: Its Uses and Rewards
Chapter 5   Labor: Its Organization and Development

The American Federationist. Washington, D.C.: American Federation of Labor and Congress of Industrial Organizations. (Published monthly)

Bowen, William G., ed. *Labor and the National Economy.* New York: W. W. Norton & Co., Inc., 1965.

Burtt, Everett J. *Labor Markets, Unions, and Government Policies.* New York: St. Martin's Press, Inc., 1963.

Dunlop, John T. *Labor Economics.* Englewood Cliffs, N.J.: Prentice-Hall, Inc., 1965.

How to Raise Real Wages. New York: Committee for Economic Development, 1961.

Perlman, Richard, ed. *Wage Determination – Market or Power Forces?* Boston: D. C. Heath and Co., 1964.

Senesh, Lawrence, and Barbara Newell. *Our Labor Force: Workers, Wages, and Unions.* Chicago: Scott, Foresman & Co., 1961.

Starr, Mark. *Labor and the American Way.* New York: Oxford Book Co., 1960.

Wages, Prices, Profits and Productivity. New York: American Assembly, 1959.

Weinstein, Paul A., ed. *Featherbedding and Technological Change.* Boston: D. C. Heath and Co., 1965.

Chapter 6   Natural Resources, Capital, and Management: Their Uses and Rewards

Bain, Joe S. *Pricing, Distribution, and Employment,* rev. ed. New York: Holt, Rinehart & Winston, Inc., 1953.

George, Henry. *Progress and Poverty.* New York: Robert S. Schalkenbach Foundation, 1954. (Originally published in 1879)

Leftwich, Richard H. *The Price System and Resource Allocation,* 3rd ed. New York: Holt, Rinehart & Winston, Inc., 1966.

Marx, Karl. *Capital* (2 vols.). New York: E. P. Dutton & Co.

Marx, Karl, and Friedrich Engels. *Communist Manifesto.* New York: International Publishers Co., Inc. (Originally published in 1848)

Stigler, George J. *Production and Distribution Theories: The Formative Period.* New York: The Macmillan Co., 1941.

Chapter 7   Government and Its Developing Role in the Economy
Chapter 8   Government and Public Finance

Allen, Frederick Lewis. *The Big Change: America Transforms Itself, 1900–1950.* New York: Harper and Row, 1952. (Also available in paperback edition: Bantam Books, Inc., New York, 1961)

Bator, Francis M. *The Question of Government Spending: Public Needs and Private Wants.* New York: Harper and Row, 1960. (Also available in paperback edition: The Macmillan Co., New York)

Bernstein, Peter L., and Robert L. Heilbroner. *A Primer on Government Spending.* New York: Random House, Inc. (Also available in paperback edition from the same publisher)

Eckstein, Otto. *Public Finance.* Englewood Cliffs, N.J.: Prentice-Hall, Inc., 1964.

Galbraith, John K. *The Affluent Society.* Boston: Houghton Mifflin Co., 1958.

Phelps, Edmund S., ed. *Private Wants and Public Needs.* New York: W. W. Norton & Co., Inc., 1964.

Taylor, Philip E. *The Economics of Public Finance,* 3rd ed. New York: The Macmillan Co., 1961.

Chapter 9   The Consumer and His Role in the American Economy

Black, Hillel. *Buy Now, Pay Later.* New York: William Morrow and Co., 1961. (Also available in paperback edition: Pocket Books, Inc., New York, 1962)

Hamilton, David. *The Consumer in Our Economy.* Boston: Houghton Mifflin Co., 1962.

Harrington, Michael. *The Other America: Poverty in the United States.* New York: The Macmillan Co., 1962. (Also available in paperback edition: Penguin Books, Inc., Baltimore)

Kreisman, Leonard T. *The Consumer in Society.* New York: The Odyssey Press, 1964.

Packard, Vance. *The Hidden Persuaders.* New York: David McKay Co., Inc., 1957. (Also available in paperback edition: Pocket Books, Inc., New York)

Packard, Vance. *The Status Seekers.* New York: David McKay Co., Inc., 1959. (Also available in paperback edition: Pocket Books, Inc., New York, 1961)

Packard, Vance. *The Waste Makers.* New York: David McKay Co., Inc., 1960. (Also available in paperback edition: Pocket Books, Inc., New York, 1963)

Schoenfeld, David, and Arthur A. Natella. *The Consumer and His Dollar.* New York: Oceana Publications, Inc., 1966.

Veblen, Thorstein. *Theory of the Leisure Class.* New York: New American Library of World Literature, 1954.

Chapter 10   Measuring the Nation's Economy

Council of Economic Advisers. *Economic Report of the President.* Washington, D.C.: U.S. Government Printing Office. (Published in January of each year)

Hansen, Alvin H. *Fiscal Policy and Business Cycles.* New York: W. W. Norton & Co., Inc., 1941.

U.S. Department of Commerce. *Do You Know Your Economic ABC's?* Washington, D.C.: U.S. Government Printing Office, 1963.

U.S. Department of Commerce. *Supplement to the Economic Indicators: Historical and Descriptive Background.* Washington, D.C.: U.S. Government Printing Office, 1964.

Wagner, Lewis E. *Measuring the Performance of the Economy.* Iowa City, Iowa: Bureau of Business and Economic Research, State University of Iowa, 1956.

Chapter 11   National Income Analysis—A New Model

Collery, Arnold. *National Income and Employment Analysis.* New York: John Wiley and Sons, Inc., 1966.

Hansen, Alvin. *The Postwar American Economy.* New York: W. W. Norton & Co., Inc., 1964.

Keynes, John Maynard. *The General Theory of Employment, Interest, and Money.* New York: Harcourt, Brace & World, Inc., 1936.

Lekachman, Robert, ed. *Keynes and the Classics.* Boston: D. C. Heath and Co., 1964.

Schultze, Charles L. *National Income Analysis.* Englewood Cliffs, N.J.: Prentice-Hall, Inc., 1964. (Also available in paperback edition from the same publisher)

Chapter 12   Money and Prices and Their Relation to the Economy
Chapter 13   Banking and the Creation of Money

American Bankers Association, Banking Education Committee. *The Story of American Banking.* New York: American Bankers Association, c 1963.

Chandler, Lester V. *The Economics of Money and Banking,* 4th ed. New York: Harper and Row, 1964.

Dean, Edwin, ed. *The Controversy over the Quantity Theory of Money.* Boston: D. C. Heath and Co., 1965.

Duesenberry, James S. *Money and Credit: Impact and Control.* Englewood Cliffs, N.J.: Prentice-Hall, Inc., 1964.

Federal Reserve System, Board of Governors. *The Federal Reserve System: Purposes and Functions.* Washington, D.C.: Board of Governors of the Federal Reserve System, 1963.

Robertson, D. H. *Money.* Chicago: University of Chicago Press, 1959.

Chapter 14 Formulating Modern Economic Policy

Bator, Francis M. *The Question of Government Spending: Public Needs and Private Wants.* New York: Harper and Row, 1960. (Also available in paperback edition: The Macmillan Co., New York)

Hamovitch, William, ed. *The Federal Deficit: Fiscal Imprudence or Policy Weapon?* Boston: D. C. Heath and Co., 1965.

Hansen, Alvin H. *Economic Policy and Full Employment.* New York: McGraw-Hill Book Co., 1947.

Lewis, Wilfred, Jr. *Federal Fiscal Policy in the Postwar Recessions.* Washington, D.C.: The Brookings Institution, 1962.

Wagner, Lewis E. *Income, Employment, and Prices.* Iowa City, Iowa: Bureau of Business and Economic Research, State University of Iowa, c 1960.

Chapter 15 International Trade and Finance

Balassa, Bela, ed. *Changing Patterns in Foreign Trade and Payments.* New York: W. W. Norton & Co., Inc., 1964. (Also available in paperback edition from the same publisher)

Ingram, James C. *International Economic Problems.* New York: John Wiley and Sons, Inc., 1966.

The International Position of the Dollar. New York: Committee for Economic Development, c 1961.

Kenen, Peter B. *Giant Among Nations: Problems in United States Foreign Economic Policy.* Chicago: Rand McNally & Co., 1963.

Krause, Lawrence B., ed. *The Common Market: Progress and Controversy.* Englewood Cliffs, N.J.: Prentice-Hall, Inc., 1964.

Chapter 16 Economic Systems Other Than Capitalism

Campbell, Robert W. *Soviet Economic Power: Its Organization, Growth, and Challenge.* Boston: Houghton Mifflin Co., 1960. (Also available in paperback edition from the same publisher)

Ebenstein, William. *Today's Isms: Communism, Fascism, Socialism, Capitalism.* Englewood Cliffs, N.J.: Prentice-Hall, Inc., 1964.

Grossman, Gregory. *Economic Systems.* Englewood Cliffs, N.J.: Prentice-Hall, Inc., 1964.

Schumpeter, Joseph A. *Capitalism, Socialism and Democracy.* New York: Harper and Row, 1962.

Turgeon, Lynn. *The Contrasting Economies.* Boston: Allyn and Bacon, Inc., 1963.

Wilcox, Clair, and others. *Economies of the World Today: Their Organization, Development, and Performance.* New York: Harcourt, Brace & World, Inc., 1962.

Chapter 17 Problems Faced by Certain Segments of Our Economy

PART A THE FARMER

An Adaptive Program for Agriculture. New York: Committee for Economic Development, 1962.

Higbee, Edward. *Farms and Farmers in an Urban Age.* New York: The Twentieth Century Fund, 1963.

Schultz, Theodore W. *Transforming Traditional Agriculture.* New Haven: Yale University Press, 1964.

PART B THE SMALL BUSINESSMAN

Stigler, George J. "The Case Against Big Business." *Fortune,* May 1952 (p. 123).

PART C THE AGED

Carlson, Valdeman. *Economic Security in the United States.* New York: McGraw-Hill Book Co., 1962.

Miller, Herman P. *Rich Man, Poor Man.* New York: Thomas Y. Crowell Co., 1964.

Will, Robert E., and Harold G. Vatter, eds. *Poverty in Affluence.* New York: Harcourt, Brace & World, Inc., 1965.

Chapter 18 Problems Faced by Our Economy as a Whole

PART A EDUCATION—INVESTMENT IN THE FUTURE

Danière, André. *Higher Education in the American Economy.* New York: Random House, Inc., 1964.

Harris, Seymour E. *More Resources for Education.* New York: Harper and Row, 1960.

Schultz, Theodore W. *The Economic Value of Education.* New York: Columbia University Press, 1963.

Silk, Leonard S. *The Research Revolution: Brains and Economic Growth.* New York: McGraw-Hill Book Co., c 1960.

PART B ECONOMIC GROWTH—THE UNITED STATES AND THE EMERGING NATIONS

Heilbroner, Robert L. *The Great Ascent: The Struggle for Economic Development in Our Time.* New York: Harper and Row, 1963. (Also available in paperback edition from the same publisher)

Randall, Laura, ed. *Economic Development: Evolution or Revolution?* Boston: D. C. Heath and Co., 1964.

Ranis, Gustav, ed. *The United States and the Developing Economies.* New York: W. W. Norton & Co., Inc., 1964.

Rostow, W. W. *The Stages of Economic Growth: A Non-Communist Manifesto.* New York: Cambridge University Press, 1960.

PART C THE PRIVATE VERSUS THE PUBLIC SECTOR—WHAT SHOULD THE BALANCE BE?

Bator, Francis M. *The Question of Government Spending: Public Needs and Private Wants.* New York: Harper and Row, 1960. (Also available in paperback edition: The Macmillan Co., New York)

Galbraith, John K. *The Affluent Society.* Boston: Houghton Mifflin Co., 1958. (Also available in paperback edition: New American Library of World Literature, Inc., New York)

Hansen, Alvin H. *Economic Issues of the 1960's.* New York: McGraw-Hill Book Co., 1961.

Phelps, Edmund S., ed. *Private Wants and Public Needs.* New York: W. W. Norton & Co., Inc., 1964.

Glossary of Economic Terms

Most of the terms appearing in this glossary are to be found in the text. If you do not think the concise definition given here is adequate, turn to the Index to find the location of the more extensive treatment given in the body of the text.

ability-to-pay principle: justification for taxing people with larger incomes a greater percentage of their income, based on the principle of diminishing marginal utility.

absolute advantage: an advantage that one nation may have over another in trade by being able to produce a good more efficiently (at less cost).

acceleration principle: the principle that a change in sales at the consumer level will bring about a greater change in sales of producer goods.

acceptability: a characteristic of money that results in individuals and businesses accepting it as a medium of exchange in a wide market.

acreage quota: the amount of land a farmer may plant and still receive benefits from government price-support programs.

administered price: a price set under conditions of imperfect competition where the individual firm has some degree of control.

administrative budget: the expected receipts and expenditures of a government, as asked for by the administrative branch. It does not include money in public trust funds. (*Cf.* cash budget.)

ad valorem taxes: tax applied to the value of that which is being taxed, particularly imports.

agency shop: a situation in which all employees in a particular bargaining unit are required to pay union dues even though they may not wish to join the union.

aggregate demand: total spending in the economy; the sum of personal consumption expenditures, business investment, and government spending.

alternative costs: *See* opportunity costs.

antitrust: of an act or a policy designed to curb monopolistic tendencies or power.

arbitration: a method of settling a labor dispute in which both parties agree to accept the decision of a third party.

assessment: for taxation purposes the official valuation of property or income.

asset: anything of value that is owned.

automatic stabilizer: a tool used to compensate for changes in the business cycle without requiring action by a public official.

automation: use of machines to replace human labor in a continuous operation of production; usually involves a feedback system.

avoidance: a legal way to reduce tax payments.

balance of payments: a statement listing all financial transactions that a nation and its people have with all other nations.

balance sheet: an itemized statement of a business showing its assets, liabilities, and net worth on a given date.

bank reserves: the amount of money a bank holds in order to meet the requirements of the Federal Reserve Bank or of a law, or the demands of its depositors. In addition to these reserves, Federal Reserve Banks hold secondary reserves in the form of securities that can be easily converted into money.

base period: a time in the past used to measure changes. It is used to measure price index.

benefit principle of taxation: justification for taxing according to the benefits received from government by the taxpayer.

bill of exchange: a written claim for foreign currency. The same as a foreign exchange check.

blacklist: a list of workers, usually union organizers, circulated by employers and designed to prevent those on the list from getting jobs.

bond: a security representing indebtedness, frequently issued in $1,000 denominations, and bearing a fixed rate of interest. Both governments and business firms issue bonds.

boycott: generally, a collective decision by one group to force action by another group. Usually used in connection with a union urging its members and others not to buy from an employer in order to force the latter to yield to its demands.

break-even point: the point at which total revenue and total expenditures equal each other.

budget: a plan of expected revenues and expenditures for a specific period of time.

business cycle: the expansion and contraction of the level of business activity at more or less regular intervals.

capital: a man-made instrument of production; a factor of production used in furthering the production process.

capital consumption: capital that is consumed in the process of production. The depreciation of capital that is subtracted from GNP to give NNP.

capital good: a good used in the production of other goods rather than to satisfy a human want directly. Same as producer good.

capitalism: an economic system in which the means of production are owned and controlled by private individuals with a minimum of government interference. Allocation of resources is determined by the market mechanism.

cash budget: total cash receipts and expenditures of a government, including those of public trust funds, such as social security. (*Cf.* administrative budget.)

check-off: an agreement between an employer and a union by which the former deducts union dues from the employees' paychecks and turns them over to the union.

closed shop: a firm in which only workers who are already union members will be hired.

collateral: something of value pledged by a borrower to secure a loan.

collective bargaining: a method of reaching an agreement in which representatives of employers and employees discuss proposed changes in the terms of the labor contract.

combination: a situation in which individuals or firms get together to influence market conditions. The most common types of industrial combinations in the United States have been pools, trusts, holding companies, mergers, and consolidations.

commercial bank: a financial institution whose primary function is to receive demand deposits and extend short-term loans to business firms.

common stock: the capital of a corporation, di-

vided into shares which usually entitle the owners to voting rights and, if voted by the board of directors, dividends. (*Cf.* preferred stock.)

communism: an economic system in which, in theory, all goods are owned collectively and in which payment of income is according to need. The term is used to describe the economy of the Soviet Union and of those nations that have similar ideologies. In practice the individual is given little freedom in determining the *What, How,* and *For Whom.*

company union: an organization of employees largely under the control of management and unaffiliated with any national or international union.

comparative advantage: the principle which explains that all nations will benefit if each concentrates its efforts on producing and exporting goods in which it has the greatest relative efficiency and on importing goods in which it has the least relative efficiency.

compensatory countercyclical policy: a program or plan designed to reverse the direction of the business cycle when it is believed that it is becoming inflationary or deflationary.

competition: a situation in which two or more parties seek to gain an advantage over the other(s). In classical capitalism it protects the consumer by assuring efficiency of production.

compulsory arbitration: enforced settlement of a dispute, as between management and a union, by law or by some government agency. It is practiced in New Zealand and Australia, but is generally frowned upon in this country.

conciliation: encouraging the settlement of a labor-management dispute by the use of a third party, who encourages discussion that will lead to a peaceful settlement.

conglomeration: a merger involving unrelated industries.

conspicuous consumption: the purchase and use of goods and services primarily for the purpose of enhancing one's social prestige rather than for satisfaction of material needs.

consumer cooperative: an association of consumers organized to purchase goods and services for its members. Profits are distributed to members on the basis of their purchases.

consumer good: an economic good used directly to satisfy human wants rather than for resale or to further production.

consumer price index: a measurement of the cost of living prepared by the U.S. Bureau of Labor Statistics.

consumer sovereignty: a central idea of the classical model that production should be determined by the market's response to consumer demand.

consumption: the utilization of goods and services to satisfy human wants.

contract: an agreement between two or more parties recognized and enforceable by law.

contraction: a decline of economic activity in the business cycle.

copyright: an exclusive right given to artists, authors, and musicians, or to their designated agents, by government to reproduce, publish, or sell what they have created.

corporate income tax: a slightly progressive tax levied on the taxable income of corporations.

corporation: an artificial person before the law; it is chartered by the state government, which allows it such powers as the right to issue stocks and bonds and to have perpetual life. The owners have only limited liability.

correspondent bank: a commercial bank that performs services for other commercial banks.

cost-push inflation: a rise in the price level that originates on the cost (or supply) side rather than because of excess demand. It occurs when economic groups try to increase their relative share of the national income.

countercyclical: reversing the direction of the business cycle.

countervailing power: the tendency of one economic group having monopolistic power to balance another group having monopolistic power, as in the case of a monopolistic producer and a monopsonistic buyer.

craft union: a union of workers having the same or similar skills, such as electricians or plumbers. It is sometimes called a trade or horizontal union. (*Cf.* industrial union.)

credit: purchasing or borrowing with the promise to pay at some later date.

creditor nation: a nation whose citizens, businesses, and government owe less to foreign creditors than foreign debtors owe to them.

credit union: a cooperative savings and loan association.

cumulative preferred stock: stock with a stated dividend that must be paid before common stockholders receive their dividends. If not paid, the amount accumulates.

currency: that part of the money supply, in the form of coins and paper bills, that is issued by the government or its agent (central bank).

customs union: an agreement between nations to eliminate duties on goods traded between them and to have a common external tariff applicable to all nonmembers.

debenture bonds: long-term promissory notes issued by a corporation and backed only by the good faith of the corporation.

debtor nation: a nation whose citizens, businesses, and government owe more to foreign creditors than foreign debtors owe to them.

decreasing costs: costs which decline per unit as production increases.

deficit financing: the condition in which government expenditures exceed government revenues, the difference being made up by borrowing. In the United States it is frequently planned by the national government to increase aggregate demand.

deflation: a decline in the general price level; it results in an increase in the purchasing power of money.

demand: the quantity of goods or services that buyers are willing to purchase at various prices at a given time.

demand deposit: a deposit on account in a commercial bank upon which checks can be written and money withdrawn without any advance notice. Demand deposits make up the largest part of our money supply.

demand-pull inflation: a rise in the price level caused by too much money pursuing too few goods. The demand for goods is greater than the ability to supply them.

depreciation: reduction in the value of capital goods because of the wear and tear on them in producing other goods. Also called "capital consumption."

depression: the period in the business cycle when most measurements of economic activity are at their lowest. Characterized by low production, low prices, and high unemployment.

derivative deposits: those deposits that come into being as a result of people's borrowing from a bank.

devaluation: a decrease in the value of the unit of money (dollars, pounds, francs, etc.) in relation to gold.

dictatorship of proletariat: according to Karl Marx and his followers, that stage in the evolution of society that follows the overthrow of capitalism, when representatives of the working class assume complete power.

diminishing marginal utility: the gradual decline in consumer satisfaction that each additional unit of consumption of a particular good or service gives.

diminishing returns, law of: when additional units of one factor of production are added to a constant quantity of other factors, eventually each additional unit added will yield less than the preceding unit.

discount: interest that is paid in advance.

discount store: a company that sells goods at less than standard list price.

discretionary policy: monetary and fiscal policy requiring action by an individual or a government agency and designed to compensate for the business cycle.

discretionary stabilizer: an economic tool, used to counter the direction of the business cycle, that requires action or decision-making on the part of some authority.

disposable income: the amount of income individuals have left to spend and save. Personal income minus personal taxes.

distribution: the marketing or merchandising of commodities. *See also* functional distribution.

dividend: the return to shareholders from their ownership in corporate stock. It is paid from profits.

divisibility: a characteristic of money that allows it to be stated and used in fractions or multiples of the unit of money.

dollar shortage: foreign nations' lack of enough dollars to buy from the United States. Caused by a steady favorable balance of payments for the United States.

domestic system: production that takes place in the home rather than at the factory. Characteristic of production before the impact of the Industrial Revolution.

double counting: in determining GNP by the income method, the taking into account more than once of the value added to products.

dumping: selling goods to other countries below cost in order to get rid of surpluses or to destroy foreign competition.

durability: a characteristic of money that permits it to be used over a long period of time or to be replaced inexpensively.

economic freedom: the principle that individuals have mobility in the economy in that they are guaranteed the right to choose their own jobs, to buy and sell property, and to enter into or dissolve a business.

economic good: a good that is relatively scarce and requires effort to obtain; broadly defined, it includes services as well as physical goods.

economic growth: increase in real per capita income.

economic indicator: a measurement of one or several parts of the economy which is useful for evaluating the entire economy and predicting its course. It may be leading, coincident, or lagging, depending on its relation to the economy as a whole.

economic profit: profit remaining after explicit and implicit costs are paid. Sometimes called pure profit.

economic rent: the difference between the income derived from using land and the cost of producing that income.

economic system: the way society organizes itself through its institutions and its guiding principles and values in answering the central and related economic questions.

economic value: the value placed on a good because of its utility and scarcity.

economics: that branch of the social sciences that concerns itself with the production, distribution, and consumption of goods and services.

elastic demand: when a small change in price will result in a considerable change in the quantity people will buy, the demand for the product is said to be elastic.

elastic supply: when a small change in price will result in a considerable change in the quantity offered for sale, the supply of the product is said to be elastic.

emerging nation: a country which is poor and is only beginning to develop its economic potential. Usually refers to nations which have only recently been given their independence.

enterprise: that factor of production which is responsible for initiating production and organizing the other factors of production. It assumes the risk and receives as its payment profit.

entrepreneur: one who assumes the responsibility of enterprise. Management has taken over many of the functions of the entrepreneur.

equation of exchange: an equation that shows the relationship between the supply of money, prices, and business activity. It is stated as $MV = PT$, where M represents the supply of money, V its velocity, P the price level, and T the number of transactions.

equilibrium: in economic theory, a condition which, once it is achieved, will continue unless one of the variables is changed or unless the changing of one variable is not offset by an equal change in another variable. Examples include: the intersection of supply and demand, the point at which aggregate demand $(C + I + G)$ crosses the 45° line, the point at which investment equals savings, and the point at which marginal cost equals marginal revenue.

escalator clause: a provision in a contract to permit changes in payment to fluctuate with changes in the general price level. Most frequently used in connection with wage payments.

escape clause: a provision to allow the United States Tariff Commission to appeal to the President to nullify a trade agreement if the Commission finds that the trade agreement may hurt a domestic industry.

estate tax: a tax placed on the value of an inherited estate.

evasion: an illegal method of reducing tax payments.

excess profits tax: a tax on business firms in addition to the normal business tax. In the United States it is levied on profits above what the law designates as normal and is usually used during wartime.

excess reserves: bank reserves that are greater than those required by the Federal Reserve.

exchange rate: the price that one nation must pay to exchange its currency for another nation's currency.

exchange value: the value placed on a good or service based on the amount of other goods and services it may be exchanged for.

excise tax: a tax placed on a good or service at the time of its sale.

expansion: that phase of the business cycle during which activity is increasing. Characterized by increasing employment and production.

explicit costs: costs that orginate outside the firm, such as wages, rent, and interest.

factors of production: those ingredients necessary for the production of any good or service. Most economists list four: land, labor, capital, and enterprise. The term *natural resources* is frequently used for land, and *management* is often used for enterprise.

fascism: a politicoeconomic system which permits private ownership but has highly centralized decision-making about economic matters and is politically a dictatorship.

favorable balance of trade: a condition in which a nation's total value of exports exceeds its total value of imports.

featherbedding: the employment of more workers than are needed for efficient operation, or placing limitations on the output of workers, according to provisions in a labor-management contract.

fiat money: money which has no precious metal backing and circulates by order of the government.

fiscal policy: planned course of action on budgetary matters by the government designed to influence economic activity.

fixed cost: cost that does not fluctuate with the volume of production.

foreign exchange: the process of settling claims, involving foreign currency, that a country has against another country.

franchise: granting by government to a firm of the right to have a monopoly or partial monopoly for a particular service.

free goods: those goods which are so abundant that they can be had without cost, e.g., air.

free trade: trade among nations in which all policy restrictions that may impede its flow are eliminated.

freedom of contract: the principle that, in the production of goods and services, individuals have the right to enter into agreements resulting in production. Such agreements must be within the framework of the law and may not be conspiracies against society.

fringe benefits: items that increase real income but are not included in the basic wage, such as sick benefits. Fringe benefits are often included in labor contracts.

full employment: a condition of the economy in which there is sufficient aggregate demand to employ all those who wish to work and are qualified to do so. In the United States it is frequently considered the condition of the economy when the unemployment rate is less than 4 percent.

functional distribution: payment — wages, rent, interest, and profit — to the factors of production according to their contribution.

general property tax: a tax on the assessed value of property; it is computed as a percentage of value. Specific types of property may be exempt.

general sales tax: a tax on most goods collected at the time of their sale. Food and medicine are frequently exempt.

gift tax: a tax on the value of property transferred primarily to avoid payment of inheritance and estate taxes.

gold certificate: in the United States, formerly, a certificate issued by the government that was redeemable in gold. Gold certificates are now issued by the Treasury and are held by the Federal Reserve Banks as evidence of their gold holdings; these are used as part of their reserves against their deposits and Federal Reserve notes.

gold exchange standard: a method by which countries which have little gold may hold currencies of other countries that are exchangeable for gold, such as Bolivia holding United States dollars.

gold-par rate of exchange: the use of a gold standard, with fixed relative values of particular currencies, as a means of facilitating currency exchange. Used primarily by the United States and western European nations before the Great Depression.

gold standard: a system in which the monetary unit is expressed in terms of gold. The government buys and sells gold freely at a fixed price.

good: when defined broadly, anything that people desire. Narrowly defined, it excludes nontangible items, which are called services.

Gresham's law: when two kinds of money are used in a country, the cheaper money will drive the relatively higher-valued money out of circulation.

gross: total amount before any deductions.

gross national debt: total indebtedness of the national government, including the debts owed by one governmental agency to another governmental agency. *Net debt* refers only to government obligations to the public.

gross national income: GNP stated as income rather than as production.

gross national product: the total retail market value of all goods and services produced in a nation during a given period, usually a year.

gross savings: the sum of capital consumption (depreciation), corporation savings, and personal savings.

guaranteed annual wage: the minimum yearly payment that an employer agrees to make to a worker. The employer agrees to employ the worker for a minimum number of weeks each year and to supplement his unemployment insurance benefits if he is laid off because of insufficient demand.

holding company: a corporation which is organized primarily to hold stock in one or more other corporations for the purpose of control.

homogeneous: a characteristic of money which refers to the fact that all similar units have similar value.

homogeneous product: a product in which all units are alike and which is therefore most suitable for achieving or maintaining pure competition. A market with homogeneous products is in contrast to the product differentiation usually found under monopolistic competition.

horizontal combination: a combination formed when two or more organizations producing the same goods or performing the same services merge.

imperfect competition: any market condition which differs from pure competition.

implicit costs: costs originating within the firm which are provided by the owner, such as time, money, or property.

import quota: a limit on the quantity of a product that may be imported during a specified period of time.

income tax: a tax on the net income of individuals or corporations, usually with progressive rates. The most important source of federal revenue.

index number: a measurement of relative change using statistical procedures.

industrial union: a labor union in which all workers in a particular industry, regardless of their jobs, are members. It is sometimes referred to as a vertical union.

industry-wide bargaining: collective bargaining in which one or several unions negotiate for a contract with virtually all the employers of an industry. In many instances a contract worked out with a particular employer sets the pattern for the entire industry.

inelastic demand: a condition in which the quantity of a product sold does not change, or changes very little, with a change in price.

inelastic supply: a condition in which the quantity of a product produced does not change, or changes very little, with a change in price.

inflation: an increase in the price level causing a decrease in the purchasing power of the monetary unit.

inheritance tax: a tax on those receiving shares of an estate.

injunction: a court order restraining an individual or a group from carrying on some kind of activity. Frequently used in connection with preventing or stopping a strike.

innovation: a new idea or method in the production process frequently involving the use of inventions in a practical way.

installment buying: acquiring goods or services by making either no down payment or a small down payment and afterwards making payments at regular intervals.

installment credit: a type of consumer credit which allows the seller to repossess the article purchased if the buyer defaults on payment.

insurance: the financial operation whereby many people contribute to a fund from which those who sustain a loss are compensated.

interest: payment for the use of capital (loanable funds).

interlocking directorate: a condition in which one or more members of a board of directors of one company are also members of the boards of directors of other companies.

intrinsic value: the market value of the material in a thing, as the value of the metal in a coin.

inventory: goods in stock and usually available for sale.

investment: when applied to an individual or a firm, the purchase of assets which will produce income. When used in macroeconomics, it refers to capital formation and capital accumulation (capital goods produced plus inventory accumulation).

investment bank: a business that specializes in underwriting and selling new issues of stocks and bonds.

invisible exports and imports: financial transactions among nations involving services or such intangibles as shipping charges, insurance, tourist spending, and the transfer of loanable funds.

jurisdictional dispute: a conflict between rival unions as to which should have control over a given job or activity and be recognized by management.

labor: one of the factors of production involving human effort in the production process. Managerial activities are frequently considered a separate factor.

labor force: includes those over 14 years of age who are working, are looking for work, or are absent from work because of such things as labor disputes, illness, vacations, etc.

labor union: an organization of employees which acts in their behalf, particularly in connection with negotiating with management.

laissez-faire: a policy associated with the classical model of capitalism suggesting that the government should not interfere with the economy.

land: the factor of production from which goods originate; natural resources before man has worked on them.

law of increasing costs: the principle that, in a production situation, average total unit cost increases as the volume of a business increases. This principle is not universally applicable, since in some industries costs are constant and in others costs decrease as volume of business increases.

legal reserve: the percentage of deposits that member banks of the Federal Reserve System are required to keep either with the Federal Reserve Bank or in their vaults.

legal tender: a form of money which the government recognizes and creditors must legally accept as payment for debts.

liability: the debt of an individual or a firm that is owed to others. Does not include capital investment by owners (stock).

limited liability: the legal exemption of stockholders in a corporation from financial liability for the debts of the company beyond the amount they have invested.

limited life: a characteristic of a single proprietorship or partnership, in both of which the business ceases to exist upon the death of the owner (or one of the owners).

liquid assets: those assets that can easily be converted into cash, such as government bonds and other easily marketable securities.

liquidity preference: the preference that people and businesses have for holding their assets in cash rather than in a less liquid form.

lockout: closing of a business by an employer in order to put pressure on a union in a labor-management dispute. The employer's counterpart of a strike.

long run: in the case of a business, a sufficiently long period of time to permit the business to develop its capacity to produce. In the long run all costs become variable.

Lorenz curve: a measuring tool for plotting the degree of inequality in the distribution of income.

macroeconomics: the study of the economy as a whole rather than as individual economic units. Sometimes referred to as aggregate economics.

maintenance-of-membership shop: a situation in which workers who are members of a union must continue their membership for the duration of the contract.

management: the factor of production that is responsible for organizing and directing the other three factors. Some economists include management with labor or call this factor the entrepreneur.

margin: in the purchase of securities, the amount of money that the buyer must deposit immediately with the broker. It is stated as a percentage of the total value of the securities.

marginal: yielding only enough value to cover the cost of production. May be used with land, labor, or a business.

marginal analysis: analysis of economic data by studying the results of the value added by an additional unit of one variable to another variable.

marginal cost: the additional cost for expanding output by one more unit.

marginal product: the additional product derived by adding one more unit (as an additional worker) of a factor of production.

marginal productivity wage theory: the principle that under competitive conditions the wages of all workers will be set by the productivity, measured in money, of the last worker hired.

marginal propensity to consume: the proportion of additional income that people spend.

marginal propensity to save: the proportion of additional income that people save.

marginal revenue: the additional revenue that a firm receives from the sale of one more unit. Under pure competition in the short run this is the same as the market price.

marginal revenue product: the additional revenue a firm receives by the addition of one more unit of a factor of production, such as an additional worker.

market: the place or situation in which buyers and sellers can meet for the purpose of exchange.

measure of value: that function of money which

provides the standard for measuring the value of production, using the monetary unit as the common denominator (such as showing the value of apples and the value of candy bars in dollars).

mediation: a method of settling labor disputes in which a third party participates in a formal way in helping to bring about an agreement among the disputants. Plans offered by the mediator are not binding.

medium of exchange: the major function of money which facilitates the exchange of goods and services. Needed by an economy which has specialization of production.

mercantilism: an economic system most popular in the 16th, 17th, and 18th centuries which was characterized by a highly controlled market with numerous regulations designed to increase the flow of precious metals into the treasury of the "mother country." This system is usually considered a precursor of the classical model.

merger: the combining of two companies into one by the dissolution of one with the sale of assets to the other.

microeconomics: the study of the economic behavior of individual units in the economy, such as business firms.

minimum wage: the lowest wage that an employer can pay an employee as set by law. Usually expressed as an hourly rate.

mixed capitalism: an economic system in which the major portion of the instruments of production is owned and operated by private enterprise and the market mechanism is the major factor in determining the allocation of resources. However, a democratic government may provide for some ownership of, and control over, enterprise as well as assume considerable responsibility for the economic well-being of the nation.

model: a theory used by social scientists to analyze economic behavior. The closer the model is to the real world the more useful it is for analysis.

monetary policy: use of the tools of the Federal Reserve System in an attempt to achieve stable prices and full employment. The tools include changing interest rates and bank reserve ratios and, indirectly, the quantity of money for the purpose of modifying the business cycle.

money: a medium of exchange that is accepted by society. In the United States the term includes currency and demand deposits.

money wages: a term used to distinguish the number of dollars received by workers as contrasted with what those dollars will buy (purchasing power).

monopolistic competition: a market situation characterized by product differentiation and the effect that each firm's actions have on all other firms.

monopoly: a market situation in which there is only one seller of a product and there are no acceptable substitutes.

monopsony: a market situation in which there is only one buyer for a product.

multiplier: the reciprocal of the marginal propensity to save. This figure relates changes in investment and spending to changes in aggregate income.

national debt: the debt owed by the federal government. Does not include the debts of state and local governments or private debt.

national income: the total income payments made to the owners of the factors of production. Sometimes used to refer to gross or net national product.

nationalize: to take for government ownership, with or without compensation, a business or other property owned and operated privately.

natural monopoly: an industry in which competition would be costly and uneconomical.

natural resources: *See* land.

near-money: highly liquid assets other than money, such as time deposits and government securities.

net: that which is left after certain designated deductions are made from the gross amount.

net national product: gross national product minus capital consumption (depreciation).

net worth: total assets minus total liabilities. Recorded in the balance sheet of a firm.

oligopoly: a market situation characterized by only a few sellers of a product.

oligopsony: a market situation characterized by only a few buyers of a product.

open-market operations: the buying and selling of securities, primarily government securities, by the Federal Reserve System, usually to carry out a monetary policy.

open shop: a business which employs workers without reference to their membership in a union.

opportunity costs: what a factor of production could return were it used in some other activity that society needed. The amount needed to get a factor of production away from some alternative use. Also called "alternative cost."

over-the-counter market: the market for securities sold by brokers outside organized stock exchanges. Over-the-counter securities are also called "unlisted."

parity: in the United States, as part of the farm

policy, a plan designed to keep purchasing power of a unit of farm production (e.g., a bushel of wheat) equal to the purchasing power of the units of production that a farmer buys in the same ratio as existed during some selected base period.

partnership: a form of business organization consisting of two or more individuals who share in the ownership and operation of the business according to a contractual arrangement. Liability is unlimited.

patent: an exclusive right, granted by the government, to make and sell inventions.

payroll tax: a tax on wages or salaries earned within the boundaries of a government, most frequently a city.

per capita output: GNP of a country divided by the country's population. Sometimes used to indicate the relative standard of living of a nation.

perfect competition: *See* pure competition.

peril point: the lowest figure at which a duty on imports can be set without threatening a domestic industry.

perpetual life: a characteristic of a corporation, in which the death of one or more owners does not automatically bring about an end to the business.

personal consumption expenditures: the money households spend for consumer goods. Disposable personal income minus savings equals personal consumption expenditures.

personal income: total money income received by individuals before the payment of personal taxes.

personal income tax: a tax on the income of individuals or families; it is usually progressive.

personal savings: the difference between disposable personal income and personal consumption expenditures.

picketing: a weapon of unions during a strike in which workers advertise their grievances by carrying signs and walking in lines in the neighborhood of a business, urging other workers not to work and customers not to buy.

piece rate: wages that are determined by the number of units produced or work done. This is contrasted with hourly wage rates, in which a fixed rate per hour is set.

portability: a characteristic of money that allows it to be carried easily.

preferential shop: a situation in which management agrees to hire union members so long as they are available.

preferred stock: that stock of a corporation that gives the owner preferential treatment in the payment of dividends and in the distribution of assets in the event the corporation is liquidated. Dividend rates are usually fixed. (*See also* common stock.)

price: the exchange value of goods and services stated in a monetary unit.

price index: a device for measuring the changing value of money over a given period of time or the average price of a number of selected commodities at a given time.

price level: the average of prices paid for goods and services in a given period.

primary deposits: those deposits made by people depositing cash in the bank.

private enterprise: organization of production in which business units are owned and operated by individuals who take risks and are motivated by the desire to make a profit. Contrasted with government or collective enterprise.

private property: property which an individual owns and over which he has the right to exercise reasonable control. Provides incentive for producing.

product differentiation: a condition in which a producer consciously tries to represent his product as different from similar products. Characteristic of monopolistic competition and some oligopolies.

production: any kind of activity which adds value to goods and services, including creation, transportation, and storage until used.

production function: use of the technical information that shows the amount of output that is capable of being performed by specific inputs (factors of production).

productivity: the output for a unit of a factor of production.

profit: payment to a business enterprise for the risks incurred. The amount left from total revenue after all costs are paid.

progressive tax: a tax in which the rate of payment increases as the tax base increases.

promissory note: a written statement agreeing to pay a certain sum of money to a specific person or firm at an indicated time.

propensity to consume: the proportion of income that people tend to spend at different levels of income.

propensity to save: the proportion of income that people tend to save at different levels of income.

proportional tax: a tax in which the rate of tax does not change with a change in the tax base.

prosperity: the uppermost phase of a business cycle.

protectionists: those who favor high tariffs and other restrictions on imports to the end that domestic goods will not have to compete with foreign goods.

protective tariff: a tax on imported goods designed to give domestic producers protection from price competition.

public utility: a business that provides essential services to the public and tends to be a natural monopoly. It must obtain a franchise from the government and is regulated by a government agency.

pure competition: a market situation in which there are a sufficient number of buyers and sellers acting independently and in which the product is a homogeneous one, so that the entry or exit of any one buyer or seller will not affect price.

pure profit: *See* economic profit.

quantity theory of money: the theory that the general price level will change in response to the money supply. Stated as the equation of exchange: $MV = PT$.

real wages: the measurement of income in dollars of purchasing power. Useful for comparing changes in the standard of living by eliminating the influence of changes in the general price level. (*Cf.* money wages.)

recession: that phase of the business cycle that shows a downswing or contraction of the economy.

recovery: that period of the business cycle which follows a depression. Also known as an upswing or expansion.

regressive tax: a tax in which the rate of payment decreases as the tax base increases.

rent: payment for the use of land. (*See also* economic rent.)

reserve ratio: the relationship of the amount of money that must be retained in a reserve account (reserve account with the Federal Reserve Bank plus vault cash) to the total demand deposits of a member bank.

retail price maintenance: the practice of permitting a manufacturer, under protection of state law, to set retail prices for his products. The laws are usually referred to as "fair-trade" laws.

revenue: the income of a government or business enterprise. When deductions are made, it is prefaced with the word *net*.

revenue tariffs: duties placed on imports with the objective of raising revenues rather than protecting domestic industries. Such tariffs rarely discourage international trade.

sales tax: a tax placed on goods at the time of their purchase.

savings: that part of income that is not spent for consumer items.

savings bank: a financial institution specializing in small time deposits that are usually held for a considerable time.

savings and loan association: a financial institution owned by share purchasers (depositors) which specializes in long-term loans to finance real estate purchases.

seasonal fluctuations: regular and predictable changes in business activity caused by changes in the season, such as the increase in construction in the spring.

secondary boycott: action by a group of workers designed to bring pressure on a firm they have a disagreement with and involving the use of third parties not involved in the dispute, such as the refusal on the part of workers to handle goods coming from a plant that is being struck.

secondary reserves: assets that banks hold other than primary reserves that can be quickly converted into cash, such as government securities or commercial paper.

single proprietorship: the oldest and most common type of business organization, in which the business is owned by an individual.

single tax: a plan, proposed by Henry George, in which all income derived from land ownership would be taxed for the full amount, thereby eliminating the need to collect other taxes.

slowdown: a weapon of labor in which workers purposely reduce the speed at which they work, resulting in increased costs to the employer.

socialism: an economic system in which much or most of the means of production is owned and controlled collectively, usually by government, and in which central planning is substituted for the market in the allocation of resources.

soil bank: in the United States, a government farm program which pays farmers for withdrawing land from cultivation.

stability of value: a characteristic of money involving little change in what a unit will buy.

stabilizer: an economic tool used to reduce business fluctuations. It may be automatic, such as unemployment insurance, or discretionary, such as increasing or decreasing government spending.

standard allowable deduction: a rate (up to a maximum amount) that is applied to gross income and that may be deducted from gross income in determining taxable income. If it is used, no itemization of deductions is necessary.

standard of deferred payment: that function of money that expresses in terms of money the amount to be repaid.

standard of living: an evaluation of the way a family or group lives with reference to the consumer goods it has.

stock: ownership of a corporation, divided into shares and represented by certificates.

stockbroker: a middleman in the buying and selling of securities.

store of value: that function of money which allows the individual to accumulate wealth or purchasing power.

strike: a weapon of labor in which workers voluntarily stop working in order to bring pressure on the employer to meet their demands.

strikebreaker: a worker hired to replace a striking worker.

structural unemployment: unemployment caused primarily by change in consumer preferences, technology, lack of skills, and loss of markets.

submarginal: yielding less than enough to cover the cost of production. May be used with land, labor, or a business

subsidy: government assistance to a program, an enterprise, or an industry in the form of a money payment that is generally made for the good of the general public. Farmers, the airlines, and the merchant marine have been subsidized at various times.

subsistence: a level of income necessary to maintain a minimum standard of living.

supply: the quantity of goods and services that sellers are willing to offer at various prices at a given time.

supramarginal: yielding more than the cost of production. Applicable to land, labor, or a business.

surplus value: in Marxian theory, the amount charged above the cost of labor. Other economic theory considers payments made to any of the factors of production, above what the market price would call for under competitive conditions, to be surplus.

tariff: a schedule of taxes on commodities imported or exported. In the United States only imported goods are affected.

tax: a compulsory charge upon individuals and businesses to pay for the cost of running a government and carrying out its policies. Designed to reallocate resources from the private to the public sector.

tax base: the commodity, income, or service on which a tax is levied; only that part of the value of an item which is taxed.

tax incidence: the businesses and/or individuals upon whom a tax finally comes to rest.

tax rate: a specified percentage of the value of a commodity, income, or service taxed.

taxable income: the amount of income remaining after subtracting all allowable deductions and exemptions and therefore subject to taxation.

technological unemployment: the displacement of workers caused by the introduction of labor-saving machinery.

technology: knowledge of the use of resources for more efficient production.

time deposit: an account in a bank on which (1) interest is usually paid, (2) the bank may legally withhold payment for a specified number of days, and (3) checks cannot be written. Sometimes called savings accounts.

token money: coins that circulate at a higher value than the market value of the commodity (metal) they are made of.

trade association: an organization of firms engaged in a common industry or business activity to promote their mutual interests.

trade union: *See* craft union.

transfer payment: money paid by one individual or institution (particularly government) to another without the rendering of services, such as social security payments.

trust: a form of business combination which became common in the 1890's in which stockholders exchange their voting shares for trust certificates for purposes of centralizing control of an entire industry in the hands of a few.

turnover tax: a form of sales tax commonly used in the Soviet Union.

underdeveloped country: technically, a nation which has realized little of its economic potential because of a lack of capital, technology, and skilled labor. More commonly it refers to countries with a relatively low per capita income.

underwrite: to guarantee to furnish a definite sum of money by a definite date to a business or government in return for securities, such as stocks and bonds.

unemployment: when referring to the economy as a whole, the difference between the number of persons in the labor force and the number of persons employed. Also refers to those who are able to work and are seeking work but cannot find jobs.

unemployment insurance: that part of our social security program that provides covered employees with insurance against the complete loss of income due to unemployment. Payment comes primarily from taxes paid by employers.

unfavorable balance of trade: the condition in which a nation's total value of imports exceeds its total value of exports.

union label: an emblem placed on a good signifying that it was made by union workers.

union shop: a business in which the employer is free to hire any worker provided that the worker is a union member or will become a union member after a specified period of time.

unit of account: the use of money as a measure or standard of value in an economy.

unlimited liability: a disadvantage of a single proprietorship and of a partnership making the owner or owners responsible (with no exclusion of their personal assets) for the firm's debts.

utility: the satisfaction that one obtains, or anticipates he will obtain, from the consumption, ownership, or use of a good or service.

variable cost: a cost that increases with increase in production.

velocity of circulation: the rate at which the supply of money is turned over (spent) for a given period of time, usually a year.

vertical combination: a business organization that combines the various stages of production of a single finished good.

wages: the prices management pays for human effort.

wealth: the total value of economic goods.

welfare capitalism: a modified form of capitalism characterized by many social welfare programs, considerable government involvement in the economy, and legislation to provide a minimum standard of living for all citizens.

wildcat strike: a work stoppage that is not sanctioned by the union.

withholding tax: a tax deducted from wages and salaries by the employer. In the United States this method is applied to personal income and social security taxes to make payments more convenient.

yellow-dog contract: a wage contract in which the worker agrees before he is hired not to join a union during his employment. Such contracts are no longer legal.

Index

460

Homeworks.